Lecture Notes in Computer Science 11867

More information about this series at http://www.springer.com/series/7412

Aythami Morales · Julian Fierrez ·
José Salvador Sánchez · Bernardete Ribeiro (Eds.)

Pattern Recognition and Image Analysis

9th Iberian Conference, IbPRIA 2019
Madrid, Spain, July 1–4, 2019
Proceedings, Part I

 Springer

Editors
Aythami Morales
Universidad Autónoma de Madrid
Madrid, Spain

Julian Fierrez
Universidad Autónoma de Madrid
Madrid, Spain

José Salvador Sánchez
Universitat Jaume I
Castellón de la Plana, Spain

Bernardete Ribeiro
University of Coimbra
Coimbra, Portugal

ISSN 0302-9743   ISSN 1611-3349   (electronic)
Lecture Notes in Computer Science
ISBN 978-3-030-31331-9   ISBN 978-3-030-31332-6   (eBook)
https://doi.org/10.1007/978-3-030-31332-6

LNCS Sublibrary: SL6 – Image Processing, Computer Vision, Pattern Recognition, and Graphics

This Springer imprint is published by the registered company Springer Nature Switzerland AG
The registered company address is: Gewerbestrasse 11, 6330 Cham, Switzerland

Preface

Now in its ninth edition, IbPRIA has become a key research event in pattern recognition and image analysis on the Iberian Peninsula organized by the national IAPR associations for pattern recognition in Spain (AERFAI) and Portugal (APRP).

Most of the research reported here therefore comes from authors from Spain and Portugal. Out of the 401 authors who presented work to IbPRIA 2019, 29% are from Spain and 20% are from Portugal. More than 50% of the authors are from another 32 countries from around the world, with high representation from countries like Algeria, Brazil, Colombia, India, Italy, or Mexico. Our efforts to strengthen the bonds between the research conducted on the Iberian Peninsula and other countries are patent in the program, which emphasizes interactive poster sessions and includes a special session dedicated to international research cooperation.

On the other hand, we are witnessing a deep transformation in our field, now increasingly dominated by advances occurring in industry. We have also tried to integrate IBPRIA in this vortex by including in the program a number of panel discussions with international research leaders from companies like Google, Microsoft, Telefonica, Vodafone, and Accenture.

IbPRIA 2019 received 137 submissions. The review process for IbPRIA 2019 was diligent and required careful consideration of more than 400 reviews from 100 reviewers who spent significant time and effort in reviewing the papers. In the end 99 papers were accepted, which is an acceptance rate of 72%. To form the final program 30 papers were selected for oral presentations (22% acceptance rate) and 69 as poster presentations.

We hope that this book will result in a valuable resource for the pattern recognition research community. We would like to thank all who made this possible, especially the authors and reviewers.

August 2019

Aythami Morales
Julian Fierrez
José Salvador Sánchez
Bernardete Ribeiro

Organization

Organizing Committee

General Chairs

General Co-chair AERFAI
José Salvador Sánchez   Universitat Jaume I, Castellón, Spain

General Co-chair APRP
Bernardete Ribeiro   University of Coimbra, Portugal

Local Chair

Julian Fierrez   Universidad Autonoma de Madrid, Spain

Program Chairs

Aythami Morales   Universidad Autonoma de Madrid, Spain
Manuel J. Marin   University of Cordoba, Spain
Antonio Pertusa   University of Alicante, Spain
Hugo Proença   University of Beira Interior, Portugal

Local Committee

Ruben Vera-Rodriguez   Universidad Autonoma de Madrid, Spain
Ruben Tolosana   Universidad Autonoma de Madrid, Spain
Javier Hernandez-Ortega   Universidad Autonoma de Madrid, Spain
Alejandro Acien   Universidad Autonoma de Madrid, Spain
Ignacio Serna   Universidad Autonoma de Madrid, Spain
Ivan Bartolome   Universidad Autonoma de Madrid, Spain

Program Committee

Abhijit Das   Griffith University, Australia
Adrian Perez-Suay   University of Valencia, Spain
Ana Mendonça   University of Porto, Portugal
Antonino Furnari   Università degli Studi di Catania, Italy
Antonio Bandera   University of Malaga, Spain
Antonio Javier Gallego   University of Alicante, Spain
   Sánchez
Antonio Pertusa   University of Alicante, Spain
Antonio-José   Universitat Politècnica de València, Spain
   Sánchez-Salmerón
António Cunha   UTAD, Spain
António J. R. Neves   University of Aveiro, Portugal

Armando Pinho	University of Aveiro, Portugal
Arsénio Reis	UTAD, Spain
Bilge Gunsel	Istanbul Technical University, Turkey
Billy Mark Peralta Marquez	Pontificia Universidad Catolica de Chile, Chile
Carlo Sansone	University of Naples Federico II, Italy
Catarina Silva	ESTG-IPLEIRIA-PORTUGAL, Portugal
Constantine Kotropoulos	Aristotle University of Thessaloniki, Greece
Cristina Carmona-Duarte	Universidad de Las Palmas de Gran Canaria, Spain
Daniel Acevedo	Universidad de Buenos Aires, Argentina
David Menotti	UFPR - DInf, Panama
Diego Sebastián Comas	UNMDP, Argentina
Enrique Vidal	Universitat Politècnica de València, Spain
Ethem Alpaydin	Bogazici University, Turkey
Fernando Monteiro	Polytechnic Institute of Bragança, Portugal
Filiberto Pla	University Jaume I, Spain
Filip Malmberg	Uppsala University, Sweden
Francesc J. Ferri	University of Valencia, Spain
Francisco Casacuberta	Universitat Politècnica de València, Spain
Francisco Herrera	University of Granada, Spain
German Castellanos	Universidad Nacional de Colombia, Colombia
Giorgio Fumera	University of Cagliari, Italy
Helio Lopes	PUC-RIo, Brazil
Hugo Jair Escalante	INAOE, Mexico
Hugo Proença	University of Beira Interior, Portugal
Ignacio Ponzoni	UNS - CONICET, Argentina
Jacques Facon	Pontifícia Universidade Católica do Paraná, Brazil
Jaime Cardoso	University of Porto, Portugal
Jesus Ariel Carrasco-Ochoa	INAOE, Mexico
Johan Prueba	Centro de Investigacion en Matematicas, Spain
Jordi Vitria	CVC, Spain
Jorge Calvo-Zaragoza	University of Alicante, Spain
Jorge S. Marques	IST/ISR, Portugal
Jose Garcia-Rodriguez	University of Alicante, Spain
Jose Miguel Benedi	Universitat Politècnica de València, Spain
Jose Salvador Sanchez	Universitat Jaume I, Spain
Jose Silvestre Silva	Academia Militar, Spain
João Carlos Neves	IT - Instituto de Telecomunicações, Portugal
João M. F. Rodrigues	Universidade do Algarve, Portugal
Juan Valentín Lorenzo-Ginori	Universidad Central Marta Abreu de Las Villas, Cuba
Kalman Palagyi	University of Szeged, Hungary
Laurent Heutte	Université de Rouen, France
Lawrence O'Gorman	Alcatel-Lucent Bell Labs, USA
Lev Goldfarb	Faculty of CS, UNB, Canada
Luis-Carlos González-Gurrola	Universidad Autonoma de Chihuahua, Mexico

Abstracts of Invited Tutorials

Machine Learning with Scikit-Learn

Gaël Varoquaux

Parietal, Inria, Inria Saclay Île-De-France, Palaiseau, France

Abstract. This tutorial briefly covered how to do machine learning with scikit-learn. The presenter did not go into detail, but rather tried to give pointers to important aspects of the software as well as key concepts in machine learning.

Computer Vision for Affective Computing

Agata Lapedriza Garcia

Universitat Oberta de Catalunya, Barcelona, Spain

Abstract. Over the past decade we have observed an increasing interest in developing technologies for automatic emotion recognition. The capacity of automatically recognizing emotions has many applications in environments where machines need to interact and collaborate with humans. However, how can machines recognize emotions? In this tutorial we gave an introduction to affective computing (also known as emotional artificial intelligence), the discipline that studies and develops systems and devices that can recognize, interpret, process, or simulate emotions or feelings. After a general introduction to affective computing, we focused on techniques for emotion recognition, paying special attention to the problem of emotion recognition from images. We reviewed some research on emotion recognition based on face and body analysis and we discussed the importance of analyzing scenes and context, in addition to faces, in order to better recognize emotions. In particular, we showed how emotion recognition can be approached from a scene understanding perspective.

Bayesian Optimization

Daniel Hernandez-Lobato

Universidad Autonoma de Madrid, Spain

Abstract. Many optimization problems are characterized by an objective function that is very expensive to evaluate. More precisely, the evaluation may involve carrying out a time-consuming experiment. This also means that the objective may lack a closed-form expression and, moreover, that the evaluation process can be noisy. That is, two measurements of the objective function at the same input location can give different results. Examples of these problems include tuning the hyper-parameters of a deep neural network, adjusting the parameters of the control system of a robot, or finding new materials for, e.g., solar energy production. Standard optimization methods give sub-optimal results when tackling this type of problem. In this tutorial, I presented a general overview of Bayesian optimization (BO), a collection of methods that can be used to efficiently solve problems with the characteristics described. For this, BO methods fit, at each iteration, a probabilistic model to the observations of the objective function. This model is typically a Gaussian process whose predictive distribution captures the potential values of the objective in regions of the space in which there are no observations. This uncertainty is then used to build an acquisition function whose maximum indicates where to perform the next evaluation of the objective with the goal of solving the problem in the smallest number of steps. Because the acquisition function only depends on the probabilistic model and not on the actual objective, it can be cheaply optimized. Therefore, BO methods make, at each iteration, intelligent decisions about where to evaluate the objective next. This can save a lot of computational time. In this tutorial, I explained in detail each of the steps performed by BO methods and, focusing on information theory-based methods, I also describe some extensions to address problems dealing with multiple evaluations in parallel, and multiple constraints and/or objectives. I conclude with a description of BO software, open problems, and future research directions in the field. The tutorial was followed by an afternoon session in which some of the concepts and methods described were put in practice. More precisely, BO software was used for tuning the hyper-parameters of machine learning algorithms.

Abstracts of Invited Talks

Building Computer Vision Systems that Really Work

Andrew Fitzgibbon

Microsoft, Cambridge, UK

Abstract. I have been shipping advanced computer vision systems for two decades. In 1999, prize-winning research from Oxford University was spun out to become the Emmy-award-winning camera tracker "boujou," which has been used to insert computer graphics into live-action footage in pretty much every movie made since its release, from the "Harry Potter" series to "Bridget Jones's Diary." In 2007, I was part of the team that delivered human body tracking in Kinect for Xbox 360, and in 2015 I moved from Microsoft Research to the Windows division to work on Microsoft's HoloLens, an AR headset brimming with cutting-edge computer vision technology.

In all of these projects, the academic state of the art has had to be leapfrogged in accuracy and efficiency, sometimes by several orders of magnitude. Sometimes that is just raw engineering, sometimes it means completely new ways of looking at the research. I talked about this interplay, between mathematics and code, and showed how each helps to understand the other. If I had to nominate one key to success, it would be a focus on, well, everything: from cache misses to end-to-end experience, and on always being willing to change one's mind.

Face Analysis for Multimodal Emotional Interfaces

Matti Pietikäinen

University of Oulu, Finland

Abstract. Emotions are central for human intelligence, and should have a similar role in artificial intelligence. There is a growing need to develop multimodal emotional interfaces, which are able to read the emotions of people and adapt their operations accordingly. Among the areas of application are emotional chatbots, personal assistants, human–robot interaction, emotion-aware games, health and medicine, on-line learning, safe car driving, security, and user/customer experience analysis. Facial image analysis will play a key role in developing emotionally intelligent systems. In this talk, first an introduction to emotions, face information, and applications of emotion analysis was presented. Then, highlights of our recent research on facial image analysis were introduced, including methods for image and video description, face and facial (micro-)expression recognition, and heart-rate measurement from face videos. Some examples of multimodal emotion analysis were presented. Finally, future challenges for building multimodal emotional interfaces were discussed.

Fun with Human–Machine Collaboration for Computer Vision

Vittorio Ferrari

Google, Zurich, Switzerland

Abstract. Training computer vision models typically requires tedious and time-consuming manual annotation, which hinders scaling, especially for complex tasks such as full image segmentation. In this talk, I presented recent human–machine collaboration techniques from my team, where the machine assists a human in annotating the training data and training a new model. These can substantially reduce human effort and also yield more interesting interfaces to interact with. The talk explored several cases, including segmentation of individual objects, joint segmentation of all objects and background regions in an image, using speech together with mouse inputs, and annotating object classes using free-form text written by undirected annotators.

Towards Human Behavior Modeling from (Big) Mobile Data

Nuria Oliver

Vodafone, Barcelona, Spain

Abstract. Human Behavior Modeling and Understanding is a key challenge in the development of intelligent systems and a great asset to help us make better decisions. Over the course of the past 23 years, I have worked on building automatic data-driven machine-learning based models of human behaviors for a variety of applications, including smart rooms, smart cars, smart offices, smart mobile phones, and smart cities.

In this talk, I described three such projects. The first project is a smartphone app to automatically detect boredom. This project received the best paper award at Ubicomp 2015. The second project, MobiScore, tackles the challenge of financial inclusion by building machine-learning-based models of credit scoring from mobile network data. MobiScore enables people who do not have a bank account and hence are excluded from the financial system to get access to credit. Finally, the third project focuses on automatically detecting crime hotspots in a city through the analysis of mobile data.

Contents – Part I

Best Ranked Papers

Towards a Joint Approach to Produce Decisions and Explanations
Using CNNs. 3
   Isabel Rio-Torto, Kelwin Fernandes, and Luís F. Teixeira

Interactive-Predictive Neural Multimodal Systems 16
   Álvaro Peris and Francisco Casacuberta

Uncertainty Estimation for Black-Box Classification Models: A Use Case
for Sentiment Analysis. 29
   José Mena, Axel Brando, Oriol Pujol, and Jordi Vitrià

Impact of Ultrasound Image Reconstruction Method on Breast Lesion
Classification with Deep Learning. 41
   Michal Byra, Tomasz Sznajder, Danijel Korzinek,
   Hanna Piotrzkowska-Wroblewska, Katarzyna Dobruch-Sobczak,
   Andrzej Nowicki, and Krzysztof Marasek

Segmentation of Cell Nuclei in Fluorescence Microscopy Images
Using Deep Learning. 53
   Hemaxi Narotamo, J. Miguel Sanches, and Margarida Silveira

Food Recognition by Integrating Local and Flat Classifiers 65
   Eduardo Aguilar and Petia Radeva

Machine Learning

Combining Online Clustering and Rank Pooling Dynamics
for Action Proposals 77
   Nadjia Khatir, Roberto J. López-Sastre, Marcos Baptista-Ríos,
   Safia Nait-Bahloul, and Francisco Javier Acevedo-Rodríguez

On the Direction Guidance in Structure Tensor Total Variation
Based Denoising. 89
   Ezgi Demircan-Tureyen and Mustafa E. Kamasak

Impact of Fused Visible-Infrared Video Streams on Visual Tracking 101
   Stéphane Vujasinović, Stefan Becker, Norbert Scherer-Negenborn,
   and Michael Arens

Model Based Recursive Partitioning for Customized Price
Optimization Analytics   113
  Jorge M. Arevalillo

3D Reconstruction of Archaeological Pottery from Its Point Cloud   125
  Wilson Sakpere

Geometric Interpretation of CNNs' Last Layer   137
  Alejandro de la Calle, Javier Tovar, and Emilio J. Almazán

Re-Weighted ℓ_1 Algorithms within the Lagrange Duality Framework:
Bringing Interpretability to Weights.   148
  Matías Valdés and Marcelo Fiori

A Note on Gradient-Based Intensity Normalization   161
  Manuel G. Forero, Carlos Arias-Rubio,
  José de Anchieta C. Horta-Júnior, and Dolores E. López

Blind Robust 3-D Mesh Watermarking Based on Mesh Saliency
and QIM Quantization for Copyright Protection   170
  Mohamed Hamidi, Aladine Chetouani, Mohamed El Haziti,
  Mohammed El Hassouni, and Hocine Cherifi

Using Copies to Remove Sensitive Data: A Case Study on Fair Superhero
Alignment Prediction.   182
  Irene Unceta, Jordi Nin, and Oriol Pujol

Weighted Multisource Tradaboost   194
  João Antunes, Alexandre Bernardino, Asim Smailagic,
  and Daniel Siewiorek

A Proposal of Neural Networks with Intermediate Outputs   206
  Billy Peralta, Juan Reyes, Luis Caro, and Christian Pieringer

Addressing the Big Data Multi-class Imbalance Problem
with Oversampling and Deep Learning Neural Networks   216
  V. M. González-Barcenas, E. Rendón, R. Alejo, E. E. Granda-Gutiérrez,
  and R. M. Valdovinos

Reinforcement Learning and Neuroevolution in Flappy Bird Game   225
  André Brandão, Pedro Pires, and Petia Georgieva

Pattern Recognition

Description and Recognition of Activity Patterns Using Sparse
Vector Fields   239
  Ana Portêlo, Andrea Cavallaro, Catarina Barata, and Jorge S. Marques

Instance Selection for the Nearest Neighbor Classifier:
Connecting the Performance to the Underlying Data Structure   249
    Vicente García, Josep Salvador Sánchez, Alberto Ochoa-Ortiz,
    and Abraham López-Najera

Modified DBSCAN Algorithm for Microscopic Image Analysis of Wood . . .   257
    Aurora L. R. Martins, André R. S. Marcal, and José Pissarra

Automatic Detection of Tuberculosis Bacilli from Microscopic Sputum
Smear Images Using Faster R-CNN, Transfer Learning and Augmentation. . .   270
    Moumen El-Melegy, Doaa Mohamed, and Tarek ElMelegy

Detection of Stone Circles in Periglacial Regions of Antarctica
in UAV Datasets.   279
    Pedro Pina, Francisco Pereira, Jorge S. Marques, and Sandra Heleno

Lesion Detection in Breast Ultrasound Images Using a Machine Learning
Approach and Genetic Optimization   289
    Fabian Torres, Boris Escalante-Ramirez, Jimena Olveres,
    and Ping-Lang Yen

Evaluating the Impact of Color Information in Deep Neural Networks.   302
    Vanessa Buhrmester, David Münch, Dimitri Bulatov, and Michael Arens

Diatom Classification Including Morphological Adaptations Using CNNs . . .   317
    Carlos Sánchez, Noelia Vállez, Gloria Bueno, and Gabriel Cristóbal

Deep Learning of Visual and Textual Data for Region Detection Applied
to Item Coding.   329
    Roberto Arroyo, Javier Tovar, Francisco J. Delgado, Emilio J. Almazán,
    Diego G. Serrador, and Antonio Hurtado

Deep Learning Versus Classic Methods for Multi-taxon
Diatom Segmentation   342
    Jesús Ruiz-Santaquitaria, Anibal Pedraza, Carlos Sánchez,
    José A. Libreros, Jesús Salido, Oscar Deniz, Saúl Blanco,
    Gabriel Cristóbal, and Gloria Bueno

Estimation of Sulfonamides Concentration in Water Based
on Digital Colourimetry.   355
    Pedro H. Carvalho, Sílvia Bessa, Ana Rosa M. Silva, Patrícia S. Peixoto,
    Marcela A. Segundo, and Hélder P. Oliveira

Characterization of Cardiac and Respiratory System of Healthy Subjects
in Supine and Sitting Position.   367
    Angel D. Ruiz, Juan S. Mejía, Juan M. López, and Beatriz F. Giraldo

Automatic Fault Detection in a Cascaded Transformer Multilevel Inverter
Using Pattern Recognition Techniques.............................. 378
   Diego Salazar-D'antonio, Nohora Meneses-Casas, Manuel G. Forero,
   and Oswaldo López-Santos

Collision Anticipation via Deep Reinforcement Learning
for Visual Navigation 386
   Eduardo Gutiérrez-Maestro, Roberto J. López-Sastre,
   and Saturnino Maldonado-Bascón

Spectral Band Subset Selection for Discrimination of Healthy Skin
and Cutaneous Leishmanial Ulcers 398
   Ricardo Franco-Ceballos, Maria C. Torres-Madronero,
   July Galeano-Zea, Javier Murillo, Artur Zarzycki, Johnson Garzon,
   and Sara M. Robledo

Data Augmentation of Minority Class with Transfer Learning for
Classification of Imbalanced Breast Cancer Dataset Using Inception-V3..... 409
   Manisha Saini and Seba Susan

Image Processing and Representation

Single View Facial Hair 3D Reconstruction 423
   Gemma Rotger, Francesc Moreno-Noguer, Felipe Lumbreras,
   and Antonio Agudo

From Features to Attribute Graphs for Point Set Registration 437
   Carlos Orrite, Elias Herrero, and Mauricio Valencia

BELID: Boosted Efficient Local Image Descriptor 449
   Iago Suárez, Ghesn Sfeir, José M. Buenaposada, and Luis Baumela

A Novel Graph-Based Approach for Seriation of Mouse Brain
Cross-Section from Images...................................... 461
   S. Sarbazvatan, R. Ventura, F. F. Esteves, S. Q. Lima, and J. M. Sanches

Class Reconstruction Driven Adversarial Domain Adaptation
for Hyperspectral Image Classification............................ 472
   Shivam Pande, Biplab Banerjee, and Aleksandra Pižurica

Multi-label Logo Classification Using Convolutional Neural Networks 485
   Antonio-Javier Gallego, Antonio Pertusa, and Marisa Bernabeu

Non-destructively Prediction of Quality Parameters of Dry-Cured Iberian
Ham by Applying Computer Vision and Low-Field MRI............... 498
   Juan Pedro Torres, Mar Ávila, Andrés Caro, Trinidad Pérez-Palacios,
   and Daniel Caballero

Personalised Aesthetics with Residual Adapters   508
Carlos Rodríguez-Pardo and Hakan Bilen

An Improvement for Capsule Networks Using Depthwise
Separable Convolution.   521
Nguyen Huu Phong and Bernardete Ribeiro

Wave Front Tracking in High Speed Videos Using a Dynamic
Template Matching   531
Samee Maharjan

An Efficient Binary Descriptor to Describe Retinal Bifurcation Point
for Image Registration   543
*Sarder Tazul Islam, Sajib Saha, G. M. Atiqur Rahaman, Deep Dutta,
and Yogesan Kanagasingam*

Aggregation of Deep Features for Image Retrieval Based
on Object Detection.   553
*Juan Ignacio Forcén, Miguel Pagola, Edurne Barrenechea,
and Humberto Bustince*

Impact of Pre-Processing on Recognition of Cursive Video Text.   565
Ali Mirza, Imran Siddiqi, Syed Ghulam Mustufa, and Mazahir Hussain

Image Feature Detection Based on Phase Congruency by Monogenic Filters
with New Noise Estimation   577
*Carlos Jacanamejoy Jamioy, Nohora Meneses-Casas,
and Manuel G. Forero*

Texture Classification Using Capsule Networks   589
*Bharat Mamidibathula, Satakarni Amirneni, Sai Shravani Sistla,
and Niharika Patnam*

Automatic Vision Based Calibration System for Planar Cable-Driven
Parallel Robots   600
*Andrés García-Vanegas, Brhayan Liberato-Tafur,
Manuel Guillermo Forero, Antonio Gonzalez-Rodríguez,
and Fernando Castillo-García*

3D Non-rigid Registration of Deformable Object Using GPU   610
Junesuk Lee, Eung-su Kim, and Soon-Yong Park

Focus Estimation in Academic Environments Using Computer Vision   620
Daniel Canedo, Alina Trifan, and António J. R. Neves

Author Index   629

Contents – Part II

Biometrics

What Is the Role of Annotations in the Detection
of Dermoscopic Structures? 3
   Bárbara Ferreira, Catarina Barata, and Jorge S. Marques

Keystroke Mobile Authentication: Performance of Long-Term Approaches
and Fusion with Behavioral Profiling. 12
   Alejandro Acien, Aythami Morales, Ruben Vera-Rodriguez,
   and Julian Fierrez

Incremental Learning Techniques Within a Self-updating Approach
for Face Verification in Video-Surveillance 25
   Eric Lopez-Lopez, Carlos V. Regueiro, Xosé M. Pardo,
   Annalisa Franco, and Alessandra Lumini

Don't You Forget About Me: A Study on Long-Term Performance
in ECG Biometrics 38
   Gabriel Lopes, João Ribeiro Pinto, and Jaime S. Cardoso

Face Identification Using Local Ternary Tree Pattern Based Spatial
Structural Components. 50
   Rinku Datta Rakshit, Dakshina Ranjan Kisku, Massimo Tistarelli,
   and Phalguni Gupta

Catastrophic Interference in Disguised Face Recognition 64
   Parichehr B. Ardakani, Diego Velazquez, Josep M. Gonfaus,
   Pau Rodríguez, F. Xavier Roca, and Jordi Gonzàlez

Iris Center Localization Using Geodesic Distance and CNN 76
   Radovan Fusek and Eduard Sojka

Low-Light Face Image Enhancement Based on Dynamic Face
Part Selection 86
   Adel Oulefki, Mustapha Aouache, and Messaoud Bengherabi

Retinal Blood Vessel Segmentation: A Semi-supervised Approach 98
   Tanmai K. Ghosh, Sajib Saha, G. M. Atiqur Rahaman, Md. Abu Sayed,
   and Yogesan Kanagasingam

Quality-Based Pulse Estimation from NIR Face Video with Application
to Driver Monitoring   108
  Javier Hernandez-Ortega, Shigenori Nagae, Julian Fierrez,
  and Aythami Morales

Handwriting and Document Analysis

Multi-task Layout Analysis of Handwritten Musical Scores   123
  Lorenzo Quirós, Alejandro H. Toselli, and Enrique Vidal

Domain Adaptation for Handwritten Symbol Recognition: A Case of Study
in Old Music Manuscripts   135
  Tudor N. Mateiu, Antonio-Javier Gallego, and Jorge Calvo-Zaragoza

Approaching End-to-End Optical Music Recognition
for Homophonic Scores   147
  María Alfaro-Contreras, Jorge Calvo-Zaragoza, and José M. Iñesta

Glyph and Position Classification of Music Symbols
in Early Music Manuscripts   159
  Alicia Nuñez-Alcover, Pedro J. Ponce de León,
  and Jorge Calvo-Zaragoza

Recognition of Arabic Handwritten Literal Amounts Using Deep
Convolutional Neural Networks   169
  Moumen El-Melegy, Asmaa Abdelbaset, Alaa Abdel-Hakim,
  and Gamal El-Sayed

Offline Signature Verification Using Textural Descriptors   177
  Ismail Hadjadj, Abdeljalil Gattal, Chawki Djeddi, Mouloud Ayad, Imran
  Siddiqi, and Faycel Abass

Pencil Drawing of Microscopic Images Through Edge
Preserving Filtering   189
  Harbinder Singh, Carlos Sánchez, Gabriel Cristóbal, and Gloria Bueno

Line Segmentation Free Probabilistic Keyword Spotting and Indexing   201
  Killian Barrere, Alejandro H. Toselli, and Enrique Vidal

Other Applications

Incremental Learning for Football Match Outcomes Prediction   217
  José Domingues, Bernardo Lopes, Petya Mihaylova,
  and Petia Georgieva

Frame by Frame Pain Estimation Using Locally Spatial
Attention Learning   229
  Jun Yu, Toru Kurihara, and Shu Zhan

Mosquito Larvae Image Classification Based on DenseNet and Guided
Grad-CAM.   239
  Zaira García, Keiji Yanai, Mariko Nakano, Antonio Arista,
  Laura Cleofas Sanchez, and Hector Perez

Towards Automatic Rat's Gait Analysis Under Suboptimal
Illumination Conditions   247
  Ana F. Adonias, Joana Ferreira-Gomes, Raquel Alonso, Fani Neto,
  and Jaime S. Cardoso

Impact of Enhancement for Coronary Artery Segmentation Based on Deep
Learning Neural Network.   260
  Ahmed Ghazi Blaiech, Asma Mansour, Asma Kerkeni,
  Mohamed Hédi Bedoui, and Asma Ben Abdallah

Real-Time Traffic Monitoring with Occlusion Handling.   273
  Mauro Fernández-Sanjurjo, Manuel Mucientes, and Víctor M. Brea

Image Based Estimation of Fruit Phytopathogenic Lesions Area   285
  André R. S. Marcal, Elisabete M. D. S. Santos, and Fernando Tavares

A Weakly-Supervised Approach for Discovering Common Objects
in Airport Video Surveillance Footage.   296
  Francisco Manuel Castro, Rubén Delgado-Escaño, Nicolás Guil,
  and Manuel Jesús Marín-Jiménez

Standard Plenoptic Camera Calibration for a Range of Zoom
and Focus Levels   309
  Nuno Barroso Monteiro and José António Gaspar

Going Back to Basics on Volumetric Segmentation of the Lungs in CT:
A Fully Image Processing Based Technique.   322
  Ana Catarina Oliveira, Inês Domingues, Hugo Duarte, João Santos,
  and Pedro H. Abreu

Radiogenomics: Lung Cancer-Related Genes Mutation Status Prediction   335
  Catarina Dias, Gil Pinheiro, António Cunha, and Hélder P. Oliveira

Learning to Perform Visual Tasks from Human Demonstrations   346
  Afonso Nunes, Rui Figueiredo, and Plinio Moreno

Serious Game Controlled by a Human-Computer Interface for Upper Limb
Motor Rehabilitation: A Feasibility Study.   359
  *Sergio David Pulido, Álvaro José Bocanegra, Sandra Liliana Cancino,
  and Juan Manuel López*

Weapon Detection for Particular Scenarios Using Deep Learning   371
  *Noelia Vallez, Alberto Velasco-Mata, Juan Jose Corroto,
  and Oscar Deniz*

Hierarchical Deep Learning Approach for Plant Disease Detection   383
  Joana Costa, Catarina Silva, and Bernardete Ribeiro

An Artificial Vision Based Method for Vehicle Detection and Classification
in Urban Traffic   394
  Camilo Camacho, César Pedraza, and Carolina Higuera

Breaking Text-Based CAPTCHA with Sparse Convolutional
Neural Networks.   404
  *Diogo Daniel Ferreira, Luís Leira, Petya Mihaylova,
  and Petia Georgieva*

Image Processing Method for Epidermal Cells Detection and Measurement
in *Arabidopsis Thaliana* Leaves   416
  *Manuel G. Forero, Sammy A. Perdomo, Mauricio A. Quimbaya,
  and Guillermo F. Perez*

User Modeling on Mobile Device Based on Facial Clustering and Object
Detection in Photos and Videos   429
  Ivan Grechikhin and Andrey V. Savchenko

Gun and Knife Detection Based on Faster R-CNN for Video Surveillance . . .   441
  M. Milagro Fernandez-Carrobles, Oscar Deniz, and Fernando Maroto

A Method for the Evaluation and Classification of the Orange Peel Effect
on Painted Injection Moulded Part Surfaces   453
  Atae Jafari-Tabrizi, Hannah Luise Lichtenegger, and Dieter P. Gruber

A New Automatic Cancer Colony Forming Units Counting Method   465
  *Nicolás Roldán, Lizeth Rodriguez, Andrea Hernandez, Karen Cepeda,
  Alejandro Ondo-Méndez, Sandra Liliana Cancino Suárez,
  Manuel G. Forero, and Juan M. Lopéz*

Deep Vesselness Measure from Scale-Space Analysis of Hessian
Matrix Eigenvalues   473
  Ricardo J. Araújo, Jaime S. Cardoso, and Hélder P. Oliveira

Segmentation in Corridor Environments:
Combining Floor and Ceiling Detection   485
    Sergio Lafuente-Arroyo, Saturnino Maldonado-Bascón,
    Hilario Gómez-Moreno, and Cristina Alén-Cordero

Development of a Fire Detection Based on the Analysis of Video Data
by Means of Convolutional Neural Networks   497
    Jan Lehr, Christian Gerson, Mohamad Ajami, and Jörg Krüger

Towards Automatic and Robust Particle Tracking
in Microrheology Studies   508
    Marina Castro, Ricardo J. Araújo, Laura Campo-Deaño,
    and Hélder P. Oliveira

Study of the Impact of Pre-processing Applied to Images Acquired
by the Cygno Experiment.   520
    G. S. P. Lopes, E. Baracchini, F. Bellini, L. Benussi, S. Bianco,
    G. Cavoto, I. A. Costa, E. Di Marco, G. Maccarrone, M. Marafini,
    G. Mazzitelli, A. Messina, R. A. Nobrega, D. Piccolo, D. Pinci, F. Renga,
    F. Rosatelli, D. M. Souza, and S. Tomassini

Author Index   531

Best Ranked Papers

Towards a Joint Approach to Produce Decisions and Explanations Using CNNs

Isabel Rio-Torto[1]([✉]), Kelwin Fernandes[3], and Luís F. Teixeira[1,2]

[1] Faculdade de Engenharia da Universidade do Porto, Porto, Portugal
icrtto@gmail.com, luisft@fe.up.pt
[2] INESC TEC, Porto, Portugal
[3] NILG.AI, Porto, Portugal
kelwin@nilg.ai

Abstract. Convolutional Neural Networks, as well as other deep learning methods, have shown remarkable performance on tasks like classification and detection. However, these models largely remain black-boxes. With the widespread use of such networks in real-world scenarios and with the growing demand of the right to explanation, especially in highly-regulated areas like medicine and criminal justice, generating accurate predictions is no longer enough. Machine learning models have to be explainable, i.e., understandable to humans, which entails being able to present the reasons behind their decisions. While most of the literature focuses on post-model methods, we propose an in-model CNN architecture, composed by an explainer and a classifier. The model is trained end-to-end, with the classifier taking as input not only images from the dataset but also the explainer's resulting explanation, thus allowing for the classifier to focus on the relevant areas of such explanation. We also developed a synthetic dataset generation framework, that allows for automatic annotation and creation of easy-to-understand images that do not require the knowledge of an expert to be explained. Promising results were obtained, especially when using L1 regularisation, validating the potential of the proposed architecture and further encouraging research to improve the proposed architecture's explainability and performance.

Keywords: Explainable AI · Explainability · Interpretability · Deep learning · Convolutional Neural Networks

1 Introduction

Deep learning changed the machine learning paradigm in recent years, significantly improving performance on tasks like classification, sometimes even outperforming humans. Due to the achieved outstanding predictive capability, deep learning methods have since been employed in tackling other problems, such

---

This work was partially funded by NILG.AI.

A. Morales et al. (Eds.): IbPRIA 2019, LNCS 11867, pp. 3–15, 2019.
https://doi.org/10.1007/978-3-030-31332-6_1

as detection and segmentation, surpassing the performance of classical machine learning models also on these tasks.

Despite this overwhelming dominance, deep learning models, and in particular convolutional neural networks (CNNs), are still considered black-box models, i.e., models whose reasons for the outputted decisions cannot be understood at a human-level. However, with the growing ubiquitousness of deep learning systems, especially in highly regulated areas such as medicine, criminal justice or financial markets [6], an increasing need for these models to output explanations in addition to decisions is arising. Moreover, the new General Data Protection Regulation (GDPR) includes policies on the right to explanation [5], thus increasing this need for explainable deep learning systems that can operate within this legal framework.

The research community has rapidly taken an interest in this topic, proposing several methods that try to meet this explainability requirement. Nevertheless, the field is still lacking a unified formal definition or possible evaluation metrics. The terms explainability and interpretability are often used interchangeably in the literature. In this work, we adopt the definition proposed by Gilpin et al. [4]. The authors loosely define interpretability as the process of understanding the model's internals and describing them in a way that is understandable to humans, while explainability goes beyond that. Briefly, an explainable model is one that can summarise the reasons for its behaviour or the causes of its decisions. In fact, for a model to be explainable, it needs to be interpretable, but also complete, i.e., to describe the system's internals accurately. As such, explainable models are interpretable by default, while the reverse may not be true. Therefore, a good explanation should be able to balance the interpretability-completeness trade-off, because the more accurate an explanation, the less interpretable it is to humans; for example, an entirely complete explanation of a neural network would consist of all the operations, parameters and hyperparameters of such network, rendering it uninterpretable. Conversely, the most interpretable description is often incomplete.

The majority of the literature focuses only on interpretability, and more specifically on post-model or post-hoc interpretability methods, i.e. methods that are applied after the model is trained. Examples range from proxy methods that approximate the original network model [9] to methods that output visual cues representing what the network is focusing on to make its decisions, such as Sensitivity Analysis and Saliency Maps [8], SmoothGrad [10], DeConvNet [17] or Layer-Wise Relevance Propagation [2].

While a few works focus on in-model approaches, in which interpretability is taken into account while building the model, these are for the most part application oriented. Some work has been developed trying to make predictions based only on patches of the input images, which limits the interpretability of the classifier. Although such in-model methods exist for models such as CNNs [11, 12], these are still not considered intrinsically interpretable, making this category still dominated by classic methods like decision trees.

In this work, we propose a preliminary end-to-end in-model approach, based on an explainer+classifier architecture. This architecture outputs not only a class label, but also a visual explanation of such decision. The classifier takes as input an image, as well as the output of the explainer, i.e. it is trained using the explanation. Therefore, the classifier focuses on the regions the explainer deemed relevant and does not take into account regions where the explanation for that class is not present. This approach aligns with the intuition that, when explaining a decision, for example, whether or not image X is an image of a car, humans tend to distinguish what is an object and what is not, and then proceed to look for patterns in the region where the object is in order to classify it correctly. Conversely, sometimes humans cannot tell if an object belongs to some class, but can tell which regions of the image do not contain said class.

We also propose a synthetic dataset generation framework, allowing for automatic image generation and annotation. The generated images consist of simple polygons, therefore easily explainable by humans, which allows for a qualitative and quantitative evaluation of the produced explanations without the need of expert knowledge, necessary in most real-world datasets.

2   Methodology

2.1   Proposed Architecture

We propose a model consisting of an explainer and a classifier, as depicted in Fig. 1. Figure 2 depicts a detailed diagram of the proposed architecture, which is a concretisation of the aforementioned model. The explainer (top row) outputs an image, which we call the explanation, with the same spatial dimensions as the input image. It is composed of a downsampling and an upsampling path. The downsampling path is a simple convolution-convolution-pooling scheme. The upsampling path follows a convolution-convolution-deconvolution scheme, where the first convolution operation is applied to the sum of the previous layer's output with the corresponding convolutional layer in the downsampling path. These connections allow for the successive layer to learn a more precise output. Also, batch normalisation is applied to the last layer of the explainer.

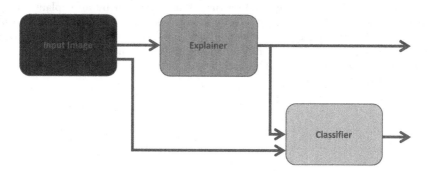

Fig. 1. Block diagram of the proposed explainer+classifier model.

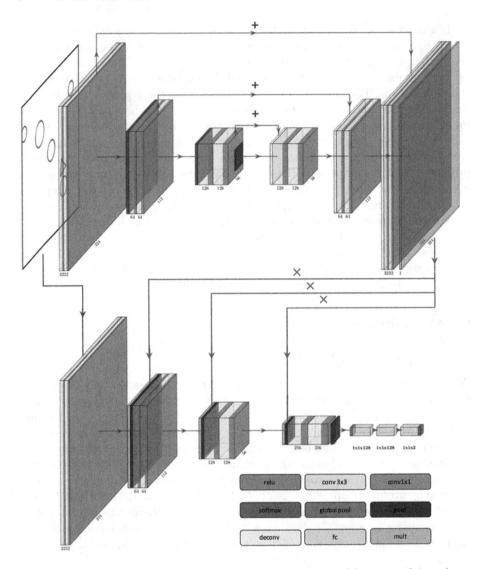

Fig. 2. Diagram of the proposed architecture. It is composed by an explainer (top row) and a classifier (bottom row). The sums correspond to the simple addition of the outputs of the respective layers. The multiplications involve the concatenation and resizing of the explainer's output before computing the element-wise multiplication with the involved classifier layer. This architecture outputs a class label, as well as an explanation for that decision.

The classifier (bottom row) is inspired by the VGG architecture [13], having 4 consecutive convolution-convolution-pool stages, ending with 2 fully connected layers, followed by a softmax layer. However, an important modification to the original VGG is made: each pooling layer takes as input the multiplication of the output of its preceding layer with the output of the explainer. This way, the classifier is trained using the outputted explanation, allowing for it to focus on the relevant parts of the input image and to discard regions where the explanation for the class being predicted is not present.

In both classifier and explainer, 3×3 kernels are used in the convolutional layers. All pooling operations resort to max pooling, downsampling by a factor of 2. The number of filters starts at 32 for the first stage and afterwards increases as a power of 2 according to its stage level.

Training involves three steps. First, only the classifier is trained, taking a "white image" as explanation, meaning that the initial explanation is the whole image. Then the explainer is trained with the classifier frozen, outputting an explanation that highlights relevant areas to the classification task. Finally, the whole architecture is fine-tuned end to end.

While the explainer is trained unsupervised, the classifier is trained using the categorical cross-entropy loss. The Keras Adadelta default optimizer was used, which employs an adaptive learning rate based on a moving window of gradient updates [16].

2.2 Synthetic Dataset

For the experimental assessment of the proposed architecture, a synthetic dataset generation framework was developed. The use of a synthetic dataset entails numerous advantages, such as:

- the ability to generate as many images as one needs
- the possibility of defining the number of instances for each class
- automatic annotation for different problems ranging from classification to detection
- definition of custom-made characteristics like overlap, occlusion, object type, object colour, image dimensions, etc.

This framework generates images consisting of several polygons, such as triangles, circles and stars. Examples of such images can be observed in Fig. 3. Moreover, for each image, an XML annotation file in PASCAL VOC format is created, containing information on how many target polygons exist in the image and their respective bounding boxes. The developed code is available at https://github.com/icrto/xML.

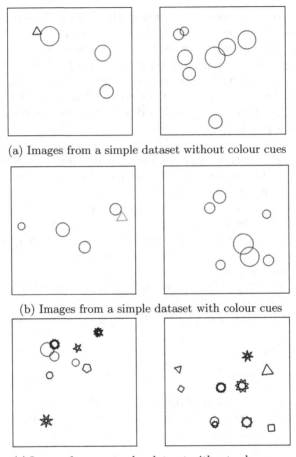

(a) Images from a simple dataset without colour cues

(b) Images from a simple dataset with colour cues

(c) Images from a complex dataset without colour cues

Fig. 3. Example images of 3 generated datasets. For each row, the left column illustrates an example of the positive class, while the right column illustrates the negative class. On the first two rows the target polygon is a triangle, while on the third row it is a 5 pointed star.

2.3   Experiments

The synthetic dataset used in the experiments consists of 1000 224×224 RGB images, each containing a triangle (target polygon) and a variable number of circles. For each image it is only taken into account the presence or absence of the target polygon, thus making these experiments binary classification tasks. The positive class has 618 instances, while the remaining 382 instances belong to the negative class. The data was split into a 75–25 training-validation partition. Each of the three training phases involved 50 epochs with 50 steps each, with a batch size of 8. The classifier was evaluated in terms of its accuracy and the explainer was qualitatively evaluated, by means of human visual inspection.

All experiments were conducted on the Google Collaboratory environment and involved applying to the explainer different L1 regularisation factors, ranging from 10^{-8} to 10^{-4}. Without regularisation, one can obtain a degraded solution, in which everything is considered an explanation. Therefore, L1 regularisation is employed, so that only a small part of the whole image constitutes an explanation.

A qualitative and quantitative comparison of the proposed architecture with various methods available in the iNNvestigate toolbox [1] is also made. This toolbox aims to facilitate the comparison of reference implementations of post-model interpretability methods, by providing a common interface and out-of-the-box implementation of various analysis methods. The toolbox is, then, used to compare the proposed architecture with methods like SmoothGrad [14], DeconvNet [17], Guided Backprop [15], Deep Taylor Decomposition [7] or Layer-Wise Relevance Propagation (LRP) [2]. In the proposed architecture, the explainer is the component that produces a visual representation of the reasoning behind the classifier's decisions, just like the analysers available in the iNNvestigate toolbox. As such, these analysis methods are applied only to the classifier of the proposed architecture, in order to compare only the explanation generators, i.e. the proposed architecture's explainer and the different analysis methods. Since these methods are applied after the model is trained, we started by training the classifier on the simple dataset without colour cues. Then, the various analysis methods are applied to the trained classifier and their generated visual explanations are compared to the ones outputted by the explainer trained in the previous experiments with 10^{-6} L1 regularisation factor. Furthermore, the classifier's accuracy with and without explainer are also compared. The obtained results are described in Sect. 3.

2.4 Experiments on Real Datasets

Experiments were also conducted on a real dataset, available at https://github.com/rgeirhos/texture-vs-shape. This dataset was created in the context of the work developed by Geirhos et al. [3], where the authors validate that Imagenet-trained CNNs are biased towards texture. In order to validate this hypothesis, the authors propose a cue conflict experiment in which style transfer is employed, introducing texture in the Imagenet images. This dataset contains 16 classes, with 80 images each. The proposed architecture was trained on this dataset without any regularisation. Results for this experiment are shown in Sect. 3.

3   Results and Discussion

For all of the following images it is worth noting that the colour code ranges from purple to yellow, where yellow represents higher pixel values. The left column corresponds to the original image, the middle column to the outputted explanation and the right column to the explanation after an absolute threshold of 0.75 is applied.

Figure 4 constitutes examples of the obtained results for simple datasets with and without a target polygon of different colour. Both images are the result of training without any kind of regularisation. For such simple datasets, it is expected that the explanation focuses on the target polygon, rendering the rest of the image as irrelevant for the predicted class.

While on the dataset with colour cues the resulting explanation consists only of the target polygon, as expected, in the slightly more complex dataset without colour cues the whole image is considered an explanation, which corroborates the need for regularising the explainer output. As stated in Sect. 2.3, we use an L1 regularisation factor, because it allows for the selection of the relevant parts of the explanation, ensuring that only a small part of the image is in fact the explanation of the classifier's decision. Thus, this regularisation ensures that the explanation is not only interpretable, but also complete, as desired.

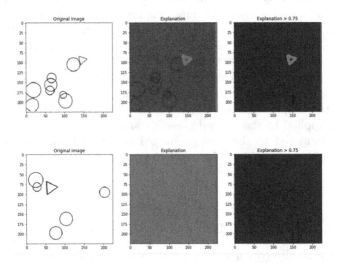

Fig. 4. Positive instance and respective explanation. These results were obtained without any kind of regularisation of the explainer's output while training on a simple dataset without (top) and with (bottom) colour cues

Figure 5 is the result of the experiments with different regularisation factors, namely 10^{-8}, 10^{-6} and 10^{-4}, on the dataset without colour cues. With a factor of 10^{-8}, not only the target polygon is considered relevant, as well as the circles, which may imply that such a small regularisation is still not enough to limit the relevant parts of the explanation. In fact, increasing L1 to 10^{-6}, produces much better results, with the target polygon clearly highlighted. Finally, increasing L1 a bit further, to 10^{-4}, proved to be too much regularisation, causing the explanation to "disappear".

Moreover, the proposed architecture was compared to several other methods available in the iNNvestigate framework [1]. As can be seen in Fig. 6, the majority of the methods are unable to produce reasonable explanations for the chosen

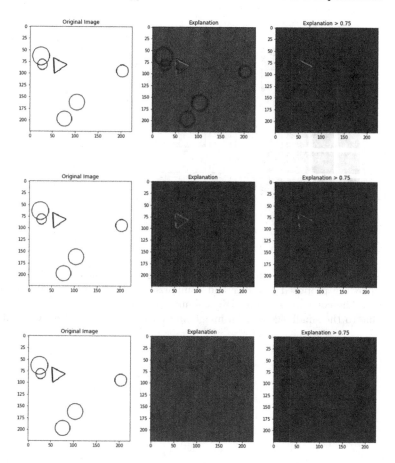

Fig. 5. Positive instance and respective explanation. These results were obtained with 10^{-8} (top), 10^{-6} (middle) and 10^{-4} (bottom) L1 regularisation of the explainer's output while training on a simple dataset without colour cues.

dataset, highlighting corners of the image, for example, while the proposed architecture is able to only highlight the relevant regions for the classifier's decision (see Fig. 5 middle). Furthermore, training only the classifier, as was done when applying the iNNvestigate toolbox's analysis methods, yields accuracies close to 62%, while the accuracy of the proposed architecture reaches 100%, as illustrated in Fig. 7. For this dataset, the proposed network not only produces explanations alongside with predictions, as well as improves accuracy, by forcing the classifier to focus only on relevant parts of the image.

Finally, Fig. 8 depicts the obtained results of the experiment on the cue conflict dataset. One can see that the generated explanations are oriented towards semantic components of the objects. For example, for the bottle case the explanations focus more on the neck of the bottle and on its label. In the car example, the explanation highlights the car's bumper and in the bicycle case, the handles

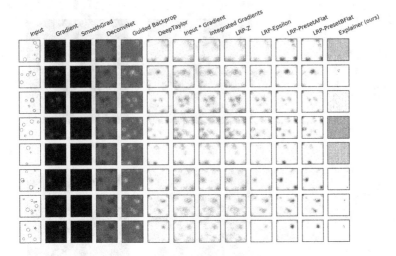

Fig. 6. Results of the application of 10 analysis methods available on the iNNvestigate toolbox [1] to the proposed classifier and comparison with the proposed end-to-end architecture. The color map of the right column's images was adjusted to help visualization due to the small size of each image and for easier comparison. (Color figure online)

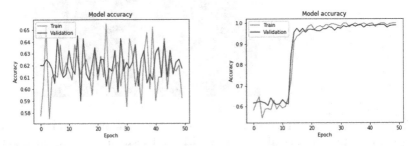

Fig. 7. Evolution of classifier accuracy per training epoch for the same classifier trained alone (left) and within the proposed explainer-classifier architecture (right).

and the seat are highlighted, while in the chair example the chair's legs are highlighted. It is worth noting that although the resulting explanations highlight different semantic components of the objects, they do not appear connected to each other (for example, the handle and the seat of the bicycle). This result hints that improving the quality of these explanations can be made by ensuring that explanations are sparse, i.e., cover a smaller part of the whole image, and also connected.

Fig. 8. Results of the cue conflict experiment.

4   Conclusion

We propose a preliminary in-model joint approach to produce decisions and explanations using CNNs, capable of producing not only interpretable explanations, but also complete ones, i.e., explanations that are able to describe the system's internals accurately. We also developed a synthetic dataset generation framework with automatic annotation.

The proposed architecture was tested with a simple generated synthetic dataset, for which explanations are intuitive and do not need to employ expert knowledge. Results show the potential of the proposed architecture, especially when compared to existing methods and when adding L1 regularisation. These also hint at the need for regularisation in order to better balance the interpretability-completeness trade off. As such, future research will study the effect of adding total variation regularisation as a way of making explanations sparse. Also, we will explore the possible advantages of supervising the explanations, as well as develop a proper annotation scheme and evaluation metrics for such task.

References

1. Alber, M., et al.: iNNvestigate neural networks! (2018)
2. Bach, S., Binder, A., Montavon, G., Klauschen, F., Müller, K.R., Samek, W.: On pixel-wise explanations for non-linear classifier decisions by layer-wise relevance propagation. PLoS One (2015). https://doi.org/10.1371/journal.pone.0130140
3. Geirhos, R., Rubisch, P., Michaelis, C., Bethge, M., Wichmann, F.A., Brendel, W.: ImageNet-trained CNNs are biased towards texture; increasing shape bias improves accuracy and robustness, November 2018. http://arxiv.org/abs/1811.12231
4. Gilpin, L.H., Bau, D., Yuan, B.Z., Bajwa, A., Specter, M., Kagal, L.: Explaining explanations: an overview of interpretability of machine learning. In: Proceedings of the 2018 IEEE 5th International Conference on Data Science and Advanced Analytics DSAA 2018, pp. 80–89 (2019). https://doi.org/10.1109/DSAA.2018.00018
5. Goodman, B., Flaxman, S.: European Union regulations on algorithmic decision-making and a "right to explanation", June 2016. https://doi.org/10.1609/aimag.v38i3.2741, https://arxiv.org/abs/1606.08813
6. Lipton, Z.C.: The Mythos of Model Interpretability (2016). https://doi.org/10.1145/3233231
7. Montavon, G., Lapuschkin, S., Binder, A., Samek, W., Müller, K.R.: Explaining nonlinear classification decisions with deep Taylor decomposition. Pattern Recognit. (2017). https://doi.org/10.1016/j.patcog.2016.11.008
8. Montavon, G., Samek, W., Müller, K.R.: Methods for interpreting and understanding deep neural networks. Digit. Signal Process. **73**, 1–15 (2018). https://doi.org/10.1016/J.DSP.2017.10.011. https://www.sciencedirect.com/science/article/pii/S1051200417302385
9. Ribeiro, M.T., Singh, S., Guestrin, C.: "Why Should I Trust You? Explaining the Predictions of Any Classifier, February 2016. http://arxiv.org/abs/1602.04938
10. Samek, W., Binder, A., Montavon, G., Lapuschkin, S., Müller, K.R.: Evaluating the visualization of what a deep neural network has learned. IEEE Trans. Neural Netw. Learn. Syst. **28**(11), 2660–2673 (2017)
11. Silva, W., Fernandes, K., Cardoso, J.S.: How to produce complementary explanations using an ensemble model. In: 2019 International Joint Conference on Neural Networks (IJCNN) (2019)

12. Silva, W., Fernandes, K., Cardoso, M.J., Cardoso, J.S.: Towards Complementary Explanations Using Deep Neural Networks (2018). https://doi.org/10.1007/978-3-030-02628-8_15
13. Simonyan, K., Zisserman, A.: Very deep convolutional networks for large-scale image recognition. arXiv preprint arXiv:1409.1556 (2014)
14. Smilkov, D., Thorat, N., Kim, B., Vi, F.: SmoothGrad: removing noise by adding noise (2017)
15. Springenberg, J.T., Dosovitskiy, A., Brox, T., Riedmiller, M.: Striving for Simplicity: The All Convolutional Net, December 2014. https://arxiv.org/abs/1412.6806
16. Zeiler, M.D.: ADADELTA: an adaptive learning rate method. arXiv preprint arXiv:1212.5701 (2012)
17. Zeiler, M.D., Fergus, R.: Visualizing and understanding convolutional networks. In: Fleet, D., Pajdla, T., Schiele, B., Tuytelaars, T. (eds.) ECCV 2014. LNCS, vol. 8689, pp. 818–833. Springer, Cham (2014). https://doi.org/10.1007/978-3-319-10590-1_53

Interactive-Predictive Neural Multimodal Systems

Álvaro Peris[(⊠)] and Francisco Casacuberta[(⊠)]

Pattern Recognition and Human Language Technology Research Center,
Universitat Politècnica de València, Valencia, Spain
{lvapeab,fcn}@prhlt.upv.es

Abstract. Despite the advances achieved by neural models in sequence to sequence learning, exploited in a variety of tasks, they still make errors. In many use cases, these are corrected by a human expert in a posterior revision process. The interactive-predictive framework aims to minimize the human effort spent on this process by considering partial corrections for iteratively refining the hypothesis. In this work, we generalize the interactive-predictive approach, typically applied in to machine translation field, to tackle other multimodal problems namely, image and video captioning. We study the application of this framework to multimodal neural sequence to sequence models. We show that, following this framework, we approximately halve the effort spent for correcting the outputs generated by the automatic systems. Moreover, we deploy our systems in a publicly accessible demonstration, that allows to better understand the behavior of the interactive-predictive framework.

Keywords: Interactive-predictive pattern recognition ·
Multimodal sequence to sequence learning · Deep learning

1 Introduction

The automatic prediction of structured objects is an extensively studied topic within the pattern recognition field. Many tasks involve the generation of a structured output, given an input object. As structure we understand a dependency across the elements of the object. Typical structured objects include sequences, trees or graphs. The application of neural networks to these problems has recently brought impressive advances. If both input and output objects are sequences, this problem is referred as sequence to sequence learning [9]. Many tasks can be posed as a sequence to sequence problem: machine translation [30],

The research leading to these results has received funding from MINECO under grant IDIFEDER/2018/025 "Sistemas de fabricación inteligentes para la industria 4.0", action co-funded by the European Regional Development Fund 2014–2020 (FEDER), and from the European Commission under grant H2020, reference 825111 (Deep-Health). We also acknowledge NVIDIA Corporation for the donation of GPUs used in this work.

A. Morales et al. (Eds.): IbPRIA 2019, LNCS 11867, pp. 16–28, 2019.
https://doi.org/10.1007/978-3-030-31332-6_2

speech recognition [5] or the automatic description of visual content, known as captioning [37,38].

Notwithstanding the important breakthroughs achieved in the last years, these automatic systems are far from being error-free [17]. However, they are useful for providing initial predictions, which are revised and corrected by a human expert. In some industries, such as machine translation, this revision procedure is widely used, as it increases the productivity with respect to performing the task from scratch [13]. This process is known as translation post-editing.

Nevertheless, this correction process can be improved in several ways. Aiming to increase the productivity of the system and seeking for a symbiotic human–computer collaboration, the so-called interactive-predictive pattern recognition was developed [3,8]. Under this paradigm, the user introduces a correction to the system prediction. Next, the system reacts to this feedback, offering a new prediction, expected to be better than the previous one, as the system has more information.

This interactive-predictive paradigm, initially devised for machine translation, can be extended to several tasks and technologies. In this work, we explore the application of this framework to several scenarios, which include data source from multiple modalities. In a nutshell, our main contributions are:

- We successfully apply the interactive-predictive protocol to the automatic captioning of image and videos and to the machine translation post-editing, using neural sequence to sequence models. To the best of our knowledge, this is the first work that delves into this topic.
- We conduct experiments on several datasets, using two common neural architectures: a recurrent neural network (RNN) with attention and a Transformer model.
- We deploy our system in a freely accessible demonstration website.
- We release all the code developed in this work, fostering the research on this topic.

The rest of the manuscript is structured as follows: in Sect. 2 we introduce the neural sequence to sequence modeling. Moreover, we describe the interactive-predictive pattern recognition framework and its implementation with neural models. Next, Sect. 2.2 details the experimental setup followed for assessing our systems. The evaluation and discussion of such systems are shown in Sect. 3. Section 4 reviews the related work. Finally, in Sect. 5 we extract conclusions and set the basis of future works.

2   Interactive-Predictive Multimodal Pattern Recognition

The pattern recognition discipline consists in automatically obtaining a prediction $\hat{y}$, given an input object $\mathbf{x}$. A common approach to pattern recognition is based its statistical formalization. Following this probabilistic framework, the goal is to obtain the most likely prediction, given the input object:

$$\hat{\mathbf{y}} = \arg \max_{\mathbf{y}} \; \Pr(\mathbf{y} \mid \mathbf{x}) \tag{1}$$

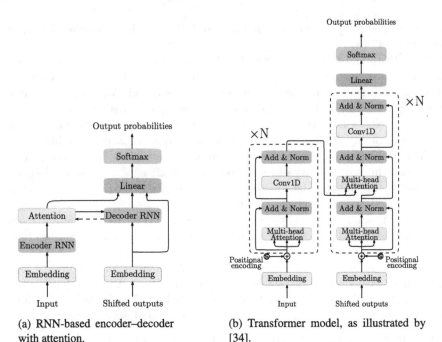

(a) RNN-based encoder–decoder with attention.

(b) Transformer model, as illustrated by [34].

Fig. 1. Different architectures for sequence to sequence learning: RNN-based (left) and Transformer models (right). Both models have the same inputs and outputs and differ on the mechanisms applied for learning their representations. In the first case, the input sequence is analyzed by an encoder RNN. The output sequence is generated, word by word, by another RNN. Both RNNs are connected through an attention mechanism. In the case of the Transformer model, the encoder and the decoder are stacks of multi-head attention mechanisms that compute different representations of the inputs. Both models have a vocabulary-sized output layer with a softmax activation, that computes a probability distribution over the output vocabulary.

Since the true probability distribution is unknown, it is approximated by a model with parameters Θ. Therefore, the prediction is given according to this model:

$$\hat{\mathbf{y}} \approx \arg\max_{\mathbf{y}} \ p(\mathbf{y} \mid \mathbf{x}; \Theta) \qquad (2)$$

As aforementioned in the previous section, we are interested in the case in which both $\mathbf{x}$ and $\mathbf{y}$ are sequences. In the last years, and framed into the resurgence of neural networks, Θ has been frequently implemented as a (deep) neural network, yielding the so-called neural sequence to sequence modeling. This neural network is usually trained on an end-to-end manner on large datasets, via stochastic gradient descent. Moreover, since performing a complete search is prohibitively expensive, the arg max is solved by applying a heuristic search method, typically, beam search [30].

2.1   Neural Architectures for Multimodal Sequence to Sequence Learning

Most neural models for sequence to sequence learning rely on the encoder–decoder paradigm: first, a neural encoder computes a representation of the input sequence. Next, a neural decoder takes this representation is then generates, element by element, the output sequence. Alternative architectures for encoder and decoder have been proposed in the literature. The most popular among them are those based on RNNs with attention [2] or those based solely on attention mechanisms [34] (the so-called Transformer models). Figure 1 depicts a schematic view of these systems. However, providing an in-depth review of these models is out of the scope of this paper. Hence, we refer the reader to the original works for a detailed explanation of these architectures.

This encoder–decoder paradigm can be applied to sequences from arbitrary sources. The only requirement is that we need to encode the input object into a low dimensional, real-valued representation. In this work, we focus on objects from three different sources: text, images and video. Hence, before being introduced to the encoder–decoder system, we need to compute an adequate representation of them. In the computer vision field, this process is known as feature extraction. Depending on the modality of the input object, we thus apply a different feature extractor:

Text: each word is mapped to a continuous representation by using an embedding matrix [30]. Hence, the sequence of input words is converted to a sequence of word embeddings. The embedding matrix is usually estimated with the rest of the parameters of the model.

Images: convolutional neural networks (ConvNets, [20]) excel in several computer vision tasks [18]. These models are also powerful feature extractors. We process the image with a ConvNet and use as features the final representation computed by the ConvNet that preserves positional information. A complete image is thus seen as a sequence of image crops. Hence, we can directly apply the sequence to sequence framework, as done by Xu et al. [37].

Videos: A video is a sequence of images. Therefore, we also rely on the usage of ConvNet for extracting the features from the each video frame. For alleviating the computational overload, we compute global features for each video image. In addition, we subsample the frames introduced to the system [38], also for reducing the computational load.

2.2   Interactive-Predictive Pattern Recognition

As discussed in the previous section, in an interactive-predictive scenario, the user introduces corrections to the predictions generated by a pattern recognition system. This correction is introduced as a feedback signal f. The systems reacts then to the introduction of the feedback, producing an alternative hypothesis, compatible with f. Considering this, the interactive-predictive framework rewrites Eq. (2) for also taking into account the user feedback signal:

$$\tilde{\mathbf{y}} = \underset{\mathbf{y} \text{ compatible with } f}{\arg\max} \ p(\mathbf{y} \mid \mathbf{x}, f; \boldsymbol{\Theta}) \tag{3}$$

Hence, the goal of an interactive-predictive system is to generate the most likely prediction that is compatible with the feedback provided by the user. Depending on the meaning conveyed by f, alternative interactive protocols can be defined. In this work, we follow the prefix-based interactive protocol. We also assume that the user introduces the corrections using a keyboard and a mouse.

The prefix-based protocol arguably is the most natural way of work. In this protocol, the user searches, from the left to the right, for the first error in the prediction given by the system and introduces the correct character. This feedback signal conveys a two-fold meaning: on the one hand, it states a correct character at a given position. On the other hand, it also validates the hypothesis up to this position. Taking this into account, a prefix-based interactive-predictive system must generate the most likely suffix, to a prefix validated by the user [3].

The implementation of this protocol in neural sequence to sequence systems requires to constrain the search [26]: the system applies a forced decoding of the feedback provided by the user. The suffix is obtained then by applying a regular search. For introducing corrections at a character level, we apply a vocabulary mask as described by [25], which ensures that the next word generated complies with the user feedback.

We evaluate our interactive-predictive framework in six different scenarios, involving three tasks and two different datasets per task. The main figures of the datasets are shown in Table 1. The tasks under study are:

Machine translation: translation of English sentences to French, on two datasets[1]: UFAL and Europarl. The first one belongs to a medical domain and the latter refers to the translation of the proceedings from the European parliament.

Image captioning: we tackled two common datasets: Flickr8k [12] and Flickr30k [27]. The goal is to generate descriptions of pictures crawled from Flickr users.

Video captioning: we tested our systems on the popular Microsoft Research Video Description (MSVD) dataset [6], a general task, relating the description of YouTube videos from multiple domains. In addition, we apply our methods to the EDUB-SegDesc dataset [4], a collection of egocentric videos and first person captions.

---

[1] Datasets available at: http://statmt.org/wmt18.

Table 1. Figures of the different datasets. M denotes millions of elements. The column #References indicates the number of different references per sample. * denotes a variable number of references. In this case, we report the average references per sample.

Task	Dataset	#Samples			#References
		Training	Validation	Test	
Machine translation	UFAL	$2.8M$	1,000	1,000	1
	Europarl	$2.0M$	3,003	3,000	1
Image captioning	Flickr8k	30,000	1,000	1,000	5
	Flickr30k	145,000	1,014	1,000	5
Video captioning	MSVD	48,779	100	670	41*
	EDUB-SegDesc	2,652	204	246	3

2.3 Evaluation Metrics

We evaluate two main aspects of our systems. On the one hand, we measure the quality of the initial predictions provided by the system. This is the most common scenario in the literature. This evaluation is carried on by comparing the predictions with the ground-truth references from each dataset. The final goal of these metrics is to correlate with the human perception of prediction quality. The metrics range from 0 (worst quality) to 100 (best quality):

BLEU [22]: Computes the geometric mean of the n-gram precision of prediction and references. In includes n-grams from order 1 to 4. It also includes a penalty for short predictions.

METEOR [19]: Computes the F1 score of precision and recall of matches between prediction and references words. To this end, it applies linguistic resources such as stemmers, paraphrase and synonym dictionaries.

On the other hand, under an interactive-predictive framework, our objective is to reduced the amount of effort spent by the user during the correction process. We follow the literature and estimate this effort as the number of keystrokes and mouse actions performed by the user during the correction process. To this end, we rely on two metrics:

CharacTER [36]: Translation edit rate computed at a character level: minimum number of character edit operations (insertion, substitution, deletion and swapping) that must be made in order to transform the hypothesis into the reference. The number of edit operations is normalized by the number of characters.

KSMR [3]: accounts for the number of keystrokes plus mouse actions involved in the interactive correction process, divided by the number of characters of the final prediction obtained.

CharacTER and KSMR are error-based metrics, hence the lower, the better. Following Zaidan et al. [39], CharacTER is an estimate of the effort of static post-edition; while the effort of interactive-predictive systems can be assessed via KSMR [3].

2.4   Usage of the System and User Simulation

Using an interactive-predictive system requires to follow the procedure described in Sect. 2: the process starts with an automatic prediction given by the system to an input object. The user then reviews the prediction, starting and the interactive-predictive process: the user searches in this hypothesis the first error, and introduces a correction. The system then reacts, providing an alternative hypothesis, considering the user feedback. This protocol is repeated until the user finds satisfactory the hypothesis given by the system. We implemented a live demonstration of this system[2].

Properly assessing interactive-predictive systems involves the experimentation with human users, which is prohibitively expensive. Hence, during the development of such systems, it is common to rely on simulated users [3,26]. We used the ground-truth samples from the different datasets as the desired outputs by our simulated users. The simulation is done by correcting the leftmost wrong character of each hypothesis from the interactive-predictive system, until reaching the desired output.

2.5   Description of the Systems

Our neural sequence to sequence systems[3] were developed with NMT-Keras [24]. This library is built upon Keras[4] and works for the Theano and Tensorflow backends. For each task and dataset, we built two models: one using RNNs with attention and another one using a Transformer architecture.

The RNN-based systems had long short-term memory units [11]. Encoder and decoder were bridged together through an additive attention mechanism [2]. We set all model dimensions to the same value. In the case of machine translation, all layers had a dimension of 512. In the case of image and video captioning, we reduced the model size to 256, since we are dealing with smaller datasets.

In the case of the Transformer models, we set two stacks of 6 layers for the encoder and the decoder. In the case of machine translation, all model dimensions were 512 and the number of attention heads was 8. This configuration is the same as the *base* model described by Vaswani et al. [34]. For the captioning tasks, we reduced again our model, to 256 dimensions on each layer.

Machine translation and image captioning systems were trained using Adam [15], with a learning rate of 0.0002. In the case of video captioning, we obtained better performance using Adadelta [40], in both datasets. In all cases, the batch

---

[2] Accessible at http://casmacat.prhlt.upv.es/interactive-seq2seq.

[3] Source code: https://github.com/lvapeab/interactive-keras-captioning.

[4] https://keras.io.

Table 2. Prediction quality for the different tasks, datasets and models. The RNN column denotes RNN-based system (Fig. 1a) and the Trans. column indicates a Transformer model (Fig. 1b)

Task	Dataset	BLEU [↑]		METEOR [↑]	
		RNN	Trans.	RNN	Trans.
Machine translation	UFAL	37.2	37.8	59.6	60.4
	Europarl	24.6	26.6	45.7	47.9
Image captioning	Flickr8k	22.1	19.6	20.8	19.8
	Flickr30k	22.2	19.3	20.0	18.5
Video captioning	MSVD	49.6	45.7	33.4	30.7
	EDUB-SegDesc	30.4	25.8	21.9	20.3

size was 64. During training, we applied an early-stopping strategy, watching the BLEU on the development set. At decoding time, we used a beam size of 6.

In the case of machine translation, the word embeddings were randomly initialized and learned together with the rest of the parameters of the system. In the case of image captioning, we extracted image features using a NASNet architecture [41], trained on the ImageNet dataset [7]. The video features were extracted with an Inception v4 network [31], also trained on the ImageNet dataset. Following Yao et al. [38], we subsampled the frames from a video, selecting 26 images per clip. Image and video feature remained static along the training process of the sequence to sequence model.

3   Results and Discussion

We show and discuss now the results obtained by our systems. First, we will assess the systems quantitatively, in terms of prediction quality and effort required during the correction stage. Next, in order to gain some insights into the behavior of the system, we analyze an image captioning example.

3.1   Quantitative Evaluation

We start by evaluating the systems in a traditional way, assessing their prediction quality. Table 2 shows the BLEU and METEOR results of the different systems for all tasks. These results are similar to those reported in the literature for each task and dataset [4,25,37,38].

It is worth to note that the Transformer model only outperformed the RNN-based systems in the case of machine translation. This model is more data-eager than RNN systems. Many of the recent advances yielded with this architecture leverage huge data collections (e.g. Radford et al. [29]). We also contrasted this fact in our experimentation: the machine translation datasets were way larger than the captioning ones (see Table 1. Hence, the Transformer model only was fully exploited in the machine translation case.

Next, we evaluate the performance of the interactive-predictive systems. To that end, we estimate the effort required for correcting the output of a static system (using CharacTER) and the effort needed by a interactive system (using KSMR). These results are shown in Table 3. The results obtained in machine translation are similar to the literature [25]. Due to the novelty of this scenario, we lack from references in the literature, regarding the other tasks.

Table 3. Effort required for correcting the outputs of static (St.) and interactive-predictive (Int.) systems, using RNN and Transformer (Trans.) models. The effort of static systems is measured in terms of CharacTER while the effort required by interactive-predictive systems is evaluated in terms of KSMR

Task	Dataset	CharacTER [↓]		KSMR [↓]	
		St. RNN	St. Trans.	Int. RNN	Int. Trans.
Machine translation	UFAL	35.7	36.5	19.0	15.9
	Europarl	53.6	51.2	30.1	29.4
Image captioning	Flickr8k	77.8	79.6	36.6	36.9
	Flickr30k	81.7	86.1	36.0	40.0
Video captioning	MSVD	58.1	64.1	36.4	40.5
	EDUB-SegDesc	72.3	71.4	40.0	38.0

Interactive-predictive systems approximately halved the amount of corrections required for correcting their outputs, with respect to traditional, static systems. The results were consistent across all tasks and for all models. Hence, these results indicate that the interactive protocol effectively achieved its goal of reducing the correction effort.

Moreover, a crucial aspect of the usability of interactive systems is their response time. Hence, it is important to keep it in adequate values. The average response time of our systems was always below 0.2 s. This provides the user of a feeling of almost instant reactivity [21].

Finally, we are aware that properly assessing the usability and effort reduction brought by these system requires a human evaluation on its usage. In this paper, we set the first step toward future developments on multimodal neural interactive-predictive pattern recognition, with positive initial results.

3.2   Qualitative Analysis and Discussion

We show and analyze an image captioning example. Other examples for the machine translation and video captioning tasks are alike. The example is taken from our multimodal showcase and shown in Fig. 2.

We can see that the caption generated by the system (at iteration 0) has an error. The user wants to indicate that the people are sitting on a bench. Hence, the feedback introduced is the character "b". The system is able to properly complete the word "bench", with this single interaction. The same happens when the user wants to introduce the clause "under a". With only typing the character "u", the system generates this clause. Finally, it is interesting to observe the behavior of the last interaction. The user introduced the character "n" to the word "a". Hence, the next word must start with a vowel. The system is able to properly account for this concordance and generates the word "umbrella". We observe that the systems also handle correctly other concordances, such as singular/plural clauses.

4   Related Work

Neural sequence to sequence learning has been a widely studied topic since its reintroduction, framed to the deep learning era [9,30]. As stated above, neural

Iter 0	System	A group of people sit on a ramp.
Iter 1	User System	*A group of people sit on a* [b]*ramp.* *A group of people sit on a* bench.
Iter 2	User System	*A group of people sit on a bench* [u]. *A group of people sit on a bench* under a building.
Iter 3	User System	*A group of people sit on a bench under a*[n]*building.* *A group of people sit on a bench under an* umbrella.
Iter 4	User	*A group of people sit on a bench under an umbrella.*

Fig. 2. Interactive-predictive session example, for correcting the caption generated for the image. At each iteration, the user introduces a character correction (boxed). The system modifies its hypothesis, taking into account this feedback: keeping the correct prefix (green) and generating a compatible suffix. Post-editing this sample in a static way, would have required the deletion of 4 characters and the addition of 23 characters (Color figure online)

machine translation [2,34] has meant a revolution in the field. Nowadays, these systems are standard in research and industry. In addition to machine translation, different tasks have been tackled following this approach: speech recognition [5], speech translation [14], syntactic parsing [35], or the already discussed image and video captioning [23,37,38].

Regarding the interactive-predictive pattern recognition framework, it has been mainly applied to machine translation. The addition of interactive protocols for fostering the productivity of translation environments have been studied for long time, for phrase-based models [3,10] and neural machine translation systems [16,26].

The interactive-predictive approach has been also previously generalized for tackling other tasks, involving multimodal signals. This is the case of the interactive transcription of handwritten text documents [32], layout detection [28], among others [33]. None of these works however, involved fully end-to-end neural multimodal systems.

5 Conclusions and Future Work

In this work, we empirically demonstrated the capabilities of the interactive-predictive framework applied to multimodal, neural sequence-to-sequence systems. We tackled a variety of tasks, using two state-of-the-art models and, in all cases, the interactive-predictive systems were able to decrease the human effort required for correcting the outputs of the system. We obtained savings of approximately a 50%. We also analyzed these systems through an online demo website. We released all source code developed.

These encouraging results open several avenues for future research. The construction of multimodal, interactive-predictive systems allow the application of this framework to other structured prediction tasks, e.g. tables to text. More precisely, this framework is directly applicable to the automatic report of medical images or to the automatic generation of life-loggers. In addition to an end application, these tools can be used by human annotators, for creating datasets on a more efficient way.

Moreover, we experimented with multimodal inputs. In a future, we want to explore the inclusion of multimodal feedback signals. This was already done for statistical models [1] and we think that neural models are able to exploit this very effectively. In addition, we used a different system for each task. In a future, we would like to explore the construction of a single multitask, multimodal system. The recent advances achieved in multitask learning [29] heavily support this research direction. Finally, for properly assessing the efficiency of this framework, we should conduct and experimentation involving human users.

References

1. Alabau, V., Sanchis, A., Casacuberta, F.: Improving on-line handwritten recognition in interactive machine translation. Pattern Recognit. **47**(3), 1217–1228 (2014)
2. Bahdanau, D., Cho, K., Bengio, Y.: Neural machine translation by jointly learning to align and translate (2015). arXiv:1409.0473
3. Barrachina, S., et al.: Statistical approaches to computer-assisted translation. Comput. Linguist. **35**(1), 3–28 (2009)
4. Bolaños, M., Peris, Á., Casacuberta, F., Soler, S., Radeva, P.: Egocentric video description based on temporally-linked sequences. J. Vis. Commun. Image Represent. **50**, 205–216 (2018)
5. Chan, W., Jaitly, N., Le, Q., Vinyals, O.: Listen, attend and spell: a neural network for large vocabulary conversational speech recognition. In: Proceedings of the ICASSP, pp. 4960–4964 (2016)
6. Chen, D.L., Dolan, W.B.: Collecting highly parallel data for paraphrase evaluation. In: Proceedings of the ACL, pp. 190–200 (2011)
7. Deng, J., Dong, W., Socher, R., Li, L.J., Li, K., Fei-Fei, L.: ImageNet: a large-scale hierarchical image database. In: Proceedings of the CVPR, pp. 248–255 (2009)
8. Foster, G., Isabelle, P., Plamondon, P.: Target-text mediated interactive machine translation. Mach. Transl. **12**, 175–194 (1997)
9. Graves, A.: Sequence transduction with recurrent neural networks (2012). arXiv:1211.3711
10. Green, S., Chuang, J., Heer, J., Manning, C.D.: Predictive translation memory: a mixed-initiative system for human language translation. In: Proceedings of the ACM UIST, pp. 177–187 (2014)
11. Hochreiter, S., Schmidhuber, J.: Long short-term memory. Neural Comput. **9**(8), 1735–1780 (1997)
12. Hodosh, M., Young, P., Hockenmaier, J.: Framing image description as a ranking task: data, models and evaluation metrics. J. Artif. Intell. Res. **47**, 853–899 (2013)
13. Hu, K., Cadwell, P.: A comparative study of post-editing guidelines. In: Proceedings of the EAMT, pp. 34206–353 (2016)
14. Jia, Y., et al.: Direct speech-to-speech translation with a sequence-to-sequence model (2019). arXiv:1904.06037
15. Kingma, D., Ba, J.: Adam: a method for stochastic optimization (2014). arXiv:1412.6980
16. Knowles, R., Koehn, P.: Neural interactive translation prediction. In: Proceedings of the AMTA, pp. 107–120 (2016)
17. Koehn, P., Knowles, R.: Six challenges for neural machine translation. In: Proceedings of the First Workshop on NMT, pp. 28–39 (2017)
18. Krizhevsky, A., Sutskever, I., Hinton, G.E.: ImageNet classification with deep convolutional neural networks. In: Proceedings of NIPS, pp. 1097–1105 (2012)
19. Lavie, A., Denkowski, M.J.: The METEOR metric for automatic evaluation of machine translation. Mach. Transl. **23**(2–3), 105–115 (2009)
20. LeCun, Y., Bottou, L., Bengio, Y., Haffner, P.: Gradient-based learning applied to document recognition. Proc. IEEE **86**(11), 2278–2324 (1998)
21. Nielsen, J.: Usability Engineering. Morgan Kaufmann Publishers Inc., Burlington (1993)
22. Papineni, K., Roukos, S., Ward, T., Zhu, W.J.: BLEU: a method for automatic evaluation of machine translation. In: Proceedings of the ACL, pp. 311–318 (2002)

23. Peris, Á., Bolaños, M., Radeva, P., Casacuberta, F.: Video description using bidirectional recurrent neural networks. In: Proceedings of the ICANN, pp. 3–11 (2016)
24. Peris, A., Casacuberta, F.: NMT-Keras: a very flexible toolkit with a focus on interactive NMT and online learning. Prague Bull. Math. Linguist. **111**, 113–124 (2018)
25. Peris, Á., Casacuberta, F.: Online learning for effort reduction in interactive neural machine translation. Comput. Speech Lang. **58**, 98–126 (2019)
26. Peris, Á., Domingo, M., Casacuberta, F.: Interactive neural machine translation. Comput. Speech Lang. **45**, 201–220 (2017)
27. Plummer, B.A., Wang, L., Cervantes, C.M., Caicedo, J.C., Hockenmaier, J., Lazebnik, S.: Flickr30k entities: collecting region-to-phrase correspondences for richer image-to-sentence models. In: Proceedings of the ICCV, pp. 2641–2649 (2015)
28. Quirós, L., Martínez-Hinarejos, C.-D., Toselli, A.H., Vidal, E.: Interactive layout detection. In: Alexandre, L.A., Salvador Sánchez, J., Rodrigues, J.M.F. (eds.) IbPRIA 2017. LNCS, vol. 10255, pp. 161–168. Springer, Cham (2017). https://doi.org/10.1007/978-3-319-58838-4_18
29. Radford, A., Wu, J., Child, R., Luan, D., Amodei, D., Sutskever, I.: Language models are unsupervised multitask learners. Technical report, Open-AI (2019)
30. Sutskever, I., Vinyals, O., Le, Q.V.: Sequence to sequence learning with neural networks. In: Proceedings of the NIPS, vol. 27, pp. 3104–3112 (2014)
31. Szegedy, C., Vanhoucke, V., Ioffe, S., Shlens, J., Wojna, Z.: Rethinking the inception architecture for computer vision. In: Proceedings of the CVPR, pp. 2818–2826 (2016)
32. Toselli, A., Romero, V., Rodríguez, L., Vidal, E.: Computer assisted transcription of handwritten text images. In: Proceedings of the ICDAR, vol. 2, pp. 944–948 (2007)
33. Toselli, A.H., Vidal, E., Casacuberta, F.: Multimodal Interactive Pattern Recognition and Applications. Springer, Heidelberg (2011). https://doi.org/10.1007/978-0-85729-479-1
34. Vaswani, A., et al.: Attention is all you need. In: Proceedings of NIPS, pp. 5998–6008 (2017)
35. Vinyals, O., Kaiser, L., Koo, T., Petrov, S., Sutskever, I., Hinton, G.: Grammar as a foreign language. In: Proceedings of NIPS, pp. 2755–2763 (2015)
36. Wang, W., Peter, J.T., Rosendahl, H., Ney, H.: CharacTer: translation edit rate on character level. In: Proceedings of the WMT, vol. 2, pp. 505–510 (2016)
37. Xu, K., et al.: Show, attend and tell: neural image caption generation with visual attention. In: Proceedings of the ICML, pp. 2048–2057 (2015)
38. Yao, L., Torabi, A., Cho, K., Ballas, N., Pal, C., Larochelle, H., Courville, A.: Describing videos by exploiting temporal structure. In: Proceedings of the ICCV, pp. 4507–4515 (2015)
39. Zaidan, O.F., Callison-Burch, C.: Predicting human-targeted translation edit rate via untrained human annotators. In: Proceedings of the NAACL, pp. 369–372 (2010)
40. Zeiler, M.D.: ADADELTA: an adaptive learning rate method (2012). arXiv:1212.5701
41. Zoph, B., Vasudevan, V., Shlens, J., Le, Q.V.: Learning transferable architectures for scalable image recognition. In: Proceedings of the CVPR, pp. 8697–8710 (2018)

Uncertainty Estimation for Black-Box Classification Models: A Use Case for Sentiment Analysis

José Mena[1,3]([⊠]) , Axel Brando[2,3] , Oriol Pujol[3] , and Jordi Vitrià[3]

[1] Eurecat, Centre Tecnològic de Catalunya, Barcelona, Spain
jose.mena@eurecat.org
[2] BBVA Analytics Data & Analytics, Madrid, Spain
axel.brando@bbvadata.com
[3] Universitat de Barcelona, Barcelona, Spain
{axelbrando,oriol_pujol,jordi.vitria}@ub.edu

Abstract. With the advent of new pre-trained word embedding models like ELMO, GPT or BERT, that leverage transfer-learning to deliver high-quality prediction systems, natural language processing (NLP) methods are reaching or even overtaking human baselines in some applications. The basic principle of these successful models is to train a model to solve a given NLP task, mainly Language Modelling, using significant volumes of data like the whole Wikipedia. The model is then fine-tuned to solve another NLP task, requiring fewer domain-specific data to achieve state-of-the-art accuracies. The method proposed in the present work assists the practitioner in evaluating the quality of the transferred classification models when applied to new data domains. In this case, we consider the original model as a black box. No matter how complex the original model may be, the method only requires access to the output layer to train a measure of the uncertainty associated with the predictions of the original model. This measure of uncertainty is a measure of how well the black-box model accommodates to the new data. Later on, we show how a rejection system can use this uncertainty to improve its accuracy, effectively enabling the practitioner to find the best trade-off between the quality of the model and the number of rejected cases.

Keywords: Sentiment analysis · Transfer learning ·
Uncertainty estimation · Natural Language Processing

1 Introduction

The application of Natural Language Processing (NLP) methods to real-world problems is gaining momentum nowadays thanks to significant advances resulting from the field of Machine Learning, and Deep Learning (DL) in particular. Recently, the appearance of new word embedding models such as BERT [16], ELMO [17] or GPT [18] has taken the quality of prediction models for tasks

© Springer Nature Switzerland AG 2019
A. Morales et al. (Eds.): IbPRIA 2019, LNCS 11867, pp. 29–40, 2019.
https://doi.org/10.1007/978-3-030-31332-6_3

such as Sentiment Analysis, Text Entailment or Question Answering, to a new level, reaching or even overtaking human baselines in some cases.

All these models share the concept of transfer learning to train models that solve a Language Modelling task to learn the fundamental structure of a given language by using vast volumes of data, like the whole Wikipedia, or a collection of News with more than 100 billion words. Once trained, they apply these models to other NLP tasks like Sentiment Analysis, fine-tuning them using a domain-specific dataset and obtaining superior accuracy metrics for the new task, thanks to the fact that the pre-trained model has already incorporated the necessary knowledge about the given language.

The success of these models is fostering the proliferation of new prediction services in the form of application programmable interfaces (API). In this scenario, one of the aforementioned generic models is trained in a given domain, e.g. movie reviews, and offered as a prediction service, e.g. as a sentiment analysis API. Take now a practitioner that wants to apply this API service in a new domain, i.e. restaurant reviews. To which extent is the API going to work in the new domain? Can the user trust the predictions of a model trained for movies? Will it be necessary to fine-tune the model for predicting reviews of restaurants?

One can foresee that fine-tuning the API for each new domain is not always possible. In the case of a third party API, one even might not have access to the model internals for such a task. In this scenario, the practitioner would most probably need some metric that evaluates the success performance, which may be directly related to the classification accuracy in the new domain. However, because domains may not be directly comparable, accuracy may not be a sufficient evaluation metric, demanding additional measures to evaluate the quality of the predictions when applying this API in the new domain.

To address this issue, probabilistic models are a natural option for evaluating confidence or uncertainty in the prediction. Given a classification problem, the output of these probabilistic models is the probability distribution of the labels given the input pattern. The analysis of this output distribution may suffice to derive prediction confidence in many cases. For example, the analysis of the entropy of the distribution or the spread of the distribution is an evident indicator of confidence. While sharper low-spread distributions suggest that the prediction has high confidence, flat distributions advocate for the opposite.

However, the former reasoning may fail in some cases when applying the black-box prediction to a new data domain. Changes in the vocabulary or the presence of new constructs (e.g. maybe the new text includes words that are not present in movie reviews but are representative of the restaurant domain, such as the words "yummy" or "tasty") may mislead the interpretation of the results. For example, giving high confidence to a wrong classification because of the lack of data support for that case. In this situation, it is important "to know what the model does not know". Fortunately, this concept is captured by the notion of uncertainty.

Previous works have analysed the role of uncertainty in deep learning, including those related to Bayesian neural networks [4], by considering the weights of the network as random variables, thus obtaining not a single model but an ensemble of them which enables the analysis of the variance of the resulting predictions. Alternatively, approximations like Variational Dropout [2] do not require to modify the model to analyse the associated uncertainty. Having a way to measure the uncertainty when applying deep learning methods to natural language processing tasks achieves three goals, namely, to increase the explainability and transparency of the models, to measure the level of confidence of the predictions, and to improve the accuracy of the models [1].

In this article, we address the problem of estimating uncertainty from a black-box model and apply it to the problem of sentiment analysis to improve its accuracy by leveraging the uncertainty in the predictions. The task of sentiment analysis is one of the most popular applications in the field of NLP. The analysis of the sentiment of textual reviews is critical to have a better understanding of customers in fields such as e-commerce [19] or tourism [20], and like other NLP tasks, Sentiment Analysis is having a sweet moment these days thanks to the advances produced in deep learning. Beyond the text feature engineering used in the past, with the advent of deep learning, embedding models like word2vec or Glove, or more recently transfer learning based models like ELMO [17], GPT [18] or BERT [16] are obtaining state of the art results that improve previous approaches by far.

The main contributions of the present work include:

- The analysis of aleatoric heteroscedastic uncertainty in deep learning classification methods, with special emphasis in NLP classification tasks.
- The development of a wrapper methodology for computing uncertainty from black-box classification models.
- The application of the uncertainty measure in a rejection framework for improving the quality of classification in a sentiment analysis domain.

The structure of the rest of the paper is as follows: Sect. 2 analyses the related work, with a particular focus in uncertainty in deep learning, sentiment analysis and rejection methods. Section 3 exposes the method proposed in the present work and Sect. 4 shows the results obtained after applying the proposed method in a practical situation. Finally, Sect. 5 sums up the work presented and points to future research directions.

2   Related Work

2.1   Uncertainty in Deep Learning

When referring to uncertainty we usually have to distinguish among the following types of uncertainty:

- **Epistemic uncertainty** corresponds to the uncertainty originated by the model. It can be explained as to which extent is our model able to describe the distribution that generated the data. In this case, we can talk of two different types of uncertainties caused by whether the model has been trained with enough data, so it has been able to learn the full distribution of the data, or whether the expressiveness of the model can capture the complexity of the distribution. When using an expressive enough model, this type of uncertainty can be reduced by showing more samples during the training phase.

– **Aleatoric uncertainty** refers to the inherent uncertainty coming from the data generation process, i.e. due to measurement noise or inherent ambiguity of the data. Adding more data to the training process will not reduce this kind of uncertainty. There are two types of aleatoric uncertainty according to the following assumptions:

  • **Homocedastic uncertainty** measures the level of noise derived from the measurement process. This uncertainty remains constant for all the data.

  • **Heteroscedastic uncertainty** measures the level of uncertainty caused by the data. For example, in the case of NLP, this can be explained by the ambiguity of some words or sentences.

Adopting a Bayesian framework, we can formalise the notion of uncertainty as follows. Let us have a training dataset, D, composed by pairs of data points and labels, $D = \{(x_1, y_1), (x_2, y_2), ..., (x_N, y_N)\}$. The goal in inference consists of estimating the label probability y^* for a new data point x^* given D, i.e. $p(y^*|x^*, D)$. By marginalizing this last quantity[1] with respect to model parameters w we obtain,

$$p(y^*|x^*, D) = \int_w p(y^*|w, x^*)p(w|D)dw \qquad (1)$$

In Eq. 1, one can see that the distribution of the output depends on two terms. The first one depends on the application of the model to the input query data. The second term measures how the model may vary depending on the training data. From this definition, we can derive that the first term is modelling aleatoric uncertainty, as it measures how the output is affected by the input data given a model, and the second term is modelling the epistemic uncertainty as it measures the uncertainty induced by the parameters of the model.

Aleatoric Heteroscedastic Uncertainty. Because we are assuming a black-box model, in this work, we are only concerned with the estimation of heteroscedastic uncertainty. Thus, we consider that we have a fixed deterministic black-box model $f^w(x)$ with undisclosed non-trainable parameters w. Our goal is to compute the variability of the term $p(y^*|w, x^*)$ in Eq. 1. For the sake of simplicity, let us assume that this conditional distribution follows a normal distribution, i.e. $y^*|w, x^* \sim \mathcal{N}(f^w(x^*), \sigma^2(x^*))$, where $f^w(x^*)$ is the black-box model evaluated at the data point x^*, and $\sigma^2(x^*)$ is a function of the input data that models the variance for that data point. In regression tasks, applying this

---

[1] We additionally assume an inductive learning approach to modelling where $p(y^*|w, x^*, D) = p(y^*|w, x^*)$ and the model parameters are independent from the test data, i.e. $p(w|D, x^*) = p(w|D)$.

approximation to the log-likelihood adds a term to the loss that depends on $\sigma(x)$ [3]. However, in classification tasks, this approximation is not as straightforward as in regression.

We consider the scenario where $f^w(x^*)$ is implemented by a deep neural network. In general, the computation of aleatoric heteroscedastic uncertainty for fully trainable networks considers the introduction of a stochastic layer to represent the output logits space. In the case that the output logits, u, of the classification model are modelled as normal distributed variables with a diagonal variance term they can be written as follows,

$$u \sim \mathcal{N}(f^w(x^*), diag(\sigma^2(x^*))) \tag{2}$$
$$p = softmax(u) \tag{3}$$
$$y \sim Categorical(p) \tag{4}$$

by reparameterizing the logits, u, we obtain,

$$u = f^w(x^*) + \sqrt{diag(\sigma^2(x^*))} \cdot \epsilon, \quad \epsilon \sim \mathcal{N}(0,1) \tag{5}$$

In its simple approach, working with this stochastic layer requires of its sampling. In general, we would need to compute the expected value by applying Monte Carlo sampling, obtaining,

$$\mathbb{E}[p] = \frac{1}{M} \sum_{m=1}^{M} softmax(u_m) \tag{6}$$

When applied to a cross-entropy loss allows us to obtain the loss we will use for the wrapper, i.e.

$$\mathcal{L}(W) = \frac{1}{N} \sum_{i=1}^{N} -\frac{1}{C} \sum_{c=1}^{C} y_{i,c} \log(p_{i,c}) = \tag{7}$$

$$\frac{1}{N} \sum_{i=1}^{N} -\frac{1}{C} \sum_{c=1}^{C} y_{i,c} \log \frac{1}{M} \sum_{m=1}^{M} softmax(u_m) \tag{8}$$

Where N is the number of examples, C is the number of classes and M is the number of Monte Carlo samples.

2.2 Rejection Methods

As outlined in the introduction, the purpose of this work is to take advantage of the uncertainty associated with classification methods, especially when using pre-trained models in new domains, to improve the quality of the resulting predictions. By using this uncertainty as a rejection metric, one can choose whether to trust or not a prediction obtained.

In the literature, we can find many approaches for classification with rejection: from the initial work presented by [21] where they minimise the classification risk by setting a threshold for rejection to more recent works where they embed the rejection option in the classifier [22]. The problem with these approaches is the fact that they need to modify the original classifier to include the rejection, which goes against the requirement of the present work of having a frozen classifier.

Moreover, many metrics used for rejection has shown some limitations. Metrics like accuracy or F1-score are used for obtaining accuracy-rejection curves (ARC) [23] or 3D ROC (receiver operating characteristic) [24]. They compare different classifiers through an analysis of the behaviour of the respective curves. The problem with this approach is that it is not able to look for the optimal rejection rate by comparing the performance of the classifiers working with different rejection rates.

In [5], they describe a set of three performance measures: non-rejected accuracy, classification quality and rejection quality. These measurements allow us to analyse different rejection metrics for a given classifier while considering different aspects of the classification, miss-classification and rejection. In the present work, we take advantage of these performance measures to evaluate the proposed rejection heuristic based on the prediction uncertainty.

3   Uncertainty Measures from Black-Box Models

In this section, we introduce the wrapping technique for obtaining aleatoric uncertainty from a black-box model. Following this, we further introduce a heuristics for measuring uncertainty from the resulting values.

3.1   A Wrapper for Computing Aleatoric Heteroscedastic Uncertainty

Given a black-box model, the goal of the wrapper is to endow this model with an aleatoric heteroscedastic uncertainty layer. For all purposes, the black box can not be modified as it is frozen and we do not have access to the internals of the model. However, we require an entry point that allows connecting the black box to the wrapper. In this work, we consider that the black box gives access to the pre-normalized logits (before the softmax) of the last layer[2]. This is a very mild requirement. It is agnostic to the particular architecture of the classifier since it does not interfere with the model internals and all models display this same structure making the wrapper generic for any architecture.

Figure 1 shows an illustration of the proposed wrapper architecture. The wrapper architecture aims at computing aleatoric uncertainty as expressed in Eq. 5. In that equation we distinguish two components: the original black-box model, shown in blue/gray in Fig. 1, corresponding to $f^w(x)$ and the trainable wrapper architecture, shown in orange/light gray in Fig. 1, that will gives us $\sigma(x)$. The first component corresponds to the logits of the original classifier, what we call μ-logits, and is the result of the last layer when applying the

---

[2] This is consistent with the former use of the notation of the model, $f^w(x)$.

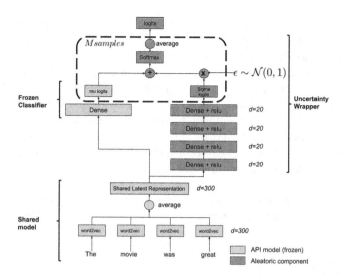

Fig. 1. Architecture of the full aleatoric model. The blue components correspond to the original classifier as exposed by the API. In orange, there is the aleatoric trainable part of the model. (Color figure online)

original classifier to the inputs. The second component, $\sigma(x)$, is the aleatoric part of the equation and will capture the variance of the predictions. We train this component using as input the same latent representation resulting from applying the frozen model to the training examples. The result of this component is what we call the σ-logits. It is worth mentioning that the composition of the μ-logits and σ-logits define a normal random variable layer. The evaluation of the network using random variables requires of its sampling. Note that the same input might generate different instantaneous predictions. Through this sampling process, we use the reparametrization trick, as described in Eq. 5 to be able to propagate gradients through the wrapper layers and infer the output distributions and statistics. In particular, by analysing the variance of these predictions, we may infer the aleatoric uncertainty that can be used as a heuristic for rejecting uncertain predictions, as shown in the next sections.

3.2 Uncertainty Heuristics

Using the former wrapper we have access to the variance of the logits. In this section, we discuss how to compute uncertainty scores based on that measure. In regression systems, it is usual to approximate the output with a Gaussian random variable. In this setting, the uncertainty score can be identified with the associated standard deviation. However, in classification systems, obtaining a single estimate is harder as the random variable is applied to the last layer logits.

For the case of classification, we find in literature [7] different ways for transforming the variance of the logits into an uncertainty score: variation ratios [8], predictive entropy [9], and mutual information [9]. The first heuristic, variation ratios, evaluates the variability of the predictions made when sampling different predictions using the aleatoric model, sort of a measure of the dispersion of the predictions around their mode. The second heuristic, predictive entropy, is based on the information theory and evaluates the average amount of information contained in the predictive distribution. Those results with lower entropy values will correspond with confident predictions, whereas a high entropy will correspond with high uncertainty. In our case, we evaluate variation ratios and predictive entropy as both can be obtained directly analyzing the output layer of the black-box model, discarding mutual information because of the complexity of its calculation.

Finally, we use the uncertainty score to reject those samples that are more uncertain, increasing thus the accuracy of the classifier for the sentiment analysis task.

4   Use Case and Results

Use Case and Datasets Description: We illustrate the feasibility of the presented method in the following use case: Consider a sentiment analysis API. In our case, this API is trained using one domain from the four used in this article. The resulting model is frozen and the internals not accessible to us except for the seam in the output layer logits for the wrapper injection. We want to apply this API to a new sentiment analysis domain. Transfer learning is not an option since we rely on a black-box non-trainable model. We will use the API in the new problem directly applying the predictions obtained. Using the uncertainty wrapper, we expect to identify where these predictions are not reliable in the product domain and apply a rejection rule in those cases.

The details on the datasets used are the following:

- Stanford Sentiment Treebank [10], SST-2, binary version where the purpose of the tasks is to classify a movie review in two categories: a positive or negative review. The dataset is split in 65,538 test samples, 872 for validation and 1,821 for testing.
- Yelp challenge 2013 [12], the goal is to classify reviews about Yelp venues where their users rated them using 1 to 5 stars. To be able to reuse a classifier trained with the SST-2 problem, we transform the Yelp dataset from a multiclass set to a binary one by grouping the ratings below three as a negative review, and positive otherwise. The dataset is split in 186,189 test samples, 20,691 for validation and 22,991 for testing.
- Amazon Multi-Domain Sentiment dataset contains product reviews taken from Amazon.com from many product types (domains) [25]. As in Yelp, the dataset consists on ratings from 1 to 5 stars that we label as positive for those with values greater or equal to 3, and negative otherwise, split into train, validation and test datasets. We use two of the domains available: music (10,595/993/2,621 examples) and computer and video games (406,035/45,093/112,794 examples).

We consider four scenarios:

- **Scenario 1:** The API is trained on Yelp venues, and applied to movie reviews.
- **Scenario 2:** The API is trained on movie reviews using SST-2, and applied to Yelp venues.
- **Scenario 3:** The API is trained on the Amazon music domain, and applied to computer and video games.
- **Scenario 4:** The API is trained on computer and video games, and applied on music reviews.

Simulating the API: In all cases, we trained sentiment analysis models using word2vec [11] to vectorize the textual reviews, as described in [6]. The idea is to obtain a sentence representation for each review by averaging the word2vec embedding of each word into a 300 summarizing vector. Using this sentence representation, we apply a classifier based on an ANN with a softmax output layer to predict whether the review is positive or negative. We simulate the black-box API by training a classifier with only one softmax layer using the Keras framework.

Uncertainty Wrapper Architecture: The wrapper architecture, shown in Fig. 1, is composed by an input layer that uses the 300 dimension vector, and four hidden layers with 20 units each. Lastly, the output layer uses a softplus activation to ensure that the outputs are positive. The wrapper is trained for 100 epochs using the Adam optimiser with a learning rate of $2e-4$.

Pre-processing: In all datasets, we pre-process the textual input that represents the corresponding reviews by tokenising it, removing HTML symbols, numbers and punctuation, also removing English stop words and contractions.

Evaluation Metrics: We apply the performance measures described in [5] to analyse how the rejection metric affects the quality of the resulting classifier, i.e.

- Non-rejected Accuracy: measures the ability of the classifier to classify non-rejected samples accurately.
- Classification Quality: measures the ability of the classifier with rejection to accurately classify non-rejected samples and to reject misclassified samples.
- Rejection Quality: measures the ability to concentrate all misclassified samples onto the set of rejected samples.

By using these performance metrics, we compare the uncertainty derived from the wrapper as a rejection heuristic with the baseline derived from directly using the entropy of the classification output logits. We compute the uncertainty heuristics based on predictive entropy and variation ratios of the aleatoric wrapper.

Experimental Results. Figure 2 displays the three rejection measures in all scenarios comparing the uncertainty derived from the predictive entropy of the output labels with the predictive entropy and variation ratios obtained using the wrapper. Observe that the aleatoric predictive entropy performs better in

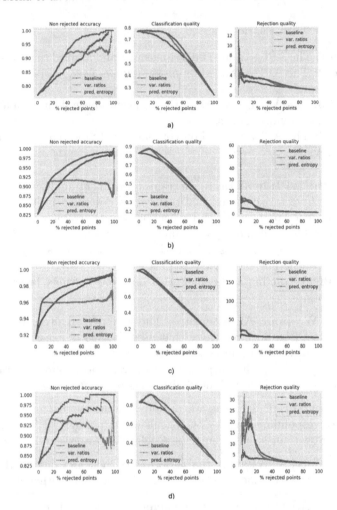

Fig. 2. Comparison of the three rejection measures where we compare the predictive entropy obtained using only the predictions of the original classifier with the predictive entropy and variation ratios obtained with the wrapper for the four experiments: (a) Yelp to SST-2; (b) SST-2 to Yelp; (c) computer reviews to music; (d) music reviews to computers.

the three performance measures. Variation ratios performs well for classification and rejection quality, but it fails to detect misclassified examples as the rejection point increases. Comparing aleatoric and non-aleatoric predictive entropies, both seem to capture wrong predictions, but the aleatoric one always outperforms the baseline in all cases.

Moreover, analyzing the non-rejected accuracy when using the aleatoric predictive entropy, the best performance is usually obtained with rejection ratios between 15% and 35%. Further, Table 1 shows that the proposed method out-

Table 1. Accuracy obtained by training an standalone classifier, applying the API and the proposed wrapper for each domain

	Standalone	API	Wrapper (20%)
Yelp	89.2%	77.1%	**92.2%**
SST-2	82.5%	82.2%	**83.7%**
Computer	85.2%	91.8%	**95.3%**
Music	93.1%	83.1%	**97.2%**

performs the accuracy resulting accuracy from training a standalone classifier using the target dataset directly. It is worth noting that we do not need a large amount of data for getting reliable uncertainty estimations. In particular, the Amazon music domain is composed of only 10k samples. The behaviour when exchanging the domains is not symmetric. We have observed that niche domains tend to display larger values of estimated sigmas when applied to more general domains. Effectively resulting in larger uncertainty estimations.

5   Conclusions

We present a method that leverages the aleatoric uncertainty to obtain a rejection metric for pre-trained classification systems. We illustrate the utility of this metric applying it to a sentiment analysis problem in four different scenarios, showing how practitioners can benefit from this method to discard those predictions that present a higher uncertainty, increasing, therefore, the quality of the prediction system.

For future work we plan to include the epistemic uncertainty, applying the method to other tasks, like language models, or work on the explainability of the uncertainty and how to identify which elements, in this case, words, are more relevant to the uncertainty obtained.

Acknowledgements. This work has been partially funded by the Spanish projects TIN2016-74946-P and TIN2015-66951-C2 (MINECO/FEDER, UE), and by AGAUR of the Generalitat de Catalunya through the Industrial PhD grant.

References

1. Xiao, Y., Wang, W.Y.: Quantifying Uncertainties in Natural Language Processing Tasks. arXiv preprint arXiv:1811.07253 (2018)
2. Gal, Y., Ghahramani, Z. Dropout as a Bayesian approximation: representing model uncertainty in deep learning. In: International Conference on Machine Learning (2016)
3. Kendall, A., Gal, Y. What uncertainties do we need in Bayesian deep learning for computer vision? In: Advances in Neural Information Processing Systems (2017)

4. Hernández-Lobato, J.M., Adams, R.: Probabilistic backpropagation for scalable learning of Bayesian neural networks. In: International Conference on Machine Learning (2015)
5. Condessa, F., et al.: Performance measures for classification systems with rejection. Pattern Recognit. **63**, 437–450 (2017)
6. Liu, H.: Sentiment Analysis of Citations Using Word2vec. CoRR abs/1704.00177, July 2017
7. Gal, Y.: Uncertainty in deep learning. Ph.D. thesis, University of Cambridge (2016)
8. Freeman, L.G.: Elementary Applied Statistics. Wiley, Hoboken (1965)
9. Shannon, C.E.: A mathematical theory of communication. Bell Syst. Tech. J. **27**(3), 379–423 (1948)
10. Socher, R., et al.: Recursive deep models for semantic compositionality over a sentiment Treebank. In: Proceedings of the 2013 EMNLP (2013)
11. Mikolov, T., et al.: Efficient estimation of word representations in vector space. In: Proceedings of Workshop at ICLR (2013)
12. Yelp Dataset Challenge. Yelp dataset challenge (2013)
13. Ranganath, R., Gerrish, S., Blei, D.: Black box variational inference. Artif. Intell. Stat. 814–822 (2014)
14. Naesseth, C.A., et al.: Variational sequential Monte Carlo. arXiv preprint arXiv:1705.11140 (2017)
15. Gal, Y., Ghahramani, Z.: A theoretically grounded application of dropout in recurrent neural networks. In: Advances in Neural Information Processing Systems (2016)
16. Devlin, J., et al.: BERT: pre-training of deep bidirectional transformers for language understanding. arXiv preprint arXiv:1810.04805 (2018)
17. Peters, M.E., et al.: Deep contextualized word representations. arXiv preprint arXiv:1802.05365 (2018)
18. Radford, A., et al.: Improving language understanding by generative pre-training (2018)
19. Pang, B., Lee, L.: Opinion mining and sentiment analysis. Found. Trends® Inf. Retr. **2**(1–2), 1–35 (2008)
20. Meehan, K., et al.: Context-aware intelligent recommendation system for tourism. In: 2013 IEEE International Conference on PERCOM Workshops. IEEE (2013)
21. Chow, C.K.: On optimum recognition error and reject tradeoff. IEEE Trans. Inf. Theory **16**(1), 41–45 (1970)
22. Yuan, M., et al.: Classification methods with reject option based on convex risk minimization. J. Mach. Learn. Res. **11**, 111–130 (2010)
23. Nadeem, M., et al.: Accuracy-rejection curves (ARCs) for comparing classification methods with a reject option. Mach. Learn. Syst. Biol. **8**, 65–81 (2010)
24. Landgrebe, T., et al.: The interaction between classification and reject performance for distance-based reject-option classifiers. Pattern Recognit. Lett. **27**(8), 908–917 (2006)
25. Blitzer, J., et al.: Biographies, bollywood, boom-boxes and blenders: domain adaptation for sentiment classification. In: ACL (2007)

Impact of Ultrasound Image Reconstruction Method on Breast Lesion Classification with Deep Learning

Michal Byra[1]([✉]), Tomasz Sznajder[2], Danijel Korzinek[2],
Hanna Piotrzkowska-Wroblewska[1], Katarzyna Dobruch-Sobczak[1],
Andrzej Nowicki[1], and Krzysztof Marasek[2]

[1] Department of Ultrasound, Institute of Fundamental Technological Research,
Polish Academy of Sciences, Warsaw, Poland
mbyra@ippt.pan.pl
[2] Department of Multimedia, Polish-Japanese Academy of Information Technology,
Warsaw, Poland

Abstract. In this work we investigate the usefulness and robustness of transfer learning with deep convolutional neural networks (CNNs) for breast lesion classification in ultrasound (US). Deep learning models can be vulnerable to adversarial examples, engineered input image pixel intensities perturbations that force models to make classification errors. In US imaging, distribution of US image pixel intensities relies on applied US image reconstruction algorithm. We explore the possibility of fooling deep learning models for breast mass classification by modifying US image reconstruction method. Raw radio-frequency US signals acquired from malignant and benign breast masses were used to reconstruct US images, and develop classifiers using transfer learning with the VGG19, InceptionV3 and InceptionResNetV2 CNNs. The areas under the receiver operating characteristic curve (AUCs) obtained for each deep learning model developed and evaluated using US images reconstructed in the same way were equal to approximately 0.85, and there were no associated differences in AUC values between the models (DeLong test p-values > 0.15). However, due to small modifications of the US image reconstruction method the AUC values for the models utilizing the VGG19, InceptionV3 and InceptionResNetV2 CNNs significantly decreased to 0.592, 0.584 and 0.687, respectively. Our study shows that the modification of US image reconstruction algorithm can have significant negative impact on classification performance of deep models. Taking into account medical image reconstruction algorithms may help develop more robust deep learning computer aided diagnosis systems.

Keywords: Adversarial attacks · Breast lesion classification · Computer aided diagnosis · Deep learning · Robustness · Ultrasound imaging · Transfer learning

Supported by the National Science Center (Poland), Grant Number UMO-2014/13/B/ST7/01271.

A. Morales et al. (Eds.): IbPRIA 2019, LNCS 11867, pp. 41–52, 2019.
https://doi.org/10.1007/978-3-030-31332-6_4

1   Introduction

Ultrasound (US) imaging is widely used for breast mass detection and differentiation in clinics. However, US data acquisition needs to be carried out by an experienced radiologist or physician who knows how to efficiently operate the ultrasound scanner. The operator has to locate the mass within the examined breast and properly record US images. Moreover, interpretation of the US images is not straightforward, but requires deep knowledge of characteristic image features related to breast mass malignancy.

Various computer-aided diagnosis (CADx) systems have been proposed to support the radiologists and improve differentiation of malignant and benign breast masses [6, 10, 11]. Currently, with the rise of deep learning methods, CADx systems based on convolutional neural networks (CNNs) are gaining momentum for breast mass classification [2–4, 13, 18, 26]. These networks process input images using convolutional filters to learn useful data representations and provide the desired output, such as a single binary decision related to the presence of particular object in the input image. However, better performing deep CNNs were developed using large sets of natural images [8]. Since medical image datasets are usually too small to train efficient CNNs from scratch, transfer learning methods are applied to develop deep learning models [20]. The aim of the transfer learning techniques is to employ a CNN model pre-trained on a large dataset of images from a different domain to address the medical image analysis problem of interest. In the case of the breast mass classification, deep models pre-trained on natural images were used to extract high level image features and utilize those to train binary classifiers, such as logistic regression or support vector machine algorithm [2–4].

In this paper we assess the usefulness of several deep learning models for transfer learning based breast mass classification. In comparison to the previous studies we investigate the impact of US B-mode image reconstruction algorithm on the classification performance [2–4, 13, 18, 26]. Our work is motivated by several studies reporting that deep learning systems can be vulnerable to adversarial examples, input images engineered to cause misclassification due to complex nonlinear behaviors of deep models [9]. Adversarial attacks can be performed by, for example, adding small artificially crafted perturbations to input image pixel intensities, which slightly modifies appearance of objects' edges and texture, and force deep model to perform wrong classification [12, 15, 16]. In medical image analysis, the vulnerability of deep learning models to adversarial attacks was demonstrated in the case of chest X-rays and dermoscopy images [9], raising concerns about the robustness of CADx systems based on CNNs [24]. Appearance of tissues in US imaging is related to applied image reconstruction algorithm. US scanners record raw radio-frequency (RF) backscattered signals and process them to reconstruct B-mode images. During routine US scanning the operator can modify scanner settings to differently reconstruct B-mode images to enhance specific B-mode image features. Due to high dynamic range RF US signals are commonly non-linearly compressed before B-mode image reconstruction. Modifications of the compression level result in different brightness levels of tissue interfaces and different speckle patterns. Here, we investigate the impact of US image reconstruction algorithm on breast mass classification with deep learning. We study whether small modifications of compression threshold levels related to applied B-mode image reconstruction may cause CNN based models to make classification errors.

2 Materials and Methods

2.1 Dataset

To develop deep learning models for breast mass classification we used an extension of the freely available breast mass dataset, the OASBUD (Open Access Series of Breast Ultrasonic Data) [5,17], which includes RF US data (before B-mode image reconstruction) recorded from breast focal masses during routine scanning performed in the Maria Skłodowska-Curie Memorial Cancer Centre and Institute of Oncology in Warsaw. The study was approved by the Institutional Review Board. The data were collected using the Ultrasonix Sonix-Touch Research ultrasound scanner with an L14-5/38 linear array transducer. The dataset includes RF signals recorded from 231 breast masses, 82 masses were malignant and 149 masses were benign. All malignant masses were histologically assessed by core needle biopsy. Benign masses were assessed either by the biopsy or a two year observation (every six months). For each scan a region of interest was determined by an experienced radiologist to correctly indicate breast mass area in B-mode image. More details regarding the dataset can be found in the original paper [17].

2.2 Ultrasound Image Reconstruction

Reconstruction scheme of a single B-mode image line is presented in Fig. 1. First, the RF signal acquired by the transducer is used to detect the envelope with the Hilbert transform. Second, since the dynamic range of US signal amplitudes is too high to fit on the screen directly, the amplitude samples are logarithmically compressed. In this work we used the following formula to compress amplitude samples:

$$A_{log} = 20log_{10}(A/A_{max}) \tag{1}$$

where A and A_{log} are the amplitude and the log-compressed amplitude of the ultrasonic signal, respectively. A_{max} indicates the highest value of the amplitude in the data. Next, the compressed amplitude samples are mapped to B-mode image pixel intensities based on a specified threshold level. Figure 2 shows three B-mode images of benign and malignant breast masses reconstructed using threshold levels of 45 dB, 50 dB and 55 dB, which are typically used in practice. Moreover, Fig. 3 shows the RF signal amplitude to pixel intensity mapping functions for these three different threshold levels. Physicians commonly select the threshold level to obtain desired image quality e.g. good speckle pattern

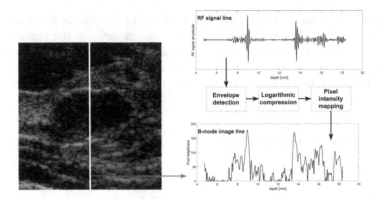

Fig. 1. Pipeline illustrating reconstruction of a single B-mode image line based on a radio-frequency ultrasound signal acquired by the transducer. The scheme includes envelope detection, logarithmic compression and mapping of compressed amplitude samples to B-mode image pixel intensities.

visibility or edge enhancement. For example, setting low threshold level results in removal of speckles that originates from US echoes of low intensities. Setting high threshold level may result in removal of important edge details.

2.3   Transfer Learning with Convolutional Neural Networks

We used three deep CNNs to perform transfer learning and classify breast masses, namely the VGG19, InceptionV3 and InceptionResNetV2 [14, 22, 23], all pre-trained on the ImageNet dataset [8] and implemented in TensorFlow [1]. These models achieved good performance on the ImageNet dataset and were used for breast mass classification with transfer learning in the previous studies [2, 4, 13]. In this work, we employed one of the most widely used transfer learning approaches, which aims to extract high level neural features from the last layers of the pre-trained model and use those to develop a classifier. In the case of the VGG19 CNN, we extracted features from the first fully connected layer. Moreover, average pooling layers of the InceptionV3 and InceptionResNetV2 CNNs were used to extract neural features.

2.4   Experiments and Evaluation

We performed several experiments to evaluate the usefulness of each CNN for the breast mass classification, and to explore the possibility of fooling the models by the compression threshold level modification. The experimental setup is presented in Fig. 4. We selected average compression threshold level of 50 dB and investigated how small perturbations (in range from 45 dB to 55 dB) can affect the classification. To assess the classification performance we applied leave-one-out cross validation. For each cross validation round, B-mode images in the training set were reconstructed using compression threshold level of 50 dB. In

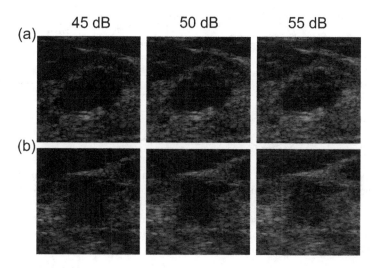

Fig. 2. B-mode images of (a) benign and (b) malignant masses reconstructed using compression threshold levels of 45 dB, 50 dB and 55 dB, respectively.

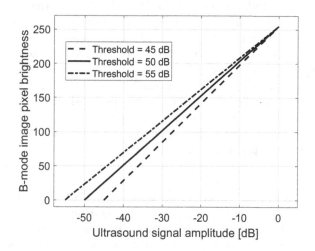

Fig. 3. B-mode image pixel brightness mapping function for logarithmic compression using compression threshold levels of 45 dB, 50 dB and 55 dB, respectively. Small modifications of the threshold level result in small change of B-mode image pixel intensities.

the case of the first experiment, each test B-mode image was reconstructed in the same way as those in the training set, using the threshold level of 50 dB. Therefore the perturbations were not applied for the first experiment. Next, to explore the possibility of fooling the models, we performed the second experiment. Again, all training B-mode images were reconstructed using the threshold level of 50 dB. But this time we reconstructed each test B-mode image using different threshold levels, ranging from 45 dB to 55 dB. Each classification model

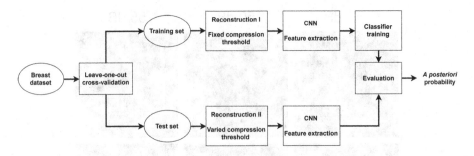

Fig. 4. Pipeline illustrating the experiments performed in our study. B-mode images for training were reconstructed using fixed compression threshold level of 50 dB. In the case of the test set, for the first experiment B-mode images were reconstructed using threshold level 50 dB, for the second (third) experiment the threshold was selected to maximally decrease (increase) the classification performance of each deep learning model. CNN - convolutional neural network.

developed on the training set was evaluated using all differently reconstructed test B-mode images, and we selected the B-mode image corresponding to the worst possible classification performance. If the test breast mass was malignant (benign), then we selected the B-mode image corresponding to the lowest (highest) obtained *a posteriori* probability of malignancy determined by the model. Studies on adversarial attacks in deep learning usually focus on efficient engineering of adversarial examples that would result in classification errors. In comparison to those studies, we also explored the possibility of using B-mode image perturbations to increase deep learning model classification performance. While the second experiment corresponded to the worst possible scenario, the third experiment corresponded to the best possible scenario. This time the test B-mode images were perturbed with the aim to increase classification performance.

To extract features for classification from deep CNNs we applied the following approach. Each B-mode image was cropped using the region on interest provided by the radiologist to contain the mass and a 5 mm band of surrounding tissues, see Fig. 2. Next, the US images were resized using bi-cubic interpolation to match the resolution originally designed for each neural network, 224×224 for the VGG19 CNN and 299×299 for the two other CNNs. Intensities of each image were copied along RGB channels and preprocessed in the same way as in the original papers [21–23]. The same approach utilizing the VGG19 CNN was employed in the previous studies on breast mass classification with transfer learning [2,3,13]. To perform binary classification we used the logistic regression algorithm. To address the problem of class imbalance, we used class weights inversely proportional to class frequencies in the training set. We used a linear classifier to omit possible issues related to the properties of non-linear classifiers, which could introduce additional non-linearity behaviors to the models in addition to those already related to deep CNNs.

To asses the classification performance we calculated the receiver operating characteristic (ROC) curves using model outputs obtained in each experiment. Next, we determined the areas under the ROC curves (AUC) for different models, the sensitivity, specificity and accuracy of the classifiers were calculated based on the ROC curve for the point on the curve that was the closest to (0, 1). The AUC value of 0.5 in the case of binary classification indicates random guessing, while the AUC value of 1 correspond to perfect classification. The AUC values of different models were compared with the DeLong test [7,19]. All calculations were performed in a programming environment including Python, R and Matlab (Mathworks, USA).

3   Results

Table 1 summarizes the classification performances obtained in all three experiments. In the case of the first experiment, for the test B-mode images reconstructed in the same way as the training images, the classification models achieved AUC values of 0.858, 0.829 and 0.860 for the VGG19, InceptionV3 and InceptionResNetV2 CNNs, respectively. There were no associated statistical differences between the AUC values obtained for the models developed using different deep CNNs (DeLong test p-values > 0.15).

In the case of the second experiment, based on the B-mode image reconstruction method modification we were able to decrease classification performance of each deep learning model. Results presented in Table 1 show that the AUC values significantly decreased (DeLong test p-values < 0.05). For the VGG19, InceptionV3 and InceptionResNet CNNs the AUC values were equal to 0.592, 0.584 and 0.687, respectively. The model trained based on features extracted from the InceptionResNetV2 CNN was less vulnerable to B-mode image modification than the other models. Figure 5 shows four adversarial examples engineered with our approach corresponding to two malignant and two benign breast masses. For example, benign breast mass present in Fig. 5a) was correctly classified as benign by all models, the corresponding *a posteriori* probabilities of malignancy were equal to 0.31, 0.38 and 0.23 for the models developed using VGG19, InceptionV3 and InceptionResNet CNNs, respectively. Due to the reconstruction threshold value modification, the corresponding probabilities increased to 0.62, 0.68 and 0.36, what caused classification errors in the case of the models developed using the VGG19 and InceptionV3 CNNs. The adversarial examples in Fig. 5 are very similar to the original B-mode images, with only slightly modified edge visibility and speckle patterns.

Additionally, Table 1 shows the results obtained in the case of the third experiment, which aimed to maximally increase classification performance by perturbing B-mode image pixel intensities. The AUC values for the VGG19, InceptionV3 and InceptionResNet CNNs significantly increased (DeLong test p-values < 0.05) to 0.970, 0.961 and 0.963, respectively.

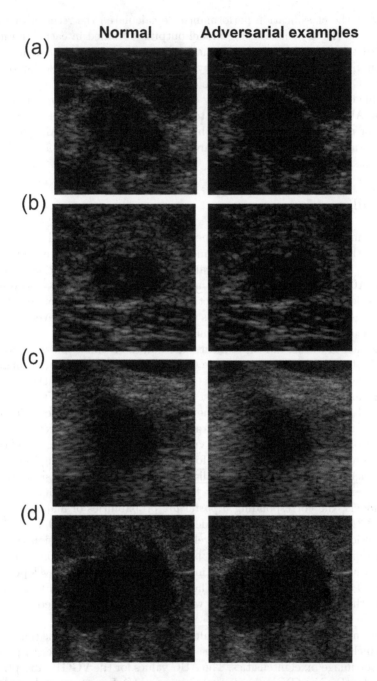

Fig. 5. Correctly classified breast mass B-mode images reconstructed using compression threshold level of 50 dB and corresponding B-mode images reconstructed to cause misclassification, (a), (b) benign masses and (c), (d) malignant masses.

Table 1. Classification performance of each deep learning model developed using transfer learning. The regular results were obtained for the models developed and evaluated using train and test B-mode images reconstructed in the same way. The worst (best) results were determined for the test B-mode images perturbed with the aim to maximally decrease (increase) classification performance. AUC - area under the receiver operating characteristic curve, standard deviations were calculated using bootstrap.

Network	Type	AUC	Accuracy	Sensitivity	Specificity
VGG19	Regular	0.858 ± 0.027	0.822 ± 0.038	0.768 ± 0.038	0.852 ± 0.034
	Worst	0.592 ± 0.034	0.649 ± 0.023	0.548 ± 0.040	0.7018 ± 0.030
	Best	0.970 ± 0.007	0.926 ± 0.015	0.890 ± 0.022	0.946 ± 0.025
InceptionV3	Regular	0.829 ± 0.028	0.757 ± 0.023	0.7682 ± 0.038	0.752 ± 0.038
	Worst	0.584 ± 0.030	0.584 ± 0.027	0.573 ± 0.062	0.590 ± 0.061
	Best	0.961 ± 0.008	0.896 ± 0.017	0.878 ± 0.026	0.901 ± 0.027
InceptionResNetV2	Regular	0.860 ± 0.026	0.792 ± 0.023	0.768 ± 0.038	0.801 ± 0.033
	Worst	0.687 ± 0.028	0.692 ± 0.028	0.573 ± 0.044	0.59 ± 0.049
	Best	0.963 ± 0.009	0.926 ± 0.023	0.890 ± 0.035	0.946 ± 0.032

4 Discussion

Our study shows the usefulness of the transfer learning with deep CNNs for breast mass classification in US. The model based on InceptionResNetV2 CNN achieved AUC value of 0.860. Our results are in agreement with those reported in the previous studies on breast mass classification with deep learning [2–4], where the authors obtained AUC values in range from 0.79 to 0.90. In [13] a specific approach to transfer learning was applied, which included fine-tuning and modification of the InceptionV3 architecture and ImageNet dataset. The authors used an ensemble of deep models for classification and reported high AUC value of 0.960. In our case, we used the InceptionV3 model for transfer learning in a more standard way following the approach proposed in [2].

Classification performance of all three developed deep learning models was sensitive to B-mode image reconstruction modifications. The decrease in classification performance was significant for all models, with the largest decrease obtained for the models developed using features extracted from the VGG19 and InceptionV3 CNNs (AUC values of 0.592 and 0.584). The model trained based on InceptionResNetV2 features was less vulnerable to US image reconstruction method modification (AUC value of 0.687). Figure 5 shows that the adversarial examples are very similar visually to the B-mode images reconstructed using threshold level of 50 dB. In comparison to the previous studies investigating how to engineer successful adversarial attacks [9], we additionally explored the possibility of manipulating image pixel intensities to artificially improve breast mass classification. By modifying the B-mode image reconstruction method we improved the performance of all models and achieved AUC values of around 0.97.

Our study depicts several important issues related to the development of CADx systems using transfer learning with deep pre-trained CNNs. First of all, the image reconstruction procedures implemented in medical scanners should be taken into account during CADx system development. It is important to know how B-mode images were acquired and reconstructed. Classification errors may result from issues related to applied B-mode image reconstruction methods, such as using non-standard scanner settings. To improve performance and make deep learning models more robust it might be necessary to develop the models based on B-mode images acquired using different scanner settings. The second possibility is to always use the same image reconstruction algorithms and scanner setting for B-mode image acquisition. In our study we used a unique dataset of RF signals collected with a research US scanner. Regular clinical US scanners, however, usually don't have access to RF data, and such data are not stored in hospital databases. Researchers, who would like to develop deep learning models based on large sets of retrospectively collected B-mode images extracted from a hospital database should take into account what apparatus and procedures were used to scan the patients. Unfortunately, usually little is known about the applied B-mode image reconstruction algorithms implemented by different US scanner manufacturers.

There are several issues related to our approach, which should be addressed in future. First, to develop the models we used one of the most widely used, but relatively simple, transfer learning method. In this case the pre-trained deep CNNs were used as fixed feature extractors. It remains to be studied whether deep learning models developed from scratch would be similarly vulnerable to B-mode image reconstruction method modifications. Second, we only explored the possibility of fooling models based on the modification of compression threshold levels, but it is also possible to modify other parameters related to the B-mode image reconstruction method. For example, perturbations of B-mode image pixel intensities can also arise from setting different logarithm base for compression. Moreover, the texture of B-mode images depends on applied beamforming technique [27] and imaging frequency [25]. Nevertheless, in the case of our study it was sufficient to modify compression threshold values to significantly change classification performance of the deep learning models.

5   Conclusions

In this work we investigated the impact of B-mode image reconstruction method on breast mass classification with deep learning. By modifying B-mode image reconstruction method we were able to significantly decrease or increase classification performance of each deep learning classifier. We believe that our work is an important step towards the development of robust deep learning computer aided diagnosis systems.

Conict of interest statement. The authors do not have any conicts of interests.

References

1. Abadi, M., et al.: TensorFlow: a system for large-scale machine learning. OSDI **16**, 265–283 (2016)
2. Antropova, N., Huynh, B.Q., Giger, M.L.: A deep feature fusion methodology for breast cancer diagnosis demonstrated on three imaging modality datasets. Med. Phys. **44**, 5162–5171 (2017)
3. Byra, M.: Discriminant analysis of neural style representations for breast lesion classification in ultrasound. Biocybern. Biomed. Eng. **38**(3), 684–690 (2018)
4. Byra, M., et al.: Breast mass classification in sonography with transfer learning using a deep convolutional neural network and color conversion. Med. Phys. **46**(2), 746–755 (2019)
5. Byra, M., Nowicki, A., Wróblewska-Piotrzkowska, H., Dobruch-Sobczak, K.: Classification of breast lesions using segmented quantitative ultrasound maps of homodyned K distribution parameters. Med. Phys. **43**(10), 5561–5569 (2016)
6. Cheng, H.D., Shan, J., Ju, W., Guo, Y., Zhang, L.: Automated breast cancer detection and classification using ultrasound images: a survey. Pattern Recognit. **43**(1), 299–317 (2010). https://doi.org/10.1016/j.patcog.2009.05.012
7. DeLong, E.R., DeLong, D.M., Clarke-Pearson, D.L.: Comparing the areas under two or more correlated receiver operating characteristic curves: a nonparametric approach. Biometrics **44**(3), 837–845 (1988)
8. Deng, J., Dong, W., Socher, R., Li, L.J., Li, K., Fei-Fei, L.: ImageNet: a largescale hierarchical image database. In: IEEE Conference on Computer Vision and Pattern Recognition, CVPR 2009, pp. 248–255. IEEE (2009)
9. Finlayson, S.G., Kohane, I.S., Beam, A.L.: Adversarial attacks against medical deep learning systems. arXiv preprint arXiv:1804.05296 (2018)
10. Flores, W.G., de Albuquerque Pereira, W.C., Infantosi, A.F.C.: Improving classification performance of breast lesions on ultrasonography. Pattern Recognit. **48**(4), 1125–1136 (2015)
11. Giger, M.L., Karssemeijer, N., Schnabel, J.A.: Breast image analysis for risk assessment, detection, diagnosis, and treatment of cancer. Annu. Rev. Biomed. Eng. **15**, 327–357 (2013)
12. Goodfellow, I.J., Shlens, J., Szegedy, C.: Explaining and harnessing adversarial examples. arXiv preprint arXiv:1412.6572 (2014)
13. Han, S., et al.: A deep learning framework for supporting the classification of breast lesions in ultrasound images. Phys. Med. Biol. **62**(19), 7714 (2017)
14. He, K., Zhang, X., Ren, S., Sun, J.: Deep residual learning for image recognition. In: Proceedings of the IEEE Conference on Computer Vision and Pattern Recognition, pp. 770–778 (2016)
15. Moosavi-Dezfooli, S.M., Fawzi, A., Frossard, P.: DeepFool: a simple and accurate method to fool deep neural networks. In: Proceedings of the IEEE Conference on Computer Vision and Pattern Recognition, pp. 2574–2582 (2016)
16. Nguyen, A., Yosinski, J., Clune, J.: Deep neural networks are easily fooled: High confidence predictions for unrecognizable images. In: Proceedings of the IEEE Conference on Computer Vision and Pattern Recognition, pp. 427–436 (2015)
17. Piotrzkowska-Wróblewska, H., Dobruch-Sobczak, K., Byra, M., Nowicki, A.: Open access database of raw ultrasonic signals acquired from malignant and benign breast lesions. Med. Phys. **44**(11), 6105–6109 (2017)
18. Qi, X., et al.: Automated diagnosis of breast ultrasonography images using deep neural networks. Med. Image Anal. **52**, 185–198 (2019)

19. Robin, X., et al.: pROC: an open-source package for R and S+ to analyze and compare ROC curves. BMC Bioinform. **12**, 77 (2011)
20. Shin, H.C., et al.: Deep convolutional neural networks for computer-aided detection: CNN architectures, dataset characteristics and transfer learning. IEEE Trans. Med. Imaging **35**(5), 1285–1298 (2016)
21. Simonyan, K., Zisserman, A.: Very deep convolutional networks for large-scale image recognition. arXiv preprint arXiv:1409.1556 (2014)
22. Szegedy, C., Ioffe, S., Vanhoucke, V., Alemi, A.A.: Inception-v4, inception-ResNet and the impact of residual connections on learning. In: Thirty-First AAAI Conference on Artificial Intelligence (2017)
23. Szegedy, C., Vanhoucke, V., Ioffe, S., Shlens, J., Wojna, Z.: Rethinking the inception architecture for computer vision. In: Proceedings of the IEEE Conference on Computer Vision and Pattern Recognition, pp. 2818–2826 (2016)
24. Topol, E.J.: High-performance medicine: the convergence of human and artificial intelligence. Nat. Med. **25**(1), 44 (2019)
25. Tsui, P.H., Zhou, Z., Lin, Y.H., Hung, C.M., Chung, S.J., Wan, Y.L.: Effect of ultrasound frequency on the nakagami statistics of human liver tissues. PLoS ONE **12**(8), e0181789 (2017)
26. Yap, M.H., et al.: Automated breast ultrasound lesions detection using convolutional neural networks. IEEE J. Biomed. Health Inform. **22**, 1218–1226 (2017)
27. Yu, X., Guo, Y., Huang, S.M., Li, M.L., Lee, W.N.: Beamforming effects on generalized Nakagami imaging. Phys. Med. Biol. **60**(19), 7513 (2015)

Segmentation of Cell Nuclei in Fluorescence Microscopy Images Using Deep Learning

Hemaxi Narotamo, J. Miguel Sanches, and Margarida Silveira(✉)

Institute for Systems and Robotics (ISR/IST), LARSyS, Instituto Superior Técnico,
Universidade de Lisboa, Lisbon, Portugal
{hemaxi.narotamo,jmrs}@tecnico.ulisboa.pt,
msilveira@isr.tecnico.ulisboa.pt

Abstract. Cell nuclei segmentation is important for several applications, such as the detection of cancerous cells and cell cycle staging. The main challenges and difficulties, associated with this task, arise due to the presence of overlapping nuclei, image intensity inhomogeneities and image noise.

Several classical methods have been proposed for cell nuclei segmentation. However, they depend strongly on manual setting of parameters and they are sensitive to noise. Recently, deep learning is becoming state-of-the-art, due to its enhanced performance in many tasks of computer vision, such as object detection, classification and segmentation. Deep learning models are robust to the presence of noise and are able to automatically extract meaningful features from the image. Although deep learning models perform significantly better than the traditional methods, they are computationally more expensive.

In this paper we present a computationally efficient approach for high throughput nuclei segmentation based on deep learning. Our approach combines the object detection capability of Fast YOLO with the segmentation ability of U-Net. We applied our method to 2D fluorescence microscopy images with DAPI stained nuclei. Our results show that our method is competitive with Mask R-CNN, but significantly faster. In fact, with our method, an image of size 1388 × 1040 is segmented in approximately 1.6 s which is about nine times faster than the Mask R-CNN (15.1 s). Additionally, our results show that the improvements in computational efficiency come at only a small cost in performance.

Keywords: Deep learning · Nuclei segmentation · Cell imaging

This work was supported by Portuguese funds through FCT (Fundação para a Ciência e Tecnologia) through the projects TRACE (PTDC/BBB-IMG/0283/2014) and reference UID/EEA/50009/2019.

A. Morales et al. (Eds.): IbPRIA 2019, LNCS 11867, pp. 53–64, 2019.
https://doi.org/10.1007/978-3-030-31332-6_5

1 Introduction

Nuclear segmentation provides valuable information about nuclei morphology, DNA content and chromatin condensation. For instance, morphological and textural features can be used for cell cycle staging [9,18] and detection of pathological mutations associated with cancer [14]. Cell overlapping, image noise and non-uniform acquisition and preparation parameters make the segmentation procedure a challenging task.

Manual segmentation is time-consuming and depends on the subjective assessment of the human operator [8]. Thus, it is not a practical approach in high-throughput applications where a huge number of nuclei need to be accurately detected. Hence, new automatic segmentation tools are needed and machine learning and computer vision approaches are the most common choices [21].

Classical approaches include Otsu's thresholding followed by watershed algorithm, graph-cuts based methods, K-means clustering and region growing [12,20]. However, these techniques often require the tuning of manual parameters, they are sensitive to noise and sometimes can be very specific for given types of images. Deep learning approaches, successfully applied in many other fields, are obvious choices for nuclei segmentation because they are robust to noise, able to learn automatically the parameters and present a good generalization capacity.

Several deep learning based approaches have been proposed for cell nuclei segmentation and it is shown that their performance is better in terms of accuracy when compared to traditional techniques mentioned above. U-Net [17], a simple and computationally efficient convolutional network, winner of the Cell Tracking Challenge in 2015, is one of the most used architectures in biomedical image segmentation and cell nuclei as well. It performs semantic segmentation, that is, it makes classification in a pixel wise basis. It is able to classify single pixels but not objects (sets of pixels). For example, if two or more nuclei are touching, it will classify them as being a single object. Since in nuclei segmentation task each nucleus needs to be identified separately, several authors proposed methods, based on U-net, to address this difficulty. Ronneberger et al. had already proposed, in the original U-net paper [17], the use of a weighted cross entropy loss function where the weight maps are created in a way to give higher weights to pixels that are closer to two or more boundaries, in that way the model can learn the separation between close objects. Other approaches convert the binary problem into a ternary one, by changing the last layer of U-Net to predict not only the nuclei but also the contour of each nucleus [5,7]. Recently, the winners of the Kaggle data competition 2018 [1,2] have shown a novel way to tackle the problem of nuclei segmentation. They changed the ground truth masks by adding a third channel that represents the touching borders between nuclei. In this way the masks contain three classes: background, nuclei and touching borders. Furthermore, they used an encoder-decoder type architecture based on U-Net and the encoder was initialized with pre-trained weights. Since then several studies [10,19] have applied similar approaches using U-Net by allowing it to predict both the nuclei and touching borders.

Recently, He et al. [11] proposed Mask R-CNN. This is an architecture designed for instance segmentation, where the main goal is to obtain a segmentation mask for each object in the image. It corresponds to the segmentation of individual objects in an image. Instance segmentation is a combination of object detection, where the goal is to identify each object's category and bounding box, and segmentation. Therefore, in instance segmentation, different instances of the same object have different labels. Mask R-CNN has essentially two stages, the first stage is a region proposal network (RPN) which generates region proposals. For each pixel, it proposes k bounding boxes and a score that tells if the bounding box contains an object or not. In the second stage, for each of the bounding boxes proposed by RPN, features are extracted and classification and bounding box regression is performed. Additionally, the mask branch generates a segmentation mask for the object enclosed in the bounding box. Although Mask R-CNN was developed for segmentation of natural images, Johnson et al. [13] have demonstrated that it can be used for the task of nuclei segmentation. Similar conclusions are drawn by Vuola et al. [19], in a study where a comparison between U-Net, Mask R-CNN and an ensemble of these two models was made. Their results showed that Mask R-CNN performs better in the nuclei detection task and U-Net performs better in the segmentation task. Finally, by combining the strengths of both models, the ensemble model performs better than both models separately. However, the main problem associated with Mask R-CNN is its high computational cost.

In this work we present an alternative to Mask R-CNN for nuclei instance segmentation. Speed is an important factor to take into consideration if the method is going to be implemented in clinical routine. We propose a deep learning based approach that achieves good segmentation results and is computationally efficient. Our approach is based on a combination of Fast YOLO for instance detection and U-Net for segmentation. According to [15], Fast YOLO can be used for real time object detection in video and it is one of the fastest object detection methods, hence its superiority compared to Mask R-CNN with respect to computational efficiency.

This paper is organized as follows: in Sect. 1 a review of the methods for cell nuclei segmentation and the goal of this work were presented. In Sect. 2 a novel deep learning approach is presented for cell nuclei instance segmentation. Section 3 describes the dataset used in this project, training of the proposed approach and evaluation metrics. In Sect. 4, the main experimental results regarding nuclei segmentation are presented as well as a comparison with some state-of-the-art methods mentioned in Sect. 1. Finally, in Sect. 5 conclusions and topics requiring future studies are presented.

2 Proposed Approach

The proposed approach for cell nuclei instance segmentation is based on a combination of two deep learning models: Fast YOLO [15] and U-Net [17], as illustrated in Fig. 1. YOLO is an architecture designed for object detection and classification, which is faster than Mask R-CNN. This is due to the fact that instead of using an RPN, which is based on a sliding window approach, YOLO applies a single network to the full image. In YOLO the image is divided into regions and then bounding boxes and class probabilities are predicted for each region. There is just one single network that divides the image and predicts objects and its corresponding classes, additionally this network can be trained end-to-end.

We used a smaller version of YOLO (Fast YOLO[1]), which has fewer convolutional layers, hence it is faster than YOLO. Nevertheless, Fast YOLO only gives a bounding box for each detected nucleus, and we want to obtain a segmentation mask for each nucleus. Therefore, we combine Fast YOLO with an U-Net trained to segment individual nuclei. We start by feeding the input image to the Fast YOLO, this will provide us bounding boxes for all detected objects in that image, steps A and B in Fig. 1, respectively. After this step, for each bounding box, the corresponding image patch is extracted and resized to a patch of size 80×80 (see step C in Fig. 1), this patch is then fed to the U-Net which will give as output a binary mask, where 0 and 1 denote pixels belonging to the background and nucleus, respectively, (step D in Fig. 1). Then, the output of the U-Net, which has size 80×80, is resized again to its original size. Finally, a spatial arrangement (step F in Fig. 1) is necessary to obtain the final segmentation mask.

The objective of the proposed approach is to first minimize the loss function of the Fast YOLO network, as described in [15], and then minimize the loss function of the U-Net, which we've defined as:

$$Loss = 0.5 \times binary\ cross\ entropy + 0.5 \times (1 - dice\ coefficient) \qquad (1)$$

where the definition of binary cross entropy (BCE) and dice coefficient (DC) is represented in Eqs. 2 and 3, respectively.[2]

$$BCE = -\sum_{i=1}^{N} y_i \times log(\hat{y}_i) + (1 - y_i) \times log(1 - \hat{y}_i) \qquad (2)$$

$$DC = \frac{2 \times |X \cap Y|}{|X| + |Y|} \qquad (3)$$

3   Experiments

In this section the dataset used in the experiments is described. Additionaly, details regarding the training of the proposed deep learning approach and evaluation metrics used to measure the performance of the model are presented.

---

[1] The architecture of Fast YOLO (illustrated in Fig. 1), is different from the one presented in the original YOLO paper [15]. In fact, the architecture of Fast YOLO used in this work is a smaller version of YOLOv2, which has some improvements over YOLO, as stated in [16].

[2] N is the total number of pixels in a given image, y_i is the true label of the pixel i and $\hat{y}_i$ denotes the predicted label for the pixel i.

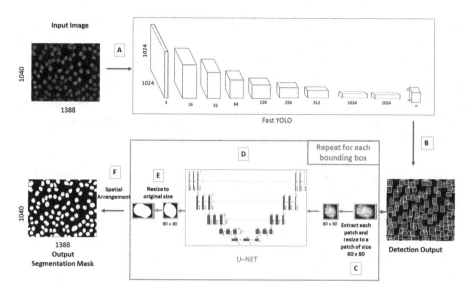

Fig. 1. Overview of the proposed approach for cell nuclei instance segmentation. The input image is fed to the Fast YOLO architecture (step A). Fast YOLO will give as output bounding boxes for all of the detected objects in the input image (step B). Afterwards, each patch inside the bounding box proposed by the previous architecture is resized to 80 × 80 (step C) and fed to the U-Net (step D). The output patch of the U-Net is then resized to the original size (step E). Finally, after spatial arrangement, the final segmentation mask is obtained, (step F).

3.1 Data

The training dataset used in the experiments consists of 130 fluorescence microscopy images of normal murine mammary gland cells stained with DAPI, with size 1388 × 1040. This dataset comes from the study presented by Ferro et al. [9]. Additionally, another dataset with one nucleus per image and patch size 80 × 80 was necessary to train the U-Net. This dataset was obtained from the original one by using the skimage tool regionprops. For each image, the ground truth mask was labeled, then regionprops tool was applied to measure the properties of the labeled mask regions, which include the bounding box coordinates for each object. This operation allows to extract one patch per nucleus, which is then resized to a patch of size 80 × 80.

3.2 Training

Fast YOLO. The implementation used for Fast YOLO is based on a publicly available implementation by Thtrieu which was released under the GNU General Public License v3.0 [3]. In order to train the Fast YOLO with our dataset, we had to generate XML files based on Pascal VOC format. These files were generated from the ground truth data using skimage tool regionprops and lxml.etree module. We've adapted the network for our problem, the number of classes in our problem is one, therefore we changed the number of filters of the last layer to 30, according to the formula $5 \times (classes + 5)$ [3]. We also changed the number of classes to 1 and resized the original image to an image of size 1024×1024. All of the other parameters remained unchanged. Finally, Fast YOLO was trained from scratch, using Adam optimizer, first it was trained for 200 epochs with learning rate 0.0001, then it was trained for another 600 epochs with learning rate 0.00001.

U-Net. We implemented the U-Net model using Keras with Tensorflow backend. The architecture of the model implemented is represented in Fig. 2. This model was trained for 100 epochs, with a learning rate of 0.001, using Adam optimizer, without dropout, with Xavier initialization and with ReLU as activation functions, except the final activation function of the last layer which is a sigmoid activation function.

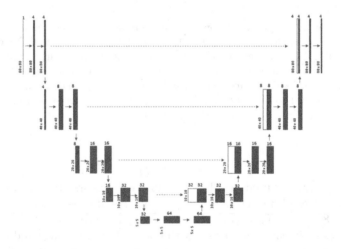

Fig. 2. U-Net architecture used for the segmentation step of the proposed approach.

3.3 Evaluation Criteria

To test the performance of the proposed segmentation model, we calculated the F1 score (see Eq. 7), at different thresholds of the intersection over union (IoU). The IoU between two objects is given by:

$$IoU = \frac{Area\,of\,overlap}{Area\,of\,union} \qquad (4)$$

For each image, an m × n matrix is built. Where m denotes the total number of objects in the ground truth mask, n the total number of objects in the predicted mask. And the component (i,j) corresponds to the IoU (Eq. 4) between object i and object j. The F1 score was calculated after applying different thresholds to this matrix. That is, the F1 score was computed by varying the IoU threshold (T) from 0.5 to 0.95, by steps of size 0.05. The F1 score requires the calculation of the precision (Eq. 5) and recall (Eq. 6). Where TP, FP and FN stand for true positives, false positives and false negatives, respectively. In one hand, a nucleus detected by an automatic technique is considered as TP if, for a given IoU threshold (T), its IoU with some ground truth nucleus is higher than T. On the other hand, if its IoU is lower than T, it is considered as FP (extra object). Finally, if for a given ground truth nucleus there isn't a corresponding detection, it will be considered as FN (miss detection).

$$Precision = \frac{TP}{TP + FP} \tag{5}$$

$$Recall = \frac{TP}{FN + TP} \tag{6}$$

$$F1\ Score = \frac{2 \times Precision \times Recall}{Precision + Recall} \tag{7}$$

3.4 Performance Comparison

We measured the performance of our approach and compared it with the performance of four approaches: Yen's thresholding plus watershed [12,22], Original U-Net [17], similar approach to the winning solution of Kaggle 2018 [2] and Mask R-CNN [11]. To simplify we denote these models as: Yen + watershed, Original U-Net, Kaggle_2018 and Mask R-CNN, respectively. To compare the performance between different models, a 13-fold cross validation was performed. In other words, for each approach, except for Yen + watershed, we've trained 13 models with 120 images each and tested their performance on 10 images. We perform leave-one-experiment-out cross-validation in order to avoid the bias introduced during the evaluation, that is, to avoid the bias that would be introduced when testing the model in images that were acquired in the same experiment as some images that were used to train this model. The final F1 Score for each approach is an average over the 13 models.

All experiments were carried out on an NVIDIA GPU GTX 1050 (4 GB) and in Python 3.6. Additionally, all implementations are based on open-source deep learning libraries Tensorflow and Keras [4,6].

4   Results

In this section, results regarding nuclei segmentation, F1 score and computational efficiency are presented. Additionally, a comparison with four state-of-the-art methods is made.

4.1   Nuclei Segmentation

We compared the performance of our approach with other state-of-the-art methods. Figure 3 shows a visual comparison between different models, regarding nuclei segmentation. The four images (in the first row) were chosen in order to emphasize the variability that exists between different input images. These images represent the blue channel of the corresponding original fluorescence images. As stated before, our dataset contains images stained with DAPI, which is a nuclear stain that binds to the DNA and emits blue fluorescence. Therefore, the blue channel of the original images contains information regarding the nuclei.

The third row in Fig. 3 shows the segmentation masks obtained by applying Yen + watershed, by observing this row it can be concluded that in some cases the segmentation masks are bigger than the ground truth masks. This is a disadvantage of the thresholding methods. Additionally, in comparison with other approaches, this is the approach that presents more merges, i.e., two or more nuclei that are joined into a big object. Results regarding Original U-Net (fourth row) and Kaggle_2018 (fifth row) show that although these approaches separate better the touching nuclei, in some cases there are gaps between these nuclei. This can be explained by our ground truth data which also has gaps between touching nuclei, in order to solve the problem as an instance segmentation problem. On the other hand, in the results obtained with Mask R-CNN and our approach those gaps disappear, since these two approaches are designed specifically to solve the problem of instance segmentation.

The last column in Fig. 3 illustrates why Mask R-CNN model outperforms all the other models. In this case there is high intensity variation along the input image and the image contains a lot of touching and occluded nuclei. Therefore, the classical method (Yen + watershed) struggles in detecting nuclei located on the left side of the image. Interestingly, our approach performs better than Yen + watershed, but still it fails to identify some of the occluded nuclei. This is due to the detection performance of Fast YOLO, which is worse than that of Mask R-CNN, specially in regions with occluded nuclei, where some of the nuclei aren't detected. Mask R-CNN is the one that provides the best segmentation mask for this input image. However, note that for the other three images the results obtained with Mask R-CNN and the ones obtained with our model are quite similar.

4.2   F1 Score vs IoU Threshold

Figure 4 shows a plot of average F1 score across increasing thresholds of IoU. The accentuated decrease of the F1 score, at $IoU \approx 0.80$, can be explained by the presence of inaccurate boundaries on our ground truth data. For example, since our ground truth masks are binary, in order to separate touching nuclei and to solve the problem as an instance segmentation problem, we have drawn lines to separate touching nuclei and considered the pixels contained in these lines as belonging to the background, (this can be observed in the second row in Fig. 3).

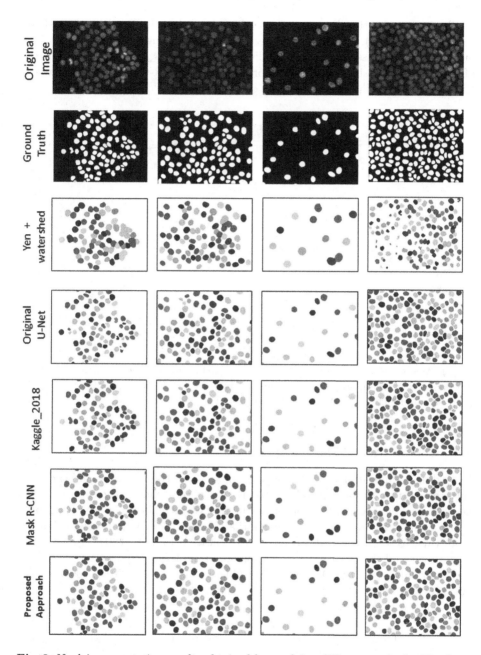

Fig. 3. Nuclei segmentation results obtained by applying different methods. The first row represents examples of the original images, for which we want to obtain the segmentation mask. The second row represents the corresponding ground truth masks. Finally, the third, fourth, fifth, sixth and seventh rows represent the corresponding segmentation results obtained by applying Yen + watershed, Original U-Net, Kaggle_2018, Mask R-CNN and the proposed approach, respectively. (Color figure online)

By comparing the deep learning approaches with the traditional method (Yen + watershed), we can conclude that deep learning models significantly outperform this classical method. Additionally, for $IoU < 0.75$ the performance of our approach is similar to the performance of Mask R-CNN and better than that of all of the other methods.

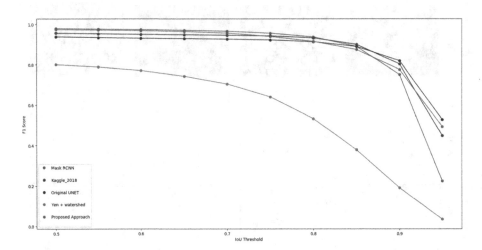

Fig. 4. Average F1-Score vs IoU threshold, comparison between different models: Yen + watershed (purple), original U-Net (green), Kaggle_2018 (blue), Mask R-CNN (red), proposed approach (yellow). (Color figure online)

4.3   Computational Efficiency

Regarding computational efficiency we compared the training time and the test time required by all the methods. Training time corresponds to the time a model needs to learn a given task, in our case, the task of nuclei instance segmentation. By observing Fig. 5(a), we can conclude that Mask R-CNN requires significantly more time to learn the task of nuclei segmentation (about 1420 min), in comparison with all the other models. Although our approach requires more time to train (450 min) than the Original U-Net (14 min) and Kaggle_2018 (100 min), it also provides better segmentation masks as illustrated in Fig. 3.

On the other hand, regarding test time, which is the time required for a model to give a segmentation prediction for an image, our results are presented in Fig. 5(b). These results show that Mask R-CNN is the model that presents the highest test time (15.1 s). Our approach in comparison with Mask R-CNN is about nine times faster. Furthermore, Yen + watershed requires 1.8 s, which is of the same order of magnitude as the test time of our approach (1.6 s), however Yen + watershed presents the worst performance, as observed in Fig. 4.

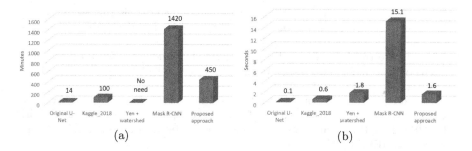

Fig. 5. (a) Training time (in minutes) associated with each model. (b) Mean test time per image (in seconds) for each model, for images of size 1388 × 1040.

5 Conclusions and Future Work

This paper addresses the important problem of nuclei segmentation for high throughput applications.

We proposed a new approach that combines the Fast YOLO architecture, specially designed for detection, with the U-Net that was conceived mainly for segmentation purposes.

The segmentation quality obtained with the proposed method is comparable to the existing deep-learning based state-of-the-art methods, e.g. Mask R-CNN, but a significant reduction of almost 10× on the segmentation time was obtained.

In the future, morphological and textural features will be extracted from the segmented nuclei for diagnosis of pathogenic mutations associated with cancer.

Acknowledgments. We acknowledge the EPIC (Epithelial Interactions in Cancer) from i3S/Ipatimup by the biological support of this research. In particular for providing the image data used in this paper.

References

1. Find the nuclei in divergent images to advance medical discovery. https://www.kaggle.com/c/data-science-bowl-2018/discussion. Accessed 20 Feb 2019
2. [ods.ai] topcoders, 1st place solution on data science bowl 2018. https://www.kaggle.com/c/data-science-bowl-2018/discussion/54741#latest-477226. Accessed 20 Feb 2019
3. Darkflow (2018). https://github.com/thtrieu/darkflow
4. Abadi, M., et al.: TensorFlow: large-scale machine learning on heterogeneous systems (2015). https://www.tensorflow.org/, software available from tensorflow.org
5. Caicedo, J.C., et al.: Evaluation of deep learning strategies for nucleus segmentation in fluorescence images. BioRxiv, p. 335216 (2019)
6. Chollet, F., et al.: Keras (2015). https://keras.io
7. Cui, Y., Zhang, G., Liu, Z., Xiong, Z., Hu, J.: A deep learning algorithm for one-step contour aware nuclei segmentation of histopathological images. arXiv preprint arXiv:1803.02786 (2018)

8. Deshmukh, B.S., Mankar, V.H.: Segmentation of microscopic images: a survey. In: 2014 International Conference on Electronic Systems, Signal Processing and Computing Technologies, pp. 362–364. IEEE (2014)

9. Ferro, A., Mestre, T., Carneiro, P., Sahumbaiev, I., Seruca, R., Sanches, J.M.: Blue intensity matters for cell cycle profiling in fluorescence DAPI-stained images. Lab. Investig. **97**(5), 615 (2017)

10. Guerrero-Pena, F.A., Fernandez, P.D.M., Ren, T.I., Yui, M., Rothenberg, E., Cunha, A.: Multiclass weighted loss for instance segmentation of cluttered cells. In: 2018 25th IEEE International Conference on Image Processing (ICIP), pp. 2451–2455. IEEE (2018)

11. He, K., Gkioxari, G., Dollár, P., Girshick, R.: Mask R-CNN. In: Proceedings of the IEEE International Conference on Computer Vision, pp. 2961–2969 (2017)

12. Irshad, H., Veillard, A., Roux, L., Racoceanu, D.: Methods for nuclei detection, segmentation, and classification in digital histopathology: a review-current status and future potential. IEEE Rev. Biomed. Eng. **7**, 97–114 (2014)

13. Johnson, J.W.: Adapting Mask-RCNN for automatic nucleus segmentation. arXiv preprint arXiv:1805.00500 (2018)

14. Mestre, T., Figueiredo, J., Ribeiro, A.S., Paredes, J., Seruca, R., Sanches, J.M.: Quantification of topological features in cell meshes to explore E-cadherin dysfunction. Sci. Rep. **6**, 25101 (2016)

15. Redmon, J., Divvala, S., Girshick, R., Farhadi, A.: You only look once: Unified, real-time object detection. In: Proceedings of the IEEE Conference on Computer Vision and Pattern Recognition, pp. 779–788 (2016)

16. Redmon, J., Farhadi, A.: Yolo9000: better, faster, stronger. In: Proceedings of the IEEE Conference on Computer Vision and Pattern Recognition, pp. 7263–7271 (2017)

17. Ronneberger, O., Fischer, P., Brox, T.: U-Net: convolutional networks for biomedical image segmentation. In: Navab, N., Hornegger, J., Wells, W.M., Frangi, A.F. (eds.) MICCAI 2015. LNCS, vol. 9351, pp. 234–241. Springer, Cham (2015). https://doi.org/10.1007/978-3-319-24574-4_28

18. Roukos, V., Pegoraro, G., Voss, T.C., Misteli, T.: Cell cycle staging of individual cells by fluorescence microscopy. Nat. Protoc. **10**(2), 334 (2015)

19. Vuola, A.O., Akram, S.U., Kannala, J.: Mask-RCNN and U-net ensembled for nuclei segmentation. arXiv preprint arXiv:1901.10170 (2019)

20. Xing, F., Yang, L.: Robust nucleus/cell detection and segmentation in digital pathology and microscopy images: a comprehensive review. IEEE Rev. Biomed. Eng. **9**, 234–263 (2016)

21. Xue, Y., Ray, N.: Cell detection in microscopy images with deep convolutional neural network and compressed sensing. arXiv preprint arXiv:1708.03307 (2017)

22. Yen, J.C., Chang, F.J., Chang, S.: A new criterion for automatic multilevel thresholding. IEEE Trans. Image Process. **4**(3), 370–378 (1995)

Food Recognition by Integrating Local and Flat Classifiers

Eduardo Aguilar[1,2]([envelope]) [iD] and Petia Radeva[2,3] [iD]

[1] Universidad Católica del Norte, Antofagasta, Chile
eaguilar02@ucn.cl
[2] Universitat de Barcelona, Barcelona, Spain
[3] Computer Vision Center, Bellaterra, Spain

Abstract. The recognition of food image is an interesting research topic, in which its applicability in the creation of nutritional diaries stands out with the aim of improving the quality of life of people with a chronic disease (e.g. diabetes, heart disease) or prone to acquire it (e.g. people with overweight or obese). For a food recognition system to be useful in real applications, it is necessary to recognize a huge number of different foods. We argue that for very large scale classification, a traditional flat classifier is not enough to acquire an acceptable result. To address this, we propose a method that performs prediction with local classifiers, based on a class hierarchy, or with flat classifier. We decide which approach to use, depending on the analysis of both the Epistemic Uncertainty obtained for the image in the children classifiers and the prediction of the parent classifier. When our criterion is met, the final prediction is obtained with the respective local classifier; otherwise, with the flat classifier. From the results, we can see that the proposed method improves the classification performance compared to the use of a single flat classifier.

Keywords: CNNs · Deep learning · Epistemic Uncertainty ·
Image classification · Food recognition

1 Introduction

Analysis of food images has been an emerging research topic in recent years within the field of Computer vision. Currently, there is a large number of food image datasets that makes possible to perform food recognition [2,3,5]. However, the food classes provided by these are still low compared to those needed for a real food recognition application. Just considering the most common foods, there will easily be thousands of different food classes in worldwide. On the other hand, models based on Convolutional Neural Networks (CNNs) have allowed to address problems of object recognition on a large-scale achieving promising results. Although it has also been shown that the number of classes that will be recognized and the number of images that belong to each one are inversely

© Springer Nature Switzerland AG 2019
A. Morales et al. (Eds.): IbPRIA 2019, LNCS 11867, pp. 65–74, 2019.
https://doi.org/10.1007/978-3-030-31332-6_6

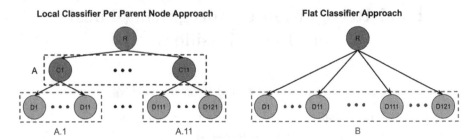

Fig. 1. Example image that illustrates the class hierarchy of the Local Classifier per Parent Node and Flat Classification approaches on MaFood-121 Dataset. A, A1-A11, B denotes the classifiers for the nodes within the respective rectangles.

proportional to the model performance [9]. Samples of this can be seen in [14], where the proposed model decreases the performance on about 10% when we compared the result on cifar-10 [7] with respect to cifar-100 [7]. In the case of food domain, a reduction of 7% is shown in [10] when we compared the result on uecfood-100 [11] with respect to uecfood-256 [5]. This suggests that the use of a single CNNs model to recognize all classes will not be enough to classify a huge amount of foods classes.

Regarding the strategies for solving classification problems, these can be grouped in two ways [12]: (1) By means of a flat classification approach, where a single classifier is used for all classes to be predicted; and (2) By means of a hierarchical classification approach, where the classes to be predicted are organized into a class hierarchy. As for the second strategy, there are three types of local classifiers to perform the predictions [12]: (2.1) Local Classifier Per Node Approach (LCN), which consists in training a binary classifier for each node of the class hierarchy; (2.2) Local Classifier Per Parent Node Approach (LCPN), which consists in training multi-class classifier for each parent node in the class hierarchy to distinguish between its child nodes; and (2.3) Local Classifier Per Level Approach (LCL), which consists of training one multi-class classifier for each level of the class hierarchy. Note that the only one hierarchical approach applied, in the context of food recognition, was proposed by [13], which incorporates in their method an LCL strategy to obtain error closer to the real class when the classification is erroneous. Focusing on the LCPN approach, the main problem is that the error in the parent local classifiers is propagated to the children. For example, in the Fig. 1, if the classifier A miss-classifies the cuisine of the image like C11, the dish recognition from the labels D111-D121 automatically will be wrong. To reduce the error propagated for the LCPN approach, we propose only to classify with this strategy those predictions that are likely well, and the remainder one to classify with a flat classification approach. To identify a good prediction, we complemented the decision of the local classifier for the parent node with the most probable child node obtained from the analysis of the Epistemic Uncertainty (EU). By definition, the EU captures the ignorance about which model generated the collected data [6]. Therefore, we expect that

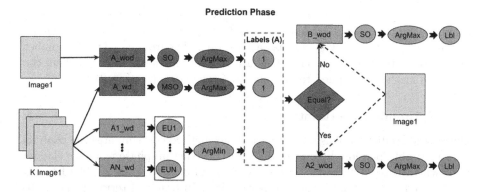

Fig. 2. Main scheme of the proposed method, which shows the procedure performed when the predictions in the first level of the hierarchy is equal to 1. The suffix wod denotes the prediction with the dropout turned off, wd denotes the prediction with the dropout turned on, the terms SO, MSO, and EU, denotes Softmax Output, Mean Softmax Output and Epistemic Uncertainty.

the correct local classifier for the child node to give a low uncertainty when the image to be predicted belongs to the classes for which it was trained.

Our main contributions in this paper are as follows: (1) we provide an epistemic uncertainty-based method, which minimizes error propagated from parents to children in the LCPN approach; (2) we propose a criterion to decide when to apply a local or flat classifier; and (3) we demonstrate that it is possible to achieve better classification results when we integrate the prediction of LCPN with flat classifier through our proposal.

The remainder of this paper is organized as follows: first, in Sect. 2, we present the proposed method; second, in the Sect. 3, we present the dataset, the experimental setup and discuss the results; finally, in Sect. 4, we describe the conclusions.

2   Proposed Method

In this section, we explain detailed the steps involved in the proposed approach, which considers local and flat classifiers to perform image predictions. In the follow subsection, we first comment the consideration in the model architecture, second we describe the equation to obtain the EU and then we explain all the components involved in our approach.

2.1   Model Setup

Every classifier trained in our proposed approach is based on the same CNNs architecture. At the top of the network, the output of the last convolution layer is flattened. Then, it is necessary to add a dropout layer after each hidden fully connected layer so that we are able to apply the Monte Carlo dropout (MC-dropout) sampling [6] to calculate the epistemic uncertainty. Finally, it is ended up with an output layer with softmax activation and neurons equal to the number of classes. Note that all the classifiers are trained independently, and then, the proposed method is applied to give the final prediction (see Fig. 2).

2.2   Epistemic Uncertainty

During the prediction phase, a key part of our method contemplates the analysis of the EU obtained for the images during the prediction phase when we classify their with the local classifier on the second level of the hierarchy. The EU can be obtained by applying MC-dropout sampling. In practical terms, it means to predict K times the same image using the model with the dropout layer turned on. Then, the EU will correspond to the predictive entropy calculated from the K predictions given.

Formally, the EU can be expressed as follows:

Let $\overline{p(y_c = \hat{y}_c|x)}$ be the average probability that the prediction y_c is equal to the ground-truth $\hat{y}_c$ given image x, calculated from K MC-dropouts simulations. Then,

$$EU(x_t) = -\sum_{c=1}^{C} \overline{p(y_c = \hat{y}_c|x_t)} \ln(\overline{p(y_c = \hat{y}_c|x_t)}), \qquad (1)$$

where

$$\overline{p(y_c = \hat{y}_c|x)} = \frac{1}{K}\sum_{k=1}^{K} p(y_c^k = \hat{y}_c^k|x). \qquad (2)$$

2.3   Prediction by Integrating Local and Flat Classifiers

The proposed method contemplates the training of LCPN and also a flat classifier, and the integration of both approaches during the prediction. The proposal is thought for two level of hierarchy, but can be easily extensible to more levels.

One problem with LCPN approach is that the error is propagated from upper to lower levels. To deal with this, in our proposal, instead of directly applying the prediction given for the local parent classifier (LPC), we propose a strategy to ensure that the prediction is very likely the correct one, and thus, minimize the error propagation. This strategy consists in three parts: (a) Get the prediction of the images using the LPC with the dropout turned off; (b) Get the mean of the predictions to send K times the images to the LPC with the dropout turned on; (c) Estimate the EU of the samples for each local child classifier (LCH) and choose the label which represents the LCH that provides the lower EU for the respective image. After that, we compared the three predictions and in the case of all of them get the same value, we apply the respective LCH using the dropout turned off. Otherwise, we classify the image with the Flat classifier with dropout turned off. In Fig. 2, we illustrated the steps involves in our proposal. In this case, all the strategies (a-c) give the same prediction, and therefore, the local classifier is chosen to give the final response.

3   Experiments

In this section, we first present the dataset used, second we describe the evaluation measures, third we present the experimental setup and last we describe the results obtained with our proposed approach.

3.1   Dataset

In order to validate the benefits of our proposed method, we chose the newly published food dataset MAFood-121 [1]. This is a multi-task food image dataset comprising 3 related tasks: (a) dish, (b) cuisine, and (c) categories/food groups. The dataset was built up taking into account the top 11 most popular cuisines collecting the images from 4 different sources, 3 public food datasets [2,3,5], and Google Search Engine. For each cuisine, 11 dishes are considered with an average of 119 images per dish with their respective annotations of food categories. In total, 21.175 images were gathered, distributed as 72.5% for training, 12.5% for validation and 15% for test. For our purpose, we only consider the single label tasks (cuisine and dish) and keep the same distribution of data for training, validation and test. An example image for each cuisine can be seen in Fig. 3.

Fig. 3. An example representative image for each cuisine belonging to MaFood-121.

3.2   Metric

In order to evaluate the performance of our approach, we used the overall Accuracy (Acc), which is a standard metric for object recognition. Formally it is defined as follows:

$$Acc = \frac{1}{T} \sum_{c=1}^{C} TP_c,\qquad(3)$$

where C is the number of classes, TP_c (True Positives) is the amount of images belonging to the class c classified correctly, and T is the total number of images evaluated.

3.3   Experimental Setup

We trained a CNN architecture based on ResNet-50 [4], using the categorical cross-entropy loss optimized with Adam. We modified this neural network by removing the output layer, and instead, we added one hidden fully connected layer of 2048 neurons, followed by a dropout layer with a probability of 0.5, and we ended up with an output layer with softmax activation and neurons equal to the number of classes of the respective subset. In this particular case, there were 121 neurons for the flat classification and 11 for the local classifiers. In total, thirteen models were trained based on the same architecture. The models are named as follows:

1. A: CNN Model trained to perform the cuisine classification.
2. $A1$–$A11$: CNN Model trained to perform the local dish classification for the following cuisines: American (A1), Japanese (A2), Italian (A3), Greek (A4), Turkish (A5), Chinese (A6), Mexican (A7), Indian (A8), Thai (A9), Vietnamese (A10) and French (A11).
3. B: CNN Model trained to perform the flat classification for all dishes.

Model B was re-trained, from a pre-trained model on ILSVRC dataset [8], during 50 epochs with a batch size of 32, and an initial learning rate of $1e-4$. With respect to models A and A1–A11, they were re-trained on the top of the networks (after the last convolutional layer) from the pre-trained model B, during 32 epoch with a batch size of 32, and an initial learning rate of $1e-5$. In all models, we applied a decay of 0.5 every 8 epochs. On the other hand, regarding the data augmentation process, for all models, the original image is re-sized to (256, 256) and then random crops with a size of (224, 224) and horizontal flip with a 50% probability are applied. The training was done using Keras with Tensorflow as backend.

3.4   Results

In this section, we present the results obtained on the MAFood-121 dataset by the Local and Flat classification approaches and our proposed method, which integrates both during the image prediction.

One of the key elements of our approach involves calculating the EU of the sample when it is sent to several local classifiers, one for each cuisine, in order to determine the cuisine to which the image belongs to. The idea behind this is that the EU is explained with enough data. Therefore, if we have an image with the features close to those learned by a model, the EU will be small, which implies that it is very likely that this image belongs to any of their classes. Figure 4 shows an example of the results obtained in terms of EU for the test set images by three local classifiers. Each color represents a different cuisine and each row corresponds to the EU obtained for the local classifiers. Note that the EU for images belonging to the type of cuisine used for the training of the first classifier (first row) is represented with the points of the first color, for the second classifier (second row) with the points of the second color and so on. As expected, when we compared the result given for a classifier with respect to the cuisine of the image (left to right) or when we compared the results for all the classifiers with respect to the images of a specific cuisine, we can see that the EU tends to be small when the test images are similar to the images used in the training of the

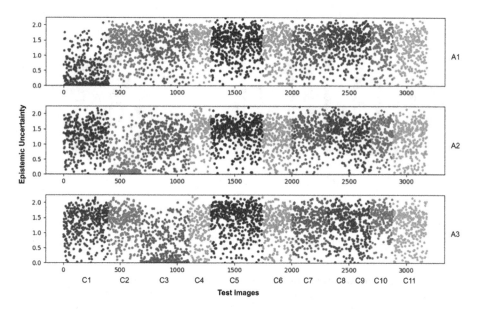

Fig. 4. Epistemic uncertainty obtained for three local cuisine classifiers in the images of the test set. Each color represents a cuisine and each subplot - the result obtained for the respective classifier. (Color figure online)

classifier. However, in some cases the minimum EU is not corresponding to the real cuisine of the image. We believe that this occurs due to the shared features among different cuisine in some cases. For this reason, we consider the analysis of the EU like a complement to the cuisine recognition classifier, instead to use directly this procedure to determine the cuisine of the image.

As for the local classifiers, we evaluate the performance applying two different training strategies: Transfer Learning from ImageNet (TLI), which consists of re-training the whole network with the food images, using as initial weight of the lower layers (before the first fully connected layer) the values obtained when the base model was trained on ImageNet dataset; and Transfer Learning from Food (TLF), which consists of freezing the lower layers and re-training only the upper layers, using as initial weight the values obtained for a model trained with the same type of data, specifically we use as a base model the flat classifier trained with all foods. The results obtained can be seen in Fig. 5a and the distribution of the test images used for each local cuisine classifiers in Fig. 5b. For all cases, using the TLF strategy we were able to improve the results of the local classifications. In particular, for the classifiers A2, A3, A6 and A9, we can see biggest increment in the performance. We believe that the improvement occurs mainly because the use of a subset of images for each classifier is not enough to avoid the overfitting of the network when we train all the layers. However, if we share the global features extracted (lower layer) from all the foods and then we only retrained

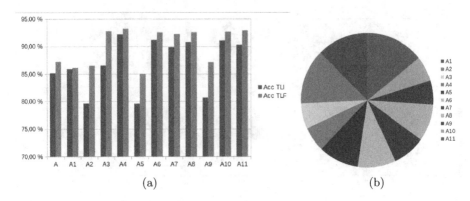

(a)   (b)

Fig. 5. From left to right: (a) the accuracy obtained for each local classifier when used Transfer Learning From ImageNet (TLI) or Transfer Learning From Food (TLF) for the training of the classifier; and (b) the distribution of the test images for each cuisine.

Table 1. Results on MaFood-121 in terms of Accuracy.

Approach	Cuisine		Local		Flat		Overall
	#Images	Acc	#Images	Acc	#Images	Acc	Acc
GT+Local	3177	100.00%	3177	89.61%	-	-	89.61%
Cuisine+Local	3177	87.19%	2770	91.71%	-	-	79.96%
Flat	-	-	-	-	3177	81.37%	81.37%
Proposed method	1579	96.96%	1531	96.08%	1598	70.21%	81.62%

the last fully connected layer, the network achieves better adjustment of the model's weights.

Finally in Table 1 we show the results achieved for four approaches: (a) GT+Local, to reflect the performance of the dish classification when we have a perfect cuisine recognition; (b) Cuisine+Local, which is the base line for dish classification when we chose the local classifier per cuisine considering the cuisine recognition performance; (c) Flat, which corresponds to classification of all the classes in the same classifier; (d) Our proposed model, which integrates the Local and Flat classifiers taking into account the EU to take the cuisine decision on the image prediction. From the results, we demonstrate that it is possible to achieve large increase in terms of accuracy when we have perfect cuisine recognition and we use an individual classifier for each cuisine type (see GT+Local). In our case, the performance of cuisine recognition is far from perfect (87.19%), and for this reason, the error propagated by these predictions produced the lowest classification accuracy (79.96%) despite the local classifier per cuisine provided 91.71% of accuracy. As for our proposed, we intend to reduce the miss-classification produced by error in the cuisine recognition complementing the prediction with the results obtained by the analysis of the EU, with which 1579 images are obtained with a high likely that the cuisine is well classified. In this subset of images, we obtain a 96.96% of accuracy on cuisine classification and 96.08% accuracy in the local classifiers per cuisine, which when combined with the Flat classifier predictions we obtain 81.62%. This result outperforms the classification obtained for the Cuisine+Local and Flat approaches.

4 Conclusions

In this paper, we proposed a new method to perform food recognition by the integration of a hierarchical with flat classifiers. In our method, we contemplated that hierarchical classification can propagate the error from parent to child nodes, and for this reason we proposed to use local classifiers only when we are sure that it is very likely that the prediction will be good. Otherwise the classification is performed with the flat classifier. To recognize good prediction, we complemented the output of the local classifier with the analysis of the EU of the images. From the results obtained, we observed that the proposed approach provides a good performance allowing us to further reduce propagation error. As a conclusion, we have shown the benefits of the proposed approach, which can be a good alternative when we have to predict a huge number of classes. As future work, we will explore the application of EU to another problems such as, novelty detection or active labeling.

Acknowledgement. This work was partially funded by TIN2015-66951-C2-1-R, 2017 SGR 1742, Nestore, Validithi, 20141510 (La MaratoTV3) and CERCA Programme/Generalitat de Catalunya. E. Aguilar acknowledges the support of CONICYT Becas Chile and M. P. Radeva is partially supported by ICREA Academia 2014. We acknowledge the support of NVIDIA Corporation with the donation of Titan Xp GPUs.

References

1. Aguilar, E., Bolaños, M., Radeva, P.: Regularized uncertainty-based multi-task learning model for food analysis. J. Vis. Commun. Image Represent. **60**, 360–370 (2019)
2. Bossard, L., Guillaumin, M., Van Gool, L.: Food-101 – mining discriminative components with random forests. In: Fleet, D., Pajdla, T., Schiele, B., Tuytelaars, T. (eds.) ECCV 2014. LNCS, vol. 8694, pp. 446–461. Springer, Cham (2014). https://doi.org/10.1007/978-3-319-10599-4_29
3. Güngör, C., Baltacı, F., Erdem, A., Erdem, E.: Turkish cuisine: a benchmark dataset with Turkish meals for food recognition. In: 2017 25th Signal Processing and Communications Applications Conference (SIU), pp. 1–4, May 2017. https://doi.org/10.1109/SIU.2017.7960494
4. He, K., Zhang, X., Ren, S., Sun, J.: Deep residual learning for image recognition. In: Proceedings of the IEEE Conference on Computer Vision and Pattern Recognition, pp. 770–778 (2016)
5. Kawano, Y., Yanai, K.: Automatic expansion of a food image dataset leveraging existing categories with domain adaptation. In: Agapito, L., Bronstein, M.M., Rother, C. (eds.) ECCV 2014. LNCS, vol. 8927, pp. 3–17. Springer, Cham (2015). https://doi.org/10.1007/978-3-319-16199-0_1

6. Kendall, A., Gal, Y.: What uncertainties do we need in Bayesian deep learning for computer vision? In: Advances in Neural Information Processing Systems, pp. 5574–5584 (2017)
7. Krizhevsky, A., Hinton, G.: Learning multiple layers of features from tiny images. Technical report. Citeseer (2009)
8. Krizhevsky, A., Sutskever, I., Hinton, G.E.: ImageNet classification with deep convolutional neural networks. In: Advances in Neural Information Processing Systems, pp. 1097–1105 (2012)
9. Luo, C., Li, X., Yin, J., He, J., Gao, D., Zhou, J.: How does the data set and the number of categories affect CNN-based image classification performance? J. Softw. **14**(4), 168–181 (2019)
10. Martinel, N., Foresti, G.L., Micheloni, C.: Wide-slice residual networks for food recognition. In: 2018 IEEE Winter Conference on Applications of Computer Vision (WACV), pp. 567–576. IEEE (2018)
11. Matsuda, Y., Hoashi, H., Yanai, K.: Recognition of multiple-food images by detecting candidate regions. In: 2012 IEEE International Conference on Multimedia and Expo, pp. 25–30. IEEE (2012)
12. Silla, C.N., Freitas, A.A.: A survey of hierarchical classification across different application domains. Data Min. Knowl. Disc. **22**(1–2), 31–72 (2011)
13. Wu, H., Merler, M., Uceda-Sosa, R., Smith, J.R.: Learning to make better mistakes: semantics-aware visual food recognition. In: Proceedings of the 24th ACM International Conference on Multimedia, pp. 172–176. ACM (2016)
14. Zagoruyko, S., Komodakis, N.: Wide residual networks. In: Proceedings of the British Machine Vision Conference (BMVC), pp. 87.1-87.12 (2016)

Machine Learning

Combining Online Clustering and Rank Pooling Dynamics for Action Proposals

Nadjia Khatir[1], Roberto J. López-Sastre[2(✉)], Marcos Baptista-Ríos[2],
Safia Nait-Bahloul[1], and Francisco Javier Acevedo-Rodríguez[2]

[1] LITIO, Department of Computer Science, University of Oran1, Ahmed Ben Bella,
Oran, Algeria
[2] GRAM, University of Alcalá, Alcalá de Henares, Spain
robertoj.lopez@uah.es
http://agamenon.tsc.uah.es/Investigacion/gram/

Abstract. The action proposals problem consists in developing efficient
and effective approaches to retrieve, from untrimmed long videos, those
temporal segments which are likely to contain human actions. This is a
fundamental task for any video analysis solution, which will struggle to
detect activities in a large-scale video collection without the proposals
step, needing hence to apply an action classifier at every time location, in
a temporal sliding window strategy, a pipeline which is clearly unfeasible.
While all previous action proposals solutions are supervised, we introduce here a novel strategy that works in an unsupervised fashion. We
rely on an online agglomerative clustering algorithm to build an initial
set of proposals/clusters. Then a novel filtering approach is proposed,
which uses the dynamics of the proposals discovered by the clustering,
to measure their actioness, and proceeds to filter them accordingly. Our
experiments show that our model improves the supervised state-of-the-
art approaches when the number of proposals is controlled.

Keywords: Action proposals · Unsupervised learning · Clustering ·
Computer vision · Action recognition

1 Introduction

In this work, we focus on the problem of localizing temporal segments in
untrimmed videos that are likely to contain human actions. This is the well-
known problem of action proposals, *e.g.* [1–6]. These proposals can speed-up
activity recognition and detection tasks, as well as retrieval and indexing in long
videos. Interestingly, in the last ActivityNet challenge [7], *all* the methods for
the task of action localization [6,8,9] have tackled the problem following a two-
stage pipeline, where the first step always consists in using an action proposal
method. So, action proposals are important.

Typically, all action proposals solutions follow a supervised approach during learning. That is, models are trained using fully annotated datasets, such

© Springer Nature Switzerland AG 2019
A. Morales et al. (Eds.): IbPRIA 2019, LNCS 11867, pp. 77–88, 2019.
https://doi.org/10.1007/978-3-030-31332-6_7

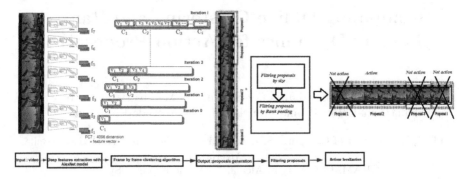

Fig. 1. We propose an unsupervised approach for action proposals. It is based on an online clustering model which works on deep features designed for object recognition. These cluster are later refined by their sizes and dynamics, using a rank-pooling based mechanism.

as THUMOS-14 [10], where for each video the time slots corresponding to each action are specified. However, the problem has not been addressed from an *unsupervised* perspective, where action proposal models can be trained without using this information. This new approach offers significant benefits. The first one is that it is not necessary to annotate videos to perform the training. Moreover, the training data becomes unlimited, and data sources such as YouTube can be used, a factor that will lead to solutions that will be able to offer a better generalization capability.

Therefore in this paper we explore if such an unsupervised perspective is viable, offering the following **contributions**. **(1)** We propose an action proposals pipeline which starts with an online agglomerative clustering algorithm (Sect. 3.2). Just using pre-computed deep features for object recognition for every video frame, our hypothesis is that we can localize actions finding clusters in this feature space. For doing so, our clustering solution must work online, *i.e.* grouping contiguous frames if they are visually similar. **(2)** We then propose two filtering mechanisms to be performed over the clusters (Sect. 3.3). One is simply based on the size of the clusters/proposals. The other uses the dynamics of the proposals identified. Dynamics should represent the video-wide temporal evolution of the appearance of the frames. In this paper we introduce an unsupervised approach. It leverages rank pooling based dynamics [11] to build an actioness module which can be used to further filter and refine the obtained proposals/clusters. **(3)** Our last contribution consists in offering a thorough experimental evaluation using the THUMOS'14 [10] dataset, with a clear evaluation protocol. This is done in Sect. 4, where we first compare the performance of our unsupervised model with state-of-the-art supervised solutions. Interestingly, when in the evaluation we control the number of proposals methods can produce, our solution reports the best results. We then analyze the precision of the action proposals, this being an aspect that has not been considered in depth before, even by supervised action proposal models, which generally tend to maximize the recall.

2   Related Work

Temporal action proposal generation has recently become of much interest since it has been demonstrated to be a crucial step for temporal action detection [12], as well as helpful at other video understanding tasks [13].

Different types of solutions have been proposed to solve this problem. On the one hand, there are works based on classifying thousands of varied-length candidate segments, being these segments extracted using the sliding window technique. Then, several classification methods have been suggested to consolidate proposals, for example the multi-stage C3D [14] network used by [15], or the dictionary-based method proposed in [1]. Additionally, the works [4,16] propose to refine segment boundaries using temporal regression to generate more precise proposals.

On the other hand, Zhao *et al.* [6] propose to build candidate segments grouping features based on their actionness score. In [3,17] we find approaches that can generate proposals in a single video pass using recurrent networks. Besides, very recent models, *e.g.* [18,19], produce proposals from temporal boundary points, instead of candidate segments. These points are combined to generate precise temporal boundaries.

All previous methods share the fact that they solve the proposal generation task from a supervised perspective. That is, they need the temporal ground truth information during training. However, our method is the first one that operates in an unsupervised fashion. We only rely on video features to generate proposals, hence addressing and proposing a more challenging task.

3   Action Proposals Generation

We here detail our novel solution for the generation of action proposals in videos. Figure 1 shows the main steps of the introduced approach: (1) video frames feature extraction; (2) online hierarchical clustering; and (3) a rank pooling dynamics based filtering.

3.1   Feature Extraction

The input of our action proposal model is a video stream. Therefore, given a video of n frames $V = \{v_1, v_2, v_3, ..., v_n\}$, we proceed to extract, for each frame $v_i \in V$, a deep feature, using any pre-trained deep model for image recognition, such as AlexNet [20]. So, a video V is mapped to a set of high-dimensional deep features, having $V = \{f_1, f_2, f_3, ..., f_n\}$.

Algorithm 1. Frame by frame (FBF) online clustering for AP

    Input: video $V = \{f_1, f_2, f_3, ..., f_n\}$;

1 threshold δ;

2 struct {float vec; int id;} leafnode;
    Output: *Cluster*

3 //Create a list of leafnodes with the features in V

4 $features \leftarrow load(V)$;

5 $L \leftarrow [leafnode(v \leftarrow array(f), id \leftarrow i) for \ i, f \ in \ enumerate(features)]$
    //Initialization

6 $Cluster \leftarrow \{\}$; $n_i \leftarrow L[0]$; $Cluster.append([n_i])$; $newvec \leftarrow n_i.vec$;

7 **for** $j \leftarrow 1$ *to* $n - 1$ **do**

8     $n_j \leftarrow L[j]$;

9     $d \leftarrow L2dist(newvec, n_j.vec)$

10   **if** $(d < \delta)$ **then**

11       $Merge(Cluster[-1], n_j)$ // Merge n_j with the last node of Cluster
         $newvec \leftarrow Cluster[-1].vec$

12   **else**

13   //Create new cluster

14       $Cluster.append([n_j])$; // n_j is appended as a new cluster
         $newvec \leftarrow n_j.vec$;

15

16 **return** *Cluster*

3.2 Online Clustering for Action Proposals

Our solution to generate action proposals is based on a clustering algorithm. The intuition behind this approach is that action video frames share a visual similarity that can be captured by deep learning features trained for object recognition. Therefore, we can localize actions finding clusters in the feature space where the video frames have been mapped to.

For doing so, it is fundamental that the solution guarantees two properties: (1) the implemented clustering must be *online*, in the sense that it tends to favour clusters with temporally close or contiguous frames; and (2) a filtering mechanism for discarding non-action clusters has to be designed. In this section, we focus on the online clustering implemented solution.

The input for our clustering solution is the set of deep learning features used to characterize every frame of a given video, *i.e.* $V = \{f_1, f_2, f_3, ..., f_n\}$. We then proceed to execute our online frame by frame (FBF) clustering algorithm in the following fashion.

First, we create a list L where each frame is assigned to a node n_i of the class *leafnode*. This class is implemented with an structure containing and index list *id*, which identifies all the features belonging to it, and a vector *vec*, which is the centroid of the cluster represented by the node. The algorithm decides whether to merge two *consecutive* pairs of nodes n_i and n_{i+1} using a distance based criterion computed over the centroids of the nodes, *i.e.* $n_i.vec$ and $n_{i+1}.vec$. Technically, we join two consecutive nodes if $dist(n_i.vec, n_{i+1}.vec) \leq \delta$. In our experiments the Euclidean distance is the one reporting the best results.

Note that our objective is to identify in the video action proposals regions. Following our online clustering solution, we consider that the frames merged in a cluster define an action proposal, the centroid being thus its representative.

If two consecutive nodes do not meet the union criterion, the cluster already formed in the first node is assigned to an action proposal. The algorithm starts again with the last analyzed node. We keep merging nodes until we go through all the frames of the video clip. Finally, our algorithm returns a list of clusters, which define the action proposals for the given video. For a detailed description of the FBF approach, we include the Algorithm 1.

Note that our online FBF model shares some similarities with an Unweighted Pair-Group Method using Centroid averages (UPGMC) for hierarchical clustering. Technically, we also follow a centroid linkage criterion. However, we do not need to perform any hierarchical search. Instead, we process the video frames in an online fashion, building clusters as soon as they occur. In our experiments, we tried other clustering approaches, like standard hierarchical clustering solutions [21] or HDBSCAN [22], but our FBF model reported the best results.

3.3   Filtering Proposals

As a result of our online FBF model, every video frame gets assigned to an Action Proposal (AP). In other words, our model fully covers the whole video with proposals. This is due to the unsupervised nature of our approach, in contrast to all the state-of-the-art models for the same problem, which are all supervised approaches. Therefore, we need to incorporate a filtering step with the objective of discarding those incorrect proposals, but again in an unsupervised way.

We first proceed to filter the proposals by their size. The idea is simple, it technically consists in filtering those proposals whose temporal length is shorter than a certain threshold α_t.

Once we have discarded the shorter APs, which typically correspond to video fragments that do not contain actions, we proceed with a novel filtering mechanism, which is based on the computation of the dynamics of the remaining proposals.

The dynamics of a video sequence are defined as the video-wide temporal evolution of the appearance of the frames. Dynamics have been previously used for action recognition, *e.g.* [11,23]. They can be seen as video representations to train a classifier for categorizing each video with an action label. We, instead, propose to use them to measure the *actioness* of a video segment, *i.e.* how likely the video is to contain an action.

For doing so, we start our reasoning with the following hypothesis. Given a video segment V_i, we can compute its corresponding dynamics vector $\mathcal{D}_i$. We now define $\widehat{V}_i$ as a randomly ordered set of frames of V_i. $\widehat{\mathcal{D}}_i$ vector represents the dynamics of this random version of V_i. If we now compute the distance between $\mathcal{D}_i$ and $\widehat{\mathcal{D}}_i$, as $d(\mathcal{D}_i, \widehat{\mathcal{D}}_i)$, we make the basic assumption that this distance will be higher for those video segments that contain actions than for those that just represent background.

Following this hypothesis, we can filter our action proposals in an unsupervised way. Technically, we proceed as follows. Let P_i be one of the proposals constructed with the FBF approach. For each proposal P_i, we build its randomly ordered version $\widehat{P}_i$. Then, as in the rank-pooling model [11], we proceed to model the video dynamics of each of these proposals solving a constrained optimization pairwise-learning-to-rank formulation [24]. In particular, we opt for a linear Support Vector Regression (SVR) based formulation. Given the set of ordered features for P_i, i.e. $P_i = \{f_1^{(i)}, f_2^{(i)}, f_3^{(i)}, \ldots, f_{n_i}^{(i)}\}$, we seek a direct mapping from the input feature vectors $f_t^{(i)}$ to a *time* variable t using a linear model with parameters $w^{(i)}$, as follows,

$$w^{(i)} = \arg\min_{w^{(i)}} \sum_t |t - w^{(i)} \cdot f_t^{(i)}|. \tag{1}$$

This SVR approach is known to be a robust point-wise ranking formulation [24]. In summary, to encode the dynamics of proposal P_i, we use the model parameters vector $w^{(i)}$. For $\widehat{P}_i$ we also compute its corresponding dynamics $\widehat{w}^{(i)}$, following the same SVR based procedure.

Once the dynamics are computed, we proceed to filter the proposals according to the Euclidean distance between these dynamics vectors. If $d_i(w^{(i)}, \widehat{w}^{(i)}) < \Delta$, then the associated proposal is discarded, because it is considered to belong to a non-action video segment.

4   Experiments

4.1   Experimental Setup

For the experiments we use the challenging dataset THUMOS-14 [10]. It contains 213 *untrimmed* test videos with temporal annotations of 20 sport action categories. Note that this dataset is also used by all state-of-the-art supervised AP methods, which allows for a direct comparison of our unsupervised model with them.

In particular, we directly compare with the following supervised AP models: DAPs [3] and Sparse-prop [1]. The authors of these papers publicly release their proposals results using THUMOS-14.

With respect to the evaluation metrics, we use two. The first one is the Average-Recall versus the Average-Number of Proposals per Video (AR-AN). This is the standard metric used by all AP models. Technically, we follow the evaluation procedure detailed in [3], where the Average Recall curve is generated for a set of Intersection over Union between 0.25 to 0.5, as a function of the number of proposals. The second metric we propose for the experimental validation is the Average Precision of the Precision-Recall curves. We follow the official implementation of Average Precision released with the THUMOS-14 benchmark [10] for action detection. Note that while with AR-AN the temporal precision of

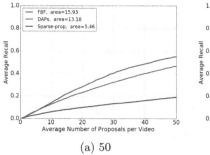
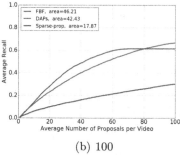

(a) 50   (b) 100

Fig. 2. Comparison of FBF with the state of the art using the AR-AN metric. Our FBF is able to improve in terms of AR when 50 and 100 average number of proposals per video are considered.

the proposals is not considered, *i.e.* just the recall is evaluated, we aim to focus the attention on the fact that precision also matters. A method that throws thousands of action proposals for each video can get an excellent recall, but very low precision, because many of those action proposals will fall into background zones, or will overlap with each other. However, our unsupervised online solution tends to generate fewer and more precise proposals, an aspect that will be shown by the Average Precision experimental evaluation.

With the aim of making our results reproducible, we detail the parameters of our solution. For the feature extraction, we proceed to extract for each video frame the last fully connected activation layer of the AlexNet CNN architecture [20], named $FC7$ (4096-dimensional), which has been pre-trained using the ImageNet database [25]. For the FBF clustering, $\delta = 100$, and we use an Euclidean distance. Then, for the filtering steps, $\alpha_t = 10$ and $\Delta = 10000$. Note that we tried to avoid any kind of manual parameter tuning as this could be considered a violation of the unsupervised character of our solution. Instead, we selected reasonable parameters in advance and held them fixed for all of the experiments.

4.2 Comparison with the State of the Art

We start with a direct comparison of our unsupervised model, with the *supervised* state-of-the-art models DAPs [3] and Sparse-prop [1]. Figure 2 shows the AR-AN curves for 50 and 100 average number of proposals per video.

Our model reports a higher AR when both 50 or 100 average number of proposals per video are considered. Note that the average number of annotations per video in the THUMOS-14 dataset is of just 15! So, this means we are giving enough margin to the models. DAPs model starts to approach to our performance (AR = 42.43) when we allow it to cast 100 proposals per video. Interestingly, Fig. 2b shows that our solution saturates at ~70 proposals per video maintaining an AR > 46. This saturation is mainly due to the clustering parameter δ used. Increasing this threshold will produce more (imprecise) proposals.

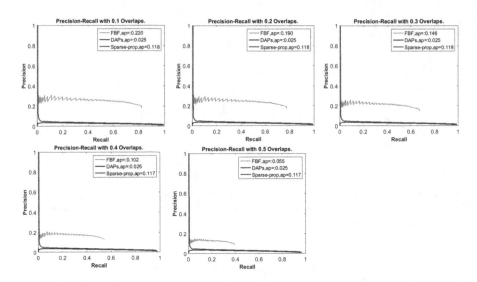

Fig. 3. Comparison of the FBF with the state of the art using Precision-Recall curves with different Intersection over Union thresholds. Our approach is able to report the best Average Precision for most of them, being trained without any supervision.

The next question that arises is: how precise are the action proposals? In other words, are the AP methods casting action proposals in temporal localizations of the videos where there are actually actions occurring? For performing this analysis, we show in Fig. 3 the Precision-Recall curves for our FBF approach and for the rest of the state-of-the-art methods. As one might expect, state-of-the-art models have been designed to maximize the recall, being their precision low. Note that we have incrementally augmented from 0.1 to 0.5 (the standard value for the object detection problem) the Intersection Over Union overlap criterion used in the Precision-Recall formulation to consider a true positive. This means that for 0.1, for instance, an AP is considered a true positive if the area of overlap between the predicted proposal and the ground truth annotation is at least of 10%. The higher this criterion, the more precise in terms of temporal location the proposals should be to be considered as correct.

DAP offers a fixed AP of 2.5% for all the overlap criteria considered, which means that the method is not able to report proposals with an overlap with the ground-truth higher than 1%. We also observe that our approach is able to report the highest Average Precision for most of the overlap criteria, all this in an unsupervised fashion, while the rest of methods are supervised.

Overall, according to the experimental evaluation designed, using the two metrics, the results show that our approach outperforms the supervised models when the number of proposal is controlled (under 100). Finally, in Fig. 4 we show some qualitative results of the action proposals obtained by our FBF method.

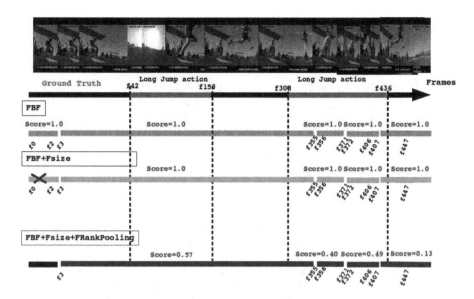

Fig. 4. Qualitative results. Set of action proposals discovered by our FBF model. The illustrative example concerns the video number 62 of the THUMOS'14 dataset which contains two actions of "Long jump" category. The first one starts from frame number 42 up to frame number 153. The second starts from frame number 308 up to frame number 436. Note that our solution FBF + Fsize + FRankPooling correctly covers the ground truth.

4.3   Ablation Study

What is the performance of our clustering based solution when no filtering mechanism is used? Do implemented filtering mechanisms really help to increase approach recall? We conclude the experiments section with an ablation study where we address these question.

Figure 5 shows the effects of the incorporation of the different filtering mechanisms in terms of AR. A first observation is that the FBF alone is able to report a decent AR. This gives us confidence that such a clustering based approach is an appropriate solution for the action proposals problem. In other words, one can use deep learning features trained for object recognition to identify groups of frames that belong to an action. Incorporating a filtering by size technique is also beneficial, note how the AR increases for FBF + Fsize. However, the greatest improvement in terms of recall is achieved thanks to the filtering based on the use of the described dynamics (+FRankPooling in Fig. 5).

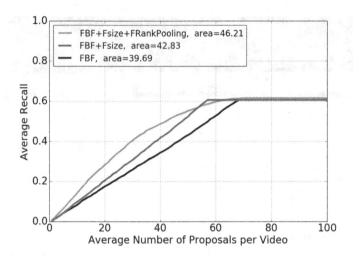

Fig. 5. Ablation study. This figure shows how the AR increases when we incorporate to our clustering solution (FBF) the filtering step using the size of the proposals (FBF + Fsize) and also the rank-pooling dynamics (FBF + Fsize + FRankPooling).

5   Conclusion

To generate action proposals is a difficult task which has not been studied from an unsupervised perspective. In this work we have presented the first attempt, to the best of our knowledge, to cast action proposals in an unsupervised fashion.

For doing so, we have introduced an approach which jointly integrates an online agglomerative clustering algorithm with a filtering mechanism that uses the dynamics of the clusters as an actioness measurement.

Our experimental evaluation shows that our model is able to outperform the average recall of supervised state-of-the-art approaches when the number of proposals is limited for all the methods. We have also shown that although our solution is unsupervised, the precision of the action proposals we generate is better than for the fully supervised models. Finally, an ablation study confirms our hypothesis and the adequateness of the designed approach.

Acknowledgments. This work is supported by project PREPEATE (TEC2016-80326-R), of the Spanish Ministry of Economy, Industry and Competitiveness. We gratefully acknowledge the support of NVIDIA Corporation with the donation of the GPU used for this research. Cloud computing resources were kindly provided through a Microsoft Azure for Research Award.

References

1. Caba Heilbron, F., Carlos Niebles, J., Ghanem, B.: Fast temporal activity proposals for efficient detection of human actions in untrimmed videos. In: CVPR, pp. 1914–1923 (2016)
2. Chao, Y.W., Vijayanarasimhan, S., Seybold, B., Ross, D.A., Deng, J., Sukthankar, R.: Rethinking the faster R-CNN architecture for temporal action localization. In: CVPR (2018)
3. Escorcia, V., Caba Heilbron, F., Niebles, J.C., Ghanem, B.: DAPs: deep action proposals for action understanding. In: Leibe, B., Matas, J., Sebe, N., Welling, M. (eds.) ECCV 2016. LNCS, vol. 9907, pp. 768–784. Springer, Cham (2016). https://doi.org/10.1007/978-3-319-46487-9_47
4. Gao, J., Yang, Z., Chen, K., Sun, C., Nevatia, R.: TURN TAP: temporal unit regression network for temporal action proposals. In: ICCV, October 2017
5. Jain, M., Van Gemert, J., Jégou, H., Bouthemy, P., Snoek, C.G.: Action localization with tubelets from motion. In: CVPR, pp. 740–747 (2014)
6. Zhao, Y., Xiong, Y., Wang, L., Wu, Z., Tang, X., Lin, D.: Temporal action detection with structured segment networks. In: CVPR (2016)
7. Ghanem, B., et al.: The ActivityNet large-scale activity recognition challenge 2018 summary. arXiv:1808.03766 (2018)
8. Lin, T., Zhao, X., Shou, Z.: Temporal convolution based action proposal: submission to activitynet 2017. arXiv preprint arXiv:1707.06750 (2017)
9. Xu, H., Das, A., Saenko, K.: R-C3D: region convolutional 3D network for temporal activity detection. In: ICCV (2017)
10. Jiang, Y., et al.: Thumos challenge: action recognition with a large number of classes (2014)
11. Fernando, B., Gavves, E., Oramas, J., Ghodrati, A., Tuytelaars, T.: Rank pooling for action recognition. IEEE TPAMI **39**(4), 773–787 (2017)
12. Alwassel, H., Caba Heilbron, F., Escorcia, V., Ghanem, B.: Diagnosing error in temporal action detectors. In: Ferrari, V., Hebert, M., Sminchisescu, C., Weiss, Y. (eds.) ECCV 2018. LNCS, vol. 11207, pp. 264–280. Springer, Cham (2018). https://doi.org/10.1007/978-3-030-01219-9_16
13. Gao, J., Ge, R., Chen, K., Nevatia, R.: Motion-appearance co-memory networks for video question answering. In: CVPR, pp. 6576–6585 (2018)
14. Tran, D., Bourdev, L., Fergus, R., Torresani, L., Paluri, M.: Learning spatiotemporal features with 3D convolutional networks. In: ICCV, pp. 4489–4497, December 2015
15. Shou, Z., Wang, D., Chang, S.F.: Temporal action localization in untrimmed videos via multi-stage CNNs. In: CVPR (2016)
16. Gao, J., Yang, Z., Nevatia, R.: Cascaded boundary regression for temporal action detection. In: BMVC (2017)
17. Buch, S., Escorcia, V., Shen, C., Ghanem, B., Niebles, J.C.: SST: single-stream temporal action proposals. In: CVPR (2017)
18. Gao, J., Chen, K., Nevatia, R.: CTAP: complementary temporal action proposal generation. In: Ferrari, V., Hebert, M., Sminchisescu, C., Weiss, Y. (eds.) ECCV 2018. LNCS, vol. 11206, pp. 70–85. Springer, Cham (2018). https://doi.org/10.1007/978-3-030-01216-8_5
19. Lin, T., Zhao, X., Su, H., Wang, C., Yang, M.: BSN: boundary sensitive network for temporal action proposal generation. In: Ferrari, V., Hebert, M., Sminchisescu, C., Weiss, Y. (eds.) ECCV 2018. LNCS, vol. 11208, pp. 3–21. Springer, Cham (2018). https://doi.org/10.1007/978-3-030-01225-0_1

20. Krizhevsky, A., Sutskever, I., Hinton, G.E.: ImageNet classification with deep convolutional neural networks. In: NIPS, pp. 1097–1105 (2012)
21. Jain, A.K., Dubes, R.C.: Algorithms for Clustering Data. Prentice-Hall, Upper Saddle River (1988)
22. McInnes, L., Healy, J., Astels, S.: HDBSCAN: hierarchical density based clustering. J. Open Source Softw. **2**(11), 205 (2017)
23. Bilen, H., Fernando, B., Gavves, E., Vedaldi, A., Gould, S.: Dynamic image networks for action recognition. In: CVPR (2016)
24. Liu, T.Y.: Learning to rank for information retrieval. Found. Trends Inf. Retr. **3**(3), 225–331 (2009)
25. Russakovsky, O., et al.: Imagenet large scale visual recognition challenge. Int. J. Comput. Vision **115**(3), 211–252 (2015)

On the Direction Guidance in Structure Tensor Total Variation Based Denoising

Ezgi Demircan-Tureyen[1,2](✉) [ID] and Mustafa E. Kamasak[2] [ID]

[1] Faculty of Engineering, Department of Computer Engineering,
Istanbul Kultur University, 34156 Istanbul, Turkey
e.demircan@iku.edu.tr
[2] Faculty of Computer and Informatics, Department of Computer Engineering,
Istanbul Technical University, 34390 Istanbul, Turkey
{edemircan,kamasak}@itu.edu.tr

Abstract. This paper introduces a new analysis-based regularizer, which incorporates the neighborhood-awareness of the structure tensor total variation (STV) and the tunability of the directional total variation (DTV), in favor of a pre-selected direction with a pre-selected dose of penalization. In order to show the utility of the proposed regularizer, we consider the problem of denoising uni-directional images. Since the regularizer is convex, we develop a simple optimization algorithm by realizing its proximal map. The quantitative and the visual experiments demonstrate the superiority of our regularizer over DTV (only for scalar-valued images) and STV.

Keywords: Image denoising · Total variation · Structure tensor · Directional total variation · Convex optimization · Inverse problems

1 Introduction

From capturing to encoding and transmission, different stages of an image acquisition pipeline produce different types of noise (additive vs. multiplicative, structured vs. random, signal dependent vs. independent, etc.). The noise existing on an image not only creates visual disruption, but also obscures significant details. Either to meet the quality expectations or to extract valuable information from the image, denoising has become an indispensable part of the processing. And yet, various denoising techniques have been proposed so far. These techniques most particularly aimed at recovering the latent signal $f \in \mathbb{R}^{NC}$ from the observation $g \in \mathbb{R}^{NC}$, by considering the forward corruption model of the form: $g = f + \eta$, where $\eta \in \mathbb{R}^{NC}$ is the additive noise that is assumed to be i.i.d. and normally distributed ($\eta \sim \mathcal{N}(\underline{0}, \sigma_\eta^2 I)$). Note that, the images are assumed to be stacked into vectors, where N and C are respectively denoting the number of pixels in a single channel, and the number of channels. For the scalar-valued images $C = 1$.

This work is supported by Istanbul Kultur University under ULEP-2018-2019/49.

The variational methods inverse the given forward model by minimizing an energy functional of the form:

$$E(f) = \frac{1}{2}\|g - f\|_2^2 + \tau R(f) \tag{1}$$

where $R(f)$ stands for the regularizer, whose role is encoding a prior on the unknown image. The prior may reflect some real characteristics, or may just presume them to reduce the size of search space. $\tau \geq 0$ is a variable used to tune the contribution of $R(f)$ to $E(f)$, and for the small values of it, the fidelity to the observed data dominates the prior. The choice of $R(f)$ is crucial. Over the years, intensive research has been pursued on designing good regularizers, which can adequately characterize the latent image in an efficiently solvable way. The concept of compressive sensing (CS) proves that the recovery of a deficient signal is possible, as long as it exhibits sparsity in a certain domain. This sparsity can be encoded by a regularizer. The total variation (TV) is such a regularizer, where the image's gradient is assumed to be sparse (yielding a piecewise constant – PWC image) as a special case of CS. It is a convex functional, thus ensures a feasible solution. TV has given rise to a diverse range of TV inspired regularizers aiming to cope with TV's limitations (especially with the staircase artifacts caused due to the PWC assumption), while preserving its convexity. One of the most popular methods is the total generalized variation (TGV) [4], which favors piecewise smoothness rather than PWC, by encoding not only first-, but also higher-order information. Another such TV variant is structure tensor total variation (STV) [8], which forms the basis for this paper together with another variant: directional total variation (DTV) [1] designed for uni-directional images. STV penalizes the non-linear combinations of the first-order derivatives within a neighborhood (i.e. eigenvalues of the structure tensor), while DTV penalizes weighted and rotated gradients of each pixel. STV applies semi-local regularization, while DTV does local. Moreover, STV can intrinsically decide and adaptively apply the dose of penalization, while DTV requires priorly determined parameters for this purpose.

STV and DTV are both analysis-based convex regularizers. Here the term *analysis-based* refers to the regularizers of the form (in discrete setting):

$$R(f) = \sum_{i=1}^{N} \phi((\Gamma f)[i]) \tag{2}$$

which directly run on the image, rather than applying the regularization in a transform domain (i.e. *sythesis-based* regularizers such as wavelet, curvelet and shearlet.) In Eq. (2), $\Gamma : \mathbb{R}^N \rightarrow \mathbb{R}^{N \times D}$ is regularization operator with $(\Gamma f)[i]$ denoting the D-dimensional i-th element of Γf mapping, and $\phi : \mathbb{R}^M \rightarrow \mathbb{R}$ is a potential function. For TV regularization, $\Gamma = \nabla$ that denotes the gradient operator, and $\phi = \| \cdot \|_p$, where $p = 2$ for the native isotropic TV [10]. There are also anisotropic alternatives, designed to catch convex shapes with angled boundaries. For example in [7], a convex TV variant that uses $p = 1$ was suggested, which was later referred to as anisotropic TV. In [6], the authors preferred using $p \in (0, 1)$, and in the recent work [9], a weighted mixed-norm design like

$\phi = w_1 \| \cdot \|_1 + w_2 \| \cdot \|_2$ was proposed. The common drawback of the last two is their non-convexity. Also, there are applications of having $p = 0$, as in [12], which is intrinsically NP-hard. This work aims at designing such a regularizer by combining the ideas behind STV and DTV regularizers, which will be introduced in the following section.

2   Background

By recalling Eq. (2), STV plugs $\Gamma = S_k$ and $\phi = \|\sqrt{\lambda(\cdot)}\|_p$. $(S_k f)[i]$ stands for the *structure tensor*, which is a symmetric positive semi-definite (PSD) matrix normally defined as $(S_k f)[i] = k_\sigma * ((Jf)[i](Jf)[i]^T)$, where k_σ is a Gaussian kernel of standard deviation σ; and λ returns the eigenvalues of the given matrix. Here J denotes the Jacobian operator defined by extending the gradient for vector-valued images: $(Jf)[i] = [(\nabla f^1)[i] \ (\nabla f^2)[i] \ \cdots \ (\nabla f^C)[i]]^T$, where superscripted f's are denoting the channels. Thus for scalar-valued images, $J(\cdot) = \nabla(\cdot)$. When compared to the local differential operators, semi-local structure tensor provides a better way to characterize the directional variations, since it also takes the neighboring pixels into account. This way lies in its rooted eigenvalues and their associated unit eigenvectors, which summarize the gradients within a patch supported by k_σ and centered at i-th pixel.

In [8], the authors also defined the structure tensor in terms of another operator that they proposed and called as *patch-based Jacobian* $J_k : \mathbb{R}^{N \times C} \mapsto \mathbb{R}^{N \times LC \times 2}$, which embodies the convolution kernel of size L. It is defined as:

$$(J_k f)[i] = [(\tilde{\nabla} f^1)[i], \ (\tilde{\nabla} f^2)[i] \ \cdots \ (\tilde{\nabla} f^C)[i]]^T \tag{3}$$

where $(\tilde{\nabla} f^c)[i] = [(\mathcal{T}_1 \nabla f^c)[i], (\mathcal{T}_2 \nabla f^c)[i], \cdots, (\mathcal{T}_L \nabla f^c)[i]]$. Each l-th entity corresponds to shifting and weighting on the gradient as $(\mathcal{T}_l \nabla f^c)[i] = \omega[p_l](\nabla f)[x_i - p_l]$, where x_i denotes the actual 2D coordinates of the i-th pixel, $p_l \in \mathcal{P}$ is the shift amount so that each $x_i - p_l$ is within the $\mathcal{P}$-neighborhood of x_i, and the weight is determined by the smoothing kernel k_σ as $\omega[p_l] = \sqrt{k_\sigma[p_l]}$. This new operator allows us to decompose the nonlinear $(S_k f)[i]$ into linear $(J_k f)[i]$'s as follows:

$$(S_k f)[i] = (J_k f)[i](J_k f)[i]^T \tag{4}$$

so that the new formulation reveals an easier way of employing optimization tools. The rooted eigenvalues of $(S_k f)[i]$ coincide with the singular values of $(J_k f)[i]$, and this paves the way of using *Schatten p-norms* to redefine STV by this time plugging $\Gamma = J_k$ and $\phi = \| \cdot \|_{S_p}$ in Eq. (2). S_p matrix norm is nothing but the ℓ_p-norm of the vector that contains the singular values of the subjected matrix, which is $(J_k f)[i]$ in our case. Therefore, STV regularizer in its first and second form is given below:

$$STV(f) = \sum_{i=1}^{N} \|\sqrt{\lambda((S_k f)[i])}\|_p = \sum_{i=1}^{N} \|(J_k f)[i]\|_{S_p} \tag{5}$$

where $\lambda((S_k f)[i]) = [\lambda^+((S_k f)[i]), \lambda^-((S_k f)[i])]^T$.

The DTV, on the other hand, simply substitutes $\Gamma = \nabla$ and $\phi = \|\Lambda_\alpha R_{-\theta}(\cdot)\|_2$, where $R_\theta = \begin{bmatrix} \cos\theta & -\sin\theta \\ \sin\theta & \cos\theta \end{bmatrix}$ and $\Lambda_\alpha = \begin{bmatrix} \alpha & 0 \\ 0 & 1 \end{bmatrix}$. Here θ corresponds to the dominant direction (that should be pre-determined), and α is used to tune the dose of penalization throughout that direction. DTV stipulates that the image to be recovered exhibits a global directional dominance. It is only designed for the scalar-valued images.

The structure tensor has the ability of capturing the first-order information within a local neighborhood. This neigborhood-awareness makes it more robust to the noise (or the other types of deterioration), when compared to the gradient. Since STV is designed by using the rooted eigenvalues of the structure tensor, it better codifies the image variation at a point than the regularizers that aims to penalize the gradient magnitude (such as TV and DTV). However, STV may not always distinguish the edges under excessive noise, thus may smooth out them. Even though DTV's preference of penalizing the gradient magnitude makes it vulnerable to the noise, it is good at struggling with it along the edges, since its gradients are rotated to a favorable direction and scaled according to a favorable dose of smoothness.

3   Method

Let us define a new operator Π (as being a composition of R_θ and Λ_α), which can act on the gradients within the patch, when applied to the patch-based Jacobian, as follows:

$$(\Pi J_k f)[i] = \begin{bmatrix} (\mathcal{T}_1 \Lambda_\alpha R_{-\theta} \nabla f^1)[i] & (\mathcal{T}_2 \Lambda_\alpha R_{-\theta} \nabla f^1)[i] & \cdots & (\mathcal{T}_L \Lambda_\alpha R_{-\theta} \nabla f^1)[i] \\ (\mathcal{T}_1 \Lambda_\alpha R_{-\theta} \nabla f^2)[i] & (\mathcal{T}_2 \Lambda_\alpha R_{-\theta} \nabla f^2)[i] & \cdots & (\mathcal{T}_L \Lambda_\alpha R_{-\theta} \nabla f^2)[i] \\ \vdots & \vdots & \vdots & \vdots \\ (\mathcal{T}_1 \Lambda_\alpha R_{-\theta} \nabla f^c)[i] & (\mathcal{T}_2 \Lambda_\alpha R_{-\theta} \nabla f^c)[i] & \cdots & (\mathcal{T}_L \Lambda_\alpha R_{-\theta} \nabla f^c)[i] \end{bmatrix} \quad (6)$$

Let it be called as *directional patch-based Jacobian*. Therefore, we propose a new regularizer of the form: DSTV functional of the form:

$$DSTV(f) = \sum_{i=1}^{N} \|(\Pi J_k f)[i]\|_{S_p} \quad (7)$$

where DSTV abbreviates the direction guided STV, here and hereafter. By means of Eq. (7), one has the chance of penalizing the eigenvalues of the structure tensor, in favor of the predetermined direction. By means of Eq. (7), the eigenvalues of the structure tensor this time summarize the rotated and scaled gradients with the incorporation of prior knowledge. Also, the presence of the $\Lambda_\alpha R_\theta$'s doesn't destroy the convexity of the regularizer.

Equation (7) can equivalently be written as a support function of the set $B_F = \{\Upsilon \in \mathbb{R}^{LC \times 2} : \|\Upsilon\|_{S_2} \leq 1\}$, which is the unit ball of S_2 (Frobenius) matrix norm and takes the shape of:

$$DSTV(f) = \sum_{i=1}^{N} \sup_{\Upsilon \in B_F} \langle (\Pi J_k f)[i], \Upsilon \rangle \tag{8}$$

where $\langle \cdot \rangle$ denotes the inner product. The right-hand side of Eq. (8) can be rewritten in the compact form of $\sup_{\Psi[i] \in B_F} \langle \Pi J_k f, \Psi \rangle$, by introducing another variable $\Psi \in \mathbb{R}^{N \times LC \times 2}$, where $\Psi[i]$ is the i-th submatrix. This expression allows us to use the available algorithms for orthogonal projection onto the convex B_F.

Therefore, a DSTV-regularized denoising problem will require to solve the following minimization problem:

$$\min_{f \in \mathcal{C}} \frac{1}{2} \|g - f\|_2^2 + \tau \sup_{\Psi[i] \in B_F} \langle \Pi J_k f, \Psi \rangle \tag{9}$$

where $\mathcal{C}$ is nothing but a set that corresponds to an additional constraint on f (e.g. box constraint), which is equal to $\mathbb{R}^N$ for unconstrained case.

Due to DSTV's nonsmoothness, solving Eq. (9) is nontrivial. But since the convexity of the STV (proven in [8]) is preserved in Eq. (8), the proximal map of DSTV corresponds to the minimizer, thus can be employed as:

$$\hat{f} = \text{prox}_{\tau DSTV(f)}(g) := \operatorname*{argmin}_{f \in \mathcal{C}} \frac{1}{2} \|g - f\|_2^2 + \tau \sup_{\Psi[i] \in B_F} \langle f, J_k^* \Pi^* \Psi \rangle \tag{10}$$

where J_k^* and Π^* arising after we leave f alone, denote the adjoints. J_k^* was defined in [8] as:

$$(J_K^* X)[k] = \sum_{l=1}^{L} -\text{div}(\mathcal{T}_l^* X[i, s]) \tag{11}$$

where $s = (c - 1)L + l$ and $k = (c - 1)N + n$ with $1 \leq n \leq N$ and $1 \leq c \leq C$. $\mathcal{T}_l^*$ corresponds to the adjoint of $\mathcal{T}_l$, which scans the $X[i, s]$ in column-wise manner, where $X[i, s] \in \mathbb{R}^2$ is the s-th row of the i-th submatrix of an arbitrary $X \in \mathbb{R}^{N \times LC \times 2}$. In Eq. (10), $X = \Pi^* \Psi$ for the operator Π^* acting the same way with Π, except that the operator pair $\Lambda_\alpha R_{-\theta}$ applied to the two-dimensional vector elements ($\Psi[i, s]$ in this case) is replaced by $R_\theta \Lambda_\alpha$. Also in Eq. (11), div is discrete divergence, whose definition depends on the discretization scheme used for the gradient. In [8], it is defined using backward differences, since the gradient is discretized using forward differences.

From now on, we will be following the fast gradient projection (FGP) method [2], which combines the dual approach introduced in [5] to solve TV-based denoising, and the convergence accelerator FISTA [3]. Equation (10) can first be expressed as a minimax problem for the objective $\mathcal{L}(f, \Psi) = \frac{1}{2} \|g - f\|_2^2 + \tau \langle f, J_k^* \Pi^* \Psi \rangle$, which is convex w.r.t. f and concave w.r.t. Ψ; thus, has a common saddle point that doesn't change when the minimum and the maximum are swapped as shown below:

$$\min_{f \in \mathcal{C}} \max_{\Psi[i] \in B_F} \mathcal{L}(f, \Psi) = \mathcal{L}(\hat{f}, \hat{\Psi}) = \max_{\Psi[i] \in B_F} \min_{f \in \mathcal{C}} \mathcal{L}(f, \Psi) \tag{12}$$

Algorithm 1. Algorithm for DSTV-based denoising

1: $\epsilon \in (0, min(1, L(d)))$, $\tau \in [\epsilon, 1]$
2: $u^{(j=1)} := [0,0]$, $t^{(j=1)} := 1$
3: **while** *Eq.* (10) is not $\epsilon - converged$ **do**
4:    $u^{(j)} \leftarrow P_{B_F}\Big(u^{(j)} + (8\sqrt{2}(\alpha^2 + 1)\tau)^{-1}\big(\Pi J_k P_C(g - \tau J_k^* \Pi^* u^{(j)})\big)\Big)$
5:    $(u^{(j+1)}, t^{(j+1)}) \leftarrow \text{FISTA}\,(t^{(j)}, u^{(j)}, u^{(j-1)})$
6: **end while**
7: $\hat{f} \leftarrow P_C(g - \gamma\tau J_k^* \Pi^* u^{(j)})$

Maximization of the dual problem $d(\Psi) = \min_{f\in C} \mathcal{L}(f, \Psi)$ at the right-hand side is same with the minimization of the primal problem at the left-hand side. When the maximizer $\hat{\Psi}$ of $d(\Psi)$ is found, it can be used to find the minimizer $\hat{f}$ of the primal problem. In order to find $\hat{\Psi}$, we first derive the minimizer $\hat{f}$, in terms of Ψ, as:

$$\hat{f} = \underset{f\in C}{\text{argmin}}\ \mathcal{L}(f, \Psi) \tag{13}$$

where $\mathcal{L}(f, \Psi) = \|f - (g - \tau J_k^*(\Pi^*\Psi))\|_2^2 - M$ is found by expanding the equation, collecting the constants at the end, and subsumed under the term M. The solution of Eq. (13) is $\hat{f} = P_C(g - \tau J_k^* \Pi^*\Psi)$, where $P_C(\cdot)$ is the orthogonal projection onto the convex set C. Then we proceed by plugging $\hat{f}$ in $\mathcal{L}(f, \Psi)$ to get the dual problem $d(\Psi) = \mathcal{L}(\hat{f}, \Psi) = \frac{1}{2}\|w - P_C(w)\|_2^2 + \frac{1}{2}(\|z\|_2^2 - \|w\|_2^2)$, where $w = g - \tau J_k^* \Pi^*\Psi$. As opposed to the primal problem, $d(\Psi)$ is smooth with a well-defined gradient:

$$\nabla d(\Psi) = \tau \Pi J_k P_C(g - \gamma\tau J_k^* \Pi^*\Psi) \tag{14}$$

obtained based on the derivation in Lemma 4.1 of [2]. From now on, finding the maximizer $\hat{\Psi}$ of $d(\Psi)$ is trivial by using the idea of the projected gradients [5]. In case of minimization, it iteratively performs decoupled sequences of gradient descent and gradient projection on a set. In our case, each $\Psi[i]$ will be projected onto the set B_F, where the projection is defined as:

$$P_{B_F}(\Psi[i]) = \frac{\Psi[i]}{\max(1, \|\Psi[i]\|_F)} \tag{15}$$

in [8], to which the readers are referred for the derivation. When it comes to gradient ascent, an appropriate step size that ensures the convergence is needed. Since Eq. (14) is a Lipschitz continuous gradient, a constant step size $1/L(d)$ can be used, where $L(d)$ is the Lipschitz constant having the upper bound $L(d) \leq 8\sqrt{2}(\alpha^2 + 1)\gamma^2\tau^2$. For the derivation, see Appendix A.

As a consequence, the overall algorithm is shown in Algorithm 1. FISTA procedure is referring to the fast iterative shrinkage-thresholding algorithm proposed in [3], and attached to Appendix B.

4   Experimental Results

In this section, we perform experiments to compare the performance of our regularizer, with its predecessor STV and its influencer DTV. Since STV's superiority over the baseline TV and the TGV has already been shown in [8], they are not included to the competing algorithms. In Fig. 1, the uni-directional grayscale and color images used in the experiments are all shown. Among those images; *reed, sea shell, cotton bud*, and *feather* were taken from Amsterdam Library of Textures (ALOT) image dataset while the others were public domain images. We use peak signal to noise ratio (PSNR) and structural similarity index (SSIM) [11] to assess the performances of the algorithms. DSTV has been implemented on top of STV, whose source code is publicly available on the author's (Lefkimmiatis, S.) website. All methods were written in MATLAB by only making use of the CPU. The runtimes were computed on a computer equipped with Intel Core Processor i7-7500U (2.70-GHz) with 16 GB of memory.

Fig. 1. Above row respectively shows the thumbnails of the grayscale *cotton bud, feather, straw*; and color *reed, grass, paper, sea shell, palm, cat fur* images of size 256 × 256 used in the experiments. (Color figure online)

For the convolution kernel k_σ of the structure tensor, we choose it to be a 5×5 pixel Gaussian window with standard deviation $\sigma = 0.5$ pixels, for both STV and DSTV. This decision is taken by prioritizing the reconstruction quality; however, by selecting a 3×3 window, the computational complexity, thus the reported runtimes can be reduced (nearly up to the DTV's runtimes) at the cost of a little loss from the quality. On the other hand, in all experiments, α for DTV and DSTV, and the regularization parameter τ for all competing regularizers are optimized, such that they yield the best possible PSNR. Furthermore, to be used by DTV and DSTV, the θ value is estimated from the observed image by computing the DTV measures for a range of angles, while keeping $\alpha > 1$ constant. The angle that yields the smallest DTV is picked as the dominant direction.

The grayscale results of the DSTV against to the DTV and the STV are reported in Table 1. The PSNR and SSIM performances are listed, along with their respective runtimes, by considering four different noise levels applied on the first three images shown in Fig. 1. Although it is obvious that the DSTV yields better recovery than the others, for the cotton bud and the feather images, DTV almost catches up DSTV, especially in terms of the PSNR measure. This is due to the fact that those images are coherently uni-directional (except the bottom left and top right corners of the feather image), with smooth, non-textural, and continuous stripes. Denoising this kind of images is a trivial task for DTV, since its enforced direction of smoothness coincides with the correct pattern. Even so,

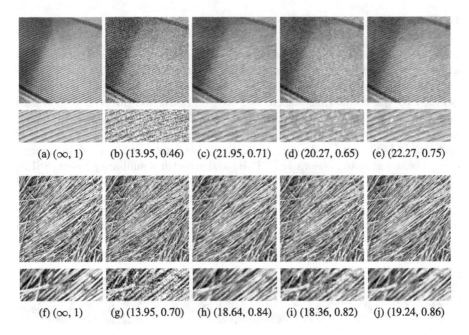

(a) (∞, 1)   (b) (13.95, 0.46)   (c) (21.95, 0.71)   (d) (20.27, 0.65)   (e) (22.27, 0.75)

(f) (∞, 1)   (g) (13.95, 0.70)   (h) (18.64, 0.84)   (i) (18.36, 0.82)   (j) (19.24, 0.86)

Fig. 2. The restored versions of the noisy ($\sigma_\eta = 0.2$) *feather* and *straw* images (col-2), by using DTV (col-3), STV (col-4) and DSTV (col-5) regularizers. The quantity pairs shown at the bottom of each image are corresponding to the (PSNR, SSIM) values. Also the detail patches cropped from each image are provided.

in higher frequency feather image, the SSIM gap between DTV and DSTV is concretely higher than the one obtained in cotton bud image. When it comes to the straw image, deviations from the dominant direction work against both DTV and DSTV. The results on straw image can better reflect the DSTV's superiority arising from the semi-localness of the structure tensor, over DTV. This semi-localness make DSTV more robust to the errors in pre-determined θ. For the visual assessment, Fig. 2 shows the restored versions of the feather and straw images by three subjected regularizers. As one can observe, STV causes to the oil-painting like artifacts on the edges, whereas it is the only regularizer that can manage to restore the texture at the bottom left corner of the feather image, where the direction does not match with the dominant one. On the other side, the DTV over-smooths by damaging rough textures on the details, which are well preserved by the DSTV (see the detail images in Fig. 2).

In Table 2 and in Fig. 3, the results obtained from the color images are reported. Since DTV is only designed for the scalar-valued images, it is excluded from these experiments. According to the results presented in the table, DSTV systematically outperforms STV for our uni-directional image denoising problem. Its superiority becomes more apparent in the high-frequency images with less deviations from the pre-determined dominant direction (e.g. palm). In sea shell image on the other hand, the PSNR and the SSIM values obtained by both

Table 1. Assessing the PSNR/SSIM performances of DTV [1], STV [8], and DSTV regularizers (along with their elapsed runtimes) on scalar-valued (grayscale) images shown in Fig. 2.

	σ_η	0.1	0.15	0.2	0.25
Cotton bud	DTV	29.80/**0.90**	27.91/0.86	26.58/0.83	25.57/0.80
		4.55 s	4.02 s	4.10 s	2.16 s
	STV	27.85/0.86	25.78/0.80	24.35/0.75	23.28/0.70
		25.08 s	29.01 s	22.70 s	28.98 s
	DSTV	**29.87/0.90**	**28.04/0.87**	**26.89/0.84**	**25.98/0.81**
		25.61 s	25.46 s	16.60 s	29.24 s
Feather	DTV	25.17/0.86	23.23/0.78	21.95/0.71	21.04/0.66
		3.06 s	4.26 s	3.92 s	4.42 s
	STV	23.83/0.82	21.69/0.72	20.27/0.65	19.30/0.56
		29.77 s	23.91 s	26.06 s	23.46 s
	DSTV	**25.60/0.87**	**27.13/0.81**	**22.27/0.75**	**21.43/0.70**
		17.82 s	23.66 s	28.50 s	31.1 s
Straw	DTV	22.59/0.93	20.19/0.89	18.64/0.84	17.51/0.79
		1.62 s	2.31 s	2.68 s	4.07 s
	STV	22.47/0.93	19.97/0.88	18.36/0.82	17.20/0.77
		27.16 s	28.45 s	30.52 s	34.48 s
	DSTV	**23.17/0.94**	**20.81/0.90**	**19.24/0.86**	**18.11/0.82**
		32.28 s	33.61 s	28.52 s	35.85 s

Table 2. Assessing the PSNR/SSIM performances of STV [8] and DSTV denoisers (along with their elapsed runtimes) on vector-valued (color) images shown in Fig. 3.

Method	STV			DSTV		
σ_η	0.1	0.15	0.2	0.1	0.15	0.2
Reed	28.31/0.95	26.73/0.93	25.62/0.92	**29.17/0.96**	**27.75/0.94**	**26.77/0.93**
	28.14 s	27.44 s	28.88 s	30.39 s	30.12 s	31.98 s
Grass	28.13/0.97	26.09/0.96	24.72/**0.95**	**29.42/0.98**	**27.26/0.97**	**25.63/0.95**
	28.52 s	31.17 s	46.52 s	29.91 s	31.12 s	30.17 s
Paper	27.38/0.95	25.03/0.91	23.47/0.88	**29.73/0.97**	**27.57/0.95**	**26.04/0.93**
	32.85 s	27.60 s	46.30 s	31.73 s	48.21 s	47.41 s
Sea shell	31.68/**0.90**	30.00/**0.87**	29.45/**0.85**	**31.72/0.90**	**30.45/0.87**	**29.54/0.85**
	33.85 s	31.46 s	28.60 s	33.50 s	37.19 s	32.29 s
Palm	24.34/0.91	22.02/0.85	20.52/0.79	**25.87/0.94**	**23.67/0.90**	**22.19/0.86**
	30.81 s	31.36 s	50.55 s	27.92 s	29.80 s	23.65 s
Cat fur	24.81/0.76	23.08/0.65	22.11/0.57	**24.87/0.77**	**23.28/0.68**	**22.31/0.60**
	30.23 s	30.85 s	30.44 s	29.83 s	27.49 s	32.75 s

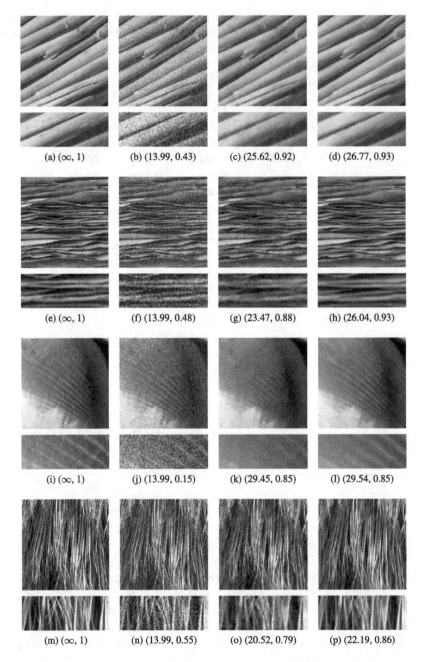

(a) (∞, 1)   (b) (13.99, 0.43)   (c) (25.62, 0.92)   (d) (26.77, 0.93)

(e) (∞, 1)   (f) (13.99, 0.48)   (g) (23.47, 0.88)   (h) (26.04, 0.93)

(i) (∞, 1)   (j) (13.99, 0.15)   (k) (29.45, 0.85)   (l) (29.54, 0.85)

(m) (∞, 1)   (n) (13.99, 0.55)   (o) (20.52, 0.79)   (p) (22.19, 0.86)

Fig. 3. The restored versions of the noisy ($\sigma_\eta = 0.2$) *reed, paper, sea shell,* and *palm* images (col-2), by using STV (col-3) and DSTV (col-4) regularizers. The quantity pairs shown at the bottom of each image are corresponding to the (PSNR, SSIM) values. Also the detail patches cropped from each image are provided. (Color figure online)

regularizers are almost same. This result is due to the smooth transitions of the stripes on the shell from one direction to another. However, for the same image, the value of DSTV can visually be seen by comparing the detail images given in Fig. 3(k) and (l). In contrast to the quantitative results, these images reflect the DSTV's ability of texture preservation. The same applies for the cat fur image, which substantially may not be categorized as a uni-directional image. Also to evaluate the DSTV's robustness to the small deviations from the dominant direction, one can observe the first row of Fig. 3. Overall, DSTV's idea of contributing STV minimization process in favor of the dominant direction succeeds denoising in more appealing way for nearly uni-directional images; while STV fails to restore high-frequency details under excessive amount of noise, since the fair contributions of the rapidly changing gradients within a neighborhood may mislead the process.

5   Conclusion and Future Work

In this paper, we discoursed the denoising problem from variational perspective, and proposed a new analysis-based regularizer to be used on uni-directional images. We utilized the DTV's idea of incorporating the prior knowledge on the directional dominance of the latent image to the inversion process, while designing our regularizer DSTV as a variant of STV. Throughout the paper, only the uni-directional images were our concern. Even though this scenario is biased to the DTV and DSTV, it provides valuable insight on how the guidance of a directional prior can improve one of the state-of-the-art regularizers. As shown by the experimental results, DSTV systematically outperformed its two predecessors. This encourages us about a possible extension to DSTV that can work with spatially varying θ's and α's, extracted from the observed image. A relevant research question is if it is possible to develop such a preprocessor algorithm that can extract robust derivative-based directional descriptors, and can feed them into DSTV-based denoising machinery.

Appendix A

In order to find an upper bound for Lipschitz constant, we follow the derivation in [2] and adapt it to our formulation.

$$
\begin{aligned}
\|\nabla d(v) - \nabla d(u)\| &= \tau \|(\Pi J_k P_C(g - \tau J_k^* \Pi^* u) - \Pi J_k P_C(g - \tau J_k^* \Pi^* v)\| \\
&\leq \tau \|\Pi J_k\| \|P_C(g - \tau J_k^* \Pi^* u) - P_C(g - \tau J_k^* \Pi^* v)\| \\
&\leq \tau \|\Pi J_k\| \|\tau J_k^* \Pi^* (u - v)\| \\
&\leq \tau^2 \|\Pi\|^2 \|J_k\|^2 \|u - v\| \\
&\leq \tau^2 \|\Pi\|^2 \|\nabla\|^2 \|T\|^2 \|u - v\|
\end{aligned}
\tag{16}
$$

where $T = \sum_{l=1}^{L}(T_l^* T_l)$. Knowing from [2] that $\|\nabla\|^2 \leq 8$, from [8] that $\|T\|^2 \leq \sqrt{2}$, and further showing that $\|\Pi^*\|^2 \leq (\alpha^2 + 1)$, we come up with the Lipschitz constant $L(d) \leq 8\sqrt{2}(\alpha^2 + 1)\tau^2$.

Appendix B

Algorithm 2. FISTA [3]

1: **function:** $(f^{(next)}, t^{(next)}) = \text{FISTA}\,(t, f^{(cur)}, f^{(prev)})$

2:    $t^{(next)} \leftarrow (1 + \sqrt{1 + 4t^2})/2$

3:    $f^{(next)} \leftarrow f^{(cur)} + (\frac{t-1}{t^{(next)}})(f^{(cur)} - f^{(prev)})$

4: **end**

References

1. Bayram, I., Kamasak, M.E.: Directional total variation. IEEE Signal Process. Lett. **19**(12), 781–784 (2012)
2. Beck, A., Teboulle, M.: Fast gradient-based algorithms for constrained total variation image denoising and deblurring problems. IEEE Trans. Image Process. **18**(11), 2419–2434 (2009)
3. Beck, A., Teboulle, M.: A fast iterative shrinkage-thresholding algorithm for linear inverse problems. SIAM J. Imaging Sci. **2**(1), 183–202 (2009)
4. Bredies, K., Kunisch, K., Pock, T.: Total generalized variation. SIAM J. Imaging Sci. **3**(3), 492–526 (2010)
5. Chambolle, A.: An algorithm for total variation minimization and applications. J. Math. Imaging Vis. **20**(1–2), 89–97 (2004)
6. Chartrand, R.: Exact reconstruction of sparse signals via nonconvex minimization. IEEE Signal Process. Lett. **14**(10), 707–710 (2007)
7. Esedoḡlu, S., Osher, S.J.: Decomposition of images by the anisotropic Rudin-Osher-Fatemi model. Commun. Pure Appl. Math. **57**(12), 1609–1626 (2004)
8. Lefkimmiatis, S., Roussos, A., Maragos, P., Unser, M.: Structure tensor total variation. SIAM J. Imaging Sci. **8**(2), 1090–1122 (2015)
9. Lou, Y., Zeng, T., Osher, S., Xin, J.: A weighted difference of anisotropic and isotropic total variation model for image processing. SIAM J. Imaging Sci. **8**(3), 1798–1823 (2015)
10. Rudin, L.I., Osher, S., Fatemi, E.: Nonlinear total variation based noise removal algorithms. Phys. D **60**(1–4), 259–268 (1992)
11. Wang, Z., Bovik, A.C., Sheikh, H.R., Simoncelli, E.P.: Image quality assessment: from error visibility to structural similarity. IEEE Trans. Image Process. **13**(4), 600–612 (2004)
12. Xu, L., Lu, C., Xu, Y., Jia, J.: Image smoothing via L_0 gradient minimization. ACM Trans. Graph. (TOG) **30**, 174 (2011)

Impact of Fused Visible-Infrared Video Streams on Visual Tracking

Stéphane Vujasinović$^{(\boxtimes)}$ ⓘ, Stefan Becker ⓘ, Norbert Scherer-Negenborn, and Michael Arens ⓘ

Fraunhofer Institute for Optronics, System Technologies, and Image Exploitation IOSB, Gutleuthausstr. 1, 76275 Ettlingen, Germany
stephane.vujasinovic@iosb.fraunhofer.de

Abstract. Currently state-of-the-art trackers rely on fully convolutional neural network (FCNN) for extracting salient features in order to create an appearance representation of the target. Ordinarily, most of them intend to work with input streams from the visible spectrum, yet how does an input stream from the infrared spectrum and a fused visible-infrared stream affect their performances and how does it benefit or detriment them? Towards this end, we compare the performance of various reference trackers utilizing FCNN for feature extraction, on visible, infrared and fused spectrums. By utilizing a carefully processed publicly available data set for the evaluation, containing visible-infrared paired sequences, we ensure to find synchronized and same attributes at the same locations, effectively studying only the impact of a spectral change. Thus, by analyzing quantitative results, we identify visual attributes which benefit or detriment from a fused approach on typical visual tracking scenarios.

Keywords: Visual tracking · Infrared imagery · Image fusion visible-infrared

1 Introduction

Tracking is an elemental task for any practical video application, requiring a level of understanding about the objects of interest. The subject has received increasing attention in recent years, where state-of-the-art trackers mainly focus on using the visible spectrum and deep neural networks. Despite the increase in accuracy and robustness, some limitations still persist. In order to overcome the constraints from a single spectral range during tracking, a multi-spectral approach can be utilized. For example, an additional infrared sensor can provide complementary information to an image obtained in the visible range. On the one hand, visible images offer rich content (i.e. colors, texture) and should be preferred when the thermal properties of an object are close to the surrounding environment, on the other hand, infrared images are better suited in case of a change in lighting conditions or gloomy environments [3,7]. This approach could

© Springer Nature Switzerland AG 2019
A. Morales et al. (Eds.): IbPRIA 2019, LNCS 11867, pp. 101–112, 2019.
https://doi.org/10.1007/978-3-030-31332-6_9

highly benefit applications such as, surveillance [1], traffic monitoring [2] and medical imaging [6].

Among some challenges arising in both domains, the potential added value is accompanied by an overhead like increased amount of raw data that needs to be processed. Therefore, an ideal fusion method should preserve the positive characteristics of the individual channels, but reduce the amount of data needed to be processed. Accordingly, all subsequent processing stages, like visual tracking should benefit from the fused input stream. However, due to an inevitable non-optimal fused image, it is not clear if the general expectation of increased performance is met. Towards this end, we evaluate the effect of current state-of-art visual trackers on fused data streams provided by current state-of-the-art fusion strategies.

The evaluation is done on typical visual tracking sequences from the Camel [9] data set. Since image fusion relies on synchronized and well-registered camera, the data set is carefully further edited to ensure best possible fusion results by still capturing different visual attributes as displayed in Fig. 1. Thereby, we can identify approaches and occurring visual attributes which can benefit from a fused input stream. This study differs from the 2015 VOT challenge [15], by only evaluating the appearance changes from one spectrum to another, by using synchronized input streams.

Fig. 1. Synchronized frames of a video stream from Camel [9] in the (from left to right) visual, infrared, addition and l1-norm subsets.

In the following Sect. 2 a short introduction of the selected trackers and fusion strategies are presented. Afterward, we describe the evaluation process and examine the quantitative results in Sect. 3 and Sect. 4 concludes the paper.

2 Visual Trackers and Fusion

2.1 Reference Trackers

Due to the potential wide range of industrial tracking-based applications, visual tracking is a very popular research area and several publicly benchmarks exist. A selection of current single-object visual trackers achieving top-ranks on most-widely used visual tracking benchmarks [14,24] is considered for the experiments presented in this paper. Furthermore, the selected tracker have to rely on an FCNN for feature extraction and operate model free. For a more detailed description and categorization, we refer to the original papers and to the corresponding benchmark papers. Following those criteria, we chose to work with:

Re^3 [10] (Real-Time Recurrent Regression Network) performs feature extraction using the CaffeNet architecture (Re-implementation of AlexNet [16] in Caffe) without the fully connected part. A regression layer is used to output the location of the object in the frame and the size of the object. The tracker uses two LSTM layers for remembering appearance changes and motion information of the target.

MBMD [27] is the winner of 2018 VOT long term challenge [14] and is composed of a bounding box regression network for identifying potential locations of the target and a verification network, identifying the target and the potential locations. Feature extraction for the regression is performed by an SSD-MobileNet [13] network and feature extraction for the verification stage is performed by a pre-trained VGG-16 [22].

DaSiamRPN [28] is the winner of the VOT real-time challenge 2018 [14] and runner up in the long term part of the challenge and is an extension of SiamRPN [18]. Feature extraction is performed using the FCNN of Bertinetto et al. [5]. In addition, it uses a local-global search region strategy for target re-detection and a distractor-aware component for catching target appearance variations and to discriminate the target against the surrounding.

MemTrack [26] is based on a dynamic memory network [17] architecture. Feature extraction is performed by the FCNN used in [5]. A soft attention mechanism [25] locates potential regions of the targets in the search area. An LSTM selects an appropriate template from stored ones based on the output of the attention mechanism, combined with a reference template, creating a residual template. Afterwards, the residual template is used for finding the location of the target in the search area.

SiamMask [23] is a recently state-of-the-art introduced tracker which produces in addition to a rotational bounding box a binary mask, classifying pixel-wise belongingness to the target. Feature extraction is performed by a variation of ResNet-50 [12]. Using a depth-wise cross correlation [4] on feature spaces and a region proposal network [21]. By examining the potential targets locations, the actual target is found and a binary mask is created.

2.2 Fusion Strategies

Image fusion strives to preserve positive characteristics of individual channels, in addition to reducing the amount of data needed for processing. Due to inevitable errors induced by image fusion and depending on specific conditions, it is unclear how beneficial this approach is for tracking applications. Before analyzing the effects, we present the main concepts on image fusion methods and the selected strategies for this study.

In multi-modal fusion, different sensors i.e. visible, infrared, are used in the process of image acquisition. The fusion process can be applied on pixel, object or on decision levels. However, in this paper, we examine only pixel level fusion, which can traditionally be divided into transformation domain methods and spatial domain methods [7,11]. These techniques can involve around simple transformations e.g. averaging, adding, subtracting, on pixel intensities, or more complex transformations e.g. Laplace pyramid, wavelet pyramid. Unlike these traditional strategies, a shift to deep learning is occurring, which are now able to achieve state-of-the-art performance. Therefore, for the experiments of this study we select the deep neural network (DNN), DenseFuse [19].

The authors of DenseFuse propose a novel deep learning architecture using convolutional layers and dense blocks. The DNN is composed of three major components. The first component is an encoder made from one convolutional layer, that extracts rough features, followed by three dense convolutional layers, enabling the network to preserve mid and deep level features better. Allowing in addition to improve information flow and diminish the overfitting problem during training. The second component is a fusion layer incorporating two fusion strategies, i.e addition strategy presented originally in DeepFuse [20] and an l1-norm strategy. This layer integrates into one feature map the pertinent features extracted by the encoder from the source images i.e from the visible and infrared images. The third part of the DNN is a decoder which re-constructs the fused visible-infrared image using convolutional layers [19].

Originally, DenseFuse fuses a grayscale image with an infrared image, but it also handles visible images, in splitting the image into separate channels, that are then passed through the DNN and fused separately with the infrared image. The final result is a combination of the three newly created fused images. Figure 1 displays the fused image using both strategies from DenseFuse, and the original visible and infrared images.

3   Evaluation

The goal of this section is to provide empirical results and discuss the benefits and detriments of a fused approach, which can lead to non-optimal output.

3.1   Data Set to Subsets

For this study, we employed the Camel [9] data set which captured 26 annotated video streams paired in the visible and infrared domain. The video streams were taken in an urban environment and captured during day and night time. Similar visual attributes from popular data set for visual object tracking challenges [8,14] are present, i.e. in-plane rotation, illumination change, scale variation, occlusion and camera motion. The data set contains 765 annotated objects in the visible domain and 787 in the infrared domain, where four different classes are present, i.e bicycle, person, vehicle and dog. In order to reduce registration errors, only a reduced subset of sequences are considered for the evaluation. The criteria are set as follows:

- We kept sequences having an Intersection over Union (IoU) over 0.7 between ground-truth bounding boxes in the visible-infrared domain and lasting at least 30 consecutive frames.

– Furthermore, in order to ensure adequate sequence length, a short drop of the IoU under 0.7 is accepted if its only for less than 10 frames and still above 0.5. Whereas an IoU under 0.5 stops the recording until the condition from stage one is valid again.

Based on the newly created domain subset, we created the two fused subsets with the available fusion strategies from DenseFuse (i.e. addition and l1-norm subsets). The ground truth annotation for the fused subsets, is simply adapted by averaging the ground truth bounding boxes from both domains, ensuring us to keep a minimal valid bounding box around the target.

The resulting 4 subsets, visible (VIS), infrared (IR), addition (Add) and l1-norm (l1) subsets used for the evaluation, contain 438 sequences, with a median sequence length of 107 frames, a median target width ratio of 0.1 and height ratio of 0.17. Example images from the four evaluation subsets are displayed in figures of Subsect. 3.5.

Although, we use a state-of-art DNN for image fusion, we can not prevent errors generated by the DNN during the fusion process, i.e. noise, registration difference between visible and infrared images. For example, the images in Fig. 2 depict a non-optimal registration between the source images.

Fig. 2. Example images from Camel [9], showing a registration problem between the synchronized frames in (from left to right) the visual and infrared domain subsets, and the final results in the addition and l1-norm subsets

In contrast to the most closely related investigations on the VOT-IR dataset, here by selecting the Camel data set, we ensure to find synchronized and same attributes at the same locations, effectively studying only the impact of a spectral change on the FCNN of the trackers.

3.2   Evaluation Metrics

Methodologies from one challenge to another differ in the evaluation process as well as the performance measures. In this paper two measures are mainly used to rank the performance: Firstly, accuracy which measures the overlap during successful tracking periods, secondly robustness, which is the number of times the tracker lost the target. We rank the tracker accordingly to their average IoU and average robustness on the whole subsets. For the evaluation, a target is considered lost when the IoU between ground truth and predicted bounding box is under 0.5 for 10 consecutive frames. If the target is lost, we initialize the tracker again on the next frame. For easier comparison between the tracker results, we combine accuracy and robustness together in on score.

3.3   Evaluation on Subsets

Since we use video streams differing domain wise, and use original implementation of the trackers, the change in performance can mainly by assigned to the extracted features. Their performances on the subsets are displayed in Fig. 3 and Table 1 resumes the results in one score.

Based on these results, the Re3, and MBMD trackers show better scores in accuracy and robustness on the visual subset compared to the infrared subset. Both also perform better on the addition subset, gaining in accuracy and robustness, whereas the usage of the l1-norm subset shows a performance drop.

The MemTrack and SiamMask trackers responded interestingly with a better score on the infrared subset than on the visible subset, but regardless of the fusion strategy employed, both achieve better results on the fused subsets. With the MemTrack achieving a slightly better score on the addition subset, and the SiamMask tracker on the l1-norm subset.

In contrast to previous trackers, the DaSiamRPN tracker, does not react as positively as expected. Indeed, the best performance is achieved on the visible subset, even though the addition subset score is close to the visible subset. The worst score for this tracker is achieved when applying the fused L1-norm subset.

Aside from the DaSiamRPN tracker, all trackers benefit from a fusion between the visible and the infrared spectrum at the input stage as shown in Table 2. We also notice that, even though the FCNN part of the tracker are different from each other, some react similarly, as Re3 with MBMD or MemTrack with SiamMask. For instance, the MemTrack and SiamMask respond very well to both fusion strategies, and Re3 displays a similar score variation as MBMD on VIS-Add.

Table 1. Average score (combination between average accuracy and robustness) for each tracker on every subsets.

Subset	DaSiamRPN	Re3	MemTrack	MBMD	SiamMask
VIS	**0.998**	0.976	**0.941**	0.883	**0.995**
IR	0.973	**0.935**	0.971	**0.878**	0.999
Add	0.981	**0.999**	**0.976**	0.905	1.015
l1	**0.972**	0.975	0.975	0.883	**1.016**

Table 2. Relative performance variation between a domain subsets (DS) and a fused subsets (FS) depending on the tracker.

DS-FS	DaSiamRPN (%)	Re3 (%)	MemTrack (%)	MBMD (%)	SiamMask (%)
VIS-Add	−1.69	2.40	3.76	2.46	2.00
IR-Add	0.89	6.84	0.61	3.09	1.57
VIS-l1	−2.64	−0.03	3.64	0.02	2.12
IR-l1	−0.08	4.30	0.49	0.64	1.69

3.4   Fused Subsets Versus Domain Subsets

Based on Table 3 we notice that the lowest score distribution occurs on the infrared subset, regardless the tracker. Indicating that the infrared subset is the most difficult one to extract an appearance model from the surrounding, which is coherent since the trackers were originally trained on visible images.

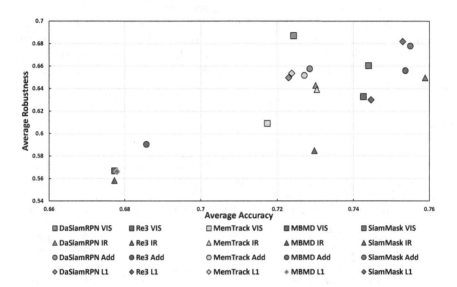

Fig. 3. Average accuracy and robustness given by reference trackers on the subsets. Tracker reaching the top-right corner of the graphic display better performance.

DaSiamPRN responds strongly on 48% video streams of the visible subset and poorly on 22%, with a standard score deviation of 0.229. Whereas, 13% video streams from the additional subset enable a high response from the tracker and only 4% a low response, with a standard score deviation of 0.196. Although, the DaSiamRPN responds stronger on a higher number of video streams from the visible subset, it also responds poorer on a higher number in comparison to the additional subset. Thus, using a fused subset enabled the tracker to track more robustly on a wider sequences diversity, even if using the fused subset did not manage to outperform the score from the visible subset.

Re3 and MBMD score better on 35% and 39% of the video streams from the additional subset, albeit Re3 also responds strongly to the same number of video streams in the visible subset. We note that both respond poorly on a low number of video streams from the addition subset, and achieving a low standard score deviation on the fused subsets. Indicating that using fused input stream enhances their performance on a larger number of streams and allows a more robust approach.

Oddly enough, MemTrack and SiamMask show a strong response on 43% video streams of the infrared subset and a poor response on 39% of it, albeit they originally were trained for visible imagery. Yet, both respond with a low amount of strong and poor scores on the video streams from the fused subsets. The standard score deviation for both trackers is also lower in the fused subsets compared to the domain subsets, even though the MemTrack has the lowest deviation on the infrared subset. Results from SiamMask indicate that using video streams from the fused subset reduce the standard score deviation, thus making the tracker more stable and also improving the results on a variety of sequences. Whereas the MemTrack, having a lower standard score deviation on the infrared domain, performs still better on the fused subsets, suggesting that the fused subset did not necessarily increase stability, but increased overall scores of the tracker on the sequences that gave previously poor scores on the domain subsets.

Table 3. Highest and lowest score distribution of trackers on video streams from the subsets and standard score deviation of the trackers on the subsets

Subset		DaSiamRPN	Re3	MemTrack	MBMD	SiamMask
	Percentage of highest scores	**48%**	**35%**	30%	13%	22%
VIS	Percentage of lowest scores	22%	26%	35%	30%	35%
	Standard score deviation	0.229	0.249	0.207	0.219	0.231
	Percentage of highest scores	17%	22%	**43%**	13%	**43%**
IR	Percentage of lowest scores	**52%**	**57%**	39%	39%	39%
	Standard score deviation	0.204	0.252	0.192	0.223	0.222
	Percentage of highest scores	13%	**35%**	17%	**39%**	9%
Add	Percentage of lowest scores	4%	9%	9%	4%	17%
	Standard score deviation	0.196	0.236	0.194	0.203	0.207
	Percentage of highest scores	22%	9%	9%	22%	13%
l1	Percentage of lowest scores	22%	9%	17%	26%	9%
	Standard score deviation	0.195	0.224	0.197	0.201	0.209

In most cases, the usage of fused subsets proved to be beneficially for stability, as the scores where more balanced and enhanced overall as a whole, rather than individual sequences.

3.5   Special Case Analysis

In this section, we look at video streams that give high score variations from a domain subset to a fused subset, regardless if positive or negative. Albeit the trackers react very differently to the video streams, there are special cases where a general tendency can be observed.

Synchronized frames of the video stream number 3 from Camel [9] are shown in Fig. 4. The video stream has a score increase on the fused subsets compared to the infrared subset, but a lower score compared to the visible subset. In these video stream, the potential targets belong to the same class and are clustered together, thus making the tracking process more challenging in the infrared domain because they all look alike in the infrared spectrum. Whereas, in the visible domain, color and texture are used to discriminate the target against the surrounding, easing the tracking process. But, depending on the fusion strategy, color and texture are removed to some extent and whitened, and useful features from the visible domain are kept to a degree, allowing a performance increase compared to the infrared domain.

Fig. 4. Synchronized frames of video stream 03 from Camel [9] in the (from left to right) visual, infrared, addition and l1-norm subset, which favours the visible domain due to the presence of color and texture in a crowded scene. (Color figure online)

Matching frames from video stream 9 from Camel [9] are displayed in Fig. 5. Contrariwise to the previous example, these video stream shows a performance gain on the fused subset compared to the visible subset and a drop compared to the infrared subset. Most of the potential targets (i.e. cars) undergo a sudden change in luminosity when passing under the shadows, which is a difficult attribute to handle for visual trackers. Whereas, on the infrared subset, the potential targets are still very clear, and since they are also clearly apart from each other, no clutter attribute is present to increase the difficulty of the tracking process in the infrared domain. By fusing both streams, the whitened target benefits from a constant white color that does not fade away under the shadows, in contrary to colors and textures.

Fig. 5. Synchronized frames of video stream 09 from Camel [9] in the (from left to right) visual, infrared, addition and l1-norm subsets, which favours the infrared domain due to the sudden illumination change. (Color figure online)

Presented in Fig. 6, are four synchronized frames from video steam number 15, which is recorded during night time in Camel [9]. Trackers show better performances on the fused subsets version of this stream than on the domain subsets.

Because of the gloomy environment, tracking in the visible domain is very difficult and naturally tracking in the infrared domain is more suited under these conditions. However, a fused version of both domains, shows a more robust alternative to the visible subset and an increase in accuracy compared to the infrared subset.

Fig. 6. Synchronized frames of video stream 15 from Camel [9] in the (from left to right) visual, infrared, addition and l1-norm subsets, favouring the fused subsets.

Synchronized frames of the video stream number 7 from Camel [9] are showed in Fig. 7. Trackers show better results on the domain subsets than on the fused versions. Due to the environment, a fused approach makes tracking more difficult since the whitening of the targets blends better with the white background and the snowy weather. Thus, tracking in the visible domain under these conditions is easier, since the tracking process can rely on color and texture features. Also, when using the infrared domain, the target is even clearer to discriminates against the surrounding background as shown in Fig. 7.

Fig. 7. Synchronized frames of video stream 07 from Camel [9] in the (from left to right) visual, infrared, addition and l1-norm subsets, where neither of the fused subset outperforms a domain subset. (Color figure online)

4   Conclusion

We present an evaluation of state-of-the-art visual trackers applied on visible, infrared, and fused input streams. In contrary to using one domain for tracking, where specific attributes to the domain can be difficult i.e. illumination change in the visible domain or clutter in the infrared domain to deal with, a fused approach at the input stage can be effective at handling those attributes. Indeed using early fused input streams indicate a tendency to enhance performance, enabling more robust and accurate tracking. In addition, allowing also to handle more robustly diverse type of sequences under various conditions and attributes. Depending on the fusion strategy, performances can improve or diminish. However an ideal fusion strategy would enable the tracker to perform on the fused subset as good as it would perform on an adequate domain subset version.

References

1. Andriluka, M., Roth, S., Schiele, B.: People-tracking-by-detection and people-detection-by-tracking. In: 2008 IEEE Conference on Computer Vision and Pattern Recognition, pp. 1–8. IEEE (2008)
2. Battiato, S., Farinella, G.M., Furnari, A., Puglisi, G., Snijders, A., Spiekstra, J.: An integrated system for vehicle tracking and classification. Expert Syst. Appl. **42**(21), 7263–7275 (2015)
3. Becker, S., Scherer-Negenborn, N., Thakkar, P., Hubner, W., Arens, M.: An evaluation of background subtraction algorithms on fused infrared-visible video streams. In: 2015 International Conference on Digital Image Computing: Techniques and Applications (DICTA), pp. 1–6, November 2015. https://doi.org/10.1109/DICTA.2015.7371229
4. Bertinetto, L., Henriques, J.A.F., Valmadre, J., Torr, P.H.S., Vedaldi, A.: Learning feed-forward one-shot learners. In: Proceedings of the 30th International Conference on Neural Information Processing Systems, NIPS 2016, pp. 523–531, Curran Associates Inc., USA (2016). http://dl.acm.org/citation.cfm?id=3157096.3157155
5. Bertinetto, L., Valmadre, J., Henriques, J.F., Vedaldi, A., Torr, P.H.S.: Fully-convolutional siamese networks for object tracking. In: Hua, G., Jégou, H. (eds.) ECCV 2016. LNCS, vol. 9914, pp. 850–865. Springer, Cham (2016). https://doi.org/10.1007/978-3-319-48881-3_56
6. Blake, A., Isard, M.: Active Contours: The Application of Techniques from Graphics, Vision, Control Theory and Statistics to Visual Tracking of Shapes in Motion. Springer, London (2012). https://doi.org/10.1007/978-1-4471-1555-7
7. Blum, R.S., Zheng, L.: Multi-Sensor Image Fusion and Its Applications. Signal Processing and Communications. Taylor & Francis, Boca Raton (2005). http://opac.inria.fr/record=b1105877
8. Fan, H., et al.: LaSOT: a high-quality benchmark for large-scale single object tracking. arXiv preprint arXiv:1809.07845 (2018)
9. Gebhardt, E., Wolf, M.: Camel dataset for visual and thermal infrared multiple object detection and tracking. In: 2018 15th IEEE International Conference on Advanced Video and Signal Based Surveillance (AVSS), pp. 1–6 (2018)
10. Gordon, D., Farhadi, A., Fox, D.: Re3: Real-time recurrent regression networks for visual tracking of generic objects. IEEE Robot. Autom. Lett. **3**(2), 788–795 (2018)
11. Goshtasby, A.A., Nikolov, S.G.: Image fusion: advances in the state of the art. Inf. Fusion **8**, 114–118 (2007)
12. He, K., Zhang, X., Ren, S., Sun, J.: Deep residual learning for image recognition. In: Proceedings of the IEEE Conference on Computer Vision and Pattern Recognition, pp. 770–778 (2016)
13. Howard, A.G., et al.: MobileNets: efficient convolutional neural networks for mobile vision applications. CoRR arxiv:abs/1704.04861 (2017)
14. Kristan, M., et al.: The sixth visual object tracking VOT2018 challenge results. In: Leal-Taixé, L., Roth, S. (eds.) ECCV 2018. LNCS, vol. 11129, pp. 3–53. Springer, Cham (2019). https://doi.org/10.1007/978-3-030-11009-3_1

15. Kristan, M., et al.: The visual object tracking vot2015 challenge results. In: Proceedings of the IEEE International Conference on Computer Vision Workshops, pp. 1–23 (2015)
16. Krizhevsky, A., Sutskever, I., Hinton, G.E.: ImageNet classification with deep convolutional neural networks. In: Pereira, F., Burges, C.J.C., Bottou, L., Weinberger, K.Q. (eds.) Advances in Neural Information Processing Systems, vol. 25, pp. 1097–1105. Curran Associates, Inc. (2012). http://papers.nips.cc/paper/4824-imagenet-classification-with-deep-convolutional-neural-networks.pdf
17. Kumar, A., et al.: Ask me anything: dynamic memory networks for natural language processing. In: Balcan, M.F., Weinberger, K.Q. (eds.) Proceedings of The 33rd International Conference on Machine Learning. Proceedings of Machine Learning Research, PMLR, vol. 48, pp. 1378–1387, New York, USA, 20–22 Jun 2016. http://proceedings.mlr.press/v48/kumar16.html
18. Li, B., Yan, J., Wu, W., Zhu, Z., Hu, X.: High performance visual tracking with Siamese region proposal network. In: The IEEE Conference on Computer Vision and Pattern Recognition (CVPR) (2018)
19. Li, H., Wu, X.: DenseFuse: a fusion approach to infrared and visible images. IEEE Trans. Image Process. 28(5), 2614–2623 (2019). https://doi.org/10.1109/TIP.2018.2887342
20. Prabhakar, K.R., Srikar, V.S., Babu, R.V.: DeepFuse: a deep unsupervised approach for exposure fusion with extreme exposure image pairs. In: 2017 IEEE International Conference on Computer Vision (ICCV), pp. 4724–4732, October 2017. https://doi.org/10.1109/ICCV.2017.505
21. Ren, S., He, K., Girshick, R., Sun, J.: Faster R-CNN: towards real-time object detection with region proposal networks. IEEE Trans. Pattern Anal. Mach. Intell. 39(6), 1137–1149 (2017). https://doi.org/10.1109/TPAMI.2016.2577031
22. Simonyan, K., Zisserman, A.: Very deep convolutional networks for large-scale image recognition. CoRR arxiv:abs/1409.1556 (2014)
23. Wang, Q., Zhang, L., Bertinetto, L., Hu, W., Torr, P.H.: Fast online object tracking and segmentation: a unifying approach. In: The IEEE Conference on Computer Vision and Pattern Recognition (CVPR) (2019)
24. Wu, Y., Lim, J., Yang, M.H.: Online object tracking: a benchmark. In: IEEE Conference on Computer Vision and Pattern Recognition (CVPR) (2013)
25. Xu, K., et al.: Show, attend and tell: neural image caption generation with visual attention. In: International Conference on Machine Learning, pp. 2048–2057 (2015)
26. Yang, T., Chan, A.B.: Learning dynamic memory networks for object tracking. In: Ferrari, V., Hebert, M., Sminchisescu, C., Weiss, Y. (eds.) ECCV 2018. LNCS, vol. 11213, pp. 153–169. Springer, Cham (2018). https://doi.org/10.1007/978-3-030-01240-3_10
27. Zhang, Y., Wang, D., Wang, L., Qi, J., Lu, H.: Learning regression and verification networks for long-term visual tracking. arXiv preprint arXiv:1809.04320 (2018)
28. Zhu, Z., Wang, Q., Li, B., Wu, W., Yan, J., Hu, W.: Distractor-aware Siamese networks for visual object tracking. In: Ferrari, V., Hebert, M., Sminchisescu, C., Weiss, Y. (eds.) ECCV 2018. LNCS, vol. 11213, pp. 103–119. Springer, Cham (2018). https://doi.org/10.1007/978-3-030-01240-3_7

Model Based Recursive Partitioning for Customized Price Optimization Analytics

Jorge M. Arevalillo[✉]

Department of Statistics, Operational Research and Numerical Analysis,
University Nacional Educación a Distancia,
Paseo Senda del Rey 9, 28040 Madrid, Spain
jmartin@ccia.uned.es

Abstract. Pricing is a relevant topic in revenue management that has awaken interest of researchers, practitioners and analysts in companies whose managerial decisions are supported by data-driven intelligent systems. This paper addresses the issue using an approach that combines model based recursive partitioning with price optimization in order to identify groups with differential price sensitivity, where optimal price allocation can be derived at a customer level. The approach is validated by application to the business case of an on-line auto lending company taking the interest rate as the price variable. The model based recursive method is used to get a tree that allows to estimate differential bid response functions across its terminal nodes; the tree is fitted on a training data set. The estimated bid response functions are combined with the bid revenue, calculated from data collected by loan applications, in order to carry out optimal price allocation maximizing the expected revenue. The expected revenue is compared on an independent test sample data set with the actual un-optimized revenue and with the revenue obtained by optimal price allocation using the standard *Logit* estimation of the bid response function; the proposed approach gives promising results that highlight new business opportunities.

Keywords: Pricing analytics · Revenue management ·
Model based recursive partitioning · Optimal price allocation

1 Introduction

Pricing analytics is a relevant issue for revenue management in organizations that aim to develop their pricing strategies on the basis of data-driven decisions that use different layers of information like product characteristics, the purchase habits of customers, their socioeconomic and demographic attributes and some other related business inputs. Due to the increasing interest among business analysts, data scientists, and financial and revenue managers in data-driven pricing approaches, the issue has become a hot study topic [4,5,13,18] with cross-sectorial applications in the banking sector [2,19], insurance [8,9],

© Springer Nature Switzerland AG 2019
A. Morales et al. (Eds.): IbPRIA 2019, LNCS 11867, pp. 113–124, 2019.
https://doi.org/10.1007/978-3-030-31332-6_10

the hospitality industry [3,10] and the airlines business [7,16,17], just to give a non-exhaustive list with a few representative business applications.

In this paper we address the issue of optimal price allocation from a data-driven viewpoint: The model based recursive partitioning (MOB) machine learning method [12,21], that allows to assess price sensitivity (PS) by means of the estimation of differential bid response functions, is used in combination with revenue optimization in order to calculate the expected revenue obtained at the optimal bid prices. The application of MOB for price sensitivity assessment is not new; actually, this paper is partially inspired in a recent work by [1] and serves as a complement of the results therein. In this paper the overall pricing picture is complemented by showing how the outputs provided by the MOB method can be used as business inputs to address the optimal price allocation problem on the basis of historical data.

The paper is organized as follows: The next section gives an overview on the decision trees, which includes classification and regression trees, conditional inference trees and the MOB method. Section 3 shows its role for addressing the optimal price allocation problem; when applied to historical data, it allows to identify groups with differential bid response functions; such differential functions will be used as inputs to solve the customized price optimization problem. In Sect. 4 we evaluate and validate the MOB approach by means of an application to an on-line auto lending company; the resulting revenue results are compared with un-optimized actual revenue and with the revenue obtained by optimal price allocation using the standard *Logit* estimation of the bid response function. The paper finishes with a section of concluding remarks that summarizes the approach and recapitulates the main findings.

2   The Decision Tree Modeling Approach

This section reviews some background about decision trees, as they are the instrumental tools of this work.

The decision tree methodology is a data-driven approach for the recursive partitioning of a data set by means of the search of splitting points within a set of segmentation variables collected in an input vector $\mathbf{Z}$. The splits are found by means of criteria that allow to quantify the relationship between the inputs and a given outcome variable Y. Essentially, the partitioning of the data responds to the construction of a segmentation guided by the outcome variable, which is carried out in a recursive fashion. Although there exists a large amount of algorithms that implement the method [15], here we focus on the classification and regression tree (CART) [6] and the conditional inference tree (CTREE) [11] algorithms, as they are two widely used tree methods.

2.1   CART Algorithm

CART is a classification and regression tree algorithm invented by [6]. The algorithm recursively segments the data through binary splits that generate a tree structure in which child nodes represent the binary partition obtained by splitting each parent node. The splits are generated by assessing the impurity of the outcome variable at parent and descendant nodes using different impurity measures [6]. CART explores the set of input variables and looks for the variable and splitting point that maximizes the impurity decrease in the left and right descendants. CART decision trees are grown in a recursive way until a large tree structure is obtained, usually a tree with a minimum number of cases in the terminal nodes; then automated pruning of such a large tree is carried out on a test sample data by means of an intelligent strategy that eliminates uninformative branches and avoids overfitting. The resulting tree is the tradeoff between model complexity and predictive accuracy.

For additional details about CART tuning controls and some other functionalities of the algorithm, the reader is referred to the pioneer monograph [6]. An easy to use implementation of CART is provided by the *rpart* R package [14].

2.2   CTREE Algorithm

One weakness of CART is its bias towards the selection of splitting variables with many categories [6]. Unlike CART, the CTREE algorithm provides an alternative approach to overcome such a bias problem [11]. It takes the p-value obtained by permutation tests that use function-based statistics of the inputs as a criterion to find the best cutoff point; the p-values are calculated by asymptotic approximations or by Monte Carlo simulations. Although CTREE can control the splitting bias, it has the disadvantage of not having a pruning strategy like CART; so usually the stopping rule must be set in advance by the expert: it may consist of a threshold for the significance level of the aforementioned tests, above which a node is declared as terminal (its default is $\alpha = 0.05$), or alternatively, a minimum size for the descendant nodes.

The *party* R package [12] provides an implementation of CTREE, along with other handy graphical functionalities of the algorithm.

2.3   Model Based Recursive Partitioning

The model based recursive partitioning method rests upon the decision tree methodology; its goal is twofold: firstly, the segmentation of a data set guided by a given outcome variable, and secondly, the fit of a parametric model in the terminal nodes derived by the tree partitioning mechanism so that the parametric fit of the model is embedded in the tree construction [21]. In order to describe the MOB method in brief, some previous notation is needed.

Let us denote by Y the outcome target variable. On the other hand, let $\mathbf{X}$ be a vector of covariates used to explain the outcome Y by means of a parametric model $\mathcal{M}(\mathbf{X}, Y; \theta)$; assume that the model is fitted by the optimization of an objective function $\Psi(\mathbf{X}, Y; \theta)$; some standard objective functions are those ones defined by the ordinary least squares (OLS) or the maximum likelihood (ML) methods. Finally, let us denote by $\mathbf{Z}$ an input vector containing a set of segmentation variables like customer attributes, product characteristics and some other business inputs.

The goal of the MOB method is the search of non-overlapping groups in the data, defined by the segmentation variables, such that the parametric model $\mathcal{M}(\mathbf{X}, Y; \theta)$ exhibits differential fits on each group. This goal is accomplished by assessing parameter model stability through fluctuation tests, which are well-established inferential tools for testing parameter stability [20, 21]. The MOB method is implemented by a greedy search algorithm that finds the segmentation variable yielding the highest instability, as assessed by the significance level of the corresponding fluctuation test. At each step, the data set is partitioned into two data subsets by a binary split in the segmentation variable which defines the rule yielding the descendant nodes; the recursive partitioning stops when the highest achievable significance for testing stability is above a specified significance level (default: $\alpha = 0.05$), in which case, the node is declared as terminal. The algorithm can be summarized by the following steps.

MOB recursive partitioning method

Set the outcome variable Y, the vector of covariates $\mathbf{X}$ and the vector $\mathbf{Z}$ of segmentation variables

Set the significance level threshold to assess parameter instability (default $\alpha = 0.05$)

Step 1. Fit the parametric model $\mathcal{M}(\mathbf{X}, Y; \theta)$ to the data (parent node)

Step 2. Test for parameter stability in the set of segmentation variables

Step 3. Find the most significant variable, say Z_l

If its significance is higher than α then stop and declare the node as terminal

else split in Z_l, by finding the cutoff point that locally optimizes Ψ, in order to get descendant nodes

Step 4. Go to step 1 and repeat the procedure for each one of the descendant nodes

---

The *partykit* R package [12] provides an easy to use implementation of the MOB method with fancy utilities for setting α and the minimal size of terminal nodes, and also for the customization of the output.

3   The MOB Method for Pricing Analytics

In the context of the pricing problem, we assume that the outcome variable Y is a binary one taking the value $Y = 1$ if a customer has accepted a bid and the value $Y = 0$ if the customer didn't accept it. Now, we consider only one covariate, X, which is the price variable. Without considering exogenous factors, we can theoretically assume that the probability of acceptance of a bid increases as the price decreases; this is a natural observation that points to the *Logit* model as a reasonable one to estimate the *bid response function* [18]. Hence, in this case the general model $\mathcal{M}(\mathbf{X}, Y; \theta)$ is given by the following equation:

$$\log \frac{P(Y = 1|X)}{P(Y = 0|X)} = \alpha_0 + \alpha_1 X. \tag{1}$$

The coefficients in (1) are fitted by the ML method. Once the model has been fitted from the data, a function of the purchase probability against the price can be obtained upon inversion of the *Logit* transform.

In this context we also consider a set of partitioning variables collected by a vector $\mathbf{Z} = (Z_1, Z_2, \ldots, Z_k)$ which may contain product characteristics, socioeconomic and demographic customer attributes, and any other related business input. When applied to pricing, the goal of the MOB method is the search of a data partition leading to segments that exhibit differential purchase sensitivities, which are described by differential fits of the *bid response function* using the *Logit* Eq. (1). Hence, its application will allow to uncover groups that can be classified in accordance to their differential PS.

The MOB method is appealing and intuitive, as it provides a customized estimate of the *bid response function* easy to interpret in terms of the segmentation variables that came up as splitters in the resulting MOB tree. For each one of the terminal nodes of the tree, the customized *bid response function* can be expressed formally as follows:

$$g(r, \mathbf{z}) = P(Y = 1 | X = r, \mathbf{Z} = \mathbf{z}) \tag{2}$$

where r and $\mathbf{z}$ are the price and the observed values of the vector of segmentation variables at a customer/bid level.

Note that for an observed instance of the segmentation variables, $\mathbf{Z} = \mathbf{z}$, we obtain a function with respect to the price r. Thus, in order to maximize the expected revenue for each bid, we state the following optimization problem.

Statement 1. *Let us assume that the vector of segmentation variables is such that $\mathbf{Z} = \mathbf{z}$. The optimal price allocation can be derived by solving the following optimization problem*

$$\max_r g(r, \mathbf{z}) R(r, \mathbf{z}) \tag{3}$$

where $R(r, \mathbf{z})$ is the revenue for a given bid with price r.

If we denote by r^* the optimal price that solves (3) then the maximum expected revenue of the bid is $g(r^*, \mathbf{z}) R(r^*, \mathbf{z})$. Now, assume that the MOB method results in a data partition with H terminal nodes, each one of size N_k, such that $N_1 + N_2 + \cdots + N_H = N$ with N the total number of cases in the data; then the overall expected revenue of the resulting MOB optimization model can be calculated as follows.

Statement 2. *Let us denote by g_j the bid response function derived by the MOB method at the jth terminal node $TN_j : j = 1, 2, \ldots, H$. Then the total expected revenue obtained by optimal price allocation is given by*

$$TotalRevenue = \sum_{j=1}^{H} \sum_{\mathbf{z}_i \in TN_j} g_j(r_i^*, \mathbf{z}_i) R(r_i^*, \mathbf{z}_i) \tag{4}$$

where r_i^* and $\mathbf{z}_i$ are the optimal price and the observed attributes for the ith bid.

4   Business Case Application

This next section gives an application of the MOB method to a real business case. The results of optimal price allocation using MOB are compared with unoptimized actual prices and with the optimal prices obtained on the basis of the *Logit* estimation of the bid response function.

4.1   Data Description

An auto lending company collected historical data from loan applications during the period from July 2002 to November 2004. The data set contains 208085 approved applications. The 47210 applications for refinancing were removed from the analysis. In addition, we only considered applications that received approval at least 45 days prior to the investigation end date because of managerial reasons. Hence, we end up with 152965 applications for which the auto lender collected several sources of information measured by the set of variables in Table 1.

Table 1. Variables collected during the period of study.

Set of variables for MOB modeling	
Tier	Classification of applicants based on FICO scores
Primary FICO	FICO score quantifying the applicant's risk in the range $[594, 854]$
Term	Loan term in months
Amount Approved	Amount of the loan in the range $[5, 100000]$
Competition rate	Interest rate of competitor
Car Type id	Type of car: new (1) or used (2)
term class	Four level segmentation of the Term variable
partnerbin	Segmentation based on partners (1: Direct. 2: Partner A. 3: Other partners)
rate	Interest rate of the application
onemonth	Prime rate
apply	Binary outcome variable with the purchase decision

4.2   MOB Modeling

The outcome Y is the *apply* variable which takes the value 1 if the applicant was funded and the value 0 otherwise. The records indicate that 26323 applications were funded; so the response rate is around 17.2%. In this case the price variable X is the interest rate (*rate* variable). On the other hand, the vector $\mathbf{Z}$ for segmentation contains the following variables: *Tier, PrimaryFICO, Term, AmountApproved, Competitionrate, CarTypeid, termclass, partnerbin*.

The MOB tree model is fit on a training sample containing 80% of the entire data set. The algorithm is parameterized using the default significance level for node splitting, $\alpha = 0.05$, and a minimum node size of 5% the size of the entire training data set. In this case, a segmentation with $H = 4$ terminal nodes is obtained; it is given by the binary rules shown in Fig. 1. The estimation of the parameters in (1) provides the *bid response functions* depicted by the plots in Fig. 2 for each terminal node; the equations of the corresponding *Logit* transforms are shown in the table aside.

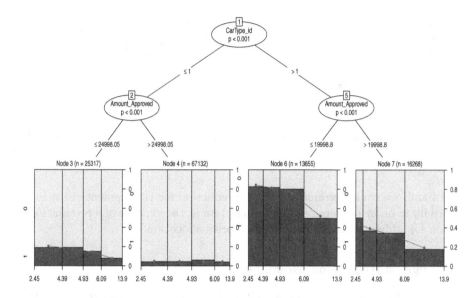

Fig. 1. Segmentation obtained by the MOB method.

Recall that the coefficient α_1 in Eq. (1) is a non-decreasing function of the odds ratio (OR), i.e. $OR = e^{\alpha_1}$. Hence, it can be interpreted as a measure for assessing PS, as it quantifies the decay of the likelihood of a positive response to the bid due to a unit price increase, with the more negative coefficients corresponding to the higher sensitivities [5]. Therefore, the resulting segments depicted by the tree of Fig. 1 can be classified as follows (see the table with the *Logit* equations of Fig. 2): The highest PS corresponds to the node 6 group, defined by loan applications for used automobiles with approved amount under $20000; the nodes 7 and 3 may be considered as moderate to high PS groups, the former corresponding to applications for used automobiles with approved amount above $20000 and the latter to loan applications for new automobiles whose approved amount is under $25000; finally, the lowest PS group appears at the node 4 which corresponds to applications for new automobiles whose approved amount is above the $25000 cutoff. Overall, we can interpret that for both new and used car applications the PS is higher for the lower approved amounts, as given by the cutoffs of about $25000 and $20000 respectively.

The results provide useful insights for undertaking managerial decisions: We could suggest a strategy for raising the price at the segments with low sensitivity, as we would expect a slight negative impact in the purchase decision; on the

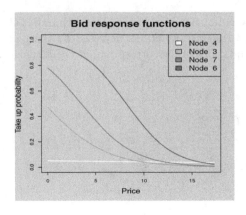

Node ID	Logit equation
3	$-0.13 - 0.31X$
4	$-2.92 - 0.02X$
6	$3.42 - 0.42X$
7	$1.27 - 0.36X$

Fig. 2. Bid response functions in the terminal nodes given by the MOB tree. The table contains the *Logit* equation at each terminal node.

other hand, we could recommend a price reduction for the segments with high sensitivity in order to increase the response rate at the expense of a revenue loss. Section 4.4 addresses the issue of optimal price allocation.

4.3   Logistic Regression Modeling

Now we succinctly review the logistic regression method and show its application to customized pricing. In this scenario the method allows to estimate the bid response function by fitting a linear model to the *Logit* of the take up probability against the price variable with the incorporation of a set of covariables [4,5]. Mathematically, the model is formulated by the following equation:

$$\log \frac{P(Y = 1 | X, \mathbf{Z})}{P(Y = 0 | X, \mathbf{Z})} = \alpha_0 + \alpha X + \alpha_1 Z_1 + \alpha_2 Z_2 + \cdots \alpha_p Z_p. \tag{5}$$

Here, X is the price variable and $\mathbf{Z} = (Z_1, \ldots, Z_p)$ is the vector of covariables that measure bid characteristics and customer attributes. The coefficients in Eq. (5) are fitted by maximum likelihood. Upon inversion of the *Logit*, we get the take up posterior probability, ensuring values in the interval $[0, 1]$.

Recall that in our business case X is defined by the interest rate. Now, we fit two *Logit* models: the first one uses as covariables the segmentation variables that came up in the MOB tree of Fig. 1; for the second fit, we include the following set of variables: *PrimaryFICO*, *Term*, *AmountApproved*, *CompetitionRate*, *CarTypeid*, *partnerbin* in the vector $\mathbf{Z}$ of covariables. The corresponding fits of model (5) lead to the *Logit* equations:

$$Logit1 = -0.5256 - 0.3150 \times rate$$
$$-0.0001 \times AmountApproved + 2.1555 \times CarTypeid \tag{6}$$

$$Logit2 = 1.5941 - 0.6022 \times rate - 0.0055 \times PrimaryFICO + 0.0473 \times Term$$
$$-0.0001 \times AmountApproved + 0.3776 \times CompetitionRate$$
$$+2.0908 \times CarTypeid - 0.2114 \times partnerbin \tag{7}$$

The next section addresses the price allocation problem for revenue optimization using the MOB modeling approach. The expected revenues resulting from MOB optimal price allocation are compared with the expected revenues obtained by price allocation on the basis of the *Logit* approach.

4.4 Optimization and Revenue Results

So far we have been concerned with the customized estimation of the *bid response function*; recall that the MOB method allowed to classify customers/bids in accordance to their PS. Now, the output given by the MOB tree is used as input to address the optimal price allocation problem and to calculate the expected revenues accordingly.

First of all, we need the revenue function $R(r, \mathbf{z})$ involved in the optimization problem (3). Since we have at our disposal the term, amount and prime rate of each bid, the revenue can be calculated by

$$R(r, \mathbf{z}_i) = DP \cdot A_i \cdot T_i \cdot \left(\frac{r/12}{1 - (1 + r/12)^{-T_i}} - \frac{pr_i/12}{1 - (1 + pr_i/12)^{-T_i}} \right) \tag{8}$$

The quantities involved in this expression denote the following business inputs: DP is the probability of default which can be set at the value $DP = 0.85$ as suggested by [5]. On the other hand, A_i. T_i and pr_i are the approved amount, term and prime rate for the ith approved bid.

If we insert (8) in expression (3) using the bid response function of the corresponding terminal node, say g_j, and solve the optimization problem, we get the optimal rate r_i^* and the expected revenue $g_j(r_i^*, \mathbf{z}_i)R(r_i^*, \mathbf{z}_i)$ for the ith bid as long as the bid belongs to the jth terminal node. The overall expected revenue can be calculated by computing (4) on an independent test sample; we also have at hand the expected revenues per node, which are given by

$$Rev_j = \sum_{\mathbf{z}_i \in TN_j} g_j(r_i^*, \mathbf{z}_i)R(r_i^*, \mathbf{z}_i) : j = 1, 2, 3, 4. \tag{9}$$

Note that the terminal nodes, $TN_j : j = 1, 2, 3, 4$, correspond to the nodes labeled by Node 3, Node 4, Node 6 and Node 7 in the tree of Fig. 1.

In order to calculate the revenue obtained from logistic regression, we must take into account that in this case there is a single bid response function, $g(r, \mathbf{z})$, defined by the fit of model (5); when inserted in (3), the overall expected revenue can be computed by

$$TotalRevenue = \sum_{i=1}^{N} g(r_i^*, \mathbf{z}_i)R(r_i^*, \mathbf{z}_i) \tag{10}$$

In our case, the function $g(r, \mathbf{z})$ will be replaced by any of the *Logit* Eqs. (6) or (7), depending on the fit we aim to use. Hence, we can compare MOB revenue results with the revenues obtained from both *Logit* models.

The results are shown by Table 2 which contains the actual revenues, corresponding to current un-optimized prices, and the expected revenues obtained by optimal price allocation derived from MOB and both *Logit* fits (percentage node revenues appear in parenthesis). The lift columns provide the increase of the expected revenue with respect to the un-optimized revenue, quantified in percentages. We can observe that the expected revenue given by MOB optimal price allocation is higher than the status quo actual revenue with an overall 39.2% revenue increase, the largest lift appearing at node 4; moreover, the other nodes also exhibit increases in revenue with lifts 8.2%, 8.2% and 18.5%. These findings reveal the usefulness of the MOB method for highlighting new business opportunities and insights. We can also note that overall, with the striking exception of node 7, the revenues resulting from MOB optimal price allocation are greater than the revenues obtained from the *Logit* approach.

Table 2. Actual un-optimized revenues and the expected revenues given by optimal price allocation from MOB and the *Logit* fits (6) and (7) are shown in the columns *Actual*, *MOB*, *Logit*1 and *Logit*2 (amounts measured in \$ millions on the test sample). Their lifts are provided by the columns $lift_{MOB}$, $lift_1$ and $lift_2$ respectively. All the values are rounded to the first decimal point.

Node ID	Actual	MOB	Logit1	Logit2	$lift_{MOB}$	$lift_1$	$lift_2$
3	255.9 (13.6%)	276.8 (10.6%)	250.7 (13.0%)	365.5 (15.2%)	8.2%	−2.0%	42.8%
4	444.6 (23.7%)	1008.6 (38.6%)	390.2 (20.2%)	601.8 (25.0%)	126.9%	−12.2%	35.4%
6	531.6 (28.3%)	630.0 (24.1%)	571.6 (29.5%)	565.1 (23.4%)	18.5%	7.5%	6.3%
7	644.3 (34.3%)	697.4 (26.7%)	722.8 (37.3%)	877.4 (36.4%)	8.2%	12.2%	36.2%
Total	1876.4	2612.8	1935.3	2409.8	39.2%	3.1%	28.4%

5   Summary and Concluding Remarks

In this paper we have addressed the customized price optimization problem. A proposal that combines the data-driven MOB method with optimal price allocation is presented using a two step price allocation strategy: firstly, differential *bid response functions* are derived using the MOB method and a segmentation with differential PS groups is obtained as a result. Secondly, optimal price allocation is carried out, taking the customized *bid response functions* as inputs for calculating the price that maximizes the expected revenue at a customer/bid level. The proposed approach was applied to the business case of an on-line auto lending company on the basis of the historical data of loan applications. A MOB tree is fitted on a training data set and the expected revenue is calculated on a test sample data set. The results show that application of the MOB optimal price allocation method may result in revenue increases with respect to the status quo scenario of un-optimized prices; the comparison with the standard *Logit* method for price allocation also reveals overall revenue gains. Future research would consist of the validation of the MOB method in other business scenarios so that it can proposed as a consistent and well-established tool for customized pricing analytics.

Acknowledgements. The author acknowledges the Center for Pricing and Revenue Management at Columbia University as the provider of the data. He is also grateful to two anonymous reviewers for their useful comments that helped to improve the paper.

Funding. This work has been funded by *UNED - Santander Bank Research and Transfer 2018 Award* with reference 2018V/PREMIO/07 under grant 18CF05.

References

1. Arevalillo, J.M.: A machine learning approach to assess price sensitivity with application to automobile loan segmentation. Appl. Soft Comput. **76**, 390–399 (2019)
2. Batmaz, İ., Danışoğlu, S., Yazıcı, C., Kartal-Koç, E.: A data mining application to deposit pricing: main determinants and prediction models. Appl. Soft Comput. **60**, 808–819 (2017)
3. Beck, J.A., Kim, M., Schmidgall, R.S.: The pricing for same-day arrival guests in the hotel industry. Int. J. Bus. Appl. Soc. Sci. **4**(1), 1–18 (2018)
4. Bodea, T., Ferguson, M.: Pricing Segmentation and Analytics. Marketing Strategy Collection. Business Expert Press, New York City (2012)
5. Bodea, T., Ferguson, M.: Segmentation, Revenue Management and Pricing Analytics. Routledge (2014). https://books.google.es/books?id=bu-buAAACAAJ
6. Breiman, L., Friedman, J., Olshen, R., Stone, C.: Classification and Regression Trees. Wadsworth and Brooks, Monterey (1984)
7. Granados, N., Kauffman, R.J., Lai, H., Lin, H.: À la carte pricing and price elasticity of demand in air travel. Decis. Support Syst. **53**(2), 381–394 (2012)
8. Guelman, L., Guillén, M.: A causal inference approach to measure price elasticity in automobile insurance. Expert Syst. Appl. **41**(2), 387–396 (2014)
9. Guelman, L., Guillen, M., Pérez-Marín, A.M.: A survey of personalized treatment models for pricing strategies in insurance. Insur. Math. Econ. **58**, 68–76 (2014)
10. Guo, X., Ling, L., Yang, C., Li, Z., Liang, L.: Optimal pricing strategy based on market segmentation for service products using online reservation systems: an application to hotel rooms. Int. J. Hospitality Manag. **35**, 274–281 (2013)
11. Hothorn, T., Hornik, K., Zeileis, A.: Unbiased recursive partitioning: a conditional inference framework. J. Comput. Graph. Stat. **15**(3), 651–674 (2006)
12. Hothorn, T., Zeileis, A.: partykit: a modular toolkit for recursive partytioning in R. J. Mach. Learn. Res. **16**, 3905–3909 (2015)
13. Kuyumcu, H.A.: Emerging trends in scientific pricing. J. Revenue Pricing Manag. **6**(4), 293–299 (2007)
14. Liaw, A., Wiener, M.: Classification and regression by randomforest. R News **2**(3), 18–22 (2002). http://CRAN.R-project.org/doc/Rnews/
15. Loh, W.Y.: Fifty years of classification and regression trees. Int. Stat. Rev. **82**(3), 329–348 (2014)
16. Morlotti, C., Cattaneo, M., Malighetti, P., Redondi, R.: Multi-dimensional price elasticity for leisure and business destinations in the low-cost air transport market: evidence from easyJet. Tourism Manag. **61**, 23–34 (2017)

17. Mumbower, S., Garrow, L.A., Higgins, M.J.: Estimating flight-level price elasticities using online airline data: a first step toward integrating pricing, demand, and revenue optimization. Transp. Res. Part A Policy Pract. **66**, 196–212 (2014)
18. Phillips, R.: Pricing and Revenue Optimization. Stanford Business Books. Stanford University Press, Palo Alto (2005)
19. Phillips, R.: Optimizing prices for consumer credit. J. Revenue Pricing Manag. **12**(4), 360–377 (2013)
20. Zeileis, A., Hornik, K.: Generalized m-fluctuation tests for parameter instability. Stat. Neerl. **61**(4), 488–508 (2007)
21. Zeileis, A., Hothorn, T., Hornik, K.: Model-based recursive partitioning. J. Comput. Graph. Stat. **17**(2), 492–514 (2008)

3D Reconstruction of Archaeological Pottery from Its Point Cloud

Wilson Sakpere[(✉)] [iD]

University of Bologna, Bologna, Italy
wilson.sakpere@unibo.it

Abstract. This paper presents a 3D reconstruction process for an archaeological pottery. Because of the shape of the pottery and its fracture, applying existing methods of registration did not yield the desired result. Thus, to improve the registration output and accuracy, a custom acquisition setup was used to acquire the point cloud data after it was calibrated. The setup was also cost effective, a consideration that is useful for archaeologists. Furthermore, the acquired point clouds were pre-processed to remove noise and outliers. Key-points were extracted from the point clouds using Principal Component Analysis (PCA) and descriptors were computed adapting the ColorSHOT descriptor. With correspondences between the key-points of point clouds established, a pairwise alignment of the point clouds was done. Finally, the global registration was done on all the point clouds, with ICP used to refine the alignment for all the point clouds. The peculiarity of the approach of this paper is in adapting and adjusting parameters as required due to the peculiar nature of the data acquired. This improved the robustness of this approach, evident in the final registration output.

Keywords: 3D reconstruction · Archaeological pottery · Potsherd · Point cloud registration

1 Introduction

From time immemorial, making and remaking objects or artefacts is an activity engaged in by people in different communities and environment. Because the objects are unique to a people or environment, it can usually be referred to as cultural heritage artefacts. To make these artefacts as intended, certain methods and processes are adhered to. They include planning, material gathering and production. These processes have been streamlined from generation to generation. By reason of use, among other reasons, these artefacts tend to degrade, wear and even break. Over time and due to the loss of civilisations, some artefacts of value are lost. One of such artefacts, that this paper focuses on, is pottery.

These artefacts, and pottery in particular, are of significant interest to certain professionals such as archaeologists. As archaeologists study the historic and prehistoric human activities through documenting discovered ancient artefacts to have a grounded understanding of the prehistoric culture, the ability to carry out accurate restorations within reasonable time become pertinent. These can then be used for further studies.

© Springer Nature Switzerland AG 2019
A. Morales et al. (Eds.): IbPRIA 2019, LNCS 11867, pp. 125–136, 2019.
https://doi.org/10.1007/978-3-030-31332-6_11

Of all the artefacts recovered from archaeological excavations, pottery is one of the most significant because of its ability not to decay when compared with other archaeological artefacts of other materials [1]. Depending on how the pottery is preserved, it could be recovered as a complete pot on site or as fragments known as potsherds. Most potsherds usually carry information such as the shape of the pottery, decoration on the pottery and colour of the pottery among others, on the inner and/or outer surfaces [2]. This information helps the archaeologist to carry out studies such as dating, and to understand the culture of the potter. However, to be able to carry out a meaningful study, there is a need to restore these potteries as much as possible for a more comprehensive understanding of what is being studied. Thus, the reconstruction problem exists.

Archaeologists have employed different time-consuming ways of studying and preserving historical relics. The methods include physical examination, classification, illustration and reconstruction of pottery through drawing. These methods are carried out manually, making the archaeologist spend time and effort to observe and possibly extrapolate from the observations [3]. As the use of computing techniques and technologies become prevalent and accessible, applying them to solve critical issues in the archaeological field become desirable. Such applications are carried out in two-dimensional (2D) space or three-dimensional (3D) space.

The 3D reconstruction of pottery, in the form of virtual digitisation, has had similar and related studies with room for improvement. To successfully reconstruct pottery, certain processes are carried out. They include data acquisition, data pre-processing, data processing and data post-processing. The data acquisition stage involves the use of tools and instruments to acquire data for pre-processing. Data pre-processing is a combination of processes to refine and analyse the data acquired to have a clean data to carry out studies. Data processing is the stage where the core of the study is carried out using the clean data. The data post-processing stage is not a compulsory stage but necessary for the archaeologist to understand what the researcher has done. How image analysis techniques could be useful in the archaeological context and how these techniques could be put to good use with pottery reconstruction is a focus in this study.

This paper approaches this challenge by presenting a path towards reconstructing archaeological pottery using point cloud data. Multiple views of the pottery were acquired as point clouds and aligned to form a whole through the registration process. To achieve this, feature detection, feature selection and feature extraction techniques have been utilised. Since the path to an optimal registration process begins with the quality of data and how it is collected, it was ensured that the point clouds were captured with the utmost accuracy. Three different objects of archaeological significance were virtualised and studied. However, the focus of this paper is on the virtualisation of one of them – an oil lamp fractured pottery and its sherd, as shown in Fig. 1. This pottery was excavated at the Claternae archaeological site of the metropolitan city of Bologna.

The remainder of the paper is structured as follows: Sect. 2 discusses previous works related to pottery reconstruction while Sect. 3 describes the data acquisition procedure. Section 4 presents the reconstruction process and the method applied. Section 5 discusses highlights of this study while Sect. 6 concludes the discussion.

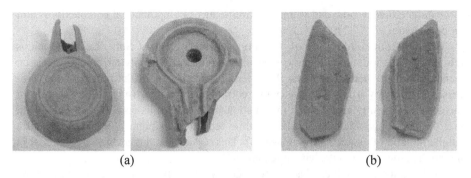

(a)   (b)

Fig. 1. (a) Oil lamp fractured pottery (b) Oil lamp sherd

2 Related Work

Many studies have attempted to solve the reconstruction problem. A well and accurately reconstructed or digitised pottery paves the way for further successful studies. For example, the study of Kampel and Sablatnig [4] developed a system that can process both complete and broken vessels. This was achieved using two reconstruction strategies known as: "shape from silhouette based method for complete vessels and a profile based method for fragments" [4]. While using these strategies have improved performance with an acceptable accuracy, it is nonetheless dependent on certain conditions being met, thus requiring further investigations that will improve accuracy.

Likewise, Smith *et al.* [5] investigated methods of classification and reconstruction of images of excavated archaeological ceramic fragments based on their colour and texture information. This was achieved by using Scale Invariant Feature Transform (SIFT) and a feature descriptor based on Total Variation Geometry (TVG) [5]. However, the performance of these descriptors was not satisfactory in terms of effectiveness and accuracy. Also, the study of Puglisi *et al.* [6] proposed a system that uses SIFT. The system uses image processing techniques to automatically identify and analyse images of the structural components of pottery through "optical microscopy". As a result, the suitable features can then be computed and analysed for classification purposes. In addition, this system aims at segmenting the acquired images and extracting their features for pottery classification. To achieve this and for the sake of better accuracy, the authors chose to use SIFT feature point method, where the feature points are extracted and matched with related pairs. While this system improves on the ones before it, it falls short in providing an optimal solution with a high accuracy, hence opening the path to further studies [6].

Furthermore, Makridis and Daras [7] focused on a technique for accurate and automatic classification of pottery. The technique was implemented in four steps namely: feature extraction, feature fusion, feature selection and classification. This approach attempted to reduce the computational complexity problem with a "bag of words (BoW)" method that uses the features extracted from the images to create a "global descriptor" vector for the images [7]. However, while this technique turned out to be quite efficient, how and if this solution reduces computational complexity is still an open issue.

Finally, Roman-Rangel *et al.* [8] proposed Histogram of Spherical Orientations (HoSO), a method for automatic analysis of pottery by applying computer vision techniques. This method analyses the external frontal view of the pottery alone, processes 3D data by using only the points coordinates without using colour, texture or faces, and efficiently encodes the information from the points coordinates. They posit that the advantages include substantial time reduction in pottery organisation and a simple method of acquiring the image [8]. This shows that advantages are inherent in the application of computer vision techniques.

In this paper, computer vision techniques were applied with a focus on working with 3D point clouds. The point clouds use the point coordinates as well as its colour and normal information. The Principal Component Analysis (PCA) technique was applied in analysing and processing the point clouds.

3   Data Acquisition

The data acquisition stage is critical to the entire stages of a study. Virtualising objects to reflect majority of its original information is important in carrying out studies. As noted by [9], when objects are virtualised without key information, data may be lost.

To attain the virtualisation process in this study, a low-cost off-the-shelf acquisition setup, consisting of a line laser, RGB camera, Arduino UNO and other embedded devices and components, was used. The line laser was set up perpendicularly to the sliding table while the camera was set up at an angle and facing the object mount or sliding table. A representation of the acquisition setup is shown in Fig. 2. The reason for using a custom setup is to allow for tuning and adjusting with ease and where necessary to get desired result. By doing so, it can be ensured that the pottery virtualisation is ideal. But the system had to be calibrated first.

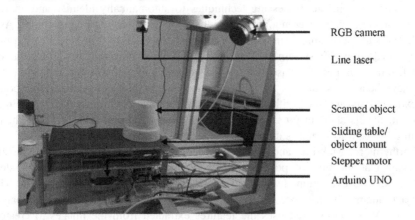

Fig. 2. Data acquisition setup

3.1 Calibration

To calibrate the system, a 1920 × 1200 pixels Daheng mercury U3V camera, a cyclic chessboard pattern and a sawtooth image were used to estimate camera intrinsic, extrinsic, and lens distortion parameters using the Brown's distortion model [10]. Twenty chessboard PNG images and four sawtooth PNG images were captured and saved, ensuring that they are within the working distance of the camera and not blurry. The images were captured at different positions and orientations within the view of the camera at an angle of 40.5° orientation. The baseline is about 221 mm, while the height of the camera to the sliding table level is about 189 mm. The working distance, which is the distance between the lens and the object mount, is about 291 mm.

A simple custom calibrator adapted from the approach of [11–14] was used for calibration. To compute the intrinsic parameters, the chessboard images were added to the calibrator and the calibration parameters (width and height of pattern and image) and distortion coefficient types were selected (2 radial and 2 tangential coefficients). The calibrator detects the centre of each circular pattern for all the images (see Fig. 3) and computes the reprojection errors. Three images were discarded for having high reprojection errors while 17 images were used to compute the intrinsic parameters.

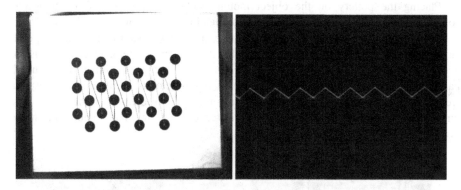

Fig. 3. Projected points on the chessboard and sawtooth images

With the intrinsic parameters computed, the sawtooth images were added to the calibrator to compute the extrinsic parameters. The pose estimation parameters (width and height of sawtooth, Gaussian values, Threshold values) were inserted. The calibrator detects the tangents of the sawtooth images (see Fig. 3) and computes the extrinsic parameters. The radial and tangential distortions can be computed using Eqs. (1) and (2) respectively [11, 12]:

$$
\begin{bmatrix} \delta u_i^{(r)} \\ \delta v_i^{(r)} \end{bmatrix} = \begin{bmatrix} k_1 \\ k_2 \end{bmatrix} \begin{bmatrix} \tilde{u}_i r_i^2 & \tilde{u}_i r_i^4 \\ \tilde{v}_i r_i^2 & \tilde{v}_i r_i^4 \end{bmatrix}
\tag{1}
$$

$$
\begin{bmatrix} \delta u_i^{(t)} \\ \delta v_i^{(t)} \end{bmatrix} = \begin{bmatrix} p_1 \\ p_2 \end{bmatrix} \begin{bmatrix} 2\tilde{u}_i \tilde{v}_i & (r_i^2 + 2\tilde{u}_i^2) \\ (r_i^2 + 2\tilde{v}_i^2) & 2\tilde{u}_i \tilde{v}_i \end{bmatrix}
\tag{2}
$$

where k_1, k_2 = coefficients of radial distortion; p_1, p_2 = coefficients of tangential distortion; u, v = image coordinates; $\tilde{u}$, $\tilde{v}$ = image projection; δu, $\delta v = u - u_0$, $v - v_0$; u_0, v_0 = image centre/principal point; $r = \sqrt{\tilde{u}^2 + \tilde{v}^2}$; i = number of the images (i.e. 1, 2, 3, ...).

As a rule, the mean reprojection errors of less than 0.2 mm are considered acceptable. The Root Mean Squared Error (RMSE), which is the metric used for the reprojection error, along the X and Y coordinates of the image are 0.0015 mm and 0.0009 mm respectively. The mean RMSE of reprojection is 0.0018 mm. The calibration report was exported as an XML file and used to compensate the effects of lens distortion during the pottery scanning process.

3.2   Scanning the Pottery

With the calibration completed and the line laser and camera synchronised, the system was ready for acquiring the data. It was ensured that the laser line was parallel to the edge of the sliding table as it reduces distortion and aids the alignment process. The goal was to acquire the pottery's point cloud as the sliding table moves from one end to another in order to get every viewing angle as much as possible as shown in Fig. 4.

Placing the pottery on the object mount, multiple exposures of the pottery's complete surface were acquired using the acquisition setup with a 16 GB RAM Core i7-6500U laptop @ 2.50 GHz. The scanning and the conversion of the data to point cloud was carried out by a script written for the Daheng camera. Due to occlusion occurring, many exposures of different viewpoints were acquired so that the occluded parts will be compensated for after registering the point clouds. While many exposures were acquired, about 24 were used for the reconstruction process. A light source was directed at the pottery at about 400 mm distance to ensure that colour and shape information are well captured.

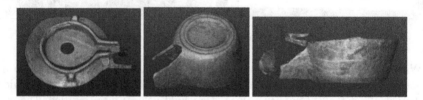

Fig. 4. Samples of the scanned pottery

4   The Registration Process

The goal of the registration process is to find the correspondence, rigid transformation and best alignment between point clouds. Given two point clouds, model $P = \{p_1, p_2, ..., p_m\}$ and target $Q = \{q_1, q_2, ..., q_n\}$, in 3D space which contain m and n points respectively. If $p \subset P$ and $q \subset Q$ are the overlapping points between the two point clouds, then a rigid transformation T applied to P such that the distance between P and Q is minimised, results in the best alignment between the point clouds and is expressed as:

$$\mathbf{y} = \mathbf{Rx} + \mathbf{t} \tag{3}$$

where $x \in p$, $y \in q$, R is the 3×3 rotation matrix and t is the 3×1 translation vector. A rigid registration can thus be found by minimising the following equation:

$$\sum_{i=1}^{M} \|Tp_i - q_i\|^2, \qquad q_i = \arg\min_{q \in Q} \|Tp_i - q\| \tag{4}$$

where p is the model point set and q is the target point set.

The registration process can be achieved with different techniques and methods as discussed by [15, 16]. But the most popular method that has formed the foundation for more improved ones is the Iterative Closest Point (ICP) algorithm [17]. However, it tends to be susceptible to local minima. Rusinkiewicz and Levoy [18] categorise the ICP process into selection of points, matching of points, weighting of pairs, rejecting pairs, error metric and minimisation. Because of the differences in objects to be registered, such as their geometry, and the unique challenges that befall them, as well as the huge point sets that might be involved, it is usually difficult to develop a "one-size-fits-all" solution for point cloud registration in general. Hence, certain works are refined or improved to suit the needs of the data that is involved [18, 19]. This has led to the basis for this study.

4.1 Data Pre-processing

The scanned point clouds, in Sect. 3.2, were processed with the CloudCompare software to obtain clean point clouds. The segmentation of the point clouds was carried out to remove unusable parts of the cloud from the useful part. The number of points of the point clouds was reduced by down-sampling. Down-sampling of the point clouds was based on space sampling, ensuring that the points are uniformly distributed to get a good estimation that contains only inliers. Points that do not have finite normal and enough neighbours in a certain radius (outliers in the scan) were removed. The outliers were removed based on the number of neighbours around a point and within a radius of 0.2 mm. The sampling or filtering approach usually affects the convergence rate of the point cloud during registration.

Also, the normal of the point clouds were computed for surface correspondence, thus ensuring a better alignment process. Principal Component Analysis (PCA) [20] was used to determine the normal vectors of the point clouds because PCA algorithms can analyse the variation of points in the three directions. The normal vector corresponds to the direction with minimum variation. From the eigen decomposition of the covariance matrix of the nearest neighbours, the eigenvector corresponding to the minimum eigenvalue represents the normal vector. The covariance matrix can be calculated from the following equation:

$$C = \frac{1}{k} \sum_{i=1}^{k} (p_i - \tilde{p})(p_i - \tilde{p})^T \tag{5}$$

where k is the number of nearest neighbours in the vicinity of p_i and $\tilde{p}$ is the mean or centroid of all k neighbours.

The pseudocode below shows how to compute the normals with PCA.

Input: d dimensional point cloud, number of neighbours
Output: vector normal
Initialize: vector normal, vector neighbours, vector neighbours mean, covariance matrix
    For each point p in P:
        Extract the neighbours using nearest neighbour search
        Calculate the centroid of the neighbours
        Compute the covariance matrix
        Compute eigenvectors and corresponding eigenvalues
        Sort eigenvectors by decreasing eigenvalues
        Extract the normal
    Return Normals
End

4.2 Features Extraction

The feature extraction entails the key-point extraction and feature description. Key-points were extracted based on distinctive properties inherent on the point cloud surface. Such properties include the colour and principal curvature of the surface normal. The largest value of the RGB components was computed by finding the products of two curvature to get the local maxima. The key-points were determined by computing the local maxima of the curvature. In essence, by analysing nearest neighbours around the point of interest within a certain radius and curvature threshold, the principal curvature for all points were computed and the covariance matrix established as stated in Eq. (5) under Sect. 4.1. For the oil lamp for example, the curvature was computed using points in a radius of 0.8 mm, and local maxima within a radius of 1 mm. This resulted in about 400–500 key-points per view.

Also, a Local Reference Frame (LRF) was computed for the key-points. The normal at the key-point was used as Z axis of the LRF, the X axis is the principal curvature direction, while the Y axis is the cross product of the Z and Y axes. This leaves the problem of "inverted" reference frames since curvature directions don't truly have a sign. However, the sign of the axis was chosen as the one where points are further away from the tangent plane defined by the normal at the key-point. This approach results in 20% of the key-points with reference frames inverted and, on average, 1.5° of error on the Z axis and 7–8° on the X and Y axes. These increases of views have a very small overlap area with large occlusion. For the oil lamp, the local reference frame was computed using points around the key-point with a maximum distance of 1.2 mm. For the sherd, the number of key-points to be extracted were increased.

Furthermore, decomposing the covariance matrix with Singular Value Decomposition (SVD) results in three eigenvalues, λ_1, λ_2, λ_3, and their corresponding eigenvectors. These eigenvalues and eigenvectors describe the neighbourhood features of the key-point that were computed using ColorSHOT descriptor [21] and the LRF at a radius of 4 μm for every key-point. ColorSHOT was chosen for its robustness and accuracy. The key-points were found on both views with descriptor distances (Euclidean distance) smaller than a threshold. The key-points that had small distances compared to most key-points were not considered. For example, two key-points with few points around them will both have descriptors full of zeros but are not necessarily the same key-point. Also, empty descriptor spatial bins were not considered when computing descriptor distances, mostly because it should make this step a little more robust to occlusion.

4.3   Correspondence Matching

Having computed the descriptors from the key-points of the point clouds, point correspondences were established using nearest neighbour search in the feature space of the key-points. Adapting the method of Lei *et al.* [22], angular vectors between the normal of the descriptor were defined and correspondences were clustered into groups. About 2,000 correspondences were established between views with large overlaps, with about 150 correspondences being correct. Likewise, about 400 correspondences were established between views with small overlaps, with about 6–7 correspondences being correct. To attempt to improve this, some basic geometry consistency criteria was imposed by forcing the same distances between correspondences to create groups from them. For example, for two point pairs (p_i, q_i) and (p_j, q_j), distance $d = \|p_i - p_j\| = \|q_i - q_j\|$ for the pairs to be valid. By creating all the possible groups with more than 1,000 correspondences, this step becomes very slow. Hence, the best correspondences were used to create a completely new group and then look for compatible correspondences among the others. The idea behind this is that if there are some correct correspondences there should be at least a couple of them among the best correspondences. ICP was then used to do a pairwise registration on the point clouds as shown in Fig. 5.

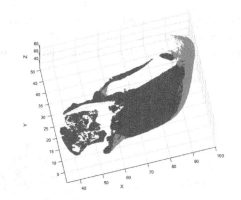

Fig. 5. Pairwise registration of two point clouds

4.4 Global Registration

With the pairwise matching of the point clouds done, a coarse alignment was done for all pairs of point clouds, resulting in a transformation that brings all the clouds to the reference frame of the "reference" view. Following the method of Pulli [23], the global registration was improved, and the registration error that was propagated and accumulated with all the registration pairs was redistributed. With this method, the pairwise registrations converge much faster than the global registration, thereby resulting in "pairwise constraints" between the point clouds. These constraints were later applied to register all the point clouds. The output is shown in Fig. 6.

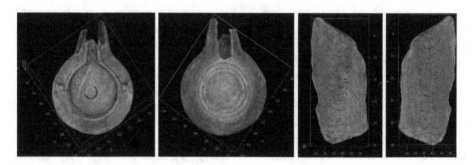

Fig. 6. Global registration of oil lamp pottery and potsherd

5 Discussion

While one solution may not solve all problems, as stated earlier, this work intended to bridge a gap that exists specifically with archaeological pottery. As was seen from the extraction of key-points from the lamp and its sherd, flexibility played a role. When present parameters did not satisfy the same goal for both lamp and sherd, the parameter was adjusted so that more key-points could be extracted from the sherd, as much as possible. Furthermore, from applying the method of [24] (see Fig. 7), it can be seen that though their method worked for their study, it did not attain accurate result with the data used in this study.

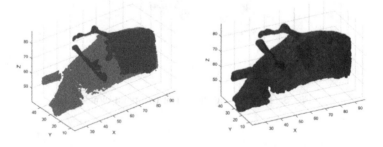

Fig. 7. Output of the method of [24]

Also, the local minimum problem was managed to a reasonable extent as a result of doing a coarse registration. This improves efficiency and robustness.

However, the time complexity of this study needs improvement and will be an area of focus on subsequent studies.

6   Conclusion

While physical documentation of artefacts is a way that archaeologists preserve artefacts, applying digital means of documentation would help in preserving artefacts much longer. The process of virtualising artefacts will play a key role in preserving and documenting valuable artefacts. The process of virtualising artefacts using point cloud data was presented in this paper. The artefact was acquired as point cloud and pre-processed to have a clean cloud. The pre-processing step includes segmentation, normal computation, down-sampling and boundary point computation. Thereafter, keypoints were detected and extracted from the point clouds, and descriptors computed using point and colour information. The approach presented in this paper focuses on improving accuracy and optimising the cost function to have an optimal result for the pottery's profile. However, while the final registration for the pottery and its sherd was successful, it was observed that the robustness of the descriptor dropped due to occlusion.

For further studies, the point clouds will be acquired to reduce noise and occlusion and increase robustness. More data of different shapes will be used to test this approach, as well as rigorous evaluation in general. Also, an attempt to reassemble the pottery and its sherd will be investigated.

Acknowledgement. This work is supported by Regione Emilia Romagna (RER), Italy. Many thanks to Professor Bevilacqua and Dr. Gherardi for their support. Thanks, also, to Roberto Togni and Marco Rovinelli for the code contribution.

References

1. Barclay, A., Knight, D., Booth, P., Evans, J., Brown, D.H., Wood, I.: A Standard for Pottery Studies in Archaeology. Medieval Pottery Research Group, London (2016)
2. Di Angelo, L., Di Stefano, P., Pane, C.: Automatic dimensional characterisation of pottery. J. Cult. Herit. **26**(2017), 118–128 (2017)
3. Drucker, J.: Humanistic theory and digital scholarship. In: Gold, M.K. (ed.) Debates in the Digital Humanities, pp. 85–95. University of Minnesota Press, Minneapolis (2012)
4. Kampel, M., Sablatnig, R.: Virtual reconstruction of broken and unbroken pottery. In: Fourth International Conference on 3-D Digital Imaging and Modeling (3DIM), pp. 318–325 (2003)
5. Smith, P., Bespalov, D., Shokoufandeh, A., Jeppson, P.: Classification of archaeological ceramic fragments using texture and color descriptors. In: 2010 IEEE Computer Society Conference on Computer Vision and Pattern Recognition Workshops (CVPRW), pp. 49–54 (2010)

6. Puglisi, G., Stanco, F., Barone, G., Mazzoleni, P.: Automatic extraction of petrographic features from pottery of archaeological interest. J. Comput. Cult. Herit. **8**(3), 13:1–13:13 (2015)
7. Makridis, M., Daras, P.: Automatic classification of archaeological Pottery Sherds. J. Comput. Cult. Herit. **5**(4), 15:1–15:21 (2012)
8. Roman-Rangel, E., Jimenez-Badillo, D., Marchand-Maillet, S.: Classification and retrieval of archaeological potsherds using histograms of spherical orientations. J. Comput. Cult. Heritage **9**(3), 17:1–17:23 (2016)
9. Gilboa, A., Tal, A., Shimshoni, I., Kolomenkin, M.: Computer-based, automatic recording and illustration of complex archaeological artifacts. J. Archaeol. Sci. **40**(2), 1329–1339 (2013)
10. Brown, D.C.: Decentering distortion of lenses. Photogramm. Eng. **32**(3), 444–462 (1966)
11. Heikkilä, J., Silvén, O.: A four-step camera calibration procedure with implicit image correction. In: IEEE Computer Society Conference on Computer Vision and Pattern Recognition (CVPR), pp. 1106–1112 (1997)
12. Zhang, Z.: Flexible camera calibration by viewing a plane from unknown orientations. In: Seventh IEEE International Conference on Computer Vision, pp. 666–673 (1999)
13. Scaramuzza, D., Siegwart, R.: A practical toolbox for calibrating omnidirectional cameras. In: Obinata, G., Dutta, A. (eds.) Vision Systems: Applications, pp. 297–310. InTech, Vienna (2007)
14. Urban, S., Leitloff, J., Hinz, S.: Improved wide-angle, fisheye and omnidirectional camera calibration. ISPRS J. Photogramm. Remote Sens. **108**, 72–79 (2015)
15. Tam, G.K.L., et al.: Registration of 3D point clouds and meshes: a survey from rigid to nonrigid. IEEE Trans. Vis. Comput. Graph. **19**(7), 1199–1217 (2013)
16. Bellekens, B., Spruyt, V., Berkvens, R., Penne, R., Weyn, M.: A benchmark survey of rigid 3D point cloud registration algorithms. Int. J. Adv. Intell. Syst. **8**(1&2), 118–127 (2015)
17. Besl, P.J., McKay, N.D.: A method for registration of 3-D shapes. IEEE Trans. Pattern Anal. Mach. Intell. **14**(2), 239–256 (1992)
18. Rusinkiewicz, S., Levoy, M.: Efficient variants of the ICP algorithm. In: Third International Conference on 3-D Digital Imaging and Modeling (3DIM), pp. 145–152 (2001)
19. Glira, P., Pfeifer, N., Christian, B., Camillo, R.: A correspondence framework for ALS strip adjustments based on variants of the ICP algorithm. Photogrammetrie Fernerkundung Geoinformation **4**, 275–289 (2015)
20. Shlens, J.: A tutorial on principal component analysis. Google Research, pp. 1–12 (2014)
21. Salti, S., Tombari, F., Di Stefano, L.: SHOT: unique signatures of histograms for surface and texture description. Comput. Vis. Image Underst. **125**, 251–264 (2014)
22. Lei, H., Jiang, G., Quan, L.: Fast descriptors and correspondence propagation for robust global point cloud registration. IEEE Trans. Image Process. **26**(8), 3614–3623 (2017)
23. Pulli, K.: Multiview registration for large data sets. In: 2nd International Conference on 3-D Digital Imaging and Modeling (3DIM), pp. 160–168 (1999)
24. Cirujeda, P., Dicente Cid, Y., Mateo, X., Binefa, X.: A 3D scene registration method via covariance descriptors and an evolutionary stable strategy game theory solver. Int. J. Comput. Vis. **115**(3), 306–329 (2015)

Geometric Interpretation of CNNs' Last Layer

Alejandro de la Calle[✉], Javier Tovar, and Emilio J. Almazán

Image Recognition Team, Nielsen,
c/Salvador de Madariaga 1, 28027 Madrid, Spain
{alejandro.delacalle.consultant,javier.tovar,
emilio.almazan}@nielsen.com

Abstract. Training Convolutional Neural Networks (CNNs) remains a non-trivial task that in many cases relies on the skills and experience of the person conducting the training. Choosing hyper-parameters, knowing when the training should be interrupted, or even when to stop trying training strategies are some difficult decisions that have to be made. These decisions are difficult partly because we still know very little about the internal behaviour of CNNs, especially during training. In this work we conduct a methodical experimentation on MNIST public database of handwritten digits to better understand the evolution of the last layer from a geometric perspective: namely the classification vectors and the image embedding vectors. The visual inspection of these vectors during training have revealed misalignment issues, which otherwise would have not being obvious to detect. We show that by constraining the norms of the classifiers during training these issues are mitigated as well as the time to converge is reduced by 40%. Within this context we present the problem of the variability across equal set-up trainings due to the random component of the initialisation method. We propose a novel approach that guides the initialisation of the parameters in the classification layer. This method reduces 12% the variability across repetitions and leads to accuracies 18% higher on average.

Keywords: Deep Learning · Convolutional Neural Networks · Image classification · Unbalanced datasets · Initialisation strategies

1 Introduction

To this day nobody doubts about the potential of Deep Learning for addressing Artificial Intelligence (AI) challenges. Moreover, the Computer Vision field has experienced a revolution where Deep Learning models have substantially outperformed the state of the art, not only in image classification and detection but also in other domains such as image processing, 3D modelling or Natural Language Processing. Despite its success, an important fraction of the community has strongly criticised the inability to provide a clear explanation of how

© Springer Nature Switzerland AG 2019
A. Morales et al. (Eds.): IbPRIA 2019, LNCS 11867, pp. 137–147, 2019.
https://doi.org/10.1007/978-3-030-31332-6_12

CNNs work inside. Important research has been conducted for the visualisation of the filters and the activations [2,10,14]. These works provide tools that enable better diagnosis for addressing issues and identifying failure modes. However, we are still far from a good understanding of neural nets, especially during training time.

Apart from high level metrics such as accuracy or cross entropy loss, we do know very little about how the dynamics of filters and classifiers of the model evolve during the course of training. For instance, it would be helpful to know information about the distribution of the image features in the latent space, or even if the parameters have been initialised to locations that can ensure good convergence. By better understanding the behaviour of the model insights and how it evolves during training we should expect better training strategies that improve the accuracy.

Latent Features and Loss Strategies. In order to extend the understanding of CNNs is common to divide the CNN into two blocks: namely the block in charge of extracting features of interest from the input image, also known as embedding or encoding, and the classifier block that receives the embedding and predicts the correct class. A well trained network is expected to generate similar embeddings for images that belong to the same class and dissimilar embeddings for different classes. Generating good representative ans discriminative features is chief to ensure good accuracies on image classification and image retrieval tasks. Training a CNN for image classification with the standard cross entropy loss does not ensure good separability of classes in the embedding space [6,7, 12]. A common approach is to train directly the embedding space using pairs of images [11] or triplets [9]. These losses tend to obtain more discriminative embeddings than the standard cross entropy loss. However, since the number of possible pairs/triplets explode with the size of the dataset, these methods require a non-trivial process of data mining to generate the pairs or triplets of interest for training. A popular approach to avoid data mining is the center loss [13] yet it requires extra computation to re-calculate the class centres and intra-class distances at every iteration. Alternatively, some researchers propose variations of the cross entropy loss that aim at reducing the intra-class distance and increasing the inter-class distance. The work of Liu et al. [6] adds a margin in the angle of the embedding vector with respect to the correct classifier, in a similar way that Hinge loss enforces maximum margins between embeddings and classifier's boundaries. Close to that approach, Wang and coworkers [12] write the softmax loss as a cosine loss by renormalizing the ℓ^2-norms of feature vectors and weights, and again introducing a margin to maximise the separability between classes. It is interesting to point out that what is common to all of these proposals and our work is the geometric formalism used to describe the latent space. Furthermore, Ranjan et al. [7] noted that the ℓ^2-norm of the feature vectors is a good indicator of the representativeness of the image to its class. They proposed the Crystal loss, which computes the cross entropy loss over features where all have the same norm. Another interesting approach was proposed by Wan et al. [12] where the embedding space is modelled as a mixture of Gaussian distributions. The loss function aims at increasing the probability of each instance to its distribution.

Parameters Initialisation. A significant amount of work has been conducted on the initialisation of parameters and how they can help on mitigating the exploding or vanishing gradients, as well as to avoid slow convergence [3,5]. In the work of Ayinde et al. [1] a study was conducted on how the initialisation methods affected the amount of redundant filters learned. These well known techniques have a random component that makes each training start from a different configuration and likely to lead to different training states. Thus, it is worth studying deeper the variability across training repetitions and how this variability can be reduced.

Using the previous research as the seed of our study we investigated how the backbone of the network and the final classification layer evolve during training. From a geometrical point of view, we treat the classifier's weights as vectors that live in the embedded space. This perspective allows us to focus on the geometrical evolution of both vectors representing the classifier weights and image embeddings. We conduct a series of ablation studies to better understand the interplay between these vectors. Moreover, we explore the variability across initialisations in unbalanced datasets with a long tail shape. Finally, we propose a novel initialisation of the classifiers vectors based on the train set distribution. Hence, this method reduces the variability in 12% across initialisations in a long-tail version of MNIST. This paper is arranged as follows: Sect. 2 introduces the geometrical approach of this study. Then in Sect. 3 we identify issues associated with standard training techniques and present a method that mitigates these issues through a guided initialization of the last layer vectors. Lastly, Sect. 4 presents the conclusions and further work.

2   Background

Convolutional Neural Networks (CNNs) can be divided in two blocks, as shown in Fig. 1a, namely the **feature extraction block** and the **classification block**:

- **The feature extraction block** receives an input image and applies a series of convolutions and pooling operations with the goal of identifying discriminative features. The output of this block is a one-dimensional vector regarded as the image encoding or embedding of the image. If it is well trained we should expect encodings from the same class to be close together. Figure 1b depicts image encodings from a subset of the train set of the MNIST dataset. Note that we use 2D vectors for visualisation purposes. Each point in the plot represents a different image and their colour corresponds to their respective ground truth label. These vectors are the input for the classification block.

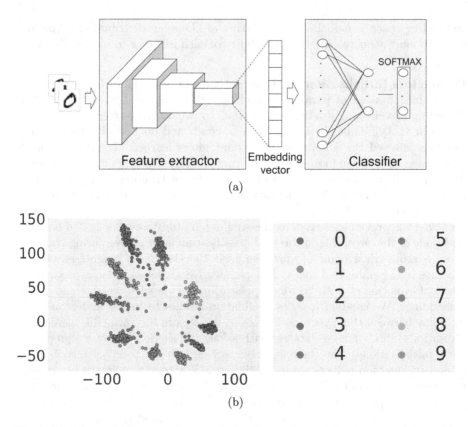

(a)

(b)

Fig. 1. (a) Schematic diagram of a convolutional neural network. The network is mainly composed by two parts: the backbone block and the classifier block. (b) Example of an embedded space for a subset of the MNIST dataset. (Color figure online)

- **The classification block** is a classifier with the softmax function. Although the classification block can in general be composed of several dense layers, we will refer to classification block as the last layer of the CNN throughout the paper. This layer calculates the class probability for the input image. It has a linear classifier that performs the linear transformation given by

$$z_c = \sum_{j=1}^{N} W_{c,j} \cdot x_j + b_c, \tag{1}$$

where $\boldsymbol{W} \in \mathbb{R}^{C \times N}$ is the classifier weight matrix with C being the number of classes and N the size of the image encoding, $\boldsymbol{b} \in \mathbb{R}^C$ is the bias term, $\boldsymbol{x} \in \mathbb{R}^N$ is the image embedding i.e. the outcome of the feature extraction block, and $\boldsymbol{z} \in \mathbb{R}^C$ is the prediction class vector. We note that the bias term $\boldsymbol{b}$ is removed throughout for simplicity. The block also uses the softmax function, which is a non-linear transformation that produces a probability distribution across all classes. This function $f(\boldsymbol{x})$ is defined as

$$[f(z)]_c = \frac{\exp(z_c)}{\sum_{c=1}^{C} \exp(z_c)}, \tag{2}$$

where $[f(z)]_c$ is the probability of the cth class. Note that the performance of the classifier block is highly dependent upon the quality of the features. The classifier will benefit from a well separated class-wise features.

During training the network tries to optimise a loss function through back-propagation and gradient descent. One of the most common objective functions is the cross-entropy loss, which measures the difference between the predicted distribution $f(x)$ and the target distribution $p(x)$ i.e. the one constructed from the ground truth. For a given instance the cross-entropy is expressed as follows:

$$\mathcal{L} = -\sum_{c=1}^{C} \left[p(x^{(i)})\right]_c \log\left[f(x^{(i)})\right]_c, \tag{3}$$

where C is the total number of classes.

2.1   Geometric Interpretation

We can express Eq. (3) using the geometric notation of the dot product as follows

$$\mathcal{L}_i = -\sum_{c=1}^{C} \left[p(x^{(i)})\right]_c \log\left[\frac{\exp\left(\|W_c\| \cdot \|x^{(i)}\| \cos\theta_c^{(i)}\right)}{\sum_{c=1}^{C} \exp\left(\|W_c\| \cdot \|x^{(i)}\| \cos\theta_c^{(i)}\right)}\right]_c, \tag{4}$$

where $\theta_c^{(i)}$ is the angle between the image encoding i with respect to the classifier vector c. Considering Eq. (4), we can see that there are two pathways to reduce the loss according to the two blocks of the network: updating the parameters of the backbone, i.e. the feature extraction block, or updating the parameters of the classifier.

- **Backbone update:** This entails updating parameters of the convolutional filters of the network, eventually leading to different encoding vectors. From the geometric perspective, in order to reduce the loss the network can reduce the angle $\theta_c^{(i)}$ for c by moving the encoding closer to its classifier.
- **Classifier update:** Updating the classifier block entails updating the classifier's vectors. The training process can yield an increase of $|W_{c,j}|$ for the correct class or/and change the direction of this vector, so the angle $\theta_c^{(i)}$ of the correct class is reduced. Likewise, it can also reduce the norm of the rest of the classifiers or/and increase their angles with the encoding by changing their directions away from it.

3   Experiments and Results

In the following experiments we study the interplay between the image encodings and the classifier layer during training. In particular, we explore these dynamics

in balanced and in unbalanced datasets. In our experiments we use as backbone
the ResNet 101 architecture [4] with an embedding of length 2, a batch size of
512, an initial learning rate of 5×10^{-4} that gets divided by 5 at epochs 15th
and 80th. We use a weight decay of 5×10^{-3}, the ADAM optimiser and Xavier
for the initialisation of parameters.

3.1   Balanced Dataset

Using the previous configuration we conduct a standard training and visualise
the evolution of the classifiers' vectors and image embeddings as the training
progresses. Figure 2a shows the state at the end of a training with an accuracy
of 0.98. It is apparent that image embeddings from the same class group together
creating clusters that fall in their corresponding class region. Moreover, the classifiers vectors span the angular domain, similarly to the hands of a clock. If we
take a closer look we observe that the classifiers vectors do not transverse their
clusters. This means that, although the accuracy is high, the dot product in the
numerator of Eq. (4) is far from being optimally maximised.

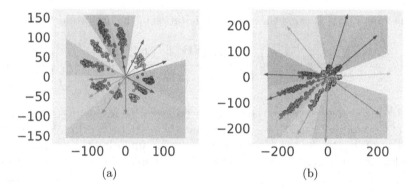

Fig. 2. Embedded space representation for a CNN trained using MNIST. The dots
and arrows represent the image encodings and the classifier vectors respectively. They
are coloured with their ground truth class. The different coloured regions represent
the locations in which the network predicts a particular class. In (a) it is shown the
embedded space for a training with no restrictions imposed, whereas in (b) it is shown
the resulting space when the classifiers vectors norm are constrained. (Color figure
online)

With the goal of reducing the angle between the classifiers vectors and their
corresponding embeddings, we constrain the norm of the classifiers during training to a fixed value of 1. Hence, only the angle can be reduced to improve the
loss. The resulting embedded space is depicted in Fig. 2b. Now the classifiers vectors traverse their corresponding clusters. Furthermore, when we constrain the
classifiers' norm the training convergence is achieved faster. We can see in Fig. 3,
the standard training reaches maximum accuracy at 10,000 iterations, while the

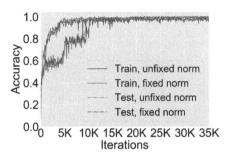

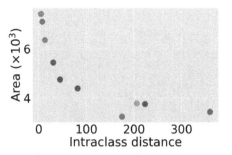

Fig. 3. Accuracy over iterations for trainings using restricted and unrestricted norms. The training when the norm is fixed converges 40% faster than the unfixed norm case.

Fig. 4. Area vs. Intra-class distance, where each dot represents a class.

constrained case achieves the same accuracy in 4,000 iterations, a reduction in time of 40%.

Another interesting observation arises from the calculation of the classification areas from each class region and the intra-class distance. These areas give us a way to measure the relative coverness of each class within the embedded space. Such areas are simply computed by integrating the surface regions of each class in a circumference of fixed radius. The surface for each class is the one in which the value of the softmax function is the highest among all classes. Also, the intra-class distance is defined as the mean distance of each instance with respect to the centroid of it's correspondent cluster. As depicted in Fig. 4, the area seem to be inversely correlated with the intra-class distance. It is left for investigation to determine whether we can manipulate the shape of encoding distributions by imposing restrictions on the classifier's norms.

Figures 5a and b correspond to the vector's configuration at the beginning and at the end of the training respectively. If we compare them, we see little variation in their directions. This confirms the importance of the classifiers initialisation. Additionally, it suggests that the influence might be more accentuated in unbalanced datasets, where high represented classes in the train set might overcome adjacent classifiers with lower presence.

3.2 Unbalanced Dataset

Unbalanced datasets, are of great interest due to its presence in real-world problems. A particular case of unbalancing is the long-tail dataset. We have modified the MNIST dataset in a way that the instances are geometrically distributed across classes following the relation $y_c^{LT} = y_c * g_c$ where y_c is the number of instances of class c in the balanced dataset, and the down-sampling factor g_c is given by

$$g_c = p(1-p)^c \quad c = 1, \dots, C. \tag{5}$$

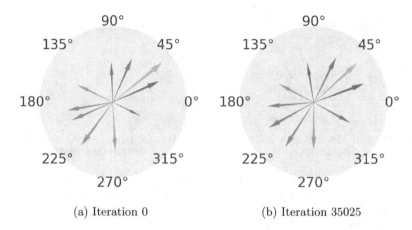

(a) Iteration 0   (b) Iteration 35025

Fig. 5. Classifier's vectors representation during training using a balanced MNIST. We show in (a) the configuration of vectors at the beginning of the training and (b) at the end. No restriction has been imposed to the classifiers vectors during this training.

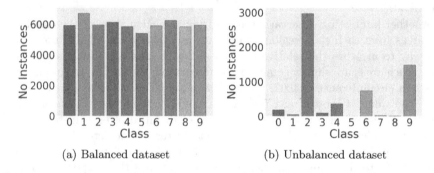

(a) Balanced dataset   (b) Unbalanced dataset

Fig. 6. Number of instances per class in the dataset, in case of (a) a balanced dataset, and (b) and unbalanced dataset.

In this study we have set $p = \frac{1}{2}$. The resulting distribution is shown in Fig. 6b. We must note that in this experiments we have unbalanced the train set whilst the test set remains balanced (Fig. 6a, as in Sect. 3.1).

Figures 7a and c show the resulting embedded space from a training with our unbalanced dataset. The single most striking observation is that some classes (i.e. 1, 5, 7 and 9) finish the training without classification area. Interestingly, these classes correspond to classes with low representation in the train set. We also observe that classes with higher presence in train tend to overcome the adjacent classes with less presence, up to a point where the minority classes are left without area.

The previous observation along with the little variation of the classification vectors during training evidence the importance of the initialisation, especially in long-tail datasets. The evolution of the accuracy for three different experiments

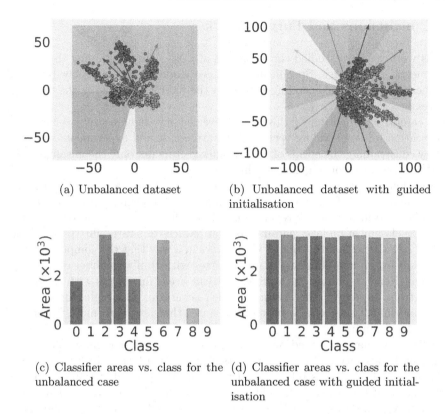

(a) Unbalanced dataset

(b) Unbalanced dataset with guided initialisation

(c) Classifier areas vs. class for the unbalanced case

(d) Classifier areas vs. class for the unbalanced case with guided initialisation

Fig. 7. (a) and (c) Embedded space and classifier areas for each class respectively, at the end of a training without restrictions for the unbalanced dataset case. (b) and (d) are the same as (a) and (c) but using guided initialisation.

that have been randomly initialised reveals high variability among repetitions, where each training leads to different accuracies, from 95% to 64% in train and from 50% to 33% in test. A difference of 31% and 17% in train and test respectively for trainings with the same set of hyperparameters and number of epochs.

To mitigate this effect, we propose a novel approach that consists on a guided initialisation where areas of classes with similar number of instances are located next to each other. This approach reduces the competition between high and low-represented classes, and therefore the areas of the former will not push out of the embedded space the areas of the latter.

In Figs. 7b and d the results of the guided initialisation are shown. We observe how the absent areas of the previous experiment are now present in the embedded space. In addition, variability among trainings has been reduced to 4% and the final test accuracies are 18% higher in average.

4   Conclusions and Future Work

In this work we have studied the dynamics of CNNs during training time from a geometric perspective. Specifically, we have explored the interplay between classification and image encoding vectors in the final layer space as the training progresses.

A careful examination of this space revealed misalignment issues between classification and embedding vectors. We have conducted experiments showing that by constraining the norms of the classifier vectors not only the misalignment is reduced but also convergence is achieved faster.

Additionally, we have shown how unbalanced datasets are highly sensitive to the randomness of the parameters initialisation, reporting up to 17% accuracy difference in test across repetitions. We proposed a novel approach to initialise the classification layer parameters that reduces this variability to 4%. This method sets the initial direction of the vectors in a way that the competition for the classification area happens between classes with similar number of training instances. Hence, minimising the risk of absent areas for classes with less presence in train. Moreover, this method yielded accuracies 18% higher in average, suggesting that it sets more robust initial states that lead with more frequency to good local minima.

Finally, we have observed an inverse correlation between the classification area of each category and the shape of its cluster. As a future work we propose to investigate further this relation and the impact of the cluster shape on the performance of the network. In addition, we are planning to extend this study to more complex datasets, such as Imagenet [8], in order to test the robustness of our proposal.

Acknowledgements. The authors would like to thank Dr. J. Javier Yebes for careful revisions and comments.

References

1. Ayinde, B.O., Inanc, T., Zurada, J.M.: On correlation of features extracted by deep neural networks. arXiv e-prints arXiv:1901.10900, January 2019
2. Binder, A., Bach, S., Montavon, G., Müller, K.-R., Samek, W.: Layer-wise relevance propagation for deep neural network architectures. In: Kim, K., Joukov, N. (eds.) Information Science and Applications (ICISA) 2016. LNEE, vol. 376, pp. 913–922. Springer, Singapore (2016). https://doi.org/10.1007/978-981-10-0557-2_87
3. Glorot, X., Bengio, Y.: Understanding the difficulty of training deep feedforward neural networks. In: Teh, Y.W., Titterington, M. (eds.) Proceedings of the Thirteenth ICAIS. Proceedings of Machine Learning Research, vol. 9, pp. 249–256. PMLR, Chia Laguna Resort, Sardinia, Italy, 13–15 May 2010. http://proceedings.mlr.press/v9/glorot10a.html
4. He, K., Zhang, X., Ren, S., Sun, J.: Deep residual learning for image recognition. arXiv e-prints. arXiv:1512.03385 (2015)

5. He, K., Zhang, X., Ren, S., Sun, J.: Delving deep into rectifiers: surpassing human-level performance on ImageNet Classification. arXiv e-prints arXiv:1502.01852, February 2015
6. Liu, W., Wen, Y., Yu, Z., Yang, M.: Large-Margin softmax loss for convolutional neural networks. arXiv e-prints arXiv:1612.02295, December 2016
7. Ranjan, R., et al.: Crystal loss and quality pooling for unconstrained face verification and recognition. arXiv e-prints arXiv:1804.01159, April 2018
8. Russakovsky, O., et al.: ImageNet large scale visual recognition challenge. Int. J. Comput. Vis. (IJCV) 115(3), 211–252 (2015). https://doi.org/10.1007/s11263-015-0816-y
9. Schroff, F., Kalenichenko, D., Philbin, J.: Facenet: A unified embedding for face recognition and clustering. In: Proceedings of the IEEE Conference on Computer Vision and Pattern Recognition, pp. 815–823 (2015)
10. Selvaraju, R.R., Cogswell, M., Das, A., Vedantam, R., Parikh, D., Batra, D.: Grad-CAM: visual explanations from deep networks via gradient-based localization. In: Proceedings of the IEEE International Conference on Computer Vision, pp. 618–626 (2017)
11. Sun, Y., Chen, Y., Wang, X., Tang, X.: Deep learning face representation by joint identification-verification. In: Advances in Neural Information Processing Systems, pp. 1988–1996 (2014)
12. Wan, W., Zhong, Y., Li, T., Chen, J.: Rethinking feature distribution for loss functions in image classification. arXiv e-prints arXiv:1803.02988, March 2018
13. Wen, Y., Zhang, K., Li, Z., Qiao, Y.: A discriminative feature learning approach for deep face recognition. In: Leibe, B., Matas, J., Sebe, N., Welling, M. (eds.) ECCV 2016. LNCS, vol. 9911, pp. 499–515. Springer, Cham (2016). https://doi.org/10.1007/978-3-319-46478-7_31
14. Zeiler, M.D., Fergus, R.: Visualizing and understanding convolutional networks. In: Fleet, D., Pajdla, T., Schiele, B., Tuytelaars, T. (eds.) ECCV 2014. LNCS, vol. 8689, pp. 818–833. Springer, Cham (2014). https://doi.org/10.1007/978-3-319-10590-1_53

Re-Weighted ℓ_1 Algorithms within the Lagrange Duality Framework
Bringing Interpretability to Weights

Matías Valdés$^{(\boxtimes)}$ and Marcelo Fiori

Instituto de Matemática y Estadística Rafael Laguardia, Facultad de Ingeniería,
Universidad de la República, Montevideo, Uruguay
{mvaldes,mfiori}@fing.edu.uy

Abstract. We consider an important problem in signal processing, which consists in finding the sparsest solution of a linear system $\Phi x = b$. This problem has applications in several areas, but is NP-hard in general. Usually an alternative convex problem is considered, based on minimizing the (weighted) ℓ_1 norm. For this alternative to be useful, weights should be chosen as to obtain a solution of the original NP-hard problem. A well known algorithm for this is the Re-Weighted ℓ_1, proposed by Candès, Wakin and Boyd. In this article we introduce a new methodology for updating the weights of a Re-Weighted ℓ_1 algorithm, based on identifying these weights as Lagrange multipliers. This is then translated into an algorithm with performance comparable to the usual methodology, but allowing an interpretation of the weights as Lagrange multipliers. The methodology may also be used for a noisy linear system, obtaining in this case a Re-Weighted LASSO algorithm, with a promising performance according to the experimental results.

Keywords: Sparsity · Weighted ℓ_1 · Lagrange multiplier · Duality · Compressed sensing · Sparse coding · LASSO · Subgradient

1 Introduction

An important problem in signal processing, particularly in the field of compressed sensing and sparse coding, is to find the "sparsest" solution of a linear system $\Phi x = b$; being $\Phi \in \mathbb{R}^{m \times n}$, $m < n$. That is: a solution with as many null coordinates as possible. This problem has applications in several areas like [9]: medical imaging, error correcting, digital cameras and wireless communication. Sparsity may be measured by the ℓ_0 pseudo-norm $||x||_0$, which counts the number of non zero coordinates. The problem of interest is then:

$$\begin{aligned} &\operatorname{argmin} \, ||x||_0. \\ &\Phi x = b \\ &x \in \mathbb{R}^n \end{aligned} \qquad (P_0)$$

© Springer Nature Switzerland AG 2019
A. Morales et al. (Eds.): IbPRIA 2019, LNCS 11867, pp. 148–160, 2019.
https://doi.org/10.1007/978-3-030-31332-6_13

This problem is NP-hard in general [8]. A usual alternative is to replace the ℓ_0 pseudo-norm by a weighted ℓ_1 norm:

$$x^w \in \operatorname{argmin} \sum_{i=1}^{n} w_i |x_i|. \qquad\qquad (P_1 W)$$
$$\Phi x = b$$
$$x \in \mathbb{R}^n$$

Problem $(P_1 W)$ is convex and so it may be solved efficiently, although it is not always equivalent to (P_0). Note that ℓ_1 minimization is obtained by using unit weights in $(P_1 W)$. For this particular case there are important results about its equivalence with (P_0), mainly due to Donoho [7] and Candès, Romberg and Tao [4]. For the general case, the task is to choose "useful weights" for $(P_1 W)$, defined as those that make x^w be a solution of (P_0). Candès, Wakin and Boyd (CWB) proposed an iterative algorithm, known as Re-Weighted ℓ_1 (RWℓ_1), to estimate useful weights [5]. The algorithm updates weights as follows:

$$w_i^{k+1} = \frac{1}{|x_i^k| + \epsilon_k}, \forall k \geq 0; \qquad\qquad (1)$$

for some $\epsilon_k > 0$ and with:

$$x^k \in \operatorname{argmin} \sum_{i=1}^{n} w_i^k |x_i|, \forall k \geq 0. \qquad\qquad (2)$$
$$\Phi x = b$$
$$x \in \mathbb{R}^n$$

In this work we propose a new methodology to estimate weights, based on the theory of Lagrange duality. Using this methodology, together with an algorithm for estimating solutions from a dual problem, we obtain a new RWℓ_1 algorithm. The methodology is also applied to a noisy linear system, obtaining in this case a Re-Weighted LASSO algorithm (RW-LASSO).

The rest of the paper is organized as follows: Sect. 2 introduces the proposed methodology in the oracle case, in which a solution of (P_0) is known. Here an oracle dual problem is obtained. Section 3 describes some solutions of this dual problem. In Sect. 4 a new RWℓ_1 algorithm is obtained by applying the proposed methodology with the subgradient algorithm. Section 5 extends the methodology and the RWℓ_1 subgradient algorithm to the non-oracle case, in which no solution of (P_0) is known. Section 6 generalizes the methodology for the case in which the linear system is affected by noise. Here a RW-LASSO algorithm is obtained. Section 7 analices the performance of the proposed RWℓ_1 algorithm in the noiseless case, and the RW-LASSO algorithm in the noisy case, both applied to random linear systems. Section 8 gives the final conclusions.

2   Methodology with Oracle

The proposed methodology is introduced in the ideal case in which a solution x^* of (P_0) is known. Consider the ideal primal problem defined as:

$$\begin{array}{c} \text{argmin} \quad 0. \\ \Phi x = b \\ |x_i| \leq |x_i^*|, \forall i \end{array} \qquad (P)$$

This is a convex problem, so it can be solved efficiently. Also, any solution of (P) is a solution of (P_0). Of course (P) is ideal, since x^* is assumed to be known, so it has no practical value. Consider the Lagrange relaxation obtained by relaxing only the constraints involving x^*. The associated Lagrangian is:

$$L(x, w) = \sum_{i=1}^{n} w_i \left(|x_i| - |x_i^*| \right) = \sum_{i=1}^{n} w_i |x_i| - \sum_{i=1}^{n} w_i |x_i^*|, \qquad (3)$$

where $w_i \geq 0$ are the Lagrange multipliers. The dual function is then:

$$d(w) := \min_{\substack{\Phi x = b \\ x \in \mathbb{R}^n}} L(w, x) = \left(\min_{\substack{\Phi x = b \\ x \in \mathbb{R}^n}} \sum_{i=1}^{n} w_i |x_i| \right) - \sum_{i=1}^{n} w_i |x_i^*|. \qquad (4)$$

This dual function involves a Weighted ℓ_1 problem, in which weights are Lagrange multipliers. This is the key idea behind the proposed methodology: identify weights of (P_1W) as Lagrange multipliers. The problem is then in the context of Lagrange duality. In particular, weights may be estimated by any algorithm to estimate multipliers. Equivalently, weights may be estimated as solutions of the dual problem, given by:

$$\begin{array}{c} \text{argmax } d(w). \\ w \geq 0 \\ w \in \mathbb{R}^n \end{array} \qquad (D)$$

This maximization problem is always concave, so it may be solved efficiently. One drawback is that usually the dual function is non differentiable, so for example gradient based algorithms must be replaced by subgradient.

3   Solutions of the Dual Problem

Now the interest is to find "useful solutions" of the dual (D). That is: $w \geq 0$ such that x^w is a solution of (P_0). This section shows that such solutions always exist, although not every solution of (D) has this property.

Proposition 1. *Primal problem (P) satisfies strong duality: $d^* = f^*$.*

Proof. The primal optimal value is clearly $f^* = 0$. By weak duality: $d^* \leq f^* = 0$. So it suffices to show that $d(w) = 0$, for some $w \geq 0$. Taking $w = \mathbf{0}$:

$$d(\mathbf{0}) = \left(\min_{\substack{\Phi x = b \\ x \in \mathbb{R}^n}} \sum_{i=1}^{n} 0|x_i| \right) - \sum_{i=1}^{n} 0|x_i^*| = 0. \tag{5}$$

$\square$

It was also shown that $w = \mathbf{0}$ is a solution of (D). Clearly $w = \mathbf{0}$ is not necessarily a useful solution, since x^0 could be any solution of the linear system:

$$x^0 \in \operatorname*{argmin}_{\substack{\Phi x = b \\ x \in \mathbb{R}^n}} \sum_{i=1}^{n} 0|x_i| = \{\Phi x = b\}.$$

A consequence of strong duality is that the set of Lagrange multipliers and of dual solutions are equal. Therefore, useful weights may be estimated as dual solutions. The following result shows that the dual problem always admits useful weights as solutions.

Proposition 2. *Let $\hat{w} \geq 0$ such that: $\hat{w}_i = 0 \Leftrightarrow x_i^* \neq 0$. Then every solution $x^{\hat{w}}$ of the problem (P_1W) associated to $\hat{w}$, is a solution of (P_0).*

Proof. Let $I = \{i/x_i^* = 0\}$. By definition of $\hat{w}$ and $x^{\hat{w}}$, and using that $\Phi x^* = b$:

$$0 \leq \sum_{i \in I} \hat{w}_i |x_i^{\hat{w}}| = \sum_{i=1}^{n} \hat{w}_i |x_i^{\hat{w}}| \leq \sum_{i=1}^{n} \hat{w}_i |x_i^*| = \sum_{i \in I} \hat{w}_i |x_i^*| = 0. \tag{6}$$

This implies: $\hat{w}_i |x_i^{\hat{w}}| = 0, \forall i \in I$. Since $\hat{w}_i > 0, \forall i \in I$, then we must have: $x_i^{\hat{w}} = 0, \forall i \in I$. So: $||x^{\hat{w}}||_0 \leq ||x^*||_0$. By definition $\Phi x^{\hat{w}} = b$, then it solves (P_0).

$\square$

4   RWℓ_1 with Projected Subgradient Algorithm

In this section we give an implementation of the proposed methodology, by using the projected subgradient algorithm for estimating solutions of the dual problem. This algorithm may be thought as a (sub)gradient "ascent", with a projection on the dual feasible set. More specifically, starting at $w^0 \geq 0$, the update is:

$$\begin{cases} w^{k+1} = w^k + \alpha_k g^k \\ w^{k+1} = \max\{0, w^{k+1}\} \end{cases}, \forall k \geq 0; \tag{7}$$

where $g^k \in \partial d(w^k)$ is a subgradient of the dual function at w^k, and $\alpha_k > 0$ the stepsize. Although this is not strictly an ascent method, it is always possible to choose the stepsize in order to decrease the distance of w^k to the dual solution set. A way for this is to update the stepsize as [3]:

$$\alpha_k = \frac{d^* - d(w^k)}{||g^k||_2^2} \geq 0, \ \forall k \geq 0. \tag{8}$$

Applying [2] [Example 3.1.2] to (P), it can be seen that a subgradient $g^k \in \partial d(w^k)$ can be obtained by solving a Weighted ℓ_1 problem:

$$
\begin{aligned}
x^k \in \ &\text{argmin} \ \sum_{i=1}^{n} w_i^k |x_i| \Rightarrow g(x^k) \in \partial d(w^k), \forall k \geq 0. \\
&\Phi x = b \\
&x \in \mathbb{R}^n
\end{aligned}
\tag{9}
$$

Note that the stepsize can now be written as:

$$\alpha_k = \frac{d^* - d(w^k)}{||g^k||_2^2} = \frac{0 - L(x^k, w^k)}{||g(x^k)||_2^2} = -\frac{\sum_{i=1}^{n} w_i^k \left(|x_i^k| - |x^*| \right)}{\sum_{i=1}^{n} \left(|x_i^k| - |x^*| \right)^2}, \forall k \geq 0. \tag{10}$$

Algorithm 1 shows a pseudocode of the proposed RWℓ_1 subgradient algorithm.

Algorithm 1. RWℓ_1 with projected subgradient (with oracle and noise-free)

Require: $\Phi \in \mathbb{R}^{m \times n}, b \in \mathbb{R}^m, w^0 \geq 0$, RWIter ≥ 0

1: $x^0 \in \underset{\substack{\Phi x = b \\ x \in \mathbb{R}^n}}{\text{argmin}} \ \sum_{i=1}^{n} w_i^0 |x_i| \quad \{(P_1 W)\}$

2:

3: $k = 0$

4: **while** $k <$ RWIter **do**

5: $\quad g_i^k = g_i(x^k) = |x_i^k| - |x_i^*| \ \{\text{subgradient at } w^k\}$

6:

7: $\quad$ Choose α_k using (10)

8:

9: $\quad w_i^{k+1} = w_i^k + \alpha_k g_i^k$

10: $\quad w_i^{k+1} = \max\left(0, w_i^{k+1}\right)$

11:

12: $\quad x^{k+1} \in \underset{\substack{\Phi x = b \\ x \in \mathbb{R}^n}}{\text{argmin}} \ \sum_{i=1}^{n} w_i^{k+1} |x_i| \quad \{(P_1 W) \text{ with warm restart } x^k\}$

13:

14: $\quad k = k + 1$

15:

16: **end while**

17: **return** x^k

---

5   Methodology and Algorithm Without Oracle

The proposed methodology is now extended to the practical case, in which no solution of (P_0) is known. A simple way for doing this is to replace x^* in the ideal constraints by its best known estimate x^k, "amplified" by some $\epsilon_k > 0$:

$$g_i^k(x) = |x_i| - (1 + \epsilon_k)|x_i^k|, \forall k \geq 0; \tag{11}$$

where x^k is calculated in the same way as in the oracle case:

$$\begin{array}{c} x^k \in \text{argmin} \sum_{i=1}^{n} w_i^k |x_i|, \forall k \geq 0. \\ \Phi x = b \\ x \in \mathbb{R}^n \end{array}$$

This gives specific constraints $g^k(\cdot)$ for each step k, and their respective primal problem:

$$\begin{array}{cc} \text{argmin} & 0. \\ \Phi x = b \\ |x_i| \leq (1 + \epsilon_k)|x_i^k|, \forall i \\ x \in \mathbb{R}^n \end{array} \tag{P^k}$$

Since x^k is always feasible at (P^k), this problem has optimal value $f^k = 0$. By relaxing its non-ideal constraints, a dual problem may be obtained. The Lagrange an dual functions are, respectively:

$$L^k(x, w) = \sum_{i=1}^{n} w_i |x_i| - \sum_{i=1}^{n} w_i (1 + \epsilon_k) |x_i^k|, \tag{12}$$

$$d^k(w) = \left(\begin{array}{c} \min_{\substack{\Phi x = b \\ x \in \mathbb{R}^n}} \sum_{i=1}^{n} w_i |x_i| \end{array} \right) - \sum_{i=1}^{n} w_i (1 + \epsilon_k) |x_i^k|. \tag{13}$$

Like in the oracle case, each dual function involves a Weighted ℓ_1 problem, with weights as Lagrange multipliers. This allows to extend the methodology, by estimating weights of (P^k) as Lagrange multipliers, or solving its dual problem:

$$\begin{array}{c} \text{argmax } d^k(w). \\ w \geq 0 \\ w \in \mathbb{R}^n \end{array} \tag{D^k}$$

Solutions of (D^k) may be analized in a similar way as for (D). In particular, it can be easily seen that (P^k) satisfies strong duality, with optimal values $f^k = d^k = 0$. It is very useful to know the optimal value d^k for (D^k), in order to compute the stepsize for the subgradient algorithm, when applied to (D^k):

$$\alpha_k = \frac{d^k - d^k(w^k)}{\|g^k(x^k)\|_2^2} = \frac{0 - L^k(x^k, w^k)}{\|g^k(x^k)\|_2^2} = \frac{1}{\epsilon_k} \frac{\|W^k x^k\|_1}{\|x^k\|_2^2} \geq 0. \tag{14}$$

Algorithm 2 shows the pseudo-code of the non-oracle RWℓ_1 method, obtained by combining the proposed methodology with the projected subgradient algorithm.

Algorithm 2. RWℓ_1 with projected subgradient (without oracle and noise free)

Require: $\Phi \in \mathbb{R}^{m \times n}$, $b \in \mathbb{R}^m$, $w^0 \geq 0$, RWIter ≥ 0

1:
2: $x^0 \in \text{argmin}_{\substack{\Phi x = b \\ x \in \mathbb{R}^n}} \sum_{i=1}^n w_i^0 |x_i|$ $\{(P_1 W)\}$

3:
4: $k = 0$
5: **while** $k <$ RWIter **do**
6:     $g_i^k = g_i(x^k) = |x_i^k| - (1 + \epsilon_k)|x_i^k| = -\epsilon_k|x_i^k|$ {subgradient of d^k at w^k}
7:
8:     Choose α_k using (14)
9:
10:    $w_i^{k+1} = \max\left(0, w_i^k + \alpha_k g_i^k\right)$
11:
12:    $x^{k+1} \in \text{argmin}_{\substack{\Phi x = b \\ x \in \mathbb{R}^n}} \sum_{i=1}^n w_i^{k+1} |x_i|$ $\{(P_1 W)$ with warm restart $x^k\}$

13:
14:    $k = k + 1$
15:
16: **end while**
17: **return** x^k

At each step of Algorithm 2, and before the projection, the update is:

$$w_i^{k+1} = w_i^k + \alpha_k g_i^k(x^k) = w_i^k - \frac{\|W^k x^k\|_1}{\|x^k\|_2^2}|x_i^k|, \forall k \geq 0;$$

so Algorithm 2 is independent of $\epsilon_k > 0$. We take $\epsilon_k = 1, \forall k \geq 0$.

6   Problem with Noise

In this section we consider the case in which the linear system is affected by noise. That is: $b = \Phi x^* + z$, where z represents the noise. The problem of interest is now:

$$\text{argmin}_{\substack{\frac{1}{2}\|\Phi x - b\|_2^2 \leq \frac{\eta^2}{2} \\ x \in \mathbb{R}^n}} \|x\|_0. \tag{P_0^η}$$

This problem is also NP-hard in general, for any level of noise $\eta \geq 0$ [8]. Replacing the ℓ_0 pseudo-norm by a weighted ℓ_1 norm, we obtain a convex alternative:

$$\underset{\frac{1}{2}\|\Phi x - b\|_2^2 \leq \frac{\eta^2}{2}}{\text{argmin}} \sum_{i=1}^{n} w_i |x_i|. \qquad (P_1^\eta W)$$

The proposed methodology is the same as in the noiseless case. Now the oracle primal problem is:

$$\underset{\substack{\frac{1}{2}\|\Phi x - b\|_2^2 \leq \frac{\eta^2}{2} \\ |x_i| \leq |x_i^*|, \forall i}}{\text{argmin}} \quad 0. \qquad (15)$$

The Lagrangian obtained by relaxing the ideal constraints is the same as for the noiseless case. The dual function is now:

$$d(w) = \left(\underset{\frac{1}{2}\|\Phi x - b\|_2^2 \leq \frac{\eta^2}{2}}{\min} \sum_{i=1}^{n} w_i |x_i| \right) - \sum_{i=1}^{n} w_i |x_i^*|. \qquad (16)$$

This is a Weighted ℓ_1 problem with quadratic constraints. Such as in the noiseless case, weights can be identified with Lagrange multipliers. So the methodology and the RWℓ_1 subgradient algorithm are the same as for the noiseless case, but replacing $(P_1 W)$ with $(P_1^\eta W)$. Going a step further, if the quadratic constraints are also relaxed, a new dual function may be obtained:

$$d(w, \lambda) = \left(\underset{x \in \mathbb{R}^n}{\min} \frac{\lambda}{2}\|\Phi x - b\|_2^2 + \sum_{i=1}^{n} w_i |x_i| \right) - \left(\frac{\lambda}{2}\eta^2 + \sum_{i=1}^{n} w_i |x_i^*| \right). \qquad (17)$$

This involves the well known Weighted LASSO problem, which is a simple generalization of the LASSO problem, introduced by Tibshirani in the area of statistics [10]. Chen, Donoho and Saunders introduced the same LASSO problem in the context of signal representation, but with the name of Basis Pursuit Denoising [6]. Note that useful weights of $(P_1^\eta W)$ can still be estimated as part of the Lagrange multipliers; which are now $w \in \mathbb{R}_+^n$ and $\lambda \in \mathbb{R}_+$. When combined with the projected subgradient algorithm, this gives a RW-LASSO algorithm, in which at each step a Weighted-LASSO problem must be solved instead of $(P_1^\eta W)$:

$$x^k \in \underset{x \in \mathbb{R}^n}{\text{argmin}} \frac{\lambda^k}{2}\|\Phi x - b\|_2^2 + \sum_{i=1}^{n} w_i^k |x_i|, \forall k \geq 0. \qquad (18)$$

Algorithm 3 shows a pseudocode for the proposed subgradient RW-LASSO algorithm.

Algorithm 3. RW-LASSO with subgradient (without oracle and with noise)

Require: $\Phi \in \mathbb{R}^{m \times n}$, $b \in \mathbb{R}^m$, $w^0 \geq 0$, $\lambda^0 \in \mathbb{R}$, $\eta \geq 0$, RWIter ≥ 0

1: $x^0 \in \operatorname{argmin}_{x \in \mathbb{R}^n} \frac{\lambda^0}{2} \|\Phi x - b\|_2^2 + \sum_{i=1}^{n} w_i^0 |x_i|$ {Weighted-LASSO}

2:

3: $k = 0$

4: **while** $k <$ RWIter **do**

5:      $g_i^k = g_i^k(x^k) = |x_i^k| - (1 + \epsilon_k)|x_i^k|$

6:      $w_i^{k+1} = \max\left(0, w_i^k + \alpha_k g_i^k\right)$

7:

8:      $g_\lambda^k = g_\lambda(x^k) = \frac{1}{2}\left(\|\Phi x^k - b\|_2^2 - \eta^2\right)$

9:      $\lambda^{k+1} = \max\left(0, \lambda^k + \alpha_k g_\lambda^k\right)$

10:

11:      $x^{k+1} \in \operatorname{argmin}_{x \in \mathbb{R}^n} \frac{\lambda^{k+1}}{2}\|\Phi x - b\|_2^2 + \sum_{i=1}^{n} w_i^{k+1}|x_i|$ {with warm restart x^k}

12:

13:      $k = k + 1$

14:

15: **end while**

16: **return** x^k

CWB RWℓ_1 algorithm can also be extended to the noisy model, by updating weights as in the noiseless case, but taking [5]:

$$x^k \in \underset{\frac{1}{2}\|\Phi x - b\|_2^2 \leq \frac{\eta^2}{2}}{\operatorname{argmin}} \sum_{i=1}^{n} w_i^k |x_i|, \forall k \geq 0. \tag{19}$$

7 Experimental Results

7.1 Results for the Noise-Free Setting

This section analyzes the performance of the proposed RWℓ_1 subgradient algorithm, when applied to a random linear system, and taking the method by CWB as reference. For a given level of sparsity s, a random linear system $\Phi x = b$ is generated, with a solution x^* such that $\|x^*\|_0 \leq s$. The experimental setting is based on [5]:

1. Generate $\Phi \in \mathbb{R}^{m \times n}$, with $n = 256$, $m = 100$ and Gaussian independent entries:

$$\Phi_{ij} \sim N\left(0, \sigma = \frac{1}{\sqrt{m}}\right), \forall i, j.$$

   Note that in particular Φ will have normalized columns (in expected value).
2. Select randomly a set $I_s \subset \{1, \dots, n\}$ of s indexes, representing the coordinates of x^* where non-null values are allowed.

3. Generate the values of $x_i^*, i \in I_s$, with independent Gaussian distribution:

$$x_i^* \sim N\left(0, \sigma = \frac{1}{\sqrt{s}}\right), \forall i \in I_s.$$

Note that in particular x^* will be normalized in expected value.

4. Generate the independent term: $b = \Phi x^* \in \mathbb{R}^m$.

For both RW algorithms, the proposed one and the method by CWB, we use $w^0 = 1$. For CWB we take $\epsilon_k = 0.1, \forall k \geq 0$. Following [5], we say x^* was recovered if:

$$\|x^{\text{RWIter}} - x^*\|_\infty \leq 1 \times 10^{-3}. \tag{20}$$

For each level of sparsity $s \in [15, 55]$, a recovery rate is calculated as the percentage of recovery over $N_p = 300$ random problems. Figure 1 shows the results for different number of RW iterations. Results for ℓ_1 minimization are also shown for reference. Considering only one RW iteration, the proposed algorithm is slightly better than CWB. This difference disappears for two or more RW iterations, where both algorithms show the same performance; with the additional interpretability of the weights in the proposed methodology.

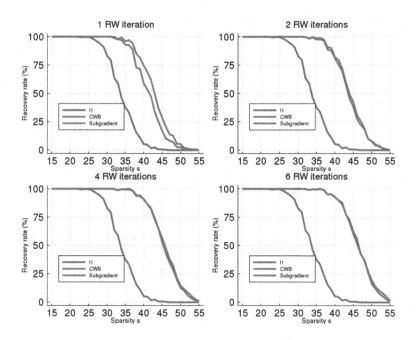

Fig. 1. Recovery rate of RWℓ_1 algorithms.

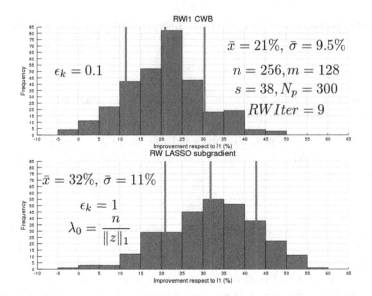

Fig. 2. Performance of RW algorithms with respect to ℓ_1 minimization (with noise). (Color figure online)

7.2 Results for the Noisy Setting

Following [5], random problems with noise are generated with $n = 256$ and $m = 128$. Φ and x^* are generated in the same way as in the noiseless case. Noise z in b is taken with Gaussian independent coordinates, and such that x^* is feasible with high probability. For this we take: $z_i = \sigma v_i, v_i \sim N(0, 1)$ independent, so:

$$\|z\|_2^2 = \sigma^2 \|v\|_2^2 = \sigma^2 \left(\sum_{i=1}^m v_i^2 \right) \sim \sigma^2 \chi_m^2. \tag{21}$$

Taking for example $\eta^2 = \sigma^2 \left(m + 2\sqrt{2m} \right)$, we have:

$$P \left(\|\Phi x^* - b\|_2^2 \leq \eta^2 \right) = 1 - P \left(\chi_{128}^2 \geq 160 \right) \simeq 0.971. \tag{22}$$

We use $w^0 = \mathbf{1}$ for both algorithms. For subgradient RW-LASSO we take $\lambda^0 = \frac{n}{\|z\|_1}$, where z is a solution of $\Phi x = b$ with minimum ℓ_2 norm. FISTA algorithm is used for solving each Weighted-LASSO problem [1]. Performance is measured by the improvement with respect to a solution $x_{\ell_1}^\eta$ of noisy ℓ_1 minimization:

$$a = 100 \times \left(1 - \frac{\|x^{RW} - x^*\|_2}{\|x_{\ell_1}^\eta - x^*\|_2} \right) \%. \tag{23}$$

Figure 2 shows the performance with noisy measures for both RW methods: the proposed RW-LASSO algorithm and the RWℓ_1 CWB algorithm. Results correspond to $N_p = 300$ tests on random problems with fixed sparsity $s = 38$. The mean improvement $\bar{x}$ is also shown (vertical red line), together with $\pm$ one standard deviation $\bar{\sigma}$ (vertical violet and green lines). CWB RWℓ_1 algorithm shows a mean improvement of 21% with respect to ℓ_1 minimization. For RW-LASSO subgradient this improvement is 32%, significantly higher than CWB.

We also considered the RW-LASSO algorithm with weights updated as CWB, but the performance was very poor. The reason for this may be that λ_k remains fixed at λ_0, as there is no obvious rule for updating it.

8 Conclusions

In this paper the important problem of finding sparse solutions of a linear system was considered. A usual alternative to this NP-hard problem is the Weighted ℓ_1 problem, where the choice of weights is crucial. A new methodology for estimating weights was proposed, based on identifying weights as solutions of a Lagrange dual problem. It was shown that this problem always admits "useful" solutions. The proposed methodology was then applied using the projected subgradient algorithm, obtaining a RWℓ_1 algorithm, alternative to the classical one, due to CWB. This new algorithm was tested on random problems in the noiseless case, obtaining almost the same performance as that of CWB, but allowing an interpretation of weights. The proposed methodology was then extended to the noisy case. Here a RW-LASSO algorithm was obtained, by introducing a new Lagrange multiplier. This last algorithm showed a considerable improvement in performance, with respect to the RWℓ_1 algorithm proposed by CWB.

Acknowledgment. This work was supported by a grant from Comisión Académica de Posgrado (CAP), Universidad de la República, Uruguay.

References

1. Beck, A., Teboulle, M.: A fast iterative shrinkage-thresholding algorithm for linear inverse problems. SIAM J. Imaging Sci. **2**(1), 183–202 (2009)
2. Bertsekas, D.P., Scientific, A.: Convex Optimization Algorithms. Athena Scientific, Belmont (2015)
3. Bertsekas, D.: Nonlinear Programming. Athena Scientific Optimization and Computation Series. Athena Scientific, Belmont (1999)
4. Candes, E., Romberg, J., Tao, T.: Robust uncertainty principles: exact signal reconstruction from highly incomplete frequency information. arXiv preprint arXiv:math/0409186 (2004)
5. Candès, E.J., Wakin, M.B., Boyd, S.P.: Enhancing sparsity by reweighted l_1 minimization. J. Fourier Anal. Appl. **14**(5–6), 877–905 (2008)
6. Chen, S.S., Donoho, D.L., Saunders, M.A.: Atomic decomposition by basis pursuit. SIAM Rev. **43**(1), 129–159 (2001)
7. Donoho, D.L., et al.: Compressed sensing. IEEE Trans. Inf. Theory **52**(4), 1289–1306 (2006)
8. Foucart, S., Rauhut, H.: A Mathematical Introduction to Compressive Sensing. Birkhäuser, Basel (2013)

9. Qaisar, S., Bilal, R.M., Iqbal, W., Naureen, M., Lee, S.: Compressive sensing: from theory to applications, a survey. J. Commun. Netw. **15**(5), 443–456 (2013)
10. Tibshirani, R.: Regression shrinkage and selection via the lasso. J. Roy. Stat. Soc.: Ser. B (Methodol.) **58**(1), 267–288 (1996)

A Note on Gradient-Based Intensity Normalization

Manuel G. Forero[1]([⊠]) [iD], Carlos Arias-Rubio[1],
José de Anchieta C. Horta-Júnior[2], and Dolores E. López[3]

[1] Facultad de Ingeniería, Universidad de Ibagué, Ibagué, Colombia
manuel.forero@unibague.edu.co, caar93@hotmail.com
[2] Anatomy Department, São Paulo State University (UNESP), Assis, Brazil
[3] Instituto de Neurociencias de Castilla y León, Universidad de Salamanca,
Salamanca, Spain

Abstract. This paper presents an improvement on gradient-based intensity normalization introduced by Sintorn et al., which is used in microscopy, especially in the evaluation of proteins and other cell elements in densitometry. In this method, images contain similar textures, but their density and intensity may vary dramatically. Two new profiles are introduced, and the Bhattacharyya distance is employed to find the best matching result. Results show the validity of the improved method.

Keywords: Intensity normalization · Bivariate histogram · Microscopy · Densitometry · Histogram profiles

1 Introduction

Densitometry is one of the most common methods employed in the evaluation of proteins and other chemical elements of cells. In this method, the optical density difference between several tissues stained with a specific marker is measured and compared. The original procedure involved exposing light-sensitive photographic films to light. Currently, films have been mostly replaced by electronic devices. Thus, to compare the intensity of different images, an initial approach consists of trying to acquire the images under similar light intensity without changing any other parameter. However, this procedure is not the best as it does not consider intensity differences due to changes in the tissue itself, differences in the quality of the staining, variations in light intensity, modification of the intensity due to the movement of the lens during focusing, and change of the distance from the lamp to the sample and the lens. Several image processing techniques have been proposed to accomplish this function. Alvarado et al. [1] proposed a simple method, which has several deficiencies that we present here. Using an image with the best quality as a reference is common in densitometry. This image normally shows the best contrast, is not saturated, and occupies all the available dynamic range $[0, L - 1]$. The other images are compared against the reference image, and transformed to resemble the original as much as possible, assuming that they have very similar tissue. Considering that all images show the same kind of tissue and are acquired under similar conditions under ideal conditions, the gray level distribution in

A. Morales et al. (Eds.): IbPRIA 2019, LNCS 11867, pp. 161–169, 2019.
https://doi.org/10.1007/978-3-030-31332-6_14

all images will be the same, and therefore the histograms should be the same. Based on this idea, several methods have been employed to match the histogram. The method proposed by Capek et al. [2] divides the histogram of the reference image in several parts and tries to transform the histogram of another image so as to resemble these parts. Another popular technique was proposed by Gonzalez et al. [3], and it uses the accumulative histogram to match the histograms of the images. More recently, Sintorn et al. [4] proposed the use of bivariate histograms, from which three profiles can be employed to match the tissues' brightness values. This method produces good results, which can be further improved. More complex techniques, not based on the histogram, have also been proposed, but they are beyond the scope of this paper and are not covered here. The described methods are based on the similarity of the histogram. In this paper, an improvement of the original Sintorn technique is proposed, including two additional profiles based on a different bivariate histogram, which in general produces better results than the original ones. Additionally, the distance between histograms is employed to compare these profiles, providing the better profile automatically.

2   Review

Alvarado et al. [1] did not give a complete mathematical formulation of their method; however, a full formulation can be extracted from it. In this method, images are modified independently without using a reference image. This method consists of two steps. From Eq. (1), the first step consists of adjusting the contrast according to the value of a variable a, based on the standard deviation of the pixels in the image or region of interest and its size

$$R(q) = P(q) \cdot a \qquad (1)$$

where $R(q)$ and $P(q)$ are the resulting image and the image to be fixed, and q is the gray level in the image. The second step is simply an expansion of the histogram to the maximum range, i.e., between 0 and $L - 1$, being L the maximum number of gray levels in the images of size 256. Clearly, the first step is useless and can in fact even degrade the image quality by introducing a quantification error. When $a < 1$, several gray levels of the original image are combined in just one gray level in the modified image. Equally, if $a > 1$ and

$$P(q) \cdot a > L - 1 \qquad (2)$$

several gray levels of the original image are saturated, and the information provided by the higher gray levels are lost in the resultant image (Eq. (2)). Subsequently, rejecting the first step, the Alvarado method consists only of a stretching step, which does not consider the reference image.

   Sintorn et al. [4] proposed the use of a bivariate histogram. The 2D histograms of the reference and input images were obtained using the gray level of the images as abscissa and their gradient as ordinate. They showed that 2D histograms exhibit more similarity between images than 1D histograms do, by providing better matching results. Once the bivariate histograms were obtained, two projections or profiles of each 2D histogram in both axes were used as new 1D profiles and employed to match the input image to the reference image. Additionally, they proposed the relation between both projections to produce a third profile. Finally, the profiles were matched; thus, the resulting transformation of the input image was now similar to the reference image. The three profiles proposed by Sintorn et al. are the following:

Ordinary Histogram Matching (OHM). The simplest profile utilizes the information from the intensity in a standard gray scale from a histogram.

$$P_i^{OHM} = \sum_{g=0}^{L-1} b_{ig} \tag{3}$$

where P_i^x is the profile derived from the bivariate histogram, each profile is a function of intensity i, and x represents the abbreviation of the current method. b_{ig} is the bivariate histogram computed as the number of occurrences of image pixels with intensity i and gradient g.

Gradient Weighted (GW). This profile combines intensity and gradient information.

$$P_i^{GW} = \sum_{g=0}^{L-1} g b_{ig} \tag{4}$$

Average Gradient (AG). The average (mean) gradient is the ratio of the first two profiles: the OHM and gradient weighted.

$$P_i^{AG} = P_i^{GW} / P_i^{OHM} \tag{5}$$

3 Material

In this study, 8 pairs of light microscopy images of rat brains with a size of 4080×3072 pixels and 25 pairs with a size of 1388×1040, 10 images of a transparent slide taken under different illumination conditions with size of 1382×1034 pixels were used, as shown in Fig. 1. Additionally, other 24 images were obtained by modifying the brightness and contrast of the light microscopy images. The image processing methods were implemented in Java as plugins for the open-access software ImageJ [5].

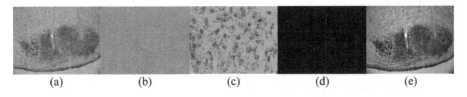

(a)   (b)   (c)   (d)   (e)

Fig. 1. Images of a rat brain and a transparent slide taken under different illumination conditions: (a, b) Original high contrast images taken as reference; (c, d) Low contrast images; (e) Modified image with doing a manual adjust of contrast.

4 Methodology

Sintorn et al. [4] proposed the use of bivariate histograms of the reference and input images, using the gradient as ordinate. Instead of the gradient, here we propose the use of a smoothed image, showing that in general, it produces better matching results, as shown in Fig. 2. In this way, two new profiles can be obtained:

Smooth Weighted (SW). This profile combines intensity and smooth information, b_{is} is the bivariate histogram with intensity i and smooth s.

$$P_i^{SW} = \sum_{s=0}^{L-1} sb_{is}. \tag{6}$$

Average Smooth (AS). Average smooth is the ratio of the two profiles: the OHM and smooth weighted.

$$P_i^{AS} = P_i^{SW}/P_i^{OHM}. \tag{7}$$

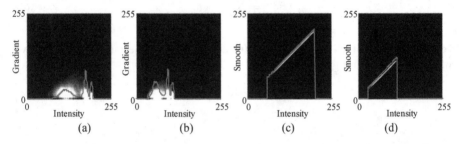

Fig. 2. Images of intensity-gradient bivariate histograms and intensity-smooth bivariate histograms: (a) intensity gradient of reference image; (b) intensity gradient of input image; (c) intensity smoothening of reference image; (d) intensity smoothening of input image.

Therefore, image processing is based on the following steps:

- Selection of the reference image and the input image, with or without ROI; both images must be in gray scale.
- Gradient image and smoothed image extraction.
- Creation of gradient-based bivariate histograms and the proposed smoothening-based histograms.
- Execute the five methods of intensity normalization, resulting in the three profiles proposed by Sintorn et al. and the two proposed herein.
- Generate the five resulting images: one from each method.
- Generate the histogram corresponding to each image and compare the distance between histograms with the reference.
- Evaluate the results to obtain the best and shows the result image.

However, a common feature of tissue images is that part of them is occupied by the background. Given that the size of the area occupied by the background changes from image to image, the shape of the histogram changes accordingly, affecting the equalization method. To reduce the error introduced by the background, we selected the region of interest more accurately and excluded the intensity normalization section of the image that was not of interest (Fig. 3). ROI selection was done manually.

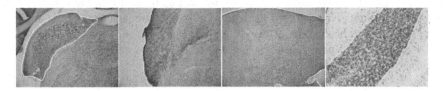

Fig. 3. Images of a rat brain with selection of ROI to exclude the background.

Saturation Correction. This step comprises stretching the histograms of the images, maximizing the dynamic range of both images. In this way, the minimal and maximal gray levels on the images become the same. However, this method has several disadvantages: if the reference image is already saturated, i.e., many pixels have minimum or maximum intensity or both, the processed image will also have a high number of saturated pixels, which is not desirable. Therefore, instead of checking if there are peaks at the maximum and minimum intensity values of the histogram, as it was proposed by Sintorn et al. [4], in the solution proposed herein, we search if the reference histogram has saturated bins at the ends of the histograms and do not consider them when fixing the input image. Instead, the first and last values of the reference histogram are modified making them equal to the second and penultimate values of the reference histogram, and this modified histogram is then used to fix the histogram of the input image.

5   Results

We evaluate images of the same tissue under different conditions of light intensity, trying to reproduce the method usually employed in densitometry before the introduction of image processing techniques. Given that each pair of images has the same content, and only the light intensity is different, the normalized histogram of the input image should be exactly equal to the histogram of the reference image. Therefore, the quality of the normalization can be assessed by measuring the difference between the histograms of the reference and normalized images. Because the images resulting from intensity normalization are very similar, determining the measure that provides the best performance is difficult. Therefore, four distances employed to compare histograms were evaluated to determine the best measure [6]. The Bhattacharyya distance, used to assess equality between two distributions, was identified as the best one. This distance is closer to zero when histograms are more similar.

Figure 4 presents the results obtained with five pairs of images. Figure 5 shows the histograms of two of the images in Fig. 4. As it can be seen in Table 1, the profile of the ordinary histogram provides the best performance with the original images (twenty-three cases), followed by the average gradient profile in five cases. The ordinary histogram profile has the best performance with the contrast modified images (fifteen cases). The use of a ROI histogram, as shown in Fig. 6, improves the result of the intensity correction, given that only the regions of interest are included in both images. Figure 7 shows the histograms of two of the images in Fig. 6. In this case, the SW profile gives the best performance in eighteen cases, followed by the ordinary histogram profile in fourteen.

Figure 8 shows the results obtained with three pairs of images of the transparent microscope slides taken under different illumination conditions and Fig. 9 shows the histograms of two of the images. As it can be seen in Table 1, the GW profile obtained the best performance in six cases, the SW profile in three cases and the ordinary profile in one. As it can be observed, the extension of the original method by Sintorn et al. provides better results in several cases, which is very important in biology to evaluate slight variations in tissues. Additionally, the use of the Bhattacharyya distance allows the automatic determination of the best profile.

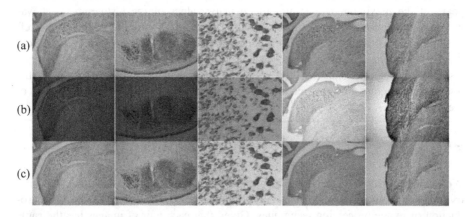

Fig. 4. Five pairs of light microscopy images of rat brains taken under different illumination conditions: (a) reference images; (b) input images; and (c) best result obtained of each one. The first three columns correspond to original images, and the last two to manually modified ones.

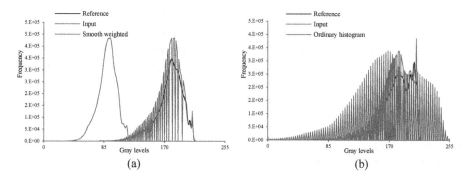

Fig. 5. Histograms of the images tested in Fig. 4, reference image in black, input image in blue, and profile of the best result in red: (a) column 1 in Fig. 4, and (b) column 5 in Fig. 4. (Color figure online)

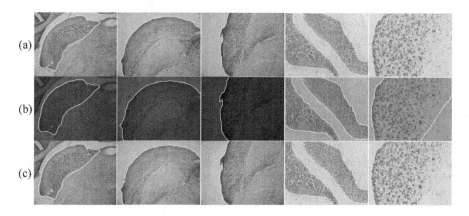

Fig. 6. Images of a rat brain with ROI: (a) reference images with ROI, (b) input images with ROI, (c) best result obtained of each one.

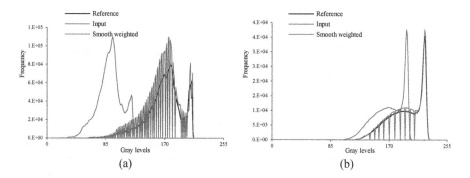

Fig. 7. Histograms of two pairs of images tested in Fig. 6, with the reference image in black, input image in blue, and profile of the best result in red: (a) column 1 in Fig. 6, (b) column 4 in Fig. 6. (Color figure online)

Table 1. Distances between histograms in all analysed images.

Images	Ordinary histogram	Gradient weighted	Average gradient	Smooth weighted	Average smooth	Total pairs of images
Original	23	0	5	4	1	33
Contrast modified	15	1	0	7	1	24
ROI selection	14	4	1	18	1	38
Transparent slide	1	6	0	3	0	10

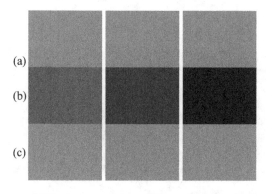

Fig. 8. Images of a transparent slide taken under different illumination conditions: (a) reference images with intensity 0.5; (b) input images with intensity 2.5, 4.5 and 6.5; (d) best result obtained of each one.

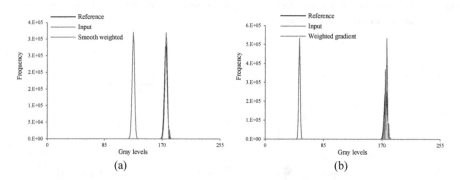

Fig. 9. Histograms of two pairs of images tested in Fig. 8, with the reference image in black, input image in blue, and profile of the best result in red: (a) column 1 in Fig. 8, (b) column 3 in Fig. 8. (Color figure online)

6 Conclusions

In this work, three improvements over Sintorn et al.'s gradient intensity normalization were introduced, including saturation correction, the selection of the region of interest, and two new profiles based on the use of a smoothening-based bivariate histogram, obtaining good results. Alvarado et al.'s method was also shown to be inappropriate for this task.

In some cases, wherein microscopic images have much non-useful information (background), the selection of the region of interest is a great alternative for optimizing the results of the intensity normalization.

One of the two proposed profiles of smoothening-based bivariate histogram, called smooth weighted, in most cases exhibited a better approximation in the intensity normalization with respect to the reference, than original proposed profiles.

Since the best profile for adjusting two images depends on the type of image, Bhattacharyya's distance is adequate for measuring the quality of the adjustment and automating this task.

Acknowledgements. This work was supported by project # 17-461-INT Universidad de Ibagué.

References

1. Alvarado, J.C., Santamaria, V.F., Henkel, C.K., Brunso-Bechtold, J.K.: Alterations in calretinin immunostaining in the ferret superior olivary complex after cochlear ablation. J. Comp. Neurol. **470**, 63–79 (2004)
2. Capek, M., Kubínová, L., Hána, K., Smrcka, P.: Compensation of the contrast and brightness attenuation with depth in confocal microscopy. In: Proceedings of the 21st Spring Conference on Computer Graphics (2005)
3. Gonzalez, R.C., Woods, R.E.: Digital Image Processing, 3rd edn. Pearson, London (2009)
4. Sintorn, M., Bischof, L., Jackway, P., Haggarty, S., Buckley, M.: Gradient based intensity normalization. J. Microsc. **240**, 249–258 (2010)
5. Rasband, W.S.: ImageJ. U. S. National Institutes of Health, Bethesda, Maryland, USA (1997–2016). https://imagej.nih.gov/ij/. Accessed 19 Mar 2019
6. Forero, M.G., Arias-Rubio, C., González, B.T.: Analytical comparison of histogram distance measures. In: Vera-Rodriguez, R., Fierrez, J., Morales, A. (eds.) CIARP 2018. LNCS, vol. 11401, pp. 81–90. Springer, Cham (2019). https://doi.org/10.1007/978-3-030-13469-3_10

Blind Robust 3-D Mesh Watermarking Based on Mesh Saliency and QIM Quantization for Copyright Protection

Mohamed Hamidi[1]([✉]), Aladine Chetouani[2], Mohamed El Haziti[1],
Mohammed El Hassouni[3], and Hocine Cherifi[4]

[1] LRIT - CNRST URAC29, Rabat IT Center, Faculty of Sciences,
Mohammed V University, Rabat, Morocco
`hamidi.medinfo@gmail.com`, `elhazitim@gmail.com`
[2] PRISME Laboratory, University of Orleans, Orléans, France
`aladine.chetouani@univ-orleans.fr`
[3] LRIT - CNRST URAC29, Rabat IT Center, FLSH,
Mohammed V University, Rabat, Morocco
`mohamed.elhassouni@gmail.com`
[4] LIB EA 7534, Université de Bourgogne, Dijon, France
`hocine.cherifi@u-bourgogne.fr`

Abstract. Due to the recent demand of 3-D models in several applications like medical imaging, video games, among others, the necessity of implementing 3-D mesh watermarking schemes aiming to protect copyright has increased considerably. The majority of robust 3-D watermarking techniques have essentially focused on the robustness against attacks while the imperceptibility of these techniques is still a real issue. In this context, a blind robust 3-D mesh watermarking method based on mesh saliency and Quantization Index Modulation (QIM) for Copyright protection is proposed. The watermark is embedded by quantifying the vertex norms of the 3-D mesh using QIM scheme since it offers a good robustness-capacity tradeoff. The choice of the vertices is adjusted by the mesh saliency to achieve watermark robustness and to avoid visual distortions. The experimental results show the high imperceptibility of the proposed scheme while ensuring a good robustness against a wide range of attacks including additive noise, similarity transformations, smoothing, quantization, etc.

Keywords: 3-D mesh watermarking ·
Quantization Index Modulation (QIM) · Copyright protection ·
Mesh saliency

1 Introduction

Due to the rapid development of digital services and the increase in network bandwidth, the transfer of multimedia contents such as image, audio, video and

A. Morales et al. (Eds.): IbPRIA 2019, LNCS 11867, pp. 170–181, 2019.
https://doi.org/10.1007/978-3-030-31332-6_15

3-D model has been increased considerably. These contents can be modified or duplicated easily. Therefore, the need to develop security methods became crucially important. Digital watermarking has been found as an efficient solution to overcome this issue. Its underlying concept is to embed an extra information called watermark into multimedia content to protect its ownership. In the last decade, 3-D meshes have been widely used in medical images, computer aided design (CAD), video games, virtual reality, etc. Each 3-D watermarking system should ensure a three major requirements: imperceptibility, capacity and robustness. The attacks can be divided into two major types. Connectivity attacks including subdivision, cropping, remeshing, and simplification. Geometric attacks that include similarity transformations, local deformation operations and signal processing manipulations. The applications of 3-D mesh watermarking include copyright protection, authentication, content enhancement, indexation, etc. We note that the proposed method aims to protect copyright. It is worth mentioning that in contrast with the maturity of image watermarking techniques [1], there are only few watermarking methods that work on 3-D meshes. In addition, the processing techniques applied to 2D images cannot be used in case of 3D meshes [2–5]. This is due to the challenges in three dimensional geometry related to its irregular topology as well as the complexity of attacks that target this kind of geometrical content [6,7]. The majority of 3-D watermarking techniques have essentially focused on the robustness against attacks. Few 3-D mesh watermarking methods based on saliency have been proposed [8]. In [9], a watermarking 3-D mesh method using the visual saliency is presented. Firstly, the perceptually conspicuous regions using the mesh saliency [10] have been identified. Secondly, the norm of each vertex is calculated and its histogram is constructed. The watermark is embedded in each bin by normalizing the associated vertex norms. Zhan et al. [11] proposed a blind 3-D mesh watermarking algorithm based on curvature. The authors calculated the root mean square curvature for all vertices of the 3-D model. The watermark is embedded by modulating the mean of the root mean square curvature fluctuation of vertices. Rolland-Neviere et al. [12] proposed a 3-D mesh watermarking method where the watermark embedding is formulated as a quadratic programming problem. Son et al. [13] proposed a 3-D watermarking method with the aim of preserving the appearance of the watermarked 3-D model. The method used the distribution of the vertex norm histogram as a watermarking primitive that is already introduced by Cho et al. [14]. The latter inserts the watermark by altering the mean or variance of the vertex norms histogram.

In this paper, a 3-D mesh blind and robust watermarking method based on mesh saliency and QIM quantization is proposed. The watermark bits are inserted in the host 3-D mesh by quantizing its vertices norms. The choice of these norms has been guided by the mesh saliency of the 3-D mesh. Taking the full advantages of QIM scheme as well as mesh saliency, the proposed method can achieve high robustness to common attacks while preserving high imperceptibility. The rest of this paper is organized as follows. Section 2 presents the background. Section 3 gives a description of the proposed method composed by embedding and extraction. The experimental setup, evaluation metrics and experimental results are discussed in Sect. 4. Finally, Sect. 5 concludes the paper.

2   Background

2.1   3-D Mesh Saliency

Mesh saliency can be defined as a measure that captures the importance of a point or local region of a 3-D mesh in a similar way to human visual perception [15]. The visual attention of Human is usually directed to the salient shape of the 3-D model. The evaluation of mesh saliency used in the proposed scheme is Lee et al. [10]. The later evaluates the saliency of each vertex using the difference in mean curvature of the 3-D mesh surfaces from those at other vertices in the neighborhood. The first step is computing surface curvatures. The computation of the curvature at each vertex v is performed using Taubin's method [16]. Let $Curv(v)$ the mean curvature of a mesh at a vertex v. The Gaussian-weighted average of the mean curvature can be expressed as follows:

$$G(Curv(v), \sigma) = \frac{\sum_{x \in N(v,2\sigma)} Curv(x) exp(\frac{-\|x-v\|^2}{2\sigma^2})}{\sum_{x \in N(v,2\sigma)} exp(\frac{-\|x-v\|^2}{2\sigma^2})} \tag{1}$$

where x is a mesh point and $N(v, \sigma)$ denotes the neighborhood for a vertex v which represents a set of points within an Euclidean distance σ calculated as:

$$N(v, \sigma) = \{x| \ \| \ x - v \ \| < \sigma\} \tag{2}$$

The saliency $S(v)$ of a vertex v is calculated as the absolute difference between the Gaussian-weighted averages computed at fine and coarse scale.

$$S(v) = |G(Curv(v), \sigma) - G(Curv(v), 2\sigma)| \tag{3}$$

(a)   (b)   (c)   (d)

Fig. 1. Saliency of 3-D meshes using Lee's method [10] (a) Flower, (b) Vase, (c) Cup, (d) Cat.

Figure 1 shows an example of mesh saliency using Lee's method [10].

2.2 Quantization Index Modulation

Quantization Index Modulation (QIM) approaches have been widely used in image, audio, and video processing. Their application to 3-D meshes is trivial since two quantifiers are needed to insert a binary message in the 3-D data [17]. QIM techniques are simple to implement and have a small complexity. In addition, they ensure a high tradeoff between robustness and capacity. Each watermark bit is associated to a quantizer in the host signal. Let $b \in (0,1)$ the watermark bit and x the host signal to be quantized. The QIM techniques operate independently on these two elements. In order to embed a bit b, two quantizers Q_0 and Q_1 are needed [18]. They can be defined as follows:

$$Q_b(x) = \Delta[\frac{1}{\Delta}(x - (-1)^b\frac{\Delta}{4}) + (-1)^b\frac{\Delta}{4}] \tag{4}$$

Where $[]$ refers to the rounding operation and Δ is the quantization step. In the extraction process the signal is re-quantized using the same family of quantizer to get the embedded bits. The recovered bits are easily calculated as follows:

$$\hat{b} = argmin \|x - Q_b(x)\| \tag{5}$$

3 The Proposed Method

In this paper, a blind robust 3-D mesh watermarking technique based on visual saliency and QIM quantization for Copyright protection is proposed. The watermark is embedded by modifying the salient vertex norms of the 3-D mesh to using mesh saliency and QIM quantization. The mesh saliency of Lee et al. [10] used to obtain candidate vertices aims to ensure high imperceptibility and to improve the watermark robustness. The choice of these points has been driven by the fact that these primitives are relatively stable even after applying several attacks including similarity transformations, noise addition, smoothing, quantization, etc. Figure 2 shows the flowchart of the proposed method. Figure 3 illustrates the Lee's [10] mesh saliency of Bimba model after applying different attacks.

3.1 Watermark Embedding

The proposed method takes the full advantage of the mesh saliency to achieve high imperceptibility. The watermarking bits are embedded by quantizying the vertex norms of the 3-D model using mesh saliency. The motivation behind using the QIM quantization is the good tradeoff between capacity and robustness [17]. In addition, QIM methods are blind. Firstly, the mesh saliency is computed and a threshold is fixed automatically to define the salient and non-salient points. In fact, for each saliency vector, the 70% maximum values represent the salient points while the other points are considered non-salient. Next, the norms of salient points are calculated according to this threshold. After, a watermark is generated using pseudo-random generator using a secret key (key1). Afterwards, two quantizers Q_{zero} and Q_{one} are calculated using Eq. 4 according to the watermark bit. Finally, starting from the modified vertex norms the new vertex coordinates are calculated using Eq. 6 in order to construct the 3-D watermarked mesh. We note that the quantization step can be considered as second secret key (key2) that will be used in the extraction step.

$$V'(x', y', z') = \frac{\|V'\|}{\|V\|} V(x, y, z) \tag{6}$$

where $V'(x', y', z')$ are the new coordinates of new vertices and $V(x, y, z)$ are the old coordinates.

3.2   Watermark Extraction

The watermark extraction is blind since only secret keys (key1 and key2) are needed. First, the mesh saliency of the 3-D watermarked model is calculated and the salient points are extracted according to the threshold used in the watermark embedding. We note that this parameter is chosen automatically since it represents the 70% maximum values of the saliency vector. Next, the norms according to the chosen vertices are calculated. The two quantizers are calculated and the extracted watermark bits are obtained using Eq. 5.

4   Experimental Results

4.1   Experimental Setup

The proposed watermarking method is tested on several 3-D meshes with different shape complexities: Flower (2523 vertices, 4895 faces), Vase (2527 vertices, 5004 faces), Cup (9076 vertices, 18152 faces), Ant (7654 vertices, 15304 faces), Bimba (8857 vertices, 17710 faces) and cat (3534 vertices, 6975 faces) where some of them are shown in Fig. 4((a), (c), (e)). It is worth noticing that for comparison purpose the imperceptibility and robustness evaluation have been performed using the 3-D models: Bunny (34835 vertices, 69666 faces), Horse (112642 vertices, 225280 faces) and Venus (100759 vertices, 201514 faces). The quantization step is chosen in such a way that ensures good tradeoff between imperceptibility and robustness. This parameter is tuned experimentally and we kept $\Delta = 0.08$. Several metrics have been used to measure the amount of distortion introduced by the embedding process. This distortion can be measured geometrically or perceptually. The maximum root mean square error (MRMS) proposed in [19] is used to calculate the objective distortion between the original meshes and the watermarked ones. The Hausdorff distance (HD) is defined as the minimum Euclidean distance between a point of one surface of the original mesh and another surface of the distorted mesh. The mesh structural distortion measure (MSDM) metric is chosen to measure the visual degradation of the watermarked meshes [20]. The MSDM value is equal to 0 when the original and

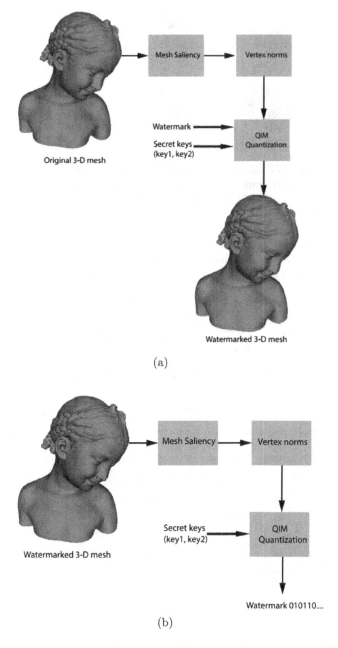

Fig. 2. Flowchart of the proposed method: (a) watermark embedding, (b) watermark extraction.

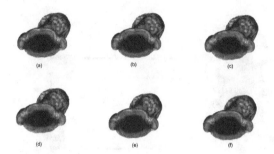

Fig. 3. Mesh saliency of Bimba before and after attacks: (a) before attack, (b) additive noise 0.3%, (c) Similarity transformation 1, (d) Simplification 10%, (e) Quantization 9 bits, (f) Smoothing $\lambda = 0.1$ (30 iterations).

watermarked 3-D objects are identical. Otherwise, the MSDM value is equal to 1 when the objects are visually very different. The robustness is measured using the normalized correlation ($Corr$) between the inserted watermark and the extracted one.

$$Corr = \frac{\sum_{i=1}^{M}(w_i' - \overline{w}^*)(w_i - \overline{w})}{\sqrt{\sum_{i=1}^{M}(w_i' - \overline{w}^*)^2 . \sum_{i=1}^{M}(w_i - \overline{w})^2}} \quad (7)$$

Where $i \in \{1, 2, \ldots, M\}$, $\overline{w}^*$ and $\overline{w}$ are the averages of the watermark bits respectively.

Table 1. Watermark imperceptibility measured in terms of MRMS, HD and MSDM.

Model	MRMS (10^{-3})	HD (10^{-3})	MSDM
Flower	0.63	4.33	0.30
Vase	0.41	3.34	0.37
Cup	0.98	2.95	0.37
Ant	0.62	4.19	0.51
Cat	0.61	1.0	0.16
Bimba	0.39	1.63	0.10
Average	0.61	2.91	0.30

4.2   Results Discussion

Imperceptibility. Figure 4 illustrates the original and watermarked 3-D meshes. We can see that the distortion is imperceptible thanks to the saliency adjustment. In addition, according to Table 1, it can be observed that the proposed method can achieve high imperceptibility in terms of MRMS, HD and

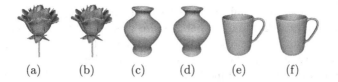

(a)   (b)   (c)   (d)   (e)   (f)

Fig. 4. (a) Flower, (b) Watermarked Flower, (c) Vase, (d) Watermarked Vase, (e) Cup, (f) Watermarked Cup.

MSDM. We believe that this performance is obtained thanks to the exploitation of mesh saliency to avoid serious distortions. It can be also observed that the imperceptibility results in terms of MRMS, HD and MSDM are different from a mesh to another. This difference is mainly due to the curvature nature of each one of these 3-D meshes.

Table 2. Watermark imperceptibility without using saliency measured in terms of MRMS, HD and MSDM compared to the proposed method.

Model	MRMS (10^{-3})	HD (10^{-3})	MSDM
Flower	0.89/**0.63**	5.03/**4.33**	0.88/**0.30**
Vase	0.58/**0.41**	4.76/**3.34**	0.76/**0.37**
Cup	1.02/**0.98**	3.45/**2.95**	0.87/**0.37**
Ant	0.83/**0.62**	4.43/**4.19**	1.0/**0.51**
Cat	1.2/**0.61**	1.9/**1.0**	0.29/**0.16**
Bimba	0.76/**0.39**	2.98/**1.63**	1.66/**0.10**
Average	0.88/**0.61**	3.76/**2.91**	0.91/**0.30**

To further evaluate the importance of using mesh saliency to improve the imperceptibility of the proposed method, we compare the obtained results with those obtained without using the saliency. Table 2 exhibits the imperceptibility performance in terms of MRMS, HD and MSDM without using the mesh saliency compared to the proposed method based on mesh saliency. We note that the obtained results of our method based on saliency are shown in bold. According to Table 2, it can be seen that the proposed method outperforms which illustrates the imperceptibility improvement achieved using the saliency aspect in the watermark embedding.

Robustness. To evaluate the robustness of the proposed scheme, 3-D meshes have been undergone several attacks. For this purpose, a benchmarking system has been used [21]. The robustness of our scheme is tested under several attacks including noise addition, smoothing, quantization, cropping, subdivision and similarity transformations (translation, rotation and uniform scaling).

Figure 5 shows the model Bimba after several attacks. To evaluate the robustness to noise addition attack, binary random noise was added to each vertex of 3-D models with four different noise amplitudes: 0.05%, 0.10%, 0.30% and 0.50%. According to Table 3, it can be seen that the proposed method is robust against noise addition four all the 3-D models.

For evaluating the resistance of the proposed scheme to smoothing attack, the 3-D models have undergone Laplacian smoothing proposed in [22] using 5, 10, 30 and 50 iterations while keeping the deformation factor $\lambda = 0.10$. Table 3 shows that our method is able to withstand smoothing operation. The robustness of the proposed scheme is evaluated against elements reordering attack called also file attack. According to Table 3 the proposed scheme can resist to element reordering. Quantization is also applied to the 3-D models to evaluate the robustness against this attack using 7, 8, 9, 10 and 11 bits. It can be concluded from Table 4 that the proposed method shows good robustness against quantization regardless of the used 3-D mesh. The robustness of our method is evaluated against similarity transformation in which 3-D models have undergone a random rotation, a random uniform scaling and a random translation. Table 4 sketches the obtained results in terms of correlation. It can be observed that our method can achieve high robustness against these attacks. The proposed scheme is tested against subdivision attack including three schemes (loop, midpoint and sqrt3). The obtained results in Table 4 in terms of correlation exhibit the high robustness against subdivision. Cropping is considered to be one of the most damaging attack since it deletes a region from the 3-D mesh and thus the useful information will be lost. It can be observed from Table 4 that the proposed method is not enough robust to cropping attacks. In fact, if the deleted surface contains salient points, the extraction process will fail. In the future work, we will search a solution to the issue related to the robustness weakness against this attack.

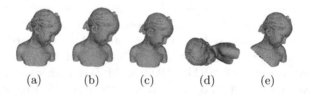

(a)   (b)   (c)   (d)   (e)

Fig. 5. Six attacks versions of Bimba: (a) noise addition 0.50%, (b) Smoothing $\lambda = 0.1$ with 5 iterations, (c) quantization 9 bits, (d) Similarity transformation, (e) Cropping ratio 10.0.

4.3   Comparison with Alternative Methods

To further evaluate the performance of the proposed scheme in terms of imperceptibility and robustness we compare it with Cho's [14], Wang's et al. [23],

Table 3. Watermark robustness against additive noise, Laplacian smoothing and elements reordering measured in terms of correlation.

Parameters	Noise addition				Laplacian Smoothing				Elements reordering		
	0.05%	0.10%	0.30%	0.50%	5	10	30	50	Type 1	Type 2	Type 3
Flower	0.98	0.94	0.89	0.81	1.0	0.99	0.98	0.89	1.0	0.95	1.0
Vase	1.0	0.91	0.85	0.71	1.0	0.98	0.97	0.86	1.0	0.96	1.0
Cup	0.96	0.93	0.83	0.78	1.0	1.0	0.90	0.87	1.0	1.0	0.98
Ant	0.97	0.95	0.86	0.77	0.99	0.97	0.93	0.85	1.0	0.98	1.0
Cat	0.99	0.91	0.88	0.73	1.0	0.95	0.95	0.90	1.0	1.0	1.0
Bimba	1.0	0.93	0.90	0.80	1.0	1.0	0.94	0.91	0.99	0.97	0.96
Average	0.98	0.93	0.87	0.77	0.99	0.98	0.94	0.88	0.99	0.97	0.99

Table 4. Watermark robustness against quantization, similarity transformations, subdivision and cropping measured in terms of correlation.

Parameters	Quantization					Similarity transformation			Subdivision			Cropping		
	11-bits	10-bits	9-bits	8-bits	7-bits	Type 1	Type 2	Type3	Loop iter 1	Midpoint iter 1	Sqrt3 iter 1	10%	30%	50%
Flower	1.0	1.0	0.98	0.91	0.80	1.0	0.95	0.98	1.0	0.93	1.0	0.56	0.44	0.28
Vase	1.0	1.0	0.98	0.91	0.78	0.92	0.94	0.98	0.98	0.87	0.96	0.59	0.31	0.12
Cup	1.0	0.99	0.97	0.93	0.83	1.0	1.0	1.0	1.0	0.84	0.94	0.67	0.37	0.16
Ant	1.0	1.0	0.97	0.92	0.77	0.94	0.96	1.0	0.94	0.91	1.0	0.61	0.45	0.21
Cat	1.0	0.97	1.0	0.93	0.76	1.0	1.0	0.96	0.95	0.94	1.0	0.58	0.30	0.22
Bimba	1.0	1.0	0.99	0.98	0.86	0.98	1.0	0.90	0.98	0.95	0.96	0.50	0.22	0.17
Average	1.0	0.99	0.98	0.93	0.80	0.97	0.97	0.97	0.97	0.91	0.97	0.58	0.35	0.19

Table 5. Imperceptibility comparison with Cho's [14], Rolland-Neviere's [12] and Son's [13] schemes measured in terms of MRMS and MSDM for Horse model.

Metric	[14]	[12]	[13]	Our method
MRMS (10^{-3})	3.17	1.48	2.90	0.53
MSDM	0.3197	0.2992	0.3197	0.2865

Zhan's et al. [11], Rolland-Neviere et al. [12] and Son's et al. [13] schemes. We note that for comparison purpose, we have tested the robustness of our method using the 3-D models Bunny, Horse and Venus.

Table 5 exhibits the imperceptibility comparison with schemes in terms of MRMS and MSDM. The obtained results demonstrate the high imperceptibility of the proposed method and show its superiority to the alternative methods. The proposed method is compared to Cho's [14] and Zhan's [11] methods in terms of imperceptibility using MRMS as well as robustness in terms of correlation against noise addition, smoothing and quantization using Bunny and Venus 3-D meshes. Table 6 sketches the robustness comparison in terms of correlation between our method and schemes [11,14]. It can be concluded from Table 6 that the proposed method is quite robust to additive noise, smoothing and quantization and outperforms the alternative methods.

Table 6. Robustness comparison with Cho's [14] and Zhan's [11] schemes against additive noise, smoothing and quantization in terms of correlation for Bunny and Venus models.

Model	Bunny									Venus								
Attack	Noise addition			Smoothing			Quantization			Noise			Smoothing			Quantization		
Intensity	0.1%	0.3%	0.5%	10	30	50	9	8	7	0.1%	0.3%	0.5%	10	30	50	9	8	7
[14]	0.72	0.72	0.66	0.84	0.60	0.36	0.73	0.58	0.17	0.94	0.87	0.27	0.94	0.63	0.45	0.87	0.48	0.07
[11]	1.0	0.91	0.80	0.92	0.85	0.44	1.0	0.91	0.58	0.95	0.95	0.79	0.95	0.93	0.78	1.0	0.83	0.73
Proposed method	1.0	0.93	0.84	0.97	0.91	0.58	1.0	0.92	0.67	1.0	0.98	0.81	1.0	0.99	0.79	1.0	0.90	0.85

5   Conclusion

In this paper, a blind robust 3-D mesh watermarking method based on mesh saliency and QIM quantization for Copyright protection is proposed. The proposed method achieves both high robustness and imperceptibility. The robustness requirement is achieved by quantizing the vertex norms using QIM while the imperceptibility achievement is ensured by adjusting the watermarking embedding according to the mesh visual saliency. The experimental results demonstrate that the proposed scheme yields a good tradeoff between the imperceptibility and robustness requirements. Moreover, experimental simulations show that the proposed method outperforms the existing methods against the majority of common attacks. In the future work, we will investigate the issue related to the robustness weakness against cropping attack.

References

1. Hamidi, M., El Haziti, M., Cherifi, H., El Hassouni, M.: Hybrid blind robust image watermarking technique based on DFT-DCT and Arnold transform. Multimedia Tools Appl. **77**(20), 27181–27214 (2018)
2. Eude, T., Cherifi, H., Grisel, R.: Statistical distribution of DCT coefficients and their application to an adaptive compression algorithm. In: Proceedings of TENCON'94-1994 IEEE Region 10's 9th Annual International Conference on: 'Frontiers of Computer Technology', pp. 427–430. IEEE (1994)
3. Rital, S., Cherifi, H., Miguet, S.: Weighted adaptive neighborhood hypergraph partitioning for image segmentation. In: Singh, S., Singh, M., Apte, C., Perner, P. (eds.) ICAPR 2005. LNCS, vol. 3687, pp. 522–531. Springer, Heidelberg (2005). https://doi.org/10.1007/11552499_58
4. Pastrana-Vidal, R.R., Gicquel, J.C., Blin, J.L., Cherifi, H.: Predicting subjective video quality from separated spatial and temporal assessment. In: Human Vision and Electronic Imaging XI, vol. 6057, p. 60570S. International Society for Optics and Photonics (2006)
5. Hamidi, M., El Haziti, M., Cherifi, H., Aboutajdine, D.: A blind robust image watermarking approach exploiting the DFT magnitude. In: 2015 IEEE/ACS 12th International Conference of Computer Systems and Applications (AICCSA), pp. 1–6. IEEE (2015)
6. Wang, K., Lavoué, G., Denis, F., Baskurt, A.: Three-dimensional meshes watermarking: review and attack-centric investigation. In: Furon, T., Cayre, F., Doërr, G., Bas, P. (eds.) IH 2007. LNCS, vol. 4567, pp. 50–64. Springer, Heidelberg (2007). https://doi.org/10.1007/978-3-540-77370-2_4

7. Hamidi, M., El Haziti, M., Cherifi, H., Aboutajdine, D.: A robust blind 3-D mesh watermarking based on wavelet transform for copyright protection. In: 2017 International Conference on Advanced Technologies for Signal and Image Processing (ATSIP), pp. 1–6. IEEE (2017)
8. Hamidi, M., Chetouani, A., El Haziti, M., El Hassouni, M., Cherifi, H.: Blind robust 3D mesh watermarking based on mesh saliency and wavelet transform for copyright protection. Information 10(2), 67 (2019)
9. Nakazawa, S., Kasahara, S., Takahashi, S.: A visually enhanced approach to watermarking 3D models. In: 2010 Sixth International Conference on Intelligent Information Hiding and Multimedia Signal Processing (IIH-MSP), pp. 110–113. IEEE (2010)
10. Lee, C.H., Varshney, A., Jacobs, D.W.: Mesh saliency. ACM Trans. Graph. (TOG) 24(3), 659–666 (2005)
11. Zhan, Y., Li, Y., Wang, X., Qian, Y.: A blind watermarking algorithm for 3D mesh models based on vertex curvature. J. Zhejiang Univ. Sci. C 15(5), 351–362 (2014)
12. Rolland-Neviere, X., Doërr, G., Alliez, P.: Triangle surface mesh watermarking based on a constrained optimization framework. IEEE Trans. Inf. Forensics Secur. 9(9), 1491–1501 (2014)
13. Son, J., Kim, D., Choi, H.-Y., Jang, H.-U., Choi, S.: Perceptual 3D watermarking using mesh saliency. In: Kim, K., Joukov, N. (eds.) ICISA 2017. LNEE, vol. 424, pp. 315–322. Springer, Singapore (2017). https://doi.org/10.1007/978-981-10-4154-9_37
14. Cho, J.-W., Prost, R., Jung, H.-Y.: An oblivious watermarking for 3-D polygonal meshes using distribution of vertex norms. IEEE Trans. Signal Process. 55(1), 142–155 (2007)
15. Song, R., Liu, Y., Martin, R.R., Rosin, P.L.: Mesh saliency via spectral processing. ACM Trans. Graph. (TOG) 33(1), 6 (2014)
16. Taubin, G.: Estimating the tensor of curvature of a surface from a polyhedral approximation. In: ICCV, p. 902. IEEE (1995)
17. Chen, B., Wornell, G.W.: Quantization index modulation: a class of provably good methods for digital watermarking and information embedding. IEEE Trans. Inf. Theory 47(4), 1423–1443 (2001)
18. Vasic, B., Vasic, B.: Simplification resilient LDPC-coded sparse-QIM watermarking for 3D-meshes. IEEE Trans. Multimedia 15(7), 1532–1542 (2013)
19. Cignoni, P., Rocchini, C., Scopigno, R.: Metro: measuring error on simplified surfaces. In: Computer Graphics Forum, pp. 167–174, vol. 17, no. 2. Wiley Online Library (1998)
20. Lavoue, G., Gelasca, E.D., Dupont, F., Baskurt, A., Ebrahimi, T.: Perceptually driven 3D distance metrics with application to watermarking. In: SPIE Optics+ Photonics. International Society for Optics and Photonics, pp. 63 120L–63 120L (2006)
21. Wang, K., Lavoue, G., Denis, F., Baskurt, A., He, X.: A benchmark for 3D mesh watermarking. In: Shape Modeling International Conference (SMI) 2010, pp. 231–235. IEEE (2010)
22. Taubin, G.: Geometric signal processing on polygonal meshes. In: Proceedings of the Eurographics State-of-the-art Reports, pp. 81–96 (2000)
23. Wang, K., Lavoué, G., Denis, F., Baskurt, A.: Hierarchical watermarking of semiregular meshes based on wavelet transform. IEEE Trans. Inf. Forensics Secur. 3(4), 620–634 (2008)

Using Copies to Remove Sensitive Data: A Case Study on Fair Superhero Alignment Prediction

Irene Unceta[1,2]🆔, Jordi Nin[1,2,3(✉)]🆔, and Oriol Pujol[2]🆔

[1] BBVA Data & Analytics, Barcelona, Spain
{irene.unceta,jordi.nin}@bbvadata.com
[2] Department of Mathematics and Computer Science,
Universitat de Barcelona, Barcelona, Spain
{irene.unceta,jordi.nin,oriol_pujol}@ub.edu
[3] ESADE, Universitat Ramon Llull, Barcelona, Spain

Abstract. Ensuring classification models are fair with respect to sensitive data attributes is a crucial task when applying machine learning models to real-world problems. Particularly in company production environments, where the decision output by models may have a direct impact on individuals and predictive performance should be maintained over time. In this article, build upon [17], we propose copies as a technique to mitigate the bias of trained algorithms in circumstances where the original data is not accessible and/or the models cannot be re-trained. In particular, we explore a simple methodology to build copies that replicate the learned decision behavior in the absence of sensitive attributes. We validate this methodology in the low-sensitive problem of superhero alignment. We demonstrate that this naïve approach to bias reduction is feasible in this problem and argue that copies can be further exploited to embed models with desiderata such as fair learning.

Keywords: Fairness · Superhero alignment · Bias reduction · Copying classifiers

1 Introduction

Machine learning is rapidly infiltrating critical areas of society that have a substantial impact on people's lives. From financial and insurance markets to medicine, citizen security or the criminal justice system, the tendency has prevailed in recent years to devolve decision making to machine learning models. This tendency is deeply rooted in the idea that algorithms provide an objective approach to social problems, as a reliable alternative to human cognitive biases.

However, while algorithms may escape prejudices, the data with which they are trained does not. Algorithms can only be as good as the data they are trained with and data is often imperfect [8]. Machine learning models that learn from labeled examples are susceptible to inheriting biases in the training data. Indeed,

© Springer Nature Switzerland AG 2019
A. Morales et al. (Eds.): IbPRIA 2019, LNCS 11867, pp. 182–193, 2019.
https://doi.org/10.1007/978-3-030-31332-6_16

they have been shown to reproduce existing patterns of discrimination [4,12]. So much so that algorithms are often biased against people with certain protected attributes like race [3,6,14,15], gender [5,7] or sexual orientation [11]. Studies on analogy generation using word embeddings have demonstrated that the popular Word2Vec space encodes gender biases that are potentially propagated to systems based on this technology [5]. Similarly, machines trained to learn word associations from written texts have been shown to display problematic attitudes towards race or gender [7]. Associations between female names and family or male names and career are particularly worrying consequences of this result. Besides these findings, examples of significant racial disparities in commercial software have also proliferated over the last years.

In light of these findings many works have studied how to create fairer algorithms [4,9,13] as well as to benchmark discrimination in various contexts. Fairness-aware learning has, as a matter of fact, received considerable attention in the machine learning community of late, with most solutions being aimed at introducing new formal metrics for fairness and ensuring that classifiers satisfy the desired levels of equity under such definitions.

Solutions to this problem often come in two types. In the first case, an exhaustive data preprocessing removes the ability to distinguish between group membership by getting rid of the sensible information in the training data [10]. This amounts to removing the sensitive attributes themselves, but also to ensuring no residual information is encoded by the remaining data. While simple, this approach often succeeds in repairing the original disparity. In the second case, unfairness is removed by adding corrective terms to the optimization function. A fairness metric [9,13] is defined and incorporated to the training algorithm. Initially biased models are therefore re-trained ensuring that the fairness measure is optimized together with the defined classification loss.

In this article we propose the use of copies as a technique to mitigate the bias of trained algorithms in circumstances where the original data is not accessible and/or the models cannot be re-trained. Copying [17] corresponds to the problem of building a machine learning model that replicates the decision behavior of another. This process not only reproduces the target decision function, but it may also be used to endow the considered classifier with new characteristics, such as interpretability, online learning or equity features. The use of copies has already been shown to improve model accuracy when ensuring decomposability of attributes in financial production environments where more explainable machine learning models are desirable [16].

Notably, in this paper we explore a potential use of copies in the context of fair prediction. In the simplest scenario, we use copies to remove sensitive attributes from the original classifier while maintaining its performance and reducing the unfairness in the resulting predictions. Further, we argue that desiderata such as equity of learning could be directly imposed upon copies to obtain more sophisticated solutions to the problem of fairness.

We validate our approach in a case study, where we obtain a new decision function from which the protected features are absent. Due to the generally sensible nature of data in this kind of studies, we carry our experiments using a proxy dataset. In particular, we use the superhero dataset [2], which contains socio-demografic data including gender and race, as well as personal traits and features in the form of superpowers for an extensive list of superheroes and villains. We use this data to predict superhero alignment. Nonetheless, the methodology proposed in this article is readily applicable to other real datasets that satisfy the same constraints (detailed in the experimental settings and discussion of the results). The main contributions of this article are the following:

- We introduce copies as a promising methodology for reducing unfairness in classification models.
- This methodology is agnostic to the internals of the classifiers and can be used in any classification setting where the model is considered as a *black-box*.
- Furthermore, we show that we can reduce the prediction bias even when original data is not available.

The rest of this paper is organized as follows. First, Sect. 2 presents a case study using the superhero dataset. Section 3 describes our proposed methodological approach. In Sect. 4, we carry out a set of experiments and in Sect. 5 we describe the results that empirically validate our theoretical proposal. Finally, the paper ends with our conclusions and future work in Sect. 6.

2   Case Study

In the following sections we explore how to reduce the bias inherited by a machine learning classifier which has been already trained using sensitive information and which cannot be modified. We do so by means of a fictitious example that nonetheless represents a use case common to many real scenarios. In particular, we use the publicly accessible superhero dataset, which contains information about a few hundred superheroes in the literature, including their physical attributes, powers and alignment. We choose this dataset in order to avoid using real sensitive data, as well as to enable an in-depth study of how the mechanism affects the different variables and instances.

This dataset serves as a good proxy to many real problems where data contains sensitive information. Among the many attributes in the superhero dataset, there are those that account for protected group features. This is the case, for example, of *gender* and *race*. Without the appropriate control, models trained on these attributes can lead to an unfair decision system. For this case study, we assume a classifier has been trained using both *gender* and *race* attributes and that it cannot be modified or re-trained to correct for any bias.

There exists many situations in which a new training may not be advisable, or even possible. This is the case, for example, of company production environments, where the predictive performance of models should be maintained in time. Another situation in which a new training is not an option is when the original training data is not available. This could either be because the data has been lost or because it is subject to privacy constrains or because the server where the data is hosted is not accessible any more. Whatever the cause of this lack of availability, the fact that the original data points are unknown, makes a new training impossible.

Under these circumstances we propose a methodology to build a copy of the trained model that is able to retain its predictive accuracy and from which we can remove the protected data attributes. Copies are new classifiers built to replicate the decision behavior of their target models. When copying, we can transfer the attributes of the original model to the copy, while at the same time including new characteristics during the process.

3   Methodological Proposal

In this section we describe our approach to mitigate the bias induced by the existence of protected data attributes in superhero alignment prediction models. We first present the copying methodology and then describe how this methodology can be exploited to remove protected attributes from copies. Note that the full theoretical background for copying is developed in [17]. We refer the reader to this reference for a full description of the different elements and processes that come into play. We here only provide an overview of this framework.

3.1   Copying Machine Learning Classifiers

Let us assume a set of data pairs $X = \{x_i, t_i\}$ for $i = 1, ..., M$, where the x_i are d-dimensional data points and t_i their corresponding labels. In the case of a binary classification problem, we assume these labels to be such that $t_i \in \{0, 1\}$. We define a classifier as a function $f : x \to t$ from input instances to targets. Under the copying framework, we refer to the set X as the *original dataset* and define the *original model*, $f_\mathcal{O}$, as a classifier trained using this data. Copying then corresponds to the problem of building a new model $f_C(\theta)$, parameterized by θ, such that it replicates the behavior of $f_\mathcal{O}$.

In order to build this new model, we do not exploit the original training data X. Instead, we refer to the original decision function $f_\mathcal{O}$. To do this we need to introduce a set of labelled pairs $Z = \{(z_j, y_j)\}$ for $j = 1, ..., N$, where $\{z_1, ..., z_N\}$ are artificially generated data points and $\{y_1, ..., y_N\}$ their labels predicted by the original, so that $y_j = f_\mathcal{O}(z_j)$. We refer to Z as the *synthetic dataset* and use it to access the information in $f_\mathcal{O}$ through its prediction $f_\mathcal{O}(z_j)$ for any given sample. The problem of copying can then be written as

$$\theta^* = \arg\max_\theta \int_{z \sim P_Z} P(\theta|f_\mathcal{O}(z))dP_Z, \qquad (1)$$

Under the empirical risk minimization framework we can cast the equation above into a dual optimization problem where we simultaneously optimize the model parameters θ, the synthetic dataset Z and a probability distribution P_Z over the sampling space. Given a defined empirical loss $R_{emp}(f_C, f_\mathcal{O})$ we can define such a problem as

$$\underset{\theta, Z}{\text{minimize}} \quad \Omega(\theta)$$

$$\text{subject to} \quad \|R_{emp}^{Pz}(f_C, f_O) - R_{emp}^{Pz}(f_C^\dagger, f_O)\| < \epsilon, \tag{2}$$

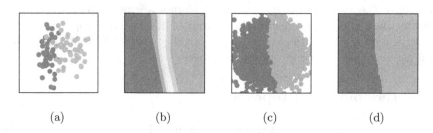

(a)   (b)   (c)   (d)

Fig. 1. Example plots for (a) the *original dataset*, (b) the *original decision function*, (c) the *synthetic dataset* and (d) the *copy decision function*.

for ϵ a defined tolerance, $\Omega(\theta)$ a measure of the capacity of the copy model and $f_C^\dagger$ the copy model obtained as a solution to the corresponding unconstrained problem. Roughly speaking, the capacity of a model describes how complex a relationship it can model. A direct way to estimate the capacity of a model is to count the number of parameters. The more parameters, the higher the capacity in general, although this rule can be wrong in many situations.

In this article we restrict to the simplest approach to this problem, the *single-pass copy* [17]. We cast the simultaneous optimization problem into one where we only use only a single iteration of an alternating projection optimization scheme. Thus, we effectively split the problem in two independent sub-problems. We first find an optimal set of synthetic data points Z^* and then optimize for the copy parameters θ^*.

In Fig. 1 we show an example of the different steps during a single-pass copy. The data points in Fig. 1(a) represent a randomly generated binary classification dataset. We learn this data using a multilayer perceptron that outputs the decision function displayed in Fig. 1(b). We sample the original attribute domain following a random normal distribution and label the resulting data points according to the predictions of the original classifier. The resulting synthetic dataset is shown in Fig. 1(c). Finally, we fit this data using a decision tree classifier. The decision function learned by this model, the form of which replicates that of the original classifier, is shown in Fig. 1(d).

3.2   Using Copies to Remove Sensitive Data

When copying, we can transfer model features from one model to another [16,17]. For one thing, we can ensure the original accuracy is retained by building a copy that replicates the original decision behavior to a high degree of fidelity. Moreover, this can be done by imposing the new characteristics such as considering only self-explanatory features or removing biased attributes upon the copy. In doing so, we can understand copying as a mechanism to correct pre-existing biases.

Our proposed solution is of particular importance when models are trained in the absence of an external auditing or which are now subject to a regulation that they were previously excluded from. Existing techniques to remove bias or correct unfairness often rely in a new training of the model: change the optimization function to ensure certain constraints are satisfied or remove sensitive variables. However, this is not always possible. For example, in models in production we may not have the specifics or even access to the original data.

In the simplest approach, in order to ensure prediction equity, we require the model not to have access to sensitive data with the additional constraint that this information not be leaked through the remaining attributes. In the copying framework this can be accomplished by changing the input space of the copy, characterized by Z. During the synthetic sample generation process, we can remove the sensitive data attributes that were present in the original training dataset X. In removing this attributes, we ensure the copy has no access no the sensitive information. Because the copying model replicates the behavior of the original black-box model one expects the copy to maximize its performance even in the lack of the sensitive data.

4   Experiments

We use superheroes dataset [1], which describes characteristics such as demographics, powers, physical attributes and studio of origin of every superhero and villain in SuperHeroDb [2]. In what follows we describe the experimental set up, including the original dataset preprocessing, original model training, synthetic sample generation and, finally, the copy model building; as well as the metrics we use to evaluate our results.

Original Dataset. The dataset contains information about 177 attributes for 660 superheroes. We remove all entries with an unknown alignment label. We also discard all attributes for which the number of missing values exceeds the 20% of the total size of the dataset. For the remaining columns, we set all missing values to the median for numerical attributes and to *other*, in the case of categorical variables. For the latter, we also group under the general category *other* all values with a count below a certain threshold. We set this threshold to 1% for variable *eye color* and to 10% for *publisher*. In the case of *race* we group all entries under the general categories *human*, *mutant*, *robot*, *extraterrestial* and *other*. Additionally, we impose that for superhero powers the sum be above the 1% of the total number of entries. Finally, we convert nominal attributes to numerical by means of one-hot encoding and re-scale all variables to zero-mean and unit variance. The resulting dataset contains 135 variables. We use this data to define a binary classification problem choosing superhero alignment as the target attribute. We label as *good* all superheroes marked as so and identify as *bad* all other entries, including those labelled as bad, neutral or unknown. In other words, we assume every superhero not explicitly labelled as good to be bad. The distribution of target labels is slightly unbalanced, with a third of the dataset belonging to the positive label, *good*, and the remaining two thirds labelled as *bad*. We split this data into stratified 80/20 training and test sets.

Original Model. We use the resulting binary classification dataset to train a fully-connected artificial neural network with 4 hidden layers, each consisting of 128, 64, 32 and 16 neurons. We use *SeLu* activations, a drop-out of 0.6 and a softmax cross entropy loss optimized using *Adam* optimizer for a learning rate equal to $1e-3$. We train the network from a random initialization of weights and without any pretraining. We use balanced batches with a fixed size of 32. We assume this model as a baseline biased model.

Synthetic Sample Generation Process. We generate the synthetic dataset using different sampling strategies for numerical and categorical attributes. For the first, we directly generate synthetic data points in the original attribute domain by sampling a random normal distribution with mean 0 and standard deviation 1. In the case of categorical variables, we sample uniformly at random the original category set. When generating new synthetic values for superhero powers, we ensure that the relationships among the original data attributes are kept. To do so, we sample uniformly at random the *n_powers* variable and then randomly distribute the total count over the individual power attributes. Following the guidelines in [17], we generate a balanced synthetic dataset consisting of $1e6$ labelled data pairs, from which we extract the two problematic attributes. We use this dataset as a training set.

Copy Model. We use the lower-dimensional synthetic dataset to learn a new artificial neural network with the same architecture and training protocol as that of the original model, with a fixed batch size to 512 and a drop-out rate of 0.9.

Performance Metrics. We measure the extent to which the copy replicates the original decision behavior following the metrics described in [17]. In particular, we report the empirical fidelity error over both the synthetic dataset, $R_{\mathcal{F}}^{\mathcal{Z}}$, and the original dataset, $R_{\mathcal{F}}^{\mathcal{X}}$; and the copy accuracy, $\mathcal{A}_{\mathcal{C}}$. The first two give a level of disagreement between original and copy over a common set of data points, while the latter corresponds to the generalization performance of the copy in the original data environment. Additionally, we measure the presence of bias by evaluating the difference in accuracy over the *gender* and *race* groups.

Validation. We run each experiment 10 times and evaluate the performance of copies using test sets comprised of $1e6$ synthetic points. For validation purposes, we assume both the original accuracy and the original dataset to be known in all cases and report average metrics over all repetitions.

5 Discussion of Results

In what follows we discuss our experimental results. We begin by checking that the problem conditions are such that the two sensitive attributes can be safely removed from the synthetic dataset. On this basis, we evaluate copy performance in terms of the defined metrics. Finally, we show how the removal of the protected variable results in a shift in the original decision boundary that mitigates the bias effect in the resulting decision behavior.

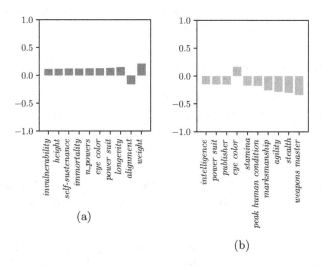

Fig. 2. Top ten ranked attributes in terms of their one-to-one correlation coefficient with (a) *gender* and (b) *race*. The ranking is computed taking the absolute value.

Hypothesis Testing. In many real scenarios, systematic bias results in individuals belonging to privileged and unprivileged groups not having access to the same resources, a reality that could very well be reflected in the data attributes of each group. Hence, before proceeding proposal, we ascertain the feasibility of our approach: we verify that the removal of the two sensitive attributes will not result in any residual leakage of information into the copies. This could happen, for example, if the remaining variables encode information that could be traced back to each superhero's *gender* or *race*, even in the absence of this data. In order to ensure that the sensitive attributes can be safely removed in our case, we first check that no other variable is correlated with *gender* and *race*.

In Fig. 2 we report the top ten ranked attributes in terms of their one-to-one correlation with these two variables. We show that at most, this correlation is equal to 0.18 in the case of variable *gender* and to 0.35 in the case of *race*. Thus, we conclude that there exist no residual information left in the synthetic dataset after the removal of these attributes and that we can therefore safely remove them without incurring in any leakage of information. Note that for this particular check we use the original dataset.

Evaluating the Copy Performance. Having established that our proposed approach is feasible, in Table 1 we report our results when replicating the original decision function using the variable-removed copies. The original network yields an accuracy, $\mathcal{A}_O$, of 0.65. The copy, in turn, obtains a copy accuracy, $\mathcal{A}_C$, of 0.65 ± 0.01 averaged over all runs. Notably, the loss in accuracy we incur when substituting the original with the copy in the original data space is close to zero in most cases. Thus, we incur in no effective loss when deploying the copy instead of the original to predict new data points.

Table 1. Performance metrics for original and copy models.

$\mathcal{A}_O$	$R^Z_{\mathcal{F}}$	$R^X_{\mathcal{F}}$	$\mathcal{A}_C$
0.65	0.059 ± 0.003	0.22 ± 0.01	0.66 ± 0.01

The empirical fidelity error measured over the synthetic dataset, $R^Z_{\mathcal{F}}$, is equal to 0.031 ± 0.001. This value represents the residual error when learning the optimal copy model parameters to fit the original decision function encoded by the synthetic data points. Finally, the mean empirical fidelity error evaluated over the original test data, $R^X_{\mathcal{F}}$, is 0.25 ± 0.01. This value corresponds to the level of agreement between original and copy when generalizing the prediction to new unobserved points in the original data environment. The value of this last error is specially relevant when understanding how the copy is able to replicate the original decision function in the absence of the sensitive information. Removal of the protected attributes from the synthetic dataset results in a certain shift in the learned decision function, with respect to the original. To better understand how this shift impacts the classification of individual data points, we further study the value of the reported performance metrics over the different groups.

Evaluating Bias Reduction. The results above confirm a good fit of the copy to the original predictive performance. On this basis, we evaluate the difference in behavior derived from the removal of the sensitive data attributes in the copy. In Table 2 we report the mean accuracies by *gender* group for original and copy. We observe that there exist significant differences in the predictive accuracy of the original model across the different gender populations. In particular, *male* superheroes are more usually wrongly classified than *female*. This is a clear sign of the presence of bias in the original classifier. Independently of whether the decision depends on the *gender* attribute it does affect the different groups in a disparate form. When compared to the results obtained by the copy, we observe that the disparity among *male* and *female* groups is notably reduced in the latter. In particular, the difference in accuracy among groups goes from 0.09 for the original to 0.03 for the copy. As a result, the decisions output by the copy have a more balanced impact on individuals in both populations.

Table 2. Accuracy by *gender* groups for original and copy models.

	Original	Copy
female	0.73	0.69
male	0.64	0.66

To better characterize the results in the table above, we further provide the confusion matrices for the two gender groups. Thus, Fig. 3(a), (b), (c) and (d) show the relation between true and false positives and negatives for data points in groups *male* and *female* for original and copy, respectively. We observe how in the case of the *male* group, the number of true positives increases for the copy, while the opposite effect is seen for the case of *female*. The net effect of this is the balancing of predictive accuracy between both groups.

Table 3. Accuracy by *race* group for original and copy models.

	Original	Copy
human	0.78	0.76
mutant	0.75	0.75
robot	0.67	0.5
extraterrestial	0.25	0.5
other	0.59	0.64

Importantly, these results are also observed for the case of the *race* attribute, albeit less strongly. As shown in Table 3, the mean accuracies by group tend to balance in the case of the copy. This is clearly observed in the two majority classes, namely *humans* and *mutants*. In the minority classes we also see the benefits of the proposal for the group *extraterrestial* which is more often incorrectly classified by the original.

We conclude that this simple approach, does result in a certain mitigation of the bias for the *gender* attribute. Moreover, it shows the potential of copies when used to tackle the issue of fair learning. These results pave the way for more complex treatments of the fairness problem by means of copies. Following our approach, one could, for example, endow copies with fairness metrics such as equity of learning or equality of odds, so that the resulting classifier retains the original accuracy while at the same time optimizing for this new measures.

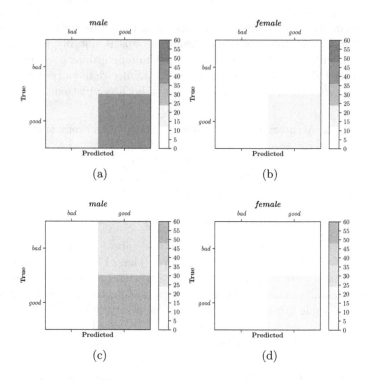

Fig. 3. Confusion matrices for *male* and *female* gender groups for (a) and (b) the original model and (c) and (d) the copy.

6   Conclusions and Future Work

In this paper we propose and validate a methodology to reduce the unfairness in machine learning classifiers by removing sensitive attributes from the training data. We present a case study using data from the SuperHero database. We train a classifier to learn the superhero alignment using all the data attributes. We then build a copy of this model by removing all the sensitive information. Our results demonstrate that this process can be performed without loss of accuracy and that it can be further exploited to mitigate biases of the original classifier with respect to sensitive attributes such as *gender* or *race*. Our proposed method allows us to redefine the learned decision function to get rid of the sensitive information without risk of leakage.

We here purposely use a fictitious dataset to conduct our experiments. Future work should focus on extending this technique to real datasets where correcting discriminative biases towards sensitive attributes may be crucial to ensure a fair classification. Importantly, this article shows the potential of copies in the study of fairness. Future research should move on from this approach to explore more complex methods for bias reduction in the presence of constraints such as the impossibility to re-train the models or access the original data.

Acknowledgment. This work has been partially funded by the Spanish project TIN2016-74946-P (MINECO/FEDER, UE), and by AGAUR of the Generalitat de Catalunya through the Industrial PhD grant 2017-DI-25. We gratefully acknowledge the support of BBVA Data & Analytics for sponsoring the Industrial PhD.

References

1. Super Heroes Dataset, Kaggle. https://www.kaggle.com/claudiodavi/superhero-set
2. Superhero Database. https://www.superherodb.com/
3. Angwin, J., Larson, J., Mattu, S., Kirchner, L.: Machine bias: there's software used across the country to predict future criminals. And it's biased against blacks. ProPublica (2016)
4. Barocas, S., Selbst, A.D.: Big data's disparate impact. Calif. Law Rev. **104**(671), 671–732 (2016)
5. Bolukbasi, T., Chang, K.W., Zou, J., Saligrama, V., Kalai, A.: Man is to computer programmer as woman is to homemaker? Debiasing word embeddings. In: Proceedings of the Conference on Neural Information Processing Systems (NIPS), pp. 4356–4364 (2016)
6. Buolamwini, J., Gebru, T.: Gender shades: intersectional accuracy disparities in commercial gender classification *. In: Proceedings of Machine Learning Research, vol. 81, pp. 1–15 (2018)
7. Caliskan, A., Bryson, J.J., Narayanan, A.: Semantics derived automatically from language corpora contain human-like biases. Science **356**(6334), 183–186 (2017)
8. Crawford, K.: The Hidden Biases in Big Data. Harvard Business Review (2013)
9. Dwork, C., Hardt, M., Pitassi, T., Reingold, O., Zemel, R.: Fairness through awareness. In: Proceedings of the 3rd Innovations in Theoretical Computer Science Conference, pp. 214–226 (2012)
10. Feldman, M., Friedler, S.A., Moeller, J., Scheidegger, C., Venkatasubramanian, S.: Certifying and removing disparate impact. In: Proceedings of the ACM SIGKDD International Conference on Knowledge Discovery and Data Mining (KDD), pp. 259–268 (2015)
11. Guha, S., Cheng, B., Francis, P.: Challenges in measuring online advertising systems. In: Proceedings of ACM International Conference on Data Communications (SIGCOMM), pp. 81–87 (2010)
12. Hardt, M.: How big data is unfair (2014). https://medium.com/@mrtz/how-big-data-is-unfair-9aa544d739de
13. Hardt, M., Price, E., Srebro, N.: Equality of opportunity in supervised learning. In: Proceedings of Conference on Neural Information Processing Systems (NIPS), pp. 3323–3331 (2016)
14. Klare, B.F., Burge, M.J., Klontz, J.C., Bruegge, R.W.V., Jain, A.K.: Face recognition performance: role of demographic information. IEEE Trans. Inf. Forensics Secur. **7**(6), 1789–1801 (2012)
15. Popejoy, A.B., Fullerton, S.M.: Genomics is failing on diversity. Nature **538**, 161–164 (2016)
16. Unceta, I., Nin, J., Pujol, O.: Towards global explanations for credit risk scoring. eprint arXiv:1811.07698 (2018). http://arxiv.org/abs/1811.07698
17. Unceta, I., Nin, J., Pujol, O.: Copying machine learning classifiers. eprint arXiv:1903.01879 (2019)

Weighted Multisource Tradaboost

João Antunes[1,2(✉)], Alexandre Bernardino[2(✉)], Asim Smailagic[1(✉)],
and Daniel Siewiorek[1(✉)]

[1] Carnegie Mellon University, Pittsburgh, PA, USA
{joaoa,ds1p}@andrew.cmu.edu, asim@cs.cmu.edu
[2] Instituto Superior Técnico, Lisboa, Portugal
alexandre.bernardino.pt@ieee.org

Abstract. In this paper we propose an improved method for transfer learning that takes into account the balance between target and source data. This method builds on the state-of-the-art Multisource Tradaboost, but weighs the importance of each datapoint taking into account the amount of target and source data available. A comparative study is then presented exposing the performance of four transfer learning methods as well as the proposed Weighted Multisource Tradaboost. The experimental results show that the proposed method is able to outperform the base method as the number of target samples increase. These results are promising in the sense that source-target ratio weighing may be a path to improve current methods of transfer learning. However, against the asymptotic conjecture of [6], all transfer learning methods tested in this work get outperformed by a no-transfer SVM for large number on target samples.

Keywords: Transfer learning · TrAdaboost · Random decision forests

1 Introduction

Most machine learning techniques are based on the PAC (Probably Approximately Correct) [7] model, which states that while operating on a learning problem the samples used for training and the samples that we want to classify follow the same probability distribution. However, this assumption does not hold in a variety of cases. Frequently, the data used for training has become obsolete (e.g. due to changes on how data was collected) or simply that the data available is not enough to train a robust classifier. Insufficient data frequently occurs in classifiers that recognize a high number of classes (e.g. in object recognition systems routinely discriminate between $\approx 10^4$ categories) [5]. In this case, machine learning techniques give very little guarantees about the generalization error obtained. Transfer Learning is an approach to address the small dataset challenge. The intuition behind transfer learning is to mimic the way humans learn. The data we acquire from all our senses is stored in our memory along with concepts and inferences we make as to how to categorize this data. This makes it so that any

A. Morales et al. (Eds.): IbPRIA 2019, LNCS 11867, pp. 194–205, 2019.
https://doi.org/10.1007/978-3-030-31332-6_17

new concept to be assimilated is not learned in isolation. Instead, we consider connections between what we already know and try to apply them to the new concept. The goal of transfer learning is to extract relevant information from data that does not need to come from the same probability distribution as the data to be classified by the final model. The ability to leverage more data during the learning process leads to more robust models since more information is used for training. In this paper, an improvement on a state-of-the-art transfer learning method is presented: Weighted Multisource Tradaboost. Our proposed approach incorporates the belief that if more target data is available, the contribution of the source data used in the model should gradually shift from model defining to fine-tuning. This is achieved with a re-weighing procedure. A comparative study is then provided between four state-of-the-art methods: Multisource Tradaboost [7], Task Tradaboost [7], Multi-KT [5], transfer learning decision forests [3], and Weighted Multisource Tradaboost. This study is evaluated on a subset of four classes of the Caltech-256 Dataset [4]. In turn, one of each of the four classes used is the target, while the other are used as sources. The classes chosen are dog, horse, leopard and zebra, chosen for empirically possessing a positive relationship with each other. The results show that our method can overcome the other methods in accuracy performance, but the higher asymptote assumption is still not achieved. This assumption states that a method employing transfer learning should outperform machine learning methods without transfer even when target data is abundant [6].

The contributions described in this paper are a comparative study exhibiting results not found in the literature, stating that the higher asymptote behavior theorized in [6] is not achieved by several state-of-the-art methods, and a novel approach for transfer learning that addresses this limitation of the methods studied. Although this limitation is not surpassed the method is showing a way to improve transfer learning approaches towards the theoretical asymptotic performance that can be applied in several transfer learning methods.

The rest of this document is organized as follows: Sect. 2 describes necessary concepts and notation introduced by transfer Learning. Section 3 describes the methods studied in this document. Section 4 describes the experiment ran, and the results obtained are discussed in Sect. 5. Finally, our conclusions and possible future research directions are presented in Sect. 6.

2   Transfer Learning

Transfer learning introduces several new concepts to machine learning. The definitions and notation described here will be used throughout this paper.

Standard machine learning tries to learn and then classify using one dataset for training and another one for testing. Both these datasets are assumed to come from the same distribution. In transfer learning information is leveraged from additional sources. The dataset that has the same distribution as the test data is called the target, and other(s) is(are) called source(s).

In this paper, the methods studied assume all datasets lie in the same feature space. This is called homogeneous transfer learning. If the feature space is

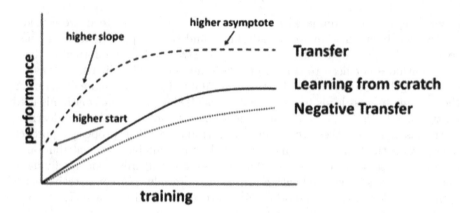

Fig. 1. Three different ways in which transfer learning may improve traditional machine learning as a function of the number of target training samples: Higher Start, Higher Slope and Higher Asymptote (See Sect. 2). Use of sources with no relation with the target may lead to the behavior described by the Negative Transfer curve. Figure adapted from [5].

different for at least one of the sources it is heterogeneous transfer learning (see MultiK-KT in [5]).

The success of transfer learning hinges on the inherent relationship between target and sources. In the case of a weak/non-existent connection between source and target the final classifier may actually be worse than its no-transfer counterpart. This phenomenon is known as negative transfer.

There are three measures by which transfer may improve learning [6] (see Fig. 1): Higher Start (better performance at the beginning of learning since source information is leveraged), Higher Slope (using the transferred knowledge the new task can be learned faster), and Higher Asymptote (since more information is being leveraged, the final system should have better performance). As shall be seen by the study presented in this paper, the Higher Asymptote hypothesis doesn't always hold true, even when a positive relationship between source and target can be established (See Sect. 5).

Finally, there is one more distinction between two types of transfer: instance transfer and task transfer. Instance transfer refers to scenarios in which some of the source data can actually be used to help train the new model. MultiSource-Tradaboost is an example of this scenario. In task transfer, the source tasks are described explicitly by models trained *a priori*. Multi-KT and TaskTradaboost are examples of this type of transfer.

3   State-of-the-Art

The methods compared in this paper comprise the recent state-of-the-art approached used in low data transfer learning. The methods are now described in detail.

3.1 Multi-KT - Support Vector Machines [5]

In 2014, Tommasi *et al.* [5] proposed a formulation for transfer learning using Support Vector Machines (SVM). Their problem setting was as follows: Assume that j old (source) models (described by $\hat{w}_j$) are available *a priori*, and that these models can be expressed as a weighted sum of kernel functions (*e.g.* obtained *a priori* from an off-the-shelf SVM package). Then, in order to leverage the information already encoded in the other models, a simple framework is presented: change the cost function of an SVM solver to include a term imposing "model fidelity" (*i.e.* the cost function of the new model w must be close to a weighted sum of the pre-existing j models) (see Eq. 1).

$$\operatorname*{argmin}_{w,b,\xi} \quad \frac{1}{2}\left\|w - \sum_{j=1}^{J}\beta_j\hat{w}_j\right\|^2 + C\sum_{i=1}^{n}\zeta_i\xi_i^2$$
$$\text{subject to} \quad y_i(w^T\phi(x_i) - b) \geq 1 - \xi_i,$$
$$\xi_i \geq 0$$

(1)

where ζ_i are used to balance the contribution of positive and negative samples, taking into account their proportion in the training set, β_i are real numbers that control the influence that each *old* model should have over the new model (estimated *via* minimizing the leave-one-out error). The rest are components that make up a standard SVM formulation (*i.e.* $\|w\|$ ensures margin maximization, $C\sum_{i=1}^{n}\zeta_i\xi_i^2$ encodes the trade-off between model fidelity and margin maximization and data fidelity; and the constraints ensure data fidelity).

3.2 Transfer Learning Decision Forests (TLDF) [3]

In 2014, Goussies *et al.* [3], proposed a method to do transfer learning using random decision forests. This is a method that uses data from several sources to shape the decision regions. Considering $N + 1$ classification tasks, $T_0, \ldots, T_N$, the goal is to solve the classification task T_0, called the target task, using the knowledge of all tasks. By leveraging information from all datasets at once, the regions generated by the decision splits of each tree in the forest will construct a classifier with a higher classification accuracy, since more information is taken into account when shaping the decision regions (see Fig. 2).

Goussies *et al.* go on to propose a mixed information gain formulation that formalizes the intuition described. For the k-th split:

$$\theta_k^* = \operatorname*{argmax}_{\theta_k}(1 - \gamma)\mathcal{I}_0(\theta_k) + \gamma\sum_{n=1}^{N}\mathcal{I}_n(\theta_k)$$

(2)

where $\mathcal{I}_0$ is the information gain on the target dataset (that stems from split θ_k) and $\mathcal{I}_n, n = 1, \ldots, N$ are the information gains on the source datasets (stemming from the same split). γ is a trade-off parameter that regulates the importance given to the information gain on the source and target datasets.

Fig. 2. Consider two tasks (red and green), each with two labels (stars and crosses for the red task, circles and squares for the green task). The red task is the target task, the green task is a source task. All three hyperplanes shown in the figure separate the target (red) dataset perfectly. The hyperplane represented in black, however, separates all the data from all the datasets simultaneously. According to the thinking presented in [3] the black hyperplane is preferable, and should be a better minimizer of the generalisation error. Image adapted from [3]. (Color figure online)

From this formulation a new problem arises: the leaf nodes of the tree are not required to have any datapoint belonging to the target. So, after creating a tree, a label propagation procedure is applied. For a given leaf node without a single target datapoint a distance vector is constructed with the distance from that node to all other leaf nodes that have at least one target datapoint. Then, the prediction made by the closest leaf node possessing at least one target datapoint is copied to the current node without target datapoints. The distance measure used is a Mahalanobis distance using the estimated mean and estimated covariance of the leaf nodes involved.

3.3 TrAdaboost

In 2007, Dai *et al.* proposed TrAdaboost [1], a transfer learning variant of AdaBoost. In 2010, Yao and Doretto [7], proposed two boosting models that perform transfer learning from multiple sources: MultiSource TrAdaboost and TaskTradaboost. Adaboost works as follows: At each iteration a weak classifier is trained. Then, the samples in the training set are re-weighted, increasing the weight of misclassified samples. This forces the next weak classifier trained to focus on getting the misclassified samples right. As such, expert models are being created for all the regions of the feature space of the dataset. Then, a final classifier is constructed by weighted majority voting of all the weak classifiers. The extensions proposed by Yao and Doretto in Tradaboost included:

MultiSource TrAdaboost [7]. For the MultiSource TrAdaboost model, proposed by Yao and Doretto [7] the availability of a very small target dataset is complemented by the availability of several larger datasets to be used as source. Information for all the datasets is leveraged by multiplexing between datasets in each iteration. When training one of the weak classifiers to boost, the target dataset is complemented by the source dataset that appears to be the most closely related to the target (*i.e.* the one that leads the weak classifier to the lowest error in the target dataset in the current iteration). Then, the weights of the datapoints in all the datasets are readjusted. However, unlike in Adaboost where misclassified points have their weight increased, the re-weighting procedure differs depending on which dataset is being used. Points in the target dataset have their weight increased if they are misclassified. On the other hand, misclassified points in any source dataset have their weight reduced. This is to express the belief that if a point in a source dataset is presenting conflicting information with the target dataset,then transfer from that datapoint should be avoided. The precise algorithm used is shown in Fig. 3, taken from [7].

Task TrAdaboost [7]. The TaskTrAdaboost performs transfer from previously available models, instead of from other datasets. It is divided in two phases.

Phase I consists of training off-the-shelf Adaboost models on each of the source datasets available.

Phase II mimics Adaboost by boosting several weak classifiers on a weighted dataset. However, in TaskTradaboost the weak models used are the Adaboost models trained on the source datasets. The weight update step in this algorithm is identical to the one in Adaboost.

Weighted Multisource Tradaboost. When using transfer learning, information from both target and source datasets is leveraged. Naturally, most strategies have some way to weigh the data according to the prior belief of how similar the target data's and the source data's distribution is (*i.e.:* the β_j in Multi-KT, the γ parameter in TLDF's, and the weight vectors $w_i^{S_k}$ and w_i^T in Tradaboost). However, to our knowledge, no method incorporates the proportion of target and source data available as prior knowledge in the mixing of target and source information in the learning stage.

We believe this approach to be sound because, if more target data is available, the contribution of the source data used in the model should gradually shift from model defining to fine-tuning. We postulate this is the case because as more target data becomes available, the model built using only target data becomes more and more robust. In that case, forcing the model to accommodate source data can actually be detrimental to the model's performance. We shall prove this with a comparative study in the results section.

Our approach follows the general method described by Tradaboost but replaces the weight update rules defined in step 10 of the algorithm (see Fig. 3) to take into account the proportion of target and source data available.

Instead, we propose:

$$w_i^{S_k} \leftarrow w_i^{S_k} e^{-\eta \alpha_S |h_t(x_i^{S_k}) - y_i^{S_k}|}$$

$$or \qquad (3)$$

$$w_i^{S_k} \leftarrow w_i^{S_k} \eta e^{-\alpha_S |h_t(x_i^{S_k}) - y_i^{S_k}|}$$

$$w_i^{T} \leftarrow w_i^{T} e^{\eta \alpha_T |h_t(x_i^{T}) - y_i^{T}|}$$

$$or \qquad (4)$$

$$w_i^{T} \leftarrow w_i^{T} \eta e^{\alpha_T |h_t(x_i^{T}) - y_i^{T}|}$$

where η is a term that depends on the amount of target and source data available for training. The same term can be used for both target and source datapoints because the weight update step (shown in Eqs. 3 and 4) inverts the signal of the exponent when switching dataset. Strategies for how to define this quantity are discussed in Sect. 4.

4   Experimental Design

We compare all the methods described in Sect. 3 with a subset of the Caltech-256 Dataset [4]. This is a dataset composed of 256 classes, with images as datapoints. The images range from high-quality pictures to poor drawings of the subject of the class. A subset of 4 classes was chosen from those available: dog, horse, leopard and zebra as well as the background class. These classes were shown to test positive transfer from empirically related classes: 4-legged animals. For these classes we downloaded the Scale Invariant Feature Transform (SIFT) features from [2] (See [2] for details). These features have a dimension of 300.

The results presented are averaged over 5 tests done with random permutations of the data. For each test, the results are averaged over 4 runs, each with a different 4-legged animal as target. As such, all experiments are averaged over twenty runs. Finally, the tests are run with the number of target points available ranging from 1 to 10.

For comparison with the no-transfer scenario, an off-the-shelf SVM classifier is trained exclusively on the target data.

4.1   Method Hyperparameters

For Multi-KT the C parameter (see Eq. 1) is chosen via cross-validation on the source data. The β_j parameters are chosen by minimizing the leave-one-out error. In [5] feature fusion is used. For fairness of comparison with the other methods only SIFT features were used.

For the Random Forests methods the parameters were decided according to the values found in the literature instead of chosen by testing different values for the parameters. This was due to the long time needed for each run of this method. The parameters used were: $\gamma = 0.8$ (Controls the influence of sources and target when calculating splits), Maximum tree depth = 10, number of trees in a forest = 3.

For MultiSource Tradaboost and Task Tradaboost the only hyperparameter is the number of iterations to run. This value was set at 50 due to computational limitations.

For Weighted Multisource Tradaboost 2 different values were empirically chosen for testing:

- $\eta = \frac{N_T * 100}{N_S}$
- $\eta = \frac{N_T^2 * 100}{N_S}$

where N_T is the number of target datapoints and N_S is the number of source datapoints. The factor of 100 inserted in the numerator describes the belief that in most transfer learning settings target data will be scarce while source data will be abundant. So both these terms enforce that the influence of source samples will be greatly diminished as more target samples become available. Each of these values was tested on both variants shown in Eqs. 3 and 4, resulting in four different tests.

For comparison with the no-transfer scenario, an off-the-shelf SVM classifier is trained exclusively on the target data. The hyperparameters for this model are the same as those used for Multi-KT but setting all the β_j to 0.

5 Results

Running the comparative study of the methods described in Sect. 3 on the Caltech-256 Dataset, the graph on Fig. 4 was drawn.

As can be observed in Fig. 4, the no transfer scenario outperforms all other approaches when 10 target samples are available. None of the methods studied are able to achieve the higher asymptote behaviour [6] (see Sect. 2).

All methods studied outperform the no-transfer approach in scenarios where the number of target samples available is very limited, up to 7 target samples.

The fact that all methods get overtaken when more target data is available suggests that once "high-quality" (target) data is available in sufficient quantity the methods are unable to extract information from the sources in a way that is not conflicting with the targets. This implies that further protection from negative transfer is required.

The TLDF method shows very unstable performance. Also, results have been found in the literature stating that this method outperforms no-transfer in cases where more target data is available. Only 1-10 target datapoints are available in our experiment, and this amount of data is not enough to populate a feature space with a dimension of 300. Since the feature space is sparsely populated, during the label propagation step the distances between leaf nodes with no target datapoints and the closest leaf node with a target can be immense, which could justify the instability found.

Algorithm 1: *MultiSourceTrAdaBoost*

Input: Source training data $D_{S_1}, \cdots, D_{S_N}$, target training data D_T, and the maximum number of iterations M

Output: Target classifier function $\hat{f}_T : \mathcal{X} \to \mathcal{Y}$

1 Set $\alpha_S \doteq \frac{1}{2}\ln\left(1 + \sqrt{2\ln\frac{n_S}{M}}\right)$, where $n_S \doteq \sum_k n_{S_k}$

2 Initialize the weight vector $(\mathbf{w}^{S_1}, \cdots, \mathbf{w}^{S_N}, \mathbf{w}^T)$, where

$\mathbf{w}^{S_k} \doteq (w_1^{S_k}, \cdots, w_{n_{S_k}}^{S_k})$, and $\mathbf{w}^T \doteq (w_1^T, \cdots, w_{n_T}^T)$ to the desired distribution

for $t \leftarrow 1$ **to** M **do**

3 $\qquad$ Empty the set of candidate weak classifiers, $\mathcal{F} \leftarrow \emptyset$

4 $\qquad$ Normalize to 1 the weight vector $(\mathbf{w}^{S_1}, \cdots, \mathbf{w}^{S_N}, \mathbf{w}^T)$

$\qquad$ **for** $k \leftarrow 1$ **to** N **do**

5 $\qquad\qquad$ Find the candidate weak classifier $h_t^k : \mathcal{X} \to \mathcal{Y}$ that minimizes the classification error over the combined set $D_{S_k} \bigcup D_T$, weighted according to $(\mathbf{w}^{S_k}, \mathbf{w}^T)$

6 $\qquad\qquad$ Compute the error of h_t^k on D_T:

$$\epsilon_t^k \doteq \sum_j \frac{w_j^T [y_j^T \neq h_t^k(\mathbf{x}_j^T)]}{\sum_i w_i^T}$$

7 $\qquad\qquad$ $\mathcal{F} \leftarrow \mathcal{F} \cup (h_t^k, \epsilon_t^k)$

8 $\qquad$ Find the weak classifier $h_t : \mathcal{X} \to \mathcal{Y}$ such that

$$(h_t, \epsilon_t) \doteq \arg\min_{(h,\epsilon)\in\mathcal{F}} \epsilon$$

9 $\qquad$ Set $\alpha_t \doteq \frac{1}{2}\ln\frac{1-\epsilon_t}{\epsilon_t}$, where $\epsilon_t < 1/2$

10 $\qquad$ Update the weight vector

$$\begin{aligned} w_i^{S_k} &\leftarrow w_i^{S_k} e^{-\alpha_S |h_t(\mathbf{x}_i^{S_k}) - y_i^{S_k}|} \\ w_i^T &\leftarrow w_i^T e^{\alpha_t |h_t(\mathbf{x}_i^T) - y_i^T|} \end{aligned}$$

return $\hat{f}_T(\mathbf{x}) \doteq \text{sign}\left(\sum_t \alpha_t h_t(\mathbf{x})\right)$

Fig. 3. MultiSource Tradaboost algorithm. Taken from [7]

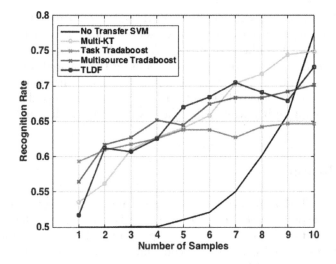

Fig. 4. Results obtained running the experiment described in Sect. 4. Each point represents the average over 20 runs with random sample and target selection

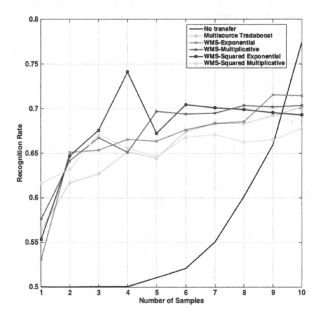

Fig. 5. Results obtained running the experiment described in Sect. 4 for Weighted Multisource Tradaboost. Each point represents the average over 20 runs with random sample and target selection

To address this limitation of failing to achieve the higher asymptote behaviour, the Weighted Multisource Tradaboost method was applied to the same dataset in the same conditions. The results obtained are shown in Fig. 5.

In this figure, WMS-Exponential and WMS - Multiplicative refer to using the linear η weight shown in Sect. 4.1 witht the weight update rules defined in Eqs. 3 and 4 respectively. WMS-Squared exponential and WMS-Squared Multiplicative correspond to the same weight update rules using the squared η weight shown in Sect. 4.1. As can be seen in Fig. 5 all attempts outperform Multisource Tradaboost except for the Squared Outside attempt. However, the failure to achieve the higher asymptote behavior still eludes us. More research is needed on this topic.

6   Conclusion

All methods studied outperform the no-transfer approach when very little target data is available only to get outperformed by it when more target data is accessible. This failure to achieve the higher asymptote behaviour theorized in [6] is an unpublished result, and is one of the contributions of this work. Our proposed attempt to improve Multisource Tradaboost to achieve the higher asymptote behaviour did not come to fruition, albeit managing to improve the classification performance. Further research is required to determine when to expect the no-transfer approach to be preferable, and how to achieve the higher asymptote. The strategies employed in this paper can be ported to other transfer learning methods, namely the Multi-KT method. Our strategy to improve transfer learning approaches towards the theoretical asymptotic performance predicted in [6] is our other contribution.

6.1   Future Work

According to the results obtained the following future research is suggested:

– Add a regularization term in the β_j calculation steps for Multi-KT that takes into account how much target data is available. This would hopefully lead the method to not be outperformed by no-transfer approaches, fusing the best of both worlds
– Further testing with the Random Forests approaches is needed in order to evaluate the performance of these methods in situations where more target data is available. Results found in the literature indicate that this research is promising.
– Test all the methods in a scenario where the classes are unrelated and test specifically for resilience against negative transfer

Acknowledgements. This work was partially supported by FCT projects AHA (CMUP-ERI/HCI/0046/2013), FIREFRONT (PCIF/SSI/0096/2017) and VOAMAIS (02/SAICT/2017/31172, PTDC/EEI-AUT/31172/2017).

References

1. Dai, W., Yang, Q., Xue, G.-R., Yu, Y.: Boosting for transfer learning. In: Proceedings of the 24th International Conference on Machine Learning, pp. 193–200. ACM (2007)
2. Gehler, P., Nowozin, S.: On feature combination for multiclass object classification. In: 2009 IEEE 12th International Conference on Computer Vision, pp. 221–228. IEEE (2009)
3. Goussies, N.A., Ubalde, S., Mejail, M.: Transfer learning decision forests for gesture recognition. J. Mach. Learn. Res. **15**, 3667–3690 (2014)
4. Griffin, G., Holub, A., Perona, P.: Caltech-256 object category dataset (2007)
5. Tommasi, T., Orabona, F., Caputo, B.: Learning categories from few examples with multi model knowledge transfer. IEEE Trans. Pattern Anal. Mach. Intell. **36**(5), 928–941 (2014)
6. Torrey, L., Shavlik, J.: Transfer learning. In: Handbook of Research on Machine Learning Applications and Trends: Algorithms, Methods, and Techniques, vol. 1, pp. 1–2 (2009)
7. Yao, Y., Doretto, G.: Boosting for transfer learning with multiple sources. In: 2010 IEEE Conference on Computer Vision and Pattern Recognition (CVPR), pp. 1855–1862. IEEE (2010)

A Proposal of Neural Networks with Intermediate Outputs

Billy Peralta[1]([image]) [image], Juan Reyes[2], Luis Caro[2] [image], and Christian Pieringer[3] [image]

[1] Andres Bello University, Santiago, Chile
billy.peralta@unab.cl
[2] Catholic University of Temuco, Temuco, Chile
jreyes2011@alu.uct.cl, lcaro@uct.cl
[3] INACAP, Santiago, Chile
cpieringer@inacap.cl

Abstract. The automatic data classification is an essential problem in machine learning, and it applies to different contexts such as people detection, health or astronomy. In recent years, deep neural networks have gained extensive attention due to their excellent performance on large and complex datasets. A neural network is a supervised method for classification, therefore typically requires a set of inputs and targets for the training process. However, it is possible to include auxiliary outputs that characterize aspects of the object of interest, which can accelerate the learning process. For example, in an image, a person may have extra outputs like attributes given by the presence of a hat or beard. However, the classical neural networks do not consider the presence of explicit auxiliary outputs. Furthermore, these outputs might be at a lower semantic level. We propose a framework that allows for using auxiliary outputs connected to hidden layers that complement the output connected to the output layer of the network. The key idea is to improve the training process of a neural network through a variant of the standard backpropagation algorithm that considers these auxiliary outputs. The article presents experimental evidence of the advantages of the proposed idea in various real datasets. Results also show new research venues and practical applications into image recognition considering a deep learning setting.

Keywords: Neural network · Data classification · Supervised learning

1 Introduction

Currently, artificial intelligence helps to perform most of the tedious tasks that involve classification, packaging and quality control, while human operators have had to change their duties and skills [14]. Every year, researchers related to Machine Learning propose novel and powerful models able to imitate human

Supported by Andres Bello University.

A. Morales et al. (Eds.): IbPRIA 2019, LNCS 11867, pp. 206–215, 2019.
https://doi.org/10.1007/978-3-030-31332-6_18

reasoning and transfer this human capability to a machine to make it able to take decisions in unstructured environments and situations.

Machine learning (ML) algorithms are increasingly present in people's daily lives. We can usually find some applications of this type of technology in most of the giant of the IT services. For example, Google applies algorithms to improves searches ranking web pages related to the content that a user entered in the search bar. Another example is Amazon, that uses a recommender system to suggest new products based on previous purchases of a user or similar items purchased by other users [15]. Furthermore, ML also allows the development of tools based on speech recognition, such as voice assistants and chatbots [3].

One of the most essential and challenging tasks in ML is the automatic classification of data. There is a vast universe of situations at different complexity levels where this task is carried out. From problems such as written digit recognition in images [1] to identifying possible implicit risks in contracts and business agreements of large companies [9]. In recent years, Artificial Neural Networks (ANNs) have gained a new attraction to solve cases like the previous ones. ANN is one of the earlier machine learning methods to solve supervised learning problems [4,12] simulating the brain connections [8]. The advances in computational hardware, optimization algorithms and the amount of data allow that ANN currently achieves high performances in classification tasks using deep variants [5,11].

Traditional ANN considers a typical set of output variables associated to a set of input variables. Nonetheless, there are cases where more than one set of output variables are associated with the set of input variables; in particular, we consider the case where one set of outputs is not in the same semantic level as the typical set of outputs. For example, we can consider the people detection task where we assume the presence of a persona in a subset of training images. But, what happens if we also have access to additional visual variables, as the presence of a hat, trousers, glasses, etc., on each training image with a person?. We can consider that these visual additional variables are in lower semantic order respect to regular output variable person because these variables are typically part of a person. Typical ANN does not contemplate to handle these auxiliary set of output variables of lower semantic order. Moreover, we can think that the auxiliary output variables are hard to assign in a particular input data, however, modern classification algorithms can be reliable in many applications (for example, deep learning techniques for visual recognition), therefore, we can apply massively these techniques to assign the required auxiliary outputs. This article proposes and explores for the first time, as far we know, the idea of modeling neural networks with intermediate outputs applied to data classification task. Particularly, we research how these auxiliary output variables affect the training process. Our motivation is the possibility of training neural networks with a reduced set of data records considering more output variables instead of massive data records with typical outputs, however, the specific exploration of this idea is left to future work.

2 Standard Neural Network

An ANN generally has an input layer, a set of hidden layers and an output layer. Figure 1 shows a diagram of an ANN, where layer 1 receives the input data. The layers share information through connections between them, for example in the same figure, each node in layer 1 has a connection with all the nodes in layer 2, and the nodes in layer 2 are connected to the single node of layer 3. Each of these connections has an associated weight, and an activation function gives the response of the node.

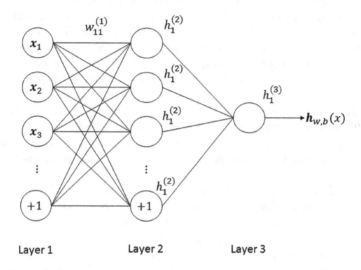

Fig. 1. Artificial Neural Network model using one hidden layer. Nodes in Layer 1 fully connect with nodes in Layer 2. Layer 3 is the output layer and concentrates all the outputs of the previous layer.

The weights associated with the links of nodes control the influence that a node in layer i has over a node in the layer $i+1$. The $w_{ij}^{(l)}$ denotes the weight that exists between the node i at layer $l+1$ and the node j at layer l (the current). The bias vector $b_i^{(l)}$ only has a direct connection with the next layer. Finally, the output node responds as $h_j^{(l)}$, where j denotes the node at layer l.

In an ANN, weights w and bias b are the parameters of the network. An optimization algorithm performs the searching and computation of parameters minimizing a loss function. A typical loss function is the Mean Square Error (MSE) computed between the real target (label) and the target predicted by the network. Let (x^i, y^i) be the record data of the input vector and its class used during training. The loss function for the instance i is:

$$J(w) = \frac{1}{m} \sum_{i=0}^{m} \frac{1}{2} \parallel y^i - h^{n_l}(x^i) \parallel^2 = \frac{1}{m} \sum_{i=0}^{m} J(W, x^i, y^i) \qquad (1)$$

Equation 1 defines the loss function for the z-th training sample, where h^{n_l} is the output at the last layer of the network. The output indicates the predicted class y_{pred} for that sample. The optimization algorithm fits iteratively the weights such that the network increases the prediction performance. Weights $w_{ij}^{(l)}$ fit following the gradient of the loss function as define:

$$w_{ij}^{(l)} = w_{ij}^{(l)} - \alpha \frac{\partial}{\partial w_{ij}^{(l)}} J(w) \qquad (2)$$

3   Proposed Method

Our idea consists of integrating a set of auxiliary output variables to an artificial neural network, where the main constraint is that these output variables are at a lower semantic level than regular output variables. Our rationale is that the intermediate layer can be semantically related to these auxiliary variables. For such reason, we propose to link the output of a particular intermediate layer to the auxiliary output variables considering a variation of the regular cost function of ANN by adding a new cost function of the output of a specific intermediate layer and the auxiliary output variables. In this work, we call these auxiliary output variables as *intermediate outputs*. The selection of the intermediate layer is relevant for this model; however, this work considers two intermediate layers in order to experiment with this architecture; in this case, we choose the later layer because we expect that the intermediate outputs have a nonlinear dependence of input variables. Next, we derive the solutions to the proposed modification of the typical cost function of a multilayer perceptron neural network.

3.1   Backpropagation Based on the Proposed Variant of Cost Function

In this case, we will assume that there is a h layer where the results of such neurons are compared with some auxiliary output variables. In the case of artificial vision, such outputs can be interpreted as visual attributes. This is reasonable since these attributes can be understood as intermediate patterns that allow objects to be recognized. Still more, we think that these intermediate outputs can give a good guide to the learning process of neural network. For this reason, we propose the following energy function considering the sum of the objective function and an auxiliary function weighted with λ:

$$E = \frac{1}{2}(y - y_{pred})^2 + \frac{\lambda}{2}(a - o^h)^2 \qquad (3)$$

In the previous equation, we consider the mean squared error cost function by the simplicity of mathematical derivation, however, the equations are similar for case of cross-entropy loss function. In relation to the proposed neural network, we note that only the weights that reach the indicated intermediate layer consider

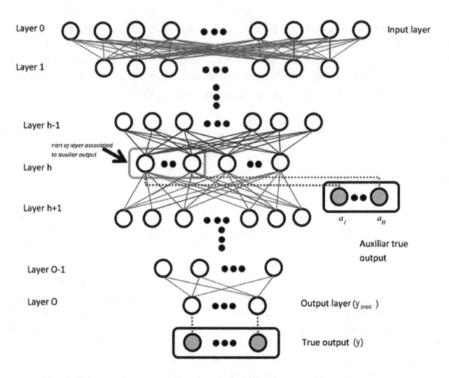

Fig. 2. Proposed variant of neural network with intermediate outputs

the error of the auxiliary output. The output layer only considers objective function error. That replicates up to layer $h + 1$. When it reaches layer h, the weights are influenced by auxiliary error (Fig. 2).

Derivating with respect to weight w_{ij} you get the same results as classical backpropagation [4] except in $\frac{\partial E}{\partial o_j}$. Again considering E as a function of output neurons and including the intermediate outputs a, we have:

$$\frac{\partial E(o_j)}{\partial o_j} = \frac{\partial E(a, net_u.net_v, ..., net_w)}{\partial o_j} \tag{4}$$

Considering the dependence on outputs a, we have:

$$\frac{\partial E}{\partial o_j} = \frac{\partial E}{\partial a} + \sum_{l \in L} \left(\frac{\partial E}{\partial net_l} \frac{\partial net_l}{\partial o_j} \right) = \sum_{l \in L} \left(\frac{\partial E}{\partial o_l} \frac{\partial o_l}{\partial net_l} w_{jl} \right) \tag{5}$$

Again we assume that the subsequent derivatives are known, then we have:

$$\frac{\partial E}{\partial w_{ij}} = \delta_j o_i \tag{6}$$

with:

$$\delta_j = \frac{\partial E}{\partial o_j} \frac{\partial o_j}{\partial net_j} = (\lambda(o_j - a_j) + \sum_{l \in L} \delta_l w_{jl})o_j(1 - o_j) \tag{7}$$

Therefore, we can integrate all cases in this way:

$$\frac{\partial E}{\partial w_{ij}} = \delta_j o_i \tag{8}$$

considering:

$$\delta_j = \frac{\partial E}{\partial o_j} \frac{\partial o_j}{\partial net_j}$$

$$= \begin{cases} (o_j - y_j)o_j(1 - o_j) & if \ j \ a \ a \ output \ neuron \\ (\sum_{l \in L} \delta_l w_{jl})o_j(1 - o_j) & if \ j \ is \ an \ intern \ neuron \\ (\lambda(o_j - a_j) + \sum_{l \in L} \delta_l w_{jl})o_j(1 - o_j) & if \ j \ is \ an \ intermediate \ output \ neuron. \end{cases} \tag{9}$$

As this method is based on an artificial neural network with intermediate outputs, we call it as **ANNIO**.

4 Experiments

In this Section, we test the performance of our proposed method ANNIO using diverse datasets. Specifically, we use four real data sets, two from the UCI Machine Learning Repository: Iris and Yeast [7] and two from attributes based datasets Yahoo Images (AYAHOO) and Pascal Images (APASCAL) [2]. We normalize all variables of these datasets to the range [0, 1]. All experiments are performed on a PC with 4.0 Ghz with Intel®CoreTM i7-4790K CPU 8 processors with 16 GB of RAM memory. We use Python with Tensorflow to code the algorithms [10]. We compare our proposed algorithm ANNIO against the regular neural network with typical Backpropagation algorithm. We compare these techniques in terms of accuracy and convergence time. In general, we use the available test partitions to validate the results of each algorithm.

We choose the aforementioned datasets because, in addition to their corresponding input and output variables, they can have a set of variables that represent the intermediate output variables present in the analyzed objects, in another case, we generate these intermediate outputs to evaluate our proposed technique considering diverse conditions. These intermediate outputs will be entered only during the training of the proposed neural network with intermediate outputs.

In the case of Iris dataset consists of flowers data with 4 input variables and 3 classes. The intermediate output is created from the width of the sepal in centimeters of each of the flowers. These intermediate outputs are based on variable *separation*, which is the most discriminative. According to fixed intervals, we build 64 binary variables. In the Yeast dataset, we have records of yeasts with 103 inputs variables and 14 classes, which can be multiple per instance. In this case, we perform multiple experiments where in each case, we assume one original class as the output variable and the others as intermediate output variables.

In relation to image databases, the Yahoo dataset corresponds to 2037 Yahoo images related to 12 animals and also has 64 semantic binary attributes associated which correspond to our intermediate outputs, for example, if the animal has hair or tail. Finally, in Pascal dataset also corresponds to a total of 12703 images with 9751 features besides having 32 classes and where again there are 64 attributes of a semantic type which are used as intermediate outputs. Both image datasets were preprocessed by using clipped bounding box information, normalizing to 500×500 pixels and extracting the HOG features [6]. In summary, the databases are described in Table 1:

Table 1. Detail of used datasets

Database	Training set	Test set	N° of classes	N° of intermediate outputs	Number of records
Iris	90	60	3	64	150
Yeast	1500	917	2	13	2417
AYAHOO	1586	1058	12	64	2644
APASCAL	6337	6347	32	64	2417

In relation to neural networks, we use full connected neural networks considering a sigmoid activation function with two hidden layers. The first hidden layer has 256 nodes and the second layer has 128 nodes. We consider a rate learning of 0.01 and 10000 training epochs. We consider this configuration for both models. In relation to ANNIO, we test by connecting the intermediate outputs to the second hidden layer, as we hypothesize a non-linear relationship between input variables and intermediate outputs.

In relation to experiments, we show the training cost for all datasets, the test accuracy and the average cost during training process. We finally evaluate the sensitivity of accuracy respect to selection of intermediate outputs and weighting parameter of intermediate outputs. In the case of the average cost of training process, it is defined as the area given by the number of epochs and cost function, in such way, we have an intuition about the learning process speed.

In general, the training process is stable for all datasets for ANNIO. For example in Fig. 3, we show the training cost evolution of ANNIO algorithm for Iris dataset, where we observe the convergence of the training process. This pattern is repeated for all datasets.

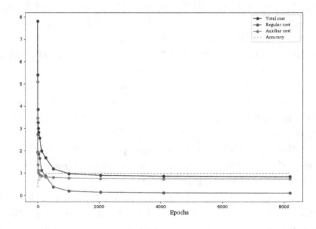

Fig. 3. Multiples costs and accuracy vs epochs for Iris dataset with ANNIO

Table 2. Results of accuracy and average training cost for all datasets

Datasets	ANN: Average cost training	ANN: Accuracy	ANNIO: Average cost training	ANNIO: Accuracy
Iris	2105	96%	1514	97%
Yeast (Class 2)	35	81%	34	93%
Yeast (All classes)	32	39%	32	46%
AYAHOO	2219	56%	1877	56%
APASCAL	5129	53%	1493	52%

We show in Table 2, we show the accuracy and the average cost of the training process obtained in all datasets considering both algorithms. We found that the reduction of the average training cost using ANNIO is significant. The results of accuracy have been variable. Particularly in Yeast dataset, ANNIO overcomes ANN by a wide 12%. In the case of image datasets, we found an acceleration of convergence but similar accuracies, however, we found that a slight tuning of weighting parameter of intermediate outputs improves ANNIO with a 2% over ANN considering APASCAL dataset as we will detail in later experiments.

We found that the use of the neural network with intermediate outputs generates a lower cost than the traditional network, obtaining a faster convergence of a correct model. Specifically, the difference of epochs for the convergence of the traditional network and the proposed network is around 128 epochs. The fact that the neural network with intermediate outputs converges early, we hypothesized that it is due to the importance of auxiliary characteristics for input data given by the weighting parameter λ, which is constrained to range $[0, 1]$.

We also explore the sensibility of accuracy respect to the number of attributes by considering only APASCAL dataset. Using Weka software [13], we rank the set of the sixty-four auxiliary attributes according to the discrimination level. Figure 4 shows the accuracy curve for both training and test partitions of APASCAL dataset. We found that the performance clearly improves in relation to the default version giving a rough improvement of 2% with respect to the total list of auxiliary attributes, which indicates that a selection of intermediate outputs can be beneficial to learning a right model. We suspect that this behaviour is originated because some attributes can produce overfitting as we can be totally uncorrelated to the classes.

Finally, we explore the cost and accuracy considering different weight parameter of intermediate outputs (λ) considering again APASCAL dataset. We use a set of auxiliary weights in the range of 0.1 to 0.9 with a step of 0.1; this set of 9 different weights was tested in ANNIO to obtain cost and accuracy curves where we showed the results in test set. The results of these experiments are shown in Table 3. We conclude that the accuracy shows an almost linear growing behaviour of the weighting parameter of intermediate outputs with respect to accuracy at least in this dataset.

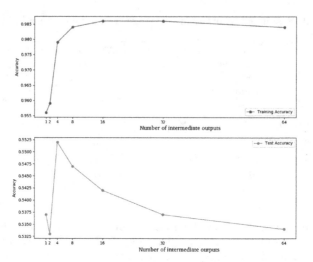

Fig. 4. Accuracy sensibility considering ordered groups of intermediate outputs.

Table 3. Sensitivity of auxiliary weights λ) respect to cost and accuracy in test set of APASCAL dataset

Weighting parameter (λ)	Cost in test set	Accuracy in test set
0.1	0.644	53.1%
0.2	0.167	54.2%
0.3	0.138	54.9%
0.4	0.133	55.3%
0.5	0.128	55.8%
0.6	0.130	55.5%
0.7	0.122	56.1%
0.8	0.128	56.0%
0.9	0.137	56.4%

5   Conclusions

In this work, we propose a variant of classical multilayer perceptron neural network where we add a set of intermediate outputs which are connected to a hidden layer. The results show that network training with auxiliary variant generally obtains best accuracy results than the classical option, furthermore, it also obtains a faster convergence than the traditional neural network.

We found that not all intermediate outputs, or auxiliary attributes, have the same level of discrimination, where some intermediate outputs affect the training process. It probably is due to a lack of correlation between these auxiliary attributes and class variables. It suggests the need for using the auxiliary attributes to have a high level of discrimination.

We also found that the weight of intermediate outputs is relevant as it ponders the importance of auxiliary attributes in the adjustment of the network weights during backpropagation process. In particular, the optimal weight is the one that generates a greater improvement in data accuracy.

Respect to the future avenues of this research, we plan to test this idea considering deep convolutional neural networks and new datasets. Another point to consider is the modification of the neural network configuration, that is, modifying the number of hidden layers, number of nodes per layer and finally modifying the layer where the auxiliary outputs are connected.

References

1. Abdul, N., Amir, N.: Handwritten recognition using SVM, KNN and neural network (2016)
2. Ali, F., Ian, E., Derek, H., David, F.: Describing objects by their attributes. In: CVPR 2009, vol. 1, no. 3 p. 3.1 May 2009. https://www.cs.cmu.edu/~afarhadi/papers/Attributes.pdf
3. Anusuya, M., Katti, S.: Speech recognition by machine: a review (2009)
4. Bishop, C.M.: Neural Networks for Pattern Recognition. Oxford University Press Inc., New York (1995)
5. Chollet, F.: Deep Learning with Python, 1st edn. Manning Publications Co., Greenwich (2017)
6. Dalal, N., Triggs, B.: Histograms of oriented gradients for human detection. In: CVPR 2005 Proceedings of the 2005 IEEE Computer Society Conference on Computer Vision and Pattern Recognition (CVPR 2005), vol. 1, pp. 886–893. IEEE Computer Society, Washington (2005). https://doi.org/10.1109/CVPR.2005.177
7. Dua, D., Graff, C.: UCI machine learning repository (2017). http://archive.ics.uci.edu/ml
8. Eluyode, O., Akomolafe, D.: Comparative study of biological and artificial neural networks (2013)
9. Gao, L.: Applications of machine learning and computational linguistics in financial economics (2016)
10. Goldsborough, P.: A tour of tensorflow (2016)
11. Goodfellow, I., Bengio, Y., Courville, A.: Deep Learning. The MIT Press, Cambridge (2016)
12. Gurney, K.: An Introduction to Neural Networks. CRC Press, Boca Raton (1997)
13. Hall, M., Frank, E., Holmes, G., Pfahringer, B., Reutemann, P., Witten, I.H.: The WEKA data mining software: an update. SIGKDD Explor. Newsl. 11(1), 10–18 (2009). https://doi.org/10.1145/1656274.1656278
14. Murphy, K.P.: Machine Learning: A Probabilistic Perspective. The MIT Press, Cambridge (2012)
15. Smola, A.: Introduction to Machine Learning (2008)

Addressing the Big Data Multi-class Imbalance Problem with Oversampling and Deep Learning Neural Networks

V. M. González-Barcenas[1], E. Rendón[1], R. Alejo[1(✉)],
E. E. Granda-Gutiérrez[2], and R. M. Valdovinos[3]

[1] Division of Postgraduate Studies and Research,
National Institute of Technology of Mexico (TecNM) Campus Toluca,
Av. Tecnológico s/n, Agrícola Bellavista, 52149 Metepec, México
ralejoe@toluca.tecnm.mx

[2] UAEM University Center at Atlacomulco, Universidad Autónoma del Estado
de México, Carretera Toluca-Atlacomulco Km. 60, 50450 Atlacomulco, México

[3] Faculty of Engineering, Universidad Autónoma del Estado de México,
Cerro de Coatepec s/n, Ciudad Universitaria, 50100 Toluca, México

Abstract. The class imbalance problem is a challenging situation in machine learning but also it appears frequently in recent Big Data applications. The most studied techniques to deal with the class imbalance problem have been Random Over Sampling (ROS), Random Under Sampling (RUS) and Synthetic Minority Over-sampling Technique (SMOTE), especially in two-class scenarios. However, in the Big Data scale, multi-class imbalance scenarios have not extensively studied yet, and only a few investigations have been performed. In this work, the effectiveness of ROS and SMOTE techniques is analyzed in the Big data multi-class imbalance context. The KDD99 dataset, which is a popular multi-class imbalanced big data set, was used to probe these oversampling techniques, prior to the application of a Deep Learning Multi-Layer Perceptron. Results show that ROS and SMOTE are not always enough to improve the classifier performance in the minority classes. However, they slightly increase the overall performance of the classifier in comparison to the unsampled data.

Keywords: Multi-class imbalance · Deep learning neural networks · Big data

1 Introduction

Big Data applications have increased importantly in recent years [23]. The volume of information, the speed of data transference, and the variety of data are the main characteristics of Big Data paradigm [8,10]. Concerning to the volume

This work has been partially supported under grants of project 5106.19-P from TecNM.

A. Morales et al. (Eds.): IbPRIA 2019, LNCS 11867, pp. 216–224, 2019.
https://doi.org/10.1007/978-3-030-31332-6_19

of information, a data set belongs to Big Data scale when it is difficult to process with traditional analytical systems [18].

In order to efficiently seize the large amount of information from Big Data applications, Deep Learning techniques have become an attractive alternative, because these algorithms generally allow to obtain better results than traditional machine learning methods [12,20]. Multi-Layer Perceptron (MLP), the most common neural network topology, has been also translated to the Deep Learning context [14].

Deep Learning MLP (DL-MLP) incorporates two or more hidden layers in its architecture [11], which increases the computational cost of processing large size and high dimension data sets. However, this disadvantage can be overtaken by using modern efficient frameworks, such as Apache-Spark [24] or Tensor-Flow [1]. Thus, the high performance, robustness to overfitting, and high processing capability of this deep neural networks can be exploited.

Nevertheless, deep learning algorithms are strongly affected by the class imbalance problem [6]. The class imbalance problem refers to situations where the number of samples in one or more classes of the data set is fewer than in another class (or classes), producing an important deterioration of the classifier performance [5]. In literature, many investigations dealing with this problem have been documented, being Random Over Sampling (ROS), Random Under Sampling (RUS) and Synthetic Minority Over-sampling Techniques (SMOTE) the most popular methods [15]. Although the results are not conclusive for the specific application in the Big Data scale, they have motivated the development of other over-sampling methods [13,17].

The KDD CUP 1999 intrusion detection data set (KDD99) was introduced at The Third International Knowledge Discovery and Data Mining Tools Competition [4]. It consists of more than 4 million instances (with 41 attributes); it is divided into twenty-three types of attacks clustered in four categories, therefore it is formally considered as Big Data [22]. Some attacks in KDD99 have less of ten instances; i.e., it is highly imbalanced and few represented, which implies a Big Data challenge with class imbalance problem [15,18].

Previous works have been focused in the study of the KDD99 dataset to probe different machine learning techniques. Nevertheless, most of them have used only a subset of it [22]. For example, in [23] KDD99 was divided into four two-class data sets and the class imbalance problem has been addressed with parallel models of evolutionary under-sampling methods based in the Map Reduce paradigm. Seo et al. [22] used a KDD99 subset of five classes: four of them were the attack categories and the fifth class was the normal connections; then, a wrapper method was proposed to find the best SMOTE ratio by identifying the best level of sampling for the minority classes.

In this paper, the whole KDD99 data set was analyzed, by using all the twenty three attacks as classes with the aim of study the performance of the classical oversampling approaches, like ROS and SMOTE, in the Big Data class imbalance context, while the Deep Learning MLP was used as base classifier.

2   Theoretical Framework

2.1   Deep Learning Multilayer Perceptron

MLP constitutes the most conventional neural network architecture. It is commonly based on three layers: input, output, and one hidden layer [14]. Thus, the MLP can be translated into a deep neural network by incorporating two or more hidden layers within its architecture, becoming a Deep Learning MLP. This allows to reduce the number of nodes per layer and uses fewer parameters, but it leads to a more complex optimization problem [11]. However, due to the availability of more efficient frameworks, such as Apache-Spark or Tensorflow, this disadvantage is less restrictive than before.

Traditionally, MLP has been trained with the back-propagation algorithm (which is based in the stochastic gradient descent) and its weights randomly initialized. However, in the late versions of DL-MLPs, the hidden layers are pre-trained by an unsupervised algorithm and the weights are optimized by the back-propagation algorithm [14].

MLP uses sigmoid activation functions, such as the hyperbolic tangent or logistic function. In contrast, DL-MLP includes (commonly) the Rectified Linear Unit (ReLU) $f(z) = \max(0, z)$ because typically learns much faster in networks with many layers, allowing training of a DL-MLP without unsupervised pre-training.

There are three variants of the descending gradient that differ in how many data are used to process the gradient of the objective function [21]: (a) Batch Gradient Descendent calculates the gradient of the cost function to the parameters for the entire training data set, (b) Stochastic Gradient Descendent performs an update of parameters for each training example, and (c) Mini-batch Gradient Descendent takes the best of the previous two and performs the update for each mini-batch of a given number of training examples.

The most common algorithms of descending gradient optimization are: (a) Adagrad, which adapts the learning reason of the parameters, making bigger updates for less frequent parameters and smaller for the most frequent ones, (b) Adadelta is an extension of Adagrad that seeks to reduce aggressiveness, monotonously decreasing the learning rate instead of accumulating all the previous descending gradients, restricting accumulation to a fixed size, and (c) Adam, that calculates adaptations of the learning rate for each parameter and stores an exponentially decreasing average of past gradients. Other important algorithms are AdaMax, Nadam and RMSprop [21].

2.2   Classical Sampling Methods Used to Deal with the Class Imbalance Problem

The class imbalance problem has been a hot topic in machine learning and data mining, and more recently in deep learning and Big Data [7,15]. Oversampling (mainly ROS and SMOTE) are the most common techniques used to face with the class imbalance problem, mainly due to their independence of the underlying classifier [17]. ROS replicates samples in the minority class biasing the discrimination process to compensate the class imbalance, while SMOTE generates artificial samples from the minority class by interpolating existing instances that lie close together [9].

Table 1. A brief summary of main characteristics of the KDD99 data set.

Attack name	Attacks in data set	Category	Class imbalance ratio
normal	972781	NORMAL	0.19859032
warezclient	1020	R2L	0.00020823
multihop	7	R2L	0.00000143
ftp_write	8	R2L	0.00000163
imap	12	R2L	0.00000245
guess_passwd	53	R2L	0.00001082
warezmaster	20	R2L	0.00000408
spy	2	R2L	0.00000041
phf	4	R2L	0.00000082
neptune	1072017	DOS	0.21884906
back	2203	DOS	0.00044974
teardrop	979	DOS	0.00019986
smurf	2807886	DOS	0.57322151
pod	264	DOS	0.00005389
land	21	DOS	0.00000429
buffer_overflow	30	U2R	0.00000612
loadmodule	9	U2R	0.00000184
rootkit	10	U2R	0.00000204
perl	3	U2R	0.00000061
portsweep	10413	PROBE	0.00212578
satan	15892	PROBE	0.00324430
ipsweep	12481	PROBE	0.00254796
nmap	2316	PROBE	0.00047280

The under-sampling methods also have shown effectiveness to deal with the class imbalance problem [13]: the RUS technique is one of the most successful under-sampling methods, which eliminates random samples from the original data set (usually from the majority class) to decrease the class imbalance. However, this method loses effectiveness when it removes significant samples [17]. To compensate this disadvantage, other important under-sampling methods include a heuristic mechanism [13].

Lately, Dynamic Sampling Methods have become an interesting alternative to sampling class imbalanced data sets because they automatically set the class imbalance sampling rate [2], and select the best samples to train the classifier [16]. The key of these methods is that they use the neural network output to identify those samples that are either close or in the decision regions of other classes; i.e., in the frontier decision or class overlap region.

3   Experimental Set-Up

KDD99 data set was used in the experimental stage, which is available from the University of California at Irvine (UCI) machine learning repository [4]. It contains about 4 million instances with 41 attributes each.

In order to deal with the Big Data multi-class imbalance problem, all the twenty-three attacks of KDD99 data set were defined as classes for this investigation. The hold–out method was used to randomly split the KDD99 data set in training (70%) and test (30%). Table 1 shows a brief summary of main characteristics of the KDD99 data set.

The main goal of this paper is to show the performance of classical oversampling approaches (ROS and SMOTE) to deal with the Big Data class imbalance problem. SMOTE and ROS were selected because they have shown their success to deal with the multi-class imbalance problem and even SMOTE is considered the "de facto" standard in the framework of learning from imbalanced data [9]. Thus, the scikit-learn library was used to perform SMOTE and ROS algorithms. Scikit-learn is a free library software for machine learning for the Python programming language [19].

Two hidden layer were used in the DL-MLP with ReLU activation functions in its nodes, and softmax function on its output layer. The configuration of each hidden layer was 30 nodes. The number of hidden layers and nodes were obtained by a trial-error strategy. DL-MLP was performed in TensorFlow framework [1], and Adam algorithm [21] was used as the training method.

The most widely used metrics on investigations to face the multi-class imbalanced problems has been the Multi-class Area Under the receiver operating characteristic Curve (MAUC) [2] and the Geometric Mean of Sensitivity and Precision (g-mean) [25]. However, these are global metrics and the evidence of the individual performance of ROS and SMOTE over the minority classes is more interesting for this paper; thus, the accuracy by-class was used instead.

Finally, in order to compute the general classification performance, the Ranks method was used. This assigns the rank 1 to the best algorithm, 2 to the second best, 3 to the third best, and so on up to the umpteenth best rank; if ties exist, then the average rank is calculated. The lesser the rank number, the better the algorithm performance.

4   Results and Discussion

Table 2 shows the accuracies by-class obtained by SMOTE and ROS in each individual class. It is organized in three parts: the first column represents the evaluated class, the second column are the number of samples classified correctly

Table 2. Back-propagation classification performance. The results represent the averaged values between ten folds and the initialization of ten different weights of the neural network. The bold numbers represent the best average MAUC values.

Class	Standard		ROS		SMOTE	
	Correct/Total	Average(%)	Correct/Total	Average(%)	Correct/Total	Average(%)
normal	**291199/291835**	**99.7**	276466/291835	94.7	290712/291835	99.6
warezclient	244/306	79.7	237/306	77.4	**263/306**	**85.9**
multihop	0/3	0	0/3	0	1/3	33.3
ftp_write	0/3	0	1/3	33.3	1/3	33.3
imap	3/4	75	3/4	75	3/4	75
guess_passwd	0/16	0	14/16	87.5	11/16	68.7
warezmaster	0/6	0	2/6	33.3	3/6	50
spy	0/1	0	0/1	0	0/1	0
phf	0/1	0	1/1	100	1/1	100
neptune	121542/321606	37.79	121419/321606	37.75	114277/321606	35.5
back	642/661	97.1	657/661	99.3	**654/661**	**98.9**
teardrop	**294/294**	**100**	294/294	100	293/294	99.6
smurf	**842317/842366**	**99.9**	312365/842366	37	312365/842366	37
pod	77/80	96.2	**80/80**	**100**	79/80	98.7
land	3/7	42.8	3/7	42.8	3/7	42.8
buffer_overflow	0/9	0	8/9	88.8	7/9	77.7
loadmodule	0/3	0	0/3	0	0/3	0
rootkit	0/3	0	0/3	0	0/3	0
perl	0/1	0	1/1	100	1/1	100
portsweep	3009/3124	96.3	2974/3124	95.2	**3070/3124**	**98.2**
satan	4683/4768	98.2	46484683/4768	97.4	**47114683/4768**	**98.8**
ipsweep	**2960/3745**	**79**	2585/3745	69	2935/3745	78.3
nmap	590/695	84.8	**681/695**	**97.9**	562/695	80.8
Average Rank		2.18		1.95		1.87

and the total of samples belonging to these class, and the third column is the average accuracy by-class. This is repeated for each sampling method: Standard (unsampled), ROS and SMOTE.

It is noticeable in Table 2 that some minority classes like *back*, *teardrop* and *pod* seem unaffected by the class imbalance problem. Another example is class *imap*, which is very poorly represented but the DL-MLP classifies correctly three of four of its samples. This confirmed the findings of others works, which affirmed that the class imbalance problem only increases the major disadvantage of the algorithms based in the back-propagation; i.e., the slow rate of convergence of the neural network and often it is the cause of the poor classification performance of the classifier, but not always [3].

It is observed also that the classifier accuracy by-class, in a few minority classes is not improved by the application of ROS or SMOTE methods. For example, the accuracy of the class *multihop* is not increased using ROS. The accuracies of the classes *spy*, *loadmodule* and *rootkit* are neither improved by ROS and SMOTE. Moreover, the classifier performance on the minority class *ipsweep* was reduced when ROS or SMOTE were applied. This could be originated by the increase of the noise or overlap in these minority classes when they are sampled.

Within the machine learning community, it is known that the class imbalance problem is severely stressed by other factors, such as class overlapping, small disjuncts, the lack of density and information, noisy data, the significance of the borderline samples and its relationship with noisy samples, and the data set shift problem [17].

All of these classes have a common feature: they are severely imbalanced, and the origin of this imbalance comes from different sources. Thus, an important question is how to deal with this problem. Maybe, the solution to this problem is not only the over-sampling of the minority classes, but heuristically sub-sampling the majority classes close to severely imbalanced minority classes, in a similar way to [3]. Then, an effective over-sampling method should be applied. However, another problem appears in the scene: how to identify the decision frontier of those minority classes. The use of the neuronal network output could be an interesting alternative [2].

Table 2 also exhibits that, in overall, the sampling methods improve the classifier performance in comparison to the unsampled data set. The average rank for both, SMOTE (1.87) and ROS (1.95), represent better results than standard rank (2.18).

In Big Data context, results from Table 2 confirm the conclusions of other investigations, which affirm that the class imbalance problem adversely affect the classifier performance, but in other situations it is not the main cause of effectiveness loss of classifier. In other words, the class imbalance problem in Big Data follows a similar behavior that the studied so far in machine learning community.

5   Conclusion

In this paper, the performance of two successful methods to deal with the multi-class imbalance problem, ROS and SMOTE, was analyzed. Results show that ROS and SMOTE are not always enough to improve the classifier performance in the minority classes, in the Big Data multi-class imbalance context. However, these oversampling methods increase the DL-MLP accuracy on most of the cases. It is considered necessary a cleaning stage before applying either SMOTE or ROS, and the neural network output could be a good alternative for this stage. Thus, further research is required to investigate the potential of recent dynamic sampling methods [2,16], which use the neural network output to identify and delete samples from majority classes that are close or in the minority classes decision regions. Subsequently, the use of SMOTE or ROS would improve the classification performance on these minority classes.

References

1. Abadi, M., et al.: Tensorflow: a system for large-scale machine learning. In: Proceedings of the 12th USENIX Conference on Operating Systems Design and Implementation. OSDI 2016, pp. 265–283, USENIX Association, Berkeley (2016). http://download.tensorflow.org/paper/whitepaper2015.pdf
2. Alejo, R., Monroy-de Jesús, J., Ambriz-Polo, J.C., Pacheco-Sánchez, J.H.: An improved dynamic sampling back-propagation algorithm based on mean square error to face the multi-class imbalance problem. Neural Comput. Appl. **28**(10), 2843–2857 (2017). https://doi.org/10.1007/s00521-017-2938-3
3. Alejo, R., Valdovinos, R., García, V., Pacheco-Sanchez, J.: A hybrid method to face class overlap and class imbalance on neural networks and multi-class scenarios. Pattern Recogn. Lett. **34**(4), 380–388 (2013)
4. Asuncion, A., Newman, D.: UCI machine learning repository (2007). www.ics.uci.edu/~mlearn/
5. Błaszczyński, J., Stefanowski, J.: Local data characteristics in learning classifiers from imbalanced data. In: Gawęda, A.E., Kacprzyk, J., Rutkowski, L., Yen, G.G. (eds.) Advances in Data Analysis with Computational Intelligence Methods. SCI, vol. 738, pp. 51–85. Springer, Cham (2018). https://doi.org/10.1007/978-3-319-67946-4_2
6. Buda, M., Maki, A., Mazurowski, M.A.: A systematic study of the class imbalance problem in convolutional neural networks. Neural Netw. **106**, 249–259 (2018). https://doi.org/10.1016/j.neunet.2018.07.011
7. Dong, Q., Gong, S., Zhu, X.: Imbalanced deep learning by minority class incremental rectification. CoRR abs/1804.10851 (2018)
8. Elshawi, R., Sakr, S., Talia, D., Trunfio, P.: Big data systems meet machine learning challenges: towards big data science as a service. Big Data Res. **14**, 1–11 (2018). https://doi.org/10.1016/j.bdr.2018.04.004
9. Fernandez, A., Garcia, S., Herrera, F., Chawla, N.V.: SMOTE for learning from imbalanced data: progress and challenges, marking the 15-year anniversary. J. Artif. Intell. Res. **61**, 863–905 (2018)
10. Fernández, A., del Río, S., Chawla, N.V., Herrera, F.: An insight into imbalanced big data classification: outcomes and challenges. Complex Intell. Syst. **3**(2), 105–120 (2017). https://doi.org/10.1007/s40747-017-0037-9
11. Goodfellow, I., Bengio, Y., Courville, A.: Deep Learning. MIT Press, Cambridge (2016)
12. Guo, Y., Liu, Y., Oerlemans, A., Lao, S., Wu, S., Lew, M.S.: Deep learning for visual understanding: a review. Neurocomputing **187**, 27–48 (2016)
13. He, H., Garcia, E.: Learning from imbalanced data. IEEE Trans. Knowl. Data Eng. **21**(9), 1263–1284 (2009). https://doi.org/10.1109/TKDE.2008.239
14. LeCun, Y., Bengio, Y., Hinton, G.: Deep learning. Nature **521**, 436–444 (2015)
15. Leevy, J.L., Khoshgoftaar, T.M., Bauder, R.A., Seliya, N.: A survey on addressing high-class imbalance in big data. J. Big Data **5**(1), 42 (2018). https://doi.org/10.1186/s40537-018-0151-6
16. Lin, M., Tang, k., Yao, X.: Dynamic sampling approach to training neural networks for multiclass imbalance classification. IEEE Trans. Neural Netw. Learn. Syst. **24**(4), 647–660 (2013). https://doi.org/10.1109/TNNLS.2012.2228231
17. López, V., Fernández, A., García, S., Palade, V., Herrera, F.: An insight into classification with imbalanced data: empirical results and current trends on using data intrinsic characteristics. Inf. Sci. **250**, 113–141 (2013). https://doi.org/10.1016/j.ins.2013.07.007

18. Oussous, A., Benjelloun, F.Z., Lahcen, A.A., Belfkih, S.: Big data technologies: a survey. J. King Saud Univ. - Comput. Inf. Sci. **30**(4), 431–448 (2018). https://doi.org/10.1016/j.jksuci.2017.06.001

19. Pedregosa, F., et al.: Scikit-learn: machine learning in Python. J. Mach. Learn. Res. **12**, 2825–2830 (2011)

20. Reyes-Nava, A., Sánchez, J.S., Alejo, R., Flores-Fuentes, A.A., Rendón-Lara, E.: Performance analysis of deep neural networks for classification of gene-expression microarrays. In: Martínez-Trinidad, J.F., Carrasco-Ochoa, J.A., Olvera-López, J.A., Sarkar, S. (eds.) MCPR 2018. LNCS, vol. 10880, pp. 105–115. Springer, Cham (2018). https://doi.org/10.1007/978-3-319-92198-3_11

21. Ruder, S.: An overview of gradient descent optimization algorithms. CoRR abs/1609.04747 (2016)

22. Seo, J.H., Kim, Y.H.: Machine-learning approach to optimize smote ratio in class imbalance dataset for intrusion detection. Comput. Intell. Neurosci. **2018**, 1–11 (2018). https://doi.org/10.1155/2018/9704672

23. Triguero, I., et al.: Evolutionary undersampling for imbalanced big data classification. In: 2015 IEEE Congress on Evolutionary Computation (CEC), pp. 715–722, May 2015. https://doi.org/10.1109/CEC.2015.7256961

24. Zaharia, M., et al.: Apache Spark: a unified engine for big data processing. Commun. ACM **59**(11), 56–65 (2016). https://doi.org/10.1145/2934664

25. Zarinabad, N., Wilson, M., Gill, S., Manias, K., Davies, N., Peet, A.: Multiclass imbalance learning: improving classification of pediatric brain tumors from magnetic resonance spectroscopy. Magn. Reson. Med. **77**(6), 2114–2124 (2017). https://doi.org/10.1002/mrm.26318

Reinforcement Learning and Neuroevolution in Flappy Bird Game

André Brandão, Pedro Pires, and Petia Georgieva$^{(\boxtimes)}$ (iD)

Department of Electronics, Telecommunications and Informatics,
University of Aveiro, Aveiro, Portugal
{andrebrandao,ptpires,petia}@ua.pt

Abstract. Games have been used as an effective way to measure the advancement of artificial intelligence. Chess, Atari2600 and Go, are some of the most mediatic demonstrations where AI computer programs defeated human players. In this paper we add the popular Flappy Bird game in the list of games to quantify the performance of an AI player. Based on Q-Reinforcement Learning and Neuroevolution (neural network fitted by genetic algorithm), artificial agents were trained to take the most favorable action at each game instant. The Neuroevolution agent outperformed by far the Reinforcement Learning agent (111 points average result) and achieved on average super-human performance of impressive score of 28700 points.

Keywords: Flappy Bird game · Reinforcement learning · Neuroevolution

1 Introduction

Nowadays, games are seen as the perfect test-bed for artificial intelligence (AI) algorithms, and are also becoming an increasingly important application area. Game AI is a broad field, covering everything from the challenge of making super-human AI for difficult games such as Go or Atari, to creative applications such as the automated game design. Over the last decade this area of research has seen massive expansion and enrichment with the inclusion of video games, and enables us to address a broader range of challenges that have great commercial, social, economic and scientific interest [1].

The mobile game Flappy Bird was released in May, 2013 [2], and right from the beginning received great popularity and many critics related to its high level of difficulty. In 2014 the game was removed from smartphones by its creator, Dong Nguyen, because it became too addictive. The game seems simple, the player has to guide a bird through the gaps between regularly disposed pipes, by taking two actions: doing nothing (the bird descend) or pressing the 'up' key

This Research work was funded by National Funds through the FCT - Foundation for Science and Technology, in the context of the project UID /CEC/00127/2013.

(the bird jumps upward). Nevertheless, the scores achieved are usually low due to the fast game dynamics, high environment variability and vast search space. Development of a computer program that can play the game requires careful feature definitions to set up the problem.

The goal of this paper is to teach an AI agent to play the Flappy Bird game better than non-expert human players and reach at least a score relevant for a platinum medal (the highest game prize).

The rest of the paper is organized as follows. Section 2 reviews related works. Sections 3 and 4 describe the training and performance evaluation of the Reinforcement Learning (RL)-based agent and the Neuroevolution(NE)-based agent respectively. Section 5 summarizes the work.

2   Related Work

In 1997, IMB's Deep Blue was the first computer to defeat the chess world champion Garry Kasparov [3]. The strategy used by the computer was a brute force approach, i.e. it analyzed millions of sequences before making a move using the alpha-beta algorithm to decrease the number of nodes in the search tree.

17 years later, in 2013, Google AI company DeepMind created the first deep learning model to successfully learn control policies directly from high-dimensional sensory input using RL [4]. One of the challenges for RL is to find the best features to feed the algorithm, therefore domain experts have to choose hand-crafted features and make a lot of tests. To overcome this problem, DeepMind researchers, trained a convolutional neural network (CNN) with a variant of Q-learning algorithm and stochastic gradient descent optimization to learn successful control policies from raw video data. The CNN allows extraction of high-level features from raw sensory data. With this approach DeepMind achieved remarkable results in six of seven games of Atari2600 (*B. Rider, Breakout, Enduro, Pong, Q*bert, Seaquest* and *Space Invaders*) using the same model with the same architecture and hyperparamenters in all games.

In [5] the NE approach was compared with the DeepMind agent on the same Atari Games. NE is motivated by the evolution of biological systems and applies a genetic algorithm to optimize the neural network (NN) architecture. The NN consists of three layers where the input layer receives the raw pixels of the game, objects information or the noise-screen state representation. The authors studied two major frameworks: Conventional Neuroevolution (CNE) with weight evolution over a topologically static NN and Neuroevolution of Augmenting Topologies (NEAT) where both the weights and NN topology have been evolved.

In 2016, DeepMind presented AlphaGo, the first computer program that has defeated a human professional player in the full-sized game of Go (best of 5 games) [6]. The Go game is one of the most challenging games for computers due to its huge search space and the difficulty of evaluating board positions and moves. To accomplish this task the model used a *value network* to predict the winner of the game and a *policy network* to give a recommendation of the best action to take. Both deep neural networks (DNNs) where trained by combining supervised learning from human expert games and RL from self-played games. Then, using a tree search to evaluate positions, the moves were selected by the DNNs, where the *policy network* helped at reducing the breadth of the tree and the *value network* the depth, thus reducing drastically the search space. This strategy of combining the two modes for training the DNNs was very innovative, because the computer has learned both from humans and from itself and achieved 99.8% winning rate against other Go programs and defeated the human European Go champion.

One year latter, in 2017, DeepMind launched a new version of AlphaGo, AlphaGo Zero [7]. In this strategy there is no human data, the policy and value networks are combined into one neural network. RL plays against itself, with an opponent that is calibrated to its current level of performance. The goal has been to build a less complex and more general model. This new version achieved a very high performance winning 100-0 against the previous version of AlphaGo.

This paper is inspired by the Stanford Institute for Computational & Mathematical Engineering (ICME) report on Playing FlappyBird with Deep Reinforcement Learning [8]. In this work a deep convolutional neural network acts as the approximate function to represent the Q-value (action value) in Q-reinforcement learning. The proposed model, coined deep Q network (DQN), consists of two convolutional layers followed by two fully connected layers. DQN learns control policies directly from image observations.

In the present paper instead of using raw pixels of the game frames as the game state we apply more domain specific feature selection and represent the current game state by the the bird velocity and the difference between the bird's position and the next lower pipe. This feature engineering approach reduces drastically the feature space and eliminates the need of deeper models to automatically extract underlying features. The agent is provided with rational human-level inputs to guide its learning. Two AI strategies are comparatively evaluated: generic RL and a standard 3 layer NN structure with genetic optimization algorithm (Neuroevolution) to learn playing the Flappy Bird game and improve progressively their performance.

3   Flappy Bird Game

The Flappy Bird game is a a side-scroller game where the player controls a bird, attempting to fly between columns of pipes without hitting them (Fig. 1(a). If the bird touches the pipes, the game is over and may restart for a new episode. The player controls the vertical position (height) of the bird, the bird is always falling and when the key (space bar or up arrow) is pressed the bird jumps. (https:// www.youtube.com/watch?v=l1gX6gMkGeg - game play example). The pipes are displayed randomly in height with always the same gap between the bottom and the upper pipe and the same horizontal distance between the current pipe and the next one. In the python code of the game we have access to the bird and pipes positions. The scatter plot in Fig. 2 represents the histogram of the following game variables: bird's coordinates (x, y), bird's vertical (y) velocity, the

(a) Game screenshot   (b) Game representation model

Fig. 1. Flappy Bird Game

closest lower pipe coordinates (x, y) and the vertical (y) position of the closest upper pipe. The x coordinates of the closest upper and lower pipes are the same. These values where recorded during a game where the player scored 64 points (number of pipes the bird passed successfully).

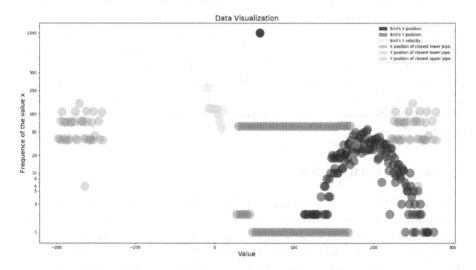

Fig. 2. Data visualization.

4   Reinforcement Learning to Flappy Bird Game

In the reinforcement learning (RL) framework the algorithm (the agent) is not provided with the 'right answer' (as with the supervised learning) instead it receives feedback in the form of rewards, that indicate to the learning agent when it is doing well, and when it is doing poorly [9]. Agent's utility is defined by the reward function. The goal of the agent is to learn to act so as to maximize the expected rewards. The RL problem defined as Markov decision process has the following elements:

- S - set of states.
- A - set of actions.
- $P(s, a)$ - state-transition probability between each state and action.
- R - reward function that returns a reward based on the current state, the action taken, and/or the next state.
- γ - discount factor (a real number between 0 and 1), represents how much value loose the future rewards according to how distant in time they are.

4.1 Q-Learning to Flappy Bird Game

In this paper we apply the Q-Learning approach of RL. Based on experience with previous games the algorithm creates the Q-table that contains the maximum expected future rewards for each action at each state. The best policy function, i.e. the function that, given a state, returns the action that maximizes the future reward, satisfies the Bellman's equation

$$Q(s, a) = R(s') + max_{a_i \in A}[\gamma \cdot Q(s', a_i)] \tag{1}$$

where s is the current state and s' is the next state after taking action a.

In our framework, the game state is represented by the difference between the bird's position and the next lower pipe (dx, dy), Fig. 1b, and the bird velocity in y axis (v_y). The possible actions in any state are *jump* or *do nothing* (the bird just falls). The reward function return $+1$ every time the agent completes a step without dying, and -100 when it dies. According to the rules of the game, the player gets a point only when the bird passes successfully between two pipes. However, over a number of frames the bird moves to find the next pipe and in order to learn if it is doing the right action our strategy rewards each step (frame) and not only the score step after the bird passes between two pipes. In the implementation of the Bellman's Eq. (1), at each iteration instead of completely replacing the previous Q value we introduced a learning rate α (a real number between 0 and 1).

$$Q(s, a) = (1 - \alpha) \cdot Q(s, a) + \alpha \cdot [R(s') + max_{a_i \in A}[\gamma \cdot Q(s', a_i)]] \tag{2}$$

4.2 Performance Evaluation

The learning rate α and the discount factor γ were chosen after a grid search over the following intervals of discrete values, $\alpha = [0.1, 0.3, 0.5, 0.7, 0.9]$ and $\gamma = [\ 0.1, 0.3, 0.5, 0.7, 0.9, 1]$. The heat map in Fig. 3a was obtained after training the RL model for each combination of parameters (30 combinations in total) over 1500 episodes. The episode ends whenever the bird hits a pipe. The

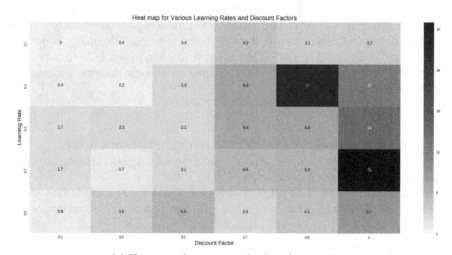

(a) Heat map for a range of values for α and γ

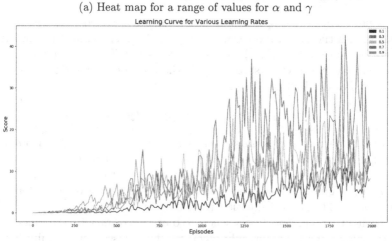

(b) Learning curves as a function of α

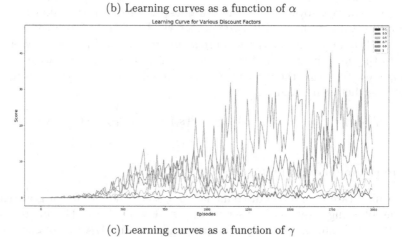

(c) Learning curves as a function of γ

Fig. 3. Learning curves - Reinforcement Learning

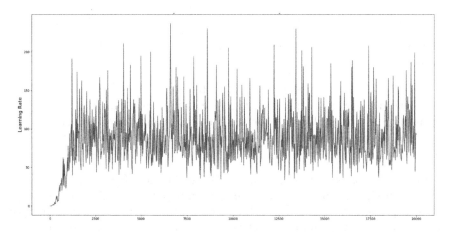

Fig. 4. RL agent with the optimal hyper-parameters: average score over sequences of 20 episodes.

values inside the rectangles, mapped by color (the darker the color, the higher the value), are the average scores of 10 consecutive episodes after training. The score over one episode corresponds to the number of pipes the bird passed before hitting a pipe. The best performance was achieved for the combination $\alpha = 0.7$ and $\gamma = 1$. Figure 3b illustrates in more details the learning curves achieved when the discount factor is set to 1 and α varies. Note that the learning rate significantly affects the score with the best performance achieved for $\alpha = 0.7$. Subsequently, the learning rate was set to its optimal values of 0.7 and the discount factor alternates between [0.1, 0.3, 0.5, 0.7, 0.9, 1]. The results shown in Fig. 3c validate $\gamma = 1$ as the most relevant choice.

The RL agent with the optimal hyperparameters was tested over 20000 episodes. In order to eliminate score fluctuations between subsequent episodes and get statistically more relevant trends in the agent performance, in Fig. 4 are shown moving average scores over sequences of 20 episodes. The AI player needs around 1000 episodes to stabilize its playing performance and then keeps the learned strategy over long number of episodes. Table 1 summarizes the scores over the last 10 episodes and the relevant statistics (average, standard deviation, best and worst score). There is not an official statistics, however 110 points in average before hitting a pipe is a respectful result, according to wikipedia players who achieve a score of forty or higher receive a platinum medal. Nevertheless, dedicated human players can achieve much better results, therefore we consider the RL agent not as a potential game winner but as a stimulating partner in AI-human competitions.

5   Neuroevolution Applied to Flappy Bird Game

Neuroevolution (NE) is an unsupervised machine learning approach to fit a neural network model based on genetic optimization algorithm [10].

5.1 Genetic Optimization

The major nature-inspired natural selection principles encoded into the genetic algorithm are:

- **Heredity** - The process for the children to inherit the parent's properties.
- **Variation** - Variety of traits must exist in the population.
- **Selection** - The probability for some of the population members become parents and pass down their genetic information (referred also as *Survival of the fittest*).

The basic steps of the NE algorithm applied to fit the NE Flappy Bird player are summarized in Algorithm 1. We start with a population of N neural network models (represented in the game by their bird avatars) with randomly generated initial properties. In our implementation, the properties that will undergo evolution are the NN weights and the number of hidden layer units. For each element of the population we evaluate its fitness (how well or bad is it in doing a given task) and its relative fitness (how well or bad is it in a given task compared to the other elements of the same population). The next step (*crossover*) is to pick two parents and combine their properties to create a child. The parents are chosen according to their relative fitness, the higher the fitness, the higher the probability of being selected. Based on a predefined mutation probability, the child's properties undergo mutation (small changes in their properties), which defines the new generation. This iterative process is repeated until we find a generation (a model) that satisfies our demands (e.g. the NE agent reaches a target score). The NE training is illustrated in Fig. 5.

Algorithm 1. Neuroevolution

1: **procedure** GENETICALGORITHM
2:     *Setup:*
3:     *population* ← Create a population of N elements (NN models) with randomly generated *properties*
4:     *Loop:*
5:     **for** *element* in *population* **do**
6:         evaluate element's fitness.
7:     *newPopulation* ← Empty population
8:     **for** $i = 0$ to N **do**
9:         *parents* ← Pick two parents according to relative *fitness(crossover)*
10:         *child* ← Create a *child* by combining the *properties* of these two parents
11:         *mutatedChild* ← Mutate the child's *properties* based on a given probability
12:         *newPopulation* ← Add mutatedChild to the new population
13:     *population* ← newPopulation
14:     **goto** *Loop.*

5.2 Performance Evaluation

The state representation of the game (the inputs of the NN model) are the same as the ones used in the RL approach, namely the difference between the bird's position and the next lower pipe (dx, dy) and the bird velocity in y axis (v_y). The NNs have three layers, the input layer has 3+1(the bias) units, the hidden layer is

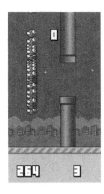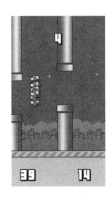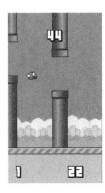

Fig. 5. Neuroevolution training stages (top number is the current score, left-bottom number is the current population size, right-bottom number is the generation number).

initialized with 4 sigmoid nodes and the output layer has one sigmoid node. The population size and the mutation probability, considered as hyperparameters of model, were chosen after a grid search over intervals of discrete values.

Figure 6(a) illustrates the learning curves when the population size is fixed to 300 birds for each generation and the mutations probability is set to (0.3, 0.5, 0.7, 0.9). The mutation probability represents the likelihood of a mutation occurring in the NN weights or in the number of the hidden layer units. Note that the mutation probability significantly affects the score with the best performance achieved for mutation probability of 0.3.

Theoretically, the higher the population size, the better are the chances to find a satisfactory NE agent, however, in practice the computational cost limits this choice. In Fig. 6(b) are shown the learning curves where the mutation probability is set to 0.3 and the population varies in the interval (50, 100, 200, 300, 500). The plots show that a population size between 100 and 200 is enough to maintain a consistent growth. In order to illustrate the trend in the learning process, the curves in Fig. 6 represent moving average scores over sequences of 5 episodes.

The NE model with the optimal hyper-parameters (mutation probability $= 0.3$, population size $= 200$) was trained and the results are shown in Fig. 6(c). After 280 generations the NE agent demonstrated a qualitative jump in its competitive properties and achieved impressive scores in the range of 10^5. The scores over the last 10 episodes are given in Table 1, with the best result of 149652 points and the average of 28694 points. At this stage, the NE agent has found the key performance parameters, the episodes has become very long before it lose and the game was stopped.

There isn't an official statistics regarding Flappy Bird competition between human players, some sources claim 1940 points as the best recorded score for the game. Even if this information may not be sufficiently reliable we believe that the average score reached by the NE agent proposed in this paper has not been ever achieved by a human.

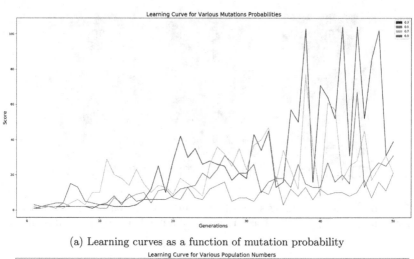

(a) Learning curves as a function of mutation probability

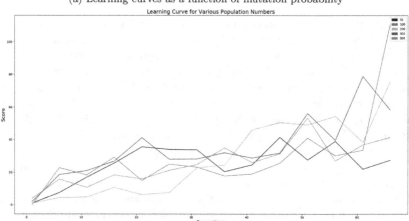

(b) Learning curves as a function of population size

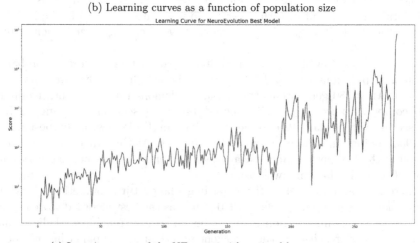

(c) Learning curve of the NE agent with optimal hyper-parameters.

Fig. 6. Learning curves - Neuroevolution

Table 1. Results.

#	RL Score	NE Score
1	120	4112
2	120	1639
3	245	2200
4	68	1812
5	70	18
6	105	21
7	100	1301
8	120	46321
9	90	79844
10	75	149652

Model	Average	SD (σ)	Best	Worst
RL	111.3	51.23	245	68
NE	28694	50235.52	149652	18

6 Conclusion

Applying AI techniques to games is a convenient way to test and compare them because we can easily quantify their performance. In this paper we compare the performance of Reinforcement Learning and Neuroevolution learning setups to play the FlappyBird game.

The key for the high scores achieved by both algorithms is their already proven ability to encode the general game logic and the feature engineering applied in this paper. In contrast to previous works where deep models need to learn relevant features on high-dimensional image data (snapshots of the game), here distance and velocity are the inputs processed by the AI agents. Further to that, NE agent got surprisingly high performance taking advantage of the good generalization capacity of NNs in the continuous state space of the game. Though RL agent was defeated by the NE agent, it achieved a platinum medal level of competitive performance.

References

1. Yannakakis, G.N., Togelius, J.: Artificial Intelligence and Games. Springer, New York (2018). https://doi.org/10.1007/978-3-319-63519-4
2. Rhiannon, W.: What is Flappy Bird? The game taking the App Store by storm. The Daily Telegraph, 30 January 2014
3. Hsu, F.-H.: IBM's deep blue chess grandmaster chips. IEEE Micro **19**(2), 70–81 (1999)
4. Mnih, V., et al.: Playing Atari with deep reinforcement learning. In: NIPS Deep Learning Workshop (2013)
5. Hausknecht, M., Lehman, J., Miikkulainen, R., Stone, P.: A neuroevolution approach to general Atari game playing. IEEE Trans. Comput. Intell. AI Games **6**(4), 355–366 (2014)

6. Silver, D., et al.: Mastering the game of go with deep neural networks and tree search. Nature **529**(7587), 484–489 (2016)
7. Silver, D., et al.: Mastering the game of go without human knowledge. Nature **550**, 354 (2017)
8. Appiah, N., Vare, S.: Playing FlappyBird with Deep Reinforcement Learning. http://cs231n.stanford.edu/reports/2016/pdfs/111Report.pdf
9. Qiang, W., Zhongli, Z.: Reinforcement learning model, algorithms and its application. In: International Conference on Mechatronic Science, Electric Engineering and Computer, 19–22 August 2011
10. Risi, S., Togelius, J.: Neuroevolution in games: state of the art and open challenges. IEEE Trans. Comput. Intell. AI Games **9**(1), 25–41 (2017)

Pattern Recognition

Description and Recognition of Activity Patterns Using Sparse Vector Fields

Ana Portêlo[1][✉], Andrea Cavallaro[2], Catarina Barata[3], and Jorge S. Marques[3]

[1] INESC-ID, Instituto Superior Técnico, Universidade de Lisboa, Lisbon, Portugal
ana.i.portelo@gmail.com
[2] Centre for Intelligent Sensing, Queen Mary University of London, London, UK
[3] Institute for Systems and Robotics, Instituto Superior Técnico,
Universidade de Lisboa, Lisbon, Portugal

Abstract. Far-field activities represented as time series or trajectories can be summarized in compact representations of frequent patterns. Popular representations such as clustering or probabilistic modeling of trajectories often do not inform about both velocity and direction of motion, which are by definition visually and quantitatively embedded in vector fields. However, a common use of vector fields may dismiss information about forbidden areas, or regions with concurrent activity patterns. To address this problem we present a non-iterative layered vector field estimation process that yields sparse vector field abstractions of activity patterns from groups of trajectories. The key feature of our approach is the estimate of the probability density function (PDF) of targets positions: it automatically tunes the cost function parameter, and serves as weights in the sparse estimation problem. We also propose a trajectory labeling algorithm that labels trajectories according to their activity patterns using the vector field abstractions. Experiments in synthetic and real trajectory data show that the proposed estimation approach yields correctly sparse vector fields, which are similar to known generating vector fields, and 5–12% higher labeling accuracy on test trajectories when compared to other generative models. Outlier trajectories are also detected.

Keywords: Activity patterns · Vector fields · Sparse optimization · Trajectory labeling · Oulier detection

1 Introduction

Far-field activities can be described by trajectories [4,10], their spatial and angular features [1,9], or by generative models [2,6,11,12]. A high-level description of the spatial distribution of frequent activity patterns can support anomaly

This work was partially supported by FCT under project SPARSIS - Sparse Modeling and Estimation of Vector Fields, contract PTDC/EEIPRO/0426/2014 and pluriannual funding UID/EEA/50009/2019 and UID/CEC/50021/2019 (INESC-ID).

A. Morales et al. (Eds.): IbPRIA 2019, LNCS 11867, pp. 239–248, 2019.
https://doi.org/10.1007/978-3-030-31332-6_21

detection [8] and accessibility planning [5], and encode semantic regions of the scene [13].

In the literature, both diffusion and probabilistic models have been used to describe frequent activity patterns and to label trajectories according to activity patterns. On the one hand, *diffusion* models such as optical flow models have been used to describe coherent motions and semantic regions [14], and heat maps based on thermal diffusion processes have been used to capture the temporal motion information of activities [7]. On the other hand, *probabilistic* models such as Hidden Markov Models have been used to detect the points of interest in a scene [11], and Dirichlet Process Mixture Models have been used to robustly label new trajectories according to their activity patterns [6]. These studies either focused on attributing a single semantic meaning to specific spatial regions [11,14], or on labelling trajectories according to their activity patterns [6,7]. However, neither of them provide straightforward information about velocity and direction of the activity patterns, and only the latter are able to describe different global activity patterns in the same region of the scene. Typically, this type of motion information is associated to vector fields which embed both the physical meaning of motion (*i.e.*, velocity and direction) and the semantic interpretation of different regions of the scene [5,12].

We propose to (i) describe multiple, complex activity patterns using layered vector fields and (ii) label test trajectories according to activity patterns using the estimated vector fields. Our approach extends that of previous studies in that: (a) it imposes data-driven sparsity to the vector field abstractions to prevent erroneous extrapolations in regions with no target data (contrarily to [5,12]); (b) it is sensitive to concurrent activity patterns (contrarily to [11,14]); and (c) it provides information on the velocity and direction of activity patterns (contrarily to [6,7]).

The proposed vector field estimation uses a cost function specifically designed to yield sparse estimates. Contrarily to other studies, which induce sparsity of the vector field estimates through the l_1-norm [3], this work does so through statistical conditioning on available data – the estimated spatial Probability Density Function (PDF) of the targets positions restricts vector field estimates to the regions where targets are observed. The proposed cost function further benefits from automatic parameter tuning using targets positions and trajectory features. Layered vector field abstractions can be obtained if the proposed approach is applied on pre-clustered trajectories with similar activity patterns. We assess the accuracy of the vector field abstractions of synthetic trajectories by comparing the estimated and generating vector fields, and the correct sparsity by comparing the estimated vector fields in regions with no target data with the null vector field. Vector field comparisons focus on the mean vector length (RMSL) and the vector similarity coefficient (R) [16].

Moreover, we propose a trajectory labeling algorithm according to activity patterns. The displacement error between test trajectories and generated trajectories using the estimated vector fields is the measure for classification. This way, test trajectories are sorted according to activity patterns or detected as outliers.

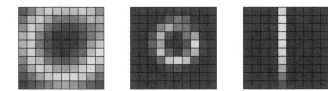

Fig. 1. Probability density functions of the targets positions for 3 different activity patterns from the synthetic data set (D_0). Gradient colours of ascending density of data points from dark blue to yellow. (Color figure online)

We assess the accuracy of the trajectory labeling algorithm by comparing the attributed and the observed activity pattern labels of test trajectories.

2   Estimation of Multiple Vector Fields

We first aim to estimate the vector field, T, that describes the activity patterns of a set of S trajectories, $\mathcal{X} = \{x_1, \ldots, x_S\}$. Let $t = 1, \ldots, L_s$ and the target position, $x_s(t)$, in the image plane of a camera be *driven* by T according to

$$x_s(t) = x_s(t-1) + T(x_s(t-1)) + w_s(t), \tag{1}$$

where $w_s(t) \sim \mathcal{N}(\mathbf{0}, \sigma^2 \mathbf{I}), \forall t$, is a white random perturbation. Let the image plane be normalized, thus $x_s(t) \in [0,1]^2 \, \forall t$.

The vector field, $T : [0,1]^2 \to \mathbb{R}^2$, is defined only at the grid nodes of an overimposed regular, uniform grid, $\mathcal{G} = \{g_n \in [0,1]^2, n = 1, 2, \ldots, N\}$, on the image plane. As the target trajectories can be defined in any image coordinate, even if it does not correspond to a grid node ($x_s(t) \notin \mathcal{G}$), we bilinearly interpolate to represent the vector field that drives the target position on any coordinate of the image plane, $x_s(t) \notin \mathcal{G}$:

$$T(x_s(t)) = \sum_{n=1}^{N} \phi_n(x_s(t)) \, t_n, \tag{2}$$

where $\phi_n(x_s(t))$ are the interpolation coefficients of the velocity vectors, t_n, at the grid nodes. The matrix of interpolation coefficients for set $\mathcal{X}$ is $\mathbf{\Phi}$.

Vector field estimation corresponds to an optimization problem where T is the minimizer of a given cost function that has to induce data-driven sparsity. To impose *sparsity* of the vector field estimates in the regions where target data does not exist, the velocity vectors in T are weighted by 1 minus the spatial probability density function (PDF) of targets positions, *i.e.*, $\mathcal{D} = \mathbf{1} - \Gamma_p$, $\Gamma_p \in \mathbb{R}^N$. Γ_p is the estimated PDF of the targets positions using the Parzen window algorithm over set $\mathcal{X}$. Then, to get its value at the grid nodes, we discretize at the desired image coordinates (Fig. 1).

The cost function is therefore defined as

$$f(T) = \|V - T\mathbf{\Phi}\|_2^2 + \alpha \|T \circ \mathbf{1}\mathcal{D}^\top\|_2^2, \tag{3}$$

where $\mathbb{1}$ is of size $[2 \times 1]$, $\|.\|_2$ defines the l_2-norm of a vector, "$\circ$" represents the Hadamard product, and $\boldsymbol{T} \in \mathbb{R}^{2 \times N}$, $\boldsymbol{V} \in \mathbb{R}^{2 \times M}$, $\boldsymbol{\Phi} \in \mathbb{R}^{N \times M}$, $M = \sum_{s=1}^{S}(L_s - 1)$, are given by

$$\boldsymbol{T} = \begin{bmatrix} \boldsymbol{t}_1 & \cdots & \boldsymbol{t}_N \end{bmatrix}, \tag{4}$$

$$\boldsymbol{V} = \begin{bmatrix} \boldsymbol{v}_1(2) \dots \boldsymbol{v}_1(L_1) \mid \dots \mid \boldsymbol{v}_S(2) \dots \boldsymbol{v}_S(L_S) \end{bmatrix}, \tag{5}$$

$$\boldsymbol{\Phi} = \begin{bmatrix} \phi_1(\boldsymbol{x}_1(1)) \dots \phi_1(\boldsymbol{x}_1(L_1 - 1)) & & \phi_1(\boldsymbol{x}_S(1)) \dots \phi_1(\boldsymbol{x}_S(L_S - 1)) \\ \vdots & \cdots & \vdots \\ \phi_N(\boldsymbol{x}_1(1)) \dots \phi_N(\boldsymbol{x}_1(L_1 - 1)) & & \phi_N(\boldsymbol{x}_S(1)) \dots \phi_N(\boldsymbol{x}_S(L_S - 1)) \end{bmatrix}, \tag{6}$$

with matrix $\boldsymbol{V}$ composed of the velocity vectors between consecutive target positions, i.e., $\boldsymbol{v}_s(t) = \boldsymbol{x}_s(t) - \boldsymbol{x}_s(t-1)$.

In Eq. (3), α is correlated with the grid resolution N. To avoid manual parameter input in every estimation procedure, we propose an *automatic tuning* based on the cardinality of the non-zero elements (i.e., $|\cdot|_{\neq 0}$), expected value (i.e., $\mathbb{E}[\cdot]$), and standard deviation [i.e., $\sigma(\cdot)$] of the estimated PDFs of target and trajectory features,

$$\alpha = 1 - \frac{|\Gamma_p|_{\neq 0}}{N}, \tag{7}$$

$$N = \max\left\{ N_{\min}, |\Gamma_c|_{\neq 0} > \mathbb{E}[\Gamma_c] + 1.5\,\sigma(\Gamma_c) \right\}, \tag{8}$$

where Γ_p is the spatial PDF of the target positions as before; $\Gamma_c \in \mathbb{R}^N$ is the average curvature of the trajectories at the grid nodes, which is estimated using the velocity angles $\theta(t) = \tan^{-1}\left(\frac{y(t) - y(t-1)}{x(t) - x(t-1)}\right)$ [1,8]; and $N_{\min}$ is the minimum grid resolution selected by the user. In (8), very curly trajectories (i.e., extreme values of the distribution of Γ_c) define the grid resolution.

Multiple vector fields can be estimated using (3) if it is applied to each set of pre-clustered trajectories $(\mathcal{X}_k)$ with similar activity patterns, e.g. using multiple features [1]. In the following, we assume that the pre-clustering step has taken place and that we have access to the sets $\mathcal{X}_k$.

3   Activity Pattern Labeling

Our second aim is to label trajectories according to their activity patterns. To achieve this aim, we first estimate the $\boldsymbol{T}_k$ following the above approach and using only trajectories from training sets $\mathcal{X}_k$. Then, we propose the following labeling algorithm:

1. Trajectory labeling:
    (a) Generate trajectories from the starting point of a given test trajectory using the estimated $\boldsymbol{T}_k$ and (1);
    (b) Compute the displacement error as the euclidean distance between the generated and the test trajectories;

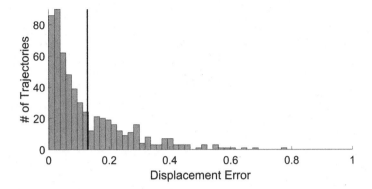

Fig. 2. Histogram of displacement errors between validation trajectories and generated trajectories using the known labels of activity patterns (vector fields). The cutoff threshold is shown in black. The validation trajectories used in this example come from the real data set D_3.

    (c) Label each test trajectory with the activity pattern (vector field abstraction) that yields the smallest displacement error.
2. Outlier detection using threshold:
    (a) Compute the cutoff threshold as the sum of the median and the median absolute deviation (MAD) of the displacement errors obtained from steps 1.(a) and 1.(b) applied on a set of validation trajectories (Fig. 2);
    (b) Label test trajectories as outliers of the labeled activity pattern from step 1.(c) if their displacement error is above the threshold.

In the Outlier detection step above, the cutoff threshold for outlier detection is the sum of the median and median absolute deviation of the displacement errors. We use the median and its absolute deviation instead of the mean and standard deviation given that the distribution of displacement errors is right skewed.

4   Experimental Results

4.1   Synthetic Data

Assessment Measures. Estimates of vector fields using synthetic data (T_{est}) are assessed regarding both the *accuracy* when compared to the known generating vector field (T_{ref}) and the correct *sparsity* compared to the null vector field (T_0) in regions where no target data is observed. Let each node on the overimposed grid be labeled according to its proximity to a given trajectory as an *active node*, if it belongs to a square of nodes containing part of a given trajectory, or a *non-active node*, if it does not belong to such a square of nodes. Thus, the region where no target data is observed is defined as the set of non-active nodes in the image plane, $\mathcal{Z}$, with respect to a given trajectory set.

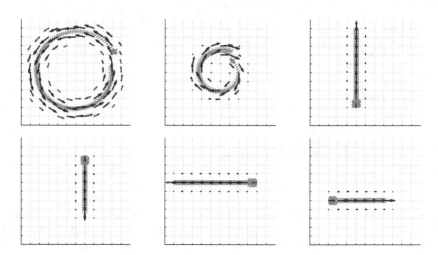

Fig. 3. Vector field estimates for the 6 activity patterns of the synthetic data set (D_0). Activity patterns are ordered across rows from left to right (top: 1, 2, 3; bottom: 4, 5, 6). Generating vector fields are shown in red, estimated vector fields in blue, generated trajectories in gray. (Color figure online)

The assessment measures compare pairs of vectors regarding the vector similarity coefficient (R), *i.e.*, the mean of the inner product of normalized vector pairs from 2 vector fields A and B, defined as [16],

$$R = \frac{1}{|\mathcal{P}|} \sum_{i \in \mathcal{P}} \hat{t}_i^A \cdot \hat{t}_i^B \; ; \tag{9}$$

and the vector root mean square length (RMSL), *i.e.*, the systematic difference in the mean vector length, defined as [16],

$$\text{RMSL} = L_V^2 = \frac{1}{|\mathcal{P}|} \sum_{i \in \mathcal{P}} \left\| t_i^A - t_i^B \right\|_2^2 \; ; \tag{10}$$

where "." is the inner product, $\hat{t} = \frac{t}{\sqrt{\|t\|_2^2}}$, $\| \cdot \|_2$ represents the l_2-norm of a vector, and $|\cdot|$ represents the cardinality of a set. In the case of *accuracy* assessment, $A = T_{\text{ref}}$, $B = T_{\text{est}}$, and $\mathcal{P} = \mathcal{G}$, the set of grid nodes. In the case of correct *sparsity* assessment, $A = T_0$, $B = T_{\text{est}}$, and $\mathcal{P} = \mathcal{Z}$, the set of non-active nodes. The optimal values for these measures are (R, RMSL)= $(1, 1)$ and RMSL= 0, respectively for accuracy and sparsity assessments.

Data Set. The synthetic data set (D_0) has 300 trajectories generated using 6 different activity patterns. We use D_0 as a proof of concept for the assessment of accuracy and correct sparsity of the estimated vector fields.

Table 1. Overall accuracy of trajectory labeling for the proposed approach and comparison with literature results [6,11,14].

Data set	Activity Patterns	traj. per Pattern	Overall accuracy (%)	
			Ours	Literature
D_0	6	50	**100.00**	–
D_1	15	18–278	**87.81**	[82.00, 86.70]
D_2	11	20	**95.45**	[86.30, 91.80]
D_3	19	100	**99.47**	[95.00, 98.00]

Results. Figure 3 shows that the vector field estimates are very similar to the generating vector fields not only in terms of magnitude (RMSL) and direction (R) but also regarding sparsity in the regions with no data, as expected. The accuracy of the estimated vector fields (activity patterns) is respectively (R, RMSL) **1:** (0.920, 0.663); **2:** (0.952, 2.305); **3:** (0.982, 0.979); **4:** (0.973, 0.723); **5:** (0.954, 9.787); **6:** (0.968, 0.763), and the RMSL of the vector field estimates corresponds to sparse vector fields, *i.e.*, all bellow 2.94e−04.

4.2 Real Data

Assessment Measures. Activity pattern labeling accuracy is computed by comparing attributed and known trajectory labels taking into account the cutoff threshold as

$$Acc = \frac{\sum \mathrm{diag}(\mathcal{M})}{\sum_{ij} \mathcal{M}_{ij}}, \tag{11}$$

where $\mathcal{M}$ is the confusion matrix in a problem with multiple activity patterns.

Data Set. The real data sets we used are: D_1 (Hu), containing 1500 trajectories with 15 activity patterns [6]; D_2 (Wang), containing 220 trajectories with 11 activity patterns [14]; D_3 (Morris), containing 1900 trajectories with 19 activity patterns [11]. We use these data sets to assess activity pattern labeling and outlier detection.

Results. Table 1 shows that overall the proposed algorithm correctly labels trajectories according to their activity patterns with an accuracy above that described in the literature. More specifically with higher accuracy than Heatmap, HMM, and DPMM, which are comparable generative models used to describe activity patterns [6,11,14,15].

Regarding outlier detection, note that the proposed algorithm always assigns an activity pattern to a trajectory – the attributed activity pattern is the one that generates trajectories with the smallest displacement error relative to the test trajectory. However, if the displacement error is above the threshold the respective trajectory is plotted in a different colour than the others and tagged

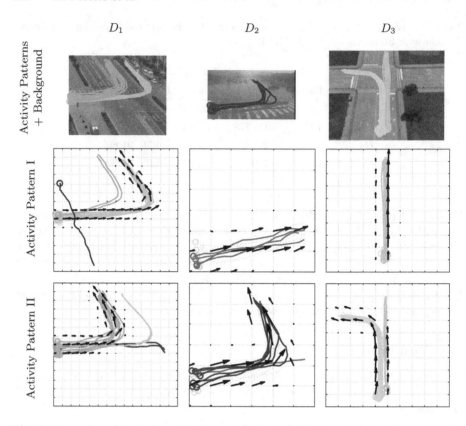

Fig. 4. Examples of trajectory labeling using the real data sets (D_1, D_2, and D_3), only two example activity patterns are shown for each data set. *Top row.* Overview of background image and test trajectories. *Middle row.* Correctly labelled trajectories and over-imposed estimated vector fields (black arrows) for Activity Pattern I. *Bottom row.* Correctly labelled trajectories, over-imposed estimated vector fields (black arrows), and outliers (shown in different colors) for Activity Pattern II. (Color figure online)

as an outlier. Figure 4 shows examples of 2 activity patterns for each real data set, which have similar motion patterns but different semantic meanings. Concerning Activity Pattern I, only D_1 has outlier trajectories from two other activity patterns (shown in different colors, Fig. 4 middle row). Concerning Activity Pattern II, all the data sets have outlier trajectories from Activity Pattern I, and D_1 also has outlier trajectories form one additional activity pattern (Fig. 4 bottom row).

The proposed approach yields vector field abstractions that can distinguish between similar activity patterns with different underlying semantics, given that for each data set, trajectories which were wrongly labelled as having one activity pattern were correctly detected as outliers of that activity pattern. For example, the green outlier trajectories from D_1 (Fig. 4 bottom left panel) are detected as outliers of that activity pattern – whereas the vector field of interest describes a left turn into the primary road, the outlier trajectories correspond to targets that instead performed a left turn into a secondary road. Similar examples for the other two data sets are shown in the bottom row of Fig. 4.

5   Conclusion

We proposed a vector field estimation approach that copes with dense trajectory data and yields compact abstractions of frequent activity patterns. The proposed approach abstracts frequently observed activity patterns and embeds data-driven sparsity, through the estimated spatial Probability Density Function (PDF) of the targets positions. Moreover, it informs about the physical and semantic meaning of the observed activity patterns. Finally, the estimated vector fields can be used to label new trajectories and detect outliers according to their activity pattern, with an improvement of about 5–12% on trajectory labeling accuracy when compared to other generative models.

References

1. Anjum, N., Cavallaro, A.: Multifeature object trajectory clustering for video analysis. IEEE Trans. Circuits Syst. Video Technol. **18**(11), 1555–1564 (2008)
2. Barão, M., Marques, J.S.: Gaussian random vector fields in trajectory modelling. In: Proceedings of the 19th Irish Machine Vision and Image Processing Conference (IMVIP), pp. 211–216 (2017)
3. Barata, C., Nascimento, J.C., Marques, J.S.: A sparse approach to pedestrian trajectory modeling using multiple motion fields. In: IEEE International Conference on Image Processing (ICIP), pp. 2538–2542 (2017)
4. Dollar, P., Wojek, C., Schiele, B., Perona, P.: Pedestrian detection: an evaluation of the state of the art. IEEE Trans. Pattern Anal. Mach. Intell. **34**(4), 743–761 (2012)
5. Ferreira, N., Klosowski, J.T., Scheidegger, C.E., Silva, C.T.: Vector field k-means: clustering trajectories by fitting multiple vector fields. In: Eurographics Conference on Visualization (EuroVis), vol. 32 (2013)
6. Hu, W., Li, X., Tian, G., Maybank, S., Zhang, Z.: An incremental DPMM-based method for trajectory clustering, modeling, and retrieval. IEEE Trans. Pattern Anal. Mach. Intell. **35**(5), 1051–1065 (2013)
7. Lin, W., Chu, H., Wu, J., Sheng, B., Chen, Z.: A heat-map-based algorithm for recognizing group activities in videos. IEEE Trans. Circuits Syst. Video Technol. **23**(11), 1980–1992 (2013)
8. Marques, J.S., Figueiredo, M.A.T.: Fast estimation of multiple vector fields: application to video surveillance. In: 7th International Symposium on Image and Signal Processing and Analysis (ISPA) (2011)
9. Mirge, V., Verma, K., Gupta, S.: Dense traffic flow patterns mining in bi-directional road networks using density based trajectory clustering. Adv. Data Anal. Classification **11**(3), 547–561 (2017)
10. Morris, B.T., Trivedi, M.M.: A survey of vision-based trajectory learning and analysis for surveillance. IEEE Trans. Circuits Syst. Video Technol. **18**(8), 1114–1127 (2008)

11. Morris, B.T., Trivedi, M.M.: Trajectory learning for activity understanding: unsupervised, multilevel, and long-term adaptive approach. IEEE Trans. Pattern Anal. Mach. Intell. **33**(11), 2287–2301 (2011)
12. Nascimento, J.C., Figueiredo, M.A.T., Marques, J.S.: Activity recognition using a mixture of vector fields. IEEE Trans. Image Process. **22**(5), 1712–1725 (2013)
13. Robicquet, A., Sadeghian, A., Alahi, A., Savarese, S.: Learning social etiquette: human trajectory understanding in crowded scenes. In: European Conference on Computer Vision (ECCV) (2016)
14. Wang, W., Lin, W., Chen, Y., Wu, J., Wang, J., Sheng, B.: Finding coherent motions and semantic regions in crowd scenes: a diffusion and clustering approach. In: European Conference on Computer Vision (ECCV), pp. 756–771 (2014)
15. Xu, H., Zhou, Y., Lin, W., Zha, H.: Unsupervised trajectory clustering via adaptive multi-kernel-based shrinkage. In: The IEEE International Conference on Computer Vision (ICCV) (2015)
16. Xu, Z., Hou, Z., Han, Y., Guo, W.: A diagram for evaluating multiple aspects of model performance in simulating vector fields. Geosci. Model. Dev. **9**(12), 4365–4380 (2016)

Instance Selection for the Nearest Neighbor Classifier: Connecting the Performance to the Underlying Data Structure

Vicente García[1], Josep Salvador Sánchez[2(✉)], Alberto Ochoa-Ortiz[1], and Abraham López-Najera[1]

[1] Universidad Autónoma de Ciudad Juárez, Ciudad Juárez, Chihuahua, Mexico
{vicente.jimenez,alberto.ochoa,abraham.najera}@uacj.mx
[2] Institute of New Imaging Technologies, Department of Computer Languages and Systems, Universitat Jaume I, Castelló de la Plana, Spain
sanchez@uji.es

Abstract. Instance selection is one of the most successful solutions to low noise tolerance of the nearest neighbor classifier. Many algorithms have been proposed in the literature, but further research in this area is still needed to complement the existing findings. Here we intend to go beyond a simple comparison of instance selection methods and correspondingly, we carry out a qualitative analysis of why some algorithms perform better than others under different conditions. In summary, this paper investigates the impact of instance selection on the underlying structure of a data set by analyzing the distribution of sample types, with the purpose of linking the performance of these methods to changes in the data structure.

Keywords: Nearest neighbor classifier · Instance selection · Editing · Sample types

1 Introduction

In supervised learning, one of the most popular models is the well-known and understood k-nearest neighbors (kNN) algorithm [6]. A query sample is assigned to the class represented by the majority of its k nearest neighbors in the training set (a collection of correctly classified instances). A particular case is when $k = 1$, in which a query sample is decided to belong to the class indicated by its closest neighbor. The 1NN classifier benefits from a number of advantages, which have made it useful and effective for many real-world problems: (i) it can be implemented easily due to its conceptual simplicity; (ii) it does not require any a priori probabilistic information relating to data; and (iii) the error rate for 1NN is at most twice the optimal Bayes error as the training set size tends to infinity.

© Springer Nature Switzerland AG 2019
A. Morales et al. (Eds.): IbPRIA 2019, LNCS 11867, pp. 249–256, 2019.
https://doi.org/10.1007/978-3-030-31332-6_22

However, the kNN algorithm suffers from some inherent weaknesses that may hinder its efficiency and effectiveness due to intensive computational requirements and extreme sensitivity to errors or noise in the training set. To tackle these issues, data reduction has been devised as a tool to obtain a reduced representation of the training set that can closely maintain the properties of the original data. Depending on the approach of the data reduction methods, these can be categorized into two groups [8]: *instance reduction* or *condensing* to lessen the size of the training set by removing redundant examples, and *instance selection* or *editing* to achieve a similar or even higher accuracy by eliminating erroneous and noisy samples. While condensing retains borderline samples (those that are close to the decision boundaries) and removes internal samples, the general strategy followed by editing is the opposite (i.e., the examples chosen to be removed are the borderline samples). In the case of editing, most studies have focused either on carrying out experimental comparisons over multiple data sets or on designing a meta-learning framework to choose the best performing algorithm through the analysis of some data characterization measures [5, 12, 14].

The aim of this paper is to contribute to further understanding of the effects of instance selection on the underlying structure of data sets and to explore for possible connections with the classification accuracy of 1NN. To this end, we will exploit local information to categorize the instances into four different groups (safe, borderline, rare, and outlier), compare their distribution in the original training set with that in the edited set, and relate the performance of some instance selection methods to changes in the data structure. Hopefully, this will allow to gain some insight into the reasons why the 1NN classification performance depends so heavily on the particular instance selection algorithm.

2   Categorization of Sample Types

In the context of learning from imbalanced data, several authors have proposed to distinguish between *safe* and *unsafe* samples according to their neighborhood [11, 15, 17]. The safe samples are placed in homogeneous regions with data from a single class and are sufficiently separated from instances belonging to any other classes, whereas the remaining samples are referred to as unsafe. The safe samples are correctly classified by most models, but the unsafe samples may make their learning especially difficult and more likely to be misclassified.

The common property of the unsafe samples is that they are located close to instances that belong to the opposite class. However, the unsafe samples can be further divided into three subtypes: *borderline*, *rare* and *outlier* [10, 15]. The borderline samples are located closely to the decision boundary between classes. The rare samples form small data structures or clusters located far from the core of their class. Finally, the outliers are single samples that are surrounded by instances from the other class. In the present work, this categorization of samples types will not be used for class-imbalanced problems, but for the analysis of instance selection methods.

A straightforward method to identify each sample type consists of analyzing the local distribution of the data, which can be modeled either by computing their k-neighborhood or through a kernel function (this consists in setting a local area around the instance and estimating the number of neighbors and their class labels within it). It has been claimed that analyzing a local distribution of instances is more appropriate than using global approaches because the minority class is often formed by small sub-groups with difficult, nonlinear borders between the classes [15,17].

Algorithm 1. Identification of sample types for multi-class data

---

1: **Input:**
2: S {Input data set}
3: k {Neighborhood size}
4:
5: **Output:**
6: $safe$ {Set of safe samples}
7: $borderline$ {Set of borderline samples}
8: $rare$ {Set of rare samples}
9: $outlier$ {Set of outlier samples}
10:
11: **for all** $z_i \in S$ **do**
12:     $neighbors \leftarrow$ computeNeighbors($z_i, S - \{z_i\}, k$)
13:     $sameClass \leftarrow$ countSameClass($y_i, neighbors$)
14:     **if** $sameClass \geq \lfloor 0.8k \rfloor$ **then**
15:         $safe \leftarrow safe \cup \{z_i\}$
16:     **else**
17:         **if** $sameClass \geq \lfloor 0.5k \rfloor$ **then**
18:             $borderline \leftarrow borderline \cup \{z_i\}$
19:         **else**
20:             **if** $sameClass \geq \lfloor 0.2k \rfloor$ **then**
21:                 $rare \leftarrow rare \cup \{z_i\}$
22:             **else**
23:                 $outlier \leftarrow outlier \cup \{z_i\}$
24:             **end if**
25:         **end if**
26:     **end if**
27: **end for**

Suppose we have a data set, $S = \{z_i = (x_i, y_i)\}$, where $x_i \in X \subset \mathbb{R}^d$ is a vector of attributes describing the i-th instance and y_i is its class label. The type of a sample z_i is often decided by comparing the number of its k nearest neighbors that belong to the class of z_i with the number of neighbors of the opposite class. Following the procedure given in Algorithm 1, which is a generalization for multiclass data of the scheme proposed by Stefanowski and Wilk [20], a safe sample is characterized by having a neighborhood dominated by instances that belong to its same class, rare samples and outliers are mainly surrounded by instances from different classes, and the borderline samples are surrounded by instances both from their same class and also from a different class. Here we have used two functions: *computeNeighbors* to search for the k nearest neighbors of a sample z_i and store them in a vector named *neighbors*, and *countSameClass* to count how many of the k nearest neighbors belong to the class of z_i.

Most authors choose a fixed size $k = 5$ because smaller values may poorly distinguish the nature of instances and higher values would violate the assumption of local neighborhood. By using $k = 5$, an instance z_i will be defined as: (i) *safe* if at least 4 neighbors are from the class y_i; (ii) *borderline* if 2 or 3 neighbors belong to the class y_i; (iii) *rare* if only one neighbor belongs to the class y_i, and this has no more than one neighbor from its same class; and (iv) *outlier* if all its neighbors are from the opposite class.

3   Databases and Experimental Setting

Experiments were conducted on the artificial data sets depicted in Fig. 1, which are all two-dimensional and correspond to well-balanced binary classification problems. Using synthetic data allows to know their characteristics a priori and analyze the results in a fully controlled environment.

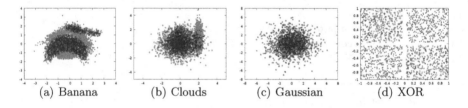

(a) Banana   (b) Clouds   (c) Gaussian   (d) XOR

Fig. 1. Artificial data sets

The Banana data set is a non-linearly separable problem with 5,300 samples that belong to two banana shaped clusters [1]. The Clouds database has 5,000 samples where one class is the sum of three different normal distributions and the other class is a single normal distribution [3]. The Gaussian database consists of 5,000 instances where one class is represented by a multivariate normal distribution with zero mean and standard deviation equal to 1 and the other by a normal distribution with zero mean and standard deviation equal to 2 in all directions [3]. In the XOR database, a total of 1,600 random bivariate samples were generated following a uniform distribution in a square of length equal to 2, centered at zero (apart from a strip of width 0.1 along both axes); the samples were labeled at each quadrant to reproduce the well-known XOR problem, that is, the label of each point (x, y) was computed as $\text{sign}(x) \cdot \text{sign}(y)$ [2].

The stratified 10-fold cross-validation method was adopted for the experiments, thus preserving the prior class probabilities of a database and the statistical independence between the training and test blocks of each fold. The experiments were carried out as follows: (i) the training sets were preprocessed by various editing techniques, (ii) the 1NN classifier with the Euclidean distance was applied using each data set, and (iii) the proportion of each sample type in both the original sets and the filtered sets was recorded. Our hypothesis is that the analysis of the distribution of sample types in a data set may allow to explain the performance of each editing algorithm.

The instance selection techniques used in the experiments were: (1) all-kNN editing (aKNN) [21], (2) Wilson's editing (WE) [23], (3) editing with estimation of class probabilities and threshold (CPT) [22], (4) modified Wilson's editing (MWE) [9], (5) model class selection (MCS) [4], (6) Multiedit (MultiE) [7], (7) editing based on nearest centroid neighborhood (NCN) [19], (8) pattern by ordered projections (POP) [16], (9) editing based on relative neighborhood graph (RNG) [18], and (10) variable-kernel similarity metric (VSM) [13].

4   Results and Discussion

For each database, the graphs in Fig. 2 display to the accuracy rates of 1NN using both the original training set with no preprocessing (the dotted horizontal lines) and the collection of edited sets (vertical bars). The results for Banana, Clouds and XOR show that all instance selection methods had a very similar behavior: leaving aside the 10-VSM method, the 1NN classifier trained with the original training sets and with the edited sets performed equally well. The most interesting results were for the Gaussian database because most algorithms improved the performance achieved by 1NN using the original sets and even more important, some differences from one algorithm to another can be seen. However, the question here was why some methods performed better than others. Thus taking care of this objective, the next step in the experiments was to analyze the underlying structure of each data set and investigate any possible link between the distribution of sample types and the performance of instance selection methods.

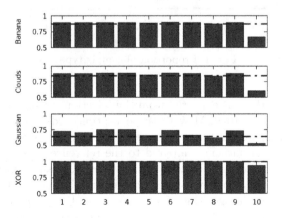

Fig. 2. Classification accuracy

The vertical bars in Fig. 3 represent the proportions of safe, borderline, rare and outlier samples in the sets after applying the editing algorithms. The dotted horizontal lines are for the proportions in the original sets, which should be interpreted as a reference value. A rapid comparison of the proportions of safe and unsafe samples in the original training sets reveal that the Gaussian database represents the most complex and interesting problem with very high class overlapping, and XOR corresponds to the easiest problem with linear class separability and no overlapping.

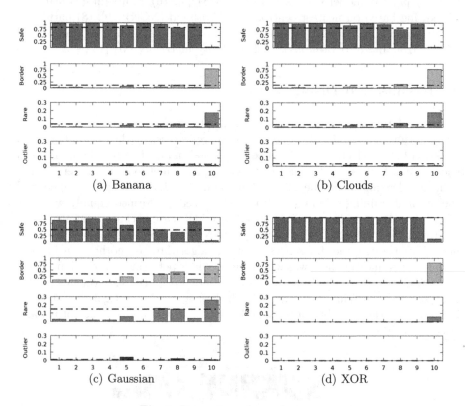

Fig. 3. Proportion of sample types

Figure 3 shows that, as expected from the selection strategy of editing, most methods (8-POP and 10-VSM were the exception) led to an increase in the proportion of safe samples and a decrease in the proportion of unsafe samples (borderline, rare and outlier) compared to the reference values (original training sets). However, paying special attention to the Gaussian problem, one can note that there exist significant differences in the data structure resulting by the application of each algorithm; for instance, 3-CPT, 4-MWE and 6-MultiE were the methods with the highest increase of safe samples and also the highest decrease of unsafe samples, while the changes produced by 5-MCS and 7-NCN were negligible. This may explain the different behavior of 1NN trained by 3-CPT, 4-MWE or 6-MultiE and that trained by 5-MCS or 7-NCN as shown in Fig. 2. This observation reinforces our hypothesis and was supported by the fact that those algorithms with the largest positive changes in the underlying structure of data sets also achieved the highest accuracy rates and therefore, it seems possible to conclude that the analysis of the distribution of sample types can be a useful tool to explain the performance of editing methods.

5 Concluding Remarks

This paper has shown that the performance of instance selection methods can be understood by analyzing the underlying structure of data sets. To this end, one can use local information to categorize the samples into different groups (safe, borderline, rare, and outlier) and compare their distribution in the original training set with that in the edited set.

The experiments have revealed that the algorithms with the highest increase of safe samples and the highest decrease of unsafe samples correspond to those with the highest improvement in 1NN accuracy. Although this work can be further extended by incorporating other techniques and some real-life databases, we believe that these initial observations could be utilized to provide a qualitative discussion of the experimental results in papers where several procedures have to be compared each other.

Acknowledgment. This work has partially been supported by the Universitat Jaume I under grant UJI-B2018-49.

References

1. Alcalá-Fdez, J., et al.: KEEL data-mining software tool: data set repository, integration of algorithms and experimental analysis framework. J. Mult.-Valued Log. S. **17**, 255–287 (2011)
2. Barandela, R., Ferri, F.J., Sánchez, J.S.: Decision boundary preserving prototype selection for nearest neighbor classification. Int. J. Pattern Recogn. **19**(6), 787–806 (2005)
3. Blayo, E., et al.: Deliverable R3-B4-E Task B4: benchmarks, ESPRIT 6891. In: ELENA: Enhanced Learning for Evolutive Neural Architecture (1995)
4. Brodley, C.E.: Adressing the selective superiority problem: automatic algorithm/model class selection. In: Proceedings of the 10th International Machine Learning Conference, Amherst, MA, pp. 17–24 (1993)
5. Caises, Y., González, A., Leyva, E., Pérez, R.: Combining instance selection methods based on data characterization: an approach to increase their effectiveness. Inf. Sci. **181**(20), 4780–4798 (2011)
6. Dasarathy, B.V.: Nearest Neighbor (NN) Norms: Nn Pattern Classification Techniques. IEEE Computer Society Press, Los Alamitos (1991)
7. Devijver, P.A.: On the editing rate of the MULTIEDIT algorithm. Pattern Recogn. Lett. **4**(1), 9–12 (1986)

8. García, S., Derrac, J., Cano, J., Herrera, F.: Prototype selection for nearest neighbor classification: taxonomy and empirical study. IEEE Trans. Pattern Anal. **34**(3), 417–435 (2012)
9. Hattori, K., Takahashi, M.: A new edited k-nearest neighbor rule in the pattern classification problem. Pattern Recogn. **33**, 521–528 (2000)
10. Krawczyk, B., Woźniak, M., Herrera, F.: Weighted one-class classification for different types of minority class examples in imbalanced data. In: Proceedings of the IEEE Symposium on Computational Intelligence and Data Mining, Piscataway, NJ, pp. 337–344 (2014)
11. Kubat, M., Matwin, S.: Addressing the curse of imbalanced training sets: one-sided selection. In: Proceedings of the 14th International Conference on Machine Learning, Nashville, TN, pp. 179–186 (1997)
12. Leyva, E., González, A., Pérez, R.: A set of complexity measures designed for applying meta-learning to instance selection. IEEE Trans. Knowl. Data Eng. **27**(2), 354–367 (2015)
13. Lowe, D.G.: Similarity metric learning for a variable-kernel classifier. Neural Comput. **7**(1), 72–85 (1995)
14. Mollineda, R.A., Sánchez, J.S., Sotoca, J.M.: Data characterization for effective prototype selection. In: Proceedings of the 2nd Iberian Conference on Pattern Recognition and Image Analysis, Estoril, Portugal, pp. 27–34 (2005)
15. Napierala, K., Stefanowski, J.: Types of minority class examples and their influence on learning classifiers from imbalanced data. J. Intell. Inf. Syst. **46**(3), 563–597 (2016)
16. Riquelme, J.C., Aguilar-Ruiz, J.S., Toro, M.: Finding representative patterns with ordered projections. Pattern Recogn. **36**, 1009–1018 (2003)
17. Sáez, J.A., Krawczyk, B., Woźniak, M.: Analyzing the oversampling of different classes and types of examples in multi-class imbalanced datasets. Pattern Recogn. **57**, 164–178 (2016)
18. Sánchez, J.S., Pla, F., Ferri, F.J.: Prototype selection for the nearest neighbor rule through proximity graphs. Pattern Recogn. Lett. **18**, 507–513 (1997)
19. Sánchez, J.S., Pla, F., Ferri, F.J.: Improving the k-NCN classification rule through heuristic modifications. Pattern Recogn. Lett. **19**(13), 1165–1170 (1998)
20. Stefanowski, J., Wilk, S.: Selective pre-processing of imbalanced data for improving classification performance. In: Proceedings of the 10th International Conference in Data Warehousing and Knowledge Discovery, Turin, Italy, pp. 283–292 (2008)
21. Tomek, I.: An experiment with the edited nearest-neighbor rule. IEEE Trans. Syst. Man Cybern. **6**(6), 448–452 (1976)
22. Vázquez, F., Sánchez, J.S., Pla, F.: A stochastic approach to Wilson's editing algorithm. In: Proceedings of the 2nd Iberian Conference on Pattern Recognition and Image Analysis, Estoril, Portugal, pp. 35–42 (2005)
23. Wilson, D.L.: Asymptotic properties of nearest neighbor rules using edited data. IEEE T. Syst. Man Cybern. **2**(3), 408–421 (1972)

Modified DBSCAN Algorithm for Microscopic Image Analysis of Wood

Aurora L. R. Martins[1] , André R. S. Marcal[1]([✉]) , and José Pissarra[1,2]

[1] Faculdade de Ciências da Universidade do Porto, Porto, Portugal
andre.marcal@fc.up.pt
[2] GreenUPorto – Research Centre for Sustainable Agrifood Production, FCUP,
Porto, Portugal

Abstract. The analysis of the intern anatomy of wood samples for species identification is a complex task that only experts can perform accurately. Since there are not many experts in the world and their training can last decades, there is great interest in developing automatic processes to extract high-level information from microscopic wood images. The purpose of this work was to develop algorithms that could provide meaningful information for the classification process. The work focuses on hardwoods, which have a very diverse anatomy including many different features. The ray width is one of such features, with high diagnostic value, which is visible on the tangential section. A modified distance function for the DBSCAN algorithm was developed to identify clusters that represent rays, in order to count the number of cells in width. To test both the segmentation and the modified DBSCAN algorithms, 20 images were manually segmented, obtaining an average Jaccard index of 0.66 for the segmentation and an average index $M = 0.78$ for the clustering task. The final ray count had an accuracy of 0.91.

Keywords: Wood anatomy · Ray width · Image processing · DBSCAN

1 Introduction

Wood identification is a relevant issue for various applications, such as illegal logging, conservation and restoration, among others [14]. Currently, there are several methods to identify wood species, including chemical, genetic and visual identification [5]. The work presented here focuses on the later, through the analysis of the intern anatomy of wood samples, using microscopic images. The microscopic identification of wood is based in three different cuts in the wood sample that form three different sections: transverse, radial and tangential. A variety of features and pattern recognition techniques can be used to analyse the images of different sections, in order to assist in the identification process.

© Springer Nature Switzerland AG 2019
A. Morales et al. (Eds.): IbPRIA 2019, LNCS 11867, pp. 257–269, 2019.
https://doi.org/10.1007/978-3-030-31332-6_23

There are two groups of woods - softwoods and hardwoods. The relevant features for each of these types are significantly different. Softwoods have simpler anatomy than hardwoods, which have many more relevant features and more variety within each feature. In Fig. 1a wood sample from hardwood is presented showing the three sections and some of the main structures found in this type of wood. Each section has important features to support an accurate identification, especially because these features may vary within species. One important feature for the hardwood species is the ray width, which can be seen in the tangential section. This criterion indicates the number of cells that compose a ray in width. These ray cells are usually oval or lens shaped objects. An example of the tangential section of a hardwood sample is presented in Fig. 1b, for a species with bi- to 3-seriate rays.

Ray width can be classified as [15]:

– Uniseriate rays - only one cell wide.
– Bi- to 3-seriate rays - most of the rays are 2–3 cells wide, but rare uni- and 4-seriate rays are present.
– 3- to 5-seriate rays - most of the rays are 3–5 cells wide, but rare uni- and biseriate rays are present.
– Uni- and multiseriate rays - in addition to numerous uniseriate rays, large rays are also present.

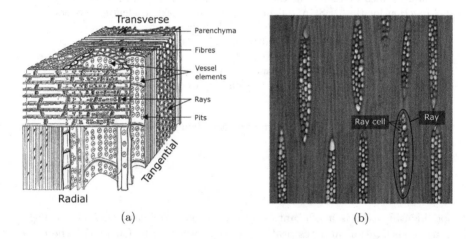

(a)   (b)

Fig. 1. (a) Hardwood anatomy, (b) Microscopic image - tangential section

Although the analysis of microscopic wood anatomy is the most reliable method nowadays to provide an initial identification, only experts can perform this task with accuracy. There are only a few wood anatomists in the world and the training needed to educate an experienced one can take decades [5], thus the importance of automation to assist in this process. In recent years there has been an increase in the work developed in this topic, but it is still an area relatively unexplored. The systems available only analyse the transverse section (ignoring the other two sections) as it is the section that contains most information. Two main tasks are included in existing systems: image processing techniques to segment objects of interest [1,2,6,8,11] and automatic feature extraction for species classification [3,9,10,13,16–18]. However, none of the available systems joins the segmentation task and the species classification task with features that are meaningful in a biological sense to perform a species identification.

This work focuses on the use of the tangential section of microscopic images of hardwood, with the aim of providing additional meaningful information for the classification process. The segmentation task is based on an edge detector method, followed by a selection of the objects of interest. In order to separate the clusters that represent the rays, a clustering algorithm is used. Since the number of clusters is unknown, a density based algorithm is used - the Density-Based Spatial Clustering of Applications with Noise (DBSCAN) [7]. A modified version of the MATLAB implementation of DBSCAN [4] was developed in order to correctly separate the different clusters by defining an alternative distance function to be used by the algorithm. Finally, the cell count is computed for each cluster.

2   Materials and Methods

2.1   Wood Anatomy Database

The database used is a portion of a larger database - the Wood anatomy of central European Species [15]. It is composed of 1908 microscopic images from 133 species, with grey scale images of 600×400 pixels from the three sections. The database has 383 tangential section images (stemwood samples with a magnification of $100\times$), from 127 species.

To evaluate the performance of the algorithms developed, 20 tangential section images were manually segmented. Four examples of each ray width class (uniseriate, bi- to 3-seriate, 3-seriate to 5-seriate, multiseriate, uni- and multiseriate) were selected. The manually segmented objects were the rays, instead of the ray cells, meaning that the contours of the ray cells are included in this image. Examples of manually segmented images of each class are present in Fig. 2, where each ray has a different colour.

2.2   Segmentation of Ray Cells

The first step is to segment the ray cells, which can have different levels of intensity. Usually these objects are very bright (white) but quite often they are not (intermediate grey levels), with the same intensity values as other objects that are not ray cells. Furthermore, there are also objects that are not ray cells but that are very bright (nearly white).

An edge detection spacial filter is used - Laplacian of the Gaussian [12] with $\sigma = 1.5$ and an 11×11 kernel, including all zero-crossings. This filter is used

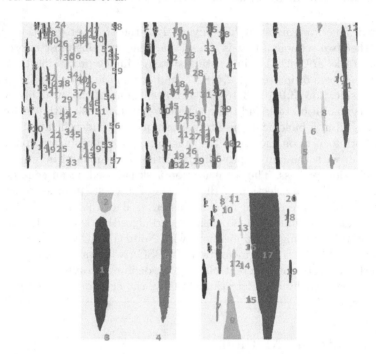

Fig. 2. Example of manually segmented images for each ray width class. From left to right - top: uniseriate; bi- to 3-seriate; 3- to 5-seriate; bottom: multiseriate; uni- and multiseriate.

because the contours are, in most cases, well defined. The zero-crossing results in closed contours on the output image, which are filled to obtain most of the closed objects of the image. Then, the objects that differ from ray cells in terms of size, shape and intensity values are removed (very large, small, elongated

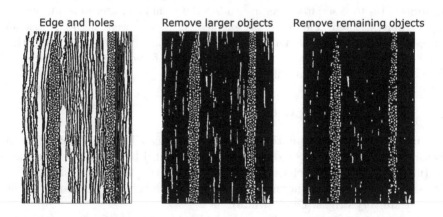

Fig. 3. Example of the 3 main segmentation processing stages.

and darker objects). Although not all the unwanted objects are eliminated and some unwanted objects are kept, the final results produced are adequate for the subsequent processing. Figure 3 presents an example of the three main steps of the algorithm.

2.3 DBSCAN

The DBSCAN algorithm [7] has two inputs: the minimum number of points a cluster needs to have in order to be considered valid and a fixed radius for the search of neighbours. Basically, the algorithm assigns points to a cluster if they are within the radius of search of at least one of the points already assigned to that cluster. If the cluster does not have the minimum number of points, then those points are considered noise. This algorithm is usually applied to numeric datasets to aggregate sets of points, but here it is applied to the ray cells' centroid coordinates.

Since the objects vary considerably in size and the distance between two objects is dependent on the radii of the two, the choice of the fixed radius needed for the DBSCAN is hard to make. An illustration of the method is presented in Fig. 4a, applied to a small portion of an image of the tangential section. The radius chosen in this case was 10 pixels, with 2 as the minimum number of points. In this example it is noticeable that a radius of 10 pixels might be too small, since many objects were considered noise (represented by a red cross) when they should not have been. However, increasing the radius would introduce real noise points inside of clusters and also join clusters that should be apart.

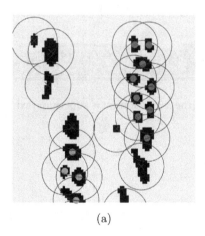 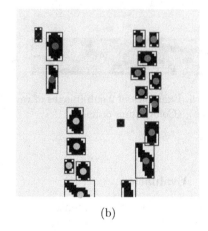

(a)   (b)

Fig. 4. Illustration of the DBSCAN method: (a) original, (b) modified version. (Color figure online)

The DBSCAN algorithm distance function was thus modified to compute the distance between the bounding boxes of the objects. In this way, instead of looking for points within a radius, it looks for objects that are closer from the left/right and up/down. A higher distance is assigned to the vertical component and a smaller one to the horizontal component because joining two clusters will only compromise the ray width if they are side by side. The accepted distance is now a two component vector with a fixed horizontal and vertical values of 2 and 10 pixels, respectively, and the minimum number of points is 2. In Fig. 4b presents the result for the same test image, using this modified version, where the bounding box for each object is represented as a red rectangle. The points that do not have neighbours closer than 10 pixel vertically and 2 pixel horizontally are considered noise (marked by a red cross).

The ability of the DBSCAN algorithm in dealing with noise is particularly useful in this context. Objects identified on the segmentation task that are not ray cells and are isolated become noise and are not considered as ray cells.

2.4   Ray Width

A binary image of each cluster is produced to analyse the number of ray cells. In the example of Fig. 5, two such images are represented with green colour, superimposed on the original grey scale images. A simple but effective approach was implemented: scan horizontal rows and count the number of times a transition from 1 (ray cell - green) to 0 (negative space - not green) occurs. To count the ray cells that are in the margins of these images, zero-padding is previously added. The ray width for each cluster is the highest number of transitions found on each row. In order to reduce the computational effort, only one out of three lines are scanned. Although this sub-sampling can affect the final number of ray cells counted per row, the differences were found to be negligible.

Fig. 5. Examples of 2 sub-images of ray clusters (the segmentation is superimposed in green). (Color figure online)

2.5   Evaluation

Since the manually segmented images contain closed regions (clusters) representing groups of rays instead of the individual ray cells (the contours of the ray cells are included), the segmented image used to compare the results should also be composed of closed objects, one for each cluster. In order to achieve such image, the contour of each cluster returned by the modified DBSCAN algorithm (excluding the points considered noise) is computed, based on the vertices of the bounding boxes of all the objects that belong to that cluster. The contour is then filled, returning an approximation of the closed object that represents

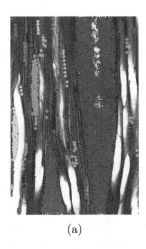

(a)   (b)

Fig. 6. Example of the computed clusters (a) which are used to create the "cluster image" (b).

the computed cluster. The image that contains all these closed objects is named "cluster image". Figure 6a shows the clustering results that are then used to create the "cluster image" presented in Fig. 6b. It should be noted that, since the "cluster image" is an approximation, some errors related to the clusters shapes are introduced on the evaluation.

To evaluate the segmentation of the image rays, the Jaccard metric is used. The Jaccard metric, or index, is also known as intersection over union (the intersection of two sets over the union of the two sets). In this case, the sets are the manually segmented image and the "cluster image".

To evaluate the results of the modified DBSCAN algorithm, the metric should be computed for each cluster, and these values then used to compute a final metric for the whole image. This can be done from the perspective of the clusters on the manually segmented image or from the clusters of the "cluster image". A one-to-one correspondence is needed between the clusters. Depending on which image we choose as reference, some clusters will be disregarded. For example, if one chooses the manually segmented image as reference, the predicted clusters that are not real ones (false clusters) are never assigned to a cluster. Instead of choosing a reference image, a metric is computed for both images (as reference) and the average result is used.

Let I_c be the "cluster image" and I_m the manually segmented image. The metric used for each cluster of the "cluster image" and for each cluster of the manually segmented image are, respectively, given by:

$$M_{c_i} = \frac{I_{c_i} \cap I_m}{I_{c_i}}, \qquad M_{m_j} = \frac{I_{m_j} \cap I_c}{I_{m_j}},$$

where I_{c_i} is the image that contains only the predicted cluster $i = 1, \dots, N_c$ and I_{m_j} is the image that contains only the manually segmented cluster

$j = 1, \ldots, N_m$. This metric evaluates how well each cluster is identified, for both the predicted ones (M_{c_i}) and for the manually segmented ones (M_{m_j}). A weighted mean is applied to the resulting metrics, according to the area of the clusters, since larger clusters are more significant than smaller ones. The final result is a single metric for each image - M_c and M_m. A geometric mean is then used to get the final overall metric: $M = \sqrt{M_c \times M_m}$ (values between 0 to 1, with 1 as the perfect result).

3   Results

To illustrate the type of results produced by the segmentation task, Fig. 7 shows one image from each of the classes considered (uniseriate, bi- to 3-seriate, 3- to 5-seriate, multiseriate, uni- and multiseriate). The figure shows the original images (masked by the manual segmentation) with the cluster image superimposed. The values of the Jaccard index are also presented for each image. Although there are some misdetection of ray cells (both false positives and false negatives), the results can be considered adequate for the subsequent processing because they generally capture the width of the rays.

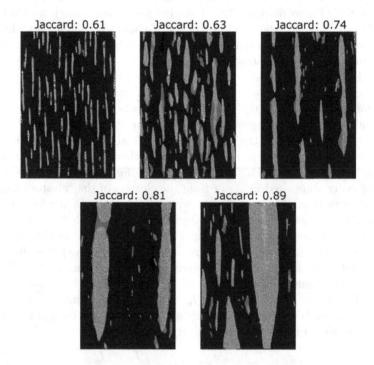

Fig. 7. Example of the segmentation results for each ray width class. From left to right - top: uniseriate; bi- to 3-seriate; 3- to 5-seriate; bottom: multiseriate; uni- and multiseriate.

Table 1. Segmentation evaluation results - Jaccard index values. O - original DBSCAN; M - modified DBSCAN (in bold when difference is ≥0.05).

Class	Image 1		Image 2		Image 3		Image 4		Mean	
	O	M	O	M	O	M	O	M	O	M
Uniseriate	0.37	**0.61**	0.12	**0.31**	0.22	**0.70**	0.05	**0.37**	0.19	**0.50**
Bi- to triseriate	0.49	**0.63**	0.45	**0.52**	0.56	**0.69**	0.22	**0.35**	0.43	**0.55**
Tri- to 5-seriate	0.77	0.74	0.50	0.53	0.82	0.80	0.80	0.76	0.72	0.71
Multiseriate	0.84	0.81	0.87	0.88	0.76	0.75	0.17	**0.92**	0.66	**0.84**
Uni- and multiseriate	0.88	0.89	0.59	0.59	0.46	**0.59**	0.39	**0.74**	0.58	**0.70**

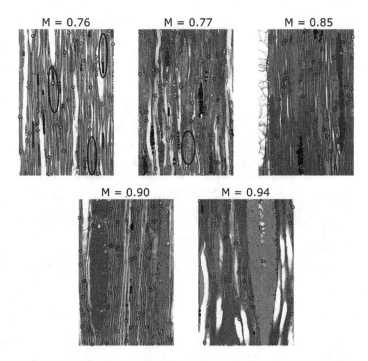

Fig. 8. Example of the clustering results for each ray width class. Top: uniseriate, bi- to 3-seriate, 3- to 5-seriate. Bottom: multiseriate, uni- and multiseriate.

The Jaccard index values for the 20 images tested (4 from each class) are present in Table 1, both for the original DBSCAN and for the modified DBSCAN, as well as the mean for each category. The index is higher for images with larger rays, possibly because the shape of smaller rays is more difficult to identify with the method used to produce the "cluster image". Other factors also have to be considered, such as the fact that darker ray cells tend to be eliminated in the process. The average index for all 20 images is 0.52 for the original DBSCAN and 0.66 for the modified version.

Table 2. DBSCAN evaluation results - M index. O - original DBSCAN; M - modified DBSCAN (in bold when difference is ≥ 0.05).

Class	Image 1		Image 2		Image 3		Image 4		Mean	
	O	M	O	M	O	M	O	M	O	M
Uniseriate	0.58	**0.76**	0.27	**0.49**	0.45	**0.82**	0.14	**0.57**	0.36	**0.66**
Bi- to triseriate	0.67	**0.77**	0.63	**0.69**	0.73	**0.81**	0.37	**0.52**	0.60	**0.70**
Tri- to 5-seriate	0.87	0.85	0.68	0.70	0.90	0.89	0.89	0.86	0.84	0.83
Multiseriate	0.91	0.90	0.93	0.93	0.87	0.86	0.41	**0.96**	0.78	**0.91**
Uni- and multiseriate	0.94	0.94	0.75	0.75	0.65	**0.74**	0.62	**0.85**	0.74	**0.82**

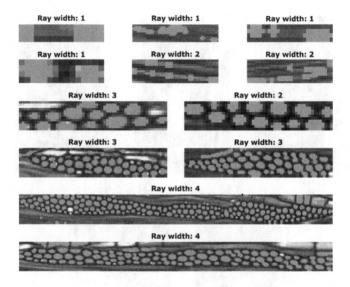

Fig. 9. Ray cells count.

Figure 8 shows the results obtained with the modified version of DBSCAN for one image of each class. The hollow red circles represent points that are considered noise, and the filled coloured circles represent the points that belong to clusters, with different colours representing different clusters. Again, the metric considered (M) is displayed for each image. Some rays are split vertically, but the ray width remains the same. The problems arise when the split is horizontal, which introduces two false ray widths. The reverse situation, where clusters are joined, is also detrimental for the vertical case because a larger cluster can hide a smaller one. In the first image we can see that some clusters were split vertically and in the second image we can see an example of two clusters that were joined horizontally, marked with a black ellipse. Fortunately, these situations were not found to be very common.

A visual inspection suggests that the results are adequate, as the clusters are mostly well identified. The quantitative results are presented in Table 2. For classes uniseriate and bi- to 3-seriate (first two rows in Table 2) the values of the M index are lower than the remaining classes. This is consistent with the segmentation results, that have a high influence on the DBSCAN results. The multiseriate images are the ones with the best performance, achieving an average M value of 0.91. In general, the results are fairly good, with an overall average of 0.78 for the modified version of DBSCAN, which is an improvement compared to the original DBSCAN that achieved 0.66.

For the ray width evaluation, clusters were individually analysed to check if the assigned ray width corresponds to the expected values (ground truth). The ray width was evaluated considering only what the algorithm should count and not the actual ray width, meaning that false rays are considered correctly classified in terms of ray width if the count is correct. Figure 9 presents examples of the sub-images obtained for some clusters of a tri- to 5-seriate species, including the predicted ray width. Some of these rays were wrongly identified, such as the first two sub-images, but their count is nevertheless correct.

A confusion matrix (Table 3) was built to compute the accuracy of the ray cells count. It shows that the misclassified cluster have an error of one unit at the most, which is mostly an underestimation. These underestimations happen because only one out of three lines are being analysed, missing the lines that have the maximum width present. The accuracy of the ray width count is 0.91.

Table 3. Confusion matrix for the ray width estimation.

Computed	Reference					
	1	2	3	4	5	>5
1	**166**	6	0	0	0	0
2	1	**40**	5	0	0	0
3	0	0	**31**	6	0	0
4	0	0	0	**16**	6	0
5	0	0	0	0	**9**	3
>5	0	0	0	0	0	**11**

4 Conclusion

A modified distance function for the DBSCAN method was developed to assist in extracting information from microscopic images of hardwoods (tangential section). The method is used to count the number of ray cells in width. It can be applied to other image processing tasks when there is a need to form an unknown number of groups from the objects present in the image.

The accuracy of the clustering task is obviously dependent on the segmentation task, since missing/additional objects will cause splitting/merging of clusters. In the experimental evaluation carried out, the average segmentation Jaccard index was 0.66 and the average DBSCAN index M was 0.78. The accuracy of the algorithm developed to identify the ray width was found to be 0.91. As future work the ray cells count may be used to extract features and train a classifier to predict the ray width given an image as input.

References

1. Arx, G.V., Dietz, H.: Automated image analysis of annual rings in the roots of perennial forbs. Int. J. Plant Sci. **166**(5), 723–732 (2005)
2. Brunel, G., Borianne, P., Subsol, G., Jaeger, M., Caraglio, Y.: Automatic identification and characterization of radial files in light microscopy images of wood. Ann. Bot. **114**, 829–840 (2014)
3. Cavalin, P.R., Kapp, M.N., Martins, J., Oliveira, L.E.S.: A multiple feature vector framework for forest species recognition. In: Proceedings of the 28th Annual ACM Symposium on Applied Computing, SAC 2013, pp. 16–20 (2013)
4. Daszykowski, M., Walczak, B., Massart, D.L.: Looking for natural patterns in data. Part 1: density based approach. Chemom. Intell. Lab. Syst. **56**, 83–92 (2001)
5. Dormontt, E.E., et al.: Forensic timber identification: it's time to integrate disciplines to combat illegal logging. Biol. Conserv. **191**, 790–798 (2015)
6. Espinosa, L.F., Herrera, R.J., Polanco-Tapia, C.: Segmentation of anatomical elements in wood microscopic images using artificial vision techniques. Maderas. Ciencia y tecnología **17**(4), 735–748 (2015)
7. Ester, M., Kriegel, H.P., Sander, J., Xu, X.: A density-based algorithm for discovering clusters in large spatial databases with noise. In: Knowledge Discovery and Data Mining, p. 226 (1996)
8. Fabijańska, A., Danek, M., Barniak, J., Piórkowski, A.: Towards automatic tree rings detection in images of scanned wood samples. Comput. Electron. Agric. **140**, 279–289 (2017)
9. Martins, J., Oliveira, L.S., Nisgoski, S., Sabourin, R.: A database for automatic classification of forest species. Mach. Vis. Appl. **24**, 567–578 (2013)
10. Martins, J.G., Oliveira, L.S., Britto, A.S.B., Sabourin, R.: Forest species recognition based on dynamic classifier selection and dissimilarity feature vector representation. Mach. Vis. Appl. **26**, 279–293 (2015)
11. Pan, S., Kudo, M.: Segmentation of pores in wood microscopic images based on mathematical morphology with a variable structuring element. Comput. Electron. Agric. **75**, 250–260 (2011)
12. Parker, J.: Algorithms for Image Processing and Computer Vision. Wiley Publishing, Inc., Hoboken (2011)
13. Rosa da Silva, N., et al.: Automated classification of wood transverse cross-section micro-imagery from 77 commercial Central-African timber species. Ann. Forest Sci. **74**, 30 (2017)
14. Ross, R.J.: Wood Handbook - Wood as an Engineering Material. Department of Agriculture, Forest Service, Forest Products Laboratory, centennial ed. general technical report fpl; gtr-190. madison, wi: u.s edn. (2010)
15. Schoch, W., Heller, I., Schweingruber, F., Kienast, F.: Wood anatomy of central European Species (2004). www.woodanatomy.ch

16. Yadav, A.R., Anand, R.S., Dewal, M.L., Gupta, S.: Hardwood species classification with DWT based hybrid texture feature extraction techniques. Sadhana **40**(8), 2287–2312 (2015)
17. Yadav, A.R., Anand, R.S., Dewal, M.L., Gupta, S.: Multiresolution local binary pattern variants based texture feature extraction techniques for efficient classification of microscopic images of hardwood species. Appl. Soft Comput. J. **32**, 101–112 (2015)
18. Zamri, M.I.P., Khairuddin, A.S.M., Mokhtar, N., Yusof, R.: Wood species recognition system based on improved basic grey level aura matrix as feature extractor. J. Robot. Netw. Artif. Life **3**(3), 140–143 (2016)

Automatic Detection of Tuberculosis Bacilli from Microscopic Sputum Smear Images Using Faster R-CNN, Transfer Learning and Augmentation

Moumen El-Melegy[1(✉)], Doaa Mohamed[1], and Tarek ElMelegy[2]

[1] Electrical Engineering Department, School of Engineering, Assiut University,
Assiut 71516, Egypt
moumen@aun.edu.eg
[2] Clinical Pathology Department, School of Medicine, Assiut University,
Assiut 71516, Egypt

Abstract. Tuberculosis (TB) is a serious infectious disease that remains a global health problem with an enormous burden of disease. TB spreads widely in low- and middle-income countries, which depend primarily on sputum smear test using conventional light microscopy in disease diagnosis, in this paper we propose a new deep-learning approach for bacilli localization and classification in conventional ZN-stained microscopic images. The approach is based on the state of the art Faster Region-based Convolutional Neural Network (RCNN) framework. Our experimental results show significant improvement by the proposed approach compared to existing methods, thus helping in accurate disease diagnosis.

Keywords: Deep learning · Faster R-CNN · Tuberculosis · Mycobacterium tuberculosis · Conventional microscopy

1 Introduction

Tuberculosis (TB) is a serious infectious disease caused by bacteria called Mycobacterium tuberculosis that is spread from one person to another through the air; it generally affects the lungs, but can also affect other parts of the body such as kidneys, liver, bones, brains and central nervous system. According to the Global TB control report of 2018 [1], worldwide TB is one of the top 10 causes of death. In 2017, an estimated 10.0 million people developed TB and 1.3 million died from the disease. Over 95% of TB deaths occur in developing countries. However TB can be treated successfully if it is diagnosed correctly at the appropriate time and there are many methods for TB diagnosis, such as chest X-ray test, blood test, skin test, and sputum smear microscopy test. Yet diagnosis remains a challenging task because some tests take a long time to obtain a result. In addition, some TB tests are not very accurate and some tests are very expensive and require complex laboratory facilities [2]. Smear microscopy of sputum is often the primary TB test to be used in countries with a high rate of TB infection because it is simple, inexpensive test and results can be available within hours.

© Springer Nature Switzerland AG 2019
A. Morales et al. (Eds.): IbPRIA 2019, LNCS 11867, pp. 270–278, 2019.
https://doi.org/10.1007/978-3-030-31332-6_24

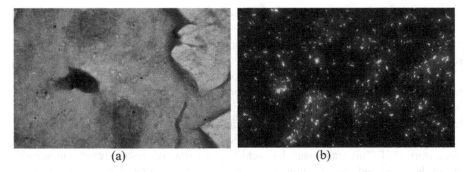

Fig. 1. Comparison between the contrast between two microscopic images of TB sputum smears. (a) Image acquired with a conventional microscope (b) Image acquired with a fluorescence microscope. Clearly the latter has a higher contrast and is easier to diagnose.

Sputum smear microscopy can be made using auramine-O stain (fluorescence microscopy) or Ziehl-Neelsen (ZN) stain (conventional light field microscopy). While fluorescence microscopy is 10% more sensitive than light field microscopy [3] (see Fig. 1) and faster than light field microscopy [4], conventional microscopy is widely used in low- and middle-income countries, where TB prevalence rate is high because it is less expensive, easier to use and maintain [3]. As such, we will focus in this work on this kind of microscopy.

Manual TB diagnosis is tedious work and prone to error due to high work load and dearth of properly trained technicians, often leading to failing to detect TB cases. As such, automatic methods are the best solution to increase accuracy of TB diagnosis. To that end, efforts have focused on automating this task by trying to detect TB bacteria (bacilli) in the microscopic images. Some authors [5–12, 18] relied on color information and hand-crafted set of shape descriptors of the bacilli, which has resulted in rather low detection accuracy.

In recent years, researchers [13–16] have started applying emerging, powerful deep learning methods which allow the learning of the discriminating features for bacilli detection and classification. The Convolutional Neural Networks (CNNs) are the main engine for all these methods. In several works, e.g., [13, 14, 16], the authors had to divide a microscopic image into smaller patches, each containing one image object of concern that possibly could be a TB bacillus. The CNN function was to decide if this object is indeed a TB bacillus or not. Accuracy as high as 99% has been reported on these image patches (but not the whole image) of the used datasets. The main shortcoming of these methods is how to split the larger microscopic image into such a way. The method performance depends to a large extent on this preliminary patching step. Some authors (e.g., [14, 16]) did not reveal the details of how this was done, whether in an automated, semi-automated or even a manual way. Trying to avoid this drawback, the recent work of [15] proposed to employ an initial stage of image binarization and pixel classification to locate foreground objects of interest (bacilli, non-bacilli, artifacts) and then create the required patches. Each patch will contain one foreground object and is sent to the CNN stage for final classification into bacilli or non-bacilli. Although this method automates the image patching step, its overall accuracy relies on the success of the binarization/pixel-classification pre-step, which is often error-prone for the challenging conventional bright-field microscopy (see the left image in Fig. 1). In addition, it suffers from touching foreground objects and over-stained images.

In this paper, we propose to use one of the state-of-the-art deep learning-based approaches that has the ability for localization and classification of TB bacilli with high performance. It can avoid all the above work difficulties, such as finding proper set of features, dividing images into patches, and detection of touching bacilli. The proposed approach is based on the Faster Region-based Convolutional Neural Network (RCNN) framework [17]. This framework has achieved the state-of-the-arts results on several object detection and classification challenges (e.g., Pascal VOC [24] and MS COCO [19]). *To the best of our knowledge, it has not been adopted before to the task at hand.* It intrinsically solves the patching step of the existing methods [13–16] because it combines region proposal and classification in one learning framework. Another contribution of this paper is that we assess and compare notable existing methods against ours on the same dataset. Previous works used different datasets and thus it is not possible to compare between the reported results.

The paper is organized as follows. In Sect. 2, the proposed approach along its implementation details is discussed. The data used in this work and the obtained experimental results are reported in Sect. 3. Finally, our conclusions are drawn in Sect. 4.

2 Proposed Approach

In this paper, we propose an automatic method for TB detection in images acquired with conventional bright field microscopy based on the Region-CNN (R-CNN) framework family. The R-CNN framework can locate and classify objects inside images by combining CNNs and region proposal methods. A region proposal method is a method that finds a set of regions, defined by bounding boxes, which might contain objects of interest. Early members of this framework used EdgeBoxes [21] or Selective Search [20]. Although it improved the previous best detection results on Pascal VOC 2012 [24] by about 30%, it was computationally slow since it processed each image many times to detect regions of interest.

After that new members of this family were proposed to solve this problem. Fast R-CNN [22] introduces a more effective method for training the CNN and adopts a bounding box regressor. The bounding box regressor is a layer that outputs the locations of bounding boxes where objects of interest might be located. Faster R-CNN [17] combines the Fast R-CNN with a RPN (Region Proposal Network). RPN is a network that uses the feature map, to generate regions of interest each with score, then fast R-CNN classifies the proposed regions and refines their locations. The time cost of generating region proposals is much smaller in RPN than selective search.

In order to share convolutional layers between the RPN and Faster R-CNN models, an algorithm of four steps was presented in [17]. In the first step, input image is passed to a conventional network which returns feature map for that image. Second step, RPN is applied to this feature map and returns object proposals with scores. Third step,

Region Of Interest (ROI) pooling layer is applied to these proposals to down sample it to the same size. In the fourth step, object proposals are passed to fully connected layer to classify and output the bounding boxes for objects. Figure 2 illustrates the four steps of the Faster R-CNN framework.

In our Implementation we depend on transfer learning where a pre-trained model can be reused as starting point for a model on another related task, which allows rapid progress and improves performance. In our faster R-CNN framework, we use a pre-trained VGG-16 net for the CNN part (see Fig. 2). VGG-16 is a 16-layer convolutional neural network consisting of five convolutional layers, each followed by max pooling layer, then three fully connected layers and a softmax layer. VGG16 has input image size of 224 × 224 × 3. Conv_1 has two convolutional layers, each followed by Relu activation function, and 64 filters. Conv_2 has two convolutional layers, each followed by Relu activation function, and 128 filters. Conv_3 has three convolutional layers, each followed by Relu activation function, and 256 filters. Conv_4 has three convolutional layers, each followed by Relu activation function, and 512 filters. Conv_5 is the same as Conv_4. All convolutional networks have a filter size 3 × 3. The VGG-16 network is pre-trained on more than million training images from ImageNet database with 100 categories [25], and then tuned on our training TB images to detect TB bacilli as described next.

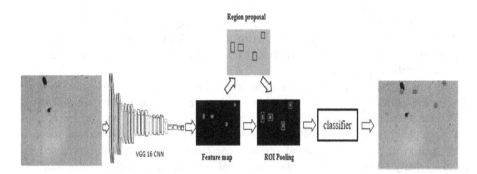

Fig. 2. Faster R-CNN is a network that combines a Convolutional Neural Network, a Region Proposal Network, a Region of Interest Pooling layer, and a classifier.

3 Experimental Results

In this section we describe the data we used for our framework training and testing and report the results obtained. We also compare the proposed approach with several existing methods in the literature on the same dataset.

All images that were used for training and evaluation are taken from ZNSM-iDB [23] public database that consists of various categories (autofocused data, overlapping objects, single or few bacilli, views without bacilli, occluded bacilli, over-stained views with bacilli and artifacts), see Fig. 3. The database consists of three divisions, each acquired with a different microscope. Our training and test data are taken from first and second divisions, the first using Labomed Digi 3 digital microscope with an iVu 5100 digital camera 5.0 megapixel (MS-1), and the second using Motic BA210 digital microscope with a type Binocular head and Moticam 2500 digital camera module 5.0 megapixel (MS-2).

The number of images we thus have is 500 with 2000 training object. Due to limited number of available TB images, we have used data augmentation to increase the number of images. Data augmentation is a technique used to overcome the problem of lack of sufficient amount of training data; it expands the size of dataset by creating modified versions of original (existing) images of the dataset. We have used several data augmentation methods: random image rotation, mirroring and random translations. This will ensure proper Faster R-CNN training and lead to more accuracy. As a result, the number of microscopic images we have used becomes 1500 images after applying data augmentation methods. 80% of them are selected in random for training and 20% for testing.

The faster R-CNN is tuned on the training dataset. Several key hyper-parameters have been tuned in this process, such as the minimum anchor box sizes (we use 3 box sizes 16^2, 24^2, and 30^2). The batch size is 4. The learning rate is 1e-5. The network is trained for 100 epochs.

To assess the performance of our approach, precision, recall and F-score metrics are calculated. To calculate these metrics, several figures are calculated: True positive (TP) which is total number of TB bacilli that are detected correctly by the approach, False Positive (FP) which is total number of non-bacilli that are detected as bacilli by the approach, and False Negative (FN) which is total number of true bacilli that are not detected by the approach.

For the sake of comparison, we have implemented the method proposed in [18]. The reason behind choosing this reference is that it uses a comprehensive set of features and several machine learning classifiers for TB bacilli detection. As such, it is considered a plethora of methods altogether. It consists of four stages: the first stage uses a combination of pixel classifiers to segment the candidate bacillus objects based on color intensity features. In stage two, shape and color features, such as color moment features, eccentricity, compactness, Fourier features, were extracted. In stage three, feature selection was applied. Classical machine learning classifiers including support vector machines (SVMs), k-Nearest Neighbor (kNN) classifiers, Linear Discriminant Analysis (LDA) and Quadratic Discriminant Analysis (QDA) have been employed for object classification in stage four.

Table 1 reports the accuracy of the proposed approach on the test dataset in comparisons to the other methods. It is clear that the proposed Faster R-CNN indeed demonstrates a higher accuracy and sensitivity in detecting TB bacilli from images as shown in Fig. 4. It successfully detects touching/overlapping bacilli as well as bacilli from over-stained images.

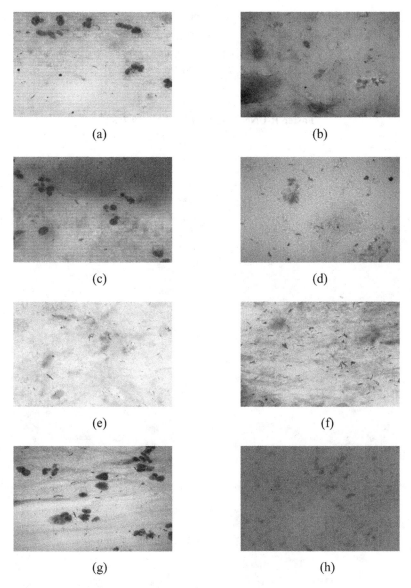

(a)

(b)

(c)

(d)

(e)

(f)

(g)

(h)

Fig. 3. Sample images from the database: (a) image from single bacilli category acquired using MS-1, (b) image from single bacilli category acquired using MS-2, (c) image from overlapping bacillus category acquired using MS-1, (d) image from overlapping bacillus category acquired using MS-2, (e) image from overlapping bacillus category acquired using MS-1, (f) image from Autofocus category acquired using MS-1, (g) 1image from overstaining bacillus category acquired using MS-2, (h) image from without bacillus category acquired using MS-1.

Table 1. Results of Proposed approach vs. other methods.

Classifier	Recall	Precision	F-score
SVM	94.6%	81.6%	88%
KNN	93.9%	80.7%	86.8%
QDA	96.3%	79.2%	86.9%
LDA	94.4%	79.4%	86.2%
Faster R-CNN	**98.3%**	**82.6%**	**89.7%**

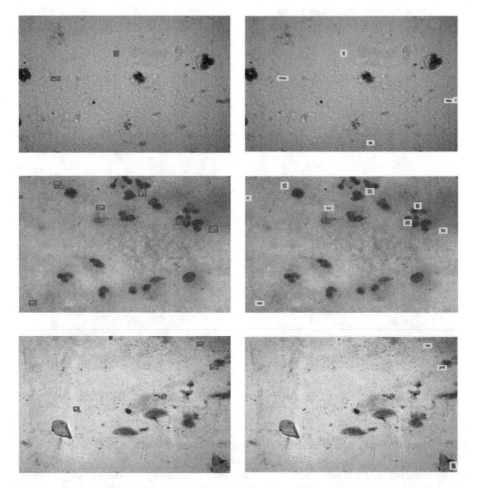

Fig. 4. Sample results by the proposed approach: left column shows ground truth images (ground-truth TB bacilli are marked in red boxed), right column shows detected TB bacilli as marked in yellow boxes. (Color figure online)

4   Conclusions

In this paper we have proposed a deep-learning approach to the detection and classification of TB bacilli in ZN-stained microscopic images. The new approach is based on the Faster Region-based Convolutional Neural Network (RCNN) framework. *To the best of our knowledge, this is the first time to apply this framework to this problem.* Our experimental results demonstrate considerable improvement by the proposed approach compared to existing methods.

Our current research is directed towards enhancing the performance of the proposed approach. To that end, we plan to increase the size of the data used for the deep network training. Since the ZNSM-iDB database [23] was the only one available to us in the public domain, we plan to collect our own samples from Assiut University Hospital and use them along with the available ZNSM-iDB data. This is expected to increase the performance of the proposed approach.

Acknowledgement. This research is supported by Information Technology Industry Development Agency of Egypt (grant # CFP139).

References

1. WHO Global tuberculosis report 2018. https://www.who.int/tb/publications/global_report/en/
2. TB facts, information about TB. https://www.tbfacts.org/tb-tests/
3. Steingart, K., et al.: Fluorescence versus conventional sputum smear microscopy for tuberculosis: a systematic review. Lancet Infect. Dis. **6**, 570–581 (2006)
4. Bhalla, M., Sidiq, Z., Sharma, P.P., Singhal, R., Myneedu, V.P., Sarin, R.: Performance of light-emitting diode fluorescence microscope for diagnosis of tuberculosis. Int. J. Mycobacteriol. **2**, 174–178 (2013)
5. Costa, M.G.F., Costa Filho, C.F.F., Sena, J.F., Salem, J., de Lima, M.O.: Automatic identification of mycobacterium tuberculosis with conventional light microscopy. In: 30th Annual International IEEE EMBS Conference, pp. 382–385 (2008)
6. Raof, R.A.A., et al.: Color thresholding method for image segmentation algorithm of Ziehl-Neelsen sputum slide images. In: 5th International Conference on Electrical Engineering, Computing Science and Automatic Control (CCE 2008), pp. 212–217 (2008)
7. Khutlang, R., Krishnan, S., Whitelaw, A., Douglas, T.S.: Automated detection of tuberculosis in Ziehl-Neelsen-stained sputum smears using two one-class classifiers. J. Microsc. **237**(1), 96–102 (2010)
8. Osman, M.K., Mashor, M.Y., Jaafar, H., Wahab, A.S.W.: Segmentation of tuberculosis bacilli in Ziehl-Neelsen tissue slide images using hybrid multilayered perceptron network. In: 10th International Conference on Information Science, Signal Processing and Their Applications (ISSPA 2010), May 2010
9. Osman, M.K., Mashor, M.Y., Saad, Z., Jaafar, H.: Segmentation of tuberculosis bacilli in Ziehl-Neelsen-stained tissue images based on KMean clustering procedure. In: International Conference on Intelligent and Advanced Systems, June 2010
10. Costa Filho, C.F.F., Levy, P.C., Xavier, C.M., Costa, M.G.F., Fujimoto, L.B.M., Salem, J.: Mycobacterium tuberculosis recognition with conventional microscopy. In: 34th Annual International Conference of the IEEE EMBS, San Diego (2012)

11. Divekar, A., Pangilinan, C., Coetzee, G., Sondh, T., Lure, F.Y.M., Kennedy, S.: Automated detection of tuberculosis on sputum smeared slides using stepwise classification. In: International Society for Optical Engineering, February 2012
12. Adi, K., Gernowo, R., Sugiharto, A., Firdausi, K.S., Adi, P., Adi, B.: Tuberculosis (TB) identification in the Ziehl-Neelsen sputum sample in NTSC channel and support vector machine (SVM) classification. Int. J. Innov. Res. Sci. Eng. Technol. 2, 5030–5035 (2013)
13. Quinn, J.A., Nakasi, R., Mugagga, P.K.B., Byanyima, P., Lubega, W., Andama, A.: Deep convolutional neural networks for microscopy-based point of care diagnostics. In: International Conference on Machine Learning for Health Care, August 2016
14. López, Y.P., Costa, C.F.F., Aguilera, L.M.R., Costa, M.G.F.: Automatic classification of light field smear microscopy patches using Convolutional Neural Networks for identifying Mycobacterium Tuberculosis. In: CHILEAN Conference on Electrical, Electronics Engineering, Information and Communication Technologies, October 2017
15. Panicker, R.O., Kalmady, K.S., Rajan, J., Sabu, M.K.: Automatic detection of tuberculosis bacilli from microscopic sputum smear images using deep learning methods. Biocybern. Biomed. Eng. 38, 691–699 (2018)
16. Kant, S., Srivastava, M.M.: Towards automated tuberculosis detection using deep learning. arXiv preprint, arXiv:1801.07080 (2018)
17. Ren, S., He, K., Girshick, R., Sun, J.: Faster R-CNN: towards real-time object detection with region proposal networks. In: Proceedings of the Advances in Neural Information Processing Systems, pp. 91–99, December 2015
18. Khutlang, R., et al.: Classification of Mycobacterium tuberculosis in images of ZN-stained sputum smears. Trans. Info. Tech. Biomed. 14(4), 949–957 (2010)
19. Lin, T.-Y., et al.: Microsoft COCO: common objects in context. In: Fleet, D., Pajdla, T., Schiele, B., Tuytelaars, T. (eds.) ECCV 2014. LNCS, vol. 8693, pp. 740–755. Springer, Cham (2014). https://doi.org/10.1007/978-3-319-10602-1_48
20. Uijlings, J.R.R., van de Sande, K.E.A., Gevers, T., Smeulders, A.W.M.: Selective search for object recognition. Int. J. Comput. Vis. 104(2), 154–171 (2013)
21. Zitnick, C.L., Dollár, P.: Edge boxes: locating object proposals from edges. In: Fleet, D., Pajdla, T., Schiele, B., Tuytelaars, T. (eds.) ECCV 2014. LNCS, vol. 8693, pp. 391–405. Springer, Cham (2014). https://doi.org/10.1007/978-3-319-10602-1_26
22. Girshick, R.: Fast R-CNN. In: Proceedings of the International Conference on Computer Vision, Santiago, Chile, pp. 1440–1448, December 2015
23. Shah, M.I., et al.: Ziehl-Neelsen sputum smear microscopy image database: a resource to facilitate automated bacilli detection for tuberculosis diagnosis. J. Med. Imaging (Bellingham, Wash.) 4(2) (2017)
24. Everingham, M., Eslami, S.M.A., Van Gool, L., Williams, C.K.I., Winn, J., Zisserman, A.: The pascal visual object classes challenge: a retrospective. Int. J. Comput. Vis. 111, 98–136 (2015)
25. Simonyan, K., Zisserman, A.: Very deep convolutional networks for large-scale image recognition. arXiv preprint arXiv:1409.1556 (2014)

Detection of Stone Circles in Periglacial Regions of Antarctica in UAV Datasets

Pedro Pina[1]([✉]), Francisco Pereira[2], Jorge S. Marques[2], and Sandra Heleno[1]

[1] CERENA, Instituto Superior Técnico, Lisbon, Portugal
ppina@tecnico.ulisboa.pt
[2] Institute for Systems and Robotics, Instituto Superior Técnico, Lisbon, Portugal

Abstract. This paper tests three methods, based on template matching, the watershed transform and the sliding band filter, for the identification of stones circles, a natural pattern formed in periglacial regions of the Earth. All the methods take advantage of the 3D shape of the structures conveyed by Digital Elevation Models (DEM). The DEMs were built from milimetric imagery captured by Unmanned Aerial Vehicles (UAV) in Barton Peninsula, King George Island, Antarctica (62°) during a field campaign developed in 2018. The best results were achieved by the sliding band filter method with a F score of 83.9%.

Keywords: Patterned ground · Antarctica · UAV · DEM · Template matching · Watershed · Sliding band filter

1 Introduction

Stone circles are a type of natural patterned ground formed in periglacial environments easily attracting the attention due to its remarkable circular geometry (Fig. 1). These metric circular shapes, occurring in clusters of tens to thousands of individuals, are formed in frost-susceptible soils due to freezing and thawing cycles [1] in a convection-like circulation of soil in the active layer of permafrost [2]. Besides their evident geomorphic importance, the periodic burial and exhumation of geological materials may play an important role in the soil carbon cycle in connection to permafrost conditions, designating the stone circles as potential paleoclimatic indicators [3]. Although the processes underlying their formation and evolution are relatively well understood [4], their geometric characteristics, dating and seasonal dynamics are supported by sampling and monitoring few circles [5], preventing obtaining robust statistics and an extended spatial analysis of large fields.

Imagery with mili - to centimetre resolution captured by UAV can greatly contribute to a much more complete geomorphic description of this type of patterned ground in large areas giving context to data built at ground-level [6]. The amount of circles involved requires the use of automated methods to make their segmentation, characterisation and also multitemporal monitoring to account for

© Springer Nature Switzerland AG 2019
A. Morales et al. (Eds.): IbPRIA 2019, LNCS 11867, pp. 279–288, 2019.
https://doi.org/10.1007/978-3-030-31332-6_25

Fig. 1. Stone circles observed from UAV in Barton Peninsula, King George Island (Antarctica), acquired by IST team in February 2018.

the dynamics of the processes involved. This paper deals only with the initial phase, that is, with the segmentation of the stone circles which, to our knowledge, is addressed for the first time.

2   Data Acquisition

The sites selected for developing the surveys are located in Barton Peninsula of King George Island (62°S), Antarctica (Fig. 1). This peninsula is an ice-free area of about 12 km^2 and one of the sites in Antarctica where these natural patterns are more ubiquitous [7]. A field campaign was developed during February 2018 by two of the authors of the current work (PP and SH) with logistics support from the Portuguese Polar Program and the Korean Polar Research Institute. The imagery was acquired with a quadcopter DJI Phantom 3 equipped with a RGB camera at low altitude flights (10 m above ground) to allow perceiving stones up to 5 mm in size. The aerial surveys were planned in a double-grid mode with a high overlap (80%) between adjacent images (lateral and frontal) to provide an increased number of views for the same point. The area surveyed in each individual flight, conditioned by battery duration, is about 80 m × 80 m and contains about 500 images. The individual images were processed with *Agisoft Photoscan* software to build orthorrectified image mosaics and digital elevation models (DEM) based on SIFT-Scale-Invariant Feature Transform and SfM-Structure from Motion technique. The resolutions obtained are 2.6 mm/pixel for the orthorectified image (typical size of 25, 000 × 25, 000 pixels) and 1.3 cm/pixel for the DEM (5000 × 5000 pixels). Smaller square regions from the global mosaic and DEM (5000 and 1000 pixels, respectively) were extracted to be processed with circles detection algorithms, as illustrated in Fig. 2.

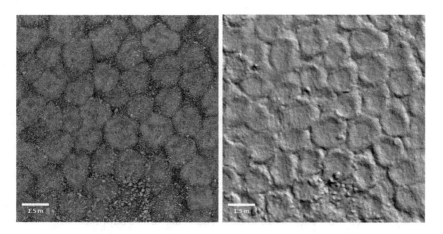

Fig. 2. Detail of orthorrectified mosaic (left) and respective DEM (right).

3   Detection Methods

Circular structures can be described by their circular shape patterns although several kinds of deformation can be observed in many images. These deformations are related to the process of structure formation along the years and to the slope of the terrain. In the sequel we will present three detection methods that take into account the 3D shape of the structures to be detected.

3.1   Template Matching

Most structures to be detected have a circular shape with a radius that is approximately constant within each site. The radius may change from site to site since it depends on the altitude and characteristics of the soils.

We will assume that the elevation image contain 3D patterns of known shape $T(x, y)$, denoted as template. The fit between the elevation image $I(x, y)$ and the sliding template $T(x, y)$ can be measured by the correlation

$$R(x_0, y_0) = \sum_{(x,y)} I(x, y) T(x - x_0, y - y_0), \tag{1}$$

that achieves a local maximum when the template is aligned with the circle. The template is chosen as a half torus (Fig. 3)

$$T(x, y) = \left(1 - \frac{(r - R)^2}{(\epsilon R)^2}\right)^+, \qquad r = \sqrt{x^2 + y^2}, \tag{2}$$

where R is the radius, ϵR is the torus width ($\epsilon = 0.2$), and $x^+ = \max(0, x)$ is the rectifier function.

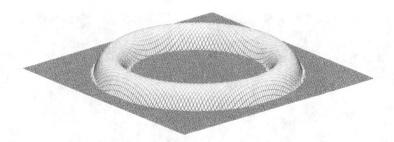

Fig. 3. Template: half torus.

The detection of circles is based on the analysis of the correlation matrix $R(x, y)$ by detecting all the local maxima (non-maximum suppression), followed by comparison with a threshold T.

Since the elevation image has some natural slope, the image I is first preprocessed by a high-pass filter. The proposed algorithm depends on two parameters (R, T), radius and threshold.

3.2 Watershed

The internal regions of the circles are relatively flat with their edges corresponding to crests in the elevation data. The watershed transform, which simulates the flooding of a surface from its minima, seems adequate to make their segmentation. The watershed (WS) of the elevation image I corresponds to the skeleton of influence zones (SKIZ) of its minima (min) [8]:

$$\mathrm{WS}(I) = \mathrm{SKIZ}(\min(I)). \qquad (3)$$

Since not all the minima from the elevation image are interesting, namely the deeper ones normally located outside the circular shapes, its filtering can be performed to leave only (ideally) the shallower ones located within each circle. This procedure is done in two steps. First by increasing the regularity of the circular structures by a morphological filter of the type closing ϕ followed by an opening γ of the elevation image I with a disk B as structuring element

$$I_f = \gamma^B(\phi^B(I)), \qquad (4)$$

and then by discarding the minima whose depth or contrast value exceeds the value h. The interesting and shallower minima ($\min_S$) of I_f are identified through the h-minima transform (HMIN) [8]

$$\min_S(I_f) = \mathrm{HMIN}_h(I_f) = R^\varepsilon_{I_f}(I_f + h), \qquad (5)$$

where $R^\varepsilon_f(I + h)$ indicates the reconstruction by erosion of the marker image $(I_f + h)$ into the mask I.

Since it is intended to delineate each circle along its crest line, the minima or seeds upon which the watershed transform will start the flooding procedure are constituted by the union of min_S and the border lines of their regions of influence, like performed in a similar delineation problem of impact craters [9].

Finally, a post-processing step based on the morphometric features of the detected objects is performed to filter out small and less circular individuals. The size threshold can be easily fixed, but the circularity C obtained by the index that relates the area A and perimeter P of an object ($C = 4\pi A/P^2$) requires some analysis. Therefore this algorithm depends also on two parameters (h, C).

3.3   Sliding Band Filter

The gradient field of natural circles exhibit radial vector patterns (see Fig. 4). To detect such patterns, we adopt a modified version of the sliding band filter (SBF) proposed in [10] for the detection of cells in microscopy images. The problem addressed in this paper is slightly different, however, since the gradient of cell images points inwards while the gradient of natural circles points inwards and outwards, depending on the distance to the center.

Let us assume that we know the center of the circle $c = [x, y]^T$ and let us define N radial directions starting from c, with angles $\theta_i = 2\pi i/N, i = 0, \ldots, N-1$. Along each direction we will measure the alignment between the gradient direction and the radial orientation θ_i, given by

$$A_i(r) = \cos(\phi_i(r) - \theta_i), \tag{6}$$

where $\phi_i(r)$ denotes the direction of the gradient field at a point $c + r[\cos(\theta_i), \sin(\theta_i)]^T$. The gradient orientation changes when the point is located at the circle boundary. To detect the boundary we will perform template matching along each direction and choose the radius r_0 that corresponds to the highest peak. Therefore, the best alignment in direction θ_i is

$$A_i = \max_{r_0}\left\{\sum_r T(r - r_0)A_i(r)\right\}, \tag{7}$$

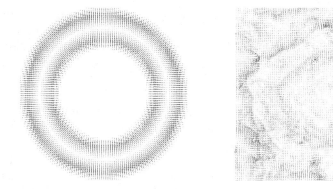

Fig. 4. Gradient field of torus (left) and natural stone circle (right).

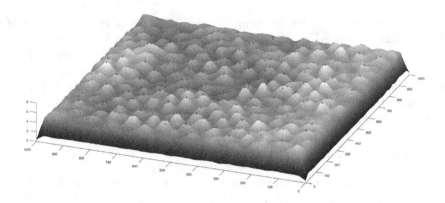

Fig. 5. Alignment score as a function of the circle center.

where $T = u(r + \Delta) - 2u(r) + u(r - \Delta)$ is the template (u(r) denotes the unit step signal). Since there are N radial directions, the global alignment is the sum of all the directional alignments

$$A = \sum_{i=0}^{N-1} A_i. \tag{8}$$

The previous expressions provide the alignment score associated to the center hypothesis $c = [x, y]^T$. In practice we do not know c. What we do is to compute the alignment score for each image point, c, and detect the circle centers by non-maximum suppression and thresholding (see Fig. 5).

To be specific, the gradient vector is computed by using Sobel masks and its magnitude is compared with a threshold: gradients with small magnitude are discarded.

4   Results

The algorithms were evaluated on a dataset of six DEMs from two sites, with size 1000×1000 pixels. These images include a variety of cases ranging from regions with a stationary quasi-periodic structure to highly unorganized regions.

4.1   Performance Measure

To evaluate the performance of the proposed algorithms, ground truth (GT) information was built by visually detecting all the circles and annotating their centers.

Since the algorithms also produce a set of centers, we need to establish a correspondence between the detected centers and the ground truth information. This was achieved by using a simple matching algorithm defined as follows. First, we build a matrix of distances from all the GT centers to all the detected centers.

Table 1. Performance measures of template matching, watershed and sliding band filter (SBF) methods: mean and standard deviation computed in six images.

Methods	Precision (%)	Recall (%)	F (%)
Template matching	69.6 (10.5)	73.8 (14.1)	70.3 (8.1)
Watershed	65.2 (12.3)	79.5 (7.0)	71.3 (9.7)
SBF	**78.5 (6.3)**	**90.5 (6.0)**	**83.9 (4.5)**

The minimum element of the matrix is found (excluding the diagonal elements) and the corresponding points are matched, provided that the minimum distance is smaller than a threshold Δ. If two points are matched they are considered as a true positive (TP) detection and the corresponding line and column are removed from the distance matrix. The process is repeated until there are no more candidates for matching. The ground truth points which were not matched are considered as false negatives (FN) and the detected points that were not matched are considered as false positives (FP).

The performance of the detection algorithm is characterized by the well known measures

$$\text{Precision} = \frac{TP}{TP + FP}, \qquad \text{Recall} = \frac{TP}{TP + FN}, \tag{9}$$

$$F = 2 \frac{\text{Precision.Recall}}{\text{Precision} + \text{Recall}}. \tag{10}$$

The F-score combines the precision and recall in a single measure.

Figure 6 shows the performance of the proposed methods in two images extracted from different sites. The example on the left is well organized and quasi-periodic while the example on the right is much more difficult. For each example we show the ground truth information (circles), the detected objects (crosses) and the TP (green), FN (yellow) and FP (red). In the case of the watershed and SBF methods, we also show the circle boundaries (yellow). All the methods detect most of the natural circles present in the image, despite the fact that the dynamic range presents small changes on the order of centimetres.

4.2 Statistical Evaluation

The parameters associated with each method were chosen experimentally: $R = 35$ pixels, $T = 0.4$ for template matching method, $h = 10\,\text{cm}$, $C = 0.70$ for watershed method, and $N = 16$, $\Delta = 7$, threshold $= 70\%$ of maximum peak amplitude for SBF method. Then, we processed the six images with the three methods and for each image we computed precision, recall and F-score. The mean and standard deviation of all these measures are shown in Table 1. The best results were obtained by SBF method which achieves a F-score $= 83.9\%$.

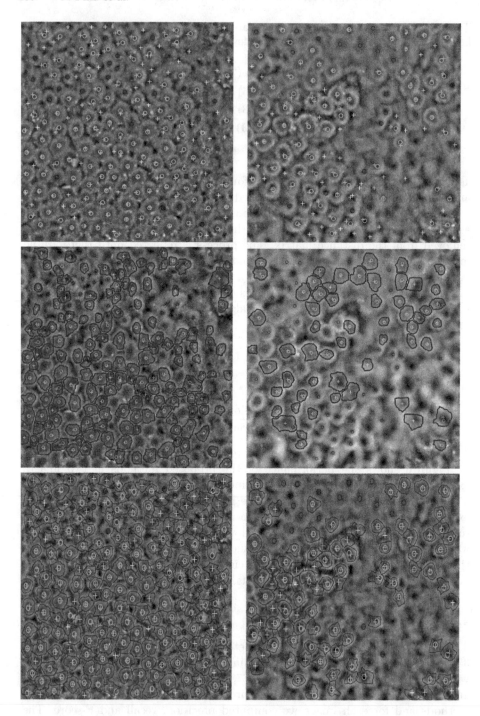

Fig. 6. Examples from 2 field sites: outputs of template matching (top), watershed (middle) and SBF (bottom). Colour code: true positives (green), false positives (red) and false negatives (yellow). (Color figure online)

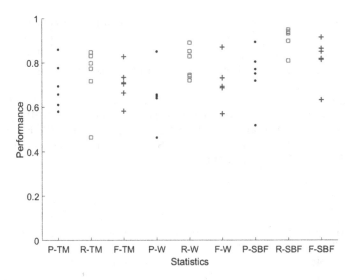

Fig. 7. Precision (blue point), recall (green square) and F score (red cross) for the three methods in each of the six images. (Color figure online)

The template matching and watershed method achieve worse performances (F-scores = 70.3% and 71.3%, respectively).

Figure 7 displays the three statistics (precision, recall and F-score) obtained by the three methods in each of the test images highlighting the superiority of SBF method.

5 Conclusions

This paper presents a new problem: the detection of stone circles in periglacial terrains. The information used to estimate such structures consists of elevation data built after optical imagery, captured by a UAV in Antarctica (Project CIRCLAR2 from the Portuguese Polar Program).

The structures have a circular shape, exhibiting several types of deformation due to the natural processes involved in their formation and development along centuries. Three automatic algorithms are described, exploiting the shape information, based on template matching, watershed transform and sliding band filter (SBF). The methods are evaluated in six elevation images (1000 × 1000 pixels) achieving an F score ranging from 70.3% to 83.9%. The best results were achieved by SBF method that clearly outperforms the other two. This is probably related to the assumptions made in each method. Template match makes strong rigidity assumptions about the object shape, the watershed-based is probably too flexible. The SBF filter presents a more appropriate trade-off between shape assumptions and deformation.

There are several open issues to be addressed in the future. One concerns shape deformation. The assumption of rigid scales adopted in template matching is perhaps too hard and should be studied. A second issue concerns multiple scales since the size of the natural circles change, depending on the type of material and altitude. One promising direction for future research concerns the combination of multiple detection algorithms and the use of multi-scale methods.

Acknowledgements. This work was supported by FCT plurianual funding (UID/EEA/50009/2019 and UID/ECI/04028/2019), project CIRCLAR2 (call 2017-2018 from PROPOLAR-Portuguese Polar Program) and KOPRI-Korean Polar Research Institute for logistics at King Sejong Station in Antarctica, and FCT project SPARSIS PTDC/EEIPRO/0426/2014.

References

1. Washburn, A.L.: Geocryology: A Survey of Periglacial Processes and Environments. Wiley, New York (1980)
2. Hallet, B.: Stone circles: form and soil kinematics. Philos. Trans. R. Soc. A **371**, 20120357 (2013)
3. Kaab, A., Girod, L., Berthling, I.: Surface kinematics of periglacial sorted circles using structure-from-motion technology. Cryosphere **8**, 1041–1056 (2014)
4. Kessler, M.A., Murray, A.B., Werner, B.T., Hallet, B.: A model for sorted circles as self-organized patterns. J. Geophys. Res.-Solid Earth **106**, 13287–13306 (2001)
5. Jeong, G.Y.: Radiocarbon ages of sorted circles on King George Island, South Shetland Islands, West Antarctica. Antarct. Sci. **18**, 265–270 (2006)
6. Pina, P., Vieira, G., Bandeira, L., Mora, C.: Accurate determination of surface reference data in digital photographs in ice-free surfaces of Maritime Antarctica. Sci. Total Environ. **573**, 290–302 (2016)
7. López-Martínez, J., Serrano, E., Schmid, T., Mink, S., Linés, C.: Periglacial processes and landforms in the South Shetland Islands (northern Antarctic Peninsula region). Geomorphology **155–156**, 62–79 (2012)
8. Soille, P.: Morphological Image Analysis. Principles and Applications, 2nd edn. Springer, Heidelberg (2003). https://doi.org/10.1007/978-3-662-05088-0
9. Pina, P., Marques, J.S.: Delineation of impact craters by a mathematical morphology based approach. In: Kamel, M., Campilho, A. (eds.) ICIAR 2013. LNCS, vol. 7950, pp. 717–725. Springer, Heidelberg (2013). https://doi.org/10.1007/978-3-642-39094-4_82
10. Quelhas, P., Marcuzzo, M., Mendonça, A.M., Campilho, A.: Cell nuclei and cytoplasm joint segmentation using the sliding band filter. IEEE Trans. Med. Imaging **29**(8), 1463–1473 (2010)

Lesion Detection in Breast Ultrasound Images Using a Machine Learning Approach and Genetic Optimization

Fabian Torres[1,2(✉)] (ID), Boris Escalante-Ramirez[1,2] (ID),
Jimena Olveres[2], and Ping-Lang Yen[3]

[1] Centro Virtual de Computación, Universidad Nacional Autónoma de México,
04510 México CDMX, Mexico
`fabian_torres@cvicom.unam.mx.com`

[2] Departamento de Procesamiento de Señales, Facultad de Ingeniería,
Universidad Nacional Autónoma de México, 04510 México CDMX, Mexico

[3] Department of Bio-Industrial Mechatronics Engineering,
National Taiwan University, Taipei, Taiwan

Abstract. Breast ultrasound has become one of the most important and effective modalities for early detection of breast cancer and it is most suitable for large scale breast cancer screening and diagnosis in low-resource countries. Breast lesion detection is a crucial step in the development of Computer Aided Diagnosis and Surgery systems based on ultrasound images, since it can be used as a seed point to subsequently initialize segmentation methods such as region growing, snakes or level-sets. Because of inherent artifacts of the ultrasound images, such as speckle, acoustic shadows and blurry edges, the detection of lesions is not an easy task. In this work we propose a machine learning based approach to locate lesions in breast ultrasound images. This approach consists on the classification of image pixels as lesion or background with a Random Forest optimized with genetic algorithms to generate candidate regions. After pixel classification the method chooses the correct lesion region by discriminating false positives using a new proposed probability approach. The pixel classification and region discrimination steps are compared with other methods, showing better results in the detection of lesions. The lesion detection was evaluated using the True Positive Fraction and the False Positives per image, having results of 84.4% and 15.6% respectively.

Keywords: Breast lesion · Ultrasound · Random Forest · Genetic algorithms

1 Introduction

Although mammography is the most used imaging method for breast tumor analysis, ultrasound has been used as one of the gold standard techniques for breast cancer imaging, since mammography may miss over 1/3 lesions in dense breast. Currently ultrasound is responsible for about 1/5 of all diagnostic images and has become an important and effective modality for early detection of breast cancer and it is most suitable for large scale breast cancer screening and diagnosis in low-income countries,

© Springer Nature Switzerland AG 2019
A. Morales et al. (Eds.): IbPRIA 2019, LNCS 11867, pp. 289–301, 2019.
https://doi.org/10.1007/978-3-030-31332-6_26

but the visualization of lesions in breast ultrasound (BUS) images is a difficult task due to some intrinsic characteristics of the images, like speckle, acoustic shadows and blurry edges [1].

Computer Aided Diagnosis and Surgery (CAD/CAS) systems based on BUS images have been developed to help the physician to have better visualization of the lesion by overcoming the considerable inter and intra-variability, since it directly affects the performance of the quantitative analysis and diagnosis of the lesions. Lesion detection is an initial state of CAD/CAS systems as a seed point to subsequently initialize segmentation methods such as region growing, snakes or level-sets. Because of the mentioned inherent artifacts in BUS images, the detection of lesions is not an easy task. Several semi-automatic and automatic methods have been proposed. Three main categories of methods for breast lesion detection can be identified: (1) Classical approaches; (2) Graph based approaches; and (3) Machine-Learning approaches [2]. Due to the challenging nature of the task, just using a single image processing technique cannot achieve desirable results. Most successful approaches employ hybrid techniques and model biological priors using pixel intensity, texture, and spatial information [3].

Machine learning methods thrive in BUS lesion detection in the last decade because they provide a good approach to integrate different levels of features. In this work we use a machine learning based approach to locate a lesion in BUS images. This approach consists on the classification of image pixels as tumor or background to generate candidate regions, and then choose the correct region where the tumor is located. To achieve this, we compare several machine learning methods, concluding that the Random Forest algorithm outperforms other machine learning algorithms in the pixel classification task. After optimization using genetic algorithms, an accuracy of 82.92% was achieved using a set of 19 texture descriptors (2 histogram, 3 co-occurrence, 4 run-length and 10 Hermite coefficients), 850 trees with $m = 10$ and a maximum of samples per leaf of 1 pixel. After pixel classification, false positive regions must be removed. Several methods have been proposed to find the correct region where the lesion is located, here we propose a new discrimination method based on a probability image build with the computed probabilities of each pixels by the RF and compare it with different approaches, by evaluating the True Positive Fraction and the False Positives per image, having results of 84.4% and 15.6% respectively.

1.1 Modeling Lesions in Breast Ultrasound Images

Successful approaches for lesion detection in BUS should model domain related priors appropriately. The main features used for modeling breast tumors in ultrasound images are: intensity; internal echo pattern (Texture); and spatial distribution.

Ultrasound gray-level intensity provide helpful information about the density of the different tissues found in the image and helps to differentiate and identify different structures. The main disadvantage of medical ultrasound images is the poor quality due to speckle noise. Speckle reduction in ultrasound images is usually done by techniques that are applied directly to the original image domain. Several methods have been proposed to address the problem of speckle noise. The speckle reduction anisotropic (SRAD) filter is an edge-sensitive diffusion for speckled images. This filter has a large potential in assisting segmentation techniques and has been used in BUS images to obtain more homogeneous regions while preserving edges [4]. On the other hand, contrast enhancement in ultrasound images has the purpose to adjust the display contrast and increase the edge sharpness of objects. Histogram equalization and stick filtering have been widely used in ultrasound breast images to improve the contrast between the lesion and the background [5].

Internal echo pattern can be described using texture. Texture information provides a way to differentiate the lesion from other objects that have similar gray intensities, like acoustic shadows. The main texture descriptors used for lesion detection in BUS images are extracted from histogram and co-occurrence matrices. First-order texture descriptors are extracted from the pixel image values. These descriptors do not consider the spatial relationship with neighborhood pixels. The most frequently used first-order texture descriptors in BUS images are central moments of the histogram. The gray-level co-occurrence matrix describes how frequently two gray-levels appear in a window separated by a given distance and a given angle. Second-order texture descriptors computed from the analysis of the co-occurrence matrices have been pro-posed by Haralick [6]. Some of these texture descriptors have been used for the segmentation and classification of breast tumors [7]. Although these descriptors consider the spatial relationship between pixels, the computational cost of computing the co-occurrence matrix is very high compared to first order descriptors. Another method to characterize texture that also takes into account the spatial relationship between pixels is based on run-lengths of image gray-levels, where the run-length matrix of an image is defined as the number of runs with pixels of equal gray level and a given run-length [8]. Although these descriptors have not been widely used as an effective texture classification and analysis method, it has been demonstrated by Tang et al. that there is rich texture information contained in this matrices [9]. On the other hand, methods that resemble the human visual system have increased in popularity because they allow images to expand into a local decomposition that describes intrinsic attributes and highlights structures that are useful for segmentation. The main advantage of the Hermite transform is the easy extraction of important details as lines, edges and texture information by applying a decomposition scheme. Hermite-based texture descriptors have been used in the segmentation of ultrasound images successfully [10].

The spatial distribution of BUS is widely used in lesion detection approaches to discriminate lesions from other tissue such as fat and glands. Breast lesions are usually located in the center of the images, while subcutaneous fat, glandular tissue and skin typically appear in the upper portion of the image. Modern ultrasound systems can acquire high-resolution images which may include other structures such as ribs, pec-toral muscle or the air in the lungs, making the lesion detection more difficult. Nowadays it is no longer necessary to place the suspected lesion at the center of the image for better visualization, hence, methodologies that assume that the lesion is centered in the image fail in more cases when using modern ultrasound systems [2].

1.2   Lesion Detection in Breast Ultrasound Images

The improvement of the performance of lesion detection is an increasingly challenge that has reach a bottleneck, and only a few new approaches were published in the last several years. BUS segmentation is a crucial step in CAD/CAS systems, since it directly affects the performance of the quantitative analysis and diagnosis of tumors. Different kinds of automatic and semiautomatic methods have been developed. Three main categories of breast tumor segmentation can be identified [11]:

Classical Approaches. Most of the classical approaches are quite simple, fast and efficient to conduct initial segmentation of BUS images using simple low-level features, but these methods are vulnerable to low image quality due to noise, inhomogeneity and low contrast. Thresholding is the most intuitive, simple and fast of these methods and it has been successfully used for BUS lesion detection [12]. Region growing methods grow regions defined by a set of pixels (seed) to bigger regions using a growth criterion. The seed can be chosen manually or automatically, and the main challenge of this techniques is to find a growth criterion that adjust correctly to noisy images. Madabhushi et al. proposed a region growing based method for breast tumor segmentation with automatic seed selection [5]. Watershed is a powerful segmentation method with better results than thresholding and region growing that could integrate domain-related priors. The main problem of watershed is finding the markers, because using the local minimum gradient as a marker usually results in over segmentation and region merging should be involved [2].

Graph Based Methods. These methods are among the earliest techniques for breast lesion detection and provide a simple way to organize task-related priors and image information in a unified framework; they are flexible, computationally efficient and suitable for expressing soft constrains between random variables, like pixels. Markov Random Fields with maximum a posteriori optimized with Iterated Conditional Model is a flexible framework for image partition. The performance of methods based on this framework usually is good but has a shortcoming because they only obtain local optimum solutions. The approaches based on graph cuts focus on designing well-defined boundary problems by using more comprehensive data and smoothness terms to deal with contrast and inhomogeneity. The main disadvantage of these approach is that they tend to generate a much shorter boundary than the real one (shrink problem). Normalized cut methods avoid the shrink problem, but it cannot integrate semantic information and user interaction is needed to achieve good performance. Although graph-based methods account for the second largest portion of BUS segmentation, these techniques fade away due to the successful application of other powerful approaches [2].

Machine Learning-Based Approaches. Image segmentation can also be viewed as a two-class classification problem (classifying pixels into lesion and background). Supervised and unsupervised learning methods have been employed in lesion detection in BUS images. The unsupervised methods aim to partition the image in disjoint regions as a preprocessing step [2]. Supervised learning methods integrate different levels of features and can learn the relation between the inputs and the target outputs. The most common supervised learning approaches used in BUS are: Naive Bayes Classifier; Support Vector Machines; and Artificial Neural Networks [3, 13–16]. These methods are used for pixel classification using a set of texture features, where the main difference between them is the set of texture descriptors used. Other machine learning methods that may be suitable for BUS images, like Random Forest, have been used for the segmentation and classification of breast tumors in mammograms. Classification methods usually cannot produce accurate tumor boundary and refinement is usually necessary [2]. After pixel classification a binary image containing the lesion region and false positive regions is obtained, several methods have been used for the discrimination of false positive regions and the detection of the lesion region. Several methods have been proposed to select the correct region including spatial information, considering that the lesion usually is found near the center of the image in the parenchyma of the breast [5, 17]; however, this assumption does not apply for images acquired with modern ultrasound systems since they may include pectoral muscles and ribs information [2]. Because of this, machine learning methods such as SVM have been used to discriminate false positive and find the correct lesion region, but extracting new features for region classification is not an easy task [18].

1.3 Optimization of Machine Learning Methods with Genetic Algorithms

Dimensionality reduction is a step commonly used in machine learning, especially when dealing with a high dimensionality space of features. A high number of features may slow down the methods while giving similar results as obtained with a smaller subset; also, not all the features used to describe the problem are necessarily relevant and beneficial for the learning task. Dimensionality reduction is usually performed by constructing a new dimension space through feature transformation or by selecting a subset of the original dimensions, like principal component analysis and feature selection respectively. Different feature selection methods have been developed and applied in machine learning following different search strategies like: Forward selection (start with an empty set and greedily add features one at a time); Backward elimination (start with a feature set containing all features and greedily add or remove features); Random mutation (start with a feature set containing randomly selected features and add, or remove randomly selected features). Also, the feature selection methods can be divided into: Filters that use an evaluation function independent of the learning algorithm; Wrappers that use the same machine learning algorithm that will be used for modeling; and Embedded approaches that perform feature selection during the model generation [19]. Genetic algorithms (GA) have been used as a Wrap random mutation approach for feature selection. GAs make it possible to explore greater range of possible solutions to a problem under controlled and well understood conditions. It has been proved theoretically and empirically that these algorithms provide a global near-optimal solution for various complex optimization problems [20].

Besides feature selection, setting the parameters of a classifier has an important influence on its classification accuracy. A common used parameter search approach is the grid search, but its search ability is low. The optimal classification accuracy of a classifier can be obtained by feature selection and optimal parameters setting. The trend in recent years is to simultaneously optimize feature selection and parameter optimization. GAs have the potential to generate both feature selection and parameter optimization at the same time [21]. Although GAs have been previously used to find the optimal features for classifying and segmenting breast tumors in ultrasound images they have not been used for parameter optimization.

2 Materials and Methods

In this work we propose an automatic lesion detection method in BUS images. The method consists on a three-step approach: (1) Preprocessing; (2) Pixel classification; and (3) Identification of the lesion region. Feature selection and parameter optimization of the machine learning method for pixel classification was performed using a simple GA to improve the accuracy of the classification.

2.1 Dataset

A public data base of 58 BUS images with a lesion, provided by the Department of Radiology of Thammasat University and Queen Sirikit center of Breast Cancer of Thailand, was used for the evaluation of the proposed method; the database includes the ground truth hand-drawn by leading radiologists of these centers [22].

2.2 Random Forest

Random Forests are a combination of tree predictors, usually CARTs, such that each tree depends on the values of a random vector sampled independently and with the same distribution for all trees in the forest [23]. RFs trains an ensemble of individual decision trees based on samples, their class designation and variables; every tree is built using a random subset of samples and variables [24].

Suppose a forest of decision trees $(RF = \{T_1(X_1), T_2(X_2), \ldots, T_B(X_B)\})$ is constructed with a training data set X with N instances, where $X = \{x_1, x_2, \ldots x_M,\}$ is a M-dimensional vector of features associated with an instance in the data set and B is the number of trees in the forest. From the training data, a randomly sampled set, X_i, with replacement (bootstrap), is extracted to grow each tree in the forest. This bootstrap set of size n, where $n < N$, usually contains about two-third of the samples in the original training set; also, a random set of features of size m, where $m < M$, extracted from X is used for each bootstrap; where the size m of the random set is usually $\sqrt{M}$ or $\sqrt{M}/2$ [25]. To classify an instance every tree in the forest records a vote for the class to which the instance belong and it is labeled as a member of the class with the most of votes. One characteristic of the random forest classifier is that not only the class of the object can be computed but also the probability of the object belonging to that class could be obtained. The standard approach to probability estimation in many areas of science relies on logistic regression. However, it is almost impossible to guarantee that a logistic model is well-specified when modern data sets with nonlinear or high dimensional structure are used. Random forest has become a widely used tool for probability estimation. After fitting a RF to training data, it is a common practice to infer conditional class probabilities for test point by simply counting the fraction of trees in the forest that vote for a certain class [26].

2.3 Genetic Algorithms

GAs are based on natural selection and sexual reproduction. Natural selection determines which members of a population survive to reproduce, and sexual reproduction ensures the mixing and recombination of the genes of their offspring. A string of bits corresponding to the presence or absence of specific features and parameter values (in binary representation) are used in GAs to describe different members of the population (individuals) [27]. Each individual in a generation is tested, looking for the optimization of an objective function as a measure of fitness. The individual fitness $F(x_i)$ is computed as the individual performance $f(x_i)$ relative to that of the whole population.

The reproduction operator used in a simple GA is a single point crossover; where individuals with a high fitness value are paired at random, exchanging a random segment between individuals to create two offspring. The mutation operation consists of flipping each bit of the individuals with lowest fitness value [28]. This is repeated through several generations until a predefined condition is satisfied.

2.4 Proposed Method

The proposed method consists in three steps:

Preprocessing. The preprocessing step consists on extracting descriptive features from BUS images that could help in the classification of pixels into lesion and background classes. An enhanced intensity image is obtained using the SRAD filter and histogram equalization. To obtain texture images that could describe the internal echo pattern of the lesion and the background a total of 29 texture descriptors extracted from histogram, co-occurrence matrices, run-length matrices and Hermite transformation were computed; using the original intensity image without any pre-processing to avoid elimination of any texture related information.

Pixel Classification. A supervised machine learning method is used to classify pixels into lesion or background classes. Gray-level intensity values, extracted from the original and preprocessed images, are used as features for the classification. During the training of the classifier a GA was used to find the optimal subset of features and parameter optimization. After pixel classification a binary image is obtained, but this binary image usually contains false positive regions and a further discrimination must be made. Along with the binary classification image a lesion probability image is generated with the probability estimated with the RF classifier. The classification and probability images are shown in Fig. 1.

Lesion Region Detection. After pixel classification the discrimination of false positive regions must be made to find the localization of the lesion region. In this work we propose a new discrimination method based on a probability image build with the computed probabilities of each pixels by the RF. First basic mathematical morphology (dilation and erosion) is applied to the classification image in order to eliminate small regions and disconnect weak connected regions. After applying mathematical

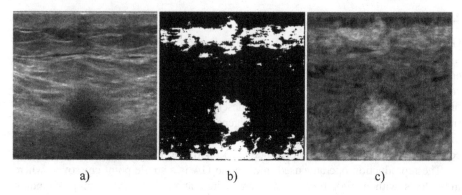

Fig. 1. Results of random forest classifier: (a) Original; (b) Classification and (c) Probability images

morphology a deletion of the candidate regions connected with the boundary of the image is done as in [17], excluding the regions that are connected with a window about half the size of the whole image and centered at the image center. After the connected-boundary regions are deleted the probability of each region is computed as the mean of all the pixels inside the region using the gray-level values of the probability image obtained with the RF classifier. The region with the highest probability is choose as the detected lesion region. This step is illustrated in Fig. 2.

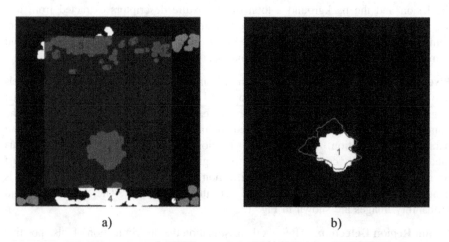

Fig. 2. Proposed method for lesion detection after classification: (a) Mathematical morphology of image 1a, deleted boundary-connected regions to be deleted are marked in red; and (b) maximum probability region chosen as lesion region. (Color figure online)

3   Experiments and Results

The proposed method was evaluated and compared against other state of the art methods for pixel classification and lesion detection. The results of these steps are explained in this section.

3.1   Pixel Classification Using Random Forest

Several machine learning methods were tested to find the classifier that has better results in the classification of pixels into lesion and background classes. A set of 31 features (original, enhanced intensity and 29 texture descriptors) were used for pixel classification. A set of pixels were extracted from the original and preprocessed images and labeled as lesion or background. A k-fold cross-validation (with k = 4) was used to find the accuracy (Eq. 1), sensitivity (Eq. 2) and specificity (Eq. 3) of the classification.

$$Accuracy = \frac{TP+TN}{TP+TN+FP+FN} \tag{1}$$

$$Sensitivity = \frac{TP}{TP+FN} \tag{2}$$

$$Specificity = \frac{TN}{TN+FP} \tag{3}$$

where *TP*, *TN*, *FP* and *FN* are the true positives, true negatives, false positives and false negatives pixels found in the classification process. The results in terms of accuracy of the classification with different classifiers is shown in Table 1.

The RF with default parameters (500 trees and $m = \sqrt{M}/2$) has a better accuracy than the other tested classifiers. After finding the best classifier a GA was used to find the optimal set of features and parameters that improves the outcome of the classification. A run of a simple GA was computed during 400 generation with a population of 15 individuals and a generational gap (number of individuals that survive to the next generation) of 5%. The accuracy error $(1 - Accuracy)$ of the RF method was used as the individual performance and it was computed using the same cross-validation method as mentioned before but using different characteristics and parameter values for the classification according to the GA individuals. After the GA run, an accuracy of 83.92% was achieved with a set of 19 features (2 histogram, 3 co-occurrence, 4 run-length and 10 Hermite coefficients), 850 trees with $m = 10$ and a maximum of samples per leaf of 1 pixel. The sensitivity and specificity are often used to complement the evaluation of segmentation algorithms; sensitivity is used to measure how many pixels in the region of interest are correctly segmented, it does not tell anything about how many pixels in the background are going to be segmented as tumor (FP); the specificity measures how many pixels in the background are correctly excluded and does not tell if a tumor pixel is going to be correctly segmented as tumor (FN). The sensitivity and specificity of the optimized RF method were 82.23% and 82.61% respectively. It can be seen in Table 1 that the tree-based methods (CART, ABoost, LBoost and RF) have better balance in terms of sensitivity and specificity.

Table 1. Pixel classification accuracy.

Classifier	Accuracy	Sensitivity	Specificity
Logistic regression	73.30 ± 0.28%	69.61%	76.97%
SVM (Gauss Kernel)	55.28 ± 0.60%	99.88%	10.86%
Naïve Bayes	68.08 ± 0.32%	62.20%	73.94%
KNN	77.22 ± 0.34%	79.26%	75.18%
CART	73.54 ± 0.40%	73.84%	73.24%
Aboost	74.86 ± 0.52%	74.81%	74.90%
LBoost	74.59 ± 0.68%	74.41%	74.59%
RF	81.14 ± 0.43%	81.00%	81.28%
RF+GA	82.92 ± 0.52%	82.23%	82.61%

3.2   Evaluation of Lesion Detection

In lesion detection current practice, a radiologist annotates a rectangular region of interest (ROI) where the lesion is located. Most of the BUS lesion detection methodologies in the literature evaluate their algorithms using the seed point as detection criterion [2]. After lesion detection with the proposed algorithm a bounding box that comprises the detected lesion region is generated. The lesion detection is considered a true positive if the center of the bounding box is placed within the bounding box of an expert radiologist and considered a false positive when the center is outside the bounding box. The True Positive Fraction (TPF, Eq. 4), and the False Positives per image are used as quantitative measurements of the sensitivity of the lesion detection technique (FPs, Eq. 5).

$$TPF = \frac{TP}{Total\ number\ of\ images}, \tag{4}$$

$$FPs = \frac{FP}{Total\ number\ of\ images}, \tag{5}$$

The proposed method results are shown in Table 2. Different methods to discriminate false positive regions were tested for comparison of the method, the results are also shown in Table 2. The result of the lesion detection in three ultrasound images using the proposed approach are shown in Fig. 3.

It can be seen in Table 2 that the proposed lesion detection method outperforms the methods used for comparation. It is important to notice that the Madabhushi [5] and Shan [17] methods relies in the assumption that the lesion is located near the center of the image and this assumption is not always true, especially when using modern ultrasound systems for acquisition. On the other hand, Yang [16] and Jiang [18] methods use machine learning to classify the regions, CART and SVM respectively. Extracting new characteristics from BUS images for region classification is not an easy task, Jiang use the results of a k-means pixel clustering algorithm as features for the classification, but this method shows poor results in the lesion detection compared with

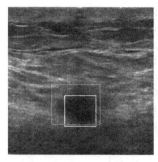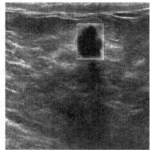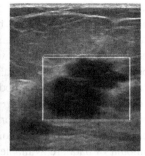

Fig. 3. Results of lesion detection in BUS images. The bounding box annotated by the experts is marked in red and the chosen by the proposed algorithm is marked in green. (Color figure online)

Table 2. Lesion detection evaluation

Classifier	TPF	FPs
Proposed method	84.48%	15.52%
Madhabushi	74.14%	25.86%
Shan	65.52%	34.48%
Jiang	68.97%	31.03%
Yang	75.86%	24.14

the proposed method. Yang proposed morphology characteristics such as size, compactness, region ratio and width height ratio as characteristics for classification; this method is not a good approach, as seen in Table 2, since breast lesions does not have a defined morphology.

4 Conclusion

In this work we present a new method for lesion detection in BUS images. The proposed method consists of three steps. In the first step preprocessing is used to extract an enhanced intensity image and texture images to be used as features for pixel classification. The second step consists of pixel classification using a random forest classifier and the extracted features from the preprocessing step. The random forest classifier was compared to other machine learning classification methods, showing better results in the classification of pixels into tumor or background classes. Also, the pixel classification method is improved using a simple GA to find an optimal subset of features and parameters. After pixel classification a false positive region discrimination must be done. In this work we proposed a new method based on a probability image generated using the probability of each pixel to belong to a lesion using the RF classifier in the second step. The proposed method was compared with four methods found in the literature, showing better results in finding the lesion region location. While lesion detection is an important step in the development of CAD/CAS systems, the segmentation of tumor boundaries could be more helpful to assist physicians in the diagnosis and treatment of breast cancer. Emerging methods such as Deep Learning could be used for feature extraction (preprocessing step), pixel classification, lesion detection and segmentation with high accuracy. Although the increasing computational power of hardware and parallel computing techniques, the development of BUS lesion detection methods using modern deep neural networks represent a challenge in terms of computational time and size of the training data sets, since modern neural networks need thousand of images for training and it is a difficult task to collect this amount of data, especially in low-income countries, and no public databases with the required amount of data are available [12, 29, 30].

Acknowledge. This work has been sponsored by UNAM grants PAPIIT IA103119 and UNAM PAPIIT IN116917. The DGAPA financial support of the postdoctoral fellowship program in the Facultad de Ingeniería is gratefully acknowledge.

References

1. Stöblen, F., Landt, S., Stelkens-Gebhardt, R., Sehouli, J., Rezai, M., Kümmel, S.: First evaluation of the diagnostic accuracy of an automated 3d ultrasound system in a breast screening setting. Int. J. Cancer Res. Treat. (2011)
2. Xian, M., Zhang, Y., Cheng, H.D., Xu, F., Zhang, B., Ding, J.: Automatic breast ultrasound image segmentation: a survey. Pattern Recogn. **79**, 340–355 (2018)
3. Liu, B., Cheng, H.D., Huang, J., Tian, J., Tang, X., Liu, J.: Fully automatic and segmentation-robust classification of breast tumors based on local texture analysis of ultrasound images. Pattern Recogn. **43**(1), 280–298 (2010)
4. Sivakumar, R., Gayathri, M.K., Nedumaran, D.: Speckle filtering of ultrasound b-scan images - a comparative study of single scale spatial adaptive filters, multiscale filter and diffusion filters. Int. J. Eng. Technol. **2**(6), 514 (2010)
5. Madabhushi, A., Metaxas, D.N.: Combining low-, high-level and empirical domain knowledge for automated segmentation of ultrasonic breast lesions. IEEE Trans. Med. Imaging **22**(2), 155–169 (2003)
6. Haralick, R.M.: Statistical and structural approaches to texture. Proc. IEEE **67**(5), 786–804 (1979)
7. Liao, Y.Y., Wu, J.C., Li, C.H., Yeh, C.K.: Texture feature analysis for breast ultrasound image enhancement. Ultrason. Imaging **33**, 264–278 (2011)
8. Selvarajah, S., Kodituwakku, S.R.: Analysis and comparison of texture features for content based image retrieval. Int. J. Latest Trends Comput. **2**(1), 108–113 (2011)
9. Tang, X.: Texture information in run-length matrices. IEEE Trans. Image Process. **7**(11), 1602–1609 (1998)
10. Estudillo-Romero, A., Escalante-Ramirez, B., Savage-Carmona, J.: Texture analysis based on the Hermite transform for image classification and segmentation, vol. 8436, p. 843619 (2012)
11. Huang, Q., Luo, Y., Zhang, Q.: Breast ultrasound image segmentation: a survey. Int. J. Comput. Assist. Radiol. Surg. **12**(3), 493–507 (2017)
12. Yap, M.H., Edirisinghe, E.A., Bez, H.E.: A novel algorithm for initial lesion detection in ultrasound breast images. J. Appl. Clin. Med. Phys. **9**(4), 2741 (2008)

13. Huang, S.-F., Chen, Y.-C., Woo, K.M.: Neural network analysis applied to tumor segmentation on 3D breast ultrasound images. In: 2008 5th IEEE International Symposium on Biomedical Imaging: From Nano to Macro, Proceedings, ISBI, pp. 1303–1306 (2008)
14. Chen, D.-R., Chang, R.-F., Kuo, W.-J., Chen, M.-C., Huang, Y.-L.: Diagnosis of breast tumors with sonographic texture analysis using wavelet transform and neural networks. Ultrasound Med. Biol. **28**(10), 1301–1310 (2002)
15. Yankaskas, B.C.: Epidemiology of breast cancer in young women. Breast Dis. **23**, 3–8 (2006)
16. Yang, M.-C., Huang, C.-S., Chen, J.-H., Chang, R.-F.: Whole breast lesion detection using naive bayes classifier for portable ultrasound. Ultrasound Med. Biol. **38**(11), 1870–1880 (2012)
17. Shan, J., Cheng, H.D., Wang, Y.: A novel automatic seed point selection algorithm for breast ultrasound images. In: 2008 19th International Conference on Pattern Recognition, pp. 1–4 (2008)
18. Jiang, P., Peng, J., Zhang, G., Cheng, E., Megalooikonomou, V., Ling, H.: Learning-based automatic breast tumor detection and segmentation in ultrasound images. In: 2012 9th IEEE International Symposium on Biomedical Imaging (ISBI), pp. 1587–1590 (2012)
19. Mladenić, D.: Feature Selection for Dimensionality Reduction, pp. 84–102. Springer, Heidelberg (2006)
20. Tsai, C.-F., Eberle, W., Chu, C.-Y.: Genetic algorithms in feature and instance selection. Knowl.-Based Syst. **39**, 240–247 (2013)
21. Zhao, M., Fu, C., Ji, L., Tang, K., Zhou, M.: Feature selection and parameter optimization for support vector machines: a new approach based on genetic algorithm with feature chromosomes. Expert Syst. Appl. **38**(5), 5197–5204 (2011)
22. Rodtook, A., Makhanov, S.S.: Multi-feature gradient vector flow snakes for adaptive segmentation of the ultrasound images of breast cancer. J. Vis. Commun. Image Represent. **24**(8), 1414–1430 (2013)
23. Breiman, L.: Random forests. Mach. Learn. **45**(1), 5–32 (2001)
24. Touw, W.G., et al.: Data mining in the Life Sciences with Random Forest: a walk in the park or lost in the jungle? Brief. Bioinform. **14**(3), 315–326 (2013)
25. Azar, A.T., Elshazly, H.I., Hassanien, A.E., Elkorany, A.M.: A random forest classifier for lymph diseases. Comput. Methods Programs Biomed. **113**(2), 465–473 (2014)
26. Olson, M.A., Wyner, A.J.: Making sense of random forest probabilities: a kernel perspective, December 2018
27. Holland, J.H.: Genetic algorithms. Sci. Am. **267**(1), 66–72 (1992)
28. Fleming, P.J., Purshouse, R.C.: Genetic algorithms in control systems engineering. Control Syst. Robot. Autom. **XVII** (1993)
29. Han, S., Kang, H.-K., Jeong, J.-Y., Park, M.-H., Kim, W., Bang, W.-C., Seong, Y.-K.: A deep learning framework for supporting the classification of breast lesions in ultrasound images. Phys. Med. Biol. **62**(19), 7714–7728 (2017)
30. Antropova, N., Huynh, B.Q., Giger, M.L.: A deep feature fusion methodology for breast cancer diagnosis demonstrated on three imaging modality datasets. Med. Phys. **44**(10), 5162–5171 (2017)

Evaluating the Impact of Color Information in Deep Neural Networks

Vanessa Buhrmester$^{(\boxtimes)}$, David Münch , Dimitri Bulatov ,
and Michael Arens

Fraunhofer IOSB, Ettlingen, Germany
vanessa.buhrmester@iosb.fraunhofer.de

Abstract. Color images are omnipresent in everyday life. In particular, they provide the only necessary input for deep neural network pipelines, which are continuously being employed for image classification and object recognition tasks. Although color can provide valuable information, effects like varying illumination and specialties of different sensors still pose significant problems. However, there is no clear evidence how strongly variations in color information influence classification performance throughout rearward layers. To gain a deeper insight about how Convolutional Neural Networks make decisions and what they learn from input images, we investigate in this work suitability and robustness of different color augmentation techniques. We considered several established benchmark sets and custom-made pedestrian and background datasets. While decreasing color or saturation information we explore the activation differences in the rear layers and the stability of confidence values. We show that *Luminance* is most robust against changing color system in test images irrespective of degraded texture or not. Finally, we present the coherence between color dependence and properties of the regarded datasets and classes.

Keywords: Color space representation · Degraded texture ·
Color dependence · Robustness of color model change ·
Image classification

1 Introduction

Color images surround us everywhere. The human visual systems has an innate ability to discern thousands of colors, but only a fraction shades of gray [19]. The reason is that we have three kinds of cone cells in the retina, which are sensitive to light of different wavelengths, recognizing the colors red, green, and blue, which are represented by these wavelengths. The visible colors arise through multiple combinations of red, green, and blue. To perceive light intensity we have only one kind of cells – the rod cells. Under bad light conditions, we cannot distinguish between colors but can still recognize light intensity, we see grayscale images then.

© Springer Nature Switzerland AG 2019
A. Morales et al. (Eds.): IbPRIA 2019, LNCS 11867, pp. 302–316, 2019.
https://doi.org/10.1007/978-3-030-31332-6_27

Commonly, regarding natural images we can easily recognize simple objects in images, independently if the images are colored or not. A simple example is a person standing in front of a building. Yet, color images contain additional information than grayscale ones, for instance to distinguish a hill in the desert from a snowy hill. Moreover, there are several color spaces, in which this information is based on, their motivation is to be sought on the one hand technically and on the other hand methodically [19]. Understanding the different color models and their color information is important in Computer Vision, e. g. for inpainting, colorization, segmentation tasks, and Convolutional Neural Networks [2]. We will focus on CNNs, which yield state of the art tools for object detection, face recognition or video analysis. To solve the basic task that is image classification, a CNN usually takes an input color image of a predetermined size $length \times height \times 3$ and returns a prediction vector of possible contents of the image. In this paper, we want to find out more about the information that is hidden in these three channels and provides a contribution to a deep neural network.

1.1 Related Work

The role of colors in face recognition was investigated by Yip and Sinha [23] in 2002. They made experiments with thirty-seven subjects and found that color images perform better than grayscale images and significantly better than grayscale images, when available shape information of both images is degraded by Gaussian blur. In 2009, Oliveira and Conci [17] showed that HSV color images are advantageous for skin detection, whereby a value H between 6 and 38 indicates skin. Li et al. [16] used different color models in vehicle color recognition using vector matching of templates in 2010. They found out that HSV is the best model for color recognition compared to RGB or YUV. Agrawal et al. [1] proposed 2011 a new approach for image classification using Support Vector Machines and compared accuracies in different color models, which depend on the classifier. One year later Kanan et al. [12] investigated different grayscale models in image recognition using Naïve Bayes Nearest Neighbor framework. They came to the result that $Intensity$ (with or without gamma correction) performs best, while $Value$ performs worse. Ruela [20] investigated different color spaces in Dermoscopy Analysis and shows that color features play a major role in this area. In 2014 Zeiler and Fergus [24] presented an impressive possibility to visualize deep neural networks and what and how they learn from color images. They used a multi-layered Deconvolutional Network, as proposed by Zeiler et al. [25] to project feature activations back to the input pixel space. The role of color distribution and illuminant estimation for color constancy was studied in 2014 by Cheng et al. [5]. They showed that spatial information does not provide any additional information that cannot be obtained directly from the color distribution. Humans are able to perceive colors constantly and independently of the illumination. In Computer Vision problems need color constancy in image processing to make sure that the objects in a scene can be recognized reliable under different illumination conditions. One year later Barron [3], Bianco et al. [4] investigated color constancy in Convolutional Neural Networks. Recent work investigated color augmentation techniques in deep skin image analysis [7], 2017. Galiyawala et al. [8] found out that the impact of color is helpful in deep-learning-based persons retrieval tasks in surveillance videos, 2018. Also with regard to CNN-based colorization [21], it could be useful to get a deeper understanding of color contribution in deep architectures.

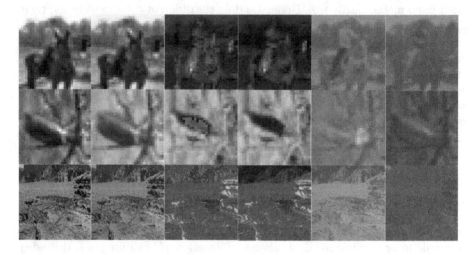

Fig. 1. Images of the different color models *Luminance, RGB, HSV, SV, YIQ, YUV*: horse (CIFAR-10), crockroach (CIFAR-100), desert (FlickrScene) shown in *RGB* representation. (Color figure online)

1.2   Contribution

Previous work examines the impact of colors only by regarding color augmentation techniques for train and test images. Because we transform the grayscale images in 3D tensors with three identical channels, we can also put them in our architecture and this makes it possible to train and test with different color models in one experimental setup. That is why we can deduce whether images are recognized or misclassified only because of their removed or added color and create statistics about these cases in the different categories. We call this property of a special class of a dataset **to be high or low (in)dependent of color information**. On the other hand we investigate degraded test images inspired by Yip and Sinha [23] to regard the coherence between color and texture. While they only used Gaussian blur to degrade edges, we add Gaussian noise on our images, too. We investigate the performance difference depending what modification is applied to the images represented to the architecture and compare the results to the dataset or classes properties. Finally, we observe the activations in higher layers and the change of confidence values under the mentioned conditions. Answers to this questions are of general interest to improve networks, but may even play an important role when classifying images of a special category or recognize something in thermal infrared images, which contain no color information.

2   Methodology

In this section, we give a short overview about CNNs. After that, we show the applied augmentation techniques and some examples of color spaces.

2.1   About CNNs

The upcoming description of those aspects of CNNs needed for our methodology will not replace an encompassing textbook [9] or article [15], therefore we assume that the reader is familiar with the basic terminology such as *loss function, max pooling* or *activation*. However in a nutshell, CNN-based image classification presupposes determination of a feature set allowing the best separation of the training data, or, equivalently, minimization of a loss function. In the simplest case, the unknowns in this function could be the weights connecting the responses of convolutions of the input image with a bunch of filters. Examples of such filters, also denoted as low-level features, are those based on color information (for example, a constant green filter could give a hint about the amount of vegetation) while others rely on textures (Gabor-like-filters). For classification problems involving many classes, these filters are propagated to deeper scales, using iterative convolutional, max-pooling, and dropout layers. For example, the widely-used VGG 16 architecture [22] diminishes the image to the scale of 32 before the fully connected layer, that is, weighted sum of filter responses to make them vote for each of the classes, is employed. On the contrary, flatter architectures are more suitable to perform classification if the number of classes is low for reasons of computational efficiency. Since for such flat architectures, the color and texture filters play a crucial, decisive part, the two goals of this work are (1) to investigate to what extent change of color space may influence the classification accuracy and (2) to find out which color space is the most robust against color and texture changes between training and test data.

2.2   Augmentation Techniques

The human brain interprets color as a physiopsychological phenomenon that is not yet fully understood. It is represented by the light that is reflected by an object and each color blends smoothly into the next, it does not end abruptly. A color model or system is a specification of a coordinate system and every color is determined by a point in that system, see [19]. Input images can be illustrated in different representations, the conversion between the descriptions is a color augmentation technique. The impact of color can be also be regarded under applied texture modifications. Therefor we add noise with several distributions, like random uniform, random gamma, or random Gaussian $\mathcal{N}(0, \sigma^2)$ with different variances $\sigma^2 \in \{3, 8.5, 12, 25, 50\}$. According to our results and regarding the work of da Costa et al. [6], who investigated several types of noise in image classification tasks, the Gaussian distribution $\mathcal{N}(0, 8.5)$ provides a medium deterioration. Another option to degrade shape is to make the images blurring employing Gaussian blur. We choose $\sigma = 0.5$ and filter size 3 inspired by Yip and Sinha [23]. Several color and texture transformations T to the input images i can be described as:

$$T: i \to T(i). \tag{1}$$

Our CNN depicts the images to a prediction:

$$\text{CNN}: i \to P, \quad \text{CNN}: T(i) \to P'. \tag{2}$$

and we are interested in the relation of P' and P.

Fig. 2. Left: Bus image in *Luminance* and *Value*, difference of both. Right: Original Car image, with noise, and Gaussian blur.

2.3   Examples of Color Spaces

This section describes the regarded color spaces of the conducted study. Let M be a tensor with entries in $\mathbb{R}$ representing a 3-channel color image. The pixels of the RGB color input image with length l and width h

$$im_{RGB} = [R, G, B] \in M^{l \times h \times 3} \tag{3}$$

are the entries of the matrices $R, G, B \in M^{l \times h}$. According to [19] an image in RGB representation can be converted to an other color model.

For a conversion into grayscale, the following coefficients, which add up to one, are tried-and-true. The model is also known as *Luminance*, and is inspired by the current spectra, which human eyes are differently sensitive to perceiving red, green, and blue:

$$L = [0.2989R + 0.5870G + 0.1140B] \in M^{l \times h} \tag{4}$$

or $G_L = [L, L, L] \in M^{l \times h \times 3}$ to get a grayscale 3D tensor. Another more simple grayscale space is the *Intensity*, mean of the RGB channels:

$$I = \frac{1}{3}[R + G + B] \in M^{l \times h} \tag{5}$$

or $G_I = [I, I, I] \in M^{l \times h \times 3}$.

To transform an image into *HSV* (*Hue, Saturation, Value*) space, we have to normalize the image and receive $R, G, B \in [0, 1]$. Sort R, G, B by size and set them $\lambda_1, \lambda_2, \lambda_3$, if two are equal set R before G before B. Now calculate

$$V = \lambda_1, \quad S = \begin{cases} 0 & ; \lambda_1 = 0 \\ \frac{\lambda_1 - \lambda_3}{\lambda_1} & ; \lambda_1 \neq 0, \end{cases}$$

$$H = \begin{cases} 0 & ; \lambda_1 = \lambda_3 \\ c + \frac{6 \cdot (\lambda_2 - \lambda_3)}{\lambda_1 - \lambda_3} & ; \lambda_1 \neq \lambda_3, \end{cases} \text{where } c = \begin{cases} 0 & ; \lambda_1 = R \\ \frac{1}{3} & ; \lambda_1 = G \\ \frac{2}{3} & ; \lambda_1 = B. \end{cases} \tag{6}$$

Carrying out equivalent transformations we can show that $H \in [0, 1), V, S \in [0, 1]$. A similar color space is *HSI*, using I instead of V. The described transformations from *RGB* to *HSV* or *HSI* are no continuous functions. To define a *grayscale* image in *HSV* mode, it is not appropriate to consider just the *Value* channel $V' = [0, 0, V]$. Kanan et al. [12] showed that *Value* performs worst of all grayscale models. Instead of this, we take G_L and considering (6) and

$$R = G = B \iff \lambda_1 = \lambda_3 \tag{7}$$

it follows that $H = S = 0, V = L, L' = [0, 0, L]$. In Fig. 2 both models are compared. Another option is to regard *SV* mode, where *Hue* is set to zero. *Grayscale* images in *HSI* mode are defined as $I' = [0, 0, I]$.

To convert an *RGB* image with $R, G, B \in [0, 1]$ into a *YUV* image (Y is the *Luminance* and U, V two *Chrominance* components), we do the following transformation, see [18]. Using (4), set

$$\begin{pmatrix} Y \\ U \\ V \end{pmatrix} = \begin{pmatrix} L \\ (B - Y) \cdot 0.493 \\ (R - Y) \cdot 0.877 \end{pmatrix}. \tag{8}$$

Grayscale images in *YUV* mode are characterized by $L' = [0, 0, L]$.

To convert an *RGB* image with $R, G, B \in [0, 1]$ into a *YIQ* image (Y is the *Luminance* and I, Q two *Chrominance* components, notice that I is redefined now) we do the following, see [10]. With (4) set

$$\begin{pmatrix} Y \\ I \\ Q \end{pmatrix} = \begin{pmatrix} L \\ 0.596R - 0.274G - 0.322B \\ 0.211R - 0.523G + 0.312B \end{pmatrix}. \tag{9}$$

The coefficients in each entry add up to zero. *Grayscale* images in *YIQ* mode are characterized by $L' = [0, 0, L]$.

The different value ranges from U, V, I, Q do not matter as we use the augmentation technique *standardization* before the images are fed into our model.

Fig. 3. PersonFinder dataset showing example images with persons (defaced) and background.

Fig. 4. Exapmples of the four categories [desert, forest, snow, urban] in FlickrScene.

3 Experiments

In the following sections we describe our experiments and explain the results.

3.1 Data

For our experiments, we consider four image datasets employed in classification tasks. The first is our own created PersonFinder dataset. It contains 15,083 color train and 793 test images with a size of $128 \times 64 \times 3$ pixels, labeled with [person, background], see Fig. 3. Second we use the custom-made FlickrScene dataset, that contains 10,000 color landscape images of size $128 \times 128 \times 3$ and four labeled categories [desert, forest, snow, urban], from which 30% were taken as test images, examples see in Fig. 4. Other datasets we worked with are the existing public datasets CIFAR-10 and CIFAR-100 [14]. Each contains 60,000 color images of 32×32 pixels, split into 50,000 train examples and 10,000 test examples, which are labeled with one of ten or hundred classes, respectively. To fit all the input images in our architecture, we down-sample them all to the same size as in the CIFAR data.

3.2 Implementation Details

As model, we use an established Convolutional Neural Network, shown in Fig. 5. We choose this rather flat architecture because the PersonFinder and CIFAR data perform well with this model and it allows us to focus on our main interest:

color and texture information. The architecture has two convolutional layers (*conv 1, conv 2*) with maxpooling (*pool 1, pool 2*) and three fully connected layers (*fc 1, fc 2*, and *softmax*) and further state-of-the-art tools like standardization, data augmentation, normalization, and dropout, see [11]. We have accordingly modified it to enter images of any color modes and to visualize the kernels, activations, confidence values and misclassified categories.

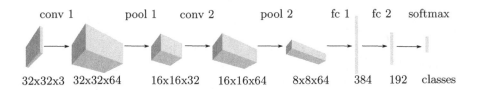

conv 1   pool 1   conv 2   pool 2   fc 1   fc 2   softmax

32x32x3 32x32x64   16x16x32   16x16x64   8x8x64   384   192   classes

Fig. 5. Graph of our Convolutional Neural Network.

3.3   Experimental Set-Up

We train our neural network with the mentioned datasets PersonFinder, CIFAR-10, CIFAR-100, and FlickrScene (all include RGB images), respectively. To compare the effects of partially lost shape information, we carry out the following experiments with three modes: normal, with noise, and blur on the images. Let $C = \{L, I, G_L, G_I, L', I', RGB, HSV, SV, HSI, YUV, YIQ\}$ be the set of representations. The value $acc(x, y), x, y \in C$ describes the test accuracy when training in x mode and testing in y mode. First, the algorithm calculates $acc(RGB, RGB)$. After that we modify the test images before evaluation and convert them into grayscale images. The results are $acc(RGB, G_L)$ and $acc(RGB, G_I)$. Now we do the training and testing with several suitable representations and evaluate $acc(x, y), x, y \in C$. Suitable means that x is the same as y or a similar color system with added or removed color information, see Fig. 6. After the evaluations we calculate the *error rates*

$$\mathrm{err}(x, y) = 1 - \frac{\mathrm{acc}(x, y)}{\mathrm{acc}(x, x)}, \tag{10}$$

$x, y \in C, x \neq y$. This relative value indicates the relative accuracy change only because of removed or added color information. A negative value indicates an improvement through the augmentation and in general is $acc(x, x) > acc(x, y) \iff err > 0$. The results of interest are given in Fig. 1.

Beside the error rates, we also accomplish a hard negative analysis to plot the classes that are mostly true negative or false positive only because of the added or removed color information in the test images, see Table 2. We call them to be *color-dependent*. Contrarily, the classes which are not recognized significantly different under color modification are called *color independent*. To investigate how color (in)dependence evolves through the architecture, we record the number of activation differences in the first fully connected layer in case of color or colorless images. We calculate the ratio of how many activations are added or lost proportionally on all output pixels and get act$(x,y), x,y \in \mathcal{C}, x \neq y$, see Table 3. Finally, we compare the different confidence values, obtained after we modified color or *Hue* information, respectively. The changing of confident values with/without color information are given as con$(x,y), x,y \in \mathcal{C}, x \neq y$, see Table 3.

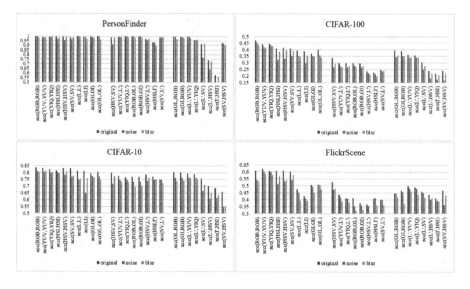

Fig. 6. Accuracies with training/test images of different color models, original, noise, and blur.

3.4   Results

Impact of Color Models on Accuracy. We first regard the experiments without noise or blurring, see Fig. 6. The reason for acc$(L', L') <$ acc$(SV, SV) <$ acc(HSV, HSV) in the last three datasets is obviously that SV color images contain more information than L' images and less than HSV. In PersonFinder, the values are similar. The fact that acc$(c,c) >$ acc(g,g) for $g \in \mathcal{G}' = \{G_L, G_I, I', L'\}, c \in \mathcal{C}' = \{RGB, HSV, HSI, SV, YUV, YIQ\}$, in each column except PersonFinder indicates that the additional information color is learned by the model to perform better than without. Depending on the used dataset, different color models perform best. In FlickrScene, it is YUV, in CIFAR-10 and CIFAR-100 it is RGB, but the results are similar in all color spaces, especially in CIFAR-10. In PersonFinder, it is *Luminance*. We have acc$(c,c) <$ acc(g,g) and the values are similar high. The model becomes color independent when applied to PersonFinder data. During training, it focuses on the special properties of the input: One the one hand, if $x \in \mathcal{G}', y \in \mathcal{C}'$ the performance differences are significantly lower because in this case the main learned properties are shape cues, edges, forms, brightness etc. and they are also useful to classify color images. On the other hand, if $x \in C', y \in G'$ the difference is higher, except Person-Finder, because the model now focuses on the colors, which is not helpful to classify grayscale test images.

Color Dependency in Different Data Sets. Furthermore we notice that the improvement of $\mathrm{acc}(c, c) > \mathrm{acc}(g, g)$ is more significant in FlickrScene and CIFAR-100 than in CIFAR-10 while $\mathrm{acc}(g, g) > \mathrm{acc}(g, c)$ is similarly low in CIFAR-10 and CIFAR-100 and higher in FlickrScene. The focus on colors during training seems to be more distinctive in FlickrScene and CIFAR-100 than CIFAR-10 and even not available in PersonFinder. To give an explanation, we compare the error rates, see Table 1. While training the neural network with color, CIFAR-10 pictures one gets the proportion $\mathrm{err}^{(c_{10})}_{(RGB, G_L)} = 0.081$. That means 8% of the before correctly classified images are now not recognized only because of the missing color information. One could say that in 8% of the images, their color provides the main information. In 92% the neural network seems to look mainly at shape cues like forms or edges and brightness. CIFAR-10 dataset differs between ten categories like vehicles, animals etc. This is what one would expect, considering humans are not reliant on colors statistically in these cases, in contrast on FlickrScene images, which seem to have much more color information. Here about 32% of the recognizable images contain necessary color information which the neural network has learned. The categories could be classified in the main colors sand for desert, white for snow, green and brown for forest and gray for urban. CIFAR-100 images rely on even more color information as this dataset has detailed subcategories, e.g. sunflowers and roses or apples and oranges. Related species of blossoms or fruits may be difficult to distinguish even for humans if only grayscale pictures are present. The error rates of PersonFinder images are very small because of the insensitivity of color modification.

Training in Grayscale. If one trains the neural network with only grayscale images but feeds in the colored ones for testing, the error rates of the first four lines are smaller, see the lower part of Table 1. Here, the algorithm learns forms, edges, and brightness and is not irritated by color test images predominantly. Maybe even test objects with extraordinary colors e.g. exotic animals like red frogs, special birds etc. in the application are recognized better. This could be explored further. In the undermost four lines when dealing with *HSV, SV,* and *HSI* model the values are out-of-band. A reason could be that some shapes change because of the discontinuity of the transformation from *RGB* to *HSV* or *HSI*, which could be also noticed in Fig. 1. In CIFAR-10 and CIFAR-100 datasets, *RGB* mode operates best while in FlickrScene *YUV, YIQ* is similar good. *HSV, SV, HSI* mode perform worse because of the above mentioned reason of lost texture. This is more crucial in CIFAR-100 images than in CIFAR-10 images or in FlickrScene images. Only in FlickrScene, $\mathrm{acc}(L, L) \approx \mathrm{acc}(G_L, G_L) \approx \mathrm{acc}(L', L') \approx \mathrm{acc}(I, I) \approx \mathrm{acc}(G_I, G_I) \approx \mathrm{acc}(I', I')$ holds. In the other datasets, the differences are higher and *Intensity* performs worse than *Luminance*. This does not confirm with the research of [12].

Table 1. Error rates heat map in %.

	PersonFinder			CIFAR-10			CIFAR-100			FlickrScene		
	original	noise	blur	original	noise	blur	origianl	noise	blur	original	noise	blur
err(HSV,SV)	0.8%	4.8%	0.5%	3.8%	8.4%	4.3%	17.5%	19.9%	24.9%	13.6%	10.8%	11.8%
err(YUV,L')	-0.3%	-0.3%	0.1%	6.6%	7.8%	10.1%	32.3%	34.3%	35.8%	29.8%	30.9%	33.6%
err(YIQ,L')	-0.3%	-0.4%	0.4%	7.3%	6.5%	9.2%	32.7%	37.6%	35.4%	32.0%	31.5%	34.1%
err(RGB,G_L)	0.3%	0.2%	0.4%	8.1%	9.9%	13.9%	36.7%	38.2%	37.8%	32.3%	34.5%	39.5%
err(RGB,G_l)	0.2%	0.3%	0.3%	8.1%	9.4%	12.9%	37.2%	41.1%	36.6%	38.3%	33.6%	38.2%
err(HSV,L')	2.7%	0.0%	1.9%	5.5%	5.7%	6.0%	42.7%	32.6%	47.1%	39.7%	33.0%	43.1%
err(HSI,I')	6.7%	3.8%	9.6%	5.4%	5.9%	5.5%	44.2%	33.1%	48.7%	32.7%	19.2%	36.3%
err(SV,L')	0.3%	-1.4%	-0.3%	9.8%	3.1%	7.2%	39.3%	33.3%	38.3%	33.1%	25.9%	37.0%
err(G_L,RGB)	0.4%	0.6%	0.0%	0.2%	1.4%	1.3%	1.3%	3.9%	-4.1%	12.4%	12.3%	11.8%
err(G_l,RGB)	0.2%	-0.3%	-0.5%	-1.1%	1.4%	3.0%	-5.4%	-0.3%	0.0%	7.5%	7.9%	17.4%
err(L',YUV)	0.4%	0.4%	0.6%	2.1%	-2.4%	-0.3%	7.4%	3.1%	0.3%	-4.6%	-6.7%	-17.0%
err(L',YIQ)	3.7%	3.8%	2.4%	2.7%	-2.1%	0.5%	8.7%	2.8%	0.6%	-2.7%	-6.7%	-10.4%
err(L',SV)	8.4%	23.1%	6.7%	6.8%	11.2%	6.5%	22.7%	28.5%	19.5%	3.4%	0.7%	-5.6%
err(L',HSV)	25.8%	35.8%	26.2%	13.5%	18.4%	13.6%	39.0%	48.1%	35.5%	7.8%	10.4%	-3.8%
err(I',HSI)	41.8%	49.2%	41.7%	15.4%	5.4%	16.2%	43.6%	41.1%	40.4%	3.5%	3.7%	0.3%
err(SV,HSV)	6.4%	5.1%	8.9%	20.6%	28.6%	28.7%	41.0%	51.9%	43.2%	22.4%	32.7%	25.3%

Degraded Images with Noise and Gaussian Blur. To understand the impact of color, it is also interesting to keep color information, but modifying the rest of the image. To do this, we add sensor noise or Gaussian blurring on our test images. As a secondary effect we receive a low-quality camera model. The accuracy is recorded in Fig. 6, the error rates are provided in Table 1. In all regarded datasets, the error rates of color model changes are similar, irrespective whether shapes are degraded or not. The colors of the heat map allow to see this. Most robust against color or texture modification is the color system *Luminance* during training. Wether one has test images in grayscale, *RGB, YUV,* or *YIQ,* they perform well.

Hard Negative Analysis. To investigate the impact of color, we regard the change of predictions when adding or removing color information of the test images in several color spaces. We count the different predicted classes caused by the modification. In Table 2, we print the normalized numbers and realize that there are several accumulations in some classes. Negative numbers indicate that the model has classified more images correctly in one category than before. Positive numbers mean a worsening.

First, we regard CIFAR-10. The category cat performs better in six of eight regarded modes of test images with less color information, the various colors of cats lead to confusions and mistakes. Contrariwise, the bad result in category deer in three of eight modes suggests that the color brown of the animal and the color green of the background was learned or needed respectively. Training with *HSV* or *HSI* system images reaches high misclassification rates in the category ship. Lost shapes and the missing background color blue is a possible explanation. Using FlickrScene, we get high values in category desert, thirteen of sixteen. This category seems to be sensitive on colors, presence of yellow, orange or sand might

Table 2. Proportion of wrongly classified test images when changing representation during testing in the different categories of CIFAR-10 [airplane, automobile, bird, cat, deer, dog, frog, horse, ship, truck] and FlickrScene [desert, forest, snow, urban]. **Highest** and lowest values highlighted. Results for CIFAR-100 and PersonFinder see text.

	CIFAR-10		FlickrScene	
mc(RGB,G$_L$)	[8, 6, 16, -3, **24**, 12, 13, 10, 11, 2]	cat, **deer**	[**84**, 22, -1, -4]	**desert**, urban
mc(RGB,G$_l$)	[7, 5, 16, -2, **26**, 10, 15, 9, 11, 2]	cat, **deer**	[**88**, 18, -1, -5]	**desert**, urban
mc(YUV,L')	[7, 5, 21, -4, **28**, 10, 15, 5, 6, 6]	cat, **deer**	[**50**, 43, -6, 14]	**desert**, snow
mc(YIQ,L')	[3, 8, **22**, -3, 21, 9, 19, 7, 8, 7]	cat, **bird**	[**83**, 19, 2, -3]	**desert**, urban
mc(HSV,L')	[13, 8, 15, 9, 9, 10, -1, 6, **23**, 7]	frog, **ship**	[**68**, 30, 5, -3]	**desert**, urban
mc(HSI,I')	[12, 9, 14, 4, 11, 6, 6, 4, **25**, 8]	horse, **ship**	[**80**, 27, -11, 3]	**desert**, snow
mc(HSV,SV)	[15, 12, 5, 11, 4, 8, -6, 3, **40**, 9]	frog, **ship**	[-8, -17, **106**, 19]	**snow**, desert
mc(SV,L')	[0, 2, 20, -13, 36, 6, **37**, 6, 4, 1]	cat, **frog**	[**99**, 34, -23, -10]	**desert**, snow
mc(G$_L$,RGB)	[14, 2, 14, -6, **22**, 13, 20, 8, 6, 7]	cat, **deer**	[28, **42**, 33, -3]	**forest**, urban
mc(G$_l$,RGB)	[**30**, 4, 28, -24, 22, 2, 20, -2, 17, 2]	cat, **plane**	[75, -39, **81**, -18]	**snow**, forest
mc(L',YUV)	[-10, 17, 37, **43**, -13, 10, 7, 0, -17, 27]	ship, **cat**	[**325**, -250, -25, 50]	**desert**, forest
mc(L',YIQ)	[**65**, -3, 38, -5, -25, -38, 10, 15, -8, 50]	dog, **plane**	[48, 13, 24, 15]	**desert**, forest
mc(L',HSV)	[7, 8, 7, 6, 11, 10, 13, 8, **18**, 11]	cat, **ship**	[**59**, 47, -17, 11]	**desert**, snow
mc(I',HSI)	[8, 10, 8, 5, 10, 9, 11, 7, **17**, 15]	cat, **ship**	[**50**, 49, -35, 36]	**desert**, snow
mc(SV,HSV)	[11, 14, 16, -3, **17**, 8, 13, 10, 13, 0]	cat, **deer**	[**207**, 78, -207, 22]	**desert**, snow
mc(L',SV)	[5, 9, 10, 6, 9, 7, 13, **16**, 13, 13]	plane, **horse**	[**75**, 59, -16, -18]	**desert**, urban

be recognized as desert. The category urban has low values because the colors of objects vary strongly. Hence the shapes and objects are more important. The impact of color is low here. Snow is classified robust against color augmentation because mainly the brightness seems to be important. We refrain from printing the CIFAR-100 results, however we evaluated them and counted the three highest and lowest numbers: Training with color and testing with grayscale images shows noticeable deterioration in the result of the classes beaver, plain, rabbit, and fox. Improvement was reached in maple, lobster, cockroach, streetcar, forest, and roses. When training with grayscale images and testing with colored ones, we obtain worse results in the categories beaver, rabbit and fox and better ones in forest, pine, sunflowers, maple, and roses. In comparison with the above results, these categories do not surprise us for they are wild animals (beaver, rabbit, fox) with similar properties as deer in CIFAR-10 and a plain landscape similar to desert in FlickrScene. Independent on color with high texture information are mainly trees and flowers. Lobster and cockroach have typical important shapes that the color is second-rate. Different streetcars may have all different colors, hence the algorithm was not learning colors and performs better with gray test images, similar to the urban category in FlickrScene. In PersonFinder, we get continuously mainly false negative results: about [1,**99**], [person, **background**] while changing the color mode from grayscale to *YIQ, SV* or *HSV*. Some persons are not detected only because of the missing or added color information, but background was mostly recognized reliable.

Table 3. Prorated differences of activations of the first fully connected layer (current left column) and confidence values (current right column) regarding without/with color information, PersonFinder, CIFAR-10, CIFAR-100, and FlickrScene. **Lowest** and highest values are highlighted.

activation/confident	PersonFinder		CIFAR-10		CIFAR-100		FlickrScene	
act, con(RGB, G_L)	0.079	0.078	0.031	0.202	0.100	0.468	0.056	0.091
act, con(G_L, RGB)	**0.024**	0.052	0.010	0.043	0.028	0.172	0.017	0.015
act, con(RGB, G_I)	0.095	0.109	0.033	0.253	0.091	0.462	0.067	0.108
act, con(G_I, RGB)	0.040	0.082	0.007	0.066	0.012	0.251	0.005	0.034
act, con(HSI, I')	0.275	0.124	0.028	0.351	0.140	0.559	0.119	0.012
act, con(I', HSI)	0.410	0.141	0.056	0.171	0.124	0.564	0.104	0.079
act, con(HSV, SV)	0.151	0.170	0.106	**0.727**	0.275	0.772	0.188	**0.387**
act, con(HSV, L')	0.219	0.237	0.026	0.377	0.140	**0.813**	0.105	0.102
act, con(L', HSV)	**0.312**	**0.451**	0.052	0.134	0.122	0.334	0.090	0.089
act, con(SV, HSV)	0.250	0.110	**0.292**	0.701	**0.366**	0.758	**0.208**	0.368
act, con(SV, L')	0.219	0.066	0.035	0.066	0.128	0.162	0.189	0.024
act, con(L', SV)	0.194	0.287	0.040	0.063	0.093	0.369	0.060	0.095
act, con(YUV, L')	0.109	0.095	0.029	0.268	0.079	0.577	0.046	0.213
act, con(L', YUV)	0.034	0.017	**0.008**	0.024	**0.018**	**0.061**	**0.006**	0.009
act, con(YIQ, L')	0.076	0.160	0.035	0.219	0.080	0.459	0.079	0.054
act, con(L', YIQ)	0.031	**0.008**	0.011	**0.013**	0.030	0.070	0.014	**0.006**

Color Dependency and Stability. In Table 3, we print first the differences of number of activations act after the first fully connected layer. The second values are the differences of the confident values con when removing or adding color information. Only the absolute differences are counted (activation or not) while the differently powerful activations remain unnoticed. The best results are small values and they are found if color information was added, more precisely, if training was executed in *Luminance* space and testing in *RGB*, *YUV*, or *YIQ* space. The worst results are found in the middle of the table, when dealing with *HSV* color images or removing color information.

In CIFAR, one notices that always act < con. Here, changing color information leads to a constant deterioration in the deep layers. In FlickrScene, this only applies to a few values and in PersonFinder, there is no regular connection to see. We have already seen that the person classifier is color independent, hence an activation difference after a rear layer because of missing or added color should not lead to a difference in the confidence value. Training in L' and testing in *HSV* or *SV* system constitutes an exception. The reason is the same as described above: deterioration of shapes in this modes.

To regard stability, we decrease *Hue* and/or *Saturation* in our input *HSV* color image in small steps. We notice only corresponding small worsening in the act and con values. All the regarded datasets seem to be stable in terms of moderate color changes.

4   Conclusions and Future Work

In this paper we investigated the impact of color depending on image quality, datasets and special classes. Our used method that makes it possible to apply test images of different color systems in the architecture is insightful. We found that, in general, color information plays an important role in image classification and its contribution becomes evident in more specialized datasets with a high number of classes or special subclasses (e. g. CIFAR-100 and FlickrScene). Furthermore, our results lead to the thesis that some categories like wild animals (deer, rabbit, fox, beaver), ship (CIFAR) or plain landscape or desert (CIFAR-100, FlickrScene) are high dependent on color information.

Regarding the application, it is more successful to train with *RGB* (CIFAR) or *YIQ* (FlickrScene) color images. Training with grayscale, especially with *Luminance* images is promising to be advantageous if the expected contribution of texture is significantly higher than that of color. This is the case in categories like trees, flowers, certain animals (cat, lobster, cockroach), persons, streetcars or urban images. An intelligent algorithm gains color independence then. This is also the case while detecting persons, because – as expected – different colors of clothes or background should not be relevant. On the opposite, *HSV* and *HSI* color spaces are interesting only if one suspects a high impact of color but a lower one of shapes. In our results, *HSV* is not suitable if texture is degraded, especially if noise is responsible for this. Regarding test images of any color space *Luminance* is the most robust color mode for training and moreover the most suitable grayscale mode, not *Intensity*, as [12] found. Anyway, the fact that one deals with smaller images and saves run-time is only a small advantage of grayscale representation. It would also be possible to perform a similar study considering state-of-the-art families of networks. Our work could be helpful if one handles with thermal infrared images [13], which include no color information, e. g. in video surveillance. It is obvious to train with grayscale images – if no suitable thermal infrared train sets are available. Our results can be applied to it.

References

1. Agrawal, S., Verma, N.K., Tamrakar, P., Sircar, P.: Content based color image classification using SVM. In: ITNG. IEEE (2011)
2. Audebert, N., Le Saux, B., Lefèvre, S.: Semantic segmentation of earth observation data using multimodal and multi-scale deep networks. In: Lai, S.-H., Lepetit, V., Nishino, K., Sato, Y. (eds.) ACCV 2016. LNCS, vol. 10111, pp. 180–196. Springer, Cham (2017). https://doi.org/10.1007/978-3-319-54181-5_12
3. Barron, J.T.: Convolutional color constancy. In: ICCV. IEEE (2015)
4. Bianco, S., Cusano, C., Schettini, R.: Color constancy using CNNs. In: CVPR Workshop. IEEE (2015)
5. Cheng, D., Prasad, D.K., Brown, M.S.: Illuminant estimation for color constancy: why spatial-domain methods work and the role of the color distribution. JOSA A **31**, 1049–1058 (2014)

6. da Costa, G.B.P., Contato, W.A., Nazare, T.S., Neto, J.E., Ponti, M.: An empirical study on the effects of different types of noise in image classification tasks. arXiv preprint arXiv:1609.02781 (2016)
7. Galdran, A., et al.: Data-Driven Color Augmentation Techniques for Deep Skin Image Analysis. arXiv preprint arXiv:1703.03702 (2017)
8. Galiyawala, H., Shah, K., Gajjar, V., Raval, M.S.: Person Retrieval in Surveillance Video using Height, Color and Gender. arXiv preprint arXiv:1810.05080 (2018)
9. Goodfellow, I., Bengio, Y., Courville, A.: Deep Learning. MIT Press, Cambridge (2016). http://www.deeplearningbook.org
10. Henning, P.: Taschenbuch Multimedia, 4th edn. Hanser, Auflage (2007)
11. Hinton, G.E., Srivastava, N., Krizhevsky, A., Sutskever, I., Salakhutdinov, R.R.: Improving neural networks by preventing co-adaptation of feature detectors. arXiv preprint arXiv:1207.0580 (2012)
12. Kanan, C., Cottrell, G.W.: Color-to-grayscale: does the method matter in image recognition? PloS One **7**, e29740 (2012)
13. Kieritz, H., Hübner, W., Arens, M.: Learning transmodal person detectors from single spectral training sets. In: Security and Defence Conference SPIE (2013)
14. Krizhevsky, A.: Learning multiple layers of features from tiny images. Technical report, University of Toronto (2009). https://www.cs.toronto.edu/~kriz/cifar.html
15. LeCun, Y., Bottou, L., Bengio, Y., Haffner, P., et al.: Gradient-based learning applied to document recognition. Proc. IEEE **86**, 2278–2324 (1998)
16. Li, X., Zhang, G., Fang, J., Wu, J., Cui, Z.: Vehicle color recognition using vector matching of template. IEEE (2010)
17. Oliveira, V., Conci, A.: Skin Detection using HSV color space. Citeseer (2009)
18. Poynton, C.: Digital Video and HDTV Algorithms and Interfaces. Morgan Kaufmann Publishers, Burlington (2003)
19. Gonzales, R.C., Richard, E.W.: Digital Image Processing, 2nd edn. Prentice-Hall, Inc., Upper Saddle River (2002)
20. Ruela, M., Barata, C., Mendonça, T., Marques, J.S.: What is the role of color in dermoscopy analysis? In: Sanches, J.M., Micó, L., Cardoso, J.S. (eds.) IbPRIA 2013. LNCS, vol. 7887, pp. 819–826. Springer, Heidelberg (2013). https://doi.org/10.1007/978-3-642-38628-2_97
21. Shinya, A., Mori, K., Harada, T., Thawonmas, R.: Potential improvement of CNN-based colorization for non-natural images. IEEE, IWAIT (2018)
22. Simonyan, K., Zisserman, A.: Very deep convolutional networks for large-scale image recognition. arXiv preprint arXiv:1409.1556 (2014)
23. Yip, A.W., Sinha, P.: Contribution of color to face recognition. Perception **31**, 995–1003 (2002). https://doi.org/10.1068/p3376
24. Zeiler, M.D., Fergus, R.: Visualizing and understanding convolutional networks. In: Fleet, D., Pajdla, T., Schiele, B., Tuytelaars, T. (eds.) ECCV 2014. LNCS, vol. 8689, pp. 818–833. Springer, Cham (2014). https://doi.org/10.1007/978-3-319-10590-1_53
25. Zeiler, M.D., Taylor, G.W., Fergus, R.: Adaptive deconvolutional networks for mid and high level feature learning. IEEE (2011)

Diatom Classification Including Morphological Adaptations Using CNNs

Carlos Sánchez[1]([✉]), Noelia Vállez[2], Gloria Bueno[2], and Gabriel Cristóbal[1]

[1] Instituto de Óptica CSIC, Serrano 121, 28006 Madrid, Spain
carlos.sanchez@io.cfmac.csic.es
[2] VISILAB Universidad Castilla La Mancha,
Av. Camilo José Cela, 13071 Ciudad Real, Spain
noelia.vallez@uclm.es
http://visilab.etsii.uclm.es

Abstract. Diatoms are a major group of aquatic microalgae. They are widely used in different fields such as environmental studies to estimate water quality. This paper presents the use of convolutional neural networks (CNNs) to identify diatoms during their life cycle. This life cycle involves morphological and other changes to the diatom frustule adding intraclass variance and making harder the classification task. The performance of CNNs is compared against a classical image classification scheme (i.e., feature extraction and classification) using a 14 classes dataset with a total number of 1085 images ranging from 40 to 120 images per class. Classification accuracy was 99.07% and 99.7% for CNNs and classical methods respectively.

Keywords: Classification · Deep learning · Diatom · Life cycle

1 Introduction

Diatoms are a group of unicellular algae that are present in a great variety of aquatic environments. It is estimated that the total number of species is more than 200,000 (although the number of species already described is about 10,000). Since diatoms can adapt themselves to the environment, they can be used as a natural water quality indicator in environmental studies [5].

Diatoms are formed by two thecae that fit together to create a capsule known as a frustule. The frustule is formed by silica and depending on its shape diatoms can be centric (rounded frustule) or pennate (elongated frustule). The reproduction of the diatoms is asexual and sexual. In the asexual stage, the frustule is separated in the two valves. Then the other half of the cell grows originating two different diatoms, one bigger than the other. These differences in size are what is called life cycle. After several generations, the size of the valve can not decrease more triggering sexual reproduction. At this point, the cell form auxospores that will form new full-size algae. This is called sexual reproduction.

© Springer Nature Switzerland AG 2019
A. Morales et al. (Eds.): IbPRIA 2019, LNCS 11867, pp. 317–328, 2019.
https://doi.org/10.1007/978-3-030-31332-6_28

Traditionally, the task of identifying diatoms in samples from different aquatic environments was made by biologists. They usually looked for different morphometric features (length, width, shape) and frustule ornamentation such as the striae density. The identification is made comparing against previously described specimens [2]. Doing this task manually involves different challenges due to inter-species similarities and intra-species dissimilarities, originated from the various stages of the life cycle.

Different attempts to automate this process has been made [3,4,22]. This task is challenging due to different factors such as to the vast number of diatom species, similarities between them and the life cycle related changes in shape and texture. Some researchers [21] used shape descriptors based on Legendre polynomials and principal component analysis (PCA) in the identification of the *Cymbella cistula* species. Others [20] applied PCA to the Fourier descriptors extracted from the contour of the *Tabellaria* group. There are also recent studies on the application of different classification methodologies and the consideration of different image features such as textures, geometry, morphology and their combination [3]. Convolutional neural networks (CNNs) have also been applied with success for a high number of taxa [22]. However, the main source of errors come from the misclassification of algae due to their life cycle.

In this paper, we present an extension of the work presented in [24]. Two different contributions are added to the previous work. The main novelty of this work resides on the one hand that the number of classes has been increased from 8 to 14 and secondly a different approach has been considered using CNNs to classify the diatoms. CNNs have been applied recently to the taxonomic identification of diatoms with a 99.51% of accuracy in 80 species. However, the dataset used by these authors contains an average of 100 samples per taxa before applying any data augmentation technique. Due to the known need of relatively large training datasets for training some architectures such as AlexNet or GoogleNet from scratch, we propose to use transfer learning techniques as a fine-tuning strategy to the complete the model or by fixing the convolutional layers to use them as feature extractor to retrain the last part of the network [30]. In both cases, the networks are initialized with the weights of their corresponding architectures previously trained on ImageNet. In this work, ResNet18, AlexNet, VGG11, SqueezeNet1.0, DenseNet121, and InceptionV3 have been compared. Finally, a comparison between the results obtained with a traditional image identification workflow (i.e., image preprocessing, segmentation, feature extraction, dimensionality reduction, and classification) and CNNs is presented.

2   Materials and Methods

2.1   Database

The database used in this work is formed by 1085 diatom images of 14 different classes distributed as in Table 1.

Table 1. Number of images per taxa.

#	Taxa	#valves
1	*Gomphonema minutum*[a]	74
2	*Luticola goeppertiana*[a]	117
3	*Nitzschia amphibia*[a]	59
4	*Nitzschia capitellata*[a]	95
5	*Eunotia tenella*[b]	68
6	*Fragilariforma bicapitata*[b]	100
7	*Gomphonema augur var augur*[b]	98
8	*Stauroneis smithii grunow*[b]	92
9	*Sellaphora pupula*[c]	40
10	*Sellaphora obesa*[c]	72
11	*Sellaphora blackfordensis*[c]	57
12	*Sellaphora capitata*[c]	120
13	*Sellaphora auldreekie*[c]	40
14	*Sellaphora lanceolata*[c]	53

[a] Available in [1]
[b] Available in [18]
[c] Available in [19]

2.2 Traditional Image Classification

The first step to carry out is image segmentation and contour extraction. Then three different sets of features are extracted to describe the segmented image and the contour. After that, all the features undergo a dimensionality reduction process. Finally, a classifier is used with this reduced set of features. The method is more extensively described in [24].

A. Segmentation and Contour Extraction. Semi-automatic global thresholding based on the Otsu method and morphological operations was used. In this process, few images were manually discarded due to inhomogeneous illumination and noise.

B. Feature Extraction. Three different descriptors have been used to describe the images. Elliptical Fourier descriptors (EFD) model the diatom contour while Gabor filters and phase congruency (PC) descriptors characterize the diatom ornamentation.

– Elliptical Fourier descriptors. The method to calculate EFD is described in [16]. It starts with a contour image and calculates the Freeman chain code. Then the x, y projections of the chain code are calculated. Finally, the Fourier coefficients are obtained from these projections. It was empirically determined that the first 30 coefficients are sufficient to represent the contour.

– Phase congruency descriptors. The phase congruency is based on the fact that all Fourier components are in phase in areas where signals occur, i.e., corners, edges, and textures of the images. PC descriptors are calculated as in [28]. Starting from the phase congruency maximum (M) and minimum (m) momentum images(described in [14]), the mean and standard deviation were calculated for both images. Those images combine the phase congruency information of each orientation. A total of 4 phase congruency descriptors are obtained.

– Gabor filters descriptors. Gabor based descriptors are calculated by the same method as in [3] and initially described in [6]. First, the log-Gabor filters are calculated as shifted Gaussians for different orientations and scales. These filters are applied to the images and then the first and second order statistics are obtained for every sub-band.

C. Dimensionality Reduction. After the feature extraction, a total of 223 features were obtained. Therefore a dimensionality reduction is needed. For such purpose, Linear Discriminant Analysis (LDA) [7] was selected as it was proven that enhances classification results over other techniques such as PCA. LDA projects the feature space into a new smaller subspace that maximizes the separation between classes. With this supervised method, the original 223 dimensions space is reduced to $N - 1$ dimensions, where N is the number of classes in the dataset ($N = 14$ in this work).

D. Classification. In machine learning, a classifier can be defined as a function that takes the values of different features of a sample and gives as an output the prediction of the class to which the sample belongs [23]. In [24], different supervised and non-supervised classifiers were tested. Among the tested algorithms, Hierarchical Agglomerative Clustering [25] was chosen as it achieved the best results with the proposed dataset. Hierarchical clustering is a machine learning algorithm to cluster unlabeled data points. It produces a set of nested clusters organized as a hierarchical tree that can be visualized using a dendogram. They may correspond to meaningful taxonomies e.g. diatom taxa. The initial phase of this algorithm states that every single observation is a different cluster. Then a distance function between clusters is computed, and the closer clusters are merged. The algorithm finishes once the number of clusters is equal to the previously defined number of clusters.

2.3 Deep Learning

The number of images contained in this dataset is reasonable for applying traditional machine learning methods but is far from the amount required by deep learning techniques as explained in [22]. This number can be decreased to 100 samples per class by using transfer learning techniques [8]. However, most of the classes have fewer samples than that, and the number should be later reduced by partitioning the dataset into training, validation and test datasets. To deal with this problem, we added a data augmentation step that performs:

1. Horizontal flip
2. Vertical flip
3. Random rotation between 0° and 90°

The combination of these three transformations is randomly applied each time a batch is requested during the training. After this process, images are resized to the network input size, i.e., 224 × 224 pixels. Figure 1 shows some examples of this process.

Fig. 1. Data augmentation examples. Note that after the size normalization the aspect ratio of the original images is not preserved. This fact will have a negative effect in the learning process reducing the final classification accuracy.

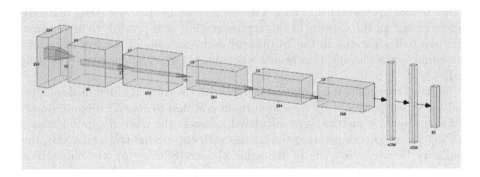

Fig. 2. Scheme of the Alexnet network tested. Source: http://alexlenail.me/NN-SVG/AlexNet.html

Since image classification is a common task, several classification network architectures have been proposed in the literature. In this case, we have tested ResNet18 [9], AlexNet [15] (see Fig. 2), VGG11 [26], SqueezeNet1.0 [12], DenseNet121 [10], and InceptionV3 [27]. To deal with convergence problems due to the low number of samples per class, two transfer learning techniques have been applied. One of them is *fine-tuning*, in which a pre-trained model in used to initialize the network and then all the weights are adjusted during training. The other one consists in using the convolutional layers as a *feature extractor* and then training only the last part of the architecture. In all cases, the model weights were initialized with the ones from their corresponding pre-trained models on ImageNet since it has demonstrated to be successful on a wide range of transfer tasks [11]. Therefore, ImageNet is only used to learn good general-purpose features as a starting point for our diatom classification task.

The dataset was split into 3 different parts to train and evaluate the models. The 80% of the images were used for training whereas the other 20% was divided into validation: 10%, and test: 10%. This was repeated 10 times following a 10 fold cross validation scheme. Data augmentation was applied after this division. Analogously to the pretrained models, the subtracted mean m and standard deviation σ used to normalize the inputs were $(m = 0.485, \sigma = 0.229)$, $(m = 0.456, \sigma = 0.224)$, $(m = 0.406, \sigma = 0.225)$ for training, validation and testing respectively.

3   Results

Two different tests were done with the dataset. In the first experiment, the images were analyzed with a traditional image classification scheme obtaining a classification accuracy of 99.7%. In the second experiment, different CNNs were tested, being *Densenet* with 99.07% accuracy the best result achieved.

Figure 3 is a representation of the clusters using t-Distributed Stochastic Neighbor Embedding (t-SNE) [17] algorithm to reduce the dimension of the feature vector. In such figure, it can be observed that the separation of the clusters allows to identify each cluster with a different class. Despite not being perfectly differentiated all the clusters in this representation, it is possible to assure that they are well separated in the 14 dimensions hyperplane of the features space according to the classification results where only 3 observations were misclassified.

Figure 4 represents the confusion matrix with the correctly identified samples and the errors produced by the classifier. In addition to classification accuracy, different objective metrics were calculated to assess the clustering performance [13,29]. These metrics measure similarities with the ground truth (RAND), the similarity between elements of the same cluster (Silhouette), the similarities between the class assignment and the ground truth classes (Adjusted Mutual Information), if a cluster contains only members of the same class (Homogeneity) and if all the members of the same class are assigned to the same cluster (Completeness) Table 2 shows the values for the metrics. The values close to 1 indicates that the clusters are separated and well defined.

Tables 3 and 4 show the accuracies of the CNN models on the test set. All architectures obtained better results with the use of fine-tuning rather than

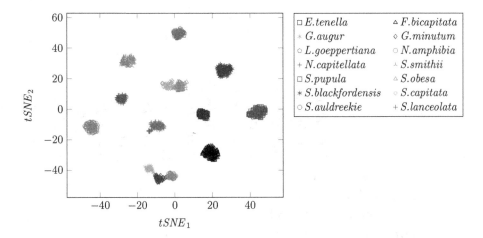

Fig. 3. Representation of the data using t-SNE algorithm for visualization. The data after the dimensionality reduction using LDA produces well separated clusters.

Table 2. Clustering metrics.

Metric	RAND	Silhouette	Adjusted mutual information	Homogeneity	Completeness
Value	0.9959	0.5173	0.9947	0.9951	0.9948

using them as a feature extractor, being the average accuracy difference between both techniques of around 11%. DenseNet, ResNet and VGG are the model architectures that provide the highest accuracy. From them, DenseNet shows the best results by achieving 99.07% of the samples correctly classified and having only one image misclassified. With the use of the convolutional layers as a feature extractor, SqueezeNet provides the best results with an accuracy of 93.52%. The differences between the two transfer learning techniques may be caused by the dissimilarity between diatoms and the classes in the ImageNet dataset. Based on that, it reasonable to have better results when the weights of the feature extractor are adjusted to the new dataset.

Regardless of the model used, the average per class accuracies show that the most challenging classes for both techniques are: *Nitzschia amphibia*, *Sellaphora blackfordensis*, and *Sellaphora pupula*. *Nitzschia amphibia* is often classified as *Gomphonema minutum*. Misclassification between them may be caused by the similarities of their lateral views as shown in Fig. 5(a)–(b). On the other hand, *Sellaphora blackfordensis* and *Sellaphora pupula* are often misclassified as *Sellaphora capitata* and *Sellaphora auldreekie*. The confusion between those classes is most likely to be caused by their high general similarity (Fig. 5(c)–(f)).

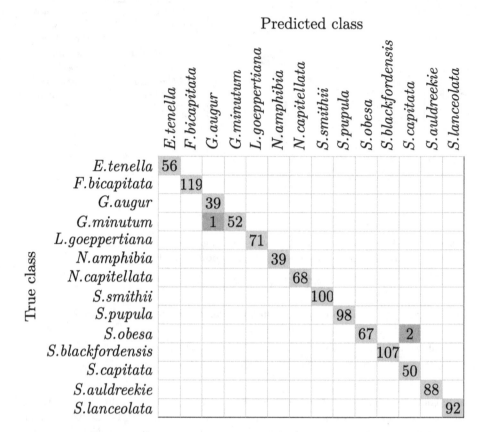

Fig. 4. Confusion matrix of the classification results obtained using hierarchical agglomerative clustering. Elements in the main diagonal represent the correct identifications while the other elements are the errors.

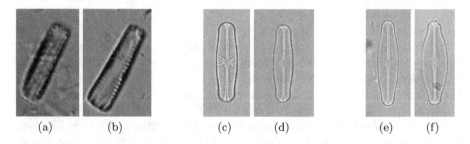

Fig. 5. Common misclassifications of the CNN models. *Nitzschia amphibia* (a) is sometimes classified as *Gomphonema minutum* (b), *Sellaphora blackfordensis* (c) as *Sellaphora capitata* (d), and *Sellaphora pupula* (e) as *Sellaphora auldreekie* (f).

Table 3. Fine tuning results

	AlexNet	DenseNet	Inception	RestNet	SqueezeNet	VGG
Eunotia tenella	100%	100%	100%	100%	100%	100%
Fragilariforma bicapitata	90%	100%	100%	100%	100%	100%
Gomphonema augur	100%	100%	100%	100%	100%	100%
Stauroneis smithii	100%	100%	100%	100%	100%	100%
Gomphonema minutum	100%	100%	100%	100%	100%	100%
Luticola goeppertiana	91.67%	100%	100%	100%	91.67%	100%
Nitzschia capitellata	100%	100%	100%	100%	100%	100%
Nitzschia amphibia	83.33%	83.33%	83.33%	83.33%	83.33%	83.33%
Sellaphora pupula	50%	100%	100%	100%	75%	100%
Sellaphora obesa	100%	100%	100%	100%	100%	100%
Sellaphora blackfordensis	83.33%	100%	83.33%	83.33%	83.33%	83.33%
Sellaphora capitata	100%	100%	100%	100%	75%	100%
Sellaphora auldreekie	100%	100%	100%	100%	100%	100%
Sellaphora lanceolata	100%	100%	100%	100%	80%	100%
TOTAL	94.44%	**99.07%**	98.15%	98.15%	92.59%	98.15%

Table 4. CNN as a feature extractor results

	AlexNet	DenseNet	Inception	RestNet	SqueezeNet	VGG
Eunotia tenella	85.71%	100%	71.43%	42.86%	100%	100%
Fragilariforma bicapitata	100%	100%	90.00%	100%	100%	100%
Gomphonema augur	100%	100%	100%	100%	100%	100%
Stauroneis smithii	100%	100%	100%	100%	100%	100%
Gomphonema minutum	85.71%	100%	100%	100%	100%	85.71%
Luticola goeppertiana	100%	100%	66.67%	91.67%	100%	100%
Nitzschia capitellata	100%	100%	100%	100%	100%	88.89%
Nitzschia amphibia	66.67%	50%	33.33%	100%	66.67%	50%
Sellaphora pupula	0.00%	100%	0.00%	25.00%	75%	50%
Sellaphora obesa	57.14%	71.43%	14.29%	100%	71.43%	100%
Sellaphora blackfordensis	33.33%	83.33%	16.67%	100%	66.67%	83.33%
Sellaphora capitata	91.67%	91.67%	41.67%	75%	100%	91.67%
Sellaphora auldreekie	100%	50%	50%	100%	100%	100%
Sellaphora lanceolata	80%	100%	60%	80%	100%	60%
TOTAL	84.26%	91.67%	65.74%	88.89%	**93.52%**	89.81%

4 Discussion

This work pursued two main purposes as a sequel of the previously presented [24]. On the one hand, use a larger dataset with more different classes for testing the method described for diatoms life cycle classification. Elsewhere, test deep learning CNNs with the same dataset to compare with the results obtained with traditional classification algorithms.

With the new dataset (14 classes), a 99.7% accuracy was obtained with classical methods, whereas a similar result than the 98% obtained with a smaller dataset (8 classes) in [24].

Despite the good results obtained for 14 classes, the dataset can be still considered small. The absence of loss of precision when some additional classes were included in the experiment needs to be corroborated in the case of considering a significantly large number of classes (e.g., 50–100) together with a sufficiently high number of samples per class. This would be a more realistic situation where a higher number of diatoms coexist in the same ecosystem.

Convolutional Neural Networks classified correctly the 99.07% of the samples in the best scenario and 65.74% in the worst case. Concerning per class accuracies, it has been shown that three classes (*Nitzschia amphibia*, *Sellaphora pupula* and *Sellaphora blackfordensis*) are the most difficult to classify independently of the learning technique. The best results were obtained using a fine-tuning strategy and thus, adjusting all the weights whereas the worst results were obtained using the first layers of the pre-trained models as fixed feature extractors. This may be caused due to the differences between the different application domains. While models trained on ImageNet learn how to classify instances from categories such as animals or objects, diatoms are very different from those. Therefore, using such models as a feature extractor do not allow to extract the needed features for diatom classification. On the contrary, models trained on ImageNet can generalize with good results to other classification problems with some adjustments.

5   Conclusions

Increasing the number of classes present in the dataset and, consequently, the number of images has not decreased the accuracy of the method based on image descriptors and a traditional classifier. It remains close to 99%. Moreover, the results obtained using Deep Learning reach also high classification rates. Although the dataset is small to train a CNN to classify diatom according to the taxa, a transfer learning procedure has been applied to obtain the 99.07% of samples correctly classified. From the two proposed techniques, fine tuning (adjusting all the network weights) achieves the best performance since diatoms differ from the objects of the categories commonly used to initialize the architectures.

Acknowledgements. The authors acknowledge financial support of the Spanish Government under the Aqualitas-retos project (Ref. CTM2014-51907-C2-R-MINECO) http://aqualitas-retos.es/en/.

References

1. Blanco, S.: Diatom life cycle images dataset (2018). https://doi.org/10.6084/m9.figshare.7077725
2. Blanco, S., Borrego-Ramos, M., Olenici, A.: Disentangling diatom species complexes: does morphometry suffice? PeerJ **5**, e4159 (2017). https://doi.org/10.7717/peerj.4159

3. Bueno, G., et al.: Automated diatom classification (Part A): handcrafted feature approaches. Appl. Sci. **7**(8), 753 (2017)
4. du Buf, H., Bayer, M.M.: Automatic Diatom Identification. Series in Machine Perception and Artificial Intelligence, vol. 51 (2002)
5. European Committee for Standardization: Water quality-guidance standard for the identification, enumeration and interpretation of benthic diatom samples from running waters. Technical report (2004)
6. Fischer, S., Šroubek, F., Perrinet, L., Redondo, R., Cristóbal, G.: Self-invertible 2D log-Gabor wavelets. Int. J. Comput. Vis. **75**(2), 231–246 (2007)
7. Fisher, R.A.: The use of multiple measurements in taxonomic problems. Ann. Eugenics **7**(2), 179–188 (1936)
8. Goodfellow, I., Bengio, Y., Courville, A.: Deep Learning. MIT Press (2016). http://www.deeplearningbook.org
9. He, K., Zhang, X., Ren, S., Sun, J.: Deep Residual Learning for Image Recognition (2015). http://arxiv.org/abs/1512.03385
10. Huang, G., Liu, Z., Weinberger, K.Q.: Densely connected convolutional networks (2016). http://arxiv.org/abs/1608.06993
11. Huh, M., Agrawal, P., Efros, A.A.: What makes ImageNet good for transfer learning? (2016). http://arxiv.org/abs/1608.08614
12. Iandola, F.N., Moskewicz, M.W., Ashraf, K., Han, S., Dally, W.J., Keutzer, K.: SqueezeNet: AlexNet-level accuracy with 50x fewer parameters and <0.5 MB model size (2016). http://arxiv.org/abs/1602.07360
13. Kassambara, A.: Practical Guide to Cluster Analysis in R: Unsupervised Machine Learning, vol. 1. STHDA (2017)
14. Kovesi, P.: Phase congruency detects corners and edges. In: The Australian Pattern Recognition Society Conference: DICTA, vol. 2003 (2003)
15. Krizhevsky, A., Sutskever, I., Hinton, G.E.: ImageNet classification with deep convolutional neural networks. In: Pereira, F., Burges, C.J.C., Bottou, L., Weinberger, K.Q. (eds.) Advances in Neural Information Processing Systems, vol. 25, pp. 1097–1105. Curran Associates, Inc. (2012). http://papers.nips.cc/paper/4824-imagenet-classification-with-deep-convolutional-neural-networks.pdf
16. Kuhl, F.P., Giardina, C.R.: Elliptic Fourier features of a closed contour. Comput. Graph. Image Process. **18**(3), 236–258 (1982)
17. Maaten, L.v.d., Hinton, G.: Visualizing data using t-SNE. J. Mach. Learn. Res. **9**(Nov), 2579–2605 (2008)
18. Mann, D., Bayer, M.: Diatom size reduction image sets for shape and appearance models (2018). http://rbg-web2.rbge.org.uk/DIADIST/
19. Mann, D.G., et al.: The Sellaphora pupula species complex (Bacillariophyceae): morphometric analysis, ultrastructure and mating data provide evidence for five new species. Phycologia **43**(4), 459–482 (2004)
20. Mou, D., Stoermer, E.F.: Separating Tabellaria (Bacillariophyceae) shape groups based on Fourier descriptors. J. Phycol. **28**(3), 386–395 (1992)
21. Pappas, J.L., Stoermer, E.F.: Legendre shape descriptors and shape group determination of specimens in the Cymbella cistula species complex. Phycologia **42**(1), 90–97 (2003)
22. Pedraza, A., Bueno, G., Deniz, O., Cristóbal, G., Blanco, S., Borrego-Ramos, M.: Automated diatom classification (Part B): a deep learning approach. Appl. Sci. **7**(5), 460 (2017)
23. Pereira, F., Mitchell, T., Botvinick, M.: Machine learning classifiers and fMRI: a tutorial overview. Neuroimage **45**(1), S199–S209 (2009)

24. Sánchez, C., Cristóbal, G., Bueno, G.: Diatom identification including life cycle stages through morphological and texture descriptors. PeerJ **7**, e6770 (2019). https://doi.org/10.7717/peerj.6770

25. Schütze, H., Manning, C.D., Raghavan, P.: Introduction to Information Retrieval, vol. 39. Cambridge University Press, Cambridge (2008)

26. Simonyan, K., Zisserman, A.: Very deep convolutional networks for large-scale image recognition. In: 3rd International Conference on Learning Representations, ICLR 2015, Conference Track Proceedings, San Diego, CA, USA, 7–9 May 2015 (2015). http://arxiv.org/abs/1409.1556

27. Szegedy, C., Vanhoucke, V., Ioffe, S., Shlens, J., Wojna, Z.: Rethinking the inception architecture for computer vision (2015). http://arxiv.org/abs/1512.00567

28. Verikas, A., Gelzinis, A., Bacauskiene, M., Olenina, I., Olenin, S., Vaiciukynas, E.: Phase congruency-based detection of circular objects applied to analysis of phytoplankton images. Pattern Recogn. **45**(4), 1659–1670 (2012)

29. Vinh, N.X., Epps, J., Bailey, J.: Information theoretic measures for clusterings comparison: variants, properties, normalization and correction for chance. J. Mach. Learn. Res. **11**(Oct), 2837–2854 (2010)

30. Weiss, K., Khoshgoftaar, T.M., Wang, D.: A survey of transfer learning. J. Big Data **3**(1), 9 (2016)

Deep Learning of Visual and Textual Data for Region Detection Applied to Item Coding

Roberto Arroyo[(⊠)], Javier Tovar, Francisco J. Delgado, Emilio J. Almazán,
Diego G. Serrador, and Antonio Hurtado

Nielsen Connect AI, Calle Salvador de Madariaga, 1, 28027 Madrid, Spain
roberto.arroyo@nielsen.com
https://www.nielsen.com/es/es.html

Abstract. In this work, we propose a deep learning approach that combines visual appearance and text information in a Convolutional Neural Network (CNN), with the aim of detecting regions of different textual categories. We define a novel visual representation of the semantic meaning of text that allows a seamless integration in a standard CNN architecture. This representation, referred to as text-map, is integrated with the actual image to provide a much richer input to the network. Text-maps are colored with different intensities depending on the relevance of the words recognized over the image. More specifically, these words are previously extracted using Optical Character Recognition (OCR) and they are colored according to the probability of belonging to a textual category of interest. In this sense, the presented solution is especially relevant in the context of item coding for supermarket products, where different types of textual categories must be identified (e.g., ingredients or nutritional facts). We evaluated our approach in the proprietary item coding dataset of Nielsen Brandbank, which is composed of more than 10,000 images for train and 2,000 images for test. The reported results demonstrate that our method focused on visual and textual data outperforms state-of-the-art algorithms only based on appearance, such as standard Faster R-CNN. These improvements are exhibited in precision and recall, which are enhanced in 42 and 33 points respectively.

Keywords: Deep learning · CNNs · OCR · Text-maps ·
Text regions detection · Item coding · Market studies

1 Introduction

The rise of artificial intelligence has revolutionized the automation of complex industrial processes. Nowadays, manual work has been complemented or even replaced by solutions based on artificial intelligence in varied environments. The automated processing of images is a field that has exponentially grown up in this sense due to the improvements in camera features and computer vision. Besides,

A. Morales et al. (Eds.): IbPRIA 2019, LNCS 11867, pp. 329–341, 2019.
https://doi.org/10.1007/978-3-030-31332-6_29

the popularization of deep learning has helped to enhance the effectiveness of these systems, that can obtain very detailed information from images [31].

In this regard, the detection of regions of interest over images has greatly improved since the success of deep learning methods based on Convolutional Neural Networks (CNNs) [12], such as Faster R-CNN [25]. However, these techniques rely on visual cues to discriminate regions and they are not expected to achieve high performance when the appearance of the regions is not discriminative. A typical example of this is the detection of regions with different categories of text, where the most distinguishing information resides in the semantic meaning of the text.

Within this context, automated item coding is a specific case in which appearance is not enough. Item coding refers to the process of transcribing the characteristics of an item into a database. The automation of this process is essential for increasing its efficiency, because manual item coding is a tedious and expensive task. For instance, a common application where automated item coding is very useful to save manual work is the extraction of data from supermarket products. As can be shown in Fig. 1, different types of textual information are commonly detected over the product packaging images, such as ingredients or nutritional facts. In this example, we can see how the textual information of the regions plays a differential role. Then, the fusion of textual representations

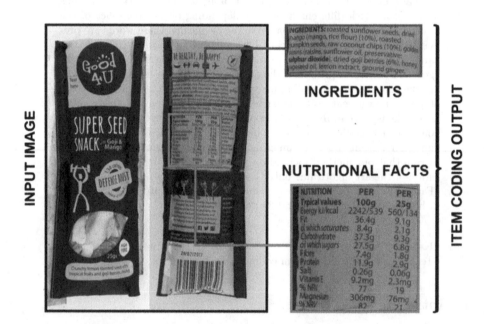

Fig. 1. A visual overview about item coding based on ingredients and nutritional facts. The diagram depicts a visual representation of a processed product packaging image jointly with the nutrition information to analyse.

with appearance-based techniques can be a promising alternative with respect to traditional computer vision approaches.

In this paper, we present a novel method for transforming textual information into an image-based representation named text-map. This concept allows a seamless integration in standard CNNs. In this sense, our approach does not modify the internal architecture because it only extends the inputs of the network, which is an advantage for adaptability to different problems, including our use case for item coding in market studies. The novelty of our solution with respect to standard state-of-the-art methods only based on visual appearance is discussed in Sect. 2. Besides, we describe in detail our CNN proposal jointly with the associated concept of text-maps in Sect. 3. After that, we present several experiments and results processed for validating our proposal in Sect. 4. Finally, we highlight the main conclusions derived from this work and some future research lines in Sect. 5.

2   Related Work

The state of the art in computer vision during the last decade can not be understood without considering the great influence of deep learning. In this regard, CNNs have helped to disseminate the application of deep learning in image processing, where seminal works considerably improved the performance of previous image classification approaches [12]. Moreover, CNNs have exhibited their successful performance in other traditional problems related to image processing, such as image retrieval [1], semantic segmentation [26] or object detection [27].

In the case of market studies, computer vision has recently demonstrated to be a useful tool for varied tasks focused on recognizing merchandise displayed in the shelves of a supermarket [22,23]. Besides, the use case of item coding for nutrition information has been also studied in works such as [19,32], where the authors define approaches for classifying images of different types of food and calculating their calories, instead of processing the text regions related to nutrition data over the product packages. In addition, there are some other works where packaging images are directly used [13,28], but they only consider standard nutritional facts tables and apply traditional computer vision techniques, which are not so accurate as a CNN-based solution.

The extraction of textual data from product packaging images usually requires effective text processing techniques [14,17,29]. The recognition of text based on Optical Character Recognition (OCR) is one of the most common methods for extracting words from images in a high variety of computer vision frameworks, such as the Google Cloud Vision API[1]. Apart from this, the detection of regions with text is another problem typically studied in the state of the art. In this sense, recent approaches have built upon techniques based on CNN solutions for differentiating text regions [18,21]. However, these solutions

---

[1] https://cloud.google.com/vision/docs/ocr.

only discern between regions with and without text, but they do not distinguish among different categories of text regions, as required in our use case for ingredients and nutritional facts regions in item coding.

Object detection based on visual appearance is also a related field where CNNs have provided a notable improvement with respect to traditional techniques, as demonstrated by methods such as Faster R-CNN [25], Yolo [24] or SSD [16]. Unfortunately, these CNN architectures are only based on appearance information, so they are not accurate for detecting regions with different types of texts, which is an essential requirement in problems such as item coding. In these cases, a CNN architecture that combines visual appearance and textual information for region detection can be an interesting solution.

In the literature of image recognition, it is common to see works that combine data from different sources, where each one provides complementary information to create a richer input data. For instance, some examples are focused on the combination of RGB with depth maps [2,5]. Besides, other approaches build upon the fusion of RGB with raw text data in varied use cases [3,21]. Our proposal for item coding is based on the fusion of RGB image information with visual representations of the semantic meaning of the processed text.

3   Our Method for Combining Appearance and Textual Information in a CNN

The key of our approach for region detection among different textual categories resides in the generation of text-maps. Then, it is essential to describe their main characteristics and how they are inputted into a CNN jointly with the RGB image information.

3.1   Generation of Text-Maps for Injecting Textual Information

We define a text-map as a visual representation of the original image where the zones that contain words are colored with different intensities depending on the relevance of the word. More specifically, the algorithm colors the text zone retrieved from a standard OCR engine according to the probability of the text to belong to a certain category of interest.

Within our item coding system, the categories of interest are ingredients and nutritional facts, as depicted in the examples presented in Fig. 2. For instance, a zone that contains the word *milk* will have a high probability of belonging to ingredients and will be brightly colored in its respective text-map. Similarly, the word *protein* will be brightly colored in the text-map corresponding to nutritional facts.

In the specific use case of our item coding approach, we use text-maps composed of 3 channels. Each channel encodes the relevance of each word based on different metrics, which are computed as follows:

- *Red channel:* A word detected by the OCR is brighter in this channel attending to a rate, which is defined as the number of occurrences of the word in the ground-truth regions divided into the total occurrences over the whole image. The computation of this channel is analogue for ingredients and nutritional facts.

– *Green channel:* It highlights punctuation signs such as commas or parentheses in the case of ingredients, because they are usually separated by these symbols. On the other hand, the case of nutritional facts in this channel is focused on numerical values of nutrients and related symbols (e.g., %).

– *Blue channel:* The rates for this channel are computed using predefined dictionaries about ingredients and nutritional facts. These dictionaries are previously generated using the ground-truth data, which contains a set of words typically appeared in products as ingredients or nutritional facts. With the aim of obtaining the rate for a specific word detected by the OCR, a Leven-

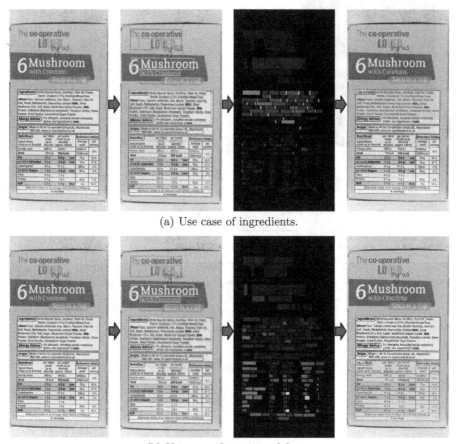

(a) Use case of ingredients.

(b) Use case of nutritional facts.

Fig. 2. Stages for obtaining the text-maps required for detecting the regions of interest. (1) Input images. (2) OCR extraction. (3) Text-maps extraction. (4) Output detection. (Color figure online)

shtein distance [15] is computed between the analyzed word and the words in the respective dictionary.

3.2 Design of the Proposed CNN Approach

After generating a text-map, it is injected into the applied CNN architecture jointly with the original RGB image to detect its specific text regions of interest. Typically, standard CNN architectures receive 3 RGB channels as input of the

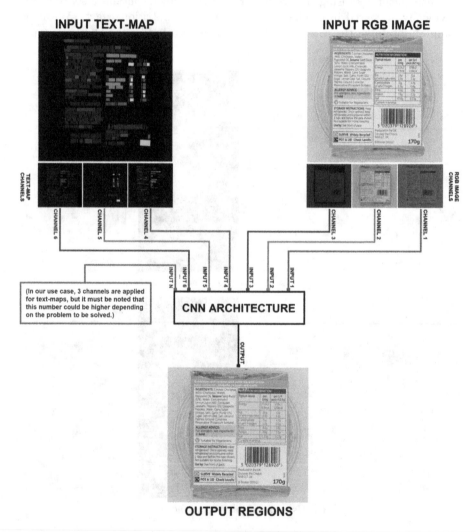

Fig. 3. Proposed CNN with RGB channels plus text-map channels. The presented example is focused on nutritional facts, but it is analog for ingredients. (Color figure online)

network. In this regard, the architecture proposed in our item coding system receives the 3 RGB channels plus 3 channels for the text-maps, so it applies 6 channels in total, as represented in Fig. 3 for the nutritional facts case (it is analog for ingredients).

The core of our CNN model can use any standard backbone network. In the case of our item coding approach, ResNet [10] exhibited a satisfactory performance as CNN backbone for the applied architecture. Obviously, the CNN model must be trained using previously labeled data for a proper performance. In this sense, the training of our models is started from pre-trained weights obtained from ImageNet [4], which is a robust dataset commonly applied in some of the most representative proposals in the state of the art [12]. Besides, several works have demonstrated the great transferability of CNN features from images belonging to different datasets and problems, as studied in [30]. This transferability is also expected for the learning of text-maps information, because mid-level image representations on large-scale datasets can be efficiently transferred to other visual recognition tasks, as evidenced in [20].

Additionally, it must be noted that after predicting the text regions of interest using the described CNN proposal, our system easily obtains the resultant ingredients and nutritional facts by post-processing the OCR previously computed for text-maps within these predicted regions. However, it is out of scope of this paper and we prefer to focus on the region detection among different text categories, which is our main contribution presented in the topic of language and vision fusion.

4   Experiments and Results

In this section, we present the main experiments carried out for evaluating our region detection method based on combined visual and textual information. The goal of these tests is to validate the improvements in performance provided by our CNN model for with respect to state-of-the-art approaches for region detection only based on visual appearance. In this case, the reported experiments are focused on the item coding system for supermarket products described along this paper.

4.1   Dataset for Item Coding

The acquisition of images and manually annotated data for evaluating our automated item coding system is a costly process. Due to this, there are not large datasets publicly available for these tasks. We found recent public datasets that are developed for the identification of merchandise in supermarkets, such as the D2S dataset [6]. Unfortunately, this dataset is not suitable for our item coding tests because of the long distance between camera and products, so ingredients and nutritional facts can not be visually distinguished and labeling for them is not available. Then, we have used our own labeled data from Nielsen Brandbank[2] to train and evaluate our automated item coding solution. This dataset is

---

[2] https://www.brandbank.com/.

composed of more than 10,000 annotated images for training and 2,000 images for validation and test.

4.2 Training and Hyperparameters

To train our CNN model, we set up an architecture based on Faster R-CNN with ResNet-101 as backbone using as input data the combination of image and text-map channels. The following main hyperparameters are applied during 10 epochs: learning rate $= 1 \cdot 10^{-5}$, weight decay $= 1 \cdot 10^{-6}$, dropout keep prob. $= 0.8$, batch size $= 1$, Adam optimizer [11] and Xavier initialization [8]. We compare our solution against a model trained with a standard Faster R-CNN only based on appearance. Analog hyperparameters are also used in this case to perform a fair comparison with respect to our approach.

4.3 Quantitative Results

Our experiments are mainly focused on precision and recall results for ingredients and nutritional facts detection. In Table 1, it can be seen how our CNN model based on text-maps clearly outperforms standard Faster R-CNN. Concretely, our approach increases precision and recall in 42 and 33 points respectively. Besides, we enhance in 38 points the total accuracy, which is calculated as the division of true positives between the sum of true positives, false positives and false negatives. According to these results, the improvements given by our solution are demonstrated for region detection among different textual categories.

Table 1. Standard Faster R-CNN vs our model with text-maps. A confidence of 0.7 is considered in these results, which is the value used in our final system.

	Faster R-CNN (3 channels)			Ours (6 channels)		
	Precision	Recall	Accuracy	Precision	Recall	Accuracy
Ingredients	0.25	0.31	0.15	**0.70**	**0.73**	**0.56**
Nutritional facts	0.34	0.57	0.27	**0.72**	**0.81**	**0.62**
Totals	0.29	0.44	0.21	**0.71**	**0.77**	**0.59**

It is important to point out that the results reported in Table 1 are calculated by considering a confidence threshold of 0.7 to discern between valid and invalid predictions. In our final item coding system, we also use this value to have an adequate precision with a minimum impact in recall. Then, the goal is to have a low number of false positive detections without increasing the amount of false negatives. Within this context, we used the precision and recall curves depicted in Fig. 4 to choose 0.7 as our preferred value for the confidence threshold. In these curves, the values for precision and recall are computed using different confidence thresholds between 0 and 1, with the aim of obtaining a proper perspective to

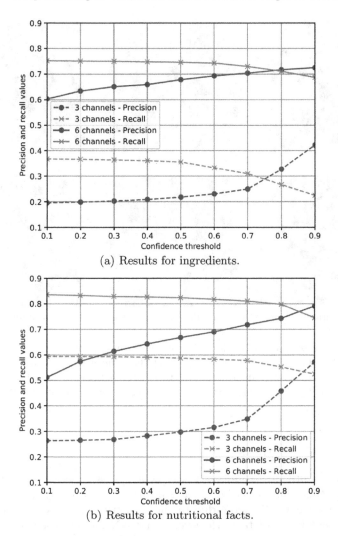

(a) Results for ingredients.

(b) Results for nutritional facts.

Fig. 4. Curves for precision and recall values over different confidence thresholds in the evaluations carried out for standard Faster R-CNN (3 channels) vs. our model with text-maps (6 channels). We present results about ingredients and nutritional facts.

fit the confidence threshold in the final system. As can be seen, these curves are represented for standard Faster R-CNN with respect to our CNN model based on text-maps. In this regard, the precision and recall curves for our approach are reaching higher values along the different confidence thresholds for both ingredients and nutritional facts cases.

(a) Detections using standard Faster R-CNN.

(b) Detections using our CNN model based on visual and textual information.

Fig. 5. A visual example of the detection of ingredients regions using a model trained with a standard Faster R-CNN vs our approach. False negatives are marked in fuchsia, false positives in blue and true positives in green. The confidences given by the networks are depicted in the upper-left corner of the detected bounding boxes. (Color figure online)

4.4 Qualitative Results

Apart from quantitative results, we also depict some qualitative visual results in Fig. 5. In this example, a lot of false positives are wrongly detected by the standard Faster R-CNN model due to the similarity of the visual appearance in the different types of text. However, our CNN model based on visual and textual information is able to correctly predict the ingredients region and false positives are not detected. These results evidence again the suitability of our CNN solution for item coding problems.

5   Conclusions and Future Works

The application of textual information as a mechanism to structure and reason about visual perception has been demonstrated along this paper, where we have described how to take advantage of visual representations derived from the semantic meaning of text.

From this point of view, our innovative CNN model enriched with text-maps has evidenced its effectiveness in detecting different categories of text, especially with respect to state-of-the-art solutions only based on visual appearance

(e. g., Faster R-CNN). We presented results associated with our specific use case for item coding in market studies, but the concept of text-maps is applicable to other problems focused on the detection of regions with different textual categories.

In further works, other text regions of interest for item coding are planned to be detected by our system, such as storage information or cooking instructions, among others. Moreover, the proposed technique for generating text-maps and the number of channels could be adapted to other text region detection challenges in future researches. Within this context, single shot scene text retrieval [9] or visual question answering [7] are some examples of active research topics that could be benefited from a model based on text-maps.

References

1. Arroyo, R., Alcantarilla, P.F., Bergasa, L.M., Romera, E.: Fusion and binarization of CNN features for robust topological localization across seasons. In: International Conference on Intelligent Robots and Systems (IROS), pp. 4656–4663 (2016)
2. Arroyo, R., Alcantarilla, P.F., Bergasa, L.M., Yebes, J.J., Bronte, S.: Fast and effective visual place recognition using binary codes and disparity information. In: International Conference on Intelligent Robots and Systems (IROS), pp. 3089–3094 (2014)
3. Bai, X., Yang, M., Lyu, P., Xu, Y., Luo, J.: Integrating scene text and visual appearance for fine-grained image classification. IEEE Access **6**, 66322–66335 (2018)
4. Deng, J., Dong, W., Socher, R., Li, L., Li, K., Li, F.: ImageNet: a large-scale hierarchical image database. In: Conference on Computer Vision and Pattern Recognition (CVPR), pp. 248–255 (2009)
5. Eitel, A., Springenberg, J.T., Spinello, L., Riedmiller, M.A., Burgard, W.: Multimodal deep learning for robust RGB-D object recognition. In: International Conference on Intelligent Robots and Systems (IROS), pp. 681–687 (2015)
6. Follmann, P., Bottger, T., Hartinger, P., Konig, R., Ulrich, M.: MVTec D2S: densely segmented supermarket dataset. In: European Conference on Computer Vision (ECCV), pp. 581–597 (2018)
7. Gao, P., et al.: Question-guided hybrid convolution for visual question answering. In: European Conference on Computer Vision (ECCV), pp. 485–501 (2018)
8. Glorot, X., Bengio, Y.: Understanding the difficulty of training deep feedforward neural networks. In: International Conference on Artificial Intelligence and Statistics (AISTATS), pp. 249–256 (2010)
9. Gomez, L., Mafla, A., Rusinol, M., Karatzas, D.: Single shot scene text retrieval. In: European Conference on Computer Vision (ECCV), pp. 728–744 (2018)
10. He, K., Zhang, X., Ren, S., Sun, J.: Deep residual learning for image recognition. In: Conference on Computer Vision and Pattern Recognition (CVPR), pp. 770–778 (2016)
11. Kingma, D.P., Ba, J.: Adam: a method for stochastic optimization. In: International Conference for Learning Representations (ICLR), pp. 1–15 (2015)
12. Krizhevsky, A., Sutskever, I., Hinton, G.E.: ImageNet classification with deep convolutional neural networks. In: International Conference on Neural Information Processing Systems (NIPS), pp. 1106–1114 (2012)

13. Kulyukin, V., Kutiyanawala, A., Zamal, T., Clyde, S.: Vision-based localization and text chunking of nutrition fact tables on android smartphones. In: International Conference on Image Processing, Computer Vision, and Pattern Recognition (IPCV), pp. 314–320 (2013)
14. Lee, C., Osindero, S.: Recursive recurrent nets with attention modeling for OCR in the wild. In: Conference on Computer Vision and Pattern Recognition (CVPR), pp. 2231–2239 (2016)
15. Levenshtein, V.: Binary codes capable of correcting deletions, insertions, and reversals. J. Sov. Phys. Dokl. **10**(8), 707–710 (1966)
16. Liu, W., et al.: SSD: single shot multibox detector. In: Leibe, B., Matas, J., Sebe, N., Welling, M. (eds.) ECCV 2016. LNCS, vol. 9905, pp. 21–37. Springer, Cham (2016). https://doi.org/10.1007/978-3-319-46448-0_2
17. Liu, Y., Wang, Z., Jin, H., Wassell, I.: Synthetically supervised feature learning for scene text recognition. In: European Conference on Computer Vision (ECCV), pp. 449–465 (2018)
18. Lyu, P., Liao, M., Yao, C., Wu, W., Bai, X.: Mask TextSpotter: an end-to-end trainable neural network for spotting text with arbitrary shapes. In: European Conference on Computer Vision (ECCV), pp. 71–97 (2018)
19. Meyers, A., et al.: Im2Calories: towards an automated mobile vision food diary. In: International Conference on Computer Vision (ICCV), pp. 1233–1241 (2015)
20. Oquab, M., Bottou, L., Laptev, I., Sivic, J.: Learning and transferring mid-level image representations using convolutional neural networks. In: Conference on Computer Vision and Pattern Recognition (CVPR), pp. 1717–1724 (2014)
21. Prasad, S., Kong, A.: Using object information for spotting text. In: European Conference on Computer Vision (ECCV), pp. 559–576 (2018)
22. Qiao, S., Shen, W., Qiu, W., Liu, C., Yuille, A.: ScaleNet: guiding object proposal generation in supermarkets and beyond. In: International Conference on Computer Vision (ICCV), pp. 1791–1800 (2017)
23. Ray, A., Kumar, N., Shaw, A., Mukherjee, D.P.: U-PC: unsupervised planogram compliance. In: European Conference on Computer Vision (ECCV), pp. 598–613 (2018)
24. Redmon, J., Divvala, S., Girshick, R., Farhadi, A.: You only look once: unified, real-time object detection. In: Conference on Computer Vision and Pattern Recognition (CVPR), pp. 779–788 (2016)
25. Ren, S., He, K., Girshick, R., Sun, J.: Faster R-CNN: towards real-time object detection with region proposal networks. In: International Conference on Neural Information Processing Systems (NIPS), pp. 91–99 (2015)
26. Saleh, F.S., Aliakbarian, M.S., Salzmann, M., Petersson, L., Alvarez, J.M.: Effective use of synthetic data for urban scene semantic segmentation. In: European Conference on Computer Vision (ECCV), pp. 86–103 (2018)
27. Sundermeyer, M., Marton, Z., Durner, M., Brucker, M., Triebel, R.: Implicit 3D orientation learning for 6D object detection from RGB images. In: European Conference on Computer Vision (ECCV), pp. 712–729 (2018)
28. Gundimeda, V., Murali, R.S., Joseph, R., Naresh Babu, N.T.: An automated computer vision system for extraction of retail food product metadata. In: Bapi, R.S., Rao, K.S., Prasad, M.V.N.K. (eds.) First International Conference on Artificial Intelligence and Cognitive Computing. AISC, vol. 815, pp. 199–216. Springer, Singapore (2019). https://doi.org/10.1007/978-981-13-1580-0_20
29. Wigington, C., Tensmeyer, C., Davis, B., Barrett, W., Price, B., Cohen, S.: Start, follow, read: end-to-end full-page handwriting recognition. In: European Conference on Computer Vision (ECCV), pp. 372–388 (2018)

30. Yosinski, J., Clune, J., Bengio, Y., Lipson, H.: How transferable are features in deep neural networks? In: International Conference on Neural Information Processing Systems (NIPS), pp. 3320–3328 (2014)

31. Zeiler, M.D., Fergus, R.: Visualizing and understanding convolutional networks. In: Fleet, D., Pajdla, T., Schiele, B., Tuytelaars, T. (eds.) ECCV 2014. LNCS, vol. 8689, pp. 818–833. Springer, Cham (2014). https://doi.org/10.1007/978-3-319-10590-1_53

32. Zhang, W., Yu, Q., Siddiquie, B., Divakaran, A., Sawhney, H.S.: Snap-n-Eat: food recognition and nutrition estimation on a smartphone. J. Diab. Sci. Technol. 9(3), 525–533 (2015)

Deep Learning Versus Classic Methods for Multi-taxon Diatom Segmentation

Jesús Ruiz-Santaquitaria[1], Anibal Pedraza[1], Carlos Sánchez[2],
José A. Libreros[3], Jesús Salido[1], Oscar Deniz[1], Saúl Blanco[4],
Gabriel Cristóbal[2], and Gloria Bueno[1(✉)]

[1] VISILAB, Universidad de Castilla-La Mancha, Ciudad Real, Spain
gloria.bueno@uclm.es
[2] Instituto de Óptica CSIC, Serrano 121, 28006 Madrid, Spain
gabriel@optica.csic.es
[3] Ing. Sistemas y Computación, Universidad del Valle, Cali, Colombia
[4] Institute of Environment, Universidad de Léon, Léon, Spain
http://visilab.etsii.uclm.es

Abstract. Diatom identification is a crucial process to estimate water quality, which is essential in biological studies. This process can be automated with machine learning algorithms. For this purpose, a dataset with 10 common taxa is collected, with annotations provided by an expert diatomist. In this work, a comparison of the classical state-of-the-art general purpose methods along with two different deep learning approaches is carried out. The classical methods are based on Viola-Jones and scale and curvature invariant ridge object detectors. The deep learning based methods are Semantic Segmentation and YOLO. This is the first time that Viola-Jones and Semantic Segmentation techniques are applied and compared for diatom segmentation in microscopic images containing several taxon shells. While all methods provide relatively good results in specific species, the deep learning approaches are consistently better in terms of sensitivity and specificity (up to 0.99 for some taxa) and up to 0.86 precision.

Keywords: Diatoms segmentation · Semantic Segmentation ·
Deep learning · YOLO ·
Scale and curvature invariant ridge object detectors · Viola-Jones

1 Introduction

Water quality in marine or freshwater areas such as rivers or lakes can be estimated through diatoms identification. Numerous studies support that biological indices based on these species help to state the ecological status of water in these environments. Nowadays, this procedure is carried out manually, which is a time-consuming and challenging task. Expert taxonomists observe the preparations of water samples through optical microscopes, to identify and quantify the diatoms

© Springer Nature Switzerland AG 2019
A. Morales et al. (Eds.): IbPRIA 2019, LNCS 11867, pp. 342–354, 2019.
https://doi.org/10.1007/978-3-030-31332-6_30

species. Thus, the implementation of automatic tools based on computer vision and machine learning techniques to perform this task is needed.

Some recent works have dealt with automatic diatom classification. These approaches try to predict the correct taxon name from image samples containing a single diatom. Some classifiers based on general handcrafted features are capable of obtaining around 98% accuracy [3], although novel techniques based on convolutional neural networks (CNN) achieve better results, above 99% accuracy [11]. However, it is common that in a single field of view (FoV) several diatoms of different taxa, sizes and shapes appear, along with other elements such as fragments or debris. In these cases, object detection or segmentation techniques are needed to locate all the regions of interest (ROI) present in the image, i.g., diatoms shells.

A recent review of phytoplankton image segmentation methods is presented in Tang et al. [16]. Most of the methods are based on classical methods such as region based segmentation [14,18], filtering [8] and active contours (AC) [6]. As far as the authors know, only two works are using deep neural network for diatom segmentation ([16] and [12]).

The performance of previous classical methods ranges from 88% to 95% accuracy. The main drawbacks are that they are sensitive to noise, like those based on region segmentation, or they need to manually set the initial curve, in the case of AC. Moreover, most of them have been demonstrated only on a single taxon and on images containing a single diatom. Only the works of Zheng et al. [17] and previous work by the authors [8] were shown on images with multi-taxon. However, the work of Zheng et al. [17] was only demonstrated for a single taxon with an average precision of 0.91 and a sensitivity of 0.81. The work by Libreros et al. [8] is dependent on the image noise and features of the ROIs.

Object detection algorithms based on deep learning have been tested on diatoms, in previous work done by the authors [12], using a Region-based Convolutional Neural Network (R-CNN) [7] and a framework called Darknet with YOLO method. In R-CNN the first step is to provide region proposals and based on these proposals a CNN extracts image features to be classified by a Support Vector Machine (SVM). In YOLO, a single neural network is applied to the whole image. The network divides the image into regions and predicts the class and the bounding box probabilities.

YOLO gives better results than R-CNN in the evaluation carried out with 10 taxa in full microscopic images with multiple diatoms [12]. This is because the model has information about the global context since the network is fed with the full image. Thus, an average F1-measure value of 0.37 with 0.29 precision and 0.68 sensitivity is obtained by the R-CNN against an average F1-measure value of 0.78 with 0.73 precision and 0.85 sensitivity obtained with YOLO. The main problem with these methods is that they do not separate the ROIs properly when overlap occurs. Therefore, the quantification of diatoms is limited.

In this work, a complete comparison of several detection and segmentation frameworks have been applied to detect and quantify diatoms of 10 different taxa. This is the first time that Viola-Jones and Semantic Segmentation techniques are used and compared for diatom segmentation in microscopic images containing several taxon shells. The paper is organized as follows. In Sect. 2, image acquisition are described. The description of the tested methods are presented in Sect. 3 and the results obtained together with the evaluation metrics used are summarized in Sect. 4. Finally, conclusions are drawn in Sect. 5.

2 Materials

A dataset with enough samples to train such a demanding resource technique as deep learning is needed. For this reason, an extensive process of data collecting, labeling and processing have been performed. The complete dataset is available under request.

2.1 Data Acquisition and Labeling

The first step is to capture images with real samples of diatoms in similar conditions as they are observed under the microscope. Therefore, it is essential to recruit expert taxonomist. In our work, the taxonomist was responsible for collecting a large number of microscopic diatom images and perform the manual identification task. Thus, 126 diatom images including 10 different taxa have been used, with variety in terms of specific features (length, internal and external shape) and diatom concentration. All the images have been taken with a Brunel SP30 microscope, using a 60x objective and an image resolution of 2592×1944 pixels.

The experts were provided with a labeling tool so that they were capable of manually label 1446 diatoms from the collected dataset. That is an average of 144 ROIs per taxa. There are many free labeling tools widely used to help in this task. VGG Image Annotator (VIA) [5] was selected in our case. VIA is an HTML file that can be opened in any standard web browser. The graphical user interface is friendly and easy to use, so once the images have been imported, the user only has to select the region and mark the points around the diatom shape. Finally, all the information can be stored in a JSON file to compose the ground truth (GT) dataset.

3 Methods

3.1 Viola and Jones

Viola-Jones is a classical detection method where the features to be learned by the detector are based on the Histogram of Oriented Gradients (HOG) [4]. This method aims to calculate the gradient (direction and magnitude) of the pixels in a region and group them in histograms. This descriptor is useful to detect shapes and contours, which is one of the most prominent features of diatom characterization. However, it is not invariant to object orientation, and this problem can be addressed with augmentation techniques such as rotation

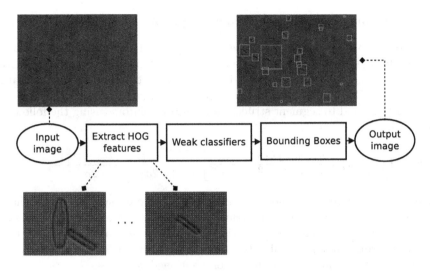

Fig. 1. Cascade object detector based on Viola-Jones algorithm.

and flips. A series of weak classifiers are trained in cascade to detect instances at different scales and positions in the image using a sliding-window approach. A general scheme of the method is presented in Fig. 1.

The development of this method is organized into three steps:

1. *Negative generation.* To improve the performance of the method, a proper set of negative images is built. To achieve that, the typical appearance of background images in diatoms slides was studied. The background usually has a small range of gray values, without any line defined. Taking this into account, an algorithm was developed to generate automatically random images that follow this appearance.
2. *Training process.* The parameters that are provided to customize the learning process are: the object training size, the negative samples factor, the number of stages, false alarm rate, and true positive rate.
3. *Model testing.* The parameters for detection are customized to prevent the over detections of artifacts, which is the main drawback of this technique. These parameters are:
   - *Minimum and Maximum bounding boxes size.* This is the minimum and maximum object size that is supposed to be found in the images.
   - *Scale factor.* This parameter determines how much the sliding-window increases its size at each iteration.
   - *Merge threshold.* This is one of the most important parameters since it is useful to tune the detection/false-alarm ratio, as according to this overlap measure, contiguous identifications are joined.

3.2 Scale and Curvature Invariant Ridge Detector

Scale and Curvature Invariant Ridge Detector (SCIRD) is based on a Gaussian non-linear transformation filter and was presented for segmenting dendritic trees and corneal nerve fibers [1]. In the context of detecting diatoms in water resources, SCIRD filters bank is applied to diatom images, following by a post-processing method to segment structures related to diatoms using the following equations:

$$F(x; \sigma; k) = \frac{1}{\sigma_2^2} \left[\frac{(x_2 + kx_1^2)^2}{\sigma_2^2} - 1 \right] exp \left[-\frac{x_1^2}{2\sigma_1^2} - \frac{(x_2 + kx_1^2)^2}{2\sigma_2^2} \right] \tag{1}$$

where (x_1, x_2) represents a point in an image coordinate system, k is a shape parameter and $\sigma = (\sigma_1, \sigma_2)$ corresponds to standard deviations in the Gaussian distribution, at each coordinate direction. k, σ_1 and σ_2 are parameters provided by a user. From Eq. 1 is possible to obtain a set of pre-defined filter banks by spanning a set of values as parameters of mentioned variables.

After generating the filters bank, by the non-linear function transformation, a convolution operation is performed using the set of filters. The final result is obtained as the maximum value at each pixel position among convolution results. Each filter represents different shapes depending on $\sigma = (\sigma_1, \sigma_2)$ values. The σ parameters must be adjusted according to image contrast, debris concentration and low noise levels [8].

3.3 YOLO

This framework is based on a fully convolutional network, a different approach than traditional R-CNN and its family (Fast/Faster-RCNN), that speeds up the running time in several orders of magnitude [13]. The above methods are based on applying the model to the input image at multiple locations and scales. However, the latter uses a single neural network to the input image, once. This one is responsible for dividing the image into candidate regions (instead of trusting on new algorithms that add extra cost). Additionally, as the whole image is fed to the network (instead of several patches), the model has global information about the context of the object, being this more suitable for accurate decisions.

In detail, this framework divides the images in a cell matrix, so each cell is responsible for proposing a fixed number of candidate regions proposals. Then, each box is moved according to a predicted offset, so that it fits in size and location to a candidate object. Along with that, the prediction also provides with confidence for both the object class and the bounding box likeliness of being an object itself. The result is that myriads of boxes are proposed, but most of them have shallow confidence, so they can be easily rejected using a threshold. A general scheme of the method is presented in Fig. 2.

The training procedure was configured with a learning rate of 0.001 and 10000 epochs. The selected optimizer was Stochastic Gradient Descent with a 0.9 of momentum coefficient. The complete dataset was divided into a training

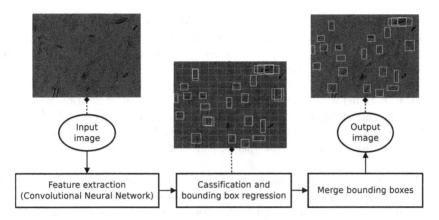

Fig. 2. YOLO architecture flowchart

subset of 105 images and a validation subset with the leaving 21 images. The
mini-batch size was configured to 4 images. After the training stage, the model
performance was evaluated using the ground truth masks.

3.4   SegNet

SegNet is a Semantic Segmentation architecture originally designed for scene
understanding applications, such as autonomous driving. For this reason, efficiency and speed at inference time are crucial. Some of the first deep learning Semantic Segmentation models tried to directly apply the deep neural network architectures designed for image classification to pixel-level classification.
However, convolution, pooling and sub-sampling operations performed by CNNs
may cause a reduction of the feature map resolution, losing spatial information
which is essential for good boundary delimitation. To solve this, novel approaches
emerged, such as Fully Convolutional Networks (FCNs) [9], DeconvNet [10], U-
Net [15] or SegNet [2]. These models share a similar architecture, with slight
differences. In this paper, SegNet is selected, due to the good accuracy and
efficiency in terms of memory and computational time.

The architecture of SegNet is formed by an encoder network, a corresponding
decoder network and a final pixel-level classification layer. The encoder network
is formed by the first 13 layers of the popular VGG16 network, pretrained on a
large image classification dataset, like ImageNet or COCO. These layers are a
combination of convolution, batch normalization, ReLU and max-pooling operations which generate the feature maps. As aforementioned, convolution and
pooling operations cause a reduction of the feature map resolution, affecting the
final segmentation accuracy. In SegNet, the fully connected layers of VGG16 are
replaced by a decoder network (one decoder for each encoder), which is responsible for upsampling the input feature maps to a higher resolution. To achieve
this, the indices of each max-pooling layer (position of the maximum feature
value) at encoding stage are stored to capture the spatial information, and, at

decoding stage, these indices are used to perform the upsampling. Finally, the output of this decoding stage (the high resolution feature maps) is the input of a softmax layer, which carries out a pixel-level classification. In Fig. 3 a general scheme of the method is presented.

At the training stage, the specific diatoms dataset is applied to adapt the pre-trained COCO network weights to our problem. Data augmentation is used to improve the size and quality of the original dataset. This process is done applying different image processing algorithms to the original dataset, like image rotations, translations, crops, mirror effects, Gaussian noise, and contrast enhancements.

The training procedure was configured with a learning rate of 0.05 and 100 epochs. The selected optimizer was Stochastic Gradient Descent with a 0.9 of momentum coefficient. The complete dataset was divided into a training subset of 105 images and a validation subset with the leaving 21 images. The images were resized to 480×360, preserving the aspect ratio, to allow a mini-batch size of 4 images. After the training stage, the model performance was evaluated using the ground truth masks.

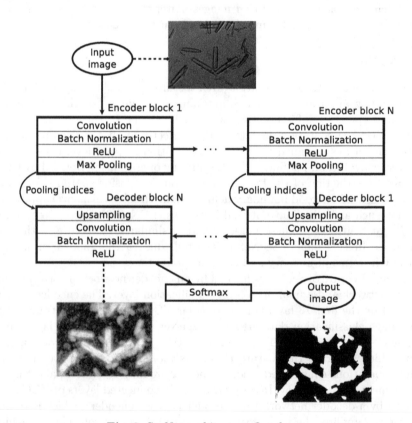

Fig. 3. SegNet architecture flowchart

4   Results

The metrics used to measure the pixel-wise detection performance are:

- *Sensitivity:* The sensitivity or recall can be measured in terms of true positives (TP) and false negatives (FN), at the pixel level, following Eq. 2. TP pixels are those that belong to the class and are predicted as positives. On the other hand, FN, also known as type 2 error, are pixels that belong to the class although are predicted as negative. This metric gives the proportion of correctly classified positives.

$$\text{Sensitivity} = \frac{\text{TP}}{\text{TP} + \text{FN}} \tag{2}$$

- *Precision:* Similar to the previous one although taking into account false positives (FP) instead of FN (Eq. 3). FP (type 1 error) pixels are those that do not belong to the ROI although they are predicted as positive. This metric gives the probability of correct detection if the prediction is positive.

$$\text{Precision} = \frac{\text{TP}}{\text{TP} + \text{FP}} \tag{3}$$

- *Specificity:* This metric gives the proportion of correctly detected negatives and follows Eq. 4. True negative (TN) pixels are those that do not belong to the ROI, and they are predicted as negatives.

$$\text{Specificity} = \frac{\text{TN}}{\text{TN} + \text{FP}} \tag{4}$$

Once the models have been trained, their performance has been evaluated using the metrics explained above over the dataset predictions. In this case, the evaluation has been done comparing the predicted bounding boxes with the GT dataset, at a pixel level. For most species, the SegNet and YOLO methods show the best results. Deep learning methods show better results than classical ones. Viola-Jones does not obtain good results for any taxa, but SCIRD obtains the best sensitivity values for some taxa. Precision is higher for the YOLO model; that is, there are few FPs compared to the other methods. However, the number of FPs is also high, and only an average precision of 0.73 is achieved. On the other hand, sensitivity is always higher for SegNet framework, indicating a low number of FNs and obtaining an average value of 0.96. Specificity is similar for SCIRD and YOLO methods with average values of 0.93 and 0.96 respectively. The average results per species with all the techniques are presented in Table 1.

Table 1. Pixel-wise detection results for each method

Species	Metric	VJ	YOLO	SCIRD	SegNet
Gomphonema rhombicum	Precision	0.46	**0.86**	0.68	0.59
	Sensitivity	0.69	0.84	0.59	**0.98**
	Specificity	0.62	**0.93**	0.86	0.70
Nitzschia palea	Precision	0.26	**0.73**	0.30	0.59
	Sensitivity	0.69	0.85	0.04	**0.87**
	Specificity	0.44	0.91	**0.97**	0.78
Skeletonema potamos	Precision	0.09	0.50	0.10	**0.63**
	Sensitivity	0.72	0.76	0.10	**0.92**
	Specificity	0.64	**0.97**	0.96	0.62
Eolimna minima	Precision	0.26	**0.64**	0.44	0.61
	Sensitivity	0.67	0.90	0.51	**0.98**
	Specificity	0.74	**0.94**	0.88	0.67
Achnanthes subhudsonis	Precision	0.31	**0.84**	0.59	0.64
	Sensitivity	0.73	0.73	0.48	**0.98**
	Specificity	0.77	**0.98**	0.95	0.70
Staurosira venter	Precision	0.08	**0.73**	0.03	0.70
	Sensitivity	0.66	0.86	0.23	**0.96**
	Specificity	0.79	**0.99**	0.83	0.72
Nitzschia capitellata	Precision	0.34	0.66	**0.80**	0.71
	Sensitivity	0.73	0.95	0.45	**0.99**
	Specificity	0.91	0.97	**0.99**	0.77
Eolimna rhombelliptica	Precision	0.23	**0.72**	0.36	0.66
	Sensitivity	0.53	0.87	0.27	**0.95**
	Specificity	0.87	**0.98**	0.96	0.70
Nitzschia inconspicua	Precision	0.24	**0.79**	0.55	0.55
	Sensitivity	0.64	0.85	0.35	**0.99**
	Specificity	0.85	**0.98**	**0.98**	0.58
Nitzschia frustulum	Precision	0.38	**0.80**	0.66	0.60
	Sensitivity	0.39	0.85	0.32	**0.98**
	Specificity	0.91	**0.97**	0.96	0.68

Finally, the bounding boxes generated by all tested methods for ten sample images of the different taxa considered are illustrated in Figs. 4 and 5. Each row shows a sample image while each column shows the results of a detection method.

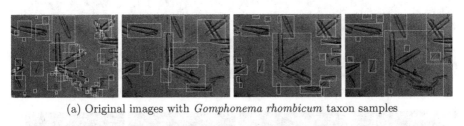

(a) Original images with *Gomphonema rhombicum* taxon samples

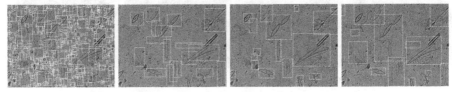

(b) Original images with *Nitzschia palea* taxon samples

(c) Original images with *Skeletonema potamos* taxon samples

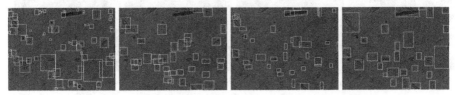

(d) Original images with *Eolimna minima* taxon samples

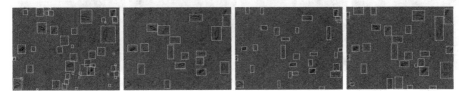

(e) Original images with *Achnanthes subhudsonis* taxon samples

Fig. 4. Example of diatoms detected by each method (I). Each column shows the results of the segmentation methods: (1st) Viola-Jones; (2nd) YOLO; (3rd) SCIRD and (4th) SegNet.

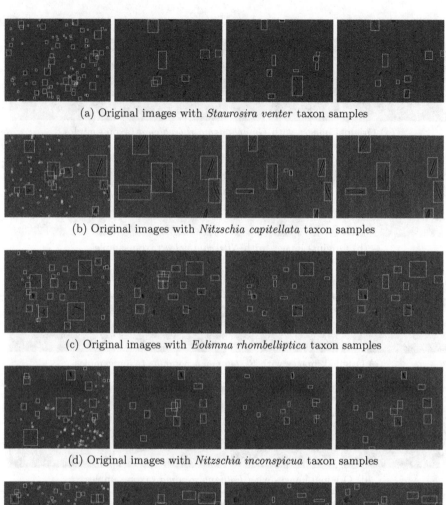

(a) Original images with *Staurosira venter* taxon samples

(b) Original images with *Nitzschia capitellata* taxon samples

(c) Original images with *Eolimna rhombelliptica* taxon samples

(d) Original images with *Nitzschia inconspicua* taxon samples

(e) Original images with *Nitzschia frustulum* taxon samples

Fig. 5. Example of diatoms detected by each method (II). Each column shows the results of the segmentation methods: (1st) Viola-Jones; (2nd) YOLO; (3rd) SCIRD and (4th) SegNet.

5   Conclusions

In this work, four different detection and segmentation frameworks have been applied to segment diatoms of 10 different taxa. This is a complex challenge due to the large variation in species and the slight differences between them. The methods are both based on classical approaches such as Viola-Jones and SCIRD, and deep learning based. Two segmentation techniques based on deep learning have been considered, that is: (i) object detection with YOLO and (ii) Semantic Segmentation by means of pixel-wise binary classification with SegNet.

This is the first time that Viola-Jones and Semantic Segmentation techniques are used and compared for multi-taxon shell segmentation, that detects different diatoms in full FoV microscopic images containing several taxon shells.

The deep learning approaches, SegNet and YOLO, showed the best results in the tests carried out. This may be due to the fact that the model has information about the global context since the network is fed with the full image. The best sensitivity is obtained with SegNet, with an average value of 0.96 versus 0.85 for YOLO. However, the best specificity is obtained with YOLO, with an average value of 0.96. SCIRD methods also achieve good specificity with an average value of 0.93. However, the precision goes down for all methods obtaining the best result by YOLO with a value of 0.73.

The sensitivity is improved with Semantic Segmentation as compared to previously published methods, but there is still room to improve the precision. The main problem with these methods is that they do not separate the ROIs properly when overlapping occurs. Therefore, the quantification of diatoms is limited. The promising results encourage us to continue working on this complex problem. The SegNet model performance can be improved by adding post-processing techniques such as morphological procedures to separate the diatom instances correctly; as well as explore new architectures based on instance segmentation.

Acknowledgements. The authors acknowledge financial support of the Spanish Government under the Aqualitas-retos project (Ref. CTM2014-51907-C2-R-MINECO).

References

1. Annunziata, R., Trucco, E.: Accelerating convolutional sparse coding for curvilinear structures segmentation by refining SCIRD-TS filter banks. IEEE Trans. Med. Imaging **35**(11), 2381–2392 (2016)
2. Badrinarayanan, V., Kendall, A., Cipolla, R.: SegNet: a deep convolutional encoder-decoder architecture for image segmentation. arXiv preprint arXiv:1511.00561 (2015)
3. Bueno, G., et al.: Automated Diatom classification (part A): handcrafted feature approaches. Appl. Sci. **7**(8), 753 (2017)
4. Dalal, N., Triggs, B.: Histograms of oriented gradients for human detection. In: International Conference on Computer Vision & Pattern Recognition (CVPR 2005), vol. 1, pp. 886–893. IEEE Computer Society (2005)
5. Dutta, A., Gupta, A., Zissermann, A.: VGG image annotator (VIA), version: 2.0.5 (2016). http://www.robots.ox.ac.uk/vgg/software/via/. Accessed 03 Apr 2019
6. Gelzinis, A., Verikas, A., Vaiciukynas, E., Bacauskiene, M.: A novel technique to extract accurate cell contours applied for segmentation of phytoplankton images. Mach. Vis. Appl. **26**(2–3), 305–315 (2015)
7. Girshick, R., Donahue, J., Darrell, T., Malik, J.: Rich feature hierarchies for accurate object detection and semantic segmentation. In: Proceedings of the IEEE Conference on Computer Vision and Pattern Recognition, pp. 580–587 (2014)

8. Libreros, J., Bueno, G., Trujillo, M., Ospina, M.: Automated identification and classification of diatoms from water resources. In: Vera-Rodriguez, R., Fierrez, J., Morales, A. (eds.) CIARP 2018. LNCS, vol. 11401, pp. 496–503. Springer, Cham (2019). https://doi.org/10.1007/978-3-030-13469-3_58

9. Long, J., Shelhamer, E., Darrell, T.: Fully convolutional networks for semantic segmentation. In: Proceedings of the IEEE Conference on Computer Vision and Pattern Recognition, pp. 3431–3440 (2015)

10. Noh, H., Hong, S., Han, B.: Learning deconvolution network for semantic segmentation. In: Proceedings of the IEEE International Conference on Computer Vision, pp. 1520–1528 (2015)

11. Pedraza, A., Bueno, G., Deniz, O., Cristóbal, G., Blanco, S., Borrego-Ramos, M.: Automated diatom classification (part B): a deep learning approach. Appl. Sci. **7**(5), 460 (2017)

12. Pedraza, A., et al.: Lights and pitfalls of convolutional neural networks for diatom identification. Opt. Photonics Dig. Technol. Imaging Appl. V **10679**, 106790G (2018)

13. Redmon, J., Farhadi, A.: YOLO9000: better, faster, stronger. arXiv preprint arXiv:1612.08242 (2016)

14. Rojas Camacho, O., Forero, M., Guillermoand Menéndez, J.M.: A tuning method for diatom segmentation techniques. Appl. Sci. **7**(17), 762 (2017)

15. Ronneberger, O., Fischer, P., Brox, T.: U-Net: convolutional networks for biomedical image segmentation. In: Navab, N., Hornegger, J., Wells, W.M., Frangi, A.F. (eds.) MICCAI 2015. LNCS, vol. 9351, pp. 234–241. Springer, Cham (2015). https://doi.org/10.1007/978-3-319-24574-4_28

16. Tang, N., Zhou, F., Gu, Z., Zheng, H., Yu, Z., Zheng, B.: Unsupervised pixel-wise classification for chaetoceros image segmentation. Neurocomputing **318**, 261–270 (2018)

17. Zheng, H., Wang, N., Yu, Z., Gu, Z., Zheng, B.: Robust and automatic cell detection and segmentation from microscopic images of non-setae phytoplankton species. IET Image Process. **11**(11), 1077–1085 (2017)

18. Zheng, H., Wang, R., Yu, Z., Wang, N., Gu, Z., Zheng, B.: Automatic plankton image classification combining multiple view features via multiple kernel learning. BMC Bioinf. **18**(16), 570 (2017)

Estimation of Sulfonamides Concentration in Water Based on Digital Colourimetry

Pedro H. Carvalho[1]($\boxtimes$), Sílvia Bessa[1,2], Ana Rosa M. Silva[1],
Patrícia S. Peixoto[3], Marcela A. Segundo[3], and Hélder P. Oliveira[1,2]

[1] INESC TEC – Institute for Systems and Computer Engineering,
Technology and Science, Porto, Portugal
pedro.h.carvalho@inesctec.pt
[2] Faculty of Sciences, University of Porto, Porto, Portugal
[3] LAQV – REQUIMTE, Faculty of Pharmacy, University of Porto, Porto, Portugal

Abstract. Overuse of antibiotics is causing the environment to become polluted with them. This is a major threat to global health, with bacteria developing resistance to antibiotics because of it. To monitor this threat, multiple antibiotic detection methods have been developed; however, they are normally complex and costly. In this work, an affordable, easy to use alternative based on digital colourimetry is proposed. Photographs of samples next to a colour reference target were acquired to build a dataset. The algorithm proposed detects the reference target, based on binarisation algorithms, in order to standardise the collected images using a colour correction matrix converting from RGB to XYZ, providing a necessary colour constancy between photographs from different devices. Afterwards, the sample is extracted through edge detection and Hough transform algorithms. Finally, the sulfonamide concentration is estimated resorting to an experimentally designed calibration curve, which correlates the concentration and colour information. Best performance was obtained using Hue colour, achieving a relative standard deviation value of less than 3.5%.

Keywords: Digital colourimetry · Colour correction ·
Image Segmentation

1 Introduction

Antibiotic resistance is becoming more common, which is a serious threat to the health of everyone in the world. The treatment of infections becomes more difficult when the microorganisms responsible are resistant to antibiotics, with increases in treatment time, risk of the spread of the infection and, ultimately, risk of death [1].

Due to the misuse and overuse of antibiotics in animal husbandry, farming and, of course, treatment of humans, environmental waters are getting polluted with them. This pollution causes bacteria to be constantly exposed to antibiotics, developing resistance to them, and subsequently disseminating antibiotic

© Springer Nature Switzerland AG 2019
A. Morales et al. (Eds.): IbPRIA 2019, LNCS 11867, pp. 355–366, 2019.
https://doi.org/10.1007/978-3-030-31332-6_31

resistant genes [2]. To monitor this pollution, several antibiotic detection methods have been developed, such as: high performance liquid chromatography tandem mass spectrometry (HPLC-MS/MS), HPLC with other detectors, electrophoresis with different detectors, immunoassays, and colourimetry [3]. These commonly used methods are expensive and difficult to use on a large scale, which discourages the deployment of them in monitoring programs. Thanks to advances made in computer vision-based analytical chemistry and the advent of the smartphone, it is now possible to create affordable and easy to use solutions for large scale environmental monitoring, based on digital colourimetry [7].

Colourimetry is the method of ascertaining the concentration of a compound in a solution by analysing its colour. Traditionally, a spectrophotometer (device that measures absorbance in a given wavelengths of UV or visible light) is used for this purpose. However, some work has been done to more easily determine compound concentrations using digital colourimetry. With image processing techniques it is quicker to analyse the colour of a solution and can be done outside of a laboratory setting. This approach, although practical, is not very precise due to photographs having device dependent colour values and changes in illumination affecting the captured colours. Therefore, a preprocessing step of colour correction is needed so that the digital colourimetry is consistent across devices. However there is not a perfect answer to this problem, since colour correction (CC) techniques use assumptions and approximations that are not always correct [4].

Concerning environmental applications, smartphone use based only in software code and application development have been proposed. For instance, exposure to air pollution considering spatially and temporally variation of population was implemented with help of mobile and wireless devices that yield information about where and when people are present. Hence, collective activity patterns were determined using counts of connections to the cellular network, allowing the estimation of population-weighted exposure to fine particulate matter (PM2.5) in New York City, USA [5]. Moreover, an application that models environmental concentrations of fine particulate matter (PM2.5), coarse particulate matter (PM10) and ozone concentrations, calculating personal health risks at the smartphone's current location, was proposed for utilisation in the state of Oregon, USA [6].

Combination of chemistry and smartphones has been underexploited in the environmental area. Evaluation of nitrite concentration and pH determination in combination with a low-cost paper-based microfluidic device has been proposed, using a dedicated application that acquires information from seven sensing areas, containing different immobilised reagents, to produce selective colour changes when a sample solution is placed in the sampling area. Under controlled conditions of light, using the flash of the smartphone as a light source, the image captured with the built-in camera is processed using a customised algorithm for multi-detection of the coloured sensing areas. The developed image processing allowed reducing the influence of the light source and the positioning of the microfluidic device in the picture, but no report about field application is given [7]. Moreover, a portable chromium(III) ion detection system based on a smartphone readout device based on ELISA protocol has been proposed without application to field analysis [8].

To the best of our knowledge, mobile devices have not been used so far for antibiotic screening in environmental waters. In this work, a new approach for antibiotic pollution monitoring is proposed, using digital colourimetry on data acquired with smartphone cameras. To estimate the concentration of sulfonamides, a calibration curve is used, correlating concentrations to the Hue colour value. The colour of the sample is corrected using a reference target, so that there is colour constancy between images of the same concentration.

2   Methodology

The objective of this work is to detect the colour of the sample in photographs taken with a smartphone and estimate its sulfonamide concentration.

Colour correction is needed to ensure colour is consistent between photographs under different illuminations or from different devices. Colour correction can be done without a reference target. Well known examples of these methods are the White Patch, Gray-World, Gray-Edge and Gamut-Mapping. However, using the colour chart usually achieves better results, since there is knowledge of what the colours of the patches should be. In this sense, in order to facilitate the colour correction, an *x-rite ColorChecker Passport* was included during the photographs acquisition. It has a few targets to use has a reference for colour correction, but, in this work, only the classic target chart with 24 patches of different colours arranged in a 6 by 4 grid, with known ground truth values, is used.

A segmentation of the *ColorChecker* patches and the sample is done, followed by a colour correction step, before extracting the colour of the sample. Finally, by comparing this colour value to a set of standard samples with known concentrations, the concentration of the sample is estimated, a method known as calibration curve in analytical chemistry. However, there are multiple colour spaces in which the colour value can be extracted, so a study between the components of the RGB, XYZ, CIELAB and HSV colour spaces is performed to find which component results in the best concentration versus colour model.

2.1   Data

For this work, a database was built with photographs of the sample next to the colour chart, set up as shown in Fig. 1. The samples vary in sulfonamide concentration, from 0 to 150 μg/L, which provide different colour in a concentration dependent manner.

For the extraction procedure of the sulfonamides, the mixed-mode ion exchange polystyrene divinylbenzene sulfonated (SDB-RPS) disk from Empore-3M (Bellefonte, PA, USA) was cut (13 mm diameter) and placed inside a polypropylene disk holder, (Swinnex R filter holder, SX0001300, EMD Millipore Corporation, Billerica, MA). Four units were attached in parallel to

Fig. 1. Example photograph from the database.

propulsion tubes (Tygon R , 1.02 mm i.d.) fitted in a peristaltic pump (Gilson Minipuls 2, Villiers-le-Bel, France). Standards and samples (10 mL) were loaded at 0.8 mL min-1. The reagent, that gives colour to the sample, used is p-dimethylaminocinnamaldehyde (DMACA). DMACA working solution (0.22 g L^{-1}) was prepared by dilution of DMACA stock solution in chloroform (1:1, v/v).

Each disk was photographed twice by three different smartphone cameras, meaning 24 photographs for each sulfonamide concentration (8 from each smartphone). The smartphones used were the *Xiaomi A1* (12 MP, f/2.2 + 12 MP, f/2.6), *Samsung Galaxy J5 2017* (13 MP, f/1.7) and *Huawei P Smart* (13 MP, AF + 2 MP, depth sensor). The photographs were captured with the default settings.

2.2 Segmentation

In order to automatically detect the colours from the reference target and the sample, a segmentation algorithm is needed to isolate both regions of interest. First, the region of the chart is detected and cropped from the initial image (see Fig. 2). Then, the 24 patches are segmented to extract their colour values (see Fig. 3). Finally the disc is detected (see Fig. 5), followed by the extraction of the sample colour (see Fig. 6).

Colour Chart: The colour chart is detected after converting the image to grayscale, using a multilevel Otsu thresholding to generate 3 thresholds and using the lowest one to binarise it (B in Fig. 2). The lowest threshold is used because, outside the patches, the colour chart is black. Afterwards the object with the larger area is chosen, in case other objects are detected. Finally, knowing the orientation in which the chart is placed, it is split in two and the desired side is kept (classic target chart with 24 patches of different colours arranged in a 6 by 4 grid), see Fig. 2.

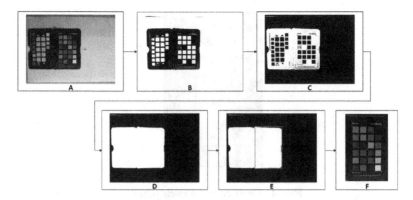

Fig. 2. Steps to isolate the classic 24 patch target. A – Original image in grayscale. B – A binarised. C – Complement of B. D – Holes filled. E – Bounding box around the desired colour target. F – Grayscale classic colour chart.

Patches: After cropping the chart from the grayscale image, it is binarised using an Otsu thresholding, followed by the exclusion of large and small objects in order to isolate all the 24 patches (C in Fig. 3). Since the patches encompass a large range of colours, it is difficult for a threshold to binarise all of them. Therefore, the missing patches are estimated by completing the missing spots in the 6 by 4 grid of patches, using the centroids of the detected patches (D in Fig. 3).

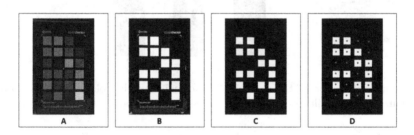

Fig. 3. Steps to estimate the centroids of the 24 patches. A – Grayscale classic colour chart. B – A binarised. C – Patches isolated. D – Estimation of missing patches centroids.

After determining the centroids for the 24 patches, a square bounding box is cropped around each one. The influence of the size of the bounding box was empirically tested and it was verified that using smaller squares does not significantly alter the colour values extracted. Therefore, since the detection of the patches might not be perfect, the bounding box is smaller than the patch, as demonstrated in Fig. 4). To extract the colour values, the median is chosen, removing the influence of outlier pixels.

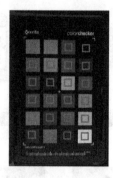

Fig. 4. Final crop for each patch.

Disk: First, the colour chart is covered, using the previous detection, so that it does not influence the sample detection. Then, a Canny edge detection is applied to detect the disk (B in Fig. 5). A dilation is applied to ensure that the edges of the disk are connected and then a fill is done so that the middle of the disk is covered (C in Fig. 5). Since this dilation greatly expands the edges, the initial segmentation is done around the disk. Figure 5 shows the initial edge detection, the result of the dilation and fill and how the disk is cropped from the initial image.

Fig. 5. Initial detection of the disk. A – Region without the colour chart. B – Edge detection. C – Edges dilated and filled. D – Disk detection bounding box. E – Cropped disk.

Sample: Using the circular Hough transform, the disk is more precisely detected (A in Fig. 6). In low concentrations of sulfonamides, the sample presents very little colour, making it hard to distinguish from the rest of the disk. To differentiate the colour in those cases, the image of the disk is converted to grayscale and normalised between 0 and 1, followed by a histogram equalisation (D in Fig. 6). Then, a binarisation is done with the lowest threshold generated from a 3-multilevel Otsu thresholding (E in Fig. 6). Figure 6 shows how the initial crop is done around the disk, followed by a more precise detection of the disk and then the sample for colour extraction, using the median of all values.

Fig. 6. Sample detection steps. A – Disk detection with Hough transform. B – Cropped disk. C – Grayscale B. D – C after normalisation and histogram equalisation. E – D binarised. F – Sample detected.

2.3 Colour Correction

In order to choose the most appropriate method for colour correction task, the following methods were compared, taken into account the standard deviation of the colour of the samples after colour correction:

* **Weighted Grey Edge (WGE).** The grey edge algorithm is based on the assumption that the average edge difference in a scene is achromatic. The weighted grey edge algorithm incorporates weighting of different types of edges (specular, shadow or material edges) [9].
* **Illuminant Estimation Using White Patch (White).** Estimating the illuminant as the colour of the white patch, since it should be white and any deviation is due to the illumination.
* **Illuminant Estimation Using Achromatic Patches (Neutral).** Same as above, but using the average colour between the 6 achromatic patches instead of just the white patch.
* **Colour Correction Matrix RGB to RGB.** This approach here presented uses the RGB values extracted from all the 24 color patches of the color rendition chart and compares them to the reference values provided by the chart's manufacturer that were precisely measured with a spectrophotometer. By performing a least square regression between these two sets of values, the parameters that will more likely approximate the measured RGB values with the reference values are estimated [10].
* **Colour Correction Matrix RGB to XYZ.** Unlike the RGB to RGB transform described before, this method uses a RGB to XYZ transformation. Therefore obtaining the colour corrected XYZ image, which is the linear, device independent version of the raw camera output [11].

3 Results

3.1 Colour Correction

Table 1 compares the colour correction methods for each colour component, using standard deviation as a metric. A low standard deviation implies a better colour correction, showing that samples with the same concentration have a similar colour. For this comparison, images of four concentrations (0, 5, 25, 100 μg/L) were selected, and manual annotation of the patches and sample was performed, so that it is independent of the segmentation algorithm.

Table 1. Comparison of standard deviations for different colour correction methods in different colour spaces.

Colour component	WGE	White	Neutral	RGB- RGB	RGB- XYZ
R	0.058	0.055	0.054	0.040	**0.016**
G	0.067	0.068	0.068	0.039	**0.021**
B	0.056	0.057	0.057	0.047	**0.023**
L	0.057	0.056	0.056	0.034	**0.017**
a^*	0.022	0.027	0.027	0.024	**0.018**
b^*	0.021	0.024	0.023	0.025	**0.017**
X	0.077	0.076	0.075	0.072	**0.025**
Y	0.080	0.081	0.081	0.072	**0.027**
Z	0.069	0.072	0.072	0.081	**0.034**
H	**0.011**	0.013	0.013	0.013	0.013
S	0.039	0.043	0.044	0.032	**0.026**
V	0.058	0.055	0.054	0.040	**0.016**
Average	0.051	0.052	0.052	0.043	**0.021**

This comparison demonstrates that the RGB to XYZ colour correction matrix is the best method overall. Figure 7 shows an example of colour correction using this method.

Fig. 7. Original image (left) and colour corrected image (right) using RGB-XYZ.

Further examination is needed to choose the best colour component, so calibration curves were plotted for each colour component and analysed.

3.2   Calibration Curves

Calibration curves were done using all the samples from the database, since their sulfonamide concentrations are known. In this step, the automatic segmentation algorithm described in Sect. 2.2 was applied, followed by the RGB to XYZ correction.

Increasing amounts of sulfonamides were retained in the solid support upon passage of more concentrated solutions. Upon addition of colour developing reagent (DMACA), the intensity of colour must be proportional to the amount of sulfonamides retained in the extracting disk. Therefore, a linear relationship between colour and concentration should exist.

Analysing the monotony of data, all colour components (in all colour spaces) showed monotony for data collected for solutions containing between 40–150 $\mu g/L$, meaning that the increase of sulfonamides retained in the solid support was correlated to an increase (or to a decrease) in the value of the component. For lower concentrations of sulfonamide (0–20 $\mu g/L$), only components G, H, a* and b* showed a monotonic behaviour. This means that these components are suitable for determination at lower concentrations, which could not be detected by analysis of other colour components.

In Fig. 8, the calibration curves for these four components are demonstrated. For each sulfonamide concentration (0, 5, 10, 15, 20, 40, 50, 100 and 150 $\mu g/L$) the average colour and the standard deviation are represented and a linear trendline is applied.

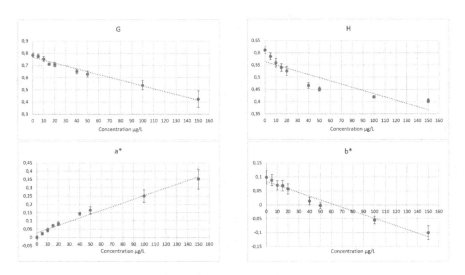

Fig. 8. Calibration curves for Green, Hue, a* and b* colour components using the RGB-XYZ method.

As Fig. 8 demonstrates, the data does not appear to be well described by a linear regression globally. Therefore, studying the data separately for the lower concentrations (0–20 $\mu g/L$) and higher concentrations (40–150 $\mu g/L$) might give better results. Figure 9 shows how this division was done using the Hue component as an example. With this, the linear approximation appears to better represent the data.

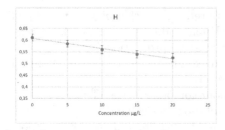 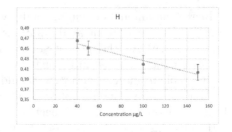

Fig. 9. Divided calibration curves for the Hue colour component using the RGB-XYZ method.

Afterwards, the relative standard deviations (RSD) were calculated for each concentration and colour component. The RSD is calculated by dividing the standard deviation by the absolute value of the mean and multiplying by 100, as shown in Eq. 1. It presents the standard deviation as a percentage of the mean. It is important for the data to have a low RSD, because it indicates a high precision.

$$RSD = \frac{std}{|mean|} * 100 \tag{1}$$

Table 2 shows that the components Green and Hue have the highest precision, although the RSD for Green becomes worse for higher concentrations, while Hue maintains its low RSD. Therefore, the concentration versus Hue calibration curve achieves the best performance. The 9694.8 RSD for a* and 427.8 RSD for b* happen because the mean is close to zero at those concentrations for those colour components.

Table 2. Relative standard deviations for each colour component and concentration.

Concentration ($\mu g/L$)	G	H	a*	b*
0	**2.1**	2.5	9694.8	24.5
5	**2.1**	2.4	38.0	22.3
10	**2.7**	3.1	26.1	24.2
15	**1.5**	2.9	12.0	27.8
20	**2.4**	3.5	14.1	31.6
40	2.9	**2.3**	6.4	95.5
50	4.1	**1.8**	13.0	427.8
100	6.7	**1.4**	15.1	25.2
150	15.8	**1.9**	16.9	24.6

4 Conclusions

This work was done with the aim of developing an algorithm to estimate sulfonamide concentration based on colour, that can be used for monitoring antibiotic pollution in environmental waters.

The methodology is composed of a segmentation, colour correction and calibration curve step. The segmentation step is split in two, colour patches and sample segmentation. The patches are necessary for the colour correction step, while the colour of the sample is needed to estimate the concentration of sulfonamides. The colour correction step uses a colour correction matrix that converts from RGB to XYZ. This colour correction method presented the best results due to using the colour chart as a known reference and converting to a device independent colour space. In order to choose which colour space and component is the best to estimate the sulfonamide concentration, an analysis of calibration curves was performed. The Hue and Green components presented the highest precision, with Hue being more consistent across all concentrations, never surpassing 3.5% relative standard deviation.

These results are promising, however there is still work to be done. New data will be acquired and used to validate the calibration curve. The developed algorithms will be incorporated in a smartphone application, so that it becomes a readily available alternative for sulfonamide detection.

Acknowledgements. This work is financed by the ERDF - European Regional Development Fund through the Operational Programme for Competitiveness and Internationalisation - COMPETE 2020 Programme and by National Funds through the Portuguese funding agency, FCT - Fundação para a Ciência e Tecnologia within project POCI-01-0145-FEDER-031756 and within PhD grant SFRH/BD/115616/2016.

References

1. World Health Organization, Drug Resistance, Antimicrobial resistance: global report on surveillance (2014). https://www.who.int/drugresistance/documents/sur-veillancereport/en/. Accessed 10 Apr 2019
2. Huerta, B., et al.: Exploring the links between antibiotic occurrence, antibiotic resistance, and bacterial communities in water supply reservoirs. Sci. Total Environ. **456**, 161–170 (2013)
3. Dmitrienko, S.G., Kochuk, E.V., Apyari, V.V., Tolmacheva, V.V., Zolotov, Y.A.: Recent advances in sample preparation techniques and methods of sulfonamides detection-a review. Analytica chimica acta **850**, 6–25 (2014)
4. Kaur, H., Sharma, S.: A comparative review of various illumination estimation based color constancy techniques. In: 2016 International Conference on Communication and Signal Processing (ICCSP), pp. 0486–0490. IEEE (2016)
5. Nyhan, M., et al.: The impact of mobile-device-based mobility patterns on quantifying population exposure to air pollution. Environ. Sci. Technol. **50**(17), 9671–9681 (2016)
6. Larkin, A., Williams, D.E., Kile, M.L., Baird, W.M.: Developing a smartphone software package for predicting atmospheric pollutant concentrations at mobile locations. Comput. J. **58**(6), 1431–1442 (2014)

7. Lopez-Ruiz, N., et al.: Smartphone-based simultaneous pH and nitrite colorimetric determination for paper microfluidic devices. Anal. Chem. **86**(19), 9554–9562 (2014)

8. Yu, S., et al.: A portable chromium ion detection system based on a smartphone readout device. Anal. Methods **8**(38), 6877–6882 (2016)

9. Gijsenij, A., Gevers, T., Van De Weijer, J.: Improving color constancy by photometric edge weighting. IEEE Trans. Pattern Anal. Mach. Intell. **34**(5), 918–929 (2012)

10. Wolf, S.: Color Correction Matrix for Digital Still and Video Imaging Systems. National Telecommunications and Information Administration, Washington, D.C. (2003)

11. Akkaynak, D., et al.: Use of commercial off-the-shelf digital cameras for scientific data acquisition and scene-specific color calibration. JOSA A **31**(2), 312–321 (2014)

Characterization of Cardiac and Respiratory System of Healthy Subjects in Supine and Sitting Position

Angel D. Ruiz[1], Juan S. Mejía[1], Juan M. López[1(✉)],
and Beatriz F. Giraldo[2]

[1] Escuela Colombiana de Ingeniería Julio Garavito, Bogotá, Colombia
{angel.ruiz,juan.mejia}@mail.escuelaing.edu.co,
juan.lopezl@escuelaing.edu.co
[2] Dept. ESAII; IBEC, Univ. Politècnica Catalunya, EEBE, Barcelona, Spain
beatriz.giraldo@upc.edu

Abstract. Studies based on the cardiac and respiratory system have allowed a better knowledge of their behavior to contribute with the diagnosis and treatment of diseases associated with them. The main goal of this project was to analyze the behavior of the cardiorespiratory system in healthy subjects, depending on the body position. The electrocardiography and respiratory flow signals were recorded in two positions, supine and sitting. Each signal was analyzed considering sliding windows of 30 s, with and overlapping of 50%. Temporal and spectral features were extracted from each signal. A total of 187 features were extracted for each window. According to statistical analysis, 148 features showed significant differences when comparing the position of the subject. Afterwards, the classifications methods based on decision trees, k-nearest neighbor and support vector machines were applied to identify the best classification model. The most advantageous performance model was obtained with a linear support vector machine method, with an accuracy of 99.5%, a sensitivity of 99.2% and a specificity of 99.6%. In conclusion, we have observed that the position of the body (supine or sitting) could modulate the cardiac and respiratory system response. New statistical models might provide new tools to analyze the behavior of these systems and the cardiorespiratory interaction complexity.

Keywords: Cardiac dynamics · Respiratory dynamics · Statistical models · Supine and sitting posture

1 Introduction

Over time, studies of the cardiac and the respiratory systems have provided a large number of tools to diagnose and improve the quality of life of the people. These contributions not only helped to deepen in the early detection of pathologies but have also generated studies of new technologies in the clinical field, and research for a better understanding of the cardiorespiratory system function [1–3].

© Springer Nature Switzerland AG 2019
A. Morales et al. (Eds.): IbPRIA 2019, LNCS 11867, pp. 367–377, 2019.
https://doi.org/10.1007/978-3-030-31332-6_32

Several studies show the relevance of the cardiac and respiratory dynamics depending on the posture [4–6], recognizing their impact on the diagnosis of some pathologies such as vertebral fracture [7, 8], how the blood pressure changes in resting conditions for hypertensive patients [9], or how the posture affects sedentary young people for the modulation of the autonomous heart rate [10]. However, to the best of the authors' knowledge, there are no studies aimed to analyze changes of features of cardiac and respiratory systems depending on posture, which may lead to specify the best position for make a clinical examination. The identification of posture, based on the analysis of the cardiorespiratory dynamics, may also be an area of interest for clinical and non-clinical applications [11–13].

This document shows a statistical analysis of respiratory flow (FLW) and electrocardiographic (ECG) features, of healthy subjects, depending on the posture. Machine learning models are proposed for the identification of the posture based only in some features from ECG and FLW.

2   Materials and Method

2.1   HealthyDB Database

ECG and respiratory flow signals of 44 healthy subjects ranging in age from 22 to 33 years old were recorded under standardized resting conditions (quiet environment, same place) using BIOPAC System Inc. MP150 equipment. All records were made considering two positions: supine (for 30 min) and sitting (for 15 min). Table 1 shows demographic information of the subjects analyzed.

Table 1. Mean ± standard deviation of the physical data of the subjects grouped by gender.

	N	Age (years)	Height (cm)	Weight (kg)	Smokers	Waist (cm)	Hip (cm)
ALL	44	27.0 ± 4.5	175.5 ± 10.5	68.0 ± 14.3	8	82.8 ± 10.9	96.5 ± 9.3
MALE	28	27.2 ± 5.4	178.7 ± 6.4	77.6 ± 8.8	7	88.8 ± 7.1	100.3 ± 7.4
FEMALE	16	26.7 ± 2.8	161.1 ± 5.5	54.3 ± 8.1	1	74.3 ± 9.6	90.9 ± 8.8

All signals were recorded simultaneously, first in supine position and then in sitting position, with a five minutes pause between each record. For each one of the 44 healthy subjects, and each position (supine or sitting), five signals were obtained: four from the ECG – monopolar leads I, II, III and chest precordial lead – with a sampling frequency of 250 Hz, and one corresponding to FLW signal with a sampling frequency of 10 Hz. Figure 1 presents an excerpt of the ECG and FLW signals of a subject in supine position.

Records were preprocessed to detect and correct artifacts and outliers. Custom algorithms were applied to detect the events of the signals. Wrong detections were manually corrected whenever necessary.

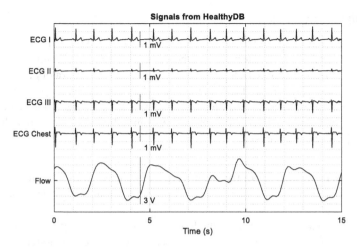

Fig. 1. Excerpt of ECG (leads I, II, III and chest) and FLW signals of a supine subject.

2.2 Signal Processing

For each subject and for each signal we extracted time and frequency domain parameters to describe cardiac and respiratory activity. For the time domain, statistical and non-linear features were extracted. In addition, machine learning models were used to classify between the sitting and supine position from the cardiac and respiratory systems. Figure 2 shows a schematic representation of the process.

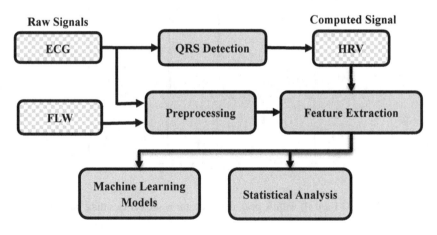

Fig. 2. Overview of the methodology used in this work.

ECG signals were pre-processed with a high pass filter with cutoff frequency of 0.2 Hz and a low pass filter with cutoff frequency of 40 Hz, to remove possible artifacts.

2.3   Temporal Features

In time domain, to characterize cardiac and respiratory dynamics, the following features were extracted: RR interval (distance between two consecutives R peaks), amplitude of R peaks from ECG signals; inspiratory time (T_I), expiratory time (T_E), and breath total time (T_{Tot}) from FLW signal. All these parameters were described in function of the mean, median, maximum, minimum, standard deviation, kurtosis and co-variance. In addition, Hjörth complexity and mobility [14], and Higuchi fractal dimension [15], were computed.

ECG

R peaks and RR intervals were the main features extracted from ECG records. These were obtained with the QRS complex detection, through Pan-Tompkins algorithm [16] (Fig. 3).

Once the R peaks were detected, the R-R intervals for each participant were found. For each R-R interval, the time of the first R peak of each one was assigned, later this signal was re-sampled at 10 Hz to obtain the HRV signal.

FLW

FLW records were analyzed taking into account three features: time of inspiration, time of expiration and total time. For these parameters, it was necessary to find the zero cuts of the signal, as can be seen in Fig. 4.

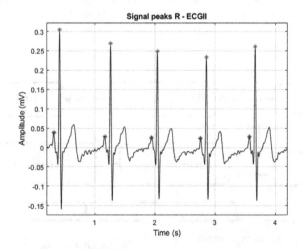

Fig. 3. ECG Lead II, with R peak detection for a subject in sitting position.

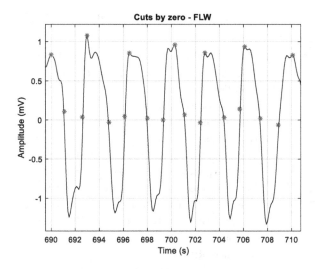

Fig. 4. Cuts by zero of the respiratory flow signal.

Complexity measurements

Complexity features allow us to obtain quantitative values related to the complex behavior of the cardiorespiratory system. These non-linear features allow an assessment of the signals which has been related with physiological and pathological states, i.e. epilepsy seizures, migraine, sustained attention, among others [17]. In particular, three features were computed: Hjörth complexity and mobility [14] and Higuchi fractal dimension [15].

2.4   Spectral Features

Power spectral density (PSD), estimated through Welch method [18], with 50% of overlapping and Hamming windowing, was computed to analyze the composition of the signal in frequency. Power of QRS (0.5 Hz to 4 Hz band), P and T waves (4 Hz to 8 Hz band) and half-power frequency in the ECG signals were obtained from PSD.

In addition, from HRV signal, very low frequency power (0 Hz to 0.004 Hz), low frequency power (0.04 to 0.15 Hz) and high frequency power (0.15 Hz to 0.4 Hz) were computed.

2.5   Statistical Analysis

Each signal was analyzed considering sliding windows of 30 s, with and over-lapping of 50%. A total of 187 features were extracted for each window. Table 2 presents the description of the temporal and spectral features extracted for each window and each signal.

Table 2. Features extracted

Signal	Domain	Features
ECG	Frequency	Relative Power of P and T wave 4 Hz – 8 Hz (PowPT)
		Relative Power of wave QRS 0.5 Hz – 4 Hz (PowQRS)
		Peak Frequency
		Peak Frequency Amplitude
		Total Power
		Half Frequency Power
		Low Frequency of RR intervals - 0.04 -0.15 Hz
		High Frequency of RR intervals - 0.15 -0.4 Hz
		Very Low Frequency of RR Intervals - 0-0.04 Hz
	Time	Average of RR Intervals, R peak and ECG signal
		Mobility RR Intervals, R peak and ECG signal
		Complexity RR Intervals, R peak and ECG signal
		Maximum RR Intervals and ECG signal
		Minimum RR Intervals, R peak and ECG signal
		Fractal Dimension RR Intervals, R peak and ECG signal
		Standard Derivation RR Intervals, R peak and ECG signal
		Median RR Intervals, R peak and ECG signal
		Kurtosis RR Intervals, R peak and ECG signal
		Covariance RR Intervals, R peak and ECG signal
FLW	Time	Inspiration Time in seconds
		Expiration Time in seconds
		Total time in seconds
		Expiration Area
		Inspiration Area
		Absolute Area
		FLW signal

In order to identify the features with statistically significant differences, a parametric t-Student test was applied, with 5% significance level.

2.6 Classification Techniques

A model was trained from the data with some spectral and temporal features extracted from signals described in the Table 2. Only the features with significant differences were fed to the models.These models a holdout validation scheme, with 80% of the samples (windows) for training and 20% of the samples for testing. Three main machine learning techniques were used: decision trees, k-nearest neighbor and support vector machines:

- *Decision trees* – Are flowchart-like structures in which each internal node represents a "test" on an attribute, each branch represents the outcome of the test, and each leaf node represents a class label, this means, decision is taken after computing all attributes. The paths from root to leaf represent classification rules [19].
  In this study, three types of decision trees were implemented: fine, with a maximum number of splits equals to 100; medium with 20 maximum splits; and coarse, with only 4 maximum number of splits.
- *K-Nearest Neighbor (KNN)* uses a predictive model. The input consists of the k closest samples in the feature space of study, and the output is a class membership. An object is classified by a proximity of its neighbors, being assigned to the class most common among its k nearest neighbors [20].
  Five different KNN models were trained: fine, medium and coarse KNN, varying the parameter k with values 1, 10 and 100. In addition, a cosine KNN (cosine distance metric) with k equals 10 and a weighted KNN (different weights based on distance) with k equals 10 were trained.
- *Support Vector Machines (SVM)* are based on transforming data into a higher dimensional space to convert a complex classification problem into a simpler one that can be solved by a linear discriminant function, known as a hyperplane, and defined by [21, 22]

$$f(x) = wz + b = \sum_{i}^{L} \alpha_i y_i K(x_i y_i) + b$$

where w is the normal vector to the hyperplane. The function $K(x_i\ y_i)$ is the Kernel function that will shape the hyperplane and αi and b define the efficiency of the classifier on the optimal values. In this study we evaluated linear and quadratic and cubic kernels.

3   Results

3.1   Statistical Analysis

Once the t-student test is done, it was obtained that 148 features present significant differences from the 187 total features.

In the bar diagram shown in Fig. 5, the average value of some of the features of interest is presented. For the implementation of a machine learning model, only those features, with significant differences were taken into account.

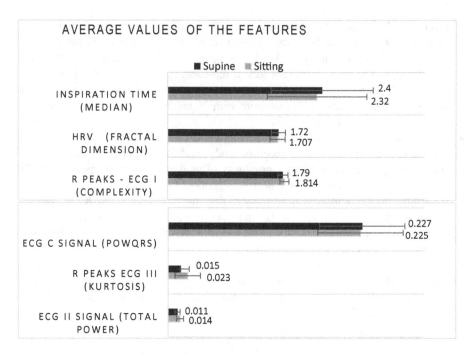

Fig. 5. Average values of the features.

As it can be seen in Fig. 5, the average values of the features do not show large differences between the sitting and supine posture, and their standard deviation is very large, however the parametric test determined that these allow to describe the physiologic behavior depending on the position, and through machine learning model corroborated that it can be determined if a subject is in a sitting or supine posture using their cardiac and respiratory signals.

3.2   Machine Learning Models

Table 3 describes accuracy scores according to trained models, and linear Support Vector Machine (SVM) shows the highest accuracy. Overall, accuracy is over 93%.

As shown in Table 3, the best performance was obtained for the linear SVM model. Its sensitivity was 99.2% and its specificity was 99.6%.

A great variety of studies have been carried out focused on the analysis of posture through the use of sensors, image capture or physiological records, and implementing models of automatic learning. Some of the applications of these models is facial recognition, classification of gestures, posture correction or monitoring while driving, among others [23–25]. However, this study seeks to determine how physiological signals can be affected by posture, and thereby may provide evidence to investigate if there is an adequate position to perform clinical studies with greater clarity.

It was also possible to train a machine learning model that allows to classify between the supine and sitting position from the cardiac and respiratory signals, in

Table 3. Accuracy scores and training time according to training models.

Classification model	Model	Accuracy	Hyperparameters	Training time (s)
Decision tree	Fine Tree	94.6%	Maximum Splits: 100	4.5
	Medium Tree	95.4%	Maximum Splits: 20	5.7
	Coarse Tree	93.6%	Maximum Splits: 4	4.3
K-Nearest Neighbor (KNN)	Fine Knn	98.5%	K: 1 Distance: Euclidean	6.4
	Medium Knn	92.4%	K: 10. Distance: Euclidean	5.2
	Coarse Knn	95.7%	K: 100. Distance: Euclidean	6.1
	Cosine Knn	97.8%	K: 10. Distance: Cosine	5.3
	Weighted Knn	99.2%	K:10. Distance: Euclidean	5.8
Support Vector Machines (SVM)	Cubic SVM	96.5%	C: 1. Kernel Scale: 1	6
	Quadratic SVM	97.3%	C: 1. Kernel Scale: 1	7.2
	Linear SVM	**99.5%**	C: 1. Kernel Scale: 1	**7.6**

order to provide monitoring tools to the medical area. In other studies, the analysis of the posture can be determined using sensors incorporated in everyday objects, in combination with machine learning models [25]; however, a continuous monitoring is not always possible.

4 Conclusions

It is possible to use statistical and computer tools for design machine learning models that allow us to identify the subject posture with an accuracy of 99.5%. Future works may use spectral and temporal analysis with other physiological signals such as Electromyography (EMG), Electrogastrography (EGG), Electroretinography, among others, in order to validate how the trace of the signal is being affected according to the posture.

A machine learning model capable of the identification of the posture of the subject based on their cardiac and respiratory signals, with an accuracy of 99.5%, provides a tool for clinical applications. For instance, in the case of a patient with restricted mobility, the proposed model may warn clinical staffs when the subject has a harmful posture. Also using the machine learning model, posture of subjects wearing intelligent garments in their house could be determined.

Acknowledgements. This work supported in part by CERCA Program, the Secretariat of Universities and Research of the Department of Economy and Knowledge of the Government of Catalonia (GRC 2017 SGR 1770) and the Spanish Ministry of Economy and Competitiveness (DPI2015-68820-R MINECO/FEDER).

References

1. Serra, M., Iturralde Torres, P., Aranda Fraustro, A.: Orígenes del conocimiento de la estructura y función del sistema cardiovascular. Arch. Cardiol. México **83**(3), 225–231 (2013)
2. Thibodeau, A., Patton, K.T.: Structure and Function of the Body, 13th edn. Mosby/Elsevier, Missouri (2008)
3. Dabbagh, A., Imani, A., Rajaei, S.: Cardiac Physiology. In: Dabbagh, A., Esmailian, F., Aranki, S. (eds.) Postoperative Critical Care for Adult Cardiac Surgical Patients, pp. 25–74. Springer, Cham (2018). https://doi.org/10.1007/978-3-319-75747-6_3
4. Madias, J.E.: Comparability of the standing and supine standard electrocardiograms and standing sitting and supine stress electrocardiograms. J. Electrocardiol **39**(2), 142–149 (2006)
5. Muehlhan, M., Marxen, M., Landsiedel, J., Malberg, H., Zaunseder, S.: The effect of body posture on cognitive performance: a question of sleep quality. Front. Hum. Neurosci. **8**, 171 (2014)
6. El-Saadawy, H., Tantawi, M., Shedeed, Howida A., Tolba, M.F.: Diagnosing heart diseases using morphological and dynamic features of electrocardiogram (ECG). In: Hassanien, A.E., Shaalan, K., Gaber, T., Tolba, Mohamed F. (eds.) AISI 2017. AISC, vol. 639, pp. 342–352. Springer, Cham (2018). https://doi.org/10.1007/978-3-319-64861-3_32
7. Tan, M.Y., Ong, T., Sivam, J., Al-Shuft, H., Sahota, O., Salem, K.: 32the role of dynamic supine-sitting spinal radiographs in the management of vertebral fragility fractures admitted to hospital. Age Ageing **47**(suppl_3), iii9–iii12 (2018)
8. Sierra-Silvestre, E., Bosello, F., Fernández Carnero, J., Hoozemans, M.J.M., Coppieters, M. W.: Femoral nerve excursion withe knee and neck movements in supine, sitting and side-lying slump: an in vivo study using ultrasound imaging. Musculoskelet. Sci. Pract. **37**, 58–63 (2018)
9. Cicolini, G., et al.: Differences in blood pressure by body position (supine, fowler's, and sitting) in hypertensive subjects. Am. J. Hypertens. **24**(10), 1073–1079 (2011)
10. Zuttin, R.S., Moreno, M.A., César, M.C., Martins, L.E.B.: Evaluation of autonomic heart rate modulation among sedentary young men, in sitting and supine postures. Braz. J. Phys. Ther. **12**(1), 7–12 (2008). Revista Brasileira de Fisioterapia, 6p. 1 Chart, 2 Graphs
11. Nemec, B., Petrič, T., Babič, J., Supej, M.: Estimation of alpine skier posture using machine learning techniques. Sensors **14**(10), 18898–18914 (2014)
12. Antunes, B.O., de Souza, H.C.D., Gianinis, H.H., Passarelli-Amaro, R.D.C.V., Tambascio, J., Gastaldi, A.C.: Peak expiratory flow in healthy, young, non-active subjects in seated, supine, and prone postures. Physiother. Theory Pract. **32**(6), 489–493 (2016)
13. Kim, Y., Son, Y., Kim, W., Jin, B., Yun, M.: Classification of children's sitting postures using machine learning algorithms. Appl. Sci. **8**(8), 1280 (2018)

14. Cecchin, T., Ranta, R., Koessler, L., Vespignani, H., Maillard, L., Caspary, O.: Seizure lateralization in scalp EEG using Hjorthparameters. Clin. Neurophysiol. **121**(3), 290–300 (2010)
15. Falconer, K.: Geometría Fractal, p. 308. Wiley, Nueva York (2003). ISBN 978-0-470-84862-3
16. Pan, J., Tompkins, W.J.: A real-time QRS detection algorithm. IEEE Trans. Biomed. Eng. **BME-32**(3), 230–236 (1985)
17. Liu, Y., Lin, Y., Wang, J., Shang, P.: Refined generalized multiscale entropy analysis for physiological signals. Phys. A Stat. Mech. Appl. **490**, 975–985 (2018)
18. Welch, P.D.: The use of fast Fourier transform for the estimation of power spectra: a method based on time averaging over short, modified periodograms. IEEE Transactions on audio and electroacoustics **15**(2), 70–73 (1967)
19. Kamiński, B., Jakubczyk, M., Szufel, P.: A framework for sensitivity analysis of decision trees. CEJOR **26**, 135–159 (2017)
20. Altman, N.: An introduction to kernel and nearest-neighbor nonparametric regression. Am. Stat. **46**, 175–185 (1992)
21. Steinwart, I., Chrismann, A.: Super Vector Machine. Information Science and Statistics. Springer, Heidelberg (2008). https://doi.org/10.1007/978-0-387-77242-4
22. Garde, A., Schroeder, R., Voss, A., Caminal, P., Benito, S., Giraldo, B.F.: Patients on weaning trials classified with support vector machines. Physiol. Meas. **31**, 979–993 (2010)
23. Vatavu, R.-D.: Beyond features for recognition: human-readable measures to understand users' whole-body gesture performance. Int. J. Hum.-Comput. Interact. **33**(9), 713–730 (2017)
24. Rasouli, M.S., Payandeh, S.: A novel depth image analysis for sleep posture estimation. J. Ambient Intell. Hum. Comput. **10**(5), 1999–2014 (2019)
25. Zemp, R., et al.: Application of machine learning approaches for classifying sitting posture based on force and acceleration sensors. Biomed. Res. Int. **2016**, 1–9 (2016)

Automatic Fault Detection in a Cascaded Transformer Multilevel Inverter Using Pattern Recognition Techniques

Diego Salazar-D'antonio[1(✉)] 🆔, Nohora Meneses-Casas[1,2] 🆔,
Manuel G. Forero[1] 🆔, and Oswaldo López-Santos[1] 🆔

[1] Facultad de Ingeniería, Universidad de Ibagué, Ibagué, Colombia
{fernando.salazar,nohora.meneses,manuel.forero,
oswaldo.lopez}@unibague.edu.co
[2] Facultad de Ciencias Naturales Y Matemáticas, Universidad de Ibagué,
Ibagué, Colombia

Abstract. Cascade transformer multilevel inverters (CT-MLI) are DC–AC converters used in medium and high power applications to provide standardized AC output. Despite their numerous advantages and robustness, these devices are highly susceptible to fault events because of their high amount of components. Therefore, early failure detection enables turning off the power system avoiding the propagation of the fault to the connected loads. Beyond that, converter operation can be reconfigured to tolerate the fault and activate a fail flag facilitating the subsequent corrective maintenance. The techniques proposed so far required several sensors, which is not practical. Therefore, in this study, we propose an automatic fault detection algorithm for cascade multilevel inverters based on pattern recognition, that only requires a sensor located at the output of the inverter. Naive Bayes, decision tree, nearest neighbor, and support vector machine were tested as classifiers using cross validation. The proposed method showed high detection accuracy when all the obtained descriptors were employed, being the K-NN the classifier showing superior performance. Furthermore, an evaluation was developed to determine the minimum number of descriptors required for the effective operation of the detection system, reducing the computational cost and simplifying its implementation. The method was validated by using simulation results obtained from a multilevel inverter circuit model.

Keywords: Automatic fault detection · Machine learning ·
Pattern recognition · Switching pattern · Multilevel inverter · Power electronics

1 Introduction

Cascaded transformer multilevel inverter (CT-MLI) topologies are structures composed by multiple stages, each one integrating a power converter and a low frequency transformer. In the majority of known topologies, the inverter stages inputs are connected in parallel to the same DC source and the outputs in serial. CT-MLI can be classified as symmetrical or asymmetrical, depending on the turns ratios of the

© Springer Nature Switzerland AG 2019
A. Morales et al. (Eds.): IbPRIA 2019, LNCS 11867, pp. 378–385, 2019.
https://doi.org/10.1007/978-3-030-31332-6_33

transformers, i.e., if they are equal or not. The building of the output signal is accomplished by stages commutating in a synchronous way named as switching pattern. According to the number of inverter stages, the turns ratios of the transformers and the switching pattern, the inverter can produce more or fewer output levels which affects directly the quality of the output signal [1–3]. Then diagnosis methods are fundamental to predict failures, avoid fault propagation, provide fault tolerant modes or isolate the system [4].

Fault diagnosis in multilevel inverters cannot rely on detection per element or stage because it is required multiple measurements, signal acquisitions, and highly complex algorithms and electronics. Therefore, many algorithms take measurement of output voltage and current and perform fault detection looking for specific anomalies in the operation of the system. Anomalies produced by power semiconductors can be attributed to a permanent state in which the control signal cannot have effect because one or more elements are damaged keeping into short circuit or open circuit. Detection of open-circuit failures is more difficult because short-circuits failures easily enforce the action of fuses and other current protection elements [5, 6]. However, considering that inverter has multiple stages and also that power levels are considerably high, in some cases short-circuit failures cannot be detected. Conventional methods operate continuously reviewing changes in the output or current waveforms that indicate the presence of a fault or using features which are computed for at least a cycle of the signal or, in best cases, involving a sliding window to increase the rapidity of the detection. The indicators mainly used are the normalized DC component or average value, the total harmonic distortion (THD), the RMS value [7–10].

Thanks to the advancements in artificial intelligence and the interest to apply these methods in diagnosis of power electronics systems, pattern recognition techniques has been also developed for multilevel inverters. Artificial neural networks (ANN) combined with discrete wavelet transform is presented in [11], where feature extraction of energy content and mean during transient is accomplished using Clark's transform. Classification and localization of faults in an induction motor drive using ANN shows a performance higher than 97.5% in a symmetric multilevel inverter of two stages where input currents are used to extract features [12].

Among the classifiers found in the literature for pattern recognition in multilevel inverters, it can be mentioned the Bayesian classifier called Naive Bayes (NB) [13], the support vector machine classifier (SVM) [14], the multiclass relevance SVM [15], and the k-Nearest Neighbors classifier (K-NN) [16]. The detection accuracy of the above-mentioned methods ranges from 85% to 99%. As a positive impact of the use of the fault detection capability of these techniques [20, 21], the control of the inverters can be complemented with fault tolerant or reconfiguration modes in which the system can temporarily operates when a failure occurs. For instance, in [17] when an inverter stage fails, the rest of the stages changes the switching pattern to obtain an output signal with reduced levels while keeping high quality. In this way, the failed stage is by-passed and the others operate with a different modulation index to compensate for the absence [18]. To potentiate the application of all these techniques in the industry context, relevant aspects are the computational cost in both memory resources and processing time, being the improvement of these features a relevant challenge for future research in this field. However, all the mentioned methods require several sensors, one located at the output of each stage, which is not practical. Therefore, in this paper, a new fault detection method based on pattern recognition is introduced, which requires sensing only the voltage output of the inverter.

The transformer based multilevel inverter in which the method is applied consists of four stages (16 power semiconductor devices, four MOSFETs for stage) and is fed by a single DC source (see more details in [19, 23]).

2   Materials

Multilevel inverters generate an AC output voltage waveform that is built using discrete amplitude steps. As the number of levels in the voltage waveform increases, higher quality is demonstrated because the total harmonic distortion (THD) decreases. A high number of levels (more than 35) may be unnecessary and unachievable, in a practical sense, because a lower amount of levels can comply with international standards which define 5% as the permissible limit level for THD. In this paper, the target inverter topology has four stages in which ratios between stages are defined as 6:7:8:9. With this ratio, the inverter can produce until 35 levels in the output signal (see more details in [19, 23]). The inverter output voltage is given mathematically by the algebraic sum of the stages output voltages.

The studied multilevel inverter uses 16 power semiconductor devices (4 for each H-bridge). Each one can suffer a breakdown that would lead to a permanent short or open circuit state. Furthermore, some failures can affect more than one semiconductor device simultaneously, thus increasing the set of potential fail events. Thereafter, the proposed automatic fault detection algorithm was designed to recognize and localize the malfunctions of the inverter. Figure 1 shows the simulated output inverted signals. Gaussian noise was added with an amplitude of 5 v and an uniform distribution, this value is higher than the noise normally found.

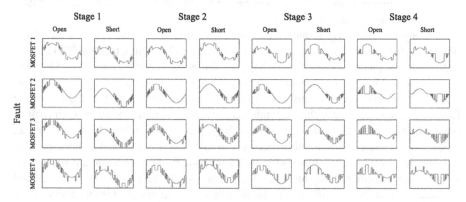

Fig. 1. CT–MLI output voltages, short circuit fail and open circuit fail.

3 Methods

The 60 Hz AC output voltage taken from the CT–MLI model was employed to construct three signal databases to train and test the machine learning-based algorithms. Each database contains a different number of sample points per signal. The first database, as is observed in Fig. 2a, is composed of 835 uniformly separated samples per cycle. The second one, as illustrated in Fig. 2b, is composed only of the samples taken at the points where there is a voltage change in the signal; it is composed of 120 nonuniformly separated samples per cycle. Finally, the third database (Fig. 2c) was a quarter of the period of the voltage signal sampled only in level change events; resulting in 30 data per cycle at 60 Hz (first quarter of the negative half-cycle was selected).

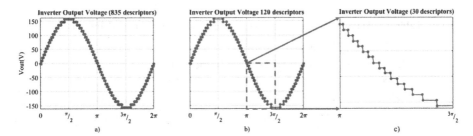

Fig. 2. The samples acquired (a) using sample time of 1 μs (835 descriptors); (b) every switching event (120 descriptors); (c) every switching event (30 descriptors).

Therefore, the database was built with 3300 signals for each sample type, used for the development and evaluation of the proposed method see Fig. 3. The first 100 signals were taken in normal operation without fails, the next signals were taken when some stage had a fault in one device H-bridge, with possibilities that device remained in open circuit or short circuit, 100 signals for each device fault in groups of 800 signals for the stage. The target data were chosen as "0" for normal operation, "1" stage 1 fault and so on.

Data	Target	Target_names
100 signals in normal operation	0	ok
400 signals with short circuit in some MOSFET 400 signals with open circuit in some MOSFET	1	inveter 1 damage
400 signals with short circuit in some MOSFET 400 signals with open circuit in some MOSFET	2	inveter 2 damage
400 signals with short circuit in some MOSFET 400 signals with open circuit in some MOSFET	3	inveter 3 damage
400 signals with short circuit in some MOSFET 400 signals with open circuit in some MOSFET	4	inveter 4 damage

3300 signals

Descriptors

Fig. 3. The database build

The study used a Apple Macbook Air model A1466 with 4 GB DDR3 of memory, a Intel Core i5 processor @ 1.3 GHz and a Intel HD 1536 MB graphics card. The signal database was acquired in PSIM and developed in Phyton 2.7. The machine learning algorithms were implemented in Phyton 2.7, using the Scikit-learn library.

4   Results

4.1   Parameter Estimation

To train the learning algorithms, 75% of the simulated data were used (2310 samples) for the estimation of the parameters using cross validation. The remaining 25% (990 samples) of the data were used to find the optimal values of each classifier according to the precision, as presented in Table 1.

Table 1. Parameters selected for the different machine learning algorithms.

Classifier	Parameter	Value
Decision tree	Number of samples per division	10
K-NN	Number of neighbors	5
SVM	Kernel	Radial basis function
	Gamma	0.001

To evaluate the methods, a second database was created. This database with more fails, two for stage and make a test with the data previously training. The build was with 400 signals for each stage. Finally, classification was performed, and the accuracy of the four methods was evaluated see Table 4.

4.2   Classification

Once the parameters of interest for each of the analyzed algorithms were selected, we proceeded with the training and precision calculations using cross validation. The times required to perform the training classification of the selected samples are shown in Tables 2 and 3 shows the performance of the classifiers in terms of accuracy for each sample size. The NB method is the least complex among the classification methods; however, it demonstrates good results and easy implementation. The K-NN results are also acceptable, but this method runs very slowly, thus increasing computation time and memory usage. The results seems to be sufficient even though only 3.6% of the original data was used.

Table 2. Classification execution per signal times in microseconds (mS)

Classifier	Time by sample 1	Time by sample 2	Time by sample 3
NB	0.07673	0.00766	0.00253
Decision tree	0.00265	0.00114	0.00079
K-NN	0.74247	0.13251	0.06057
SVM	1.74362	0.12284	0.02383

Table 3. Classifier accuracy according to datatype.

Classifier	Sample 1	Sample 2	Sample 3
NB	0.82	0.6948	0.7239
Decision tree	1	1	1
K-NN	0.9997	0.9991	0.9982
SVM	1	1	1

Table 4. Classifier accuracy for more fails for stage according to database.

Classifier	Sample 1	Sample 2	Sample 3
NB	0.5	0.5	0.75
Decision tree	0.5	0.5	0.75
K-NN	1	1	1
SVM	1	0	0

Like Lilula et al. [22], who proposed a fast and reliable power island detection method based on the wave coefficients of the transient waveforms, it was found, as it is shown in Table 3, the decision tree classifier produced the best accuracy.

5 Discussion

Table 2 show that the pattern recognition classification time is much smaller than the period time per cycle, it means that in one cycle the fail will be detected, also in Table 3 can be observe that accuracy to classification is superior to 70%. Decision Trees, K-NN and SVM are roughly equal. However, the presented methods are computationally efficient because it does not require higher training and does not require a large amount of memory and computer resources. In addition, it presented the highest precision of the studied algorithms. Among the other methods, the SVM presented the highest precision, even though it requires a long analysis time. The Decision Trees, conversely, was the fastest algorithm and had a precision better to that of the SVM, making this case the best option for this type of method. Additionally, in Table 4 is observed that despite without database training the accuracy is acceptable by sample 3 using NB, Decision Tree, and K–NN classifiers.

6 Conclusions

In this study, a new pattern recognition algorithm for automatic detection and location of faults in cascaded multilevel inverters was proposed and validated. The four tested and compared classifiers, namely NB, decision tree, K-NN and SVM show good accuracy in failure detection. The decision tree classifier showed the best results regardless of the number of descriptors, followed by SVM method which runs very slowly, which increases the calculation time and the memory usage. Furthermore, it was observed that a similar performance was obtained using the complete set of samples taken from a cycle of the output voltage waveform (120 descriptors) and the second half of the negative half cycle (30 descriptors) in all classifiers, except in NB. By summarizing, although there are more powerful techniques for pattern recognition, the K-NN classifier shows good performance and accuracy detecting and locating faults in the studied multilevel inverter. This work is being currently extended by involving more possible failure events with the aim to provide information to correctly reconfigure the inverter in a fault tolerance mode.

Simulated results using an inverter model were obtained, demonstrating the feasibility of the proposal. The effectiveness and performance of the method were assessed with tested with four different classifiers: NB, decision trees, K-NN and SVM. It was also observed the number of descriptors can be reduced without affecting the detection accuracy, which demonstrates the quality of the proposed classifier.

Acknowledgment. This research was developed with partial support of the Departamento Nacional de Ciencia, Tecnología e Innovación COLCIENCIAS under contract CT-018-2016 and the Universidad de Ibagué under project 18–543–INT. Authors want to express their gratitude to previous experimental developments of the Research Hotbed on Control for Energy Processing (SICEP), Research Group D + TEC, Universidad de Ibagué.

References

1. Rodriguez, J., Lai, J.-S., Zheng, F.: Multilevel inverters: a survey of topologies, controls, and applications. IEEE Trans. Ind. Electron. **49**, 724–738 (2002). https://doi.org/10.1109/TIE. 2002.801052
2. Panda, A.K., Suresh, Y.: Performance of cascaded multilevel inverter by employing single and three-phase transformers. IET Power Electron. **5**(9), 1694–1705 (2012). https://doi.org/ 10.1049/iet-pel.2011.0270
3. Farakhor, A., Reza-Ahrabi, R., Ardi, H., Najafi-Ravadanegh, S.: Symmetric and asymmetric transformer based cascaded multilevel inverter with minimum number of components. IET Power Electron. **8**, 1052–1060 (2015). https://doi.org/10.1049/iet-pel.2014.0378
4. Raj, N., George, S., Jagadanand, G.: Open transistor fault detection in asymmetric multilevel inverter. In: IEEE International Conference Signal Processing, Informatics, Communication and Energy Systems (SPICES), pp. 1–5 (2015). https://doi.org/10.1109/spices.2015. 7091480
5. Ge, X., Pu, J., Gou, B., Liu, Y.-C.: An open-circuit fault diagnosis approach for single-phase three-level neutral-point-clamped converters. IEEE Trans. Power Electron. **33**, 2559–2570 (2018)
6. Mukherjee, S., Zagrodnik, M.A., Wang, P., Royce, R.: Fast fault detection of open power switch in cascaded h-bridge multilevel inverters. In: IEEE Transportation Electrification Conference Expo (ITEC), pp. 1–5 (2016)
7. Ventura, R.P.S., Mendes, A.M.S., Cardoso, A.J.M.: Fault detection in multilevel cascaded inverter using park's vector approach with balanced battery power usage. In: Proceedings 14th European Conference Power Electronics and Applications, pp. 1–10 (2011)
8. Anand, A., Raj, N., Saly, G., Jadaganan, G.: Open switch fault detection in cascaded H-bridge multilevel inverter using normalized mean voltages. In: IEEE 6th International Conference on Power Systems (ICPS), New Delhi, pp. 1–6 (2016). https://doi.org/10.1109/ icpes.2016.7584128

9. Mhiesan, H., et al.: A method for open-circuit faults detecting, identifying, and isolating in cascaded H-bridge multilevel inverters. In: IEEE International Symposium Power Electronincs Distributed Generation Systems (PEDG), Charlotte, NC, pp. 1–5 (2018). https://doi.org/10.1109/pedg.2018.8447855

10. Hedesh, S.H.M., Zolghadri, M.R.: Open-circuit fault detection and localization in five-level active NPC converter. In: Proceedings 43rd Annual Conference of the IEEE Industrial Electronics Society (IECON), pp. 4763–4768 (2017). https://doi.org/10.1109/iecon.2017.8216821

11. Rohan, A., Kim, S.H.: Fault detection and diagnosis system for a three-phase inverter using a DWT-based artificial neural network. Int. J. Fuzzy Log. Intell. Syst. **16**, 238–245 (2016)

12. Khomfoi, S., Tolbert, L.M.: Fault diagnostic system for a multilevel inverter using a neural network. IEEE Trans. Power Electron. **22**(3), 1062–1069 (2007). https://doi.org/10.1109/TPEL.2007.897128

13. Chen, D., Ye, Y., Hua, R.: Fault diagnosis of three-level inverter based on wavelet analysis and Bayesian classifier. IEEE Trans. Power Electron. **33**, 2559–2570 (2018). https://doi.org/10.1109/CCDC.2013.6561798

14. Wang, T., Qi, J., Xu, H., Wang, Y., Liu, L., Gao, D.: Fault diagnosis method based on FFT-RPCA-SVM for cascaded-multilevel inverter. ISA Trans. **60**, 156–163 (2016)

15. Wang, T., Xu, H., Han, J., Elbouchikhi, E., El Hachemi, M.: Cascaded H-bridge multilevel inverter system fault diagnosis using a PCA and multiclass relevance vector machine approach. IEEE Trans. Power Electron. **30**, 7006–7018 (2015)

16. Kuraku, N.V.P., Ali, M., He, Y.: Open circuit fault diagnosis of cascaded H-Bridge MLI using k-NN classifier based on PPCA. In: Hassanien, A.E., Tolba, Mohamed F., Elhoseny, M., Mostafa, M. (eds.) AMLTA 2018. AISC, vol. 723, pp. 426–436. Springer, Cham (2018). https://doi.org/10.1007/978-3-319-74690-6_42

17. Barriuso, P., Dixon, J., Flores, P., Morán, L.: Fault-tolerant reconfiguration system for asymmetric multilevel converters using bidirectional power switches. IEEE Trans. Ind. Electron. **56**, 1300–1306 (2009)

18. Khomfoi, S., Tolbert, L.M.: Fault diagnosis and reconfiguration for multilevel inverter drive using AI-based techniques. IEEE Trans. Ind. Electron. **54**, 2954–2968 (2007). https://doi.org/10.1109/TIE.2007.906994

19. Lopez-Santos, O., Corredor-Ramirez, J.R., Salazar-Dantonio, D.F.: Computational tool for simulation and automatic testing of a single-phase cascaded multilevel inverter. Commun. Comput. Inf. Sci. **812**, 1–20 (2018)

20. Zhang, N., Wu, L., Yang, J., Guan, Y.: Naive Bayes bearing fault diagnosis based on enhanced independence of data. Sensors **18**(2), 463 (2018)

21. Venkatasubramanian, V., Rengaswamy, R., Kavuri, S.N., Yin, K.: A review of process fault detection and diagnosis: PART III: PROCESS history based methods. Comput. Chem. Eng. **27**(3), 327–346 (2003)

22. Lidula, N.W.A., Rajapakse, A.D.: Fast and reliable detection of power islands using transient signals. In: 2009 International Conference on Industrial and Information Systems (ICIIS), pp. 493–498, (December 2009)

23. Lopez-Santos, O., Jacanamejoy-Jamioy, C.A., Salazar-D'Antonio, D.F., Corredor-Ramírez, J.R., Garcia, G., Martinez-Salamero, L.: A single-phase transformer-based cascaded asymmetric multilevel inverter with balanced power distribution. IEEE Access **7**, 98182–98196 (2019)

Collision Anticipation via Deep Reinforcement Learning for Visual Navigation

Eduardo Gutiérrez-Maestro, Roberto J. López-Sastre[(✉)], and Saturnino Maldonado-Bascón

GRAM, University of Alcalá, Alcalá de Henares, Spain
robertoj.lopez@uah.es
http://agamenon.tsc.uah.es/Investigacion/gram/

Abstract. Visual navigation is the ability of an autonomous agent to find its way in a large and complex environment based on visual information. It is indeed a fundamental problem in computer vision and robotics. In this paper, we propose a deep reinforcement learning approach which is able to learn to navigate a scene to reach a given *visual* target, but anticipating the possible collisions with the environment. Technically, we propose a map-less-based model, which follows an actor-critic reinforcement learning method where the reward function has been designed to be collision aware. We offer a thorough experimental evaluation of our solution in the AI2-THOR virtual environment, where the results show that our proposed method: (1) improves the state of the art in terms of number of steps and collisions; (2) is able to converge faster than a model which does not care about the collisions, simply searching for the shortest paths; and (3) offers an interesting generalization capability to reach visual targets that have never been seen during training.

Keywords: Visual navigation · Deep reinforcement learning · Robotics · Computer vision

1 Introduction

We need robots to learn to navigate as we humans do: taking into account the environment and objects that surround us. This is the main objective of our work. The problem of navigation has been addressed in great depth in recent years. Most of the navigation solutions are considered as map-based methods, that is, a map of the environment is needed in order to make decisions for navigation (*e.g.* [1,2]). Others autonomously reconstruct a map of the environment on the fly and use it to navigate, *e.g.* [3–5], or use a human-guided experience to build the map, *e.g.* [6,7]. Finally, we find the map-less approaches, *e.g.* [8], which do not require a map as they do not have any assumption on the landmarks of the scenes.

© Springer Nature Switzerland AG 2019
A. Morales et al. (Eds.): IbPRIA 2019, LNCS 11867, pp. 386–397, 2019.
https://doi.org/10.1007/978-3-030-31332-6_34

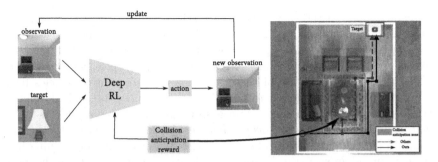

Fig. 1. Would a human in the virtual environment shown in the figure opt to follow the blue or the green path? We propose a deep reinforcement learning model which is designed to learn to navigate towards a visual target in a human-like way. Our model has to look for short trajectories, but also for paths where the collisions can be anticipated, maintaining a reasonable separation margin with the objects in the surroundings. (Color figure online)

Our approach follows this map-less principle, and we present a visual navigation solution which combines recent advances in deep and reinforcement learning. The main goal of our work is to boost robotic navigation towards a human-like behaviour. With this aim, the next question immediately arises: *how does a human learn to navigate within an indoor environment?* Look at Fig. 1. Would a human follow the blue or green path to reach the lamp? We believe that we humans tend to navigate avoiding possible collisions, anticipating them. In other words, we move trying to maintain a margin of separation with the possible obstacles of the environment that surround us.

In this paper we propose a deep reinforcement learning approach which is designed to navigate towards visual targets selecting the shortest path that is separated from possible obstacles. The **scientific contributions** of this work are as follows: **(1)** We introduce a deep reinforcement learning collision aware solution, by the appropriate design of a novel reward function, which enables to minimize the number of steps and to anticipate and avoid the collisions; **(2)** Our thorough experimental evaluation shows that our solution improves the state of the art in the AI2-THOR virtual environment in terms of number of steps and collisions; **(3)** Furthermore, results confirm that the proposed collision aware solution exhibits a better generalization capability and that is able to converge faster than a model which does not explicitly consider collisions during learning.

2   Related Work

The evolution of technology in the field of computer vision has seen breathtaking changes, many of which have to do with the use of reinforcement learning based methods. Reinforcement Learning (RL) has experienced an increasing use in different applications. In [9], a RL-based solution is proposed for the real world problem of elevator dispatching. In [10], it is made use of RL to facilitate an autonomous flight. In [11], a vision-based method using RL is used to teach a robot to shoot a ball into a goal. In [12], it is investigated this type of algorithms in order to provide to a four-legged robot a walking behaviour.

We have also the family of methods that combine deep learning with RL. In [13], the authors make use of these methods to learn control policies from high-dimensional sensory inputs to play ATARI games. In [14], it is developed a system able to detect objects within a scene, in which the agent can find a specific bounding box by using deep reinforcement learning during the agent's training. In [8], the authors introduce a visual-based algorithm for learning how to navigate in indoor scenarios by using a virtual environment to train the models. Our approach directly leverages the model described in [8], to propose a novel visual-navigation solution able to anticipate collisions, hence providing the agent the knowledge to navigate in a secure way. We do this by integrating a collision aware reward function into an actor-critic deep RL model.

3   Navigation with Collision Anticipation

3.1   Navigation Problem

The navigation solution proposed in this work is inspired by the hypothesis that we humans navigate trying to maintain a margin of separation with the possible obstacles of the environment that surround us (see again Fig. 1).

In this work, we propose a system with this ability. We make use of deep reinforcement learning, designing a reward function which is able to transfer to the agent the policy knowledge that maps the visual sensory input into actions in a 3D world, so that both the number of steps and the number of collisions are minimized.

3.2   Model Formulation

To achieve our goal we use a model based on deep reinforcement learning. This section details the different components of our approach to provide a solution that anticipates collisions in indoor environments while the agent moves.

As it is shown in Fig. 1, the inputs to our model are just two images. Technically, we feed a deep siamese network, i.e. with shared weights, with both agent's observation and navigation goal images. This way, the target is implicitly in the input data.

We now define the three key parts of our deep reinforcement learning approach: (i) action space; (ii) observation and goal; and (iii) reward function.

Action Space. The objective of our visual navigation model is to map a high-dimensional 2D input into an action in a 3D space. Here we define the actions that our agent will take according to the input data. All the indoor environments used in this work have been discretized, so that, a *grid* of the world is created. For each cell within this grid, the agent is able to take four different actions: move forward, turn right, turn left, move backward.

Observation and Goal. The agent is provided with a first-person-view camera. Note that each of the observations of the agent represents a state s_t at time t of all possible states S within the environment. The agent must navigate towards the position where the target image has been taken.

Reward. In reinforcement learning, the reward is defined as the feedback by which the success or failure of an agent's action is measured. Every time the agent selects an action, the environment returns a reward r_t at time t. In this work we propose a collision aware reward function, so that the agent is able to learn to anticipate collisions while it navigates. We first define the four main states that guide our reward assignment process. Our first state is called s_{step}, which corresponds to every time the agent executes an action in the navigation environment, i.e. it moves to a position in the grid, but considering the following exceptions. If the agent arrives to the target, the state is called s_{terminal}. If the agent is in a cell with an object or wall that could cause a collision by moving forward or backward, the state is named $s_{\text{collision}}$. Finally, if the agent is in a cell previous to a $s_{\text{collision}}$ state, i.e. in two cells before a collision could occur, we call it $s_{\text{collision}-1}$. Note how these last two states allow the agent to anticipate possible collisions with objects in the environment.

Our reward must be collision aware. Therefore, we design the following reward function that returns a different numerical value depending on the new state induced by the action taken by the agent at a certain time, i.e. s_t:

$$f(s_t) = \begin{cases} 10 & \text{if} \quad s_t = s_{\text{terminal}} \\ \alpha & \text{if} \quad s_t = s_{\text{step}} \\ \beta & \text{if} \quad s_t = s_{\text{collision}} \\ \gamma & \text{if} \quad s_t = s_{\text{collision}-1} \end{cases} . \tag{1}$$

The terminal state receives the maximum reward, indicating to the algorithm that the agent has arrived to the target. For the rest of states we assign different negative small values, being $\alpha = -0.01$, $\beta = -0.02$ and $\gamma = -0.011$. Note that for the collision anticipation states their associated negative values are higher than for the step stage. Our intention is that the agent learns to navigate away from those $s_{\text{collision}-1}$ and $s_{\text{collision}}$ states. In other words, the agent learns to anticipate the states where a collision could occur, which results in a safer navigation. Another way to understand the function of these states is shown in Fig. 1. There, one can observe the top-view of a scene, where there are some red-shadowed areas. These are the zones we do not want our agent to navigate. This fact does not mean that the agent cannot navigate through those states, since the proposed algorithm of deep RL uses *cumulative* rewards. That is, we want the agent to find the combination of states that, at the end of the episode, arises the highest reward as possible. In other words, in certain situations the agent will decide to navigate through these states previously mentioned, so that the target will be achieved earlier. Thus we leave it to the RL model to decide which is the best option autonomously.

According to the model described, at each time step t, our agent receives a representation of the state of the environment, i.e. $s_t \in S$. Based on that

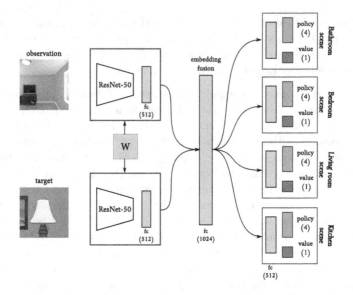

Fig. 2. Here it is shown the deep siamese network used in our work, which is fed by the agent's observation and the navigation target. Siamese layers are ResNet-50 features (truncated the softmax layer) pre-trained on ImageNet. ResNet parameters are frozen during the training stage. It can be appreciated the shared weights updated by each of the trained agents in the global network. At the right side of the figure, we have the specific network layers, which output the policy and value according to the visual sensory input for each particular type of scene.

information the agent selects an action, $a_t \in \mathcal{A}(s_t)$, where $\mathcal{A}(s_t)$ represents all possible actions for state s_t. As a consequence of the action taken, the agent receives a reward, $r_t \in \mathcal{R}$, and discovers a new state s_{t+1}. The way an agent selects an action according to the current state follows a learning *policy*, which is denoted by π_t. Therefore, $\pi_t(s_t, a_t)$ indicates the probability of the agent selecting the action a_t if the agent's state is s_t. The agent changes its policy through a reinforcement learning method, so that the agent gets the best amount of reward in each training episode.

Technically, we propose to follow an actor-critic learning model known as Asynchronous Advantage Actor-Critic (A3C) [15]. A3C is able to use multiple independent agents (in our case, deep networks) with their associated weights. These agents interact in parallel with different copies of the learning environment. In our case, each agent learns to navigate in the same environment but to a different target. Therefore, every agent is trained in parallel and updates in an asynchronous way the weights of a global network, which holds the shared parameters. Specifically, for the deep network of the agent we follow the siamese architecture proposed in [8], see Fig. 2. Our objective is to use a deep siamese actor-critic network to capture the relations between the current agent's location and the target's location, by projecting them to the same embedding space.

Therefore, we need the inputs of the two siamese networks to be the observation of the agent and the visual target. The features learned by the siamese networks are fused to build the joint representation that is used by the final scene specific layers, which are in charge of generating the policy and value outputs of the actor-critic A3C algorithm.

4 Experiments

4.1 Experimental Setup

Dataset. We obtain the data to train and evaluate our model from AI2-THOR [16]. It is a framework that provides environments that look similar to real world scenes: a total of 120 different scenes covering four different categories (kitchens, living rooms, bedrooms, and bathrooms). It also includes actionable objects that an AI agent can interact with. For our *learning to navigate* objective, AI2-THOR results an excellent resource to provide our learning model with photo-realistic pictures of indoor domestic environments where our agent can learn to move. Technically, we follow the experimental setup released in [8], which comprises 4 different scenes, one for each room category.

Evaluation Metric. To evaluate the navigation performance, we use, as in [8]: (1) the number of steps needed by the agent to reach the targets; and (2) the number of collisions during the navigation. For both metrics, the lower the better. We also propose a generalization experiment where we aim to evaluate if the agent is able to navigate to unseen targets during training. For this second experiment we use the success score (sc). This score is defined as follows. Given a scene and a target for that scene, with a fixed number of episodes, we compute sc as the number of episodes for which the agent is able to reach the target with a number of steps that is lower than 500. Since for each target we test the model one hundred times, the resulting sc measures the percentage of times that the agent reaches the goal below a fixed threshold of 500 steps.

4.2 Navigation Results

Navigation Experiment. We compare our collision anticipation model with the state-of-the-art navigation model of Zhu *et al.* [8]. Note that in [8] the authors do not consider collisions during learning, optimizing the agent to find the shortest paths towards the targets only. Table 1 shows the main results.

First, one observes that the number of collisions considerably decreases (an order of magnitude) following our approach. This fact validates the proposed reward function integrated in the reinforcement learning approach. However, it is worth to note that our solution not only minimizes the number of collisions, but also the number of steps. In other words, our model is able to jointly seek the shortest trajectories with the fewest collisions.

Table 1. Navigation results.

	Scene	Bathroom	Bedroom	Living_room	Kitchen	Average
Zhu [8]	Steps	7.17	14.82	15.2	21.38	14.7
	Collisions	0.04	0.12	0.25	0.2	0.15
Ours	Steps	7.33	14.81	14.9	20.83	**14.47**
	Collisions	0.03	0.04	0.15	0.12	**0.082**

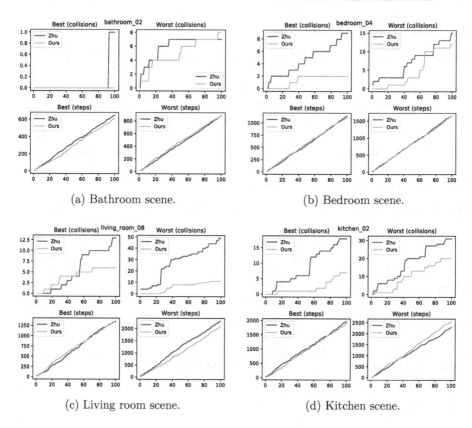

(a) Bathroom scene.   (b) Bedroom scene.

(c) Living room scene.   (d) Kitchen scene.

Fig. 3. Number of steps and collisions accumulated during the evaluation phase for each scene. We show the best and worst cases for each model.

In Fig. 3 we show how the number of collisions and number of steps are accumulated over 100 navigation episodes. For both methods (ours and Zhu [8]) we show the best and the worst cases. In terms of number of steps, we can conclude that both models obtain similar solutions. Since the agent starts the training in random positions within the scene, and taking into account the size of the scenes, which differs among the different categories, to outperform the state-of-the-art model proposed by Zhu *et al.* [8] in terms of number of steps is more complicated. However, our model is below this result as reported in table 1.

But if collisions are considered, our agent clearly performs better, even for the worst cases. Finally, we show qualitative results in the following video[1].

Fast Convergence Experiment. While training our model we are able to examine how the reward function evolves over time, and there is a fact that catches our attention: our model is capable of converging at least to a suboptimal solution much faster than the approach of Zhu *et al.* [8].

To prove this in a quantitatively way, we proceed to evaluate the navigation performance of the models for 5 millions and 10 millions training frames. Figure 4 shows the average for the number of steps and collisions. One can conclude that our approach learns faster. Interestingly, in our model the number of steps reported for 5M is pretty close to the final one reported for 10M. And with respect to the collisions, it is worth to note that although the model of Zhu *et al.* [8] is able to also indirectly minimize them, our model drastically reduces them even for the initial stages of the learning process. As a conclusion: our collision anticipation navigation solution not only outperforms the results in terms of steps and collisions, but also learns faster.

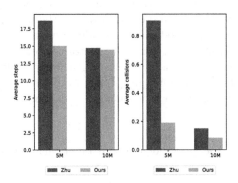

Fig. 4. Average steps and collisions for the fast convergence experiment.

Hard Targets Experiment. For all the previous navigation experiments we strictly follow the original experimental setup provided by Zhu *et al.* [8], using the fixed set of 5 different targets per scene selected by the authors. We here propose to perform an evaluation when a different set of targets is considered. We choose the new set of targets, with the aim of giving robustness to the main objective of our work: collision anticipation for visual navigation systems. For this purpose, in this experiment we select 5 targets per scene, which in terms of collisions and navigation, are harder to reach.

---

[1] https://www.youtube.com/watch?v=Eyxw-FY-iM0.

394   E. Gutiérrez-Maestro et al.

Table 2. Evaluation of the model for the hard targets navigation experiment. 10M training frames.

	Scene	Bathroom	Bedroom	Living_room	Kitchen	Average
Zhu [8]	Steps	7.43	13.76	1323.88	19.17	341.06
	Collisions	0.06	0.15	247.78	0.30	62.07
Ours	Steps	7.29	14.63	568.78	18.89	152.39
	Collisions	0.03	0.08	61.66	0.25	15.5

The results obtained for this experiment are shown in Table 2. Interestingly, the performance of both models, in terms of steps and collisions, decreases, a fact that confirms that the selected targets are actually harder than the original ones. Note that for the evaluation, the agent is thrown into random positions on the scenes, and we measure the number of collisions and steps until he reaches the target. The living room scene contains different objects (sofa, table, chairs, etc.) that difficult the navigation of both models, clearly. One can observe that the performance of our model for the living room class is much better, making the difference between Zhu's model and ours. However, the number of steps needed for this scene is higher than 500 for our model. Overall, there is a huge gap between our model and Zhu *et al.* [8]: the trajectories obtained by our model are shorter and contain less collisions on average. If the methods want to report a similar performance to the original one (shown in Table 1, for the original easy targets), they must be trained for twice as many iterations (for 20M), as Table 3 reveals.

Table 3. Evaluation of the model for the hard targets navigation experiment. 20M training frames.

	Scene	Bathroom	Bedroom	Living_room	Kitchen	Average
Zhu [8]	Steps	7.46	13.92	18.12	18.03	14.38
	Collisions	0.04	0.12	0.2	0.19	0.14
Ours	Steps	7.16	14.15	17.73	17.86	14.225
	Collisions	0.01	0.03	0.05	0.07	0.04

4.3 Target Generalization Experiments

The generalization ability of deep reinforcement learning models is an interesting aspect to evaluate. So, the question here is: are our agents able to navigate towards targets that have *not* been considered during training? We design the following experiments with the objective of evaluating whether our collision anticipation navigation model generalizes appropriately.

We propose two different experiments. The first one evaluates the navigation of our model toward targets that are at 1, 2, 4 and 8 steps away from the

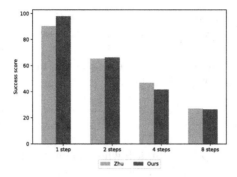

Fig. 5. Success score of the target generalization experiment.

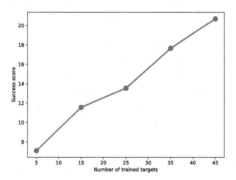

Fig. 6. Evolution of the success score obtained as the number of trained targets is increased.

original trained targets. In other words, what we have done here is to use the model trained for the original targets, whose results were reported in Table 1, but now, the evaluation is performed using *only* the new set of unseen targets. We measure the *sc* of the four scenes, and provide the average.

Figure 5 shows the main results. As expected, the higher the number of steps with respect to the trained targets, the lower the success score, since the problem becomes more difficult. If we compute the average for the 4 situations (1 step, 2 steps, 4 steps and 8 steps) for every method, the model proposed by Zhu *et al.* [8] obtains $sc = 57, 4\%$, while our model reports $sc = 58, 1\%$.

Our second experiment aims to evaluate how the number of objectives used during training affects the ability to generalize. Technically, we select five different fixed targets per scene to evaluate the model. Then, we proceed to train our model for 5, 15, 25, 35 and 45 targets that are incrementally generated. We guarantee that the test targets are never included in the training sets, *i.e.* they always remain unseen during learning.

Figure 6 shows the *sc* of our model as the number of training targets increases. As expected, the *sc* increases when more and more training targets are considered. In conclusion, the generalization ability of the proposed deep RL navigation model needs of some improvements. A simple solution could consist on enriching the training set of targets, as this last experiment has confirmed. But, in any case, further efforts will be necessary in order that the agents achieve new targets, requiring a minimum adjustment of the parameters, or even that they can navigate in scenes never seen before.

5   Conclusions

This work proposes a deep RL approach whose main goal is to learn to navigate towards visual targets selecting the shortest path that is separated from possible obstacles, and hence anticipating collisions. According to the results shown in this work, we expose the following contributions. We have introduced a deep RL collision aware solution, by the appropriate design of a novel reward function. We have done an extensive experimental evaluation showing that our solution improves the state of the art in the AI2-THOR virtual environment in terms of number of steps and collisions. Results also confirm that our model is able to learn faster than a model which does not explicitly consider collisions during learning. Finally, the results show that the proposed collision aware solution exhibits a generalization capability that has to be improved to incorporate both new targets and scenes in the navigation.

Acknowledgments. This work is supported by project PREPEATE (TEC2016-80326-R), of the Spanish Ministry of Economy, Industry and Competitiveness. We gratefully acknowledge the support of NVIDIA Corporation with the donation of the GPU used for this research.

References

1. Borenstein, J., Koren, Y.: Real-time obstacle avoidance for fast mobile robots. IEEE Trans. Syst. Man Cybern. **19**(5), 1179–1187 (1989)
2. Borenstein, J., Koren, Y.: The vector field histogram - fast obstacle avoidance for mobile robots. IEEE Trans. Rob. Autom. **7**, 278–288 (1991)
3. Wooden, D.: A guide to vision-based map building. IEEE Rob. Autom. Mag. **13**(2), 94–98 (2006)
4. Davison, A.J.: Real-time simultaneous localisation and mapping with a single camera. In: ICCV, vol. 2, pp. 1403–1410 (2003)
5. Tomono, M.: 3-d object map building using dense object models with sift-based recognition features. In: 2006 IEEE/RSJ International Conference on Intelligent Robots and Systems, pp. 1885–1890, (October 2006)
6. Kidono, K., Miura, J., Shirai, Y.: Autonomous visual navigation of a mobile robot using a human-guided experience. Rob. Auton. Syst. **40**(2), 121–130 (2006). Intelligent Autonomous Systems - IAS -6
7. Royer, E., Bom, J., Dhome, M., Thuilot, B., Lhuillier, M., Marmoiton, F.: Outdoor autonomous navigation using monocular vision. In: 2005 IEEE/RSJ International Conference on Intelligent Robots and Systems, pp. 1253–1258, (August 2005)

8. Zhu, Y., et al.: Target-driven visual navigation in indoor scenes using deep reinforcement learning. In: IEEE International Conference on Robotics and Automation (2017)
9. Crites, R.H., Barto, A.G.: Improving elevator performance using reinforcement learning. In: Proceedings of the 8th International Conference on Neural Information Processing Systems. NIPS 1995, pp. 1017–1023. MIT Press, Cambridge (1995)
10. Ng, A.Y., et al.: Autonomous inverted helicopter flight via reinforcement learning. In: Ang, M.H., Khatib, O. (eds.) Experimental Robotics IX. STAR, vol. 21, pp. 363–372. Springer, Heidelberg (2006). https://doi.org/10.1007/11552246_35
11. Asada, M., Noda, S., Tawaratsumida, S., Hosoda, K.: Purposive behavior acquisition for a real robot by vision-based reinforcement learning. Mach. Learn. **23**(2), 279–303 (1996)
12. Kimura, H., Yamashita, T., Kobayashi, S.: Reinforcement learning of walking behavior for a four-legged robot. IEEE Trans. Electron. Inf. Syst. **122**(3), 330–337 (2002)
13. Mnih, V., et al.: Playing atari with deep reinforcement learning. In: NIPS Deep Learning Workshop (2013)
14. Caicedo, J.C., Lazebnik, S.: Active object localization with deep reinforcement learning. In: The IEEE International Conference on Computer Vision (ICCV), (December 2015)
15. Mnih, V., et al.: Asynchronous methods for deep reinforcement learning. In: 33rd International Conference on International Conference on Machine Learning. ICML 2016, JMLR.org, pp. 1928–1937 (2016)
16. Kolve, E., et al.: AI2-THOR: An Interactive 3D Environment for Visual AI. arXiv (2017)

Spectral Band Subset Selection for Discrimination of Healthy Skin and Cutaneous Leishmanial Ulcers

Ricardo Franco-Ceballos[1]([⊠]), Maria C. Torres-Madronero[1]([⊠]),
July Galeano-Zea[2], Javier Murillo[3], Artur Zarzycki[2,4],
Johnson Garzon[5], and Sara M. Robledo[3]

[1] Research group on Automatic, Electronic and Computational Science,
Smart Machines and Pattern Recognition Laboratory,
Instituto Tecnologico Metropolitano, Medellin, Colombia
rfrancoce@gmail.com, mariatorres@itm.edu.co
[2] Research group on Advance Materials and Energy MatyEr,
Instituto Tecnologico Metropolitano, Medellin, Colombia
[3] Program for the Study and Control of Tropical Diseases-PECET-School
of Medicine, University of Antioquia, Medellín, Colombia
[4] Research group on Automatic, Electronic and Computational Science,
Robotics and Control System Laboratory, Instituto Tecnologico Metropolitano,
Medellin, Colombia
[5] Grupo de Optica y Espectroscopia, Universidad Pontificia Bolivariana,
Medellin, Colombia

Abstract. Leishmaniasis is a parasitic disease, transmitted by the bite of an insect that has previously fed on an infected host. One of its clinical forms is Cutaneous Leishmaniasis - CL and due to its increasing incidence, it is necessary to create effective and easy-use diagnostic methods. In this paper, we assess two unsupervised band-selection algorithms that allow the dimensional reduction of hyperspectral data taken from CL ulcers, maintaining a high classification accuracy. This is an important task for the development of an non-invasive system based on multispectral imaging, that support the diagnosis and treatment follow-up of cutaneous ulcer caused by Leishmaniasis. Spectral data was obtained in golden hamsters subjected to varying conditions of infection. Two algorithms, one based on similarity and the other based on singular values decomposition, are implemented using MATLAB functions and are applied to the spectral data. The selected subsets of bands are used to classify the spectra into healthy skin, border and ulcer centers using support vector machines - SVM and neural networks - NN. The obtained results are represented in precision tables and allow to observe that both methods achieve an appropriate dimensional reduction of multispectral data without losing key information for their subsequent classification.

Supported by Departamento Administrativo de Ciencia y Tecnologia de Colombia - COLCIENCIAS-, Instituto Tecnológico Metropolitano, Universidad de Antioquia, Universidad Pontificia Bolivariana, and Kinetics Systems S.A.S (Medellin-Colombia), under the project number 57186.

A. Morales et al. (Eds.): IbPRIA 2019, LNCS 11867, pp. 398–408, 2019.
https://doi.org/10.1007/978-3-030-31332-6_35

At the end, we show that it is possible to obtain a subset of spectral bands to discriminate between healthy skin and cutaneous ulcers caused by Leishmaniasis.

Keywords: Leishmaniasis · Hyperspectral data ·
Unsupervised band selection · Spectral reduction · Classification

1 Introduction

Leishmaniasis is a disease caused by protozoan parasites of the genus Leishmania, transmitted by the bite of an infected insect. There are two clinical presentations: Visceral Leishmaniasis (VL) and Cutaneous Leishmaniasis (CL). VL is the most serious and can be fatal. CL does not cause death, but it represents a large burden due to social stigma. Also, CL is related with psychological effects and decreasing of productivity of patients. Since the incidence of this disease is growing, it is necessary to develop new techniques for its diagnosis [1,2,10,11].

Some studies propose the use of spectral data for the diagnosis of skin diseases. Spectral data is refereed to spectral signatures obtained by spectrophotometer, as well as, multispectral or hyperspectral imagery collected by cameras. Spectral system measures the reflected and emitted energy by a surface along the electromagnetic spectrum. Spectral data from skin can provide accurate information to develop non-invasive techniques for the diagnosis of skin diseases. For example, Vyas et al. [14] proposed a non-invasive estimation of skin thickness from hyperspectral imaging; Attia et al. [4] developed a non-invasive real-time characterization of non-melanoma skin cancer; and [6] reviewed several non-invasive techniques for diagnosis of skin cancer, including some based on spectrophotometry data. Despite the advance in this field, more methodologies and techniques are necessary in order to characterize skin ulcers in their different phases of formation and treatment follow-up.

This paper presents results from a project that seeks to develop a portable non-invasive system based on multispectral imaging for the diagnosis and monitoring of skin ulcer treatments caused by Leishmaniasis. For the development of a new multispectectral system, we need to understand the spectral signature of both healthy skin and CL ulcers. An animal model for CL using golden hamsters was employed to build an spectral library. These include several spectra with nearly 2000 bands between 400 nm to 800 nm from healthy skin and ulcers in different phases. In this paper, we presents the evaluation of two unsupervised band selection algorithms, the first based on similarity [7] and the second based on singular value decomposition (SVD) [3]. These algorithms select the most relevant bands for the discrimination of healthy skin and leishmanial ulcers. The comparison of the unsupervised band selection algorithms is performed by using two classifiers: neural network (NN), and support vector machine (SVM).

2   Spectral Band Subset Selection Algorithms

In the literature, several algorithms for band subset selection - BSS can be found. These methods are known as dimensional reduction approaches, which select a set of bands according to a separability criteria. The difference between BSS algorithms with other dimensional reduction approach, such as principal component analysis, is that BSS selects bands from the measured spectrum, allowing the characterization of the materials, and opening the possibility to build low-cost sensing system using the selected bands. For this work, we select two unsupervised BSS algorithms with low computational complexity: similarity-based band selection [7] and singular value decomposition - SVD based band subset selection [3].

2.1   Similarity-Based Band Selection

Du and Yang [7] proposed two unsupervised methods: Linear Prediction - LP and Orthogonal Subspace Projection - OSP, whose basic idea is to look for the most distinctive bands, but ensuring that the selected bands also are the most informative ones. For this paper, we use the LP algorithm, since both algorithms offer the same results, but LP is computationally more efficient by operating relatively smaller matrices. For both, LP and OSP, the hyperspectral data must go through a pre-processing to eliminate water absorption and low signal-to-noise ration bands [7]. Once these bands are removed, a noise whitening is applied. This whitening is easily achieved thanks to the self-decomposition of the covariance matrix, using the method presented in [12].

The algorithm begins with the combination of the two best bands, and this combination increases consecutively until the desired number of bands is selected. The authors suggest a random selection of the first band and then, a projection of the additional bands in the orthogonal subspace of the first band, this to select the bands most dissimilar to each other. However, we chose a different selection method for the first band seeking to improve the performance of this algorithm. Since the LP algorithm seeks also for the most informative ones, we choose the band with the highest variance as the first one. Then, the next band is selected such that it is the most distant from the first one using the euclidean distance [7].

The LP algorithm assumes two bands, B_1 and B_2, belonging to the subset φ, which contains the selected bands, with N pixels each one. To find the band most dissimilar to B_1 and B_2, these bands are used to estimate a third band B using Eq. 1.

$$B' = a_0 + a_1 \, B_1 + a_2 \, B_2 \tag{1}$$

where B' is the linear estimation of B using B_1 and B_2, and a_0, a_1 and a_2 are the parameters that minimize the error of the linear prediction: $e = \parallel B - B' \parallel$. The parameter vector will be $a = (a_0, a_1, a_2)$, which can be determined using the least squares solution shown in 2.

$$a = (X^T \, X)^{-1} X^T y \tag{2}$$

In 2, X is a matrix N x 3 where the first column is one, the second column includes the N pixels of B_1 and the third column includes the pixels of B_2, and y is a vector of N x 1 with the pixels from the band that is being compared. The band B with the minimum error e is the most closely to the band B', and then it is chosen as B_3. This process is iteratively repeated until reaching the desired number of bands. A seudo-code for this procedure is presented in the Algorithm 1.

Algorithm 1. Similarity Band Selection Pseudo-code

1: **function** SUBSETBANDSELECTION (hsi,bands)
2:     $bandSubset(1) \leftarrow$ find max std band of hsi
3:     $bandSubset(2) \leftarrow$ most distant band to $bandSubset(1)$ with euclidean norm
4:     $n \leftarrow$ number of pixels of each hsi bands
5:     **for** $i = 3$ to $bands$ **do**
6:         $X \leftarrow$ Matrix with a ones $nx1$ column vector and each band of
                $bandSubset$ as column vector
7:         **for** each B band in hsi **do**
8:             **if** B is in $bandSubset$ **then**
9:                 $error(index$ of $B) \leftarrow$ -∞
10:            **else**
11:                $A \leftarrow (X'X)^{-1}Xb$
12:                $B' \leftarrow XA$
13:                $error(index$ of $B) \leftarrow \|B - B'\|$
14:            **end if**
15:        **end for**
16:        $bandSubset(i) \leftarrow$ band-index with max $error$
17:    **end for**
18:    **return** $bandSubset$
19: **end function**

2.2   SVD-Based Band Subset Selection

Velez and Jiménez [3] proposed an unsupervised method based on the singular value descomposition - SVD. This method combines the SVD with the revealing range QR factorization and allows to obtain a subset of bands that retain the data meaning without a transformation [3]. The method used the strongly restricted projection of a matrix A (see Eq. 3).

$$A = P \begin{bmatrix} I_p \\ 0 \end{bmatrix} \tag{3}$$

where A is a n x p matrix with $p < n$ and $A^T A = I_P$, and P is a permutation matrix. To compute the permutation matrix, first it is calculate the covariance Σ_{data} for the hyperspectral data. Then, the QR factorization with pivoting is used to compute the matrix V_1^T where V_1 is formed by the first p eigenvectors of Σ_{data}. The pivot matrix P that results from this factorization is the permutation matrix for the Eq. 3. Finally, the first p elements of $\overline{x}$ are the selected bands [3]. A seudo-code for this procedure is presented in the Algorithm 2.

Algorithm 2. SVD-Based Band Subset Selection Pseudo-code

1: **function** SUBSETBANDSELECTION ($hsi, bands$)
2:     $\Sigma_{data} \leftarrow$ covariance of hsi
3:     $p \leftarrow$ desired length of band-subset given in $bands$
4:     $V_1 \leftarrow$ first p eigenvectors of Σ_{data}
5:     $Q,R,P \leftarrow$ QR Factorization wit Pivoting of V_1^T
6:     $\overline{x} \leftarrow P * hsi$
7:     $bandSubset \leftarrow$ first p elements of $\overline{x}$
8:     **return** $bandSubset$
9: **end function**

---

3   Spectral Classification

Classification is a process during which each sample is labeled as a class [8], by applied decision rules, either in the multispectral or spatial domain. Classification process can be done through supervised or unsupervised approaches. Supervised classification uses a prior information to learn the decisions rules. Instead, unsupervised approaches seek for patterns in the data using some similarity criterion. In this paper, we used two supervised classification methods: support vector machines - SVM and neural networks - NN. Both methods are selected for their high performance documented in the literature with spectral data.

3.1   Support Vector Machines - SVM

SVMs are a useful technique for data classification. The objective of using SVM for classification is to find a optimal decision hyperplane to separate unknown data in two or several classes. A kernel can be used to solve the problem for non-linear separable data. Most used kernels for hyperspectral data are polynomial and radial basis function kernel [9].

3.2   Neural Networks - NN

Neural networks are a learning paradigm based on the human brain. These networks are composed of individual units that process information through highly interconnected individual nodes. NN models are useful algorithms for cognitive tasks, such as classification [8]. In this document, an NN classification was implemented with a network formed by a hidden layer of five neurons (nodes).

4   Experimental Procedure

4.1   Data Set

Animal models are widely used to analyze new drugs and treatments. For CL studies, golden hamsters are recommended due to the similarity of their skin structure with human skin [5,13]. Diffuse reflectance spectral from healthy and CL ulcers were acquired using a spectrometer Ocean Optics HR4C3337. The acquired spectra were calibrated using white and black diffuse reflectance standards. A total of 39 golden hamsters, distributed in 18 females and 21 males, were used. Hamsters are subject to several conditions of infection and treatment. For this paper, we used only spectral signatures acquired before treatment. From the 39 golden hamsters, 27 were infected with Leishmaniasis Braziliensis (LB), while 4 were hamsters infected with Leishmaniasis Panamensis (LP), and 8 hamsters were in the control group (i.e. without CL).

Spectral signatures of each hamster's skin are obtained each fifteen days. The first measure is taken before the inoculation of CL, then two more measures are taken during the development of the ulcers. In each date, up to 12 spectra are measured for each area: healthy skin, border and ulcer center. This data collection allows an exhaustive analysis of the evolution of the disease, from the inoculation process followed by the analysis of ulcer development. This protocol had the approval from the Universidad de Antioquia animal ethics committee.

Figure 1 presents the average signatures from healthy skin, ulcer border and ulcer center between 400 nm and 800 nm. After 750 nm, the signature noise increased. We can also see that the spectral response from the ulcer center is lower that from healthy skin; but, the spectral signature from the ulcer border is very similar to healthy skin.

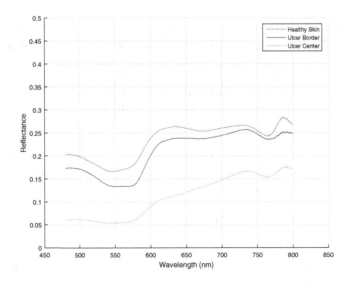

Fig. 1. Average spectral signatures of healthy skin, ulcer border and ulcer center from golden hamsters infected infected with Leishmaniasis

4.2 Experiments

For the evaluation of both BSS algorithms, we used spectral signatures of healthy skin, border and ulcer center captured from Golden hamsters. First, a mean filter with a sliding window of 3 points is applied to each of the captured signatures, in order to reduce noise. Since the bands from 750 nm present higher noise than lower bands, we defined two experiments to analyze the spectral signatures. The first experiment applied the BSS algorithms to spectral signatures between 480 nm to 750 nm, eliminating upper bands for reducing the noise. The second experiment takes all bands between 750 nm to 800 nm. For both BSS algorithms, we select 10 bands. This number is chosen since the selected bands will be used in the development a portable system, and commercial filter wheels for 10 filters are very common. Both experiments applied the two BSS methods: SVD and Similarity-Based band selection. Bands subsets are converted into its respective commercial filter, to evaluate a real configuration for a multispectral system.

The evaluation of the selected bands is performed using supervised classification. SVM and NN are used to evaluated the capability of the selected bands to improve the discrimination of healthy skin, border and ulcer center. The parameters of both classifiers are optimized to obtain the highest overall accuracy. For SVM, a radial basis function kernel is used. For NN, a configuration with a hidden layer of 5 neurons provided the best performance. For training, 30 samples are randomly selected for each class. Since border signatures are close to healthy skin signatures, as shown in Fig. 1, we first classify only healthy skin and ulcer center. Then, we performed the classification process using the three class. Each experiment is repeated 100 times to obtain the general classification accuracy.

5 Results

The selected bands from the BSS algorithms using the signatures between 480 nm to 750 nm are presented in Fig. 2. The spectral signature (blue signal) presented in Fig. 2 is the average of the all spectra used in the experiment. We can note that the selected bands by both algorithms are very close. Then, when we identify the corresponding commercial filters, many spectral bands become the same from both BSS approaches. Values of the commercial filters are presented in the table inside Fig. 2.

The selected bands from the BSS algorithms using the signatures between 480 nm to 800 nm are presented in Fig. 3. Values of the commercial filters also are presented in the table inside Fig. 3. Comparing these results with the first experiment, we note that two bands are selected between 750 nm to 800 nn for both algorithms. In these bands (785 nm and 800 nm) we can see a interesting behavior of healthy skin, border and ulcer center (see Fig. 1), that can be helpful for the discrimination process.

Once the band subsets are experimentally obtained, these are classified using SVM and NN. First, a two-class classification is performed, using only healthy skin and ulcer center signatures. A classification baseline is obtained by using

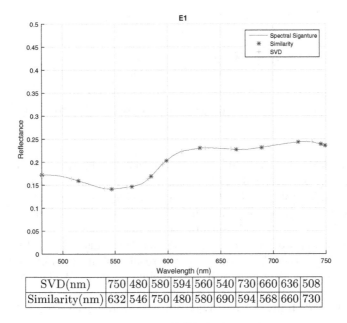

| SVD(nm) | 750 | 480 | 580 | 594 | 560 | 540 | 730 | 660 | 636 | 508 |
| Similarity(nm) | 632 | 546 | 750 | 480 | 580 | 690 | 594 | 568 | 660 | 730 |

Fig. 2. Selected spectral bands for spectral signatures between 480 nm to 750 nm using SVD (∗) and similarity-based (+) Band Subset Selection. Table shows the equivalent commercial filters. (Color figure online)

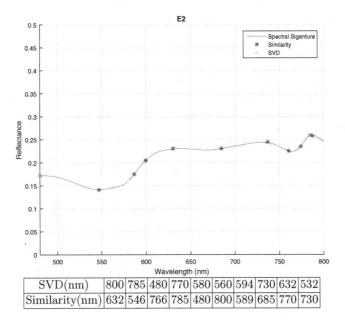

| SVD(nm) | 800 | 785 | 480 | 770 | 580 | 560 | 594 | 730 | 632 | 532 |
| Similarity(nm) | 632 | 546 | 766 | 785 | 480 | 800 | 589 | 685 | 770 | 730 |

Fig. 3. Selected spectral bands for spectral signatures between 480 nm to 800 nm using SVD (∗) and similarity-based (+) Band Subset Selection. Table shows the equivalent commercial filters.

Table 1. Overall classification accuracy for two-class problem: healthy skin and ulcer center

	480 nm to 750 nm		480 nm to 800 nm	
	SVM	NN	SVM	NN
Similarity	95.89% ± 2.41	94.32% ± 3.80	95.25% ± 2.89	93.36% ± 5.47
SVD	95.74% ± 2.83	93.85% ± 4.81	95.94% ± 2.02	91.93% ± 5.98

all spectral bands (nearly 2000). For the two-class problem, we obtain an average accuracy of 44.66% (±30.43%) using SVM and 58.06% (±13.96%) by NN using all bands. Table 1 shows the overall classification accuracy for the two-class problem using the spectral band subsets. Using the selected bands from 480 nm to 750 nm, the best classification is obtained from the subset selected by similarity-based approach and using SVM classifier. This configuration obtained a overall accuracy of 95.89%. However, the result obtained using the band subset selected by the SVD approach is very similar (95.74%). The NN classifier obtained lower overall accuracies for both subset (similarity and SVD). Using the selected bands from 480 nm to 800 nm, the overall accuracies are very close to the first experiment. Also, best performance was obtained using SVM than NN.

For three-class problem, the baseline accuracy was so low as 26.63% (±20.84%) using SVM and 74.06% (±18.89%) using NN with all the spectral bands. Table 2 shows the overall classification accuracy for the three-class problem using the spectral band subsets. We can note that for the three-class problem, the overall classification accuracy decrease for all configuration in comparison with two-class results. The best performance in this case is obtained using the spectral signatures from 480 nm to 800 nm with the band subset selected by SVD approach and using NN (82.60%). Then, the two bands selected between 750 nm to 800 nm are relevants for the discrimiantion between border and healthy skin. This can also be noted in Fig. 1.

Table 2. Overall classification accuracy for three-class problem: healthy skin, ulcer center and ulcer border

	480 nm to 750 nm		480 nm to 800 nm	
	SVM	NN	SVM	NN
Similarity	77.58% ± 4.36	77.21% ± 14.25	75.13% ± 4.60	76.02% ± 14.03
SVD	77.15% ± 4.78	76.32% ± 12.60	75.49% ± 5.15	82.60% ± 4.81

Finally, Table 3 shows the confusion matrix for the best result from the three-class problem (band subset selected by SVD and NN classifier). This confusion matrix allows determining that the ulcer border zone is the most sensitive to classification and tends to have a variability such that, depending on the location, it may have a reflectance like areas of healthy skin or ulcer center.

Table 3. Confusion matrix for the best result using the three classes: band subset selected SVD-based algorithm from bands between 480 nm to 800 nm and NN classifier

	Healthy Skin	Center	Border	Accuracy(%)
Healthy Skin	241	1	23	91.67%
Center	2	51	6	86.44%
Border	7	2	26	74.24%
Accuracy(%)	96.70%	94.44%	47.27%	

6   Conclusions

In this article, we presented the evaluation of two band-selection algorithms: the first based on similarity measures and the second based on SVD. These algorithms were applied to spectral data captured from cutaneous ulcers caused by leishmaniasis on golden hamsters. The results shows that both algorithms allows to obtain an appropriate dimensional reduction of spectral signatures without losing key information for their subsequent classification. From the spectral range analyzed, best results are obtained using 480 nm to 800 nm for the discrimination of healthy skin, border and ulcer center. Ulcer border area is highly sensitive and represents a challenge for the classification, as this area tends to be confused with ulcer center and healthy skin.

Since, the band subset selected allows a suitable discrimination of healthy skin and cutaneous ulcers caused by leishmaniasis, this can be used to develop an portable multispectal imaging system, that support the diagnosis and follow-up of treatment of CL. As future work, the selected bands can be evaluated using images and combining spectral-spatial methods, helping to improve the overall classification accuracies.

References

1. Alvar, J., et al.: Leishmaniasis worldwide and global estimates of its incidence. PLoS ONE **7**(5), e35671 (2012). https://doi.org/10.1371/journal.pone.0035671
2. Alvar, J., Yactayo, S., Bern, C.: Leishmaniasis and poverty. Trends Parasitol. **22**(12), 552–557 (2006). https://doi.org/10.1016/j.pt.2006.09.004
3. Arzuaga-Cruz, E., Jimenez-Rodriguez, L.O., Vélez-Reyes, M.: Unsupervised feature extraction and band subset selection techniques based on relative entropy criteria for hyperspectral data analysis. Proc. SPIE-Int. Soc. Opt. Eng. **5093**(September), 462–473 (2003). https://doi.org/10.1117/12.485942

4. Attia, A.B.E., et al.: Noninvasive real-time characterization of non-melanoma skin cancers with handheld optoacoustic probes. Photoacoustics **7**, 20–26 (2017). https://doi.org/10.1016/j.pacs.2017.05.003

5. Avci, P., et al.: Animal models of skin disease for drug discovery. Expert Opin. Drug Discov. **8**(3), 331–355 (2013). https://doi.org/10.1517/17460441.2013.761202

6. Calin, M.A., Parasca, S.V., Savastru, R., Calin, M.R., Dontu, S.: Optical techniques for the noninvasive diagnosis of skin cancer. J. Cancer Res. Clin. Oncol. **139**(7), 1083–1104 (2013). https://doi.org/10.1007/s00432-013-1423-3

7. Du, Q., Yang, H.: Similarity-based unsupervised band selection for hyperspectral image analysis. IEEE Geosci. Remote Sens. Lett. **5**(4), 564–568 (2008). https://doi.org/10.1109/LGRS.2008.2000619

8. Gao, J.: Digital Analysis of Remotely Sensed Imagery. McGraw Hill Professional, New York (2009)

9. Gholami, R., Fakhari, N.: Support vector machine: principles, parameters, and applications. In: Handbook of Neural Computation (1st edn.). Elsevier Inc. (2017). https://doi.org/10.1016/B978-0-12-811318-9.00027-2

10. Hotez, P.J., Bottazzi, M.E., Franco-Paredes, C., Ault, S.K., Periago, M.R.: The neglected tropical diseases of Latin America and the Caribbean: a review of disease burden and distribution and a roadmap for control and elimination. PLoS Negl. Trop. Dis. **2**(9) (2008). https://doi.org/10.1371/journal.pntd.0000300

11. Hotez, P.J., Remme, J.H.F., Buss, P., Alleyne, G., Morel, C., Breman, J.G.: Combating tropical infectious diseases: report of the disease control priorities in developing countries project. Clin. Infect. Dis. **38**(6), 871–878 (2004). https://doi.org/10.1086/382077

12. Ren, H., Chen, H.T.: Background whitened target detection algorithm for hyperspectral imagery. J. Mar. Sci. Technol. (Taiwan) **25**(1), 15–22 (2017). https://doi.org/10.6119/JMST-016-0630-1

13. Robledo, S. M., et al.: Cutaneous Leishmaniasis in the dorsal skin of hamsters: a useful model for the screening of Antileishmanial Drugs. J. Vis. Exp. (62) (2012). https://doi.org/10.3791/3533

14. Vyas, S., Meyerle, J., Burlina, P.: Non-invasive estimation of skin thickness from hyperspectral imaging and validation using echography. Comput. Biol. Med. **57**, 173–181 (2015). https://doi.org/10.1016/j.compbiomed.2014.12.010

Data Augmentation of Minority Class with Transfer Learning for Classification of Imbalanced Breast Cancer Dataset Using Inception-V3

Manisha Saini[(✉)] and Seba Susan

Delhi Technological University, Delhi, India
manisha.saini44@gmail.com

Abstract. In this paper, deep learning based experiments are conducted to investigate the effect of data augmentation on the minority class for the imbalanced breast cancer histopathology dataset (BREAKHIS). Two different pre-trained networks are fine-tuned with the minority-augmented dataset. The pre-trained networks were already trained on the well-known ImageNet dataset comprising of millions of high resolution images belonging to multiple object categories. The model so trained is further subjected to transfer learning, to correctly classify cancerous pattern from non-cancerous conditions, in a supervised manner. Our experiments were carried out in two phases. Phase-I investigates the effect of data augmentation applied on minority class for the Inception-v3 and ResNet-50 pre-trained networks. Results of phase-I are further enhanced in phase-II by the transfer learning approach in which features extracted from all layers of Inception-v3 are learnt by the SVM and weighted SVM classifiers. From experimental results, it was found that the pre-trained Inception-v3 model with data augmentation on minority class outperforms other network types. Results also indicate that Inception-v3 with data augmentation of minority class and transfer learning with weighted SVM gives the highest classification accuracies.

Keywords: Data augmentation · Imbalanced dataset · ResNet-50 · Inception-v3 · SVM

1 Introduction

Breast Cancer is a commonly found cancer related disease in women which leads to a high increase in the death rate every year [1]. So it is essential to detect and diagnose cancer at an early stage to begin with the right treatment. Even so, it was found that breast cancer histopathology dataset (BREAKHIS) is an imbalanced image dataset. Hence, this imbalanced breast cancer dataset is challenging to deal with because of the disproportionate number of samples in each class respectively [2]. It is important to recognize cancer (Malignant) class from non-cancer (Benign) class correctly so that an appropriate diagnosis of cancer is done at the right stage. It is often observed that most real-world problems involve imbalanced datasets. The imbalanced nature of such a

© Springer Nature Switzerland AG 2019
A. Morales et al. (Eds.): IbPRIA 2019, LNCS 11867, pp. 409–420, 2019.
https://doi.org/10.1007/978-3-030-31332-6_36

dataset yields results that are biased towards the majority class and the minority class is left undetected. An investigation is conducted in our work using the breast cancer dataset, to effectively discriminate minority class samples from the majority class through deep learning based experiments. A data augmentation based approach using pre-trained networks and transfer learning is used to correctly classify cancerous pattern from non-cancerous conditions. The transfer learning approach is used in the experiment to transfer the knowledge from one domain to another domain for performing a two-class classification task to segregate Benign from Malignant class. Transfer learning is a way of transferring knowledge from one specific domain or task to another task [3]. There are multiple advantages of using transfer learning approach (1) Firstly, model is already trained on a large scale dataset, and we are using the already existing model along with predefined weights for our own classification task, which saves a lot of computational processing time. (2) Secondly, we can transfer the knowledge from large scale dataset and perform classification well even with the small dataset. Pre-trained networks are trained on a large scale dataset such as ImageNet, which is composed of millions of high-resolution images belonging to multiple categories or classes (approximately 1.4 million images and 1000 classes).

Data augmentation [4] is the process of synthetically increasing the number of samples in the dataset, which helps to resolve the overfitting problem that arises due to inadequate number of samples in the dataset. There are several transform operations which can be applied for data augmentation such as scaling, rotation, horizontal and vertical flip, etc. This transformation help in increasing the number of samples of minority class as well as majority class so that we are able to correctly detect the minority class while performing the classification task. This paper is ordered into following subsequent sections. Section 2, discusses related work. In Sect. 3, the methodology for extracting features using pre-trained networks along with the data augmentation approach is described. Sections 4 and 5 discuss about the dataset and the experimental work conducted respectively. Finally, the conclusion is inferred in Sect. 5.

2   Literature Survey

BREAKHIS involves the imbalanced dataset having an unequal class distribution with the number of Benign samples significantly lesser than Malignant class. A large flux is observed in these images. Several studies have been conducted in order either to resolve the issue or study the effect of the imbalance. Gardner & Nicholas (2017), experiment on satellite images by implementing a Convolution Neural Network (CNN) model to perform multi-label classification through a comparison between VGG-16, Inception-v3, ResNet-50 and ResNet-50 with data augmentation. Best performance is achieved with ResNet-50 model after combination with data augmentation and ensemble technique by using various evaluation parameters such as F1-score, precision and recall [5]. Wang et al. (2017) proposed a method called neural augmentation which allows a neural net to learn augmentations that improve the classifier performance and comparison was carried out with traditional approaches used for data augmentation in the image classification task. Results state that a combination of traditional augmentation followed by neural augmentation further improves the classification strength [6].

In data science, sampling is the most popular remedy for the class imbalance problem. Chawla (2009), described in detail about changes that can be performed at data level or algorithmic level to overcome the class imbalance issue, such as sampling techniques at data level i.e., oversampling, undersampling, SMOTE and even variants of SMOTE such as SMOTEBOOST etc [7]. Hybrid strategies that combine oversampling of the minority class with the undersampling of the majority class have been proposed [21, 22]. In the field of computer vision, data augmentation has proved to mitigate the imbalance problem to a certain extent, and hence it is the approach used in our deep learning experiment to counter the class imbalance.

Chen, et al. (2012) conducted an experiment by applying data augmentation on various pre-trained networks such as VGG16, ResNet-50, and DenseNet for satellite images. From the experimental results, it was found that the best performance is achieved in case of the ensemble model which is formed after a combination of the results obtained from three DenseNet121 models with VGG-16 model [8].

3 Proposed Methodology and Techniques Used

Following the cue from the existing work, our work induces data augmentation [4], however on the minority class only, similar to the oversampling step in [21]. The minority augmented dataset, which is in essence balanced, is then applied for transfer learning through pre-trained networks and eventually classified using Weighted Support Vector Machine (SVM).

3.1 Data Augmentation of the Minority Class

The following data augmentation operations were applied on the minority class for the complete dataset: shear with range of 10, upper and lower zoom with the range of 20 percent and horizontal flip, along with resizing and pre-processing operations. Instances from the augmented minority set are shown in Fig. 1.

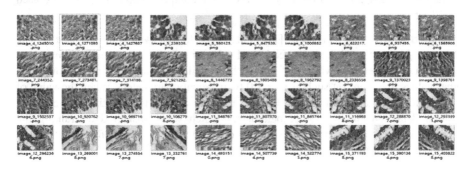

Fig. 1. Illustration of data augmentation applied on the minority class (Benign)

3.2   Phase I: Classification Using Pre-trained Networks

The pre-trained model was used for performing the classification experiment [19]. The pre-trained networks used for our experiment are described below.

(i) ResNet-50:- Architecture of ResNet-50 [5] consists of various residual blocks. Each residual block consists of a set of repeated layers. ResNet-50 architecture basically consists of 50 layers comprising of repeated convolution and pooling layers along with fully connected layers.

(ii) Inception-v3:- GoogleNet introduced the first Inception model. With time span, various other versions of Inception were introduced such as Inception-v2, Inception-v3, and Inception-v4. For our experiment, we have used Inception-v3, which has factorization as the main idea along with batch Normalization [8]. Inception-v3 architecture basically consist of 42-layer architecture, having fewer parameters, and more computational efficiency in comparison to previous Inception architectures.

Global Average Pooling 2D is added along with the dense layers [11], and Sigmoid and RELU activation functions are used.

3.3   Phase II: Deep Feature Extraction and Transfer Learning

Phase II, comprises of deep feature extraction from the pre-trained model fine-tuned with the minority augmented dataset. The deep features are extracted from all the layers of the Inception-v3 pre-trained model taken in the right order. The classifiers used for our experiment involving transfer learning based on the deep feature extracted are explained below:-

SVM. SVM classifier can be used for linearly separable and non-separable problems based upon the type of kernel used. The kernel is the parameters set to change/transform the dimension of input feature space from low to high. The kernel can be selected as 'Linear', 'Polynomial', 'rbf' etc., based upon the task performed. SVM [9, 10] is commonly used as a classifier to solve numerous tasks by selecting optimal decision boundary or hyperplane. Selected optimal decision boundary helps to segregate the samples from the two classes. For the experimental task, we have used 'rbf' kernel.

Weighted SVM. Weighted SVM [11] is also used for the evaluation in Phase II. The class weight is assigned the balanced kernel value in order to deal with the imbalanced dataset. The kernel used while performing the classification task is 'linear' along with other values that were set such as C = 1.0 (C is penalty parameter). When the value of C is set to 1, it indicates that the classifier is easily able to tolerate the wrong classification data items/points. Other parameters which was considered in training the classifier was a random state which was set equal to zero and probability is set as true while performing the experiment.

4   Experimental Results and Discussions

For the purpose of our deep learning experiments, the popular python framework Keras v2.1.6 has been used. It uses a Tensorflow backend to perform all its internal computations. The model will be trained across 3 epochs with 29 steps in each epoch. While training the pre-trained network, sparse categorical cross-entropy is used as the loss function for each fold along with Adam optimizer (Adaptive Moment Estimation), batch size set as 32 in each fold, with RELU activation function [12] in dense layer, is used for the experiment.

4.1   Dataset

Images present in the BREAKHIS dataset belong to of four different magnification factors i.e. 40X, 100X, 200X and 400X [18, 20]. Experimental evaluation was performed using 400X magnification factor images. Dataset comprises of 5,88 Benign and 1,232 Malignant images as shown in Table 1. Random sampling is applied in order to segregate testing images from training images, such that 100 samples each from Malignant and Benign class will be used for testing. Whereas the remaining number of the sample is kept for training purpose. Each input image was resized into 224 × 224 size before performing the experiment. For the experiment, five-fold cross-validation technique has been used in Phase I.

Table 1. Imbalanced image dataset of a patient having cancer and those not suffering from cancer obtained from 400 X magnification factor in training and testing dataset.

	Dataset		Train dataset	Test dataset
Class	Magnification factor	No of images		
Benign	400 X	588	488	100
Malignant	400 X	1232	1132	100

4.2   Performance Evaluation

Several studies show that accuracy is not always a reliable parameter to be used to determine the model performance while dealing with the imbalanced dataset. Accuracy illustrates how proficiently classifier is able to classify the samples in the different classes. Precision denotes the fraction of relevant samples which are correctly classified from the total number of samples. Recall denotes the fraction of samples which are correctly classified from the correct samples. F-Measure/F1-score is obtained from the combination of both recall and precision as shown in Eq. 1. Whereas the ROC curve is the graph plotted between the true positive rate and false negative rate.

$$F1 - score = \frac{2 * (Precision * Recall)}{(Precision + Recall)} \tag{1}$$

Classification report has been generated using the scikit-learn package in python for analyzing the performance of the model with precision, recall, F1-score [16] and ROC curve (Receiver Operating curve).

4.3   Results and Discussions

4.3.1   Phase I Experiments

From the experimental analysis, it was found that there is a huge difference between test and train accuracy. As average train accuracy in case of Inception-v3 is approximately between 70 to 80% range with and without data augmentation. Whereas, average test accuracy has improved from 47 to 50% as shown in Table 3. Experiments performed using Inception-v3 pre-trained networks with and without data augmentation are shown in Tables 2 and 3. From the experimental evaluation, it was found that Inception-v3 is unable to detect minority class. Whereas experiments conducted by applying data augmentation technique on minority class separately are effectively able to detect the minority class, as illustrated in Table 2 and Fig. 2. According to the literature, it was found that while dealing with the imbalanced dataset, results are biased towards the majority class. Figure 3 depicts the test samples tested on Inception-v3 pre-trained network after applying data augmentation on minority class using one of the best fold out of the average (Avg) five-fold. Whereas, data augmentation applied separately on the minority is able to detect minority class efficiently in comparison to Inception-v3 pre-trained network after data augmentation is applied on both classes. Figure 4 represents sample test images without applying data augmentation. Similar experiment was conducted with ResNet-50 architecture to measure the performance of data augmentation technique as illustrated in Tables 4 and 5. From experiment results, it was found that Inception-v3 outperforms ResNet-50 in all the cases.

Table 2. Comparison of Performance evaluation on the basis of Precision, Recall, and F1-score using cancer dataset in case of Inception-v3 pre-trained network.

Classes	Inception-v3 [14]		Inception-v3 (with data augmentation on both class) [15]		Proposed Inception-v3 (with data augmentation on minority class)	
	Benign	Malignant	Benign	Malignant	Benign	Malignant
Avg precision (five-fold)	0.076	0.49	0.05	0.49	0.46	0.44
Avg recall (five-fold)	0.006	0.48	0.002	0.99	0.56	0.35
Avg F1-score (five-fold)	0.012	0.66	0.004	0.66	0.50	0.39
Support	100	100	100	100	100	100

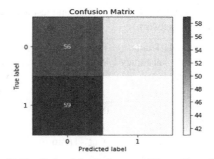

(i) Confusion Matrix in case of Inception-v3

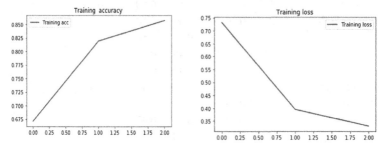

(ii) Accuracy and loss obtained while training the Inception-v3 pre-trained network

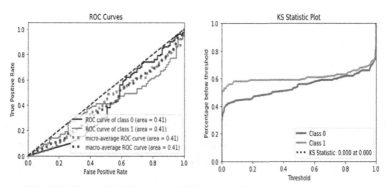

(iii) ROC Curve (iv) KS statistic Plot in case of Inception-v3 pre-trained
Network

Fig. 2. Various visualization Curves demonstrates from (i) to (iv) in case of Inception-v3 pre-trained networks after applying data augmentation on Minority class with 4 fold validation

Table 3. Comparison of performance evaluation of train and test accuracy using cancer dataset in case of Inception-v3 pre-trained network.

Pre-trained networks	Fold	Train accuracy (%)	Train loss	Test accuracy (%)	Avg test accuracy (five-fold)	Avg train accuracy (five-fold)
Inception-v3 [14]	1	0.80	0.46	0.50	0.49	0.78
	2	0.77	0.46	0.50		
	3	0.78	0.47	0.49		
	4	0.88	0.44	0.49		
	5	0.78	0.47	0.48		
Inception-v3 with data augmentation on both the classes [15]	1	0.74	0.51	0.50	0.49	0.77
	2	0.80	0.44	0.50		
	3	0.76	0.49	0.50		
	4	0.76	0.48	0.50		
	5	0.80	0.42	0.50		
Inception-v3 with data augmentation on minority class	1	0.83	0.38	0.46	0.47	0.83
	2	0.84	0.34	0.48		
	3	0.82	0.4	0.47		
	4	0.85	0.33	0.48		
	5	0.83	0.36	0.46		

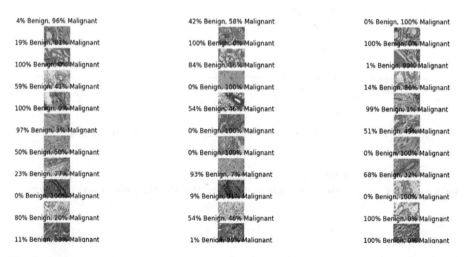

Fig. 3. Samples tested on Inception-v3 pre-trained network after applying data augmentation on minority class

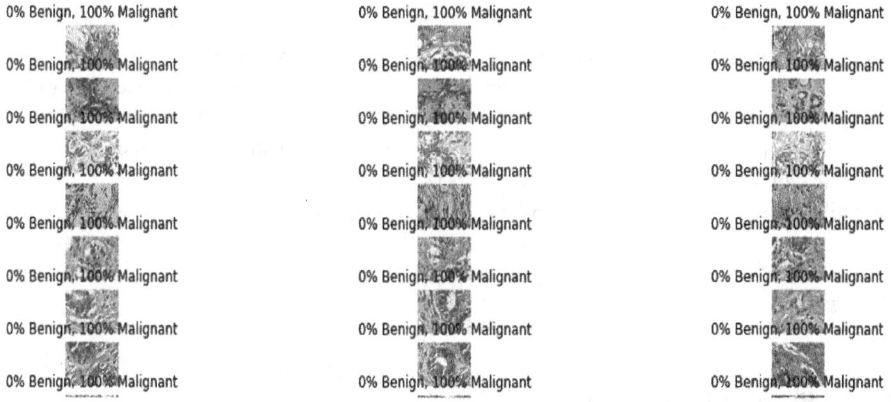

Fig. 4. Samples tested on Inception-v3 pre-trained network without applying data augmentation

Table 4. Comparison of performance evaluation on the basis of precision, recall, and F1-score using cancer dataset in case of ResNet-50 pre-trained network.

Classes	ResNet-50 [5]		ResNet-50 (with data augmentation on both class) [16]		ResNet-50 (with data augmentation on minority class)	
	Benign	Malignant	Benign	Malignant	Benign	Malignant
Avg precision (five-fold)	0.20	1.00	0.20	0.50	0.00	0.50
Avg recall (five-fold)	0.002	1.00	0.002	1.00	0.00	1.00
Avg F1-score (five-fold)	0.004	0.67	0.008	0.67	0.00	0.67
Support	100	100	100	100	100	100

Table 5. Comparison of performance evaluation of train and test accuracy using cancer dataset in case of ResNet-50 pre-trained network.

Pre-trained networks	Fold	Train accuracy (%)	Train loss	Test accuracy (%)	Avg test accuracy (%) (five-fold)	Avg train accuracy (%) (five-fold)
ResNet-50 [5]	1	0.93	0.16	0.50	0.50	0.92
	2	0.92	0.19	0.50		
	3	0.93	0.18	0.50		
	4	0.91	0.21	0.50		
	5	0.92	0.17	0.50		
ResNet-50 with data augmentation on both the classes [16]	1	0.79	0.71	0.50	0.50	0.82
	2	0.86	0.31	0.50		
	3	0.89	0.26	0.50		
	4	0.69	0.49	0.50		
	5	0.88	0.27	0.50		

(*continued*)

Table 5. (*continued*)

Pre-trained networks	Fold	Train accuracy (%)	Train loss	Test accuracy (%)	Avg test accuracy (%) (five-fold)	Avg train accuracy (%) (five-fold)
ResNet-50 with data augmentation on minority class	1	0.93	0.15	0.50	0.50	0.93
	2	0.93	0.16	0.50		
	3	0.96	0.10	0.50		
	4	0.93	0.15	0.50		
	5	0.93	0.15	0.50		

4.3.2 Phase II Experiments

Experiments were conducted to evaluate the performance of Inception-v3 under different conditions on the basis of various parameters such as precision, recall, F1-score and accuracy to evaluate the performance of the model. The comparison was done between Inception-v3 with data augmentation applied on minority class, obtained as the best result in Phase I experiment, with the features extracted from Inception-v3 pretrained model and trained on the SVM and weighted SVM classifiers. From the experimental analysis, it was found that Inception-v3 with weighted SVM and data augmentation applied on the minority class outperforms other Inception-v3 based experiments, as shown in Table 6 and Fig. 5.

Table 6. Comparison of Performance evaluation of techniques applied on the minority class

Classes	Inception-v3 [14]		Inception-v3 + SVM [17]		Proposed inception-v3 + weighted SVM			
	Data augmentation on minority class				Without data augmentation		Proposed method with data augmentation on minority class	
	Benign	Malignant	Benign	Malignant	Benign	Malignant	Benign	Malignant
Precision	0.49	0.48	0.00	0.50	0.66	0.58	0.68	0.59
Recall	0.56	0.41	0.00	1.00	0.44	0.77	0.46	0.78
F1-score	0.52	0.44	0.00	0.67	0.53	0.66	0.55	0.67
Accuracy	0.48	0.48	0.5	0.5	0.60	0.60	0.62	0.62
Support	100	100	100	100	100	100	100	100

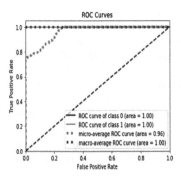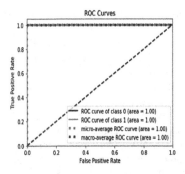

Fig. 5. (i) ROC curve in case of Inception-v3 with weighted SVM (ii) ROC Curve in case of Inception-v3 with weighted SVM and data augmentation applied on the minority class

5 Conclusion

A solution for countering class imbalance in deep learning is proposed in this work specifically for BREAKHIS breast cancer dataset. It is proved that we cannot only rely on accuracy for the identification of imbalanced dataset. Various other parameters need to be considered such as F1-score, Precision, Recall, and ROC. We have conducted experiments in two phases. Phase-I investigates the effect of data augmentation technique when applied on minority class only for the pre-trained networks Inception-v3 and ResNet-50. Results obtained are found better with the application of data augmentation on the minority class in Inception-v3 pre-trained model. In Phase-II, features were extracted from all layers of Inception-v3 and learned by the SVM and weighted SVM classifiers. Results show that Inception-v3 with data augmentation on minority class works best with transfer learning using weighted SVM as compared to other networks. However, it was also observed that despite having high test accuracy, if the model is unable to give correct predictions and the results are biased towards the majority class then the minority class is left undetected and the model will evaluate every sample image from test data as non-cancerous even though the person is having cancer. So, it is important to consider model performance using all the described parameters instead of using only accuracy as the evaluation criteria. Future work involves using ensemble deep feature approach to extract a new set of features to effectively distinguish the minority class from the majority class using pre-trained models.

References

1. Parkin, D.M., Bray, F., Ferlay, J., Pisani, P.: Global cancer statistics, 2002. CA Cancer J. Clin. **55**(2), 74–108 (2005)
2. Estabrooks, A., Jo, T., Japkowicz, N.: A multiple resampling method for learning from imbalanced data sets. Comput. Intell. **20**(1), 18–36 (2004)

3. Ferlaino, M., et al: Towards deep cellular phenotyping in placental histology. arXiv preprint. arXiv:1804.03270 (2018)

4. Kumar, A., Kim, J., Lyndon, D., Fulham, M., Feng, D.: An ensemble of fine-tuned convolutional neural networks for medical image classification. IEEE J. Biomed. Health Inf. **21**(1), 31–40 (2017)

5. Gardner, D., Nichols, D.: Multi-label Classification of Satellite Images with Deep Learning, p. 2017 (2017)

6. Liu, W., Wang, Z., Liu, X., Zeng, N., Liu, Y., Alsaadi, F.E.: A survey of deep neural network architectures and their applications. Neurocomputing **234**, 11–26 (2017)

7. Chawla, N.V.: Data mining for imbalanced datasets: an overview. In: Data Mining and Knowledge Discovery Handbook, pp. 875–886. Springer, Boston (2009). https://doi.org/10.1007/978-0-387-09823-4_45

8. Chen, Y., Dong, F., Ruan, C.: Understanding the Amazon from Space, pp. 1–9 (2012)

9. Vapnik, V., Isabel, G., Hastie, T.: Support vector machines. Mach. Learn. **20**(3), 273–297 (1995)

10. Camps-Valls, G., Gomez-Chova, L., Muñoz-Marí, J., Vila-Francés, J., Calpe-Maravilla, J.: Composite kernels for hyperspectral image classification. IEEE Geosci. Remote Sens. Lett. **3**(1), 93–97 (2006)

11. https://chrisalbon.com/machine_learning/support_vector_machines/imbalanced_classes_in_svm/

12. Kim, M., Zuallaert, J., De Neve, W.: Towards novel methods for effective transfer learning and unsupervised deep learning for medical image analysis. In: Doctoral Consortium (DCBIOSTEC 2017), pp. 32–39 (2017)

13. Niu, X.-X., Suen, C.Y.: A novel hybrid CNN–SVM classifier for recognizing handwritten digits. Pattern Recogn. **45**(4), 1318–1325 (2012)

14. Chang, C., Lin, C.: LIBSVM : A Library for Support Vector Machines, pp. 1–39 (2013)

15. Nguyen, G.H., Bouzerdoum, A., Phung, S.L.: Learning pattern classification tasks with imbalanced data sets. In: Pattern Recognition. IntechOpen (2009)

16. Ramcharan, A., Baranowski, K., McCloskey, P., Ahmed, B., Legg, J., Hughes, D.: Using transfer learning for image-based cassava disease detection. arXiv preprint. arXiv:1707.03717 (2017)

17. Barai, M., Heikkinen, A.: Impact of data augmentations when training the inception model for image classification (2017)

18. Xie, J., Liu, R., Joseph Luttrell, I.V., Zhang, C.: Deep learning based analysis of histopathological images of breast cancer. Front. Genet. **10**, 80 (2019)

19. Kieffer, B., Babaie, M., Kalra, S., Tizhoosh, H.R.: Convolutional neural networks for histopathology image classification: training vs. using pre-trained networks. In: 2017 Seventh International Conference on Image Processing Theory, Tools and Applications (IPTA), pp. 1–6. IEEE (2017)

20. https://web.inf.ufpr.br/vri/databases/. Accessed 10 May 2019

21. Susan, S., Kumar, A.: Hybrid of intelligent minority oversampling and PSO-based intelligent majority undersampling for learning from imbalanced datasets. In: Abraham, A., Cherukuri, A.K., Melin, P., Gandhi, N. (eds.) ISDA 2018 2018. AISC, vol. 941, pp. 760–769. Springer, Cham (2020). https://doi.org/10.1007/978-3-030-16660-1_74

22. Susan, S., Kumar, A.: SSOMaj-SMOTE-SSOMin: three-step intelligent pruning of majority and minority samples for learning from imbalanced datasets. Appl. Soft Comput. **78**, 141–149 (2019)

Image Processing and Representation

Single View Facial Hair 3D Reconstruction

Gemma Rotger[1]([⊠]), Francesc Moreno-Noguer[2], Felipe Lumbreras[1], and Antonio Agudo[2]

[1] Computer Vision Center and Departament Ciències de la Computació, UAB, Birmingham, Spain
grotger@cvc.uab.es
[2] Institut de Robòtica i Informàtica Industrial, CSIC-UPC, Barcelona, Spain

Abstract. In this work, we introduce a novel energy-based framework that addresses the challenging problem of 3D reconstruction of facial hair from a single RGB image. To this end, we identify hair pixels over the image via texture analysis and then determine individual hair fibers that are modeled by means of a parametric hair model based on 3D helixes. We propose to minimize an energy composed of several terms, in order to adapt the hair parameters that better fit the image detections. The final hairs respond to the resulting fibers after a post-processing step where we encourage further realism. The resulting approach generates realistic facial hair fibers from solely an RGB image without assuming any training data nor user interaction. We provide an experimental evaluation on real-world pictures where several facial hair styles and image conditions are observed, showing consistent results and establishing a comparison with respect to competing approaches.

Keywords: 3D vision · Shape reconstruction · Facial hair modeling

1 Introduction

In the last years, computer-generated characters are provided of an increasing level of realism, heightening the standards of the film and video game industry. Hair plays an essential role to build convincing digital humans and fulfill them with an identity. Pessig *et al.* [17] advised that the eyebrows alone may be the most relevant feature for facial recognition. Unfortunately, it is well known that retrieve hair geometry solely from images is a challenging task due to its structural complexity. Although several image-based methods are capable to create high-quality reconstructions [4,13–16,18], they require specialized and expensive hardware. Furthermore, except [4] none of them proved any accomplishment over facial hair.

Recently, the earliest models handling hair reconstruction from a single RGB image have emerged. The first approaches [5,7] required several user interactions. Particularly, in [5] was required depth information and a user to annotate the

© Springer Nature Switzerland AG 2019
A. Morales et al. (Eds.): IbPRIA 2019, LNCS 11867, pp. 423–436, 2019.
https://doi.org/10.1007/978-3-030-31332-6_37

hair, as well as head-region annotations in the image. In [7] was expected the user to define sparse strokes in order to determine the local direction ambiguity. It dropped to new data-driven solutions [11], which reduced the required volume of user interaction but not omitted. Later, remarkable results have been achieved with the use of structured light patterns [8] and electro-luminescent wires [9]. Unfortunately, no achievement was reported over facial hair. Similarly, deep-learning approaches contributed to the field as hair growing direction estimation [6] and hair-style parametrization [21] amongst others. However, these approaches tended to be highly data demanding, and active methods required expensive hardware setups.

In this paper, we present a novel optimization framework that uses the texture information in an RGB image to predict the facial hair fibers geometry in 3D. We take advantage of orientation analysis texture methods [15] to detect the fibers. Later, we track across this detection the individual fibers at pixel-level, splitting connections when their orientation significantly varies. Similar to [4], we allow hair crossings to be detected by connecting fibers which are close in the space and have a similar overall orientation. Afterward, we parametrize our hair generation model by minimizing a set of four different energies that take into account different 2D detection properties. To improve the computation efficiency, we arranged the detected hair fibers in different groups according to their 2D properties (these are position, length, and orientation), obtaining a different parametrization per group. More specifically, eyelashes and eyebrows require to be studied separately due to the evident differences regarding beard and mustache fibers. Finally, we enhanced more realism by adding hair density and small random noise.

Our main contribution is to propose a model for growing 3D hair fibers together with a 3D face model from a single RGB image, providing hair fibers with high resolution. To this end, no further information, user interaction, or training data is required. We demonstrate the effectiveness of our method over a wide variety of facial hair styles and geometries. Our approach is extensively evaluated on real high-quality RGB images from the Internet, proving the suitability of our framework to reconstruct plausible 3D facial hairs directly form pictures.

2   Related Work

The 3D reconstruction of realistic faces has prevailed a topic of interest [1,2,12]. Concerning the recovering of human hair fibers as an essential step to realism and verisimilitude, several methods addressed the problem from different perspectives [4–6,8,9,13,15,18,21]. While there exist a wide range of methods reconstructing a hairstyle as a parametric model [10,11,14,19,20], unfortunately, the area of research studying hair reconstruction fiber-by-fiber from a single view is shorter.

In particular, fiber-by-fiber was tackled from the perspective of multi-view stereo. The work of [15] presented a fiber-by-fiber reconstruction approach by

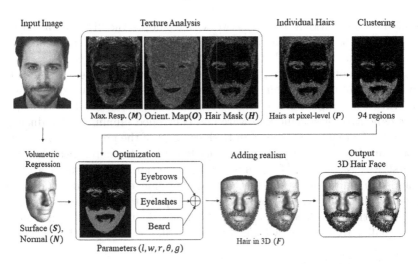

Fig. 1. An overview of our pipeline. From a single image, our approach first retrieves a 3D facial model (coded by N and S) by applying a volumetric regression CNN approach [12]. Later, a hair map is detected over the image via Gabor texture analysis, where some attributes are obtained: the maximum response and the maximum orientation response (every orientation is represented by a different color) are denoted as M and O, respectively, obtaining the final hair detection in the binary matrix H. Next, we trace individual hair fibers via pixel-connectivity, orientation differences, and endpoints distance in P. As different areas (beard and mustache, eyebrows, and eyelashes), need a different parametrization due to their variability, hair fibers are grouped in 94 different regions according to their location, orientation, and 2D length, which are included in one of the previous macro-classes. For these macro-classes, model parameters are estimated by optimization. Eventually, we append the results and add small random variations in the hair length and orientations as well as density to increase the realism. Red and blue lines represent the estimated and computed hairs, respectively. (Color figure online)

growing hair within the restrictions established by the visual hull. In a similar practice, in [18] was synthesized the hair fibers from local image orientations. In [13] was presented a new setup to capture hair arrangement fiber-by-fiber, and in [4] was proposed the first approach to reconstruct facial hair fibers. Lately, active-light methods established their solutions in the field. In [8] was proposed a novel robust strip-edge-based coding method, based on a projection pattern. In [9] was introduced a novel method for braid acquisition and 3D guide hair reconstruction based on electro-luminescent wires.

Deep-learning methods have contributed to the topic providing solutions from a single RGB image. For instance, in [5] was introduced a 3D helical hair prior that captures the geometrical structure of the hair from a single image, but it required manual hair segmentation and direction guidance. In [6] user interactions were overcome with a novel hierarchical deep-neural network for automatic hair segmentation and hair growth direction estimation. Additionally, in [21] was presented a convolutional neural network that adopts the 2D orientation fields of the image as input and generates a strand feature. The resulting parametrizations allowed interpolating between several hairstyles. However, deep-learning approaches do not handle fiber-by-fiber retrieving, recalling these methods ineffective for accurate facial hair reconstruction. Further, they are demanding in data terms. On the other side of multi-view and active-light based methods, they require expensive or specific hardware and controlled illumination, reducing its applicability in real-world scenarios. Besides, most of the previous works had not demonstrated its suitability to reconstruct facial hair fibers but head hair fibers or hairstyles. We find in [4] an interesting exception. It consists of a coupled hair and skin multi-view stereo method based on images acquired in a controlled studio. In this paper, we present a similar concept but using a single-view image under uncontrolled lighting. Our method can handle hair fibers estimation from a good quality RGB image without requiring training data or other setups.

3   Our Approach

This section describes the computation of the 3D hair strands from a single RGB image, and the final post-processing step to add further realism to the reconstruction.

First, our approach detects hair fibers in the RGB image via Gabor texture analysis. After that, based on an orientation analysis, the full facial hair is outlined from its root to the tip at pixel-level and group them in a cluster of hairs with similar properties to speed up the optimization process. In combination with the estimated 3D facial model [12], we solve a set of optimizations to find the parameters that better model each cluster of hair. Finally, we append all the computed hairs and provide further realism by adding small random variations in length and root orientation. Figure 1 depicts a schematic of the overall approach, and how every part is connected. In the remaining of this section, each step is illustrated in detail.

3.1   2D Hair Detection

Texture Analysis. Our first observation is that human hair may vary in a considerable range of tones and shapes, making the problem harder to address. Therefore, we notice that the RGB space is not suitable to achieve a proper texture analysis. For this reason, we convert the initial image to the HSV color space and only consider the saturation and value channels to exploit the greater uniformity of the hair fibers, together with a significant difference with regards to the skin pixels. The hue channel is employed to identify the inner part of the eyes and the mouth where the texture is not analyzed. It is well known that these regions do not hold hair roots. However, they can contain other features that can be confused with hair fibers in the texture analysis such as veins, or strong lip textures. For this, and similar to [4], we consider convenient not to analyze the texture on these specific areas.

As it can be analyzed in [4,15], orientation responses are suitable to estimate hair in images. Formally, they use a filter kernel K_θ for different θ orientations, at every $10°$, and keep the orientation that produces the largest score in the function $F(x,y) = |K_\theta * V|_{(x,y)} + |K_\theta * S|_{(x,y)}$, at a pixel (x,y), for the value V and saturation S channels. In a similar manner, we apply the real part of a Gabor filter bank consisting of 5 different wavelengths $\lambda = \{2, 2.5, 3, 3.5, 4\}$ and 18 orientations θ (from 0 to 170, at each $10°$). For each pixel, we hold the maximum response of the filter $M(x,y)$ and the orientation of the maximum response $O(x,y)$ which later will allow us to detect individual hair fibers. Both are defined as:

$$M(x,y) = \max(F(x,y)), \tag{1}$$

$$O(x,y) = \theta_{\max(F(x,y))} . \tag{2}$$

Next, we binarize the maximum response by applying a simple threshold τ to exclude low-confidence responses. To this end, we define a binary hair mask H as:

$$H(x,y) = M(x,y) > \tau . \tag{3}$$

Individual Hair Trace. Let us define a hair at a pixel level as P^h, and the set of all the pixels in a hair as $p_i^h \in P^h$ with $p_i^h = (x_i^h, y_i^h)$. The goal in this stage is to transform the different blobs in H into an ordered set of pixels $p_i^h \in P^h$ where p_0^h is the hair root and p_L^h the hair tip, where L denotes the length of the fiber.

We manage the hair map H regard to 8-connected region analysis techniques to find connected pixels. However, due to hair constitution, crossings, and strong shading, different samples can be grouped as a single detection. To determine a single hair fiber trace, we study the orientation map O and ensure all the pixels in the same connected region has an orientation difference with respect to the following pixel is smaller than $10°$. When this does happen, i.e., $|O(p_i^h) - O(p_{i+1}^h)| > 10$, we detach the connection.

The previous step results in small regions equivalent to visible hair fibers in the image. However, due to shadows and intersections, hair can split into several detections. In [4] was pointed that hair fibers can be re-joined in 3D if they satisfy three conditions: (1) their endpoints are unconnected, (2) they are close in the space (or overlapped), and (3) the orientation variation is lower than $20°$. We adopt a similar setup in 2D, limiting the angle to $10°$ to be consistent with our previous step. A maximum distance limit for re-connect the endpoints equal to three pixels. For all combinations of hairs, we accept those satisfying the previous conditions. We additionally allow more than two hairs to join in the same section if the overall of the segments fulfills the orientation restriction and their endpoints are allowed to connect in a two-by-two association. The relevance of this step is imperative since the estimation of the resulting 3D hair properties is directly related to the measures extracted from visible 2D hair segments.

Endpoint Labeling. In this step, we determine if a hair fiber has its endpoints (root and tip) in the proper order. This step is essential since the hair model presented in the following sections is implemented over the root position and grows unto the tip location. We employ certain facial landmarks extracted with [3]. These landmarks include the nose tip for beard, mustache, and eyebrows, and the averages of the eye landmarks as the central eye-points. We define the growth direction determining the root as the endpoint with the minimum Euclidean distance value with respect to the corresponding landmark, and the tip as the endpoint with the maximum value, such as:

$$
\begin{aligned}
\boldsymbol{p}_{root}^h &= \min(d(\boldsymbol{p}_i^h, (x_j^l, y_j^l))), \\
\boldsymbol{p}_{tip}^h &= \max(d(\boldsymbol{p}_i^h, (x_j^l, y_j^l))),
\end{aligned}
\tag{4}
$$

where (x_j^l, y_j^l) denotes the landmarks. In case the endpoints are reversed, we shift the entire $\boldsymbol{P}^h$ values to satisfy the new endpoint labeling.

3.2   A Simple Hair Growing Parametric Model

When an incipient hair shaft grows, it follows the normal surface direction. However, after reaching a determined length, its trajectory is affected by other factors, for instance, the shaft weight, the gravity effect, and the follicle cross-section, which determines the shaft thickness and the curliness. The length of the shaft also affects the curvature in a two-dimensional plane, since the longer the hair becomes, the more burden the tip of the hair shaft supports, so the greatest is the gravity effect over the fiber. However, the curliness cannot be represented as deformation in a two-dimensional plane but as a 3D local helix.

To overcome all these possible variations, we have determined a hair model that ensures local coherence and smoothness. Further, it represents both the curliness as a 3D local helix and a gravity-like effect. Our model has five different parameters that control the hair growing conditions and provide hair fiber-like results. These parameters define the size (length l, and width w), the curliness (radius r, angle θ) and a gravity-like effect (g) that avoids shafts to lie suspended in the air. s is the last parameter of the model, which determines the resolution of the generated hairs. It is defined in advance by the user according to the requirements of the desired solution. The greater the value, the larger the resolution, and the slower to perform all the computations and visualizations. In our experiments, we adopted a value of $s = 25$ for all the estimations.

Let us consider $\boldsymbol{F}^h(\boldsymbol{p}^h, \boldsymbol{n}^h, l, w, r, \theta, g)$ the parametrization of a hair fiber, where $\boldsymbol{p}^h$ denotes the 3D position and $\boldsymbol{n}^h$ the 3D growing direction. In Fig. 2, we show several examples of how our model acts as a function of the parameters. Since the image is aligned with the initial 3D, the detections over the image are likewise aligned. For each detected root $\boldsymbol{p}_0^h$ we can interpolate the three closets mesh vertices and obtain $\boldsymbol{p}^h$ as the average of the positions and $\boldsymbol{n}^h$ as the average of the vertex normals. With these considerations and the parameters explained above we can define our facial hair model as:

$$
\boldsymbol{F}_i^h(\boldsymbol{p}^h, \boldsymbol{n}^h, l, w, r, \theta, g) = \boldsymbol{p}_0^h + \boldsymbol{R}(\boldsymbol{n}^h)\frac{(i-1) \cdot l}{s}Hx(r, \theta, i) - Gy(g, i),
\tag{5}
$$

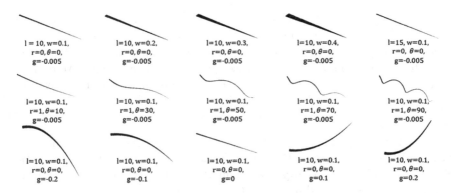

Fig. 2. Parametric Hair Model. Our parametric model depends on five parameters: length l, width w, the curliness parameters r and θ, and the gravity coefficient g. As it can be seen in the figure, thanks to our model we can obtain a wide variety of fibers. Top: Some instances varying l and w. Middle: Some instances as a function of the curliness parameters. Bottom: Modifying the gravity-like parameter.

where i denotes the i-th point in the hair fiber, $\boldsymbol{R}(n^h)$ represents the rotation matrix, which adjusts the 3D helix's direction with the corresponding normal vector at the given position.

The 3D helix is defined over the x-axis as follows:

$$Hx(r, \theta, i) = (i - 1, r \cdot \sin(\theta \cdot (i - 1)), r \cdot \cos(\theta \cdot (i - 1))), \tag{6}$$

where $Hx(r, \theta, i)$ represents the function producing the 3D coordinates of the 3D helix at the i-th point. r is the radius and θ the angle between two consecutive points.

The gravity-like effect is computed as follows:

$$Gy(g, i) = \boldsymbol{v} \cdot (i - 1) \cdot \left(\cos(\alpha), -\frac{g(i - 1)^2}{2}, \sin(\alpha)\right), \tag{7}$$

where $Gy(g, i)$ represents the effect of a gravity-like function at the i-th point of the helix. After several tests, we define $\boldsymbol{v} = [\frac{1}{\alpha}, 1, \frac{1}{\alpha}]$, being $\alpha = 10°$ as are the values that adapt better the hair fibers behavior.

Finally, we compose a cylinder over each segment of $\boldsymbol{F}^h$. Where the initial width in $\boldsymbol{F}_0^h$ is defined beside the parameter w, and it decreases consistently unto the last point $\boldsymbol{F}_l^h$ where the cylinder width is $w = 0$.

3.3   3D Growing via Energy Minimization

Hair geometry is locally consistent, yet it has different properties according to face regions. For instance, eyebrows are not similar to beard fibers, but, each is similar within the same class. To consider these different behaves, we have defined three different optimization groups. The first corresponds to beard and mustache and clusters a total of 70 groups with similar length, position, and orientation via K-means. The second group distinguishes the hairs belonging to the subject eyelashes, in total four clusters corresponding to each of the eye lines upper and lower of both eyes. The third group corresponds to the eyebrows, and it has ten clusters per eyebrow, likewise arranged with K-means. We optimize each of the 94 clusters separately to satisfy the following energy minimization:

$$\mathcal{E}_{total} = \mathcal{E}_{len} + \mathcal{E}_{ori} + \mathcal{E}_{tip} + E_{cur} . \tag{8}$$

Length Term $\mathcal{E}_{len}$. The length energy term is a direct segment longitude comparison. We use the sum of Euclidean distances from the root pixel detection $\boldsymbol{p}_0^h$ to the tip pixel detection $\boldsymbol{p}_l^h$ and compare it upon the same distance in the xy-plane for the estimated hair root $\boldsymbol{f}_0^h$ and tip $\boldsymbol{f}_l^h$.

$$\mathcal{E}_{len} = \sum_h \|(\boldsymbol{p}_l^j - \boldsymbol{p}_0^h) - (\boldsymbol{f}_l^h - \boldsymbol{f}_0^h)\|_2^2 . \tag{9}$$

Orientation Term $\mathcal{E}_{ori}$. It encourages hair fibers to have similar orientations than the detected in the given image. In practice, the global 3D orientation is determined by the surface normal, though, the gravity-like parameter can force the fiber to grow in a different orientation.

$$\mathcal{E}_{ori} = \sum_h \|\tan^{-1}\left(\frac{p_{ly}^h - p_{0y}^h}{p_{lx}^h - p_{0x}^y}\right) - \tan^{-1}\left(\frac{f_{ly}^h - f_{0y}^h}{f_{lx}^h - f_{0x}^h}\right)\|_2^2 . \tag{10}$$

Tip-to-tip Term $\mathcal{E}_{tip}$. Tip-to-tip cost encourages hairs fibers to have the tip projection on the 2D plane close to the tip detection in the image.

$$\mathcal{E}_{tip} = \sum_h \|(\boldsymbol{p}_l^h - \boldsymbol{f}_l^h)\|_2^2 . \tag{11}$$

Curviness Term $\mathcal{E}_{cur}$. It limits the hair to coincide barely with root and tip but fail in the remaining pixels. It computes the perpendicular distance from each fiber point to the closest point in the root-tip segment and compares the equivalent procedure with the detected hair on the image.

$$\mathcal{E}_{cur} = \sum_h \sum_i \|\frac{|(\boldsymbol{p}_l^h - \boldsymbol{p}_0^h) - (\boldsymbol{p}_0^h - \boldsymbol{p}_i^h)|}{(\boldsymbol{p}_l^h - \boldsymbol{p}_0^h)} - \frac{|(\boldsymbol{f}_l^h - \boldsymbol{f}_0^h) - (\boldsymbol{f}_0^h - \boldsymbol{f}_i^h)|}{(\boldsymbol{f}_l^h - \boldsymbol{f}_0^h)}\|_2^2 . \tag{12}$$

Optimization. We solve Eq. (8) over the different groups in parallel, by using the non-linear least squares. Toward the eyelash optimization, the procedure is equivalent though we force the detected roots to move along the spline formed by the eyelid landmarks. While the eyebrows optimization differs from the rest since we force the hair fibers to grow in the tangent direction instead of the normal one.

3.4 Adding Density and Further Realism

We found that estimating the hair parameters with large clusters even when they have related properties we lose significant realism. To address this issue, we propose a post-processing step which involves two actions: adding density to the retrieved result and adding further realism by appending random small variations to the final 3D hairs.

Adding Density. When we explore the individual hair fibers in 2D, we may discard hairs with severe occlusions and reject sections with poor connections. In this post-processing step, we aim to estimate the missed detections as a combination of the closest visible hairs. We compare the binary mask generated by the orthographic projection of the computed hair elements $\pi(\boldsymbol{F})$, with the initial hair map $\boldsymbol{H}$. To avoid false positives in the estimation, we expand the mask generated by $\pi(\boldsymbol{F})$ with morphological operators and estimate new hair only on the resulting region:

$$G = \sum_i \sum_j (\boldsymbol{H}(i,j) - \pi(\boldsymbol{F})(i,j)) \cdot (\pi(\boldsymbol{F}) \oplus \boldsymbol{D})(i,j), \tag{13}$$

where G represents the number of available pixels to grow a new hair, $\boldsymbol{D}$ is a binary 5×5 dilation mask, and $\oplus$ represents the binary dilation operator. G is a positive integer if the further density is required, and a negative integer if we added more than necessary hair fibers. If G is equal to zero, it implies that there is the exact amount of pixels in the hair map than projections of $\boldsymbol{F}$.

For each new hair, we grow a new hair fiber $\boldsymbol{F}^k$ as a combination of the three closest hairs. This is achieved by averaging the parameters of the hair strand or the equivalent, averaging all the j-th points in $\boldsymbol{F}_j^k = \frac{1}{3}\sum_{i=1}^{3} \boldsymbol{F}_j^i$ where i denotes each of the three nearest neighbors. The process is iterated until G is equal or slightly lower to zero.

Adding Small Random Variations. The estimation of a group of hairs with similar parametrization leads to homogeneous hair in small areas and consequently lack of realism. To overcome this situation, we add small random noise to the resultant length $\lambda_l \in [-0.05, 0.05]$ and a small random rotation amongst all the axes $\boldsymbol{\lambda}_r \in [-1, 1]$, where $\dim(\boldsymbol{\lambda}_r) = 3$. Both variations $\boldsymbol{\lambda}_r$ and λ_l are summed to the fiber estimated parameters to generate a hair shaft such as:

$$\boldsymbol{F}^h(\boldsymbol{p}^h, \boldsymbol{n}^h + \boldsymbol{\lambda}_r, l + \lambda_l, w, r, \theta, g), \tag{14}$$

where $\boldsymbol{\lambda}_r$ adjusts the orientation given by $\boldsymbol{n}^h$ and λ_l the fiber length given by l.

4 Experimental Evaluation

We now present our experimental results for different types of pictures, including several hairstyles for both genders, obtained from Pexels platform. Additionally, we also present a qualitative comparison with respect to [4].

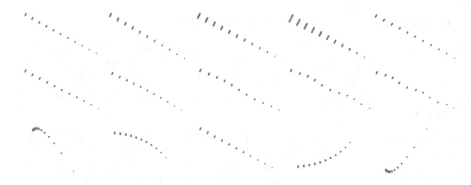

Fig. 3. Qualitative Evaluation of Several Hair Fibers. We depict the average amongst all the hairs in a single hair. Green circles represent the ground truth, and red dots our estimation. Best viewed in color. (Color figure online)

Table 1. Quantitative evaluation of several hair fibers and time budget. 3D errors of the hair fibers depicted in Fig. 3, and the corresponding computation time in seconds. The last column represents the average error for all the points in the 150 hairs.

(row,col)	(1,1)	(1,2)	(1,3)	(1,4)	(1,5)	(2,1)	(2,2)	(2,3)	(2,4)	(2,5)	(3,1)	(3,2)	(3,3)	(3,4)	(3,5)	**Average**
error 3D	0.027	0.004	0.006	0.014	0.017	0.014	0.013	0.017	0.015	0.013	0.002	0.002	0.006	0.003	0.008	0.011
time (s)	40.443	40.936	50.613	51.977	40.996	52.167	52.873	62.767	51.463	51.853	40.443	59.267	61.289	61.311	64.152	52.170

First, we had evaluated our method quantitatively with synthetic samples. To this end, we have generated a total of 150 synthetic hairs over half sphere and recovered the parameters from their 2D coordinates. Our goal is to reconstruct the 3D hairs with those parameters and obtain the 3D error between points in the initial and the reconstructed hairs. For completeness, we have used the configurations that were described in Fig. 2. Table 1 reports the 3D errors as an average of the 3D error amongst all the points. Figure 3 depicts the average hair, displaying where these errors are located. As it can be observed, in both cases our method presents very competing results and provides accurate hair reconstructions.

To show the effectiveness of our approach on real scenarios, we first consider from short to full beards and mustaches. Some results are displayed on Fig. 4, where we can observe how our method produces realistic solutions on challenging scenarios with short and long beards, mustache, eyebrows, and eyelashes. Further, it works satisfactorily with partial occlusions, as self-occluding beards (see subjects (2,1) and (3,1) on the previous figure). We also report some numbers regarding these experiments in Table 2, where the number of hair fibers is included. As it can be observed, our approach is available to recover a large number of hair fibers in different areas.

In addition, we also consider some cases over subjects with eyebrows and eyelashes, including a challenging case concerning a subject with eyeglasses. Particularly, the subject (5,2) represents a challenging scenario due to the poor

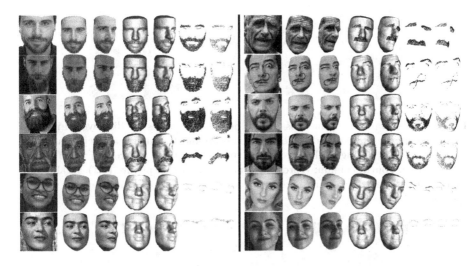

Fig. 4. Face reconstruction with different facial hair styles. In both sides, we represent the same information. First column: Input image. Second and third columns: Frontal and side views of our 3D hair + face reconstruction over a textured face. The hair fibers are represented by red lines. Fourth and fifth columns: Frontal and side views of our estimated geometry, without considering any texture. Sixth and seventh columns: Just observing our hair estimation. (Color figure online)

Table 2. Number of reconstructed hair fibers for pictures on Fig. 4. We report for every picture on Fig. 4, its resolution, and the number of retrieved hairs on the upper/lower parts of the face, showing in parenthesis the added hairs in the post-processing step. To this end, we consider the location of every picture on the figure, indicating its row and column position.

(row,col)	(1,1)	(2,1)	(3,1)	(4,1)	(5,1)	(6,1)	(1,2)	(2,2)	(3,2)	(4,2)	(5,2)	(6,2)
im res.	849×1273	1024×768	1200×825	1600×2400	4000×6000	393×588	1265×1920	845×650	1760×2640	1750×1168	3999×3999	5075×5760
hairs up	766(61)	62(2)	72(6)	181(19)	804(6)	168(13)	551(63)	609(55)	66(9)	334(67)	7132(238)	162(7)
hairs lo	10251(510)	9575(155)	17874(408)	4647(41)	0(0)	0(0)	6250(212)	7332(746)	7733(440)	9384(361)	0(0)	0(0)

texture produced by makeup. Fortunately, our approach is able to detect small pieces of eyebrow hair instead of full hairs owing to the large image resolution and quality. Another example, it is the subject (6,1), Frida Kahlo, where our approach is evaluated for a low-resolution picture. As in the previous case, our approach also produces a visually realistic solution. Again, some numbers about these experiments are reported in Table 2. In Fig. 5 we show some detailed close-ups, where it can be observed the realism we achieve with our approach.

In all cases, we use un-optimized Matlab code on an Intel(R) Xenon(R) CPU ES-1620 v3 at 3.506 GHz. The full pipeline run-time depends on the amount and complexity of the hairs to recover. It takes from 15 min to recover examples with upper hair only to 10 h to recover the subject (3,1) in Fig. 4, where the hair density is extremely large.

Fig. 5. Close-up results. Some close-ups of detailed instances are displayed. First and second column: eyelashes and a piece of beard around the mouth are represented for the subject (1,1) on Fig. 4. Third column: unveils the thick eyebrow of Frida Kahlo, subject (6,1). Fourth column: represents a man's mustache, picture (4,1). In all cases, we can observe how the hair fibers are successfully recovered, and they are visually coherent.

Fig. 6. Qualitative comparison on 3D hair + face reconstruction. First column: input RGB image for our approach. It is worth noting that the solution in [4] requires 14 cameras along with 4 flashes, i.e., a very constrained calibration is demanded. Second and third column: frontal and side views using [4]. Fourth and fifth column: our solution.

Finally, we also establish a qualitative comparison with respect to [4]. In this case, it is worth mentioning that while our approach only needs an RGB image under general and uncontrolled lighting conditions as input, [4] requires a calibrated multi-camera system. Despite this disadvantage in terms of hardware resources, our approach obtains competing results (see Fig. 6 for a qualitative comparison). As it can be observed, our method is effective in locating the hair fibers and optimizing their parametrization.

Discussion: Regardless of the surpassing performance in terms of single image facial hair fiber capture, our method works better in the presence of short and scattered hairs on high-resolution pictures. Similarly, we find helpful clear and noiseless textures with high contrast between skin and face. Although our method can reconstruct like-wise facial hairs when the previous scenarios are not favorable, we find the hair fibers with big orientation changes are difficult to be recovered (see Dali's example in Fig. 4), since our approach is not able to fully trace individual hairs with angles larger than $10°$. Moreover, the hair should be evident at pixel-level in order to be detected.

5   Conclusion

In this paper, we have proposed a framework that successfully recovers 3D facial hair from a single RGB image without any training data. To this end, we proposed a facial hair parametric model based on 3D helixes and a set of energies which rely on 2D hair detections over different face areas to estimate the parameters directly from the image. Furthermore, it does not require any training data, user interaction, or any specific setup. We have extensively validated our approach over a collection of several images with uncontrolled illumination and show consistent and realistic results even in challenging cases as thick beards, eyeglasses, low-resolution pictures, and eyebrow makeup. Further, we compare our approach with the current state of the art, where our procedure retrieves competing results despite the clear disadvantage in terms of hardware and single-image versus multiview setups. Facial hair is an essential step in the reconstruction of realistic faces. For this reason, future research lines are to join different procedures to retrieve various aspects of detail in human faces without delimiting the face area but the full head structure including the neck, which is a plausible spot for men to have hair.

Acknowledgments. This work has been partially supported by the Spanish Ministry of Science and Innovation under projects FireDMMI TIN2014-56919-C3-2-R, BOSSS TIN2017-89723-P, and HuMoUR TIN2017-90086-R; by the Spanish State Research Agency through the María de Maeztu Seal of Excellence to IRI MDM-2016-0656, and by the CSIC project R3OBJ 2018501099.

References

1. Agudo, A., Moreno-Noguer, F.: Combining local-physical and global-statistical models for sequential deformable shape from motion. IJCV **122**(2), 371–387 (2017)
2. Agudo, A., Moreno-Noguer, F.: Force-based representation for non-rigid shape and elastic model estimation. TPAMI **40**(9), 2137–2150 (2018)
3. Amos, B., Ludwiczuk, B., Satyanarayanan, M., et al.: Openface: a general-purpose face recognition library with mobile applications. CMUSCS (2016)
4. Beeler, T., et al.: Coupled 3D reconstruction of sparse facial hair and skin. TOG **31**(4), 117 (2012)
5. Chai, M., Luo, L., Sunkavalli, K., Carr, N., Hadap, S., Zhou, K.: High-quality hair modeling from a single portrait photo. TOG **34**(6), 204 (2015)
6. Chai, M., Shao, T., Wu, H., Weng, Y., Zhou, K.: AutoHair: fully automatic hair modeling from a single image. TOG **35**(4) (2016)
7. Chai, M., Wang, L., Weng, Y., Jin, X., Zhou, K.: Dynamic hair manipulation in images and videos. TOG **32**(4), 75 (2013)
8. Chen, Y., Song, Z., Lin, S., Martin, R.R., Cheng, Z.-Q.: Capture of hair geometry using white structured light. Comput.-Aided Des. **96**, 31–41 (2018)
9. Hachmann, H., Awiszus, M., Rosenhahn, B.: 3D braid guide hair reconstruction using electroluminescent wires. Vis. Comput. **34**, 793–804 (2018)
10. Hu, L., Ma, C., Luo, L., Li, H.: Robust hair capture using simulated examples. TOG **33**(4), 126 (2014)
11. Hu, L., Ma, C., Luo, L., Li, H.: Single-view hair modeling using a hairstyle database. TOG **34**(4), 125 (2015)
12. Jackson, A.S., Bulat, A., Argyriou, V., Tzimiropoulos, G.: Large pose 3D face reconstruction from a single image via direct volumetric CNN regression. In: ICCV (2017)

13. Jakob, W., Moon, J.T., Marschner, S.: Capturing hair assemblies fiber by fiber. TOG **28**(5), 164 (2009)
14. Luo, L., Li, H., Rusinkiewicz, S.: Structure-aware hair capture. TOG **32**(4), 76 (2013)
15. Paris, S., Briceño, H.M., Sillion, F.X.: Capture of hair geometry from multiple images. TOG **23**(3), 712–719 (2004)
16. Paris, S., et al.: Hair photobooth: geometric and photometric acquisition of real hairstyles. TOG **27**(3), 30 (2008)
17. Peissig, J., Goode, T., Smith, P.: The role of eyebrows in face recognition: with, without, and different. J. Vis. **9**(8), 554–554 (2009)
18. Wei, Y., Ofek, E., Quan, L., Shum, H.-Y.: Modeling hair from multiple views. TOG **24**(3), 816–820 (2005)
19. Yu, X., Yu, Z., Chen, X., Yu, J.: A hybrid image-CAD based system for modeling realistic hairstyles. In: SIGGRAPH (2014)
20. Zhang, M., Chai, M., Wu, H., Yang, H., Zhou, K.: A datadriven approach to four-view image-based hair modeling. TOG **36**(4), 156 (2017)
21. Zhou, Y., et al.: HairNet: single-view hair reconstruction using convolutional neural networks. In: ECCV (2018)

From Features to Attribute Graphs for Point Set Registration

Carlos Orrite$^{(\boxtimes)}$, Elias Herrero, and Mauricio Valencia

Instituto de Investigacion en Ingenieria de Aragon, University of Zaragoza,
Zaragoza, Spain
{corrite,jelias}@unizar.es, A01136483@itesm.mx
http://i3a.unizar.es/

Abstract. The traditional approach for point set registration is based on matching feature descriptors between the target object and the query image and then the fundamental matrix is calculated robustly using RANSAC to align the target in the image. However, this approach can easily fail in the presence of occlusion, background clutter and changes in scale and camera viewpoint, being the RANSAC algorithm unable to filter out many outliers. In our proposal the target is represented by an attribute graph, where its vertices represent salient features describing the target object and its edges encode their spatial relationships. The matched keypoints between the attribute graph and the descriptors in the query image are filtered taking into account features such as orientation and scale, as well as the structure of the graph. Preliminary results using the Stanford Mobile Visual search data set and the Stanford Streaming Mobile Augmented Reality Dataset show the best behaviour of our proposal in valid matches and lower computational cost in relation to the standard approach based on RANSAC.

Keywords: Graphs · Matching · RANSAC

1 Introduction

A large number of vision applications, such as visual correspondence, object matching, 3D reconstruction and motion tracking, rely on matching keypoints across images. Effective and efficient generation of keypoints from an image is a well-studied problem in the literature and is the basis of many Computer Vision applications. In spite of the large literature dealing with this issue, it remains a challenging topic for achieving stable and reliable matching results in a complex situation, facing illumination variation, shape and scale change, background clutter, appearance change, partial occlusions, etc.

The standard approach for feature matching relies on some steps. The first one is to find feature points in each image. Next, keypoint descriptors are matched for each pair of images using the approximate nearest neighbour (ANN). After matching features for an image pair the fundamental matrix is robustly

© Springer Nature Switzerland AG 2019
A. Morales et al. (Eds.): IbPRIA 2019, LNCS 11867, pp. 437–448, 2019.
https://doi.org/10.1007/978-3-030-31332-6_38

Fig. 1. Point set registration found with RANSAC. Feature descriptors are represented by a circle, pointing to the scale, and an arrow indicating the orientation. Inlier matches are represented in yellow, while the outliers are in red. (Color figure online)

estimated for the pair using Random Sample Consensus (RANSAC) algorithm [1] in order to determinate in-liners. Although RANSAC works well in many cases, there is no guarantee that it will obtain a reasonable solution even if there exists one. It can also be hard to determine if there is no solution at all.

Matching between images is accomplished by feature descriptors. It provides a list of candidate matching points between the object and the descriptors in the image. However, there exists some other keypoint attributes, such as scale or orientation, useful for pruning false matches. Inspired in fingerprint recognition we follow a similar feature matching process to remove wrong correspondences. So, when matching keypoints the correspondence among them has to be in accordance with the change of scale and orientation between both images. Figure 1 shows the matches after RANSAC between two images where some outliers are still present. Feature points in both images are represented by a circle, whose size is proportional to its scale, and an arrow that shows the main orientation of the descriptor. It is easily seen how the extreme outlier, depicted in red, can be removed as it does not exhibit a similar change in scale or orientation between both images.

However, this filtering process may be not enough as it is based on point to point correspondences without taking into account the overall structure of the object. Some authors propose the modelling of the object by an attribute graph, where keypoints provided by the feature detector constitute the vertices of the graph. The topological relationship of these keypoints are preserved by the edge interconnections. The structure of the graph has itself a relevant information about the object and can be useful for filtering mismatches as we propose in this paper. Figure 3 shows a mismatch between three points. Orientation and change in scale is similar for the matched points, as they correspond to a similar cloud in the image. However, from a structural point of view, both triangles are not matched as they correspond to a different graph structure.

The main contributions of this paper are: the generation of an Attribute Graph (AG) and a matching filtering based on attribute and structure which overcome the limitations of RANSAC, mainly to assess if there is no matching between two images.

2   Related Work

2.1   Local Features from Images

Feature detection aims at finding some interesting points (features) in the image such as corners. On the other hand, descriptor extraction aims to represent those interesting points to later compare them with other interesting points (features) in a different image. Current methods for feature matching rely on well-known descriptors for detection and matching as the SIFT and SURF keypoint detector and descriptor, or more recent descriptors such as BRIEF or BRISK which exhibit an acceptable performance with the benefit of a low computational cost, see [2] for a deeper insight in comparison of feature detectors and descriptors for object class matching. Those sparse methods that find interest points and then match them across images become the de facto standard [3].

In recent years, many of these approaches have been revised using deep networks [3,4], which has led to a revival for dense matching [5,6]. Despite the great expectation raised by dense methods, they still tend to fail in complex scenes with occlusions.

Regardless the learning procedure used to get local features, sparse or dense methods, this paper tackles with the problem of how to combine them in a higher structure to cope with the limitations that both approaches still suffer.

2.2   Image-to-Image Alignment

Another problem that has attracted increasing attention over the past years is the localization problem, i.e. estimating the position of a camera giving an image. Several approaches have been suggested to solve this problem. Many of them have adopted an image retrieval approach, where a query image is matched to a database of images using visual features. Sometimes this is combined with a geometric verification step, but in many cases the underlying geometry is largely ignored, see [7].

Some works afford the representation of the target object by an attributed graph, where its vertices represent feature descriptors and its edges encode their spatial relationship which has already been proposed in [8]. The authors propose an attribute graph to represent the structure of a target object in the problem of tracking it along time. The structure of the model yields in the change of shape when the object moves, adapting continuously to the edge ratio in each triangle of the graph. As in many other computer vision problems when adapting the model according to the appearance of the object it can easily be degenerated to loose the target when the model no longer fit to the object.

2.3   Filtering Correspondences

Image alignment and structure-from-motion methods often use RANSAC to find optimal transformation hypotheses [1]. In the last decades many variants of the original RANSAC procedure have been proposed, we refer the reader to [9] for a performance evaluation of these methods.

A major drawback of these approaches is that they rely on small subsets of the data to generate the hypotheses, e.g., the 5-point algorithm or 8-point algorithm to retrieve the essential matrix. It requires that most false matches have to be removed in advance. As image pairs with large baselines and imaging changes will contain a large percentage of outliers, it makes RANSAC to fail in these kind of situations.

Recent works try to overcome this limitation by simultaneously rejecting outliers and estimating global motion. GMS [10] divides the image into multiple grids and forms initial matches between the grid cells. Although they show improvements over traditional matching strategies, the piecewise smoothness assumption is often violated in practice.

As mentioned previously, traditionally hand-crafted feature descriptions have been replaced by deep learning ones, which can be trained in an end-to-end way. However, RANSAC has not been used as part of such deep learning pipelines, because its hypothesis selection procedure is non-differentiable. As far as our knowledge, DSAC [11] is the only work to tackle spare outlier rejection in a differentiable way. However, this method is designed to mimic RANSAC rather than to outperform it, as we propose in this paper. Furthermore, it is specific to 3D to 2D correspondences, rather than point set registration [12].

3   Our Approach

3.1   Attribute Graph

Given a target image and a set of keypoints and its corresponding descriptors we first model the target by an attribute graph. Triangles are 2D entities that are able to describe the geometry of planar objects and more complex objects by a triangle mesh. In our approach, the object is modelled by a triangle mesh where each point in the mesh corresponds to a keypoint, which has associated a feature descriptor.

Formally speaking, an attributed graph G consists of a set of vertices V, which are connected via a set of edges E. The edges E are inserted following the rules of the Delaunay triangulation. Hence, there is also a set of triangles F, where $c : F \longrightarrow V^3; c(f) = \{v_1, v_2, v_3\}$. The model stores attributes with vertices and triangles.

Attributes of Vertices: Each vertex $v \in V$ stores a set of attributes $\{\mathbf{p}, \beta, s\}$.
    p: $\mathbf{p}(v) = \{x, y\}^T$ is the 2D position of vertex v.
    β: $\beta(v)$ is the orientation provided by the feature detector for this vertex.
    s: $s(v)$ is the scale provided by the feature detector for this vertex.

Attributes of Triangles: Each triangle $f \in F$ stores a set of vertices $c(f) = \{v_1, v_2, v_3\}$ and barycentric angles A.

A: $A(f) = \{\alpha_1, \alpha_2, \alpha_3\}^T$ are the angles between any vertex and the barycentric, see Fig. 2.

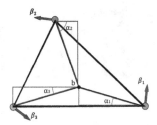

Fig. 2. Attributes for vertices and triangle.

3.2 Attribute Filtering

The standard approach for feature matching basically relies on three steps. The first one is to find feature points in each image (keypoints). Next, for each pair of images, keypoint descriptors are matched for each pair of images using the approximate nearest neighbour. After matching features for an image pair the fundamental matrix is robustly estimated for the pair using RANSAC, removing outliers.

In our proposal we follow the first two steps, i.e., feature detection and matching based on kd-tree and then use the graph structure to remove false matchings. We carry out two filtering processes one after the other. The first one is based on attributes and the other one on structure.

Matching between images is accomplished by feature descriptors. It provides a list of candidate matching points between the object and the descriptors in the image. However, other keypoint attributes, such as scale or orientation, useful for pruning false matches exist.

To recover the orientation between the model and the image the most probable orientation difference is found. The median is obtained and all the correspondences higher, or lower, a threshold from this value are rejected. To do so, the circular statistic is used due to the inherent nature of the data.

Afterwards, the same process is carried out using the scale attribute. For those correspondences exhibiting a difference in scale attribute higher or lower than the median are removed. In this paper we consider a scale threshold corresponding to the double or the half of the median scale change.

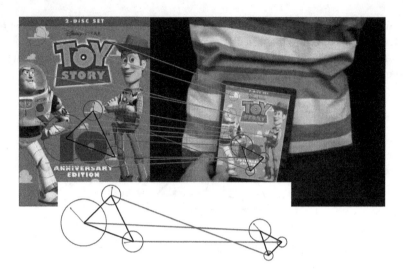

Fig. 3. Mismatch points filtered by structure.

3.3 Structure Filtering

In spite of the attribute filtering some mismatch points, with similar change in orientation and scale, might remain, see Fig. 3 where a solid triangle suffers from a projective change. The structure filtering takes into account the Delaunay triangulation in the graph to analyse the consistency of the matching from a structural point of view. For every triangle in the graph the barycentric is calculated. Afterwards, for each vertex in the triangle we compute the angle between the vector given by the descriptor orientation and the vector joining the vertex with the barycentric. In a similar way, we compute the angle between the orientation of the descriptor in the image and the vector joining that keypoint and the coordinates of its barycentric. Computing the angle descriptor in relation to the barycentric vector is similar to a normalization process and therefore, the difference between both keypoints in the image and the target should be close to 0.

For the example shown in Fig. 3, it can be easily verified that the ordination of the points is not preserved, and therefore, the change of orientation between both triangles will not pass the structure filtering. Next step consists in identifying which is the wrong point in the triangle, or could be more than one. As every triangle is not isolated, but it belongs to a graph, we check for each vertex if it is or not in accordance with its neighbour triangles in the graph. In this way, we obtain a list of triangle orientation for any point in relation to its neighbours. Now we apply the voting rule, so that the point which has received more mismatches will be rejected. The process carries on till all vertices pass the triangle orientation exam.

Fig. 4. Object detection in presence of scale and orientation changes, background clutter and partial occlusions for The Stanford Streaming Mobile Augmented Reality Dataset. From left to right: Barry White Moving, Chris Brown Moving, Toy Story Moving and Titanic Moving. At the top, the original DVD covers. Following rows show some frames suffering from different partial occlusions (first frame of the sequence on the middle row, last frame on the bottom row. The rectangular DVD cover is depicted in yellow after the four corners are detected.

4   Experiments

Next, we describe a set of experiments used to verify our theoretical results. We use two datasets: The Stanford Streaming Mobile Augmented Reality Dataset and The Stanford Mobile Visual Search data set. For the former dataset we report the mean error in the estimation of the target bounding box as well as the computational cost to carry out the object location. For the last dataset we report the image match accuracy.

All experiments have been implemented in Matlab. For both datasets we use the SIFT descriptor, running the code provided by [13]. The algorithm provides a feature vector of salient keypoints. For every keypoint the x and y coordinates, the scale and the orientation are given. Additionally, the code provides a 128-d histogram as feature descriptor for every keypoint. It is well known that Hellinger measures outperform Euclidean distance when comparing histograms. So, in our experiments we follow the so called RootSIFT approach proposed by [15] to improve the matching. As the Hellinger distance goes from 0 to 1, we use a 0.95 value as a threshold to valid the feature descriptor matching. Approximated nearest neighbour (ARR) is computed by kd-tree.

In these experiments we compared the performance of the proposed algorithm to that of RANSAC and a couple of its variants, i.e., MSAC, and MLESAC. For all these methods, the number of iterations was set to 100, and in each iteration the fundamental matrix was calculated using the eight-point algorithm, the Chi squared probability threshold for inliers is set to 0.99 and the noise standard

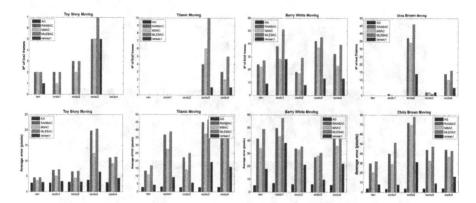

Fig. 5. Top: lost frames in any dataset. Bottom: average error for the four corners obtained from the right matched frames.

deviation to 2, see [14]. Additionally, we use another implementation of RANSAC provided by [16], that we denoted as ransac1.

4.1 The Stanford Streaming Mobile Augmented Reality Dataset

The Stanford Streaming Mobile Augmented Reality Dataset [17] contains 23 different objects of interest, divided to four categories: Books, CD covers, DVD covers and Common Objects.Each video is 100 frames long, recorded at 30 fps with resolution 640 × 480. For each video, we provide a clean database image (no background noise) for the corresponding object of interest. In our experiments we use those videos corresponding to moving objects recorded with a moving camera, i.e., Barry White Moving, Chris Brown Moving, Toy Story Moving, Titanic Moving. These videos help to study the effect of background clutter when there is a relative motion between the object and the background. The dataset authors provide the ground-truth localization information for these videos, where they manually define a bounding quadrilateral around the object of interest in each video frame. To make the experiments even more challenging we have simulated the partial occlusion of the object using a square with a texture similar to that of the target. As the object is being moved along the scene, we check the behaviour of all approaches considering four different occlusion placements, see Fig. 4.

Figures 5 (bottom) show the number of frames where the matching has failed or the error in any of the four corners is longer than the maximum image size, as well as, the mean error, given in pixels, for the four corners corresponding to the correct frames (on the top). Some conclusions can be drawn from this Figure. The most relevant one is that our approach, based on an Attribute Graph (AG) and filtering, outperforms the results provided by the RANSAC algorithm and its variants. No frame is lost in our approach. Besides, the average error for all frames in any dataset, for all occlusions, is lower in AG.

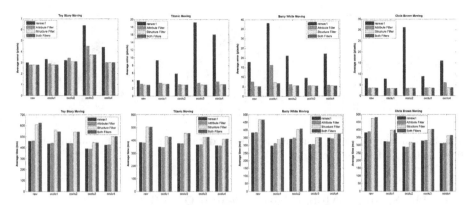

Fig. 6. Applying the attribute and structural filters after RANSAC. On the top: the average error (in pixels) for all datasets. On the bottom: the average computational cost (in ms) taken by any of the proposals.

Fig. 7. Landmark dataset. The query image (top), the reference image (bottom)

In relation to the RANSAC algorithms taken from the literature we have found that the so called ransac1 exhibits the best performance among them. Therefore, we have run a second experiment to check the improvement of this algorithm in conjunction with our approach. Figure 6 shows on the top the average error for four different situations: (a) running the RANSAC algorithm alone, (b) applying afterwards the attribute filter or (c) the structure filter and (d) both filters after RANSAC. It is noticeable how the average error of RANSAC is highly reduced after applying our filtering approach.

Figure 6 on the bottom shows the average time (in ms) taken to compute any of these four experiments. As it can be seen, the RANSAC algorithm consumes most of the time, being the attribute filter practically negligible. Therefore, we can pay for a low increase in computational cost to obtain a lower error in localization.

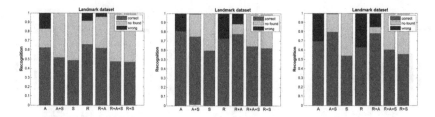

Fig. 8. Matching accuracy for the Landmark dataset for three different thresholds: 0.95; 0.90, 0.85 from left to right

4.2   The Stanford Mobile Visual Search Data Set

Outdoor applications pose additional challenges to those shown in the previous experiments where highly textured rigid planar objects taken under controlled lighting conditions were used. Buildings, on the other hand, tend to have fewer features, exhibit repetitive structures and their 3-D geometric distortions are not captured by simple affine or projective transformations. In order to check our proposal for this kind of applications we have selected The Stanford Mobile Visual Search data set, which exhibits some characteristics lacking in the previous data sets: rigid objects, widely varying lighting conditions, perspective distortion, foreground and background clutter and query data collected from heterogeneous low and high-end camera phones, [18]. The Landmarks dataset has been used for the experiments as it constitutes one of the most challenging dataset in relation to image registration. Figure 7 shows some examples.

By this new set of experiments we intend to asses the performance of the matching filtering processes discussed in this paper, i.e., orientation+scale attribute filtering, structure filtering and RANSAC. In this regard, we run a set of experiments denoted as: A (Attribute filtering); S (Structure filtering); A+S (Structure filtering after Attribute filtering); R (RANSAC); R+A (Attribute filtering after RANSAC); R+S (Structure filtering after RANSAC); R+A+S (Structured filtering after Attribute after RANSAC).

We run a new experiment with the Lanmark dataset for image retrieval taking a query image from the query subset and see which one corresponds to the reference subset. Taking into account the eight-point problem, we consider that if there are not at least eight point correspondences between the query and the reference image we label it as no found. Both subsets, query and reference, have the same number of pictures ($N = 501$). So far, we have performed several experiments using the Hellinger distance for feature matching with a threshold value equal to 0.95. This parameter can be relevant when dealing with outdoor images which tend to have fewer features and lighting conditions can change significantly at different times of the day. Therefore, in the new experiments three different values have been used, i.e., 0.95, 0.90 and 0.85.

Figure 8 shows the results for the three thresholds under consideration for all the filtering combinations previously mentioned. In order to analyse these graphs we have to consider two aspects: on the one hand, the recognition matching has to be the highest possible and on the other hand, the wrong mismatches have to be the lowest. In this regards we can notice that the attribute filtering and the RANSAC filter exhibit the highest number of wrong mismatches of all approaches. It is worth noticing that the combination of structure filtering after attribute filtering improve the results provided by the structure filtering alone. We can see how A+S outperforms S approach and the same can be said for R+A+S in relation to R+S. Finally, it is shown that the A+S approach outperforms the R+A+S for this dataset.

5   Conclusions

In this paper we have tackled with the problem of feature matching for object detection by modelling the object as an attribute graph. Keypoints provided by the feature detector constitute the vertices of the graph. The topological relationship of these keypoints is preserved by the edge interconnections. Matching filtering takes into account attributes of the nodes, such as orientation or scale, as well as the structure of the graph.

Experiments with the Stanford Streaming Mobile Augmented Reality Dataset have confirmed the better performance of our approach in relation to traditional methods based on RANSAC and variants. Moreover, the matching filtering approach based on attributes and structure has even worked well for matching outdoor images, such as landmarks, where their 3-D geometric distortions are not captured by simple affine or projective transformations. One of the most remarkable property of our approach is that it does not generate false image correspondences, as other RANSAC-based approaches do.

Acknowledgmentes. This work was supported by the Spanish project TIN2017-88841-R (Ministerio de Economa Industria y Competitividad/FEDER, UE).

References

1. Fischler, M.A., Bolles, R.C.: Random sample consensus: a paradigm for model fitting with applications to image analysis and automated cartography. Commun. ACM **24**, 381–395 (1981)
2. Hietanen, A., Lankinen, J., Buch, A.G., Kämäräinen, J.-K., Küger, N.: A Comparison of feature detectors and descriptors for object class matching. Neurocomputing **184**, 3–12 (2016)
3. Ono, Y., Trulls, E., Fua, P., Yi, K.M.: LF-Net: learning local features from images. NIPS 6234–6244 (2018)
4. Detone, D., Malisiewicz, T., Rabinovich, A.: Superpoint: self-supervised interest point detection and description. In: CVPR Workshop on Deep Learning for Visual SLAM (2018)
5. Vijayanarasimhan, S., Ricco, S., Schmid, C., Sukthankar, R., Fragkiadaki, K.: SfM-Net: learning of structure and motion from video. arXiv:1704.07804 (2017)
6. Zhou, T., Brown, M., Snavely, N., Lowe, D.G.: Unsupervised learning of depth and ego-motion from video. In: CVPR-2017 (2017)

7. Svärm, L., Enqvist, O., Oskarsson, M., Kahl, F.: Accurate localization and pose estimation for large 3D models. In: CVPR-2014 (2014)
8. Artner, N.M., Kropatsch, W.G.: Structural cues in 2D tracking: edge lengths vs. barycentric coordinates. In: Ruiz-Shulcloper, J., Sanniti di Baja, G. (eds.) CIARP 2013. LNCS, vol. 8259, pp. 503–511. Springer, Heidelberg (2013). https://doi.org/10.1007/978-3-642-41827-3_63
9. Choi, S., Kim, T., Yu, W.: Performance evaluation of RANSAC family. In: BMVC, pp. 1–12 (2009)
10. Bian, J., Lin, W., Matsushita, Y., Yeung, S., Nguyen, T., Cheng, M.: GMS: grid-based motion statistics for fast, ultra-robust feature correspondence. In: CVPR (2017)
11. Brachmann, E., et al.: DSAC - differentiable RANSAC for camera localization. ARXIV (2018)
12. Moo Yi, K., Trulls, E., Ono, Y., Lepetit, V., Salzmann, M., Fua, P.: Learning to find good correspondences. In: CVPR-2018 (2018)
13. Vedaldi, A., Fulkerson, B.: VLFeat: an open and portable library of computer vision algorithms (2008). http://www.vlfeat.org/
14. Zuliani, M.: RANSAC toolbox for matlab (2008)
15. Arandjelović, R., Zisserman, A.: Three things everyone should know to improve object retrieval. In: CVPR (2012)
16. Kovesi, P.: RANSACFITFUNDMATRIX fits fundamental matrix using RANSAC (2005). http://www.csse.uwa.edu.au/
17. Makar, M., Tsai, S.S., Chandrasekhar, V., Chen, D.M., Girod, B.: Inter-frame coding of canonical patches for mobile augmented reality. In: Proceedings of IEEE International Symposium on Multimedia (ISM) (2012)
18. Chandrasekhar, et al.: The stanford mobile visual search data set. In: Proceedings of the Second Annual ACM Conference on Multimedia Systems, pp. 117–122 (2011)

BELID: Boosted Efficient Local Image Descriptor

Iago Suárez[1,2]([⊠]) [iD], Ghesn Sfeir[1] [iD], José M. Buenaposada[3] [iD],
and Luis Baumela[1] [iD]

[1] Departamento de Inteligencia Artificial, Universidad Politécnica de Madrid,
Campus Montegancedo s/n, 28660 Boadilla del Monte, Spain
g.sfeir@alumnos.upm.es, lbaumela@fi.upm.es
[2] The Graffter, Campus Montegancedo s/n, Centro de Empresas UPM,
28223 Pozuelo de Alarcón, Spain
iago.suarez@thegraffter.com
[3] ETSII, Universidad Rey Juan Carlos, C/Tulipán, s/n, 28933 Móstoles, Spain
josemiguel.buenaposada@urjc.es

Abstract. Efficient matching of local image features is a fundamental task in many computer vision applications. Real-time performance of top matching algorithms is compromised in computationally limited devices, due to the simplicity of hardware and the finite energy supply. In this paper we present BELID, an efficient learned image descriptor. The key for its efficiency is the discriminative selection of a set of image features with very low computational requirements. In our experiments, performed both in a personal computer and a smartphone, BELID has an accuracy similar to SIFT with execution times comparable to ORB, the fastest algorithm in the literature.

Keywords: Computer vision for smartphones ·
Feature descriptors extraction · Learned descriptors · Boosting

1 Introduction

Local image representations are designed to match images in the presence of strong appearance variations, such as illumination changes or geometric transformations. They are a fundamental component of a wide range of Computer Vision tasks such as 3D reconstruction [1,20], SLAM [14], image retrieval [16], tracking [17], place recognition [15] or pose estimation [31]. They are the most popular image representation approach, because local features are distinctive, view point invariant, robust to partial occlusions and very efficient, since they discard low informative image areas.

To produce a local image representation we must detect a set of salient image structures and provide a description for each of them. There is a plethora of very efficient detectors for various low level structures such as corners [18], segments [28], lines [23] and regions [11], that may be described by real valued [3,10]

© Springer Nature Switzerland AG 2019
A. Morales et al. (Eds.): IbPRIA 2019, LNCS 11867, pp. 449–460, 2019.
https://doi.org/10.1007/978-3-030-31332-0_39

or binary [5,8,19] descriptors, being the binary ones the fastest. In this paper we address the problem of efficient feature description.

Although the SIFT descriptor was introduced twenty years ago [9,10], it is still considered the "golden standard" technique. The recent HPatches benchmark has shown, however, that there is still a lot of room for improvement [2]. Modern descriptors based on deep models have boosted the mean Average Precision (mAP) in different tasks [2] at the price of a sharp increase in computational requirements. This prevents their use in hardware and battery limited devices such as smartphones, drones or robots. This problem has been studied extensively and many local features detectors [18,19,28] and descriptors [5,8] have emerged. They enable real-time performance on resource limited devices, at the price of an accuracy significantly lower than SIFT [32].

In this paper we present an efficient descriptor. Our features use the integral image to efficiently compute the difference between the mean gray values in a pair of image square regions. We use a boosting algorithm [26] to discriminatively select a set of features and combine them to produce a strong description. In our experiments we show that this approach speeds up the computation and achieves execution times close to the fastest technique in the literature, ORB [19], with an accuracy similar to that of SIFT. Specifically, it provides an accuracy better than SIFT in the patch verification and worse in the image matching and patch retrieval tasks of the HPatches benchmark [2].

2   Related Work

SIFT is the most well-known descriptor algorithm [10]. It is widely used because it has a good performance in many Computer Vision tasks. However, it is computationally quite demanding and the only way to use it in a real-time system is using a GPU [4].

A number of different descriptors, such as SURF [3], BRIEF [5], BRISK [8] and ORB [19], have emerged to speed up SIFT. BRIEF, BRISK and ORB use features based on the comparison of pairs of image pixels. The key for their speed is the use of a limited number of binary comparisons. BRIEF uses a fixed size (9×9) smoothing convolution kernel before comparing up to 512 randomly located pixel value pairs (see Fig. 1). BRISK uses a circular pattern (see Fig. 1), smoothing the image with gaussian filters with increasing standard deviation the further away from the center. The ORB descriptor is an extension of BRIEF that takes into account different orientations of the detected local feature. In this case the smoothing is done with an integral image with a fixed sub-window size. It uses a greedy algorithm to uncorrelate the chosen pixel pairs (see Fig. 1). The main drawback of these methods is that they trade accuracy for speed, performing significantly worse than SIFT.

Descriptors based on learning algorithms may further improve the performance. To this end they learn the descriptor hyper parameters, DAISY [25], and select the most discriminative features using Boosting, BinBoost [26], or Convex Optimization [22]. More recently, the use of Deep Learning has enabled

BRIEF   BRISK   ORB   BinBoost   BELID

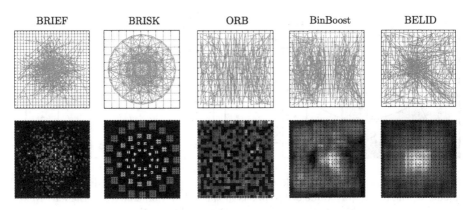

Fig. 1. Visualization of the sampling pairs of pixel locations (first row) and spatial weight heat maps (second row) employed by BRIEF, BRISK, ORB, BinBoost and our BELID trained on the Notre Dame patches dataset. BELID learns a well distributed set of point pairs giving most importance to the center area, making it close to a gaussian weight distribution. BRIEF, BRISK, ORB and BinBoost images taken from [26].

end-to-end learning of descriptors. All CNN-based methods train using pairs or triples of cropped patches. Some train Siamese nets [6], use L2 and hard negative mining [24] or modified triplet-based loss [13]. Other methods optimize a loss related to the Average Precision [7] or an improved triplet loss to help focus on hard examples in training [29]. These methods have improved by a large margin the performance of SIFT in the HPatches benchmark. However, all of them incur in a much larger computational cost.

In this paper we present BELID, a descriptor trained with Boosting that is able to select the best features for the task at hand. Like BRIEF, BRISK and ORB, our features are based on differences of gray values. However, in our descriptor, we compute the difference of the mean gray values within a box. The box size represents a scale parameter that improves the discrimination. Another important difference is that in BELID the search for the best features is guided by a discriminative objective.

3 Boosted Efficient Local Image Descriptor (BELID)

In this section we present an efficient algorithm for describing image local regions that is as fast as ORB and as accurate as SIFT. The key for its speed is the use of few, fast and discriminatively selected features. Our descriptor uses a set of K features selected using the BoostedSCC algorithm [21]. This algorithm is a modification of AdaBoost to select the weak learner (WL) that maximizes the difference between the True Positive Rate (TR) and the False Positive Rate (FP).

Let $\{(\mathbf{x}_i, \mathbf{y}_i, l_i)\}_{i=1}^{N}$ be a training set composed of pairs of image patches, $\mathbf{x}_i, \mathbf{y}_i \in \mathcal{X}$, and labels $l_i \in \{-1, 1\}$. Where $l_i = 1$ means that both patches

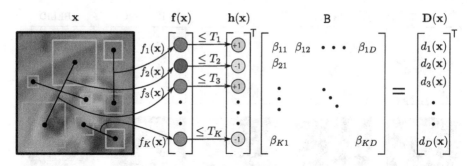

Fig. 2. Descriptor extraction workflow: To describe an image patch BELID efficiently calculates the mean gray value of the pixels in the red and blue boxes in the left. Next, for each pair of red-blue boxes (weak learner) we subtract the red box average gray value from the blue one average, obtaining $\mathbf{f(x)}$. We apply a set of thresholds to these values obtaining $\mathbf{h(x)}$ and finally we multiply by matrix $\mathbf{B}$, to produce the descriptor $\mathbf{D(x)}$. (Color figure online)

correspond to the same salient image structure and $l_i = -1$ if different. The training process minimizes the loss

$$\mathcal{L}_{BSCC} = \sum_{i=1}^{N} \exp\left(-l_i \sum_{k=1}^{K} \alpha_k h_k\left(\mathbf{x}_i\right) h_k\left(\mathbf{y}_i\right)\right), \tag{1}$$

where $h_k(\mathbf{z}) \equiv h_k(\mathbf{z}; f, T)$ corresponds to the k-th WL that depends on a feature extraction function $f : \mathcal{X} \to \mathbb{R}$ and a threshold T. Given f and T we define our weak learners by thresholding $f(\mathbf{x})$ with T,

$$h(\mathbf{x}; f, T) = \begin{cases} +1 & \text{if } f(\mathbf{x}) \leq T \\ -1 & \text{if } f(\mathbf{x}) > T \end{cases} \tag{2}$$

3.1   Thresholded Average Box Weak Learner

The key for efficiency is selecting an $f(\mathbf{x})$ that is both discriminative and fast to compute. We define our feature extraction function, $f(\mathbf{x})$,

$$f(\mathbf{x}; \mathbf{p}_1, \mathbf{p}_2, s) = \frac{1}{s^2}\left(\sum_{\mathbf{q} \in R(\mathbf{p}_1, s)} I(\mathbf{q}) - \sum_{\mathbf{r} \in R(\mathbf{p}_2, s)} I(\mathbf{r})\right), \tag{3}$$

where $I(\mathbf{t})$ is the gray value at pixel $\mathbf{t}$ and $R(\mathbf{p}, s)$ is the square box centered at pixel $\mathbf{p}$ with size s. Thus, f computes the difference between the mean gray values of the pixels in $R(\mathbf{p}_1, s)$ and $R(\mathbf{p}_2, s)$. The red and blue squares in Fig. 2 represent, respectively, $R(\mathbf{p}_2, s)$ and $R(\mathbf{p}_1, s)$. To speed up the computation of f, we use the integral image S of the input image. Once S is available, the sum of gray levels in a square box can be computed with 4 memory accesses and 4 arithmetic operations.

Detectors usually compute the orientation and scale of the local structure. To make our descriptor invariant to euclidean transformations, we orient and scale our measurements with the underlying local structure.

3.2   Optimizing Weak Learner Weights

The BoostedSCC algorithm selects K weak learners with their corresponding weights. The loss function optimized by BoostedSCC in Eq. 1 can be seen as a metric learning approach in which the metric matrix $\mathtt{A}$ is diagonal

$$
\mathcal{L}_{BSCC} = \sum_{i=1}^{N} \exp\left(-l_i \mathbf{h}(\mathbf{x}_i)^\top \underbrace{\begin{bmatrix} \alpha_1^2 & & \\ & \ddots & \\ & & \alpha_K^2 \end{bmatrix}}_{\mathtt{A}} \mathbf{h}(\mathbf{y}_i) \right), \tag{4}
$$

where $\mathbf{h}(\mathbf{w})$ is the vector with the responses of the K weak learners for the image patch $\mathbf{w}$. In this case we are not considering the dependencies between different weak learners responses. At this point the BELID-U (un-optimized) descriptor of a given image patch $\mathbf{w}$ is calculated as $\mathbf{D}(\mathbf{w}) = \mathtt{A}^{\frac{1}{2}} \mathbf{h}(\mathbf{x})$, where $\mathtt{A}^{\frac{1}{2}}$ is such that $\mathtt{A} = \mathtt{A}^{\frac{1}{2}} \mathtt{A}^{\frac{1}{2}}$.

Further, estimating the whole matrix $\mathtt{A}$ improves the similarity function by modeling the correlation between features, $s(\mathbf{x}, \mathbf{y}) = \mathbf{h}(\mathbf{x})^\top \mathtt{A} \mathbf{h}(\mathbf{y})$. FP-Boost [26] estimates $\mathtt{A}$ minimizing

$$
\mathcal{L}_{FP} = \sum_{i=1}^{N} \exp\left(-l_i \sum_{k,r} \alpha_{k,r} h_k\left(\mathbf{x}_i\right) h_r\left(\mathbf{y}_i\right) \right) = \sum_{i=1}^{N} \exp\left(-l_i \mathbf{h}(\mathbf{x})^\top \mathtt{A} \mathbf{h}(\mathbf{y}) \right). \tag{5}
$$

It uses Stochastic Gradient Descent to estimate a symmetric $\mathtt{A}$. Jointly optimizing $\mathtt{A}$ and $h_i(\mathbf{x})$ from scratch is difficult. Thus the algorithm starts from the K weak learners and α's found by BoostedSCC. This second learning step is quite fast because all weak learners responses can be pre-computed.

As in the case of the un-optimized descriptor we have to factorize the similarity function $s(\mathbf{x}, \mathbf{y})$ to compute the independent descriptors for $\mathbf{x}$ and $\mathbf{y}$. Given that $\mathtt{A}$ is a symmetric matrix we can use its eigen-decomposition selecting the D eigenvectors with largest eigenvalues

$$
\mathtt{A} = \mathtt{B} \mathtt{W} \mathtt{B}^\top = \sum_{d=1}^{D} w_d \mathbf{b}_d \mathbf{b}_d^\top, \tag{6}
$$

where $\mathtt{W} = \mathrm{diag}([w_1, \cdots, w_D])$, $w_d \in \{-1, 1\}$, $\mathtt{B} = [\mathbf{b}_1, \cdots, \mathbf{b}_D], \mathbf{b} \in \mathbb{R}^K$, and $D \leq K$. The final descriptor of a given image patch $\mathbf{w}$ is given by $\mathbf{D}(\mathbf{w}) = \mathtt{B}^\top \mathbf{h}(\mathbf{w})$ (see Fig. 2). It will be denoted using the final dimension D, as BELID-D (e.g. BELID-128 when $D = 128$).

454 I. Suárez et al.

4 Experiments

In our experiments we use the popular dataset of patches[1] from Winder *et al.* [30] for training. It consists of 64×64 cropped image patches from three different scenes: Notre Dame cathedral, Yosemite National Part and Liberty statue in New York. The patches are cropped around local structures detected by SIFT.

We compare the performance using three measures:

- **FPR-95.** This is the False Positive Rate at 95% of recall in a patch verification problem (*i.e.* given two patches deciding if they are similar - positive class - or not). When we develop a descriptor, we want to be able to match most of the local structures, lets say a 95% of recall, but with the lowest possible number of false positives. Thus, a descriptor is better the lower FPR-95 it achieves in the patch verification problem.
- **AUC.** Area Under the ROC Curve in a patch verification problem. It provides a good overall measurement, since it considers all the operation points of the curve, instead of just one as in the FPR-95 case.
- **mAP.** Mean Average Precision, as defined in the HPatches benchmark [2] for each of the three tasks: patch verification, image matching and patch retrieval.

We have implemented in Python BoostedSCC, FP-Boost and the learning and testing part of the Thresholded Average Box weak learner of Sect. 3.1. For optimizing the A matrix we use the Stochastic Gradient Descent algorithm with a fixed learning rate of 10^{-8} and a batch size of 2000 samples. We have also implemented in C++, using OpenCV, the descriptor extraction algorithm to process the input images (i.e. not cropped patches). We use this implementation to measure the execution time of BELID in different platforms.

4.1 Patch Verification Experiments

Here we first explore the effect of the number of dimensions, K, in BELID-U and D in BELID (optimized) descriptors. In Fig. 3 we show the AUC and FPR-95 values as a function of the number of dimensions ("N Dimensions"). In the case of BELID, we use $K = 512$ weak learners and compute B to reduce from 512 dimensions to the one given in the plots.

We train using a balanced set of 100 K positive and 100 K negative patch pairs from the Yosemite sequence. The testing set comprises 50 K positive and 50 K negative pairs from the Liberty statue. We first run BoostedSSC selecting 512 weak learners. We change the number of dimensions of the BELID-U curve in Fig. 3 by removing the last weak learners from this initial set. For BELID, we discard the last columns of B, that correspond to the scaled eigen-vectors associated with the smallest eigenvalues.

We can see in Fig. 3 that the boosting process selects features that, up to one point, contribute to the final discrimination. After 128 weak learners the

---

[1] http://matthewalunbrown.com/patchdata/patchdata.html.

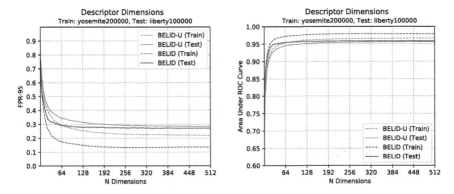

Fig. 3. BELID-U and BELID, training and testing, AUC ("Area Under the ROC Curve") and FPR-95 ("Error") as a function of the number of dimensions in a patch verification problem.

improvement provided by each new feature is very small. After 256 we do not get any improvement at all, which means that the last ones are redundant. The performances of the optimized BELID are always better than those of BELID-U. This proves the interest of the optimization process. BELID gets the lowest FPR-95 at 128 dimensions that, interestingly, is the same number of dimensions used by SIFT. In consequence, BELID-128 is our best descriptor.

In the next experiment we compare our descriptor with SIFT, the "golden standard", and ORB, a representative of the descriptors developed for computational efficiency. We also evaluate LBGM [27], a descriptor using more informative, but computationally expensive, features based on the gradients orientation and the optimization in Sect. 3.2 to estimate A. For these features we use the implementations in OpenCV. We have trained in the 200 K patch balanced set from Notre Dame and tested in the 100 K patch balanced set from the Liberty statue datasets (see Fig. 4 left). We have also trained in the 200 K patch balanced set from Yosemite sequence and tested with the 100 K patch balanced set from Notre Dame (see Fig. 4 right). Figure 4 shows the ROC curves for the testing sets. In terms of accuracy, ORB is the worst descriptor. BELID-128 is better than SIFT and marginally worse than LBGM and BinBoost, both using the same boosting scheme for selecting gradient-based features. Comparing different versions of our algorithm, we can see that BELID-U gets slightly higher FPR-95 values than BELID (as we have seen in the previous experiments) when training and testing sets are from the same domain (Notre Dame/Liberty) and a comparable FPR-95 when they are from different ones (Yosemite/Notre Dame).

4.2 Experiments on the Hpatches Dataset

The recent HPatches benchmark [2] solves some of the shortcomings of previous data sets in terms of data and task diversity, evaluation metrics and experimental reproducibility. The benchmark provides patches taken from images of different

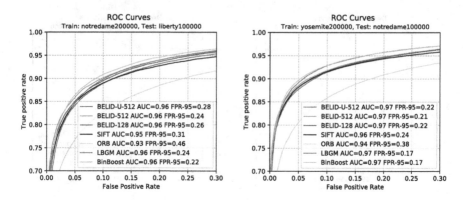

Fig. 4. Test sets ROC curves for the patch verification experiments.

scenes under real and varying capturing conditions, that are tested in patch verification, image matching and patch retrieval problems. We have trained with the balanced 200 K patches pairs from Notre Dame and evaluated on the testing HPatches dataset using the Python code provided by the authors.

Figure 5 shows the results of various BELID configurations and those of other competing approaches obtained with the HPathces tool. In the patch verification problem, the one we use to optimize our descriptor, we get the same situation of the previous experiments. All BELID configurations are better than SIFT, 69.57 vs 63.35, and much better than ORB, 58.21. However, in the other two tasks our descriptor is falling behind SIFT. This is an expected result since we are not optimizing our descriptor for these tasks. Altogether, depending on the configuration considered, BELID may provide results close to SIFT and better than ORB in all tasks.

We have added to Fig. 5 Hardnet [13], a representative CNN-based descriptor. Hardnet beats by a large margin all handcrafted (BRIEF, ORB, SIFT) and Boosting-based descriptors (BinBoost [26], BELID), but it has a much higher computational and energy requirements.

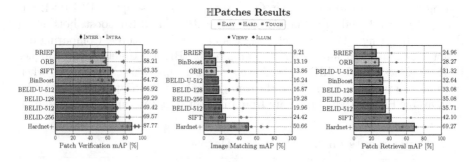

Fig. 5. Comparison in the HPatches dataset for three different tasks.

4.3   Execution Time in Different Platforms

In the last experiment we test our C++ implementation of BELID process-ing images (i.e. no cropped patches) in a desktop CPU, Intel Core i7-6700HQ at 2.60 GHz and 16 GB RAM, and in the limited CPU, Exynox Octa 7870 at 1.59 GHz and 2 GB RAM of a Samsung Galaxy J5-2017 smartphone. We report the execution time in the Mikolajczyk [12] dataset composed by 48 800 × 640 images from 8 different scenes. We detect a maximum of 2000 local structures per image with SURF.

We compare the execution time with other relevant descriptors in the OpenCV library. To this end we use the C++ interface. Specifically we run ORB [19], SIFT [10], LBGM [27] and BinBoost [26]. In Table 1 we show the size of the descriptors in terms of the number of components that can be floating point numbers (f) or bits (b) and the average execution time per image in the experiment.

In terms of speed, BELID-U (without optimization) is comparable to ORB. In fact, BELID-U is as fast as ORB in desktop (0.41 ms vs 0.44 ms) and faster in the limited CPU (2.54 ms vs 6.49 ms). This was expected since both use as features a set of gray value differences. LBGM uses the same feature selection algorithm as BELID, but with slower features. Thus, this descriptor requires the same processing time as SIFT in the desktop setup (19.77 ms vs 22.22 ms) with a slightly better FPR-95 (see Sect. 4.1).

BELID-128 takes only 3.08 ms in the desktop CPU, around 7× the time of BELID-U and ORB. In the Exynos Octa smartphone CPU the time of BELID-128 is also around 7× slower than BELID-U, as expected.

These results support the claim that our descriptor if a faster alternative to SIFT that is able to run in real-time on low performance devices, while preserving the accuracy.

Table 1. Average execution time per image of various descriptors.

	Size	Intel Core i7	Exynox Octa
SIFT	128f	22.22 ms	163.2 ms
ORB	256b	0.44 ms	6.49 ms
LBGM	64f	19.77 ms	64.24 ms
BinBoost	256b	12.57 ms	42.39 ms
BELID-512	512f	10.48 ms	61.47 ms
BELID-128	128f	3.08 ms	17.13 ms
BELID-U	512f	**0.41 ms**	**2.54 ms**

5   Conclusion

In this paper we presented BELID, an efficient learned image descriptor. In our experiments we proved that it has very low computational requirements, similar to those of ORB, the fastest descriptor in the literature. This is due to the use of very fast image features, based on gray value differences computed with the integral image. In terms of accuracy BELID is better than ORB and close to SIFT, the golden standard reference in the literature. We believe this is due to the discriminative scheme used to select the image features and the possibility of learning the best smoothing filter scale, represented in BELID by the feature box sizes. Our feature selection scheme optimizes a patch verification problem. This is why BELID achieves better accuracy than SIFT in the HPatches patch verification task and worse in the image matching and patch retrieval tasks.

As discussed in the introduction, feature matching is required in many other higher level computer vision tasks. In most of them it is a mid-level process often followed by model fitting, e.g. RANSAC. This robust fitting step fixes the errors occurred in the matching procedure. This is possibly one of the reasons why SIFT is still the most widely used descriptor. Although it is not the best performing approach in terms of accuracy, it provides a reasonable trade-off between accuracy and computational requirements. In the context of real-time performance on computationally limited devices, BELID represents also an excellent trade-off.

There are various ways to improve the results in this work. First we may change the feature selection process to optimize the performance not only in a patch verification task but also in image matching and patch retrieval. We may also binarize the output descriptor to decrease the model storage requirements and achieve higher matching speed. Finally, we also plan to improve the implementation to optimize speed in different types of processors.

Acknowledgments. The following funding is gratefully acknowledged. Iago Suárez, grant Doctorado Industrial DI-16-08966; José M. Buenaposada and Luis Baumela, Spanish MINECO project TIN2016-75982-C2-2-R.

References

1. Agarwal, S., Snavely, N., Simon, I., Seitz, S.M., Szeliski, R.: Building Rome in a day. In: 2009 IEEE 12th International Conference on Computer Vision, pp. 72–79. IEEE (2009)
2. Balntas, V., Lenc, K., Vedaldi, A., Mikolajczyk, K.: Hpatches: a benchmark and evaluation of handcrafted and learned local descriptors. In: Proceedings of the IEEE Conference on Computer Vision and Pattern Recognition, pp. 5173–5182 (2017)
3. Bay, H., Tuytelaars, T., Van Gool, L.: SURF: speeded up robust features. In: Leonardis, A., Bischof, H., Pinz, A. (eds.) ECCV 2006. LNCS, vol. 3951, pp. 404–417. Springer, Heidelberg (2006). https://doi.org/10.1007/11744023_32
4. Björkman, M., Bergström, N., Kragic, D.: Detecting, segmenting and tracking unknown objects using multi-label MRF inference. Comput. Vis. Image Underst. **118**, 111–127 (2014). https://doi.org/10.1016/j.cviu.2013.10.007. http://www.sciencedirect.com/science/article/pii/S107731421300194X
5. Calonder, M., Lepetit, V., Strecha, C., Fua, P.: BRIEF: binary robust independent elementary features. In: Daniilidis, K., Maragos, P., Paragios, N. (eds.) ECCV 2010. LNCS, vol. 6314, pp. 778–792. Springer, Heidelberg (2010). https://doi.org/10.1007/978-3-642-15561-1_56

6. Han, X., Leung, T., Jia, Y., Sukthankar, R., Berg, A.C.: Matchnet: unifying feature and metric learning for patch-based matching. In: The IEEE Conference on Computer Vision and Pattern Recognition (CVPR) (June 2015)
7. He, K., Lu, Y., Sclaroff, S.: Local descriptors optimized for average precision. In: Proceedings of the IEEE Conference on Computer Vision and Pattern Recognition, pp. 596–605 (2018)
8. Leutenegger, S., Chli, M., Siegwart, R.: Brisk: binary robust invariant scalable keypoints. In: 2011 IEEE International Conference on Computer Vision (ICCV), pp. 2548–2555. IEEE (2011)
9. Lowe, D.G.: Object recognition from local scale-invariant features. In: Proceedings of the International Conference on Computer Vision-vol. 2, p. 1150. ICCV 1999, IEEE Computer Society, Washington, DC (1999). http://dl.acm.org/citation.cfm?id=850924.851523
10. Lowe, D.G.: Distinctive image features from scale-invariant keypoints. Int. J. Comput. Vis. 60(2), 91–110 (2004)
11. Matas, J., Chum, O., Urban, M., Pajdla, T.: Robust wide baseline stereo from maximally stable extremal regions. In: Proceedings of BMVC, pp. 36.1–36.10 (2002). https://doi.org/10.5244/C.16.36
12. Mikolajczyk, K., Schmid, C.: A performance evaluation of local descriptors. IEEE Trans. Pattern Anal. Mach. Intell. 27(10), 1615–1630 (2005)
13. Mishchuk, A., Mishkin, D., Radenovic, F., Matas, J.: Working hard to know your neighbor's margins: local descriptor learning loss. In: Advances in Neural Information Processing Systems, pp. 4826–4837 (2017)
14. Mur-Artal, R., Montiel, J.M.M., Tardós, J.D.: Orb-slam: a versatile and accurate monocular slam system. IEEE Trans. Robot. 31(5), 1147–1163 (2015). https://doi.org/10.1109/TRO.2015.2463671
15. Mur-Artal, R., Tardós, J.D.: Fast relocalisation and loop closing in keyframe-based SLAM. In: 2014 IEEE International Conference on Robotics and Automation (ICRA), pp. 846–853 (May 2014). https://doi.org/10.1109/ICRA.2014.6906953
16. Nister, D., Stewenius, H.: Scalable recognition with a vocabulary tree. In: 2006 IEEE Computer Society Conference on Computer Vision and Pattern Recognition (CVPR 2006), vol. 2, pp. 2161–2168 (June 2006)
17. Pernici, F., Del Bimbo, A.: Object tracking by oversampling local features. IEEE Trans. Pattern Anal. Mach. Intell. 36(12), 2538–2551 (2014)
18. Rosten, E., Drummond, T.: Machine learning for high-speed corner detection. In: Leonardis, A., Bischof, H., Pinz, A. (eds.) ECCV 2006. LNCS, vol. 3951, pp. 430–443. Springer, Heidelberg (2006). https://doi.org/10.1007/11744023_34
19. Rublee, E., Rabaud, V., Konolige, K., Bradski, G.R.: ORB: an efficient alternative to SIFT or SURF. In: ICCV, vol. 11, p. 2. Citeseer (2011)
20. Schonberger, J.L., Frahm, J.M.: Structure-from-motion revisited. In: Proceedings of the IEEE Conference on Computer Vision and Pattern Recognition, pp. 4104–4113 (2016)
21. Shakhnarovich, G.: Learning task-specific similarity. Ph.D. thesis. Massachusetts Institute of Technology (2005)
22. Simonyan, K., Vedaldi, A., Zisserman, A.: Learning local feature descriptors using convex optimisation. IEEE Trans. Pattern Anal. Mach. Intell. 36(8), 1573–1585 (2014)
23. Suarez, I., Muñoz, E., Buenaposada, J.M., Baumela, L.: FSG: a statistical approach to line detection via fast segments grouping. In: 2018 IEEE/RSJ International Conference on Intelligent Robots and Systems (IROS), pp. 97–102 (October 2018). https://doi.org/10.1109/IROS.2018.8594434

24. Tian, Y., Fan, B., Wu, F.: L2-net: deep learning of discriminative patch descriptor in euclidean space. In: 2017 IEEE Conference on Computer Vision and Pattern Recognition (CVPR), pp. 6128–6136 (July 2017). https://doi.org/10.1109/CVPR. 2017.649

25. Tola, E., Lepetit, V., Fua, P.: A fast local descriptor for dense matching. In: 2008 IEEE Conference on Computer Vision and Pattern Recognition, pp. 1–8. IEEE (2008)

26. Trzcinski, T., Christoudias, M., Lepetit, V.: Learning image descriptors with boosting. IEEE Trans. Pattern Anal. Mach. Intell. **37**(3), 597–610 (2015)

27. Trzcinski, T., Christoudias, M., Lepetit, V., Fua, P.: Learning image descriptors with the boosting-trick. In: Advances in Neural Information Processing Systems, pp. 269–277 (2012)

28. Von Gioi, R.G., Jakubowicz, J., Morel, J.M., Randall, G.: LSD: a fast line segment detector with a false detection control. IEEE Trans. Pattern Anal. Mach. Intell. **32**(4), 722–732 (2010)

29. Wei, X., Zhang, Y., Gong, Y., Zheng, N.: Kernelized subspace pooling for deep local descriptors. In: 2018 IEEE/CVF Conference on Computer Vision and Pattern Recognition, pp. 1867–1875 (June 2018). https://doi.org/10.1109/CVPR. 2018.00200

30. Winder, S.A., Brown, M.: Learning local image descriptors. In: 2007 IEEE Conference on Computer Vision and Pattern Recognition, pp. 1–8. IEEE (2007)

31. Wohlhart, P., Lepetit, V.: Learning descriptors for object recognition and 3D pose estimation. In: Proceedings of the IEEE Conference on Computer Vision and Pattern Recognition, pp. 3109–3118 (2015)

32. Yan, W., Shi, X., Yan, X., Wang, L.: Computing OpenSURF on OpenCL and general purpose GPU. Int. J. Adv. Robot. Syst. **10**(10), 375 (2013)

A Novel Graph-Based Approach for Seriation of Mouse Brain Cross-Section from Images

S. Sarbazvatan[1]([⊠]) , R. Ventura[1] , F. F. Esteves[2] ,
S. Q. Lima[2] , and J. M. Sanches[1]

[1] Institute for Systems and Robotics (ISR/IST), LARSyS,
Instituto Superior Técnico, Universidade de Lisboa,
Av. Rovisco Pais, 1049-001 Lisbon, Portugal
s.sarbaz@ua.pt
[2] Programa Champalimaud de Neurociências, Champalimaud Research,
Avenida Brasilia, 1200-038 Lisbon, Portugal

Abstract. This paper addresses the problem of automatic seriation of mouse brain cross-sections stained with green-florescence protein (GFP). This is fundamental for the neuroscience community to help in the processing and analyzing the huge amount of experimental data. It is also a challenging problem since, during the manual procedure of cutting the brains and acquiring hundreds of images, the human operator can unwittingly change its natural sequence, loose data, induce large morphological distortions, or introduce artifacts. Most image seriation methods are two-step: firstly, a distance matrix is obtained from image processing, and secondly, the optimal seriation method is determined for this matrix. However, these methods are very sensitive to noise, distortion, and missing data, since the optimal solution for the matrix does not match the true seriation. Instead, we propose a graph-based method where the images are iteratively revisited and the image similarity information is refined, until a linear graph representing the seriation is obtained. This similarity information is based on Histogram Oriented Gradient (HOG) features, computed from random locations at the images in each iteration/revisitation. Experimental results based on both synthetic and real data are used to validate and illustrate the application of the method. It is showed that the proposed method outperforms the other state-of-the-art methods used for comparison purposes in this specific type of data.

Keywords: Seriation · (dis)similarity matrix · Mouse brain · Graph · HOG

1 Introduction

Seriation, also known by ranking, ordination or sequencing, is a general procedure that aims at linearly ordering a set of elements in a dataset. The central assumption in this type of problems, where a distance metric function is defined, is the following [1]: there

---

This work was supported by Portuguese funds through FCT (Fundação para a Ciência e Tecnologia) through the projects SENSE (PTDC/BIM-ONC/0281/2014) and reference UID/EEA/50009/2019.

© Springer Nature Switzerland AG 2019
A. Morales et al. (Eds.): IbPRIA 2019, LNCS 11867, pp. 461–471, 2019.
https://doi.org/10.1007/978-3-030-31332-6_40

is a natural order of the objects where the total distance between adjacent elements is minimized. The seriation results strongly depend on the distance metric and in the way the similarity matrix is computed. Seriation is a transversal problem in many scientific and technological fields, such as archeology [2], genomics and proteomics, paleonto-logical data and network analysis [3]. It can be formulated and solved by using several techniques based on linear algebra, graph or optimization theory [4–6]. Popular and well-studied approaches to address this problem were developed in the scope of the C1P and 2-SUM problem. In this formulation, the rows and columns of a binary similarity matrix are permuted in order to estimate the correct order of the objects that minimizes a given distance criterion. For a complete survey about seriation methods see [1, 7, 8]. A Greedy optimization method over Robinsonian matrices, based on graph-theory, have been used with success in several low dimension and topologic complexity problems [1, 5, 9]. Another popular set of seriation methods are formulated as a combinatorial optimization problem. In this class of methods, heuristic solutions are obtained by using the simulated annealing and dynamic programming algorithms [10]. The performance and accuracy of these methods are compromised with noisy data and the processing time explode exponentially with the dimension of the problem, making the computation of the solution harder. As well as, seriation of the objects in a dataset at the presence of the noise as a challenging problem has been considered [11]. From the perspective of clustering and classification theories, a seriation results interprets as a chain of objects with an optimum length [7]. Seriation of the objects from (dis)similarity matrix associated with a dataset can be considered as a one-mode two-way clustering problem [1, 8]. However, the clustering of the objects in a unique group can be translated to the language of seriation easily. A nice interpretation between clustering and seriation has been defined by [7, 12, 13] in a way that, from clustering perspective, the matrix permutation is a procedure to order the clusters at each level so that the objects on the edge of each cluster are adjacent to that object outside the cluster to which it is nearest. From the perspective of seriation, the result is an optimal ordering procedure, but with an additional grouping conditions for identi-fying the clusters and their boundaries. Since the matrix permutation approach on the seriation algorithms has some advantage to the clustering, such as, non-destructing the data by transformation or reduction, we preferred to address the problem as a seriation approach [7]. We propose here an iterative robust method where, in each iteration, the accuracy of the solution improves by local optimization of the Hamiltonian path. With permuting the complex node on the minimum spanning tree regarding to the acyclic Hamiltonian path, we are able to obtain more accurate and robust result when com-pared with the classical seriation problem solvers.

2   Problem Definition

The goal of this work is to reorder a set of images of mouse brain cross-sections obtained through a manual process of cutting. The corresponding fluorescence images of these cross-sections are noisy and distorted. The digitalization procedure of hundreds of these thin slices involves a time consuming and exhaustive manual work prone to errors during the fixation of the slices into the microscope slides and coverslips. The visual ordering of these images with high morphological similarity is challenging work.

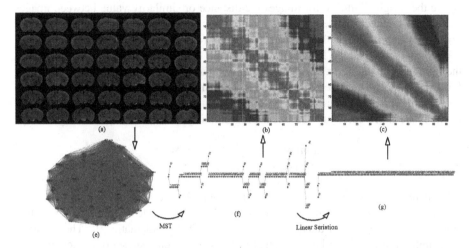

Fig. 1. Seriation method for mouse brain microscopic images. (a): Sample of montaged images, (b): pre-R distance matrix of the data, (c): shading distance matrix after seriation, (d): graph of connected images base on similarity index, (e): minimum spanning tree of data computed from HOG based (dis)similarity matrix (f): linear seriation by applying HOG_OLP method.

This process gets harder when the technician loses the correct order of cross sections during staining. In order to the reconstruction of a 3D digital atlas of the mouse brain, section-to-section registration of slices with reference images and sorting of them are essential. In this study, we aim to reorder totally 91 shuffled adult mouse brain sections that have been disordered in the lab. We applied a new seriation method based on local optimal leaf permuting over the minimum spanning tree of data to reorder the rank of images. We compared our results with other classical seriation methods that shows a competitive and accurate results. Reordering of the mouse brain section images with the morphological distortion can be addressed as a seriation problem with noisy similarity matrix. The systematic and physical damages of slices as a soft tissue on the neuroscience laboratories, decreases the efficiency of global image similarity indexes such as Euclidean distance or mutual information. We used a Histogram of Oriented Gradient base image descriptor with a various window size to build the (dis)similarity matrix in this work [14].

3 Materials and Methods

Traveling Salesman Problem (TSP) is a classical approach to formulate the seriation problems where tries to find a linear order of objects in a dataset regarding their similarities [7, 9, 15]. The optimum solution of this method for a noiseless similarity matrix at the most the times is accurate where this method finds the best solution between all possible permutation with minimizing the Hamiltonian path [16]. TSP can be formulated as a graph problem also. Here G = {V, E, W} represents a graph with vertex (cities), V = {1, 2,..., n} and $e_i \in E$ are the edges that associated with weight w_i, where the weights indicate for images the distance or similarity value between images i and other connected objects. The Hamiltonian cycle is defined to calculate the minimum distance in a tour that connects all cities (objects) exactly once to each other. This formulation leads to find the minimum path between the objects with computing the minimum spanning tree (MST) for the optimal tour. Many algorithms as a solver for TSP has been suggested in the last decades. Since TSP is NP-complete problem to decrease the computational costs for large datasets, linear and dynamic programming methods are more efficient. The linear programming formulation of TSP is given by:

$$\begin{array}{ll} minimize & \sum_{i=1}^{m} w_i x_i = \mathbf{w}^T \mathbf{x} \\ subjectto & x \in S \end{array} \tag{1}$$

Where m is the number of edges on the graph G, $w_i \in \mathbf{w}$ is the weight of edge e_i and $\mathbf{x}$ is the incidence vector of a tour. $\mathbf{x}$ contains all possible Hamiltonian cycle that connects all objects on a data set that make the TSP problematic [9]. The dynamic programming method can be formulated as follows: Given a subset of objects indicate $S \subset \{2, 3,..., n\}$ and $l \subset S$, let $d^*(S, l)$ where represents the length of the shortest path from city one to the city l that crossing from all cities on S exactly once. For subset of $S = \{l\}, d^*(S, l)$ is defined as d_{1l}. The shortest path for larger sets with $|S| > 1$ can be denoted as:

$$d^*(S, l) = min_{m \in S \setminus \{l\}} (d^*(S\{l\}, m) + d_{ml}) \tag{2}$$

The minimum tour length for a complete tour including the first node is as follows:

$$d^{**} = min_{l \in \{2,3,...,n\}} (d^*\{2, 3, ..., n\}, l) + d_{l1}) \tag{3}$$

The quantity of $d^*(S, l)$ can be estimated recursively by using the last two equation which leads to find the optimal tour d^{**}. On the second step the optimal permutation of $\pi = \{1, i_2, i_3, ..., i_n\}$ computes the order of objects reversely starting with i_n into i_2. The last notation shows that the permutation π is optimal if:

$$d^{**} = d^*(\{2, 3, ..., n\}, i_n) + d_{i_n 1} \tag{4}$$

For $2 \leq p \leq n - 1$ we have:

$$d^*(\{i_2, i_3, ..., i_p, i_{p+1}\}, i_{p+1}) = d^*(\{i_2, i_3, ..., i_p\}, i_p) + d_{i_p i_{p+1}} \tag{5}$$

For a large dataset, other formulation approaches by using relaxation for the linear programming method can give the solution for TSP. However, for a small number of objects in a dataset, the dynamic program is so fast and more efficient [1, 9]. To measure the accuracy of the results of seriation methods, we used two distance parameters, Kendall τ and Spearman's ρ [6, 17]. Nevertheless, the TSP solver as a seriation method using the Hamiltonian path, but for the noisy dataset does not meet the path graph correctly, while the path of the minimum spanning tree and TSP solution for the noiseless case is the same [15]. The proposed method starts with the construction of (dis) similarity matrix over the dataset. Employing HOG descriptor with different cell size for the images and calculation of the linear correlation coefficient between the feature vectors give a set of minimum spanning trees. The desired path is a tree with two nodes of vertex degree one and the rest nodes of vertex degree two. A noiseless similarity matrix leads to a MST that fit a path graph, while in a noisy case does not meet the same result. By measuring the complexity of each MST with counting the degree of the nodes in a tree, we are able to choose an appropriate tree that has maximum consistency with the path graph. Applying a permutation function over complex nodes with degree greater than two minimizes the differences between the tree and ground truth. This process repeats with re-computing the Hamiltonian path between the complex node and the neighbors by keeping the rest of the vertices constant. We applied a standard deviation filter over the images and random window size for the HOG to converge the result for the local permutation. The permuted nodes relocate on the global tree iteratively. This procedure continues unless the complexity parameter for the tree meets the maximum value $n-2$. The details of each step have been described separately.

3.1 Similarity and Distance Matrix

The pre-processing step for resizing and cleaning of the images is crucial before building the similarity matrix. The true seriation in an image-based dataset with morphological deformation has the main role while the Euclidian distance shows a poor effort mostly. We used the Histogram Oriented Gradient (HOG) as an image descriptor to get feature vector of the images in this paper [14]. To obtain (dis)similarity matrix in our dataset, firstly, we aligned all slices with a template image of multiple neighbors rigidly. To speed up the computation process and reduce the morphological deformation effects where mostly on the edges of slices, we selected a region of interest about fifty percent as a bounding box of image sizes from the image center. Then we used the morphological features of images obtained by applied HOG descriptor to construct the similarity matrix. We estimated the linear correlation coefficient between feature vectors pair-wisely. Let us consider a data set with n images. The feature matrix, $F_{n \times m}$ represents the dimension of data set with size equal n and the length of normalized gradient histogram of image equal m respectively. We use L2-norm Euclidian distance $f = v\left(\|v\|_2^2 + \varepsilon^2\right)^{-1/2}$ to normalize of vector raw feature vector v where collected form each image. The length of vector f changes with the size of detection windows for HOG normally that gives a set of pre-R similarity matrix [2]. The linear dependency of two vectors with m elements on the feature matrix can be defined as Pearson's correlation coefficient:

$$\rho\left(f_i, f_j\right) = \frac{1}{n-1} \sum\nolimits_{k=1}^{n} \left(\frac{f_{ik} - \bar{\mu}_{f_i}}{\sigma_{f_i}}\right) \left(\frac{f_{jk} - \bar{\mu}_{f_j}}{\sigma_{f_j}}\right) \qquad (6)$$

Where $\bar{\mu}$ and σ are the mean and standard deviation of vectors. For each pairwise vector of feature matrix, f_i and f_j the linear correlation coefficient defines as:

$$r_{ij} = \begin{pmatrix} 1 & \rho_{ij} \\ \rho_{ji} & 1 \end{pmatrix}. \tag{7}$$

Where ρ_{ij} is the correlation coefficient between image i and j. Since the pre-R similarity matrix, in this case, are symmetrical so it's easy to conclude that $\rho_{ij} = \rho_{ji}$. For similarity and dissimilarity matrixes $\mathbf{S}$ and $\mathbf{D}$ with n objects, we define $\mathbf{S} = \mathbf{R}^{\circ 2}$ and $\mathbf{D} = \mathbf{J} - \mathbf{R}^{\circ 2}$ where $\mathbf{J}$ is the all-ones matrix with a dimension of n^2 and $\mathbf{R}^{\circ 2}$ that is the squared matrix of entry-wise product for all images with elements $R_{ij} = \rho_{ij}^2$. The (dis) similarity matrix for mouse brain images satisfies the following conditions:

$$\begin{cases} S_{ii} = 1 & , & S_{ij} = S_{ji} \\ D_{ii} = 0 & , & S_{ij} = S_{ji} \end{cases} \quad and \quad \begin{cases} tr(\mathbf{D_n}) = 0 \\ tr(\mathbf{S_n} - \mathbf{I_n}) = 0 \end{cases} \tag{8}$$

where $\mathbf{I_n}$ is the $n \times n$ identity matrix.

3.2   Optimal Leaf Permutation Method

HOG based Optimal Leaf Permutation (HOG_OLP) method includes three main functions, dis(similarity) matrix construction, MST selection, and leaf permutation respectively. For dissimilarity matrix D, first, we choose detection window size randomly for HOG iteratively to get the best topological MST with less complexity. The range of window size is limited between a 4×4 pixel and forty percent of image size. We generated the minimum spanning tree for each dissimilarity matrix associated with different windows size of HOG where give the opportunity to use a relaxation parameter to select the best MST. With maximizing g, a new relaxation parameter that represents the number of leaves with degree two. This parameter as an index helps the algorithm to find the best topological MST for leaf permutation where:

$$g_m = \max\{g_1, g_2, \ldots, g_l | g_i = \#deg_2(T_i)\} \tag{9}$$

The desired minimum spanning tree is a tree with $g = (n - 2)$, where n is the number of nodes on the tree (see Fig. 1(e) and (f)). After finding the suitable MST, we apply an optimal permutation functions locally over complex nodes where tries to reorder the nonlinear leaves and relocate on the main tree. Let us denotes a features matrix $f(v_i, l)$ which are connected with vertex i as the neighbors with length l. The $I\{v_i\}$ indicates the images related to the node i with weight w_{ij} as dissimilarity value between image i and j. We estimate starting and ending vertex on the MST with calculation longest path in each iteration over distance matrix. The following algorithm explains how our method reduces the complexity of a spanned tree with the permutation of the leaves. The function return to a minimum spanning tree, T_{sl} with degrees less than three $1 \leq deg\{v_i\} \leq 3$. This iterative process will continue unless all complex nodes with degree greater than two connected with two nodes only (linear tree see Fig. 1(f)). A local permutation function using the sub-similarity matrix where builds from extracting more features by HOG method with applying median and standard deviation filters. There-fore, for each complex node and the first degree neighbors, the sub-similarity matrix is different from the global one. To keep the global seriation result, we always update and restore the similarity values when each complex node and its neighbors are aligned on the main similarity matrix. The final tree has the optimal length path between other solutions however this path is not the minimal path necessarily.

HOG based Optimal Leaf Permutation (HOG-OLP) algorithm

$set\ f \leftarrow \emptyset\quad, w_{ij} \leftarrow 0\quad and\quad \{s,e\} \leftarrow \emptyset$

$\{s,e\} \leftarrow find\ longest\ path\ between\ nodes$

$find\ all\ nodes\ with\ degree\ equal\ 1:\quad v = \{deg_1(T_m)\} - \{s,e\}$

$find\ the\ neighbours\ of\ node\ i\ \ v_i:\quad v_i' = \{v_i, l\}$

$\quad for\ all\ v_i'\ with\quad deg(T_m, v_i) \geq 3\ do$

$\quad\quad find\quad v_i'' \leftarrow \{T_m, v_i'\}$

$\quad\quad sT_i'' \leftarrow MST\{v_i''\}$

$\quad\quad while\ \#deg_1(sT_i'') \neq 2\quad do$

$\quad\quad\quad apply\ median\ and\ std\ filters\ to\ I\{v''\}$

$\quad\quad\quad update\ dissimilarity\ matrix\ \mathbf{D}\ and\ f$

$\quad\quad\quad update\ \ sT_i'' \leftarrow MST(sT_i'')$

$\quad\quad end\ of\ while$

$\quad relocate\ sT_i''\ on\ T_m$

$\quad set\ w_{ij} \leftarrow 1$

$\quad update\ \{s,e,v_i'\}$

$\quad end\ of\ for$

$return\ T_{sl} \leftarrow T_m$

---

4 Results

We tested the proposed algorithm with two types of datasets. First we applied this method over hundred teapot images and compared the results with other seriation algorithms from the literature [18]. The tests with mouse brain dataset were also performed and the results are displayed in the Figs. 2 and 3 and the Table 1. Since the teapot images are not affected by any kind of morphological deformation or noise the resulting similarity matrix is clean and straightforward. Therefore, all seriation methods tested with this type of synthetic data where able to produce the ground-truth result (100% accuracy). The different methods only differ on the estimated starting and ending images of the final sequence. In fact, all methods are not able to estimate these parameters without any additional or prior information, which is not considered in this work. A dataset of 91 images of microscopy were used to illustrate the application of the proposed methodology to real data. This sequence was unwillingly shuffled at the lab and it was manually reorder by visual inspection to generate the ground-truth. The resorting operation and ground-truth defi-nition were performed by neuroscientist that by visual comparison with the Allen Brain

Atlas references images [19]. We tested the proposed method with other 32 methods of seriation described in the literatures [1] and [8]. Most of them that failed to give acceptable results, were excluded from the comparison test. Only the following four seriation methods were included in this paper: Single linkage of Hierarchical Clustering (HC_Single), Gruvaeus and Wainer seriation method (GW_Single), Optimal Leaf Ordering (OLO_Single) and TSP solver. A good survey and review over all seriation methods can be find here [7, 8]. The Kendall τ and Spearman distances, computed for the mouse brain dataset (see Table 1) shows that the proposed algorithm.

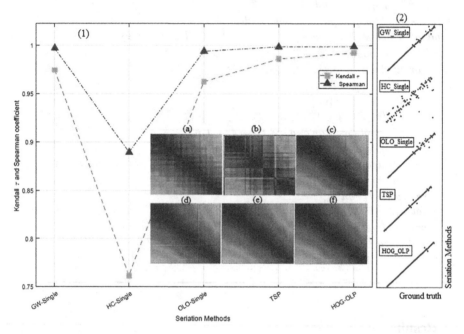

Fig. 2. plot (1) indicates the Kendall τ and Spearman's measurement for five seriation methods. The shading distance matrices (a–f) are for 91 mouse brain images includes GW single linkage, Hierarchical Clustering (HC), Optimal Leaf Ordering (OLO), TSP solution and HOG base Optimal Leaf Permuting (HOG_OLP) method respectively. Plots (2) illustrates the overlap-based similarity matrix for mouse brain dataset, x and y-axes indicate the ground truth and seriation results.

(HOG_OLP) reorders more images correctly comparing to the others. The hierarchical clustering method, with permitting the leaves in a dendrogram structure without changing the main clusters, tries to find the optimum results that for noisy similarity matrix case failing to give correct enumeration. In other hand optimal leaf ordering method by starting with hierarchical clustering and permuting the leaves have better efficiency. Employing GW method over images leads to higher accuracy comparing to other two methods. Whereas the Kendall and Spearman coefficients for this method raised to 0.9746 and 0.997 out of one respectively that are higher than HC and GW methods.

Table 1. The results of seriation accuracy for 91 mouse brain images

Seriation methods/measuring P.	Kendall's τ	Pearsman's ρ
GW_Single	0.9746	0.997
HC_Single	0.7617	0.8892
OLO_Single	0.9624	0.9942
TSP Solver	0.9863	0.9987
HOG_OLP	0.9927	0.9993

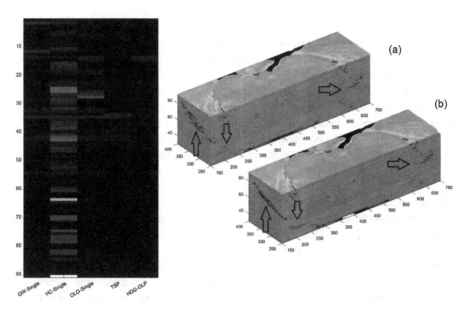

Fig. 3. The left image shows the absolute value of difference between ground truth and seriation results. The dark era illustrates that the seriation reordered successfully. The right images are a 3D blocks of 91 mouse brain before (up) and after (down) reordering respectively.

The solution of TSP among all other methods has better effort. Two measuring parameters for TSP solver are 0.9863 and 0.9987 which indicates that more images sorted correctly comparing to other three methods. However, the TSP solver normally gives the minimum path length for applied distance matrix but for noisy similarity matrix the minimum shortcut path is not the correct results therefore we need more robust and optimum results. Applying our method for this dataset gives more robust results comparing to others. The values of Kendall tau for our method is 0.9927 and Spearman's coefficient is 0.9993 that shows better efficiency see Table (1). Figure 2 shows the measuring parameters for all seriation methods as well as shading distance matrix. All the plots show the HOG_OLP method has better effort comparing to the others. On the same figure, plots (2) represents the seriation results with ground truth. The correct results should be straight line where spied dots distribution out of straight line shows the error of seriation methods. Hierarchical clustering method among other methods has more error which means could not seriate the images successfully. Figure (3) left image shows the absolute differences between ground truth and the results of seriation methods. The dark background means the image ranks is completely matched with the ground truth. Finally, the right image on the same figure shows a 3D volumetric slice of mouse brain before and after seriation. The slices have been seriate with our algorithm that the black arrows on the images show the results of reordering and consistency of the tissue.

5   Conclusion

In this paper we propose, a graph-based seriation algorithm for noisy similarity matrix to increase the robustness of seriation problem. HOG_OLP is a method consists of two main steps: similarity matrix construction and leaves permuting. At the first step, the similarity matrix calculated from the linear correlation coefficient between the feature vectors obtained by HOG method. We applied the cell size to extract the feature of the mouse brain images as a parameter to get a set of (dis)similarity matrix. Minimizing the Hamiltonian path over noisy dissimilarity matrix by using minimum spanning tree provides a set of complex MST. In the second step, we identify the best MST for local permutation by measuring the nodes of vertex degree as a complexity parameter of a tree. A tree with a maximum number of the nods with degree two is more consistency of a path graph. The complex nodes within the first rank of the neighbors reorder by a local permutation function. With keeping the global order of the nodes and applying the appropriate imaging filters to the corresponding images and following the same procedure to obtain the local MST in a loop, the complex nodes meet the desired path graph. By relocating linearized complex nodes on the main tree regarding the optimal path iteratively, we obtain the final order of the images. The measuring parameters between the results of the proposed method and the other seriation algorithms with the ground truth show a better and competitive effort. Our results demonstrate that this approach can be used for the seriation of image-based datasets with high morphological deformation or noisy similarity matrix.

References

1. Hahsler, M.: An experimental comparison of seriation methods for one-mode two-way data. Eur. J. Oper. Res. **257**(1), 133–143 (2017)
2. Robinson, W.S.: A method for chronologically ordering archaeological deposits. Am. Antiq. **16**(4), 293–301 (1951)
3. Garriga, G.C., Junttila, E., Mannila, H.: Banded structure in binary matrices. Knowl. Inf. Syst. **28**(1), 197–226 (2011)
4. Barnard, S.T., Pothen, A., Simon, H.: A spectral algorithm for envelope reduction of sparse matrices. Numer. Linear Algebra Appl. **2**(4), 317–334 (1995)
5. Fulkerson, D., Gross, O.: Incidence matrices and interval graphs. Pac. J. Math. **15**(3), 835–855 (1965)
6. Kendall, D.G.: Abundance matrices and seriation in archaeology. Probab. Theory Relat. Fields **17**(2), 104–112 (1971)

7. Liiv, I.: Seriation and matrix reordering methods: an historical overview. Stat. Anal. Data Min. ASA Data Sci. J. **3**(2), 70–91 (2010)
8. Hahsler, M., Hornik, K., Buchta, C.: Getting things in order: an introduction to the R package seriation. J. Stat. Softw. **25**(3), 1–34 (2008)
9. Hahsler, M., Hornik, K.: TSP-infrastructure for the traveling salesperson problem. J. Stat. Softw. **23**(2), 1–21 (2007)
10. Brusco, M.J., Köhn, H.F., Stahl, S.: Heuristic implementation of dynamic programming for matrix permutation problems in combinatorial data analysis. Psychometrika **73**(3), 503 (2008)
11. Ghandehari, M., Janssen, J.: An optimization parameter for seriation of noisy data. SIAM J. Discrete Math. **33**(2), 712–730 (2019)
12. Gruvaeus, G., Wainer, H.: Two additions to hierarchical cluster analysis. Br. J. Math. Stat. Psychol. **25**(2), 200–206 (1972)
13. Arabie, P., Hubert, L.J., Schleutermann, S.: Blockmodels from the bond energy approach. Soc. Netw. **12**(2), 99–126 (1990)
14. Dalal, N., Triggs, B.: Histograms of oriented gradients for human detection. In: International Conference on Computer Vision and Pattern Recognition (CVPR 2005), vol. 1, pp. 886–893. IEEE Computer Society (June 2005)
15. Balakrishnan, J., Jog, P.D.: Manufacturing cell formation using similarity coefficients and a parallel genetic TSP algorithm: Formulation and comparison. Math. Comput. Model. **21**(12), 61–73 (1995)
16. Askin, R.G., Cresswell, S.H., Goldberg, J.B., Vakharia, A.J.: A Hamiltonian path approach to reordering the part-machine matrix for cellular manufacturing. Int. J. Prod. Res. **29**(6), 1081–1100 (1991)
17. Best, D.J., Roberts, D.E.: Algorithm AS 89: the upper tail probabilities of Spearman's rho. J. Roy. Stat. Soc.: Ser. C (Appl. Stat.) **24**(3), 377–379 (1975)
18. Weinberger, K.Q., Saul, L.K.: Unsupervised learning of image manifolds by semidefinite programming. Int. J Comput. Vis. **70**(1), 77–90 (2006)
19. Allen Institute for Brain Science: Allen Brain Atlas API (2015). brain-map.org/api/index.html

Class Reconstruction Driven Adversarial Domain Adaptation for Hyperspectral Image Classification

Shivam Pande[1(✉)] [iD], Biplab Banerjee[1(✉)] [iD], and Aleksandra Pižurica[2(✉)] [iD]

[1] Center of Studies in Resources Engineering,
Indian Institute of Technology Bombay, Mumbai, India
184314002@iitb.ac.in, getbiplab@gmail.com
[2] Department of Telecommunications and Information Processing,
Ghent University, Ghent, Belgium
Aleksandra.Pizurica@ugent.be

Abstract. We address the problem of cross-domain classification of hyperspectral image (HSI) pairs under the notion of unsupervised domain adaptation (UDA). The UDA problem aims at classifying the test samples of a target domain by exploiting the labeled training samples from a related but different source domain. In this respect, the use of adversarial training driven domain classifiers is popular which seeks to learn a shared feature space for both the domains. However, such a formalism apparently fails to ensure the (i) discriminativeness, and (ii) non-redundancy of the learned space. In general, the feature space learned by domain classifier does not convey any meaningful insight regarding the data. On the other hand, we are interested in constraining the space which is deemed to be simultaneously discriminative and reconstructive at the class-scale. In particular, the reconstructive constraint enables the learning of category-specific meaningful feature abstractions and UDA in such a latent space is expected to better associate the domains. On the other hand, we consider an orthogonality constraint to ensure non-redundancy of the learned space. Experimental results obtained on benchmark HSI datasets (Botswana and Pavia) confirm the efficacy of the proposal approach.

Keywords: Domain adaptation · Adversarial training · Hyperspectral images

1 Introduction

The current era has witnessed the acquisition of a large volume of satellite remote sensing (RS) images of varied modalities, thanks to several national and international satellite missions. Such images showcase relevance in a range of important applications in areas including urban studies, disaster management, national security and many more. One of the major applications in this regard concerns

© Springer Nature Switzerland AG 2019
A. Morales et al. (Eds.): IbPRIA 2019, LNCS 11867, pp. 472–484, 2019.
https://doi.org/10.1007/978-3-030-31332-6_41

the analysis of (i) images of a given area on ground but acquired at different time instants, and (ii) images of different geographical areas but composed of similar land-cover types. Usually, it is non-trivial to generate training samples for all the images and hence it is a common practice to reuse the training samples obtained from images with *similar* characteristics to new images for carrying out the supervised learning tasks. To this end, the paradigm of inductive transfer learning, in particular domain adaptation, is extremely popular.

By definition, the unsupervised domain adaptation (UDA) techniques typically consider two related yet diverse data domains: a source domain S equipped with ample amount of training samples, and a target domain T where the test samples are accumulated. Since the data distributions are different for the two domains: $P(S) \neq P(T)$, the classifier trained on S fails to generalize for T following the probably approximately correct (PAC) assumptions of the statistical learning theory [17, 18].

Traditional UDA techniques can broadly be classified into categories based on: (i) classifier adaptation, and (ii) domain invariant feature space learning. In particular, a common feature space is learned where the notion of domain divergence is minimized or a transformation matrix is modelled to project the samples of (source) target domain to the other counterpart [4, 13]. Some of the popular ad hoc methods in this category include transfer component analysis (TCA) [15], subspace alignment (SA) [6], geodesic flow kernel (GFK) [9] based manifold alignment etc. Likewise, UDA approaches based on the idea of maximum mean discrepancy (MMD) [20] learn the domain invariant space in a kernel induced Hilbert space. Recently, the idea of adversarial training has become extremely popular in UDA. Specifically, such approaches are based on a min-max type game between two modules: a feature generator (G) and a discriminator (D). While D tries to distinguish samples coming from S and T, G is trained to make the target features indistinguishable from S [11]. The RevGrad algorithm is of particular interest in this respect as it introduces a gradient reversal layer for maximizing the gradient of the D loss [7]. This, in turn, directs G to learn a domain-confused feature space, thus reducing the domain gap substantially. Adversarial residual transform networks (ARTN) [3] is another notable approach that uses adversarial learning in UDA. Besides, the use of generative adversarial networks (GAN) have been predominant in the recent past for varied cross-domain inference tasks: image style transfer, cross-modal image generation, to name a few. Some of the GAN based endeavors in this regard are: DAN [8], CycleGAN [5] and ADDA [19].

As the UDA problem is frequently encountered in RS, the aforementioned ad hoc techniques have already been explored in the RS domain [18]. A recent example [1] proposes a hierarchical subspace learning strategy which considers the semantic similarity among the land-cover classes at multiple levels and learns a series of domain-invariant subspaces. The use of a shared dictionary between the domains is also a popular practise for HSI pairs [21]. As far as the deep learning techniques are concerned, the use of GAN or domain independent convolution networks are also explored in this regard [2].

In this work, we specifically focus on the domain classifier (DC) based adversarial approach towards UDA. Precisely, the DC based UDA approaches simultaneously train the domain classifier and a source specific classifier using the feature generator-discriminator framework. While the domain classifier is entrusted with the task of making the domains overlapping, the source classifier helps in avoiding any trivial mapping. However, we find the following shortcomings of the standard DC based approaches: (i) the learned space does not encourage discriminativeness. In particular, the notion of intra-class compactness is not explicitly taken into account, which may result in overlapping of samples belonging to fine-grained categories. (ii) the learned space is ideally unbounded and does not convey any meaningful interpretation and may be redundant in nature.

In order to resolve both the aforementioned issues, we propose an advanced autoencoder based approach as an extension to the typical DC based UDA. In addition to jointly training the binary domain classifier and the source-specific multiclass classifier, we specifically add two other constraints on the learned latent space for the source specific samples. The first one is the reconstructive constraint that is directed to reconstruct one sample from another sample from S both sharing the same class label. This essentially captures the classwise abstract attributes better than a typical autoencoder setup. Further, this loss helps in concentrating the samples from S at the category level. The other one is the orthogonality constraint to ensure that the non-redundancy of the reconstructed features in the source domain. Optimization of all four loss measures together is experimentally found to better correspond S and T. The main contributions of this paper are:

- We introduce a class-level sample reconstruction loss for the samples in S in a typical DC based UDA framework. This makes the learned space constrained and bounded.
- We enforce an orthogonality constraint over the source domain to keep the reconstructed features in the source domain non-redundant.
- Extensive experiments are conducted on the Botswana and Pavia HSI datasets where improved classification performance on T can be observed.

The subsequent sections of the paper discuss the methodology followed by the experiments conducted and concluding remarks.

2   Methodology

In this section, we detail the UDA problem followed by our proposed solution.

Preliminaries: Let $\mathcal{X}_S = \{(\mathbf{x}_i^s, y_i^s)\}_{i=1}^{N_S} \in X_S \otimes Y_S$ be the source domain training samples with $\mathbf{x}_i^s \in \mathbb{R}^d$ and $y_i^s \in \{1, 2, \ldots, C\}$, respectively. Likewise, let $\mathcal{X}_T = \{(\mathbf{x}_j^t)\}_{j=1}^{N_T} \in X_T$ be the target domain samples obtained from the same categories as of $\mathcal{X}_S$. However, $P_S(X_S) \neq P_T(X_T)$. Under this setup, the UDA problem aims at learning $f_S : X_S \to Y_S$ which is guaranteed to generalize well for $\mathcal{X}_T$.

In order to learn an effective f_S, we propose an end-to-end encoder-decoder based neural network architecture comprising of the following components: (i) a feature encoder f_E, (ii) a domain classifier f_D, (iii) a source specific classifier f_S, and (iv) a reconstructive class-specific decoder f_{DE}. Note that the feature encoder is typically implemented in terms of the *fully-connected* (fc) layers with non-linearity. For notational convenience, we denote the encoded feature representation corresponding to an input $\mathbf{x}$ by $f_E(\mathbf{x})$.

We elaborate the proposed training and inference stages in the following. A depiction of our model can be found in Fig. 1.

2.1   Training

Given the encoded feature representations, the proposed loss measure is composed of the losses from the following components in the decoder:

Source Classifier f_S: The mapping, f_S is a multiclass softmax classifier trained solely on $\mathcal{X}_S$. We express the corresponding loss in terms of the cross-entropy that is defined as the log-likelihood between the training data and the model distribution [10]. Specifically, we deploy an empirical categorical cross-entropy based loss,

$$\mathcal{L}_S = -\mathbb{E}_{(\mathbf{x}_i^s, y_i^s) \in \mathcal{X}_S}[y_i^s \log f_S(f_E(\mathbf{x}_i^s))] \tag{1}$$

where $\mathbb{E}_{\mathcal{D}}$ denotes the empirical expectation over domain $\mathcal{D}$.

The Class-Specific Source Reconstruction f_{DE}: Note that f_S ensures better inter-class separation of the source domain samples in the learned space. However, it does not consider the notion of intraclass compactness which is essential for demarcating highly overlapping categories. In addition, we simultaneously require the learned space to be meaningful and to capture the inherent class-level abstract features of both $\mathcal{S}$ and $\mathcal{T}$.

To this end, let us define two data matrices $X_S \in \mathbb{R}^{N_S \times d}$ and $\hat{X}_S \in \mathbb{R}^{N_S \times d}$ from X_S in such a way that the ith row of both the matrices refers to a pair of distinct data points obtained from a given category. Under this setup, f_{DE} aims to reconstruct $\hat{X}$ in the decoder branch given $f_E(X_S)$. We formulate the corresponding loss as:

$$\mathcal{L}_R = \sum_{i=1}^{N_S} \|\tilde{X}_S - \hat{X}_S\|_F^2 \tag{2}$$

Note that $\tilde{X}_S$ denotes the projected $f_E(X_S)$ onto the decoder. Since we perform cross-sample reconstruction in this encoder decoder branch (f_E and f_{DE}), f_E essentially captures abstract class-level features of $\mathcal{X}_S$. Besides, $\mathcal{L}_R$ further ensures within-class compactness. As a whole, the joint minimization of $\mathcal{L}_S$ and $\mathcal{L}_R$ ensures that f_E essentially learns a space which is simultaneously discriminative and meaningful.

Domain Classifier f_D: The role of f_D is to project the samples from $\mathcal{S}$ and $\mathcal{T}$ onto the shared space modelled by $\triangle f_E$. Let us assign the domain label 0 to all the source samples X_i^s and label 1 to all the target samples X_i^t. We define $X_D = [X_S, X_T]$ and $Y_D = [\hat{Y}_S, \hat{Y}_T]$ where $\hat{Y}_S = \mathbf{0}$ is an all zero vector of size N_S

and $\hat{Y}_T = 1$ of size N_T. Given that, f_D maximizes a typical binary cross-entropy based classification error through a min-max game between f_E and f_D in such a way that the learned space becomes highly domain invariant. Formally we define the loss measure for f_D as:

$$\mathcal{L}_D = -\mathbb{E}_{(\mathbf{x}_k^D, y_k^D) \in (X_D, Y_D)}[y_k^D \log f_D(f_E(\mathbf{x}_k^D))] \tag{3}$$

Orthogonality Constraint: An additional orthogonality constraint over the reconstructed source domain features is added to the total loss to ensure their non-redundancy. The constraint is given as:

$$f_{DE}(X_S)^T f_{DE}(X_S) = I \tag{4}$$

However, Eq. (4) imposes a hard constraint over the optimization problem, so instead of incorporating it in the total loss, we minimize a softer version given as:

$$\mathcal{L}_O = f_{DE}(X_S)^T f_{DE}(X_S) - I \tag{5}$$

where I denotes identity matrix.

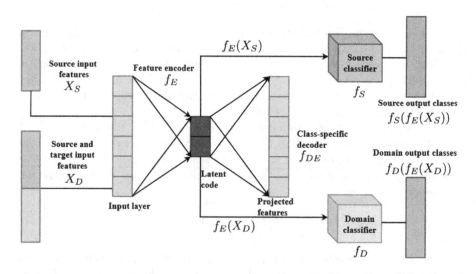

Fig. 1. Schematic flow of the proposed UDA model.

In Fig. 1, the source features X_S are encoded as $f_E(X_S)$ and then are sent to source classifier f_S. In addition, $X_D = [X_S, X_T]$ is encoded as $f_E(X_D)$ and sent to domain classifier f_D. The reconstruction loss and orthogonality constraints are applied of the reconstructed source features $f_{DE}(X_S)$.

2.2   Optimization and Inference

Based on the Eqs. (1), (2), (3) and (5), the overall loss function $\mathcal{L}$ can be represented as a two stage optimization process:
   Stage 1:

$$\mathcal{L}_1 = \min_{f_S, f_E} \mathcal{L}_S + \mathcal{L}_R + \mathcal{L}_O \tag{6}$$

   Stage 2:

$$\mathcal{L} = \min_{f_S, f_E} \max_{f_D} \mathcal{L}_1 - \mathcal{L}_D + \lambda \mathcal{R} \tag{7}$$

where λ denotes the weight of the regularizer $\mathcal{R}$ on the learnable parameters. We follow the standard alternate stochastic mini-batch gradient descent approach to optimize $\mathcal{L}$. We find that the order of optimization of the individual terms does not matter in this case.
   During testing, the target samples are assigned labels through $f_S(f_E(X_T))$.

3   Experiments

3.1   Datasets

Two benchmark hyperspectral datasets have been considered to validate the efficacy of our approach.
   The first dataset is the Botswana hyper-spectral imagery (Fig. 2) [14]. The satellite imagery was acquired by NASA EO-1 satellite in the period 2001–2004 using the Hyperion sensor with the spatial resolution of 30 m spanning over 7.7 km strip. The imagery consists of 242 bands that covering the spectral range of 400–2500 nm. However in the current study, a preprocessed version of the dataset is used that comprises 10 bands obtained following a feature selection strategy.
   Fourteen classes that correspond to land cover features on the ground are identified for the dataset. Many of the classes are fine-grained in nature with partially overlapping spectral signatures, causing the adaptation task extremely difficult. The source dataset (SD), consisting of 2621 pixels and target dataset (TD), containing 1252 pixels are created from spatially disjoint regions within the study area, leading to subtle differences in $\mathcal{S}$ and $\mathcal{T}$, respectively.
   The second dataset consists of two hyperspectral imageries, one over the Pavia City Center and the other over the University of Pavia (Fig. 3) [16]. The imageries captured from Reflective Optics Spectrographic Image System (ROSIS). The Pavia City Center image consists of 1096 rows, 492 columns and 102 bands while the University of Pavia image consists of 610 rows, 340 columns and 103 bands. Seven common classes are identified in both the images out of which few share similar spectral properties thus making their classification challenging. We use Pavia University as the source dataset while Pavia City Center as the target dataset. Since Pavia City Center image consists of 102 bands, the same number of bands are used for Pavia University image as well where the last band is dropped.

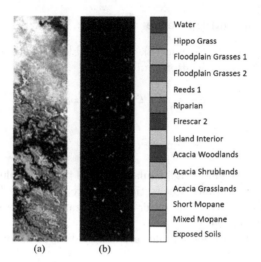

Water
Hippo Grass
Floodplain Grasses 1
Floodplain Grasses 2
Reeds 1
Riparian
Firescar 2
Island Interior
Acacia Woodlands
Acacia Shrublands
Acacia Grasslands
Short Mopane
Mixed Mopane
Exposed Soils

(a)   (b)

Fig. 2. Botswana dataset with (a) colour composite of first three bands and (b) ground truth. (Color figure online)

3.2   Protocols

The entire network is constructed in terms of fully-connected neural network layers. In particular, f_E has two hidden layers with the dimensions of the final latent layer being 50. On the other hand, a single layer neural network is used for both the source-centric classifier and the domain classifier with the required number of output nodes. $Relu(\cdot)$ non-linearity is used for all the layers. The weights for the loss terms are fixed through cross-validation and Adam optimizer [12] is considered with an initial learning rate of 0.001.

We report the classification accuracy at T and compare the performance with the following approaches from the literature: TCA, SA, GFK, and RevGrad for Botswana dataset. However, for Pavia dataset, only GFK and RevGrad have been used for comparison since the accuracies obtained from other classifiers were quite insignificant. Note all the considered techniques aim to perform UDA in a latent space and RevGrad acts like the benchmark: it implicitly showcases the advantage of the proposed reconstructive loss term $\mathcal{L}_R$. In addition, we also carried out ablation study on our proposed method by eliminating reconstruction loss and orthogonality constraint one at a time.

3.3   Discussion

Tables 1 and 2 depict the quantitative performance evaluation and comparison to other approaches for Botswana and Pavia datasets respectively. The highest accuracy by a classifier for a given class is represented in bold.

For Botswana dataset, it can be inferred that the proposed approach outperforms the others with an overall classification accuracy of 74.5%. The RevGrad

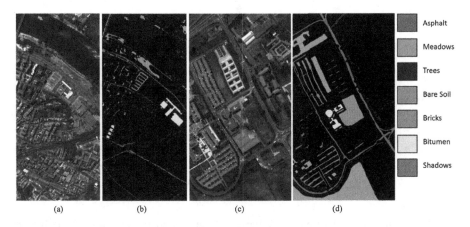

Fig. 3. Pavia dataset (a) colour composite and (b) the ground truth for the image of Pavia City Center(c) colour composite and (d) the ground truth for the image of the University of Pavia. (Color figure online)

Table 1. Performance evaluation on the Botswana dataset (in %).

Land-cover classes	Pixel counts for SD	Pixel counts for TD	TCA [15]	SA [6]	GFK [9]	RevGrad [7]	Proposed method
Water (1)	213	57	60.0	46.0	43.0	**75.0**	61.0
Hippo grass (2)	83	81	**100.0**	**100.0**	75.0	97.0	92.0
Floodplain grasses 1 (3)	199	75	56.0	59.0	69.0	67.0	**74.0**
Floodplain grasses 2 (4)	169	91	75.0	80.0	**88.0**	79.0	76.0
Reeds (5)	219	88	78.0	**83.0**	81.0	67.0	75.0
Riparian (6)	221	109	58.0	72.0	**84.0**	65.0	70.0
Firescar 2 (7)	215	83	98.0	**100.0**	**100.0**	97.0	**100.0**
Island interior (8)	166	77	62.0	48.0	60.0	66.0	**81.0**
Acacia woodlands (9)	253	67	27.0	40.0	44.0	47.0	**50.0**
Acacia shrublands (10)	202	89	40.0	50.0	62.0	48.0	**71.0**
Acacia grasslands (11)	243	174	79.0	**92.0**	**92.0**	73.0	74.0
Short mopane (12)	154	85	89.0	**93.0**	91.0	73.0	79.0
Mixed mopane (13)	203	128	48.0	61.0	65.0	**77.0**	73.0
Exposed soil (14)	81	48	85.0	**100.0**	**100.0**	79.0	77.0
Overall accuracy (OA)	–	–	61.0	65.0	70.0	69.0	**74.5**

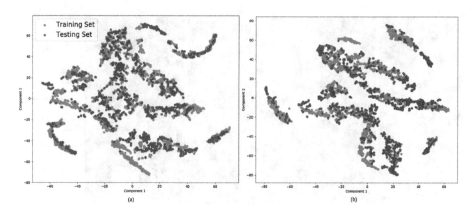

Fig. 4. Two dimensional t-SNE of Botswana's source and target datasets (a) before domain adaptation (b) after domain adaptation.

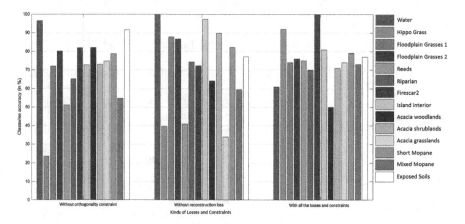

Fig. 5. Bar chart for ablation study comparing effects of exclusion of different losses on the classes of Botswana dataset.

technique on the other hand, produces an overall performance of 69%, thus implying that an overall domain alignment (without class) is not suitable for this dataset. The proposed method produces significant improvement in identifying island interior (OA = 81%), acacia woodlands (OA = 50%) and acacia shrublands (OA = 71%). These classes are difficult to handle having similar spectral properties with other classes and the ad hoc approaches considered for comparison mostly failed to identify them. For other classes, the results are comparable to the other techniques. Figure 4 shows the 2-D t-SNE comparing the source and target features (before training) with projected source and target features obtained after training.

The ablation study conducted on Botswana dataset showed that an OA of 65% is achieved when the reconstruction loss is not considered during while an

Table 2. Performance evaluation on the Pavia dataset (in %).

Land-cover classes	Pixel counts for SD	Pixel counts for TD	GFK [9]	RevGrad [7]	Proposed method
Asphalt (1)	6631	7585	50.0	64.0	**86.0**
Meadows (2)	18649	2905	47.0	61.5	**92.0**
Trees (3)	3064	6508	92.0	**94.0**	84.0
Baresoil (4)	5029	6549	**97.0**	72.5	53.0
Bricks (5)	3682	2140	62.0	67.0	58.0
Bitumen (6)	1330	7287	41.0	51.0	**57.0**
Shadows (7)	947	2165	**97.0**	83.5	95.0
Overall accuracy (OA)	–	–	66.0	70.5	**74.0**

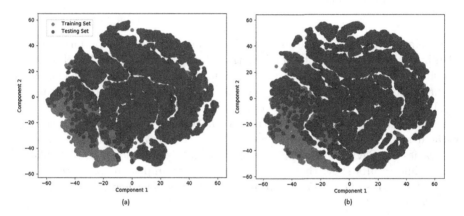

Fig. 6. Two dimensional t-SNE of Pavia's source and target datasets (a) before domain adaptation (b) after domain adaptation.

OA of 64% is recorded in absence of orthogonality constraint. Figure 5 presents the accuracies obtained while conducting the ablation study on Botswana dataset. Significant improvement is observed in the accuracy of hippo grass, reeds and firescar 2 when all the losses and constraints are considered. It is also observed that the accuracy water class is decreased considerably for the same case. The accuracies for other classes are more or less same.

The similar trend is observed for Pavia dataset as well where our method surpasses the other classifiers with an OA of 74%, while the benchmark RevGrad classifier gives an OA of 70.5%. This affirms the inefficiency of domain alignment (without class) on the Pavia dataset as well. In addition, there is a significant improvement in classification of asphalt (OA = 86%) and meadows (OA = 92%) classes. The spectral signature of meadows class overlaps with that of that of

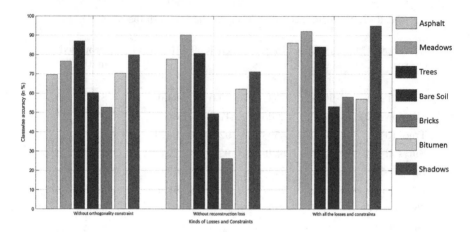

Fig. 7. Bar chart for ablation study comparing effects of exclusion of different losses on the classes of Pavia dataset.

trees (since both are a subset of vegetation), but our classifier performs well in identifying meadows much better than the other classifiers. For other classes, the classification accuracies are more or less similar to those from other classifiers. Figure 6 shows the t-SNEs of source and target features before and after training.

The ablation study on Pavia dataset showed an overall accuracy of 65% when the classifier was trained without orthogonality constraint while training without reconstruction loss gave an OA of 71%. Figure 7 compares the classwise accuracies for Pavia dataset against different losses considered in our ablation study. The results show that there is a significant improvement in the identifying of shadows (OA = 95%) and asphalt (OA = 86%) when all the losses are considered.

4   Conclusions

We propose a cross-domain classification algorithm for HSI based on adversarial learning. Our model incorporates an additional class-level cross-sample reconstruction loss for the samples in S within the standard DC framework in order to make the learned space meaningful and classwise compact and an additional orthogonality constraint over the source domain to avoid any redundancy within the reconstructed features. Several experiments are conducted on the Botswana and Pavia datasets to assess the efficacy of the proposed technique. The results clearly establish the superiority of our approach with respect to a number of existing ad hoc and neural networks based methods. Currently, our method only relies on the spectral information. We plan to introduce the spatial aspect for improved semantic segmentation of the scene by distilling the advantages of convolution networks within the model.

References

1. Banerjee, B., Chaudhuri, S.: Hierarchical subspace learning based unsupervised domain adaptation for cross-domain classification of remote sensing images. IEEE J. Sel. Top. Appl. Earth Obs. Remote Sens. **10**(11), 5099–5109 (2017)
2. Bejiga, M.B., Melgani, F.: Gan-based domain adaptation for object classification. In: Proceedings of the IGARSS 2018 - 2018 IEEE International Geoscience and Remote Sensing Symposium, pp. 1264–1267. IEEE (2018)
3. Cai, G., Wang, Y., Zhou, M., He, L.: Unsupervised domain adaptation with adversarial residual transform networks. arXiv preprint arXiv:1804.09578 (2018)
4. Chen, H.Y., Chien, J.T.: Deep semi-supervised learning for domain adaptation. In: Proceedings of the 25th IEEE International Workshop on Machine Learning for Signal Processing (MLSP), pp. 1–6 (2015)
5. Chen, Y., Xu, W., Sundaram, H., Rikakis, T., Liu, S.M.: A dynamic decision network framework for online media adaptation in stroke rehabilitation. ACM Trans. Multimed. Comput. Commun. Appl. (TOMM) **5**(1), 4 (2008)
6. Fernando, B., Habrard, A., Sebban, M., Tuytelaars, T.: Unsupervised visual domain adaptation using subspace alignment. In: Proceedings of the IEEE International Conference on Computer Vision, pp. 2960–2967 (2013)
7. Ganin, Y., Lempitsky, V.: Unsupervised domain adaptation by backpropagation. arXiv preprint arXiv:1409.7495 (2014)
8. Ganin, Y., et al.: Domain-adversarial training of neural networks. J. Mach. Learn. Res. **17**(1), 1–35 (2016)
9. Gong, B., Shi, Y., Sha, F., Grauman, K.: Geodesic flow kernel for unsupervised domain adaptation. In: Proceedings of the IEEE Conference on Computer Vision and Pattern Recognition (CVPR), pp. 2066–2073 (2012)
10. Goodfellow, I., Bengio, Y., Courville, A., Bengio, Y.: Deep Learning, vol. 1. MIT Press, Cambridge (2016)
11. Goodfellow, I.J., Shlens, J., Szegedy, C.: Explaining and harnessing adversarial examples. arXiv preprint arXiv:1412.6572 (2014)
12. Kingma, D.P., Ba, J.: Adam: a method for stochastic optimization. arXiv preprint arXiv:1412.6980 (2014)
13. Li, S., Song, S., Huang, G., Ding, Z., Wu, C.: Domain invariant and class discriminative feature learning for visual domain adaptation. IEEE Trans. Image Process. **27**(9), 4260–4273 (2018)
14. Neuenschwander, A.L., Crawford, M.M., Ringrose, S.: Results from the EO-1 experiment—a comparative study of Earth Observing-1 Advanced Land Imager (ALI) and Landsat ETM+ data for land cover mapping in the Okavango Delta, Botswana. Int. J. Remote Sens. **26**(19), 4321–4337 (2005)
15. Pan, S.J., Tsang, I.W., Kwok, J.T., Yang, Q.: Domain adaptation via transfer component analysis. IEEE Trans. Neural Netw. **22**(2), 199–210 (2011)
16. Qin, Y., Bruzzone, L., Li, B., Ye, Y.: Tensor alignment based domain adaptation for hyperspectral image classification. arXiv preprint arXiv:1808.09769 (2018)
17. Sohn, K., Shang, W., Yu, X., Chandraker, M.: Unsupervised domain adaptation for distance metric learning. In: Proceedings of the International Conference on Learning Representations (ICLR) (2018)
18. Tuia, D., Persello, C., Bruzzone, L.: Domain adaptation for the classification of remote sensing data: an overview of recent advances. IEEE Geosci. Remote Sens. Mag. **4**(2), 41–57 (2016)

19. Tzeng, E., Hoffman, J., Saenko, K., Darrell, T.: Adversarial discriminative domain adaptation. In: Proceedings of the Computer Vision and Pattern Recognition (CVPR), vol. 1, p. 4 (2017)
20. Yan, H., Ding, Y., Li, P., Wang, Q., Xu, Y., Zuo, W.: Mind the class weight bias: Weighted maximum mean discrepancy for unsupervised domain adaptation. In: Proceedings of the IEEE Conference on Computer Vision and Pattern Recognition (CVPR), vol. 3 (2017)
21. Ye, M., Qian, Y., Zhou, J., Tang, Y.Y.: Dictionary learning-based feature-level domain adaptation for cross-scene hyperspectral image classification. IEEE Trans. Geosci. Remote Sens. **55**(3), 1544–1562 (2017)

Multi-label Logo Classification Using Convolutional Neural Networks

Antonio-Javier Gallego$^{(\boxtimes)}$, Antonio Pertusa , and Marisa Bernabeu

University Institute for Computing Research (IUII),
University of Alicante, San Vicente del Raspeig, Spain
jgallego@dlsi.ua.es

Abstract. The classification of logos is a particular case within computer vision since they have their own characteristics. Logos can contain only text, iconic images or a combination of both, and they usually include figurative symbols designed by experts that vary substantially besides they may share the same semantics. This work presents a method for multi-label classification and retrieval of logo images. For this, Convolutional Neural Networks (CNN) are trained to classify logos from the European Union TradeMark (EUTM) dataset according to their colors, shapes, sectors and figurative designs. An auto-encoder is also trained to learn representations of the input images. Once trained, the neural codes from the last convolutional layers in the CNN and the central layer of the auto-encoder can be used to perform similarity search through kNN, allowing us to obtain the most similar logos based on their color, shape, sector, figurative elements, overall features, or a weighted combination of them provided by the user. To the best of our knowledge, this is the first multi-label classification method for logos, and the only one that allows retrieving a ranking of images with these criteria provided by the user.

Keywords: Logo image retrieval · Multi-Label Classification · Convolutional Neural Networks

1 Introduction

The detection and recognition of logos is an important task at the industrial level due to the need to find unauthorized usage of company logos, and also for trademark registration, where it needs to be verified that there are no similar existing logos within the same sector. However, there is not much research regarding this topic [5,9]. The reason may be because some years ago most logo datasets were not publicly available [3], but nowadays both the European Union Intellectual Property Office (EUIPO) and the United States Patent and Trademark Office (UPSTO) share their images and metadata.

Most previous computer vision works on logos are focused on Trademark Image Retrieval (TIR), i.e. similarity search to obtain the most similar logos to a query image. This is a very relevant task due to the volume of trademark

© Springer Nature Switzerland AG 2019
A. Morales et al. (Eds.): IbPRIA 2019, LNCS 11867, pp. 485–497, 2019.
https://doi.org/10.1007/978-3-030-31332-6_42

registration applications and the size of the databases containing existing trade-marks, as it is almost impossible for humans to make all the comparisons visually [8]. Traditional methods addressed TIR by extracting hand-crafted features and then matching them with the prototypes of a dataset by using kNN to obtain a ranking of the most similar ones. Features used to represent logos include color histograms [3], texture descriptors, shape [10], a combination of them [4,6], or local descriptors such as SIFT [1]. In most cases, the feature dimensionality is reduced with a clustering method such as Bag of Words [5]. Finally, the processed characteristics are usually matched with those from a ground-truth dataset by using distance metrics or more complex methods such as template matching [9].

Recent TIR works such as [1] make use of deep neural networks. A combi-nation of CNN pre-trained with ImageNet is employed in [8], fine-tuning their weights with two logo similarity datasets. Once the models are trained, authors extracted neural codes (NC) from different layers and compared them with the logo prototypes using cosine distance. For training these networks, one of the datasets used (DBc) contained a classification of figurative elements based on UPSTO with classes such as human beings, plants or foodstuffs in a multi-class setup.

Excepting the work in [8], which to the best of our knowledge is the only one using figurative classes, most TIR methods use datasets with logos that are only labeled by brand, assuming that images from a same brand would be similar. The fact that one brand may have different logo versions over time with changes in background, color, texture or shape (e.g. Disney has changed its logo more than 30 times [5]) is used to build labeled logo datasets. Examples of these are the METU dataset [12] which contains 32 classes (brands) in the query set with 10 images each, or Logos in the Wild [13], in which images are labeled with 871 brands. However, it must be noted that sometimes there are strong changes in the designs from the same brand, making them very different in appearance, therefore relying on visual similarity of logos from the same brand is not always reliable.

In addition to the trademark they belong to, logos can also be classified using different criteria, such as color, shape, sector or semantics. In this case, samples usually have more than one simultaneous label (for example, they may contain several colors or figurative elements), making this a Multi-Label Classification (MLC) task. MLC is different than traditional multi-class classification, as in the latter class labels are treated as independent target variables (relying on their mutually exclusive assumption), which is clearly suboptimal for MLC as the dependencies among classes cannot be leveraged.

In addition to MLC, there exist another task related to supervised learning from multi-label data [11]: Label Ranking (LR). The main difference is that MLC is concerned with learning a model that outputs a bipartition of the set of labels into relevant and irrelevant with respect to a query instance, while LR is concerned with learning a model that outputs a ranking of class labels according to their relevance to a query instance.

To the best of our knowledge, multi-label classification of logos remains unexplored. In this work we perform MLC and LR on logos using a large image dataset labeled with figurative elements, colors, shapes and sectors. Individual classifiers are trained for each of these tasks, together with an auto-encoder for the reconstruction of the input images. Then, the trained networks can be used for classification, but also for similarity search using kNN on the neural codes (NC) extracted from the last convolutional layers of the CNN or from the middle layer of the auto-encoder. This allows us to perform logo retrieval by mixing different criteria according to the user.

2 Dataset

For training the models we use the European Union TradeMark (EUTM) dataset, which gives owners an exclusive right in the 28 Member States from European Union. Original data was downloaded from the European Union Intellectual Property Office (EUIPO) website[1], selecting a subset of 11,000 logos corresponding to the year 2018 for experiments.

The EUTM dataset uses the Vienna Classification, a hierarchical system which proceeds from the general to the specific, dividing all elements into 29 main categories as can be seen in Table 1, that are subdivided into more specific elements (subcategories). The characteristics used in this work are the following:

- **Figurative.** In the scope of this work, we call figurative designs to those codes between 1 a 24, as they are related to the particular objects that can be found in the image logo. The figurative subcategories were not used since they are too specific (for example, 10.1.2. Cut tobacco, 10.1.3 Cigars, 10.1.5 Cigarettes, or 10.1.7 Tobacco in any other form) and the number of classes could be very large. The codes from 25 to 29 are related to the background, shape, text and color and, therefore, we did not include them for figurative classification. Codes 26 (shape) and 29 (color) were used separately as can be seen below.
- **Colors.** The 13 color codes used in this work are shown in Table 2 (left). Vienna classification also includes codes related to the number of colors (e.g., 29.01.12 means that there are two predominant colors), although they were not used.
- **Shapes.** Table 2 (right) shows the different shapes used for classification, including circles, triangles, lines, etc.
- **Sectors.** Trademarks have also the associated goods and/or services to be covered by the mark. For this, EUIPO has adopted the Nice Classification[2] that divides goods and services into 45 subcategories[3], not shown here due to space limitations, from two main sectors: goods (from codes 1 to 34), and

---

[1] https://euipo.europa.eu/ohimportal/en/open-data.

[2] https://euipo.europa.eu/ohimportal/en/nice-classification.

[3] https://www.wipo.int/classifications/nice/nclpub/en/fr/20180101/classheadings/ explanatory_notes=show&lang=en&menulang=en.

Table 1. Vienna labels [14]. In the scope of this work, figurative elements are those with codes from 1 to 24. Codes from 25 onwards are related to shape, text and color, and were not used for figurative classification.

Code	Description
1	Celestial Bodies, Natural Phenomena, Geographical Maps
2	Human Beings
3	Animals
4	Supernatural, Fabulous, Fantastic or Unidentifiable Beings
5	Plants
6	Landscapes
7	Constructions, Structures for Advertisements, Gates or Barriers
8	Foodstuffs
9	Textiles, Clothing, Sewing Accessories, Headwear, Footwear
10	Tobacco, Smokers' Requisites, Matches, Travel Goods, Fans, Toilet Articles
11	Household Utensils
12	Furniture, Sanitary Installations
13	Lighting, Wireless Valves, Heating, Cooking or Refrigerating Equipment, Washing Machines, Drying Equipment
14	Ironmongery, Tools, Ladders
15	Machinery, Motors, Engines
16	Telecommunications, Sound Recording or Reproduction, Computers, Photography, Cinematography, Optics
17	Horological Instruments, Jewelry, Weights and Measures
18	Transport, Equipment for Animals
19	Containers and Packing, Representations of Miscellaneous Products
20	Writing, Drawing or Painting Materials, Office Requisites, Stationery and Booksellers' Goods
21	Games, Toys, Sporting Articles, Roundabouts
22	Musical Instruments and their Accessories, Music Accessories, Bells, Pictures, Sculptures
23	Arms, Ammunition, Armour
24	Heraldry, Coins, Emblems, Symbols
25	Ornamental motifs, Surfaces or backgrounds with ornaments
26	Geometrical figures and Solids
27	Forms of writing, Numerals
28	Inscriptions in various characters
29	Colors

services (from 35 to 45). The goods sector includes chemicals, medicines, metals, materials, machines, tools, vehicles, instruments, etc., while services include advertising, insurance, telecommunications, transport and education, among others. In this work we use both sectors and sub-sectors.

Table 2. Vienna codes used in this work for colors (code 29 in Table 1), and shapes (code 26 in Table 1).

Code	Color
29.01.01	Red
29.01.02	Yellow
29.01.03	Green
29.01.04	Blue
29.01.05	Violet
29.01.06	White
29.01.07	Brown
29.01.08	Black
29.01.95	Silver
29.01.96	Gray
29.01.97	Gold
29.01.98	Orange
29.01.99	Pink

Code	Shape
26.1	Circles, ellipses
26.2	Segments or sectors of circles or ellipses
26.3	Triangles, lines forming an angle
26.4	Quadrilaterals
26.5	Other polygons
26.7	Different geometrical figures, juxtaposed, joined or intersecting
26.11	Lines, bands
26.13	Other geometrical figures, indefinable designs
26.15	Geometrical solids

000141922461.JPG	000141935610.JPG	000142006416.JPG	000142042708.JPG	000142000637.JPG
FIGURATIVE 01 - 18	FIGURATIVE 01 - 24	FIGURATIVE 01	FIGURATIVE 01	FIGURATIVE 03
COLOR 29.01.01	COLOR 29.01.03	COLOR 29.01.03 - 29.01.08	COLOR 29.01.04	COLOR 29.01.03
SHAPE 26.01	SHAPE 26.03	SHAPE 26.01	SHAPE 26.15	SHAPE 26.01
SECTOR 12 - 35 - 40	SECTOR 16 - 25 - 36	SECTOR 35 - 37 - 38	SECTOR 07	SECTOR 29

Fig. 1. Some trademark examples in the EUTM dataset.

2.1 Preprocessing

The EUTM metadata is stored in XML format. The XML files have fields with the categories and subcategories of the trademark, and the corresponding logo image path. We extracted these fields from each XML file and separated them in figurative (codes from 1 to 24), color (codes 29.xx.xx), shape (codes 26.xx), and sector (codes for goods and/or services). Only those trademarks that have all these fields were selected. Then, all the images related to the processed data were downloaded. Notice that a trademark can have two or more codes associated to each field, and some information is not always labeled, specially in the color and shape fields where not all elements are described, as can be seen in Fig. 1.

Regarding the color category in Fig. 1, we can see in the first example image that only red color was annotated, although it also has black and blue. In the third logo, green and black were labeled, whereas in the forth and fifth ones, which have three colors, only one of them was detailed. Meanwhile, only circles were annotated as shapes in the first, third and fifth images, although they also contain other shapes. The forth, which is also circular, was classified as geometrical solid.

The logo images were also preprocessed. First they were crop to eliminate the borders containing background. In this dataset, all the logos have a white background but the size of its border is variable, and in some cases too large. For this reason, images were crop by eliminating white borders so that all the logos

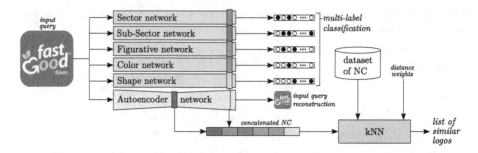

Fig. 2. Scheme of the proposed method.

occupied all the available space of the image. Once this process was completed, images were scaled to a size of 256×256 pixels, and their values were normalized into the range $[0, 1]$ to feed the networks.

3   Method

Figure 2 shows the scheme of the proposed approach. The CNNs are trained on each characteristic using an MLC setup with a sigmoid activation instead of a softmax in the last layer, as shown in Table 3. This activation function models the probability of each class as a Bernoulli distribution, where each class is independent of the others unlike it happens with softmax. Therefore, the output is a multi-label classification for each of the considered characteristics.

In addition, an auto-encoder was also trained to reconstruct the input image in order to get the NC from the middle layer. These codes are a low-dimensionality representation of the main characteristics of the image, which allows to perform similarity search with kNN. Once all networks are trained, NC are extracted from the CNNs and the auto-encoder on the input image. The size of the NC extracted from the CNNs is 128, and for the auto-encoder is 256. The NC are combined into a single vector of characteristics, which is the one used to perform similarity search. An ℓ_2-norm is applied to normalize the concatenated feature vector before searching for the most similar prototypes, since this technique usually improves the results [2].

We use a weighted distance to search for the nearest neighbors, allowing the user to adjust the search criteria modifying the weight assigned to each characteristic. We use the following equation to calculate the distance between two vectors of characteristics A and B:

$$d(A, B) = \frac{\sum\limits_{c \in \mathcal{C}} w^c d(A^c, B^c)}{\sum\limits_{c \in \mathcal{C}} w^c} \tag{1}$$

where $\mathcal{C}$ is the set of all the possible characteristics to be classified, A^c and B^c represent the subset of features corresponding to the characteristic c, w^c is the weight assigned to that characteristic, and $\forall c \in \mathcal{C} : w^c \in [0, 1]$.

Table 3. CNN and Auto-Encoder (Encoder+Decoder) architectures. Notation: Conv(f, $w \times h$) stands for a layer with f convolutional operators of size $w \times h$; ConvT(f, $w \times h$) stands for a layer with f transposed convolutional operators of size $w \times h$; MaxPool($w \times h$) stands for the Max-Pooling operator with a $w \times h$ kernel; Drop(d) refers to Dropout with ratio d; FC(n) is a Fully-Connected layer with n neurons. The NC were extracted from the layers marked in bold.

CNN configuration					
Conv(32,11×11)	Conv(32,9×9)	Conv(64,7×7)	Conv(64,5×5)	Conv(128,3×3)	Flatten()
BatchNorm	BatchNorm	BatchNorm	BatchNorm	BatchNorm	**FC(128, ReLU)**
Act ReLU	Act ReLU	Act ReLU	Act ReLU	Act ReLU	BatchNorm
MaxPool(2×2)	MaxPool(2×2)	MaxPool(2×2)	MaxPool(2×2)	MaxPool(2×2)	Drop(0.5)
Drop(0.1)	Drop(0.2)	Drop(0.3)	Drop(0.4)	Drop(0.5)	FC(n, Sigmoid)
Encoder configuration					
Conv(128,3×3)	Conv(64,3×3)	Conv(64,3×3)	Conv(64,3×3)	**Conv(1, 3×3)**	
Stride(2×2)	Stride(2×2)	Stride(2×2)	Stride(2×2)		
BatchNorm	BatchNorm	BatchNorm	BatchNorm		
Act ReLU	Act ReLU	Act ReLU	Act ReLU		
Drop(0.25)	Drop(0.25)	Drop(0.25)	Drop(0.25)		
Decoder configuration					
CnvT(64,3×3)	CnvT(64,3×3)	CnvT(64,3×3)	CnvT(128,3×3)	Conv(3,3×3)	
Stride(2×2)	Stride(2×2)	Stride(2×2)	Stride(2×2)	Act Sigmoid	
BatchNorm	BatchNorm	BatchNorm	BatchNorm		
Act ReLU	Act ReLU	Act ReLU	Act ReLU		
Drop(0.25)	Drop(0.25)	Drop(0.25)	Drop(0.25)		

3.1 Training Process

The training of the networks is carried out by means of standard backpropagation using Stochastic Gradient Descent (SGD) and considering the adaptive learning rate method proposed in [15]. In the backpropagation algorithm, *binary crossentropy* was used as the loss function between the CNN output and the expected result. The training lasted a maximum of 200 epochs with *early stopping* when the loss did not decrease during 15 epochs. The mini-batch size was set to 32 samples.

In addition, data augmentation was performed on the training images by adding random rotations, horizontal and vertical flips, scale and shear transformations.

4 Evaluation

This section presents the metrics used for evaluation and the obtained results. For evaluation we have used the dataset described in Sect. 2. From the 11,000 logo images, 80% were selected for training and the remaining samples for test.

4.1 Metrics

In multi-label learning each sample can have any number of ground truth labels associated. In this work we use the following multi-label metrics [11]:

Table 4. Results obtained with the CNNs for the different tasks.

Network	CE	LRL
Color	2.4397	0.0399
Shape	2.4751	0.1326
Sector	1.6619	0.2345
Sub-sector	16.2427	0.2120
Figurative	2.0170	0.0616

Coverage Error (CE). This is an MLC metric which computes the average number of labels that have to be included in the final prediction such that all true labels are predicted. This is useful to know how many top-scored-labels must be predicted in average without missing any true one. The best value of this metrics is thus the average number of true labels. Formally, being N the total number of samples and L the number of labels, given a binary indicator matrix of the ground truth labels $y \in \{0,1\}^{N \times L}$ and the score associated with each label $\hat{f} \in \mathbb{R}^{N \times L}$, the coverage is defined as:

$$\text{CE}(y, \hat{f}) = \frac{1}{N} \sum_{i=0}^{N-1} \max_{j:y_{ij}=1} \text{rank}_{ij} \tag{2}$$

where $\text{rank}_{ij} = \left| \left\{ k : \hat{f}_{ik} \geq \hat{f}_{ij} \right\} \right|$.

Label Ranking Loss (LRL). This LR metric computes the ranking which averages over the samples the number of label pairs that are incorrectly ordered (true labels with a lower score than false labels), weighted by the inverse of the number of ordered pairs of false and true labels. The lowest achievable label ranking loss is zero.

$$\text{LRL}(y, \hat{f}) = \frac{1}{N} \sum_{i=0}^{N-1} \frac{1}{\|y_i\|_0 (L - \|y_i\|_0)} \left| \left\{ (k,l) : \hat{f}_{ik} \leq \hat{f}_{il}, y_{ik} = 1, y_{il} = 0 \right\} \right| \tag{3}$$

where $|\cdot|$ calculates the cardinality (number of elements) of the set, and $\|\cdot\|_0$ is the ℓ_0-norm which computes the number of nonzero elements in a vector.

4.2 Results

The results of the different CNNs can be seen in Table 4. The best results using the LRL metric are obtained by the color classifier, followed by the main sector (note that it only has two labels), the figurative designs, and the shape, with fairly close results. The worst results are obtained for the sub-sector, possibly because it is the characteristic with the largest number of classes (45). In addition, it must be borne in mind that, while color and shape are objective characteristics, the sector, sub-sector and figurative design may be subjective, and in some cases the same design can be used for different sectors or sub-sectors.

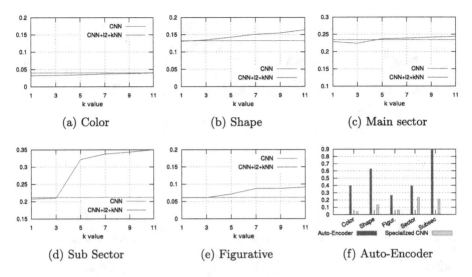

(a) Color   (b) Shape   (c) Main sector

(d) Sub Sector   (e) Figurative   (f) Auto-Encoder

Fig. 3. LRL results for each characteristic using kNN on the NC (lower values are better). In the case of the auto-encoder, results are evaluated regarding all the other possible characteristics.

With respect to the results obtained by the auto-encoder for the validation set, we obtain a binary crossentropy loss of 0.3992 and a Mean Squared Error (MSE) of 0.0687 for reconstruction. In this case, it is not possible to calculate the other metrics since the auto-encoder is trained in an unsupervised way.

Regarding similarity search with kNN, Fig. 3 shows the results obtained (using the LRL metric) for each individual characteristic. In this experiment, the value of k was evaluated in the range $k \in [1 - 11]$ to assess its impact. As can be seen in Figs. 3a–e, the best results are obtained with low k values, slightly improving the CNN result when using 1 or 3 neighbors. Although the results are similar to those from the CNN, using kNN on the NC allows us to perform similarity search. Finally, Fig. 3f shows the results obtained using the NC extracted from the auto-encoder to classify the different characteristics considered (color, shape, etc.). In this way we can analyze what the characteristics learned by the auto-encoder represent. As can be seen, the auto-encoder focuses slightly on each of the characteristics, obtaining the best results when classifying the figurative design, followed by the main sector, color, and shape, and obtaining the worst results for the sub-sector.

Figure 4 shows an example query and the most similar results using the NC of the color classifier. As seen, colors of the retrieved results are correctly matched, even when they are multiple, independently of other characteristics such as the shape. Figure 5 shows that shapes are also correctly detected. Figurative designs (see Fig. 6) are more complicated to retrieve. The first example shows a plant, and most retrieved results are correct, although there are also unrelated logos retrieved. The second example contains an animal, but the first and last retrieved results do not.

Fig. 4. Color retrieval example with kNN. The first logo is the query. (Color figure online)

Fig. 5. Shape retrieval example with kNN. The first logo is the query.

Fig. 6. Figurative design retrieval example with kNN. The first logo is the query.

Fig. 7. Sector retrieval example with kNN. The first logo is the query.

Sector is very difficult to retrieve properly, moreover when there are only two classes that do not strongly depend on visual information: goods and services. The first row in Fig. 7 shows an example of a goods logo that was correctly

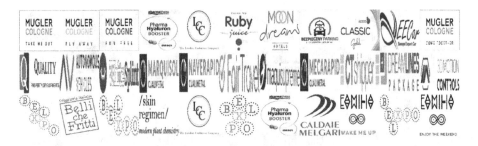

Fig. 8. Sub-sector retrieval example with kNN. The first logo is the query.

Fig. 9. Auto-encoder retrieval example with kNN. The first logo is the query.

retrieved, and the second is related to services. In the case of sub-sector (Fig. 8), the first query corresponds to a cosmetics brand. As can be seen, nearest logos are also related, and also the most visually similar are found. The second example corresponds to a brand from the construction sub-sector, and most retrieved elements are correct. The third row shows that even when logos have similar features but layout changes (BelXPo brand), they are retrieved properly.

As can be seen in Fig. 9, the auto-encoder mainly focuses on spatial distributions (the logo layout), in some cases taking also into account the colors.

Figure 10 shows the results when using the weighted distance. In this example, the characteristics of color and shape are used, comparing the result obtained by assigning 70% of the weight to the color and 30% to the shape, and vice versa. As can be seen, by increasing the weight of color, retrieved images have a similar color and slightly similar shapes (unlike the results shown in Fig. 4, in which the shape varies greatly). By inverting the weights and giving more importance to the shape, Fig. 10 shows images with more similar shapes but slightly different colors. Analyzing the results of the last row (brand "Acute angle") we can see that by giving more weight to the color only appears a completely triangular shape, since there are no more triangular logos labeled with the same color. If we compare these results with those obtained in the first row of Fig. 5 for the same mark, we can see how we also obtain only triangular shapes but with a different arrangement, in which when weighed the distance giving a certain weight to the color appears as a second result an inverted triangular shape, but with the same color.

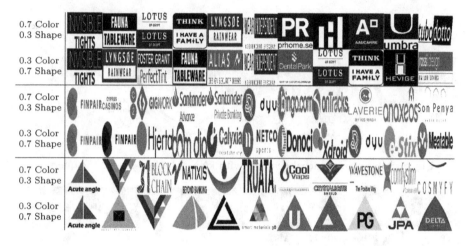

Fig. 10. Results obtained using the weighted distance with color and shape. In the first column the applied weights are shown, and the first image is the query. (Color figure online)

5   Conclusions

In this work, several multi-label CNNs were trained for the classification of logo images according to their color, figurative designs, shape, and sector. The NC extracted from internal layers were used for similarity search using kNN with optional user-driven weights for each characteristic. In addition to the NC, an auto-encoder was also trained to extract a compact representation of the logo which contains its overall appearance, and that can also be used for similarity search. To the best of our knowledge, there are no previous works addressing multi-label logo classification, with these amount of characteristics that can be used to search similar images, and allowing weighting the characteristics.

Results show that the method is reliable for retrieving logos that are similar in color or shape. Worse results are obtained using sector, sub-sector and figurative elements, as these features are much more general. However, as can be seen in the example figures, most retrieved logos are visually similar.

The design of a logo is subjective and, in addition, it is not always made by a professional designer. Moreover, there are design criteria that depend on certain factors such as the sector, since logos of the same sector often share similar features (for instance, car brand logos usually contain metallic shapes and colors). An advantage of using deep neural networks is that these models learn the most frequent designs for each sector and this can serve, in addition to looking for similar logos, as an indication of whether the logo is appropriate or not for a particular activity.

As future works, it is planned to further explore the NC, for example from color and shape, using t-Distributed Stochastic Neighbor Embedding (t-SNE [7]). This would enable us to cluster samples of similar logos visually. Also, we plan to explore more specific categories for figurative elements such as "cheese" (instead of the main categories such as "food") to obtain similar logos more accurately, although this would require to train the classifiers with many more images. In addition, an evaluation of the logo retrieval results could also be performed by expert designers.

Acknowledgments. This work is supported by the Spanish Ministry HISPAMUS project with code TIN2017-86576-R, partially funded by the EU.

References

1. Chiam, J.H.: Brand logo classification. Technical report, Stanford University (2015)
2. Gallego, A.J., Pertusa, A., Calvo-Zaragoza, J.: Improving convolutional neural networks' accuracy in noisy environments using k-nearest neighbors. Appl. Sci. **8**(11), 2086 (2018)
3. Ghosh, S., Parekh, R.: Automated color logo recognition system based on shape and color features. Int. J. Comput. Appl. **118**(12), 13–20 (2015)
4. Guru, D.S., Vinay Kumar, N.: Interval valued feature selection for classification of logo images. In: Abraham, A., Muhuri, P.K., Muda, A.K., Gandhi, N. (eds.) ISDA 2017. AISC, vol. 736, pp. 154–165. Springer, Cham (2018). https://doi.org/10.1007/978-3-319-76348-4_16
5. Iandola, F.N., Shen, A., Gao, P., Keutzer, K.: DeepLogo: hitting logo recognition with the deep neural network hammer. CoRR abs/1510.02131 (2015)
6. Kumar, N.V., Pratheek, Kantha, V.V., Govindaraju, K., Guru, D.: Features fusion for classification of logos. In: Internetional Conference on Computational Modelling and Security (CMS), vol. 85, pp. 370–379 (2016)
7. van der Maaten, L., Hinton, G.: Visualizing high-dimensional data using t-SNE. J. Mach. Learn. Res. **9**(Nov), 2579–2605 (2008)
8. Perez, C.A., et al.: Trademark image retrieval using a combination of deep convolutional neural networks. In: International Joint Conference on Neural Networks (IJCNN), pp. 1–7, July 2018
9. Pornpanomchai, C., Boonsripornchai, P., Puttong, P., Rattananirundorn, C.: Logo recognition system. In: ICSEC 2015, pp. 1–6 (2015)
10. Qi, H., Li, K., Shen, Y., Qu, W.: An effective solution for trademark image retrieval by combining shape description and feature matching. Pattern Recogn. **43**(6), 2017–2027 (2010)
11. Tsoumakas, G., Katakis, I., Vlahavas, I.: Mining multi-label data. In: Data Mining and Knowledge Discovery Handbook, pp. 667–685 (2010)
12. Tursun, O., Aker, C., Kalkan, S.: A large-scale dataset and benchmark for similar trademark retrieval. CoRR abs/1701.05766 (2017)
13. Tüzkö, A., Herrmann, C., Manger, D., Beyerer, J.: Open set logo detection and retrieval. In: International Joint Conference on Computer Vision, Imaging and Computer Graphics Theory and Applications (VISIGRAPP) (2018)
14. World Intellectual Property Organization: International Classification of the Figurative Elements of Marks: (Vienna Classification). WIPO Publication, World Intellectual Property Organization (2002)
15. Zeiler, M.D.: ADADELTA: an adaptive learning rate method. CoRR abs/1212.5701 (2012)

Non-destructively Prediction of Quality Parameters of Dry-Cured Iberian Ham by Applying Computer Vision and Low-Field MRI

Juan Pedro Torres[1] , Mar Ávila[1] , Andrés Caro[1(✉)] ,
Trinidad Pérez-Palacios[2] , and Daniel Caballero[3]

[1] Media Engineering Group, School of Technology, University of Extremadura,
Av. Ciencias S/N, 10003 Cáceres, Spain
{juanp,mmavila,andresc,dcaballero}@unex.es
[2] Food Technology Department, Research Institute of Meat and Meat Product,
University of Extremadura, Av. Ciencias S/N, 10003 Cáceres, Spain
triny@unex.es
[3] Chemometrics and Analytical Technology, Department of Food Science,
University of Copenhagen, Rolighedsvej 26, 1958 Frederiksberg, Denmark
caballero@food.ku.dk

Abstract. Computer vision algorithms and Magnetic Resonance Imaging (MRI) have been proposed to obtain quality traits of Iberian hams, due to the non-destructive, non-ionizing and innocuous nature of these approaches. However, all the proposals have been based on high-field MRI scanners, which obtain high quality images but also involve very high economical costs. In this paper, low-field MRI devices and three classical texture algorithms were used to predict quality traits of Iberian ham. Prediction equation of quality features were obtained, which estimate the quality parameters as a function of computational textures. The texture features were obtained by applying three well-known classical texture algorithms (GLCM - Gray Level Co-occurrence Matrix, GLRLM - Gray Level Run Length Matrix and NGLDM - Neighbouring Gray Level Dependence Matrix) on low-field MRI. Being the first approach that exploits this type of scanner for this purpose in dry-cured meat, the predicted elements were compared and correlated to the results obtained by means of traditional physico-chemical methods. The obtained correlation were higher than 0.7 for almost all the quality traits, reached very good to excellent relationship. These high correlations between both sets of data (traditional and estimated results) prove that low-field MRI combined with texture algorithms could be used to estimate the quality traits of meat products in a non-destructive and efficient way.

Keywords: MRI · Texture algorithms · Prediction · Quality parameters

© Springer Nature Switzerland AG 2019
A. Morales et al. (Eds.): IbPRIA 2019, LNCS 11867, pp. 498–507, 2019.
https://doi.org/10.1007/978-3-030-31332-6_43

1   Introduction

Computer vision techniques have been widely applied in many industrial processes and several engineering fields such as robotics, industrial image processing, food processing and other fields. Some advantages that promote computer vision techniques in food engineering are the possibilities for non-destructive evaluations, easy procedures for applications, quickness when performing the analysis process [1–3]. Computer vision algorithms extract information from the images by using different methods. Among all of them, texture algorithms can obtain information from the images that can be used to evaluate features described by the textures, by using co-occurrence matrix (GLCM), differences of neighbourhoods matrix (NGLDM) and run-length matrix (GLRLM) [4].

Magnetic Resonance Imaging (MRI) and computer vision techniques have been proposed as an alternative to the traditional analytical methods for determining physico-chemical traits related to dry-cured hams. These traditional procedures are laborious, time and solvent consuming and require the destruction of the meat sample, in contrast to MRI, which is non-destructive, non-invasive, non-ionizing and innocuous. Several studies have been carried out to evaluate the quality characteristics of dry-cured products by MRI, most of them on hams, allowing to monitor the ripening process of Iberian [5], Parma [6], and San Daniele [7] hams.

The extraction of textural information is very common to explore parameters related to meat quality. Ávila [8] analyzed marbling and fat level in Iberian loin based on texture features of MRI. Recently, Pérez-Palacios applied texture analysis to predict moisture and lipids content of hams [9] and classified different Iberian hams as a function of the feeding background of the iberian pigs [10,11]. Jackman et al. [12,13] proved the efficiency of the computer vision techniques to solve problems related to food technology.

In several of these studies on hams, high-field MRI scanners were used to acquire the images from the ham [9–11]. This type of scanners provide a high quality image but they also have a very high cost. Low field systems are cheaper but give lower signal to noise ratio. In order to maximize the quality of the images, an adequate configuration of the image acquisition must be done previously [14].

The objective of this paper is the prediction of quality traits of Iberian ham, based on studying the texture features obtained from MRI by using a low field scanner. The results of this computational prediction will be compared to the quality results obtained by traditional techniques, expecting that correlations between both sets of results were reasonably high. Noting that this is the first study carried out on Iberian hams by using a low-field MRI scanner.

This paper is organized as follows: Sect. 2 presents the materials used in this work. Section 3 shows the methods applied in this work. Section 4 describes the obtained results and their discussion. Section 5 draws the main conclusions and their implications.

2   Materials

MRI images from one hundred and twenty dry-cured Iberian hams were acquired, which were divided in ten different batches as shown in Table 1, as a function of the feeding background of the Iberian pigs. The images were acquired at the Animal Source Foodstuffs Innovation Services (SiPA, Cáceres, Spain). A low-field MRI scanner (ESAOTE VET-MR E-SCAN XQ 0.18 T) was used with a back coil. Sequences of Spin Echo (SE) weighted on T1 were applied with a echo time (TE) of 26 ms, repetition time (TR) of 910 ms, field of view (FOV) of 150×150 mm^2, slice thickness of 4 mm, a matrix size of 240×240 and 17 slices per sample were obtained. Two thousand and forty MRI images were obtained. All images were acquired in DICOM format, with a 512×512 resolution and 256 gray levels. The MRI acquisition was performed at 23 °C.

Physico-chemical analysis on hams were determined by traditional techniques in order to obtain values of the following quality traits: moisture, water activity, instrumental color coordinates (L, a*, b*) and salt content. Those values indicate the quality of the hams and were obtained to test the ability of the low-field MRI systems in order to non-destructively evaluate the quality of the dry-cured hams.

Table 1. Distribution of Iberian dry-cured hams and the feeding background of the pigs for each batch.

Batch	Samples	Feeding
1	10	ACORN 50%
2	10	ACORN 100%
3	10	ACORN 50%
4	10	ACORN 50%
5	10	ACORN 50%
6	10	ACORN 50%
7	10	ACORN 50%
8	24	ACORN 50%
9	8	ACORN 50%
10	18	ACORN 50%
	120	

3   Methods

Figure 1 illustrates the experimental design of this study. MRI were acquired from the Iberian hams, and then were preprocessed to recognize different muscles of the hams. Particularly, the *biceps femoris* muscle was selected for the experiments in this study [15,16]. When all the MRI were acquired from the hams, physico-chemical analysis were performed on the hams as described in Sect. 3.1, obtaining a database of *traditional* results.

On the other hand, texture features of hams were estimated by using the GLCM, NGLDM, and GLRLM algorithms [4] on the pre-processed MRI as explained in Sect. 3.2. These results were stored on a database of *computational* results.

Finally, predictive techniques were applied on the *traditional* and *computational* data, to obtain prediction equations that allow computing the quality parameters from the *computational* features. Section 3.3 explains this procedure.

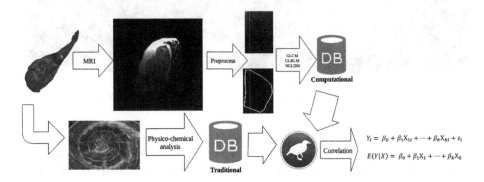

Fig. 1. Experimental design

3.1 Physico-Chemical Analyses

The physico-chemical attributes of dry-cured Iberian hams were determined by means of traditional physico-chemical analysis methods in order to obtain values for moisture [17] and salt content [17]. The water activity was determined by applying the system Lab Master-aw (NOVASINA AG, Switzerland) and the instrumental color coordinates (L, a* and b*) were measured by using a Minolta CR-300 colorimeter (Minolta Camera Corp., U.S.A.).

3.2 Computer Vision Techniques

As mentioned before, this is the first study on dry-cured Iberian hams using MRI images from a low-field scanner. The quality difference between the images from high-field and low-field scanners implies that the preprocessing stage must be mandatory before the application of the texture algorithms. Those differences can be seen in Fig. 2.

For the preprocessing stage, the images for each batch were separated. After applying several segmentation techniques, a set of contours was obtained. The selection of all countours was carried out by using the most generic template in the next step.

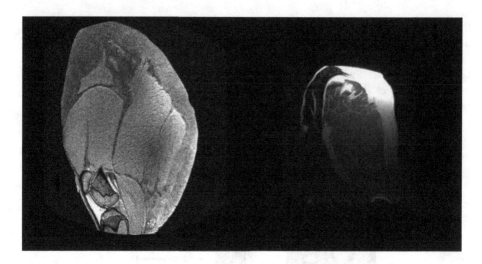

Fig. 2. High-field Image on the left, low-field on the right

An application was developed for extracting for each image the *biceps femoris* and its contour. This application load a generic contour from a set of contours obtained in a preliminary study and allows the user to manipulate it. The user can modify the size or rotate the contour template to fit better the image. In Fig. 3 it can be see how this application looks like.

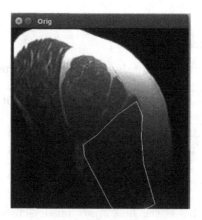

Fig. 3. Screenshot from the application

After this process, the image of the *biceps femoris* and its contour are used to obtain the largest rectangle inside the biceps, that will be the region of interest (ROI) for the application of the texture algorithms [15].

GLCM [18] was computed by counting the number of times that each pair of gray levels occurred at a given distance d in all directions. In this matrix, each item p(i, j) denotes the number of times that two neighbouring pixels separated by distance d (d = 1 in this case) occur on the image, one with gray level i and the other with gray level j, in all 2D directions: 0°, 45°, 90° and 135°. These co-occurrences are accumulated into a single matrix, from which all the textural features are extracted. The features were: energy, entropy, Correlation, Haralick's Correlation, IDM (inverse difference moment), inertia, CS (cluster shade), CP (cluster prominence), Contrast and Dissimilarity.

NGLDM uses angular independent features by considering the relationship between an element and all its neighbouring elements at one time rather than one direction at a time [21]. In this method, the neighbouring are square and the dimension of these square are 3×3 and the distance d (d = 1) between neighbouring pixels. This process eliminates the angular dependency while simultaneously reducing the calculations required to process an image. It is based on the assumption that the gray-level spatial dependence matrix of an image can adequately specify this texture information. The measures were: SNE (small number emphasis), LNE (large number emphasis), NNU (number non-uniformity), SM (second moment) and ENT (entropy).

GLRLM [19] includes runs into the image, i.e., a set of consecutive pixels in the image with the same gray level value. A large number of neighbouring pixels of the same gray level represents a coarse texture, a small number of these pixels represents a fine texture, and the lengths of the texture primitives in different directions can serve as texture description [20]. The runs with the same gray level were computed in four different directions: 0°, 45°, 90° and 135°. The features applied were: SRE (short run emphasis), LRE (long run emphasis), GLNU (gray level non-uniformity), RLNU (run length non-uniformity), RPC (run percentage), LGRE (low grey-level run emphasis), HGRE (high grey-level run emphasis), SRLGE (short run low grey-level emphasis), SRHGE (short run high greylevel emphasis), LRLGE (long run low grey-level emphasis), and LRHGE (long run high grey-level emphasis).

Table 2 shows the texture features that will be extracted and used for the prediction stage.

Table 2. Texture features for each algorithm.

Alg	Features
GLCM	Energy, Entropy, Correlation, Haralick, IDM, Inertia, CS, CP, Contrast, Dissimilarity
NGLDM	SNE, LNE, NNU, SM, ENT
GLRLM	LRE, SRE, GLNU, RLNU, RPC, LGRE, HGRE, SRLGE, SRHGE, LRLGE, LRHGE

3.3   Predictive Techniques

Predictive techniques of data mining were applied on a database constructed with results from physico-chemical analyses and computational texture features. The free software WEKA was used (Waikato Environment for Knowledge Analysis - Available for downloading from: https://www.cs.waikato.ac.nz/~ml/weka/downloading.html - last access: April 2019).

Multiple linear regression (MLR) was applied, which models the linear relationship between a target variable and more independent prediction variables [22]. The M5 method of attribute selection and a ridge value of 1×10^{-4} were applied [23]. It is based on stepping throughout the attributes, being the one with the smallest standardized coefficient removed until no improvement is observed in the estimation of the error.

To validate the prediction of the quality traits, the 10-fold cross-validation was used, and the correlation coefficient R was calculated to evaluate the goodness of the obtained equations.

4   Results and Discussion

Table 3 shows the correlation coefficients (R) of the prediction equations obtained by applying MLR for moisture, water activity, NaCl and instrumental color coordinates (L, a*, b*). These results were analyzed taking into account the rules given by Colton [24], who considered correlation values between 0 and 0.25 as little degree of relationship, from 0.25 to 0.50 as a fair degree of relationship, from 0.50 to 0.75 as moderate to good relationship and between 0.75 and 1 as very good to excellent relationship.

Table 3. Correlation coefficients for each quality trait studied.

Trait	R
Moisture	0.7878785529
NaCl	0.6923428350
Aw	0.7490669733
L	0.7063934756
a*	0.6926237835
b*	0.4872936492

As can be seen in Table 3, according to Colton [24], the moisture and the water activity reached values close to 0.75 would indicate that are very good correlated with the features of the images, the salt content, L and a* achieved a good relationship and a fairly correlationship on the b* instrumental color values.

Table 4 shows the prediction equations of the quality traits of hams as a function of the texture features obtained from GLCM, NGLDM, and GLRLM. As can be seen, each equation use around fifteen independent variables except for the moisture one that uses twenty and the salt content that uses twelve. In addition, twenty five different texture features from the total of twenty six texture features are used.

Table 4. Prediction equations for each quality trait studied.

Equations
Moisture (%) = (-10.5694 * SRE + 10.6374 * GLNU + 2.069 * RLNU + 0.4672 * RPC $-$ 8.338 * SRLGE $-$ 8.0859 * LRLGE + 4.5243 * LRHGE + 10.6169 * energy $-$ 17.5758 * entropy $-$ 10.6843 * correlation + 12.5645 * Haralick $-$ 6.99 * IDM + 12.7776 * CS $-$ 18.3662 * CP + 3.1844 * contrast $-$ 1.4421 * dissimilarity $-$ 3.265 * SNE $-$ 2.5107 * LNE + 8.2148 * NNU $-$ 11.5711 * SM + 67.2451)
NaCl (%) = (0,946 * RLNU + 0,8646 * RPC $-$ 0,9471 * SRLGE + 1,7948 * SRHGE $-$ 5,3481 * LRHGE + 3,4329 * correlation + 2,7352 * CS $-$ 7,1104 * CP + 4,1419 * SNE + 1,6906 * LNE $-$ 3,8738 * NNU $-$ 6,2528 * SM + 8,7971)
Aw = (0.0499 * LRE + 0.0733 * GLNU $-$ 0.059 * RLNU $-$ 0.0153 * RPC $-$ 0.0268 * SRHGE + 0.1073 * LRHGE $-$ 0.0346 * energy $-$ 0.025 * correlation + 0.0518 * inertia + 0.0187 * CS $-$ 0.0258 * CP $-$ 0.0152 * contrast $-$ 0.0327 * dissimilarity $-$ 0.0626 * LNE + 0.0585 * NNU + 0.8617)
L = ($-3,9384$ * RLNU $-$ 1,7442 * RPC + 4,0152 * HGRE + 6,3846 * LRLGE + 12,0199 * energy + 3,997 * entropy + 5,5445 * correlation + 2,9649 * inertia $-$ 5,5408 * CS + 12,4346 * CP $-$ 2,4383 * contrast + 12,9324 * SNE + 2,3271 * NNU $-$ 11,4367 * SM + 24,1802)
a* = ($-1,1568$ * LRE + 6,9131 * GLNU $-$ 5,4206 * RLNU $-$ 7,7057 * SRLGE $-$ 4,6581 * LRHGE + 6,126 * energy + 0,3643 * correlation + 8,139 * Haralick + 6,0313 * inertia + 1,2156 * CS $-$ 1,7246 * CP + 0,8103 * dissimilarity + 2,3772 * SNE + 4,8215 * LNE $-$ 3,2866 * SM + 1,7179 * ENT + 11,6899)
b* = ($-0,8317$ * SRE $-$ 3,6757 * GLNU + 0,6651 * RPC + 3,2273 * SRHGE $-$ 2,3148 * LRHGE + 4,2509 * energy $-$ 0,8522 * entropy $-$ 2,0777 * correlation $-$ 0,5907 * inertia $-$ 1,4403 * CS + 3,0224 * CP + 2,0108 * contrast $-$ 1,5118 * LNE + 1,5824 * NNU + 6,2644)

5   Conclusion

This work firstly demonstrates the capability of using low-field MRI for the image acquisition of dry-cured Iberian hams as it is the first time this type of scanner is used to this purpose. The analysis of these MRI images by computational texture features and the application of data mining techniques allow the prediction of moisture, salt and water activity with good results. Therefore, the use of this approach could be suitable for the meat industries in order to characterize meat products in a non-destructive, effective, efficient and accurate way.

In further researches, different computer vision algorithms will be tested to improve the results of the predictions of the quality traits, moreover, the number of quality traits predicted could be increased.

Acknowledgments. The authors wish to acknowledge the funding received from both Junta de Extremadura (Regional Government Board) European Regional Development Fund (GRU18138), and Research Project IB16089. Daniel Caballero thanks Junta de Extremadura for the post-doctoral grant (PO17017). We also wish to acknowledge the Animal Foodstuffs Innovation Service (SiPA, Cáceres, Spain) from the University of Extremadura.

References

1. Mahendran, R., Jayashree, G.C., Alagusundaram, K.: Application of computer vision technique on sorting and grading of fruits and vegetables. J. Food Process. Technol. S1-001 (2012)
2. Brosnan, T., Sun, D.-W.: Improving quality inspection of food products by computer vision - a review. J. Food Eng. **61**, 3–16 (2004)
3. Gunasekaran, S.: Computer vision technology for food quality assurance. Trends Food Sci. Technol. **7**, 245–256 (1996)
4. Caballero, D., et al.: Comparison of different image analysis algorithms on MRI to predict physico-chemical and sensory attributes of Loin. Chemometr. Intell. Lab. Syst. **180**, 54–63 (2018)
5. Antequera, T., Caro, A., Rodríguez, P.G., Pérez-Palacios, T.: Monitoring the ripening process of Iberian ham by computer vision on magnetic resonance imaging. Meat Sci. **76**, 561–567 (2007)
6. Fantazzini, P., Gombia, M., Schembri, M., Simoncini, N., Virgili, R.: Use of magnetic resonance imaging for monitoring parma dry-cured ham processing. Meat Sci. **82**, 219–227 (2009)
7. Manzoco, L., Anese, M., Marzona, S., Innocente, N., Lazagio, C., Nicoli, M.C.: Monitoring dry-curing of San Daniele ham by magnetic resonance imaging. Food Chem. **141**, 2246–2252 (2013)
8. Ávila, M.M., Durán, M.L., Antequera, T., Palacios, R., Luquero, M.: 3D reconstruction on MRI to analyse marbling and fat level in Iberian Loin. In: Martí, J., Benedí, J.M., Mendonça, A.M., Serrat, J. (eds.) IbPRIA 2007. LNCS, vol. 4477, pp. 145–152. Springer, Heidelberg (2007). https://doi.org/10.1007/978-3-540-72847-4_20
9. Pérez-Palacios, T., Caballero, D., Caro, A., Rodríguez, P.G., Antequera, T.: Applying data mining and computer vision techniques to MRI to estimate quality traits in Iberian hams. J. Food Eng. **131**, 82–88 (2014)
10. Pérez-Palacios, T., Antequera, T., Durán, M.L., Caro, A., Rodríguez, P.G., Ruiz, J.: MRI-based analysis, lipid composition and sensory traits for studying Iberian dry-cured hams from pigs fed with different diets. Food Chem. **126**, 1366–1372 (2010)
11. Pérez-Palacios, T., Antequera, T., Durán, M.L., Caro, A., Rodríguez, P.G., Palacios, R.: MRI-based analysis of feeding background effect on fresh Iberian ham. Food Res. Int. **43**, 248–254 (2011)
12. Jackman, P., Sun, D.W.: Recent advances in the use of computer vision technology in the quality assessment of fresh meat. Trends Food Sci. Technol. **22**(4), 185–197 (2011)

13. Jackman, P., Sun, D.W.: Recent advances in image processing using image texture features for food quality assessment. Trends Food Sci. Technol. **19**, 35–43 (2013)
14. Pérez-Palacios, T., Caballero, D., Antequera, T., Durán, M.L., Ávila, M.M., Caro, A.: Optimization of MRI acquisition and texture analysis to predict physicochemical parameters of Loins by data mining. Food Bioprocess Technol. **10**, 750–758 (2017)
15. Molano, R., Rodríguez, P.G., Caro, A., Durán, M.L.: Finding the largest area rectangle of arbitrary orientation in a closed contour. Appl. Math. Comput. **218**(19), 9866–9874 (2012)
16. Caro, A., Rodríguez, P.G., Duran, M.L., Antequera, T.: Active contours for real time applications. In: Flournier, M.D. (ed.) Perspectives on Pattern Recognition, pp. 173–186. Nova Science Publishers Inc., New York (2012)
17. Association of Official Analytical Chemists (AOAC): Official Method of Analysis of AOAC International, 17th edn. AOAC International, Gaithersburg (2000)
18. Haralick, R.M., Shanmugam, K., Dinstein, I.: Textural features for image classification. IEEE Trans. Man Cybern. **3**(6), 610–621 (1973)
19. Galloway, M.M.: Texture classification using gray level dependence matrix. Comput. Vis. Image Process. **4**, 172–179 (1975)
20. Ávila, M.M., Caballero, D., Durán, M.L., Caro, A., Pérez-Palacios, T., Antequera, T.: Including 3D-textures in a computer vision system to analyze quality traits of Loin. In: Nalpantidis, L., Krüger, V., Eklundh, J.-O., Gasteratos, A. (eds.) ICVS 2015. LNCS, vol. 9163, pp. 456–465. Springer, Cham (2015). https://doi.org/10. 1007/978-3-319-20904-3_41
21. Sun, C., Wee, G.: Neighbouring gray level dependence matrix. Comput. Vis. Image Process. **23**, 341–352 (1982)
22. Witten, I.H., Frank, E.: Data Mining: Practical Machine Learning Tools and Techniques with Java Implementations. Morgan-Kauffmann, San Francisco (2005)
23. Grossman, R., Seni, G., Elder, J., Agarwal, N., Liu, H.: Ensemble Methods in Data Mining: Improving Accuracy Through Combining Predictions. Morgan & Claypool Publishers, Williston (2010)
24. Colton, T.: Statistics in Medicine. Little Brown and Co., New York (1974)

Personalised Aesthetics with Residual Adapters

Carlos Rodríguez-Pardo[1,2](✉) and Hakan Bilen[2]

[1] Seddi Labs, Madrid, Spain
carlos.rodriguezpardo.jimenez@gmail.com
[2] School of Informatics, University of Edinburgh, Edinburgh, UK

Abstract. The use of computational methods to evaluate aesthetics in photography has gained interest in recent years due to the popularization of convolutional neural networks and the availability of new annotated datasets. Most studies in this area have focused on designing models that do not take into account individual preferences for the prediction of the aesthetic value of pictures. We propose a model based on residual learning that is capable of learning subjective, user-specific preferences over aesthetics in photography, while surpassing the state-of-the-art methods and keeping a limited number of user-specific parameters in the model. Our model can also be used for picture enhancement, and it is suitable for content-based or hybrid recommender systems in which the amount of computational resources is limited.

1 Introduction

The perception of aesthetics in photography, as in many art forms, is typically considered to be subjective. This puts limits on the kind of features that computational models can use in order to predict the aesthetic value of any given picture. There are several factors that influence humans' perception of beauty and aesthetics in art, such as their past experiences, social influences, the situation that surrounds them, their mood or the characteristics of the piece of art itself [18]. The features in which the piece of art can be described with will, therefore, explain only a small part of the preferences of human perceivers over aesthetics in art. Nevertheless, it has been suggested that there is some shared perception of beauty and aesthetics in art [11], which suggests that there are features that computational models can learn which account for this shared perception of beauty.

The evaluation of aesthetics in photography using machine learning models has gained popularity in the literature in recent years, due to the creation of new annotated datasets and the progress made on computer vision models. The automatic evaluation of aesthetics in photography has many applications, such as automatic image enhancement, the creation of content-based recommender systems or the development of aesthetics-aware image search engines. Most of

---

C. Rodríguez-Pardo—Work performed at the University of Edinburgh.

© Springer Nature Switzerland AG 2019
A. Morales et al. (Eds.): IbPRIA 2019, LNCS 11867, pp. 508–520, 2019.
https://doi.org/10.1007/978-3-030-31332-6_44

the progress in this field has been made on building models that can predict a mean aesthetics score of any given picture. Although this approach is certainly powerful, it does not take into account individual preferences over aesthetics in photography, which limits its potential.

The problem of taking into account subjective preferences on image aesthetics prediction is referred to as *personalized image aesthetics* [27]. Most recent approaches to image aesthetics evaluation have used different deep-learning models, which require a significant amount of annotated data for their training and evaluation. In real-world situations, it is unrealistic to assume that we will have thousands of annotated examples of rated images for any given user. This puts limits on the use of deep learning models for personalized image aesthetics prediction.

In order to train a machine learning model capable of taking into account individual preferences over aesthetics in photography, an annotated dataset with the identities of the raters of each picture is needed. One example of this kind of dataset is the *FLICKER-AES* dataset, presented by Ren et al. [27], which contains over 40000 images rated by more than 200 different human raters. Their study provides, along with this dataset (and another, smaller, dataset), a residual-based learning model capable of taking into account user-specific preferences over aesthetics in photography.

We build on their work, and propose an end-to-end convolutional neural network model capable of modelling user-specific preferences with different levels of abstraction, while keeping a reduced number of user-specific parameters within the model. Our method models user-specific preferences by using residual adapters, which were presented in [25,26] and have shown success in multi-domain learning. The main difference between our model and Ren et al.'s is that they model user-specific preferences by first training a *generic aesthetics network*, which predicts a mean aesthetic score, and computes a user-specific offset by training a Support Vector Regressor using the predicted content and some manually-defined attributes of the picture as its input; whereas our model embeds the user-specific parameters in different layers of the neural network, therefore allowing the model to find user-specific features with different levels of abstraction, and which do not necessarily depend on the contents and a fixed set of attributes of the pictures.

Our main contributions are as follows: First, we propose an end-to-end deep neural network architecture capable of surpassing the state-of-the-art results in personalized image aesthetics prediction, while keeping a reduced number of user parameters. Second, we compare different strategies to modelling user-specific preferences over aesthetics in photography using deep learning. Finally, we show how our model can be used for personalized image enhancement, by taking a gradient-ascent approach. For reproducibility reasons, we share our code and trained models in a public repository[1].

---

[1] Please visit https://github.com/crp94/Personalised-aesthetic-assessment-using-residual-adapters for our implementation in PyTorch.

2   Related Work

2.1   Computational Aesthetic Assessment in Photography

The use of computational methods for the evaluation of image aesthetics has gained popularity recently due to at least two factors. First, deep convolutional neural networks (CNN) have created the possibility of learning aesthetic-related features from annotated data. They allow the creation of models that can analyze any picture and predict their aesthetic value, without the need for any annotated data about its contents; and without making use of hand-crafted features. Some examples of the use of CNNs for image aesthetics prediction and related topics can be found in [2,4,6,9–11,17,20,33,35]. Some of those papers make use of information about the contents of the pictures to improve the predictions of the models. Despite the increasing popularity of deep CNNs for image aesthetics evaluation, there are several studies that use different machine learning algorithms to solve this problem, such as [3,7,14,15,21,23,32,34]. Nevertheless, they usually require a significant effort in manually crafting features, which is not a limitation of CNN-based models.

The second factor that allowed the emergence of computational methods for automatic aesthetics assessment in photography is the creation of new and larger datasets. The most popular dataset in the literature of this topic is the *Aesthetic Visual Analysis* (AVA) dataset, which was proposed in [22] and which contains around 250000 pictures, each with an associated histogram of ratings. Nevertheless, there are other datasets that have been used to study this problem, such as *CUHX-PQ* [31], *DPChallenge* [8], or *Photo.Net* [16].

Even so, none of the studies or datasets mentioned above allows the creation of models that account for user-specific preferences. Examples of studies that actually take into account those kinds of preferences can be found in [12,13, 24,28,29]. However, to our knowledge, the most powerful and innovative study in this field is Ren et al.'s paper [27], which not only proposes one CNN-based model, but it also publishes two datasets with the information on how each user rated each picture. Their work is important because they show that deep-learning-based models allow the learning of user-specific features, and the two datasets they introduced allow the comparison between models, so that we can empirically analyze which model is more appropriate for this problem. A main limitation of their model, one which we wanted to address, is that the user-specific preferences are learned by a Support Vector Regressor that only takes into account features related to the contents and some other manually-chosen attributes of the images.

2.2   Transfer Learning

One way to overcome the need for huge amounts of data of deep-learning systems is to make use of transfer learning. Usually, transfer learning [5] involves the use of a model that was trained on one task as a starting point to solve another, usually related, task. This method has gained popularity in computer vision problems, as the features learned by CNNs are, to some extent, largely reusable to many different tasks. Closely related to transfer learning, *Multi-domain learning* is concerned with the problem of using a single machine learning model that is capable of solving the same task in different domains. To solve this problem, we can find the solution proposed in [25, 26], which is referred to as *residual adapters*. This method consists of the addition of a set of small (usually with a kernel size of 1) domain-specific convolutional layers in parallel to the convolutional layers of a bigger, domain-agnostic, convolutional neural network. The idea is that most of the features in the network are embedded by the domain-agnostic part of the network, and the domain-specific layers compute a small adaptation of the features in the domain-agnostic part of the network. This methodology heavily exploits parameter reuse, and allows the training of deep learning models in situations in which there is only a limited amount of data available for each domain. We believe that those adapters can effectively model user-specific preferences over aesthetics.

3   Dataset Description

To train and evaluate our models, we choose the *FLICKR-AES* dataset, which contains around 40500 images rated from 1 to 5 by 210 users. The dataset provides the anonymised identity of the user that gave each rating. Each picture is rated by, on average, around 4.9 users (standard deviation of 1.87), with a maximum of 48 and a minimum of 1. The dataset contains pictures with a wide variety of styles and contents, which allows our models to find features that generalize to any style or content. To create our train and test sets, we perform a very similar division to what was done by Ren et al. (we were not able to exactly replicate their train and test division), so that our results are comparable. More precisely, we select the ratings made by 37 users as our test set. Each of those 37 users rated from 105 to 171 images (mean of 137), for a total of 4737. Our train set is composed by the ratings of the remaining 173 workers, and we made sure that the images in the train set did not overlap with the images in the test set, so that our model generalized not only to different users but also to different images. This division was performed so our results could be compared with the baseline model. The ratings were normalized to a 0-mean, unit-variance distribution.

As in [27], we evaluate our models using the Spearman's ranking correlation (ρ) as our main evaluation metric. It is defined as follows: $\rho = 1 - \frac{6 \times \sum_{i=1}^{N} r_i - \hat{r}_i}{N^2(N-1)}$. This metric is bounded in the $[-1, 1]$ range, and measures the correlation between the real ranking r_i of the picture i and its predicted ranking $\hat{r}_i$. Higher values of ρ indicate a better performance of our model.

4   Experiments

To design our model, we first create a baseline model that is capable of predicting a mean aesthetic score for each picture, and then we study ways of embedding user-specific preferences to this model. The models are trained using Adam as the learning rule and make use of mini-batches. Images in the training set are preprocessed for each mini-batch as follows: First, as is standard in many computer vision models, they are re-scaled to a 256×256 square picture, then they are horizontally flipped with a probability of 0.5 and a random subsection of 224×224 pixels is cropped (this is the image size that Residual Networks are trained on), then normalized. It can be argued that using data augmentation methods such as random cropping or random flipping can alter the aesthetic value of pictures, but we found that the use of these methods increased the generalization capability of our models. The learning rate was set to 0.001 for every experiment, and exponentially decayed by a factor of 90% every two epochs. The loss function used was the mean squared error (MSE), measuring the squared difference between predicted and real rating for each picture.

4.1   Generic Aesthetics Prediction Model

We chose a modified version of a ResNet-18 [1] as our baseline model. Residual networks have shown success in many computer vision tasks, and we chose this shallow version because it was easy to train than deeper versions of this kind of architecture. Instead of randomly initializing the weights of the network, we chose a pre-trained network (trained on the ImageNet dataset). This transfer learning method was also used in [27] and, as was argued before, it can exploit parameter reuse. We added 3 blocks of fully-connected layers to the pre-trained Resnet-18. Each block is composed by 1000 hidden PReLU units ($\alpha = 0.25$), a dropout ($p = 0.5$) *layer* and a batch normalization layer each. This showed a better performance than using the baseline ResNet-18 model. The final layer outputs 1 value, which is the normalized rating prediction. This network is trained using every picture in the training set and evaluated using the ratings and pictures in the test set.

4.2   Modelling User-Specific Preferences

To test how user-specific preferences can be embedded in the network, we assume two situations:

10 Images per User. First, we assume that, for each of the 37 users in the test dataset, we observe 10 ratings. Those 10 pictures are chosen at random, and we fine-tune the bottleneck of our baseline model (the three fully connected blocks) using those 10 images. We perform a 10-fold cross-validation experiment for each user (we choose 10 random images, 10 times) and evaluate on the remaining ratings for each user. We do not perform additional experiments using only 10 images as they are not enough for the training of more complex models.

100 Images per User. In our second set of experiments, we assume that we can observe 100 ratings for each user in the test dataset. Using 3-fold validation (doing a 10-fold configuration was computationally too heavy for those experiments), we perform 3 sets of experiments. First, as in the previous section, we only fine-tune the bottleneck of the network. Second, we fine-tune every layer of the network. This method is computationally heavy and it does not allow to have a reduced number of user-specific parameters. However, it can be seen as a baseline from which to compare other models. Third, we study the use of residual adapters as a way of embedding user-specific preferences in the network. The inclusion of residual adapters in the network allows the learning of user-specific preferences with different levels of abstraction while keeping a smaller number of user-specific parameters than fine-tuning the whole network would need to use.

To study the best way of using the residual adapters for this particular task, we perform 5 different experiments. First, as was suggested in [26], we add the adapters in parallel to all the 3×3 convolutional layers in the ResNet-18 architecture. Additionally, we also experiment on the addition of these adapters only in the last 3 blocks of convolutional layers in the network (with 128, 256 and 512 kernels per layer). This is motivated by the fact that the first block of layers typically learns low-level features, which should be more generalizable for different users than higher level features, usually learned in deeper layers of the network. Finally, we test a simple method of reducing the dimensionality of the adapters by transforming them to a simple $K \times K_1 \times K$ series of small convolutional layers. The value of K_1 is the number of user-specific filters $(K : 1 < K)$ that we allow the network to learn, and K refers to the number of filters that

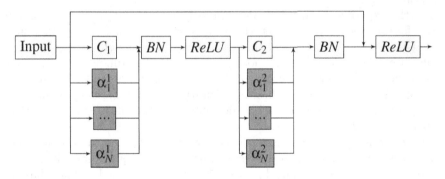

Fig. 1. Representation of the residual adapters that were tested in this paper. Each of the α_j^i is a set of K 1×1 convolutional filters, where K is the number of 3×3 kernels in the C_i layer, and is uniquely trained for each of the 37 users j in our test set. For our second set of experiments with residual adapters, the α_i layers are actually a series of three layers of 1×1 convolutional filters: first, a layer of K upcoming feature maps which outputs K_1 maps. Second, a layer that receives those K_1 feature maps and outputs other K_1 maps; and finally a layer that receives K_1 maps and outputs K maps. A weight decay of 0.005 was used on those adapters, to avoid over-fitting and to keep the adapters' initial weights close to 0. It is worth noting that, if the parameters encoded in the adapters are all equal to 0, the network with the adapters is essentially the same as a network without adapters.

the adapters receive as an input. Therefore, all the adaptation occurs at the K_1 filters. We test three configurations: $K_1 = 1$, $K_1 = \frac{K}{2}$ and $K_1 = \frac{K}{4}$. The smaller the value of K_1, the lower the complexity that the adapters will have, which can have a positive influence on the generalization capability of the network. During training time, we only train the bottleneck of the network, as well as the adapters for each particular user. The parameters in the batch normalization *layers* are also trained during training time (Fig. 1).

5 Results

Our baseline mean aesthetics prediction network obtained a correlation of $\rho = 0.491$ when predicting the relative ranking of all the pictures of the test set at once. When considering the ratings of each user in the test set separately, and then averaging their correlations, the model obtained a $\rho = 0.531$. For the personalized aesthetics methods, we randomly selected N ratings for each user and evaluated on the rest of ratings available for that user, averaging the results for the cross-validation experiments, as described in the previous section.

In the experiments where 10 ratings by each user in the test set are available, when fine-tuning the bottleneck of the network, we obtain an average correlation of 0.575. This shows that, even with a limited amount of information about the preferences of each user, a simple fine-tuning method can learn some adjustments of the weights of the network so that the preferences of each user can be better represented.

For the experiments in which we assumed that we had the ratings of 100 images for each user in the test set, the results were as follows. We saw that simply fine-tuning the bottleneck of the network was not enough, as it performed significantly worse than other methods $\rho = 0.584$. By fine-tuning all the parameters in the network for each user, we obtained a mean ρ of 0.632. When using the adapters, we saw that the best configuration was the baseline adapters in parallel to each layer in the network, which obtained a ρ of 0.639 (and fine-tuning the bottleneck) (Table 1).

We confirmed the results of [26], which showed that removing the adapters from the first block of layers in the residual network did not improve the performance of the model (we obtained $\rho = 0.637$) compared to the baseline adapters model. Finally, we could not confirm that the $K \times K_1 \times K$ adapters worked any better than the baseline adapters, so there is no evidence that justifies their use if the goal is to maximize the generalization capability of the model. Nonetheless, we saw that the model in which $K_1 = \frac{K}{4}$ performed considerably worse than when $K_1 = 1$ or $K_1 = \frac{K}{2}$. Interestingly, when $K_1 = \frac{K}{4}$, the results were even worse than the model in which we only fine-tuned the bottleneck of the network (Fig. 2).

Despite the fact that the network with the baseline adapters in parallel to each layer has obtained the best mean, median and maximum correlation of all the models that were tested, its results are not significantly different to the results of the network without adapters in which all the parameters in the network

Table 1. Comparison of the performance on unseen data for each of the methods studied. In **bold**, the best result for each category. The value of N is the number of pictures used to learn the preferences of each user in the test set. The experiment named $N = 100$, *last layers*, refers to the experiment in which only the bottleneck of the network was trained, whereas $N = 100$, *all layers* refers to the experiment in which all the network was fine-tuned for each user. All the other $N = 100$ experiments use residual adapters, in the ways described in the previous section. When the value of K_1 is specified, we refer to the results of the experiments using the *reduced* adapters, whereas the *adap. late* and *adap. all* experiments refer to the baseline adapters positioned in the last 3 blocks of layers and in every block of the network, respectively.

Model	$\sigma(\rho)$	Med. ρ	Min. ρ	Max. ρ
Baseline	0.118	0.561	0.186	0.692
$N = 10$	0.122	0.604	0.217	0.750
$N = 100$ last layers	0.118	0.593	0.274	0.778
$N = 100$ all layers	0.088	0.623	**0.458**	0.828
$N = 100$, adap. late	0.112	0.623	0.436	0.937
$N = 100$, adap. all	0.115	**0.631**	0.445	**0.941**
$N = 100$, $K_1 = 1$	0.106	0.601	0.392	0.986
$N = 100$, $K_1 = \frac{K}{4}$	0.09	0.576	0.348	0.682
$N = 100$, $K_1 = \frac{K}{2}$	0.093	0.546	0.429	0.863

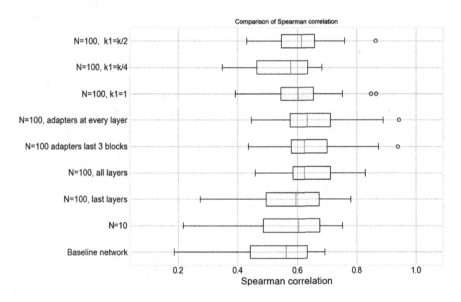

Fig. 2. Visualization of the distributions of the Spearman's ρ for each of the 37 workers in the test dataset on unseen data.

were fine-tuned. Nevertheless, we argue that the network with the adapters is preferable as it uses less user-specific parameters, thus reducing the amount of memory needed for each user. In other words, by fine-tuning the whole network, we would need a whole network for each user in the test set, whereas by using the adapters, we would need only one full network for all the users in the test set, and the set of adapters and bottleneck for each of the users in the test set. This difference can be crucial in systems with a large number of users.

6   Gradient-Ascent Picture Enhancement

Given any trained personalized neural network of those specified above, it is possible to use gradient ascent to enhance pictures in a way that the expected rating of the *enhanced* picture is greater than the expected rating of the original picture. To do so, we compute the gradient of the loss function with respect to the input image. By performing this operation: $X_{enhanced} = X_{original} + \epsilon \times \nabla_x J(X)$, where ϵ controls the intensity of the change of the picture and $J(X)$ is the loss function (the prediction of the aesthetic quality of the image), we can obtain an enhanced picture in a considerably fast way. More specifically, the gradient $\nabla_x J(X)$ is computed with respect to the input data and back-propagated to the input image. Then, a small portion (ϵ) of this gradient is added to each of the pixels, which represents the change in each pixel that would maximally increase the expected rating of the picture. One main advantage of this enhancement method is that it does not require a specific architecture for picture enhancement, as it is valid for any deep convolutional neural network that has been trained to predict aesthetic scores in photography. It does not change the style or contents of the picture in any way (Fig. 3).

So that the model could improve pictures of any kind of resolution or proportions (the baseline Res-net only allows $224 \times 224 \times 3$ images as input), we added an adaptive average pooling layer [19] to the start of the network so it adapts any image into the desired input size. Our method can be added to the literature of fast perceptual enhancement using neural networks, a topic studied by other authors [30]. In sum, our trained network can be used for both evaluating the aesthetic quality of a picture using only a feed-forward pass through the network, and for improving the quality of said picture by back-propagating once the gradient of the loss function, making the enhancement close to real-time (the whole algorithm, takes less than 1 s to process for images of 1920×1080 pixels using a GeForce 1050 GPU, and we believe this time can be reduced if the code was optimized). Please see the images above for examples of the enhancements that our method is capable of performing.

This algorithm can be easily extended so that individual preferences can be taken into account, by using each user's individual personalized network. Consequently, for each user in the dataset, the enhancement that the algorithm will make to each picture will be different. This method creates the potential of personalized picture filters that learn from the past preferences of the users, in a computationally light way.

Fig. 3. Original (left) and enhanced (right) images obtained with our enhancement algorithm and our modified Resnet-18 network. The two original pictures were taken by the authors of this paper using smart-phones, using the HDR configuration. All the enhanced images had a greater expected rating (around 10% bigger) than their corresponding original pictures. The value of α was set to 0.5 so as to make the differences more visible. It can be seen that the algorithm works for pictures taken under many different lightning conditions. Additional figures are found in our repository. (Color figure online)

7 Conclusions and Future Work

In this paper, we have shown that there are deep-learning based methods that are capable of modelling personalized preferences on aesthetic perception in photography, which do not require an explicit modelling of the contents of the pictures or the use of hand-crafted features related to aesthetics or beauty in photography. We have compared different algorithms and ways of modelling said subjective preferences. Our main addition is the proposed residual adapters model, which surpasses the state-of-the-art models in this problem, while keeping a reduced number of user-specific parameters, making our model scalable to real-world applications with a big number of pictures and/or users. We also confirm the results in the literature [26] regarding the configuration and position of those adapters, and we add some additional information about what way of reducing the dimensionality of those adapters works best. This is valuable for the transfer learning and multi-domain learning literature. The usage of our method in photography recommender systems could be studied in the future.

Our method can be improved in several ways. We used a simple Resnet-18 architecture as the basis for our models. The usage of Inception blocks or other improved architectures can be of interest for this problem, as well as the usage of any optimization algorithms that will be proposed in the future. Data augmentation issues could also be addressed to improve the generalization capabilities of the model, as well as other fine-tuning and other transfer learning methodologies. When new datasets become available, we could also test our hypothesis with more data, as well as improving the network's modelling of aesthetics in photography.

Finally, we also proposed a novel gradient-ascent method capable of performing personalized picture enhancements. Our contribution has been limited to proposing the algorithm and showing preliminary results. However, we believe this method can be studied further and has potential in image quality enhancement problems, which has many applications in research and user applications.

References

1. Alif, M.A.R., Ahmed, S., Hasan, M.A.: Isolated Bangla handwritten character recognition with convolutional neural network. In: 2017 20th International Conference of Computer and Information Technology (ICCIT), pp. 1–6. IEEE, December 2017. http://ieeexplore.ieee.org/document/8281823/
2. Shaji, A.: Understanding aesthetics with deep learning (2016). https://devblogs.nvidia.com/understanding-aesthetics-deep-learning/
3. Bhattacharya, S., Sukthankar, R., Shah, M.: A framework for photo-quality assessment and enhancement based on visual aesthetics. In: Proceedings of the International Conference on Multimedia - MM 2010, p. 271. ACM Press, New York (2010). http://dl.acm.org/citation.cfm?doid=1873951.1873990
4. Bianco, S., Celona, L., Napoletano, P., Schettini, R.: Predicting image aesthetics with deep learning. In: Blanc-Talon, J., Distante, C., Philips, W., Popescu, D., Scheunders, P. (eds.) ACIVS 2016. LNCS, vol. 10016, pp. 117–125. Springer, Cham (2016). https://doi.org/10.1007/978-3-319-48680-2_11
5. Browniee, J.: A gentle introduction to transfer learning for deep learning (2017). https://machinelearningmastery.com/transfer-learning-for-deep-learning/
6. Chen, Y.L., Huang, T.W., Chang, K.H., Tsai, Y.C., Chen, H.T., Chen, B.Y.: Quantitative analysis of automatic image cropping algorithms: a dataset and comparative study. In: Proceedings - 2017 IEEE Winter Conference on Applications of Computer Vision, WACV, pp. 226–234 (2017). https://arxiv.org/pdf/1701.01480.pdf
7. Datta, R., Joshi, D., Li, J., Wang, J.Z.: Studying aesthetics in photographic images using a computational approach. In: Leonardis, A., Bischof, H., Pinz, A. (eds.) ECCV 2006. LNCS, vol. 3953, pp. 288–301. Springer, Heidelberg (2006). https://doi.org/10.1007/11744078_23
8. Datta, R., Li, J., Wang, J.Z.: Algorithmic inferencing of aesthetics and emotion in natural images: an exposition (2008). http://riemann.ist.psu.edu/
9. Deng, Y., Loy, C.C., Tang, X.: Image aesthetic assessment: an experimental survey. IEEE Signal Process. Mag. **34**(4), 80–106 (2017). https://arxiv.org/pdf/1610.00838.pdf
10. Denzler, J., Rodner, E., Simon, M.: Convolutional neural networks as a computational model for the underlying processes of aesthetics perception. In: Hua, G., Jégou, H. (eds.) ECCV 2016. LNCS, vol. 9913, pp. 871–887. Springer, Cham (2016). https://doi.org/10.1007/978-3-319-46604-0_60

11. Hayn-Leichsenring, G.U., Lehmann, T., Redies, C.: Subjective ratings of beauty and aesthetics: correlations with statistical image properties in Western oil paintings (2017)

12. Hong, L., Doumith, A.S., Davison, B.D.: Co-factorization machines. In: Proceedings of the Sixth ACM International Conference on Web Search and Data Mining - WSDM 2013, p. 557. ACM Press, New York (2013). http://dl.acm.org/citation.cfm?doid=2433396.2433467

13. Isinkaye, F., Folajimi, Y., Ojokoh, B.: Recommendation systems: principles, methods and evaluation. Egypt. Inform. J. **16**(3), 261–273 (2015). https://www.sciencedirect.com/science/article/pii/S1110866515000341

14. Jiang, W., Loui, A.C., Cerosaletti, C.D.: Automatic aesthetic value assessment in photographic images. In: 2010 International Conference on Multimedia and Expo, pp. 920–925. IEEE, July 2010. http://ieeexplore.ieee.org/document/5582588/

15. Jin, X., Zhao, M., Chen, X., Zhao, Q., Zhu, S.-C.: Learning artistic lighting template from portrait photographs. In: Daniilidis, K., Maragos, P., Paragios, N. (eds.) ECCV 2010. LNCS, vol. 6314, pp. 101–114. Springer, Heidelberg (2010). https://doi.org/10.1007/978-3-642-15561-1_8

16. Joshi, D., et al.: Aesthetics and emotions in images. IEEE Signal Process. Mag. **28**(5), 94–115 (2011). http://ieeexplore.ieee.org/document/5999579/

17. Kong, S., Shen, X., Lin, Z., Mech, R., Fowlkes, C.: Photo aesthetics ranking network with attributes and content adaptation (2016). https://arxiv.org/pdf/1606.01621.pdf

18. Leder, H., Belke, B., Oeberst, A., Augustin, D.: A model of aesthetic appreciation and aesthetic judgments. Br. J. Psychol. **95**(4), 489–508 (2010). https://doi.org/10.1348/0007126042369811

19. Liu, Y., Zhang, Y.M., Zhang, X.Y., Liu, C.L.: Adaptive spatial pooling for image classification. Pattern Recogn. **55**(C), 58–67 (2016). https://linkinghub.elsevier.com/retrieve/pii/S0031320316000510

20. Lu, X., Lin, Z., Jin, H., Yang, J., Wang, J.Z.: Rapid: rating pictorial aesthetics using deep learning. In: Proceedings of the ACM International Conference on Multimedia - MM 2014, pp. 457–466 (2014). http://dl.acm.org/citation.cfm?doid=2647868.2654927

21. Luo, Y., Tang, X.: Photo and video quality evaluation: focusing on the subject. In: Forsyth, D., Torr, P., Zisserman, A. (eds.) ECCV 2008. LNCS, vol. 5304, pp. 386–399. Springer, Heidelberg (2008). https://doi.org/10.1007/978-3-540-88690-7_29

22. Murray, N., Marchesotti, L., Perronnin, F.: AVA: a large-scale database for aesthetic visual analysis. http://refbase.cvc.uab.es/files/MMP2012a.pdf

23. Niu, Y., Liu, F.: What makes a professional video? A computational aesthetics approach. IEEE Trans. Circuits Syst. Video Technol. **22**(7), 1037–1049 (2012). http://ieeexplore.ieee.org/document/6162974/

24. O'Donovan, P., Agarwala, A., Hertzmann, A.: Collaborative filtering of color aesthetics. In: Proceedings of Workshop Computational Aesthetics - CAe 2014, pp. 33–40. ACM Press, New York (2014). http://dl.acm.org/citation.cfm?doid=2630099.2630100

25. Rebuffi, S.A., Bilen, H., Vedaldi, A.: Learning multiple visual domains with residual adapters (2017). http://arxiv.org/abs/1705.08045

26. Rebuffi, S.A., Bilen, H., Vedaldi, A.: Efficient parametrization of multi-domain deep neural networks (2018). http://arxiv.org/abs/1803.10082

27. Ren, J., Shen, X., Lin, Z., Mech, R., Foran, D.J.: Personalized image aesthetics. In: Proceedings of the IEEE International Conference on Computer Vision, October 2017, pp. 638–647 (2017)
28. Rothe, R., Timofte, R., Van Gool, L.: Some like it hot-visual guidance for preference prediction. Technical report (2016). http://hotornot.com
29. Schafer, J.B., Frankowski, D., Herlocker, J., Sen, S.: Collaborative filtering recommender systems. In: Brusilovsky, P., Kobsa, A., Nejdl, W. (eds.) The Adaptive Web. LNCS, vol. 4321, pp. 291–324. Springer, Heidelberg (2007). https://doi.org/10.1007/978-3-540-72079-9_9
30. de Stoutz, E., Ignatov, A., Kobyshev, N., Timofte, R., Van Gool, L.: Fast perceptual image enhancement, December 2018. http://arxiv.org/abs/1812.11852
31. Tang, X., Luo, W., Wang, X.: Content-based photo quality assessment. IEEE Trans. Multimed. **15**(8), 1930–1943 (2013). http://ieeexplore.ieee.org/document/6544270/
32. Vogel, D., Khan, S.S.: Evaluating visual aesthetics in photographic portraiture. In: Proceedings of Eighth Annual Symposium on Computational Aesthetics in Graphics, Visualization, and Imaging, p. 128 (2012). https://dl.acm.org/citation.cfm?id=2328898
33. Wang, W., Shen, J.: Deep cropping via attention box prediction and aesthetics assessment. In: Proceedings of the IEEE International Conference on Computer Vision, October 2017, pp. 2205–2213 (2017)
34. Ke, Y., Tang, X., Jing, F.: The design of high-level features for photo quality assessment. In: 2006 IEEE Computer Society Conference on Computer Vision and Pattern Recognition (CVPR 2006), vol. 1, pp. 419–426. IEEE (2006). http://ieeexplore.ieee.org/document/1640788/
35. Yu, W., Chen, X.: Aesthetic-based clothing recommendation 2 (2018)

An Improvement for Capsule Networks Using Depthwise Separable Convolution

Nguyen Huu Phong$^{(\boxtimes)}$ and Bernardete Ribeiro

CISUC, Department of Informatics Engineering,
University of Coimbra, Coimbra, Portugal
{phong,bribeiro}@dei.uc.pt

Abstract. Capsule Networks face a critical problem in computer vision in the sense that the image background can challenge its performance, although they learn very well on training data. In this work, we propose to improve Capsule Networks' architecture by replacing the Standard Convolution with a Depthwise Separable Convolution. This new design significantly reduces the model's total parameters while increases stability and offers competitive accuracy. In addition, the proposed model on 64×64 pixel images outperforms standard models on 32×32 and 64×64 pixel images. Moreover, we empirically evaluate these models with Deep Learning architectures using state-of-the-art Transfer Learning networks such as Inception V3 and MobileNet V1. The results show that Capsule Networks can perform comparably against Deep Learning models. To the best of our knowledge, we believe that this is the first work on the integration of Depthwise Separable Convolution into Capsule Networks.

Keywords: Capsule Networks · Depthwise Separable Convolution · Deep Learning · Transfer Learning

1 Introduction

In our previous research, we performed experiments to compare accuracy and speed of Capsule Networks versus Deep Learning models. We found that even though Capsule Networks have a fewer number of layers than the best Deep Learning model using MobileNet V1 [2], the network performs just slightly faster than its counterpart.

We first explored details of MobileNet V1's architecture and observed that the model utilizes Depthwise Separable Convolution for the speed improvement. The layer comprises of a Depthwise Convolution and Pointwise Convolution which sufficiently reduces the model size and computation. Since Capsule Networks also integrate a Convolution layer in its architecture, we propose to replace this layer with the faster Convolution.

At the time this article is being written, there are 439 articles citing the original Capsule Networks paper [5]. Among these articles, a couple of works attempt to improve speed and accuracy of Capsule Networks. For example, the

© Springer Nature Switzerland AG 2019
A. Morales et al. (Eds.): IbPRIA 2019, LNCS 11867, pp. 521–530, 2019.
https://doi.org/10.1007/978-3-030-31332-6_45

authors [1] propose Spectral Capsule Networks which is composed by a voting mechanism based on the alignment of extracted features into a one-dimensional vector space. In addition, other authors claim that by using a Convolutional Decoder in the Reconstruction layer could decrease the restoration error and increase the classification accuracy [4].

Capsule Networks illustrated its effectiveness on MNIST dataset, though much variations of background to models e.g. in CIFAR-10 probably causes the poorer performance [5]. To solve this problem, we argue that primary filters to eliminate such backgrounds should be as important as other parts of Capsule Networks' architecture. Just, improvements on speed and accuracy of these Convolution layers can be bonus points for the network.

After a thorough search of relevant literature, we believe that this is the first work on the integration of Depthwise Separable Convolution into Capsule Networks.

The rest of this article is organized as follows. In Sect. 2, we highlight our main contributions. Next, we analyse the proposed design in Sect. 3. Following, the design of Deep Learning models for the purpose of comparison is illustrated in Sect. 4. Experiments and results are discussed in Sect. 5 accordingly. Finally, we conclude this work in Sect. 6.

2   Contribution

Our main contributions are twofold: first, on the replacement of Standard Convolution with Depthwise Separable Convolution in Capsule Networks' Architecture and, second, on the empirical evaluations of the proposed Capsule Networks against Deep Learning models.

Regarding the design of Capsule Networks, we found that the integration of Depthwise Separable Convolution can significantly reduce the model size, increase stability and yield higher accuracy than its counterpart.

With respect to experimental evaluations of Capsule Networks versus Deep Learning models, the Capsule models perform competitively both on model size and accuracy.

3   Integration of Depthwise Separable Convolution and Capsule Networks

As mentioned in the previous Section, we propose to substitute a Standard Convolution (SC) of Capsule Networks with a Depthwise Separable Convolution (DW). Figure 1 illustrates the architecture of the proposed model. Additionally, we apply this architecture for an American Sign Language (ASL) dataset with 29 signs. We discuss about this dataset more details in Sect. 5.1.

We divide this architecture into three main layers including Initial Filter, Depthwise Separable Convolution Layer and Capsules Layer. In principle, we can change the first Standard Convolution with a Depth Separable Convolution.

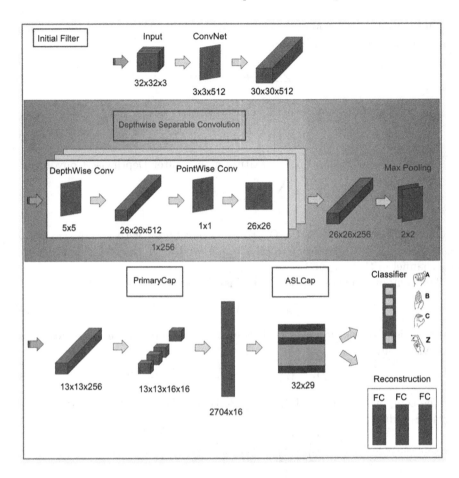

Fig. 1. Depthwise separable convolution capsule architecture.

However, the Input images have only three depth channels which require fewer computations than in the second layer so that we keep the first Convolution intact. The reduction of computation cost using DW is formulated as follows.

An SC takes an input $D_F \times D_F \times M$ feature map F and generates $D_G \times D_G \times N$ feature map G where D_F is the width and height of the input, M is the number of input channels, D_G is the width and height of the output, and N is the number of output channels.

The SC is equipped with a kernel of size $D_K \times D_K \times M \times N$ where D_K is assumed to be a spacial square. M and N are the number of input and output channels as mentioned above.

The output of the feature map G using an SC with kernel stride is 1 and same padding (or padding in short):

$$G_{k,l,n} = \sum_{i,j,m} K_{i,j,m,n} \cdot F_{k+i-1,l+j-1,m} \tag{1}$$

The computation cost of the SC can be written as:

$$D_K \cdot D_K \cdot M \cdot N \cdot D_F \cdot D_F \tag{2}$$

For one channel, the output of feature map $\hat{G}$ after Depthwise Convolution:

$$\hat{G}_{k,l,m} = \sum_{i,j,m} \hat{K}_{i,j,m} \cdot F_{k+i-1,l+j-1,m} \tag{3}$$

where $\hat{K}$ is the denotation of a Depthwise Convolution with kernel size $D_K \times D_K \times M$ and this Convolution applies m_{th} filter to m_{th} channel of F yields the m_{th} channel in the output.

The computation cost of the Depthwise Convolution is written as:

$$D_K \cdot D_K \cdot M \cdot D_F \cdot D_F \tag{4}$$

Pointwise Convolution uses 1×1 Convolution, therefore, the total cost after Pointwise Convolution:

$$D_K \cdot D_K \cdot M \cdot D_F \cdot D_F + M \cdot N \cdot D_F \cdot D_F \tag{5}$$

The computation cost of Depthwise Separable Convolution after two convolutions is reduced as:

$$\frac{D_K \cdot D_K \cdot M \cdot D_F \cdot D_F + M \cdot N \cdot D_F \cdot D_F}{D_K \cdot D_K \cdot M \cdot N \cdot D_F \cdot D_F}$$
$$= \frac{1}{N} + \frac{1}{D_K^2} \tag{6}$$

For more details of these computations, please refer to the MobileNet V1 article [5].

In Fig. 1, we show a sample where colour images have a size of $32 \times 32 \times 3$ and filtered by a ConvNet which is equipped with a 3×3 kernel and 512 filters. If the DW Conv is applied in this layer, then the cost of computation can be reduced between 8 and 9 times. Though the input image has a depth of only 3, the reduction of computation cost in this layer is unmatched with hundreds of channels in the second layer.

4 Deep Learning Models

For the purpose of comparison, we also briefly discuss the Deep Learning's architecture as shown in Fig. 2. As we can see from the Figure, this architecture comprises of several crucial layers including Transfer Learning, Multilayer Perceptron (MLP) and Long Short Term Memory (LSTM) layers. In Transfer Learning

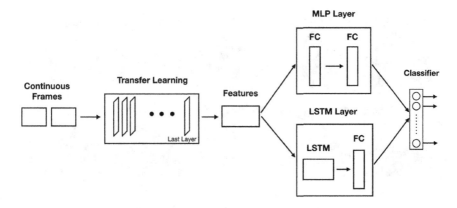

Fig. 2. Deep Learning architecture

layer, we utilize one of the models including Inception V3 [7], DenseNet V201 [3], NASNetMobile [8], MobileNet V1 [2] and MobileNet V2 [6] to extract features from input ASL signs. We then use MLP Layer as a baseline to compare with LSTM Layer. The MLP Layer includes two Fully Connected (FC) Neural Networks each with 512 neurons whereas the LSTM Layer contains one LSTM with 2048 units and one FC. More detail of the architecture can be referred to our earlier work.

5   Experiments and Results

In this section, we first discuss an ASL Dataset that will be used as our testbed. Then we setup experiments to compare our proposed Capsule's architecture using Depthwise Separable Convolution against typical Convolution Networks. Next, we analyse performances of Transfer Learning models including Inception V3, DenseNet V201, NASNet, MobileNet V1 and MobileNet V2 using MLP and LSTM. Finally, we pickup the best of Capsule Networks and challenge the best of Deep Learning models.

5.1   ASL Dataset

For the purpose of comparison with our previous work, we use the same ASL dataset for fingerspelling. The dataset was obtained from Kaggle website and includes 26 signs for letters A to Z with 3 additional signs using in other cases. Each sign contains 3000 samples (200×200 pixels), totally 87000 samples for all signs. Figure 3 shows 10 random samples from this dataset. In these experiments, we use half of the number of samples since the accuracy are similar to that of using all dataset and this also reduces the training time by half. We divide the data into a train set and a test set with the ratio 70 and 30.

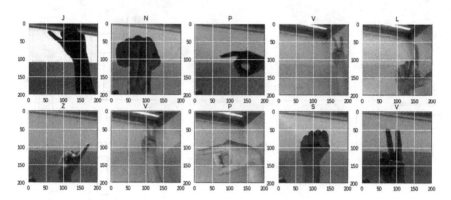

Fig. 3. Random samples from the ASL dataset

5.2   Experiment 1: DW Capsules vs SC Capsules

In this experiment, we perform experimental evaluations of DW Capsules against SC Capsules. First, we vary the size of Convolution's kernel including 9×9, 7×7, 5×5 and 3×3 using the Input image's size of 32×32. Then we add one more ConvNet in the first layer in the Capsule Networks's architecture as shown in Fig. 1. We also provide two variations of Capsule Networks, one for scaling down the total number of model parameters by adding a Max Pooling after the second ConvNet (Mini version) and, another, which increases Input image sizes to 64×64 (Max version).

Figure 4b and d show that DW Capsules perform equivalently or even better on accuracy than SC Capsules. Additionally, SC Capsules seems to be unstable and fluctuating based on kernel's size. Figure 4a shows a similar trend when SC Capsules are more likely to volatile when a half of SC Capsules are outperformed by DW Capsules. Only in Fig. 4c, all SC Capsules achieve higher accuracy than that of DW Capsules. Though this can be a trade of between training epoch and training speed.

5.3   Experiment 2: Deep Learning Models Using MLP and LSTM

In this section, we perform experiments of Deep Learning models using MLP and LSTM on variations of the ASL dataset including $\frac{1}{16}$, $\frac{1}{8}$, $\frac{1}{4}$, $\frac{1}{2}$ and the whole dataset.

Due to the limited number of pages allowed, we excerpt results from most of all Deep Learning models and preserve only one model for mobile devices and one model for powerful computers i.e. MobileNet V1 and Inception V3. We select MobileNet V1 because of its best accuracy and Inception V3 since the model is faster than DenseNet V201.

The Fig. 5a shows that Inception V3 Transfer Learning model when integrated with LSTM outperforms its version on MLP in all sets of data. Similarly, MobileNet V1 LSTM achieves a higher accuracy than MobileNet V1 MLP.

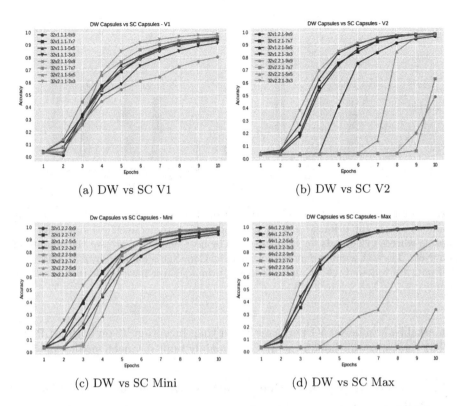

(a) DW vs SC V1

(b) DW vs SC V2

(c) DW vs SC Mini

(d) DW vs SC Max

Fig. 4. DW Capsules (blue) vs SC Capsules (cyan). The numbers 32 and 64 denote Input image sizes 32×32 and 64×64, respectively; v1 stands for DW Capsule whereas v2 stands for SC Capsule. The next number expresses the amount of ConvNets. The last number denotes whether the ConvNet is followed by a Max Pooling (1 if not, 2 if followed). All ConvNets in the primary layer have the kernel sizes vary from 9×9, 7×7, 5×5 to 3×3. (Color figure online)

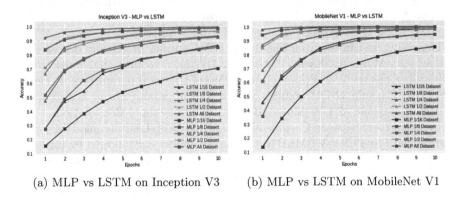

(a) MLP vs LSTM on Inception V3

(b) MLP vs LSTM on MobileNet V1

Fig. 5. Comparisons of MLP and LSTM on Deep Learning models.

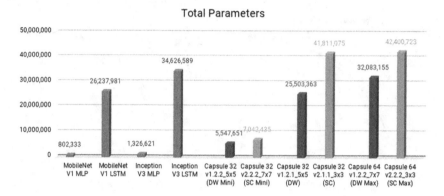

Fig. 6. Total parameters of Capsule Networks and Deep Learning models. The numbers 32 and 64 denote Input image sizes 32×32 and 64×64, respectively; v1 stands for DW Capsule whereas v2 stands for SC Capsule. The next number expresses the amount of ConvNets. The last number denotes whether the ConvNet is followed by a Max Pooling (1 if not, 2 if followed). All ConvNets in the primary layer have the kernel sizes vary from 9×9, 7×7, 5×5 to 3×3.

Remarkably, MobileNet V1 performs better than Inception V3 on both MLP and LSTM versions even though the model is mainly built for much smaller devices.

5.4   Capsule Networks vs Deep Learning Models on Model Size and Accuracy

In this Section, we analyse Capsule Networks and Deep Learning Models with respect to the total size of these models as well as accuracy. We select the best DW Capsules and SC Capsules including: (1) Input image size 32×32 pixel followed by two ConvNets and a Max Pooling (Fig. 4c), (2) Input image size 32×32 pixel one for the best accuracy SC (Fig. 4a) and one for the best accuracy DW (Fig. 4b), (3) Input image size 64×64 pixel integrated with two ConvNets and one Max Pooling (Fig. 4d). These Capsule Networks are denoted as DW Mini, SC Mini, DW, SC, DW Max and SC Max, respectively.

Generally, we can see from Fig. 6 that DW Capsules drastically decrease the models' size. More specifically, Capsule 32 DW Mini reduces the model size by 21% while Capsule 64 DW Max shrinks 25% of the total parameters. It can be noted that Capsule 32 DW reduces the number of parameters by 40% which is more than Capsule 32 DW Mini and Max due to one more Convolutions.

In comparison between Capsule Networks and Deep Learning models, we can observe that MobileNet V1 MLP has a smallest model size followed by Inception V3 MLP. Additionally, Capsule 32 DW and Capsule 64 DW Max have smaller sizes than MobileNet LSTM and Inception V3 LSTM.

In terms of accuracy, MobileNet V1 LSTM outperforms all other models. In spite of that, Capsule 64 DW Max reaches the second position and performs better than MobileNet V1 MLP after 10 epochs. In addition, Capsule 64 DW

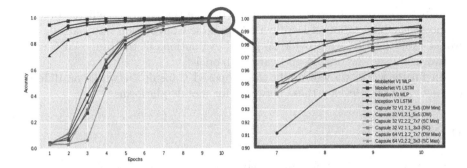

Fig. 7. Capsule Networks vs Deep Learning models

Max outperforms both versions of Inception V3 LSTM and MLP by a large extent. Though Capsule 64 DW has 40 times larger model size than MobileNet V1 MLP and 20% more than MobileNet V1 LSTM, its total parameter is less than that of Inception V3 LSTM Fig. 7.

It can be noticed that Capsule 32 DW Mini though having the smallest size among all Capsule Networks but is outperformed by MobileNet V1 MLP with regards to accuracy. However, when we perform these experiments with more epochs, this gap can be eliminated as Capsule 32 DW Mini yields the accuracy of MobileNet V1 MLP (0.9928) after 17 epochs. A similar trend also occurs to Capsule 32 SC Mini as it reaches the accuracy of MobileNet V1 LSTM (0.9986) after 18 epochs (approximately 1 h training on Tesla K80).

6 Conclusions

In this research, we first propose to replace Standard Convolution in Capsule Networks' Architecture with Depthwise Separable Convolution. Then we perform empirical comparisons of the best Capsule Networks with the best Deep Learning models.

The results show that our proposed DW Capsules remarkably decrease the size of models. Among the chosen Capsule Networks, the total parameters had shrunk roughly by an amount between 21%–25%.

In terms of accuracy, Capsule 64 DW Max performs better than other Capsule models. Though Capsule 32 SC Mini can be a trade-off between the accuracy and the number of parameters.

In comparison with Deep Learning models, Capsule 32 DW Mini has a larger number of parameters, yet it achieves the accuracy of MobileNet V1 after a few more epochs. Meanwhile, Capsule 32 SC Mini can attain that of MobileNet V1 LSTM's accuracy with 3 to 4 times smaller in the number of parameters.

Capsule 32 DW Mini and 64 DW Max outperform Inception V3 MLP and LSTM on accuracy. Moreover, Capsule 64 DW Max occupies 5% less the number of parameters than Inception V3 LSTM though Capsule 32 DW Mini has 4 times larger size than Inception V3 MLP.

After a thorough literature search, we believe that this is the first work that proposes the integration of Depthwise Separable Convolution into Capsule Networks. Additionally, we provide empirical evaluations of the proposed Capsule Networks versus the best Deep Learning models.

In future work, we will apply the proposed Capsule Networks on different datasets and will develop these networks for mobile platforms.

References

1. Bahadori, M.T.: Spectral capsule networks. In: 6th International Conference on Learning Representations (2018)
2. Howard, A.G., et al.: MobileNets: efficient convolutional neural networks for mobile vision applications. arXiv Preprint arXiv:1704.04861 (2017)
3. Huang, G., Liu, Z., Van Der Maaten, L., Weinberger, K.Q.: Densely connected convolutional networks. In: 2017 IEEE Conference on Computer Vision and Pattern Recognition (CVPR), pp. 2261–2269. IEEE (2017)
4. Mobiny, A., Van Nguyen, H.: Fast CapsNet for lung cancer screening. arXiv Preprint arXiv:1806.07416 (2018)
5. Sabour, S., Frosst, N., Hinton, G.E.: Dynamic routing between capsules. In: Advances in Neural Information Processing Systems, pp. 3856–3866 (2017)
6. Sandler, M., Howard, A., Zhu, M., Zhmoginov, A., Chen, L.C.: MobileNetV2: inverted residuals and linear bottlenecks. arXiv Preprint arXiv:1801.04381 (2018)
7. Szegedy, C., Vanhoucke, V., Ioffe, S., Shlens, J., Wojna, Z.: Rethinking the inception architecture for computer vision. In: Proceedings of the IEEE Conference on Computer Vision and Pattern Recognition, pp. 2818–2826 (2016)
8. Zoph, B., Vasudevan, V., Shlens, J., Le, Q.V.: Learning transferable architectures for scalable image recognition. In: Proceedings of the IEEE Conference on Computer Vision and Pattern Recognition, pp. 8697–8710 (2018)

Wave Front Tracking in High Speed Videos Using a Dynamic Template Matching

Samee Maharjan$^{(\boxtimes)}$

Department of Process, Energy and Environmental Technology,
University of South-Eastern Norway (USN), Notodden, Norway
samee.maharjan@usn.no

Abstract. In recent years, image processing has been evolving as an important tool to estimate the properties of a generated wave during a gas experiments. The wave properties were estimated by tracking a wave fronts in the images of a high speed video, captured during the experiment. In this work, we purposed a dynamic template matching method, based on the mean square error (MSE) between the intensity values of a template and its foot print in an image to track the wave front. At first, a dynamic template of a predefined size [5 × 20] was created, whose values varies according to the minimum and maximum intensity of the considered image. Secondly to reduce the processing time, a bounding box was set around the area of interest in the considered image, such that the matching process is limited within the area covered by the bounding box. The purposed method was tested for four different high speed videos from four different gas experiments conducted two different experimental set-ups. All the results from the purposed method are within an acceptable accuracy.

Keywords: Image processing application · Dynamic template · Front tracking

1 Introduction

Template matching or pattern matching is an image processing method to detect the desired object in an image by using a predefined template. A template matching starts with creating a template of relatively smaller size whose one or multiple features matches with the features of the desired object. Then, the created template is slid in a pixel-by-pixel basis, computing the similarity between the template features and its footprint in the image [1]. The few common features that are used for calculating a similarity while matching are, normalized cross correlation (NCC), the sum of absolute difference (SAD), the sum of squared error (SSD), mean square error (MSE) [2]. In this work, we took the template matching based on MSE, due to its simplicity and fast processing. The MSE takes a mean of the squared difference between the intensity of each pixel in the

© Springer Nature Switzerland AG 2019
A. Morales et al. (Eds.): IbPRIA 2019, LNCS 11867, pp. 531–542, 2019.
https://doi.org/10.1007/978-3-030-31332-6_46

template and the corresponding pixel in its footprint in the image. Assuming template T of size [m × n] slides over an image I, then at each position (x,y) in I, MSE is estimated as in (1). The template matches the best in the image pixel where MSE is the minimum.

$$MSE(x,y) = \frac{1}{no.of pixel} \sum_{k=1}^{m} \sum_{e=1}^{n} [I(x+k, y+e) - T(k,e)]^2. \tag{1}$$

In general, a gas explosion can be defined as a process where combustion of a premixed gas cloud, i.e. fuel-oxidiser is causing a rapid increase in pressure in a close vessel or confined area due to any kind of external energy. When the pressure exerted inside the vessel is higher than the vessel can hold then it explodes producing extremely powerful and destructive waves [3]. The most common approach to study these geberated waves and estimate their characteristics are by using the pressure transducers in the experimental area and/or computer simulations [4]. However, in recent years, the estimation of wave characteristics using the high speed videos and image processing have been emerging [5–7]. A high speed video captured during the gas experiment was later processed using image processing technologies to track the wave front in the images of the video. By tracking the wave front in these images, the wave characteristics like speed, temperature and pressure were estimate.

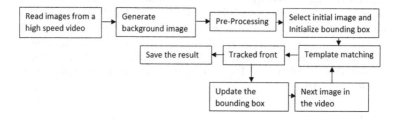

Fig. 1. Block diagram of the framework.

However, due the poor quality of images in a high speed videos, most of the image processing framework consists of multiple processing units, which not only cost a computational time but also require manual interference. One of the previous work that used template matching for front tracking can be read [8]. The tracking was done in the raw images with two predefined templates: one for a straight wave and one for the tilted (oblique wave) in a single image (refer to Fig. 2 second row). The framework then use a post-processing for finding the optimum result from both templates. The matching was based on the predefined average intensity of the template for an individual video. Even though, the framework works fine with some manual input, the sliding of a template in an overall image along with post-processing takes a high computational time. In this work, we purpose a new method of creating a dynamic template and sliding the created template within a certain region in an image bounded by a bounding box. As, we are working with a set of images from a multiple high speed videos, whose intensities varies with each image, we create a template with a fixed size but with a varying value depending in the intensity of each image to be matched.

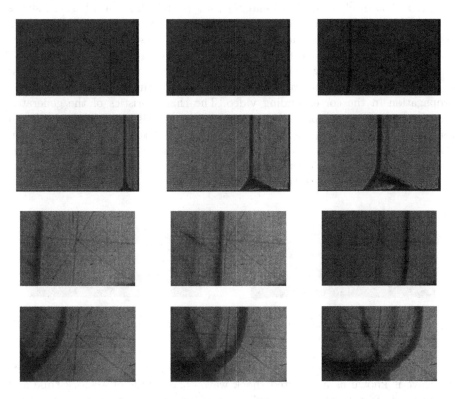

Fig. 2. Some of the images from different gas experiments chronologically sorted from left to right. An arrowhead points towards the direction of the wave propagation in the corresponding video. From top to bottom row: N_2, CO_2, H_2 and $H_2 + air$ experiment.

The rest of the paper is organized as follows. Section 2 gives a brief description on the high speed videos and the methodology of template creation, setting bounding box and matching the created template in the area surrounded by the bounding box. The results from the purposed method with some discussion are presented in Sect. 3. Lastly, the conclusion and some possible further work is discussed in Sect. 4.

2 Materials and Methods

The block diagram presented in Fig. 1 depicted the work flow of the overall framework. More on the each part are described in following sub-sections.

2.1   High Speed Videos

The four high speed videos captured during four different gas experiments were processed in this work. The experiments were conducted with N_2 (Exp.2534), CO_2 (Exp.2558), H_2 (Exp.0016) and $H_2 + air$ (Exp.0022) gases. Figure 2 shows the wave propagation during the considered four gas experiments. The images in each row are from an individual experiment and are presented in chronologically order from left to right. All the upcoming figures in this paper with four rows follows the structure row wise i.e. from top to bottom row: N_2, CO_2, H_2 and $H_2 + air$ experiment. An arrowhead points towards the direction of the wave propagation in the corresponding video. The characteristics of the generated wave during any gas explosion depends on the characteristics of the gas itself and the initial conditions like initial pressure and temperature. Due to this reason, the structure of wave is different in each experiments. The objective of this work is to design a single framework, which track the wave front in all these images/videos regardless of their structure.

Fig. 3. Background image created for left: CO_2 and right: H_2 experiments.

The first two experiments were conducted in a shock tube and the propagating wave is known as a reflected shock wave. The details of a shock tube and the method of capturing high speed video while experimenting in a shock tube can be read in [5]. The bottom two experiments were conducted in an open end experimental tube and the propagating wave is known as a detonation wave [10]. A schlieren technique [12] of imaging was used for capturing all the videos, and a special high speed camera called 'Kirana' was operated with the frequency of 500,000 frames per second. Each high speed video consists of 180 images of size [768 × 924] pixels ≈ [70 × 100] mm. However, some part of the image contains capturing window, which was cropped appropriately before processing. The final size of images for respective experiments are: N_2 and CO_2 is [400 × 910], H_2 is [356 × 631] and $H_2 + air$ is [356 × 640].

2.2   Pre-processing/Filtering

Due to the high frame rate of the camera and the ongoing chemical reactions during the experiment, the images in the high speed videos are generally with

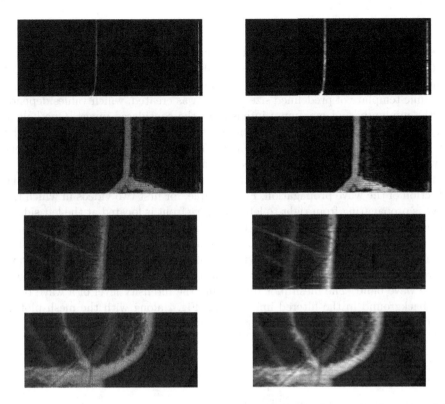

Fig. 4. Result of pre-processing, right column: result after background subtraction, left column: respective filtered image after LPF.

high amount of noise. Therefore, it is preferred to pre-process the images before further processing. The pre-processing of an image in the current framework consists of a background subtraction followed by a low pass frequency filtering. For background subtraction, a background image was created by taking average intensity values of the initial images which doesn't consists of the visual wave front. The background image created for the high speed videos of CO_2 and H_2 experiments are shown in Fig. 3. After that, the created background image was subtracted from each image with the visual front or which needs to be procressed. The remaining noise in the background subtracted image was then removed by using a low pass filter with the threshold frequency of 50 Hz. The examples of the background subtraction in the images from high speed videos is presented in Fig. 4 left column, and the right column shows their respective low pass filtered images. The process of the frequency filtering in the images and its benefits can be read on [15].

2.3 Template Creation

The close look of the intensity difference between wave band and background in the background subtracted images suggested that the waveband contains of bright pixels where as background contains of dark pixels. With this reference, a dynamic template of predefined size $[5 \times 20]$ was created, which values depends on the minimum and maximum intensity of the considered image. One half of the template, contains the minimum intensity value which should technically be the intensity of a background, while another half contains the maximum intensity value which should technically be the intensity of the wave band. However, which side of template takes the minimum and maximum value depends on the direction of the wave propagation. For example, for first two videos in which the wave is propagating from right to left, the wave front is located at the left side of the wave band. Therefore, the right half of the template contains the maximum intensity value (wave) and left half contains minimum (background). The values in the template for the bottom two videos would be exactly opposite as the wave is propagating in an opposite direction and the wave front lies at the right side of the wave band. The mesh plot illustrating the intensity level of a wave band and background in the filtered images from Fig. 4 along with the mesh plot of their respective created templates are presented in Fig. 5.

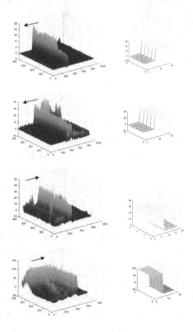

Fig. 5. The mesh plot showing the intensities. Left: the filtered images and right: a template created for the corresponding images (right).

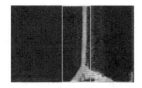 

Fig. 6. Template matching process left: a filtered image from CO_2 experiment with a bounding box for matching, center: MSE calculated from matching within the bounding box, right: the result of choosing the minimum MSE in each row presented by the green curve in a raw image of the same image in left. (Color figure online)

2.4 Bounding Box

As it can be seen in all the images presented in previous sections, the wave actually stands in the small part of image. Hence, sliding a template all over the image will only increase the processing time. Therefore, to minimize the processing time, a bounding box was created around the area of interest (wave) such that the sliding of template occurs only inside the bounding box. The height of bounding box is always the number of rows in the image, whereas the width varies depending on the horizontal span of wave band in the image. For the initial image, the bounding box was set at the side of image where, the wave originates and then it moves along the direction of wave propagation with each consecutive images. The movement of the bounding box was governed by the values of the previous tracked front.

Lets take an example of the CO_2 experiment, the bounding box was set initially at the right end of the image where the wave originated. The right end of the bounding box was set at the right end of image itself, whereas the left side was set 200 columns ahead of the right end. After the first front was tracked, the position of the bounding box was updated according to the position of the tracked front. As the wave was always going forward (towards left), the right side of the bounding box was updated with the median value of the first tracked front while keeping the width of the bounding box constant. The choice of 200 columns as the width of the bounding box came from the a priori visualization of the high speed video which gave rough idea about the total wave span (refer to Fig. 2 second row). Similarly for the H_2 experiment, the bounding box with the width of 100 was initially set at the left side of the image. After first tracking, the left side of the bounding box was then updated with the median of the first tracked front keeping the width as it is. However, in $H_2 + air$ experiment to accommodate the shape of the wave, the bounding box of width 200 was set with the median value of last 50 rows. One of the raw images from CO_2 and H_2 experiment are presented in the left image of Figs. 6 and 7 respectively. The width of bounding box for the N_2 experiment are 50.

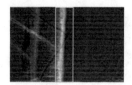

Fig. 7. Template matching process left: a filtered image from H_2 experiment with a bounding box for matching, center: MSE calculated from matching within the bounding box, right: the result of choosing the minimum MSE in each row presented by the green curve in a raw image of the same image in left. (Color figure online)

2.5   Template Matching

The sliding of the template always started from the top left of the bounding box and moved towards top right. For example, a bounding box in Fig. 6 spreads from top to bottom (all rows) and column 350 to 550. The first matching took place at top left of bounding box i.e. 1st row and 350th column of the image and the template slide along each column calculating MSE at each pixel till 531th column. After, it reached 531th column, it slide to 2nd row 350th column and continued till 531th column and so on. Four pixels at the bottom and 19 pixels at left of bounding box was exempted due to boundary adjustment. At each position, MSE between the template and its footprint in the image was estimated as in (1), such that $x = 1 : 396, y = 350 : 531$. After completing calculating MSE in one image, a pixel with the least MSE was picked out in each row. Please note that the actual front position is in the middle of the template, such that the minimum MSE pixel in any row gives the front position at 2 rows below. The position of the wave front is then 10 columns behind actual column of MSE pixel. For example, the minimum MSE point in a 1st row is at lets say column y_m actually gives the front position in 3rd row which will be in column $y_m + 10$. Hence, there was no front tracked for top 2 and bottom 2 rows.

3   Results and Discussion

A created bounding box of width 200 pixels, the result of template matching within the bounding box and the position of front in one of the raw image from CO_2 experiment is shown in Fig. 6. Similarly, the image from H_2 experiment with a bounding box of width 100 pixels, the calculated for the bounding box and result from the minimum is presented in Fig. 7. Figure 8 summarizes the results of a dynamic template matching based on MSE for tracking wave fronts in four different high speed videos. The first and second column presents the result in an individual images while, third columns shows all the tracked fronts with their respective position in the image. High speed video of N_2 and CO_2 are comparatively with less background noise than the $H_2 + air$ and H_2 experiment.

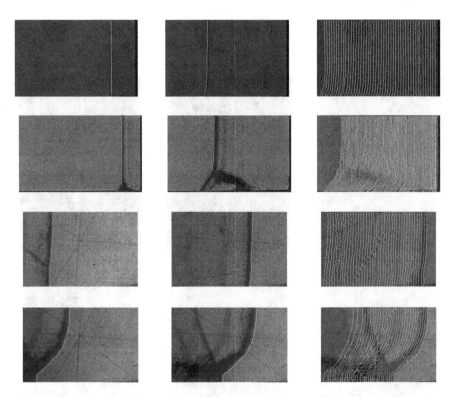

Fig. 8. Template matching process left: a filtered image from H_2 experiment with a bounding box for matching, center: MSE calculated from matching within the bounding box, right: the result of choosing the minimum MSE in each row presented by the green curve in a raw image of the same image in left. (Color figure online)

The tracked fronts are therefore with less or no distortion as seen in top two rows. However, few distortions can be seen in the results from $H_2 + air$ experiment, the noise within the bounding box is matched more than the actual front. In such cases, some post processing should be performed, as simple one can be the smoothing of the front or piecewise line fitting.

The framework/matching process also tested in the raw images as well as the background subtracted images from the high speed videos. For better illustration in Fig. 9, one image from each experiment are presented in a raw, background subtracted and filtered form with the respective front tracked by the method in the same images. For better quality video with N_2, the results are almost same for all type of images. For the H_2 experiment, the results are smoother and better with each step of pre-processing. In contrast, for $H_2 + air$ and CO_2 the worst results is while using background subtracted image as the noise in the background subtraction enhanced a background noise as line structure inside the wave band.

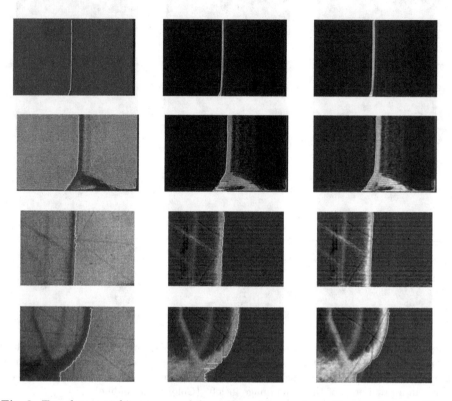

Fig. 9. Template matching process left: a filtered image from H_2 experiment with a bounding box for matching, center: MSE calculated from matching within the bounding box, right: the result of choosing the minimum MSE in each row presented by the green curve in a raw image of the same image in left. (Color figure online)

Figure 10 shows the result of using 'prewitt' edge detection method from Matlab image processing toolbox corresponding to right bottom image in Fig. 4. Some of the available edge detection methods in various processing toolboxes were able to detect the edges, however they did not provide the required precision of front position. The red curve is plotted with the first white pixel from right and green one is from the template matching. This shows the importance and the advantage of using a robust method like template matching in order to track the exact front position.

Fig. 10. The result of using 'prewitt' edge detection method corresponding to right bottom image in Fig. 4. Red curve - first white pixel from right and green curve - the template matching. (Color figure online)

4 Conclusion

A dynamic template with the predefined size and varying value was created to track the wave front the high speed videos. A bounding box which size varies with the size of the wave in the image was set in the images for sliding the created dynamic template to minimize the processing time. The use of bounding box has minimize the processing time by more than 1/3 times. The time of execution of one image from H_2 is 0.440 s while using bounding box while took 1.839 s while not using bounding box. However, the setting and the movement of the bounding box depends upon the wave propagating direction and structure of the wave, so a prior information about the structure of the wave in an image is necessary. Visually, all the results are within a acceptable accuracy and a purposed method of template matching have a huge potential for tracking various kinds of wave. The purposed method can also be used without any pre-precessing, however, the tracked fronts would be rougher hence, some post processing are suggested.

Acknowledgment. The experiments processed in this paper were conducted at California Institute of Technology (Caltech). Author would like to thank Prof. J.E. Shepherd and Dr. L. Boeck form Caltech and Prof. Ola Marius Lysaker from USN for their valuable contribution.

References

1. Brunelli, R.: Template Matching Techniques in Computer Vision: Theory and Practice. Wiley, Hoboken (2009)
2. Ouyang, W., Tombari, F., Mattoccia, S., Stefano, L.D., Cham, W.K.: Performance evaluation of full search equivalent pattern matching algorithms. IEEE Trans. Pattern Anal. Mach. Intell. **34**(1), 127–143 (2012)
3. Bjerketvedt, D., Bakke, J.R., Wingerden, K.V.: Gas explosion handbook. J. Hazard. Mater. **52**, 1–150 (1997)
4. Tseng, T.I., Yang, R.J.: Simulation of the Mach reflection in supersonic flows by the CE/SE method. Shock Waves **14**(4), 307–311 (2005)
5. Damazo, J.S. : Planar reflection of gaseous detonations. Doctoral Thesis, California Institute of Technology, Pasadena, California (2013)
6. Maharjan, S., Gaathaug, A.V., Lysaker, O.M.: Open active contour model for front tracking of detonation waves. In: Proceedings of the 58th Conference on Simulation and Modelling, pp. 174–179. Linkoping University Electronic Press, Sweden (2017)

7. Maharjan, S., Bjerketvedt, D., Lysaker, O.M.: An image processing framework for automatic tracking of wave fronts and estimation of wave front velocity for a gas experiment. In: Chen, L., Ben Amor, B., Ghorbel, F. (eds.) RFMI 2017. CCIS, vol. 842, pp. 45–55. Springer, Cham (2019). https://doi.org/10.1007/978-3-030-19816-9_4

8. Siljan, E., Maharjan, S., Lysaker, O.M.: Wave front tracking using template matching and segmented regression. In: Proceedings of the 58th Conference on Simulation and Modelling, pp. 326–331. Linkoping University Electronic Press, Sweden (2017)

9. Akbar, R.: Mach reflection of gaseous detonations. California Institute of Technology, Pasadena (2013)

10. Gaathaug, A.V., Maharjan, S., Lysaker, O.M., Vaagsaether, K., Bjerketvedt, D.: Velocity and pressure along detonation fronts - image processing of experimental results. In: Proceedings of the Eighth International Seminar on Fire and Explosion Hazards (ISFEH8), pp. 133–149 (2016)

11. Law, C.K.: Combustion Physics. Cambridge University Press, New York (2010)

12. Settle, G.H.: Schlieren and Shadowgraph Techniques. Springer, Heidelberg (2001). https://doi.org/10.1007/978-3-642-56640-0

13. Liepmann, H.W., Roshko, A.: Elemnents of Gasdynamics. Dover Publications Inc., New York (2014)

14. Settle, G.S., Hargather, M.H.: A review of recent developments in schlieren and shadowgraph techniques. Meas. Sci. Technol. **28**, 042001 (2017)

15. Maharjan, S., Bjerketvedt, D., Lysaker, O.M.: Study of a reflected shock wave boundary layer interactions based on image processing. Blind Review Process

An Efficient Binary Descriptor to Describe Retinal Bifurcation Point for Image Registration

Sarder Tazul Islam[1], Sajib Saha[2(✉)], G.M. Atiqur Rahaman[1], Deep Dutta[1], and Yogesan Kanagasingam[2]

[1] Computational Color and Spectral Image Analysis Laboratory,
Computer Science and Engineering Discipline, Khulna University,
Khulna, Bangladesh
tazulcseku@gmail.com, gmatiqur@gmail.com, duttadeep.ku.cse14@gmail.com
[2] Australian E Health Research Centre,
Commonwealth Scientific and Industrial Research Organisation (CSIRO),
Perth, WA, Australia
{Sajib.Saha,Yogi.Kanagasingam}@csiro.au

Abstract. Bifurcation points are typically considered as landmark points for retinal image registration. Robust detection, description and accurate matching of landmark points between images are crucial for successful registration of image pairs. This paper introduces a novel descriptor named Binary Descriptor for Retinal Bifurcation Point (BDRBP), so that bifurcation point can be described and matched more accurately. BDRBP uses four patterns that are reminiscent of Haar basis function. It relies on pixel intensity difference among groups of pixels within a patch centering on the bifurcation point to form a binary string. This binary string is the descriptor. Experiments are conducted on publicly available retinal image registration dataset named FIRE. The proposed descriptor has been compared with the state-of-the art Li Chen et al.'s method for bifurcation point description. Experiments show that bifurcation points can be described and matched with an accuracy of 86–90% with BDRBP, whereas, for Li Chen et al.'s method the accuracy is 43–78%.

Keywords: Bifurcation point · Binary descriptor ·
Haar feature · Hamming distance · Image registration

1 Introduction

Retinal image registration is a process of establishing pixel-to-pixel correspondence between two or more retinal images from different time, viewpoints and sources [1,2]. Registration of retinal images generally has three different forms, namely, cross-modality registration, spatial registration and temporal registration. The need for cross-modality registration arises when the ophthalmologists want to use two different imaging modalities (such as fluorescein angiography

© Springer Nature Switzerland AG 2019
A. Morales et al. (Eds.): IbPRIA 2019, LNCS 11867, pp. 543–552, 2019.
https://doi.org/10.1007/978-3-030-31332-6_47

and optical photography images) to get complementary information about retinal vessel disorder. When the ophthalmologists wish to combine narrow-field images together to produce a wider field view of the retina, spatial registration is considered. The need for temporal registration arises when it is required to track the changes of retina over time. Temporal registration facilitates estimating the severity of the disease or therapeutic progress.

Retinal image registration methods are typically divided into two categorizes - pixel/voxel based method and feature/landmark based method. Feature based approaches are typically preferred [1]. Feature based techniques first detect the landmark points in the image, and then compute features to represent the landmark points. Features across images are finally matched to find the transformation parameters to perform the registration. Robust detection, description of landmark points and accurate matching of landmark points between images are crucial for successful registration of image pairs [3]. Vessel bifurcation and cross-over points are typically considered as landmarks by most of the retinal image registration methods, since it is a prominent indicator of vasculature. Figure 1 shows example bifurcation, cross-over and terminal points in retinal image registration context.

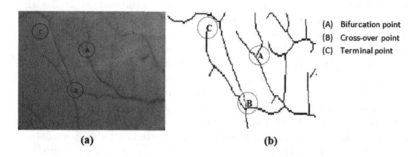

Fig. 1. (a) Retinal vasculature. (b) Vessel centerlines.

While bifurcation points can be detected reasonably reliably these days, precise description of bifurcation points still remains a challenge [1]; specially due to the difficulties of modality- and time-varying intensities of retinal images [4].

On that perspective, in this paper we propose a novel descriptor named Binary Descriptor for Retinal Bifurcation Point (BDRBP), so that bifurcation points can be described precisely and matched more accurately. BDRBP relies on Haar basis functions to form pixels grouping, whose intensities are then compared to form a binary string, representing the patch surrounding the bifurcation point. Hamming distance is used to compare/match the descriptors. Experiments on publicly available retinal image registration dataset show that bifurcation points can be described and matched more accurately with BDRBP than the state-of-the-art method.

2   Literature Review

Retinal image registration remains an active area of research over the last decade. An extensive number of methods are proposed. An interesting review about these methods are provided in [2]. Here, we provide a brief review of some of most prominent and recent ones.

In [5], Can et al. proposed a retinal image registration technique by modelling the retina as a rigid quadratic surface with unknown parameters. The algorithm uses hierarchical approach to solve the problem of one to multiple matching bifurcation points. The correspondences are refined gradually from the coarse translation model to higher order quadratic model. Stewart et al. in [6] extended the idea of Can et al. and proposed the dual-bootstrap ICP algorithm which is able to register images with as low as one initial matching points. Staring from the initial match the algorithm iteratively bootstraps both the region and the transformation model. The bootstrap region is expanded based on transformation estimate. Model bootstrapping starts from a simple model (such as translation) and gradually evolves a higher order model (such as quadratic), as the bootstrap region grows to cover the entire image overlap region. In [7], Fang et al. proposed a retinal image registration technique based on Fast chamfer matching and non-parametric elastic matching. Adal et al. [8] considered hierarchical coarse-to-fine approach to estimate the parameters of the global quadratic transformation model for registering pair of retinal images. In [9], Ghassabi et al. proposed respectively an improved scale-invariant feature transform and region detector method to identify adequate, stable and distinctive key-points aiming at robust retinal image registration for high-resolution and low-contrast images. Hernandez-Matas et al. [10] considered SURF [11] key-points and SURF features to register retinal image pairs. Saha et al. [1] proposed a two-step approach for registration of retinal images that are collected over time. In the first step a pre-registration is performed using SURF keypoints and features and in the second step fine registration is performed using BRIEF [12] descriptor. Realizing the shortcoming of available descriptors to describe bifurcation points uniquely, these methods mainly focused on refining the correspondences so that false and ambiguous matches can be minimized. Only a few attempts are made to describe bifurcation points more precisely and uniquely. To describe retinal bifurcation points more uniquely Chen et al. [4,13] computed bifurcation structure. The bifurcation structure is composed of a master bifurcation point and its three connected neighbours. The characteristic vector of each bifurcation structure consists of the normalized branching angle and length, which is invariant against translation, rotation, scaling, and even modest distortion. Ramli et al. [14] used D-Saddle feature to for precise description of Saddle keypoints to perform retinal image registration. Chen et al.'s method is simple yet efficient and has been considered as the state-of-the-art method here.

3 Binary Descriptor for Retinal Bifurcation Point (BDRBP)

BDRBP considers a patch around the bifurcation points which are then described using binary string relying on pair wise intensity comparisons. It is inspired by the earlier works in [12,15] and [16]. In [12], it has been shown that image patches could be described by binary values on the basis of pair-wise intensity comparisons. In [15], it was discussed about different types of patterns that can be used to make comparison inside an image patch. In [16], authors proposed to use Haar features using integral image to detect faces. Hence, the idea of this paper is to generate descriptor using binary values from the comparison of different pixels groups determined by a set of Haar like patterns.

3.1 Descriptor Generation

BDRBP uses the intensity difference test between two pixel groups to define each bit of the descriptor, where pixel groups are defined using some specific patterns that are reminiscent of Haar basis function.

Each test T on patch P of size $S \times S$ is mathematically defined as

$$T(P,X,Y) = \begin{cases} 1; \text{ if } P_x \geq P_y \\ 0; \text{ Otherwise} \end{cases} \tag{1}$$

where P_x and P_y represent the sum of intensities of two different pixel groups X and Y.

In order to perform a plurality of test T BDRBP considers a set of 4 patterns as depicted in Fig. 2. In addition to that tests are performed at 4 different levels. In the first level a 32×32 patch is considered around the bifurcation point, and 4 bit vector is generated based on 4 intensity tests.

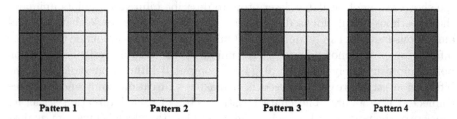

Pattern 1   Pattern 2   Pattern 3   Pattern 4

Fig. 2. 4×4 pixel pattern to calculate BDRBP for an image patch. For each pattern the dark portion will be compared with the bright portion.

At second level the patch is divided into 4 equal sub-patches of size 16×16. A 4 bit vector is generated for each of these sub-patches. Thus in the second level a total of 16 ($=4 \times 4$) bit values is generated. In the third level each of the previous level patches is further divided four equal sized sub-patches and a total of 64 (=16 × 4) bit values is generated. By following this process at level-4 a total of 256 (=64 × 4) bit values is generated. BDRBP is defined as the concatenation of the 85 (1+4+16+64) bit strings issued from the original patch and the 84 derived sub-patches. Thus the final length of BDRBP becomes 340 (=1 × 4 + 4 × 4 + 16 × 4 + 64 × 4) bits.

A pictorial description about the patch decomposition to generate BDRBP is provided in Fig. 3.

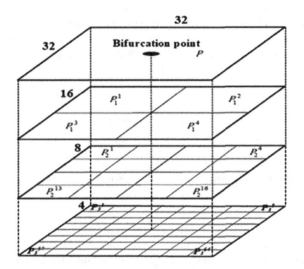

Fig. 3. Main patch decomposition in 4 levels which creates 84 sub-patches where keypoint is the bifurcation point.

3.2 Descriptor Matching

Hamming distance [12], which measures the minimum number of substitutions required to change one string into the other, is used to measure the similarity between two BDRBPs. The Hamming distance between two bit strings S and T of length N can be mathematically computed as:

$$H(S,T) = \sum_N h(S[i], T[i])$$

$$\text{where } h(x,y) = \begin{cases} 0; & \text{if } x = y \\ 1; & \text{Otherwise} \end{cases} \tag{2}$$

The lower the Hamming distance, the more similar they are. It is worth mentioning Hamming distance can be computed very efficiently with a bitwise XOR operation followed by a bit count on current processor architecture.

4   Experiments and Results

Experiments are conducted on publicly available fundus image dataset named FIRE [17]. FIRE is purposely built and specifically designed to evaluate the performance of retinal image registration methods. The dataset contains 134 image pairs (i.e. 268 retinal images in total) that were acquired at the Papageorgiou Hospital, Aristotle University of Thessaloniki, Thessaloniki, Greece. The images were captured by a Nidek AFC-210 fundus camera and the resolution of each image is 2912×2912. The dataset contains two binary mask images and ten sets ground truth points for each registration pair to evaluate registration performance. The image pairs were already classified into three categories – 'A', 'P' and 'S', depending on their characteristics. Table 1 summarizes these categories.

Table 1. Characteristics of FIRE dataset.

	Category S	Category P	Category A
Image pair	71	49	14
Approximate overlap	>75%	<75%	>75%
Anatomical changes	No	No	Yes

'P' category images show minimal overlap, at the same time reference and test images are rotated to a significant scale. Since, BDRBP is not designed to be rotation invariant, 'P' category images are not used in the experiment.

The proposed method has been compared against Chen et al.'s method [4]. Matching accuracy defined as below is used to evaluate the performance of the methods.

$$\text{Matching Accuracy} = \frac{Number\ of\ Correctly Matched\ Pairs}{Total\ Number\ of\ Pairs} \times 100\%$$

Matching accuracy is computed in two different scenarios – (1) for 20 best selected matching pairs with varying threshold, and (2) for varying number of best selected matching pairs with fixed threshold.

4.1   Matching Accuracy for 20 Best Selected Pairs

For each image pair the 10 pairs of ground truth points are used to generate the transformation matrix M. Then for each of the methods we select the best 20 matching pairs returned by the method in consideration. We consider a match as accurate if $\| P_T - M \times P_R \| \leq thr$, where P_T is the point in the test image, P_R is the matched point (determined by the method) in the reference image, and thr is the threshold. Euclidian distance is used to compute the difference between two points. We have computed matching accuracy for different threshold 5, 10, 15, 20, 25 and 30 as proposed in [17]. Figure 4 shows the average matching accuracy obtained by the proposed and Li Chen et al.'s methods.

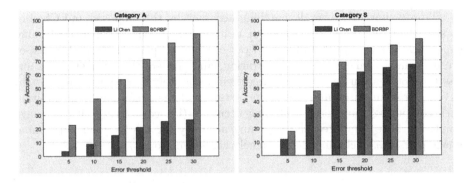

Fig. 4. Average matching accuracy for category 'A' and 'S' images.

4.2 Matching Accuracy for Varying Number of Best Selected Matching Pairs

Likewise in Sect. 4.1, here also for each image pair first we have generated the transformation matrix M from the 10 pairs of ground truth points. We consider a match as accurate if $\| P_T - M \times P_R \| \leq 10$, where P_T is the point in the test image, and P_R is the matched point (determined by the method) in the reference image. We have computed matching accuracy by varying the number of matching pairs – 10 pairs, 20 pairs, 30 pairs and 40 pairs, as proposed in [17]. Figure 5 shows example matching pairs determined by using BDRBP and Chen et al.'s methods.

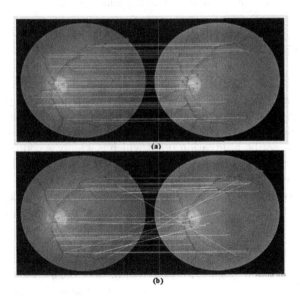

Fig. 5. Best 30 matching points using (a) BDRBP descriptor, (b) Chen et al.'s method.

Figure 6 shows the overall matching accuracy by the proposed and Chen et al.'s methods for different number of best matching pairs. Worth mentioning experimentally we have found that 57 out of 85 image pairs of the FIRE dataset are extremely challenging for registration, and state-of-the-art methods show less than 50% accuracy in registering them accurately [17]. Hence, in order to have a fair comparison and better understating of the performance, in addition with computing the overall matching accuracy (i.e. considering all the image pairs), we have computed the matching accuracy for the 28 good performing image pairs (i.e. excluding the extremely challenging pairs).

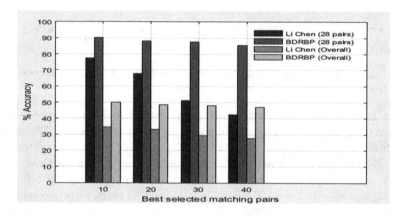

Fig. 6. Matching accuracy by the proposed and Chen et al.'s methods computed on the 28 good performing image pairs, and all the image pairs.

5   Conclusion

This paper introduces BDRBP, a memory efficient binary descriptor to facilitate retinal image registration. BDRBP relies on Haar-like pixel patterns define within an image patch and performs intensity difference test to encode the image patch into a binary string. BDRBP has been favorably compared with Chen et al.'s method to describe bifurcation point which is widely accepted as simple yet efficient approach. Extensive experiments on FIRE dataset reveals that BDRBP outperforms Chen et al.'s method with a significant margin.

Worth clarifying, while we have used the same image pairs and evaluation metrics of FIRE [17], direct comparisons of the experimental results with [17] is not appropriate here. In [17], they are evaluating registration methods, whereas, in this paper we are comparing retinal keypoint descriptors. Registration methods perform a preliminary screening of the matching pairs (depending on whether they satisfy a minimum geometric transform or not) prior to use them to compute transformation matrix for registration. Many false matches are removed through preliminary screening; hence, for fair comparisons of descriptors they need to be compared before preliminary screening. Undoubtedly, with preliminary screening of the matching pairs or in other words as complete registration methods, higher registration accuracy will be observed for both of the proposed and Chen's et al.'s methods.

Several perspectives for improvements of BDRBP can be envisioned. The decomposition of the main patch, the number of pixel patterns and the patterns themselves could for instance be optimized in order to improve the current results.

Further work should also incorporate orientation and scale invariance into BDRBP so that it can compete with other existing descriptors in a wider set of situations. Finally, even though majority of the descriptors are based on intensity information of the images, the introduction of color information while calculating BDRBP is also an interesting perspective for future improvements.

References

1. Saha, S.K., Xiao, D., Frost, S., Kanagasingam, Y.: A two-step approach for longitudinal registration of retinal images. J. Med. Syst. **40**(12), 277 (2016)
2. Saha, S.K., Xiao, D., Bhuiyan, A., Wong, T.Y., Kanagasingam, Y.: Color fundus image registration techniques and applications for automated analysis of diabetic retinopathy progression: a review. Biomed. Sig. Process. Control **47**, 288–302 (2019)
3. Saha, S.K., Xiao, D., Frost, S., Kanagasingam, Y.: Performance evaluation of state-of-the-art local feature detectors and descriptors in the context of longitudinal registration of retinal images. J. Med. Syst. **42**(4), 57 (2018)
4. Chen, L., Xiang, Y., Chen, Y., Zhang, X.: Retinal image registration using bifurcation structures. In: 2011 18th IEEE International Conference on Image Processing (ICIP), pp. 2169–2172. IEEE (2011)
5. Can, A., Stewart, C.V., Roysam, B., Tanenbaum, H.L.: A feature-based, robust, hierarchical algorithm for registering pairs of images of the curved human retina. IEEE Trans. Pattern Anal. Mach. Intell. **24**(3), 347–364 (2002)
6. Stewart, C.V., Chia-Ling, T., Roysam, B.: The dual-bootstrap iterative closest point algorithm with application to retinal image registration. IEEE Trans. Med. Imaging **22**(11), 1379–1394 (2003)
7. Fang, B., Hsu, W., Lee, M.L.: Techniques for temporal registration of retinal images. In: 2004 International Conference on Image Processing, ICIP 2004, vol. 2, pp. 1089–1092. IEEE (2004)
8. Adal, K.M., et al.: A hierarchical coarse-to-fine approach for fundus image registration. In: Ourselin, S., Modat, M. (eds.) WBIR 2014. LNCS, vol. 8545, pp. 93–102. Springer, Cham (2014). https://doi.org/10.1007/978-3-319-08554-8_10
9. Ghassabi, Z., Shanbehzadeh, J., Mohammadzadeh, A., Ostadzadeh, S.S.: Colour retinal fundus image registration by selecting stable extremum points in the scale-invariant feature transform detector. IET Image Process. **9**(10), 889–900 (2015)
10. Hernandez-Matas, C., Zabulis, X., Argyros, A.A.: Retinal image registration based on keypoint correspondences, spherical eye modeling and camera pose estimation. In: 2015 37th Annual International Conference of the IEEE Engineering in Medicine and Biology Society (EMBC), pp. 5650–5654. IEEE (2015)
11. Bay, H., Tuytelaars, T., Van Gool, L.: SURF: speeded up robust features. In: Leonardis, A., Bischof, H., Pinz, A. (eds.) ECCV 2006. LNCS, vol. 3951, pp. 404–417. Springer, Heidelberg (2006). https://doi.org/10.1007/11744023_32

12. Calonder, M., Lepetit, V., Strecha, C., Fua, P.: BRIEF: binary robust independent elementary features. In: Daniilidis, K., Maragos, P., Paragios, N. (eds.) ECCV 2010. LNCS, vol. 6314, pp. 778–792. Springer, Heidelberg (2010). https://doi.org/10.1007/978-3-642-15561-1_56

13. Chen, L., Huang, X., Tian, J.: Retinal image registration using topological vascular tree segmentation and bifurcation structures. Biomed. Sig. Process. Control. **16**, 22–31 (2015)

14. Ramli, R., et al.: Feature-based retinal image registration using D-Saddle feature. J. Healthc. Eng. **2017**, 1–15 (2017)

15. Saha, S., Démoulin, V.: ALOHA: an efficient binary descriptor based on Haar features. In: 2012 19th IEEE International Conference on Image Processing (ICIP), pp. 2345–2348. IEEE (2012)

16. Viola, P., Jones, M.: Rapid object detection using a boosted cascade of simple features. In: Proceedings of the 2001 IEEE Computer Society Conference on Computer Vision and Pattern Recognition, CVPR 2001, vol. 1, p. I. IEEE (2001)

17. Hernandez-Matas, C., Zabulis, X., Triantafyllou, A., Anyfanti, P., Douma, S., Argyros, A.A.: FIRE: fundus image registration dataset. J. Model. Ophthalmol. **1**(4), 16–28 (2017)

Aggregation of Deep Features for Image Retrieval Based on Object Detection

Juan Ignacio Forcén[1]([✉]), Miguel Pagola[2], Edurne Barrenechea[2],
and Humberto Bustince[2,3]

[1] Das-Nano — Veridas, Noain, Spain
jiforcen@das-nano.com
[2] Dpto Estadística, Matemáticas e Informática and Institute of Smart Cities,
Universidad Pública de Navarra, Pamplona, Spain
[3] King Abdullazid University, Jeddah, Saudi Arabia

Abstract. Image retrieval can be tackled using deep features from pre trained Convolutional Neural Networks (CNN). The feature map from the last convolutional layer of a CNN encodes descriptive information from which a discriminative global descriptor can be obtained. However, this global descriptors combine all of the information of the image, giving equal importance to the background and the object of the query. We propose to use an object detection based on saliency models to identify relevant regions in the image and therefore obtain better image descriptors. We extend our proposal to multi-regional image representation and we combine our proposal with other spatial weighting measures. The descriptors derived from the salient regions improve the performance in three well known image retrieval datasets as we show in the experiments.

Keywords: Image retrieval · Feature aggregation · Saliency

1 Introduction

Visual image search has been evolved from variants of the bag-of-words model [10] based on local features, typically SIFT [11], to approaches based on deep neural network features [21]. The first contributions in image retrieval using deep features from Razavian et al. [16] and Babenko et al. [20] proposed different aggregation strategies for deep features and demonstrated state-of-the-art performance in popular benchmarks. Based on these results, recent contributions have been made in order to improve the quality of the final image representation. Representations for image retrieval need to be compact i.e., representations around a few hundred dimensions, while retaining most of the details of the images.

Some approaches like [2] have tried to fine-tune the CNN with training datasets related to test datasets. Others methods as, [19] or [6], have focused in the methodology of feature extraction from the layers of the network. Fine-tuning approaches improve results in particular datasets, but have drawbacks of

© Springer Nature Switzerland AG 2019
A. Morales et al. (Eds.): IbPRIA 2019, LNCS 11867, pp. 553–564, 2019.
https://doi.org/10.1007/978-3-030-31332-6_48

requiring training datasets with expensive annotations depending on a category of the test dataset.

We place this work as pre-trained single-pass category of CNN-based approaches, defined by Zheng et al. [21]. We encode images into compact feature vectors using an off-the-shelf CNN, commonly known as a general feature extractor. Kalantidis et. al. [6] established a straightforward way of creating powerful image representations by means of multidimensional aggregation and weighting. In Fig. 1 is depicted the basic process of this methodology. An image is processed by a CNN, from which we get the tensor X, i.e. the activation maps of the last convolution layer. These convolutional features can be weighted channel-wise by a vector β and spatially by a matrix α to obtain a weighted feature matrix X'. These weighted features X' are pooled to derive a final feature vector, i.e. the image representation.

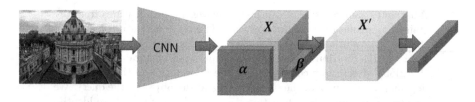

Fig. 1. Methodology to obtain image representations by multidimensional weighting and aggregation.

In this work we follow such methodology to obtain compact image representations. Our objective is to propose a spatial weight matrix α such a way we focus on the relevant object of the image and therefore remove non discriminative information providing better results in image retrieval applications. Basically, we propose to use object detection based saliency measure [22] to identify relevant regions in the image. The contributions of this paper can be summarized as follows:

- We propose a weighting approach based on object detection, over off-the-shelf CNN convolutional features for image retrieval.
- We extend the weighting methodology to multi-regional image representation.
- In the experimental results we demonstrate the effectiveness of our method to well-known image retrieval datasets, and compared it to the state-of-the-art techniques that are in the category of "pre-trained single-pass".

This work is divided in the following sections: first, in Sect. 2, related works with our proposal are recalled. In Sect. 3 we give a detailed explanation of our proposal followed by the experimental results Section. Finally the conclusions and future work are presented.

2   Related Work

CNN-based retrieval methods have been developed in recent years and are replacing the classical local detectors and descriptors. Several CNN models serve as good choices for extracting features, including AlexNet [8], VGGNet [18] or ResNet [8]. Based on the transfer learning principle, the first idea was to extract an image descriptor from a fully-connected layer of the network, however, it has been observed by [19] that the pooling layer after the last convolutional layer (e.g., pool5 in VGGNet), usually yields superior accuracy than the fully-connected descriptors and other convolutional layers. Basically, in [16] and [19], was proposed a feature aggregation pipeline using max-pooling that, in combination with normalization and whitening obtained state-of-the-art results for low dimensional image codes. Following these results, research efforts have been focused on the aggregation of the features from the pre-trained CNNs. Taking into the account Fig. 1, the research within the "pre-trained single-pass" methods, is devoted to study the aggregation procedure to get the final vector. This means, to identify a proper channel weighting vector β, a proper spatial weighting matrix α and select the correct aggregation function, for example, maximum or sum, to obtain a low dimensional image representation. In Babenko et. al. [20] is used a global sum pooling with a centering priority. Kalantidis et. al. [6] proposed a non-parametric spatial weighting method focusing on activation regions and a channel weighting related to activation sparsity with global sum pooling. Similarly, Cao et al. [1] proposed a method to derive a set of base regions directly from the activations of the convolutional layer. An extension to global pooling is the Regional-Maximum Activation of Convolutions (R-MAC) [20] where the image is divided into overlapped square regions of specific scales. R-MAC performs a max pooling for all regional feature maps and a standard post-processing such as l2-normalization and PCA-whitening. The global feature vector is obtained by sum pooling of the region vectors, followed by l2-normalization. Jimenez et al. [5] studied the Class Activation Maps (CAMs) to improve over the fix region strategy of R-MAC.

The notion of saliency in CNN-based image retrieval works has referred to the most active regions of the image. Two different types of saliency measures have been used in the literature. The first saliency measures are calculated from the same CNN from which image representations are extracted. For example, Lanskar and Kannala [9] used a saliency measure directly derived from the convolutional features to weight the contribution of the regions of R-MAC prior to aggregation. Their proposed saliency measure consists in sum aggregating the feature maps over the channel dimension. Similarly, the work of Simeoni et al. [17] propose using a saliency measure based on the k nearest neighbours regions of an image dataset. Other works proposed saliency models trained by an auxiliary network [7].

Other type of saliency measures are human-based saliency models, such as those derived from the popular Itti and Koch model [3]. In [12], different human-based saliency measures are compared when the final feature vector is created by means of bags of local convolutional features (BLCF).

However, all these methods do not take into account that within the query image the most important region of the image (what we are looking for) usually is the main object of the image. Saliency measures based of activations should prioritize important regions for classification, while human based measures focus on important details for eye-recognition. But, in order to improve the final accuracy in the image search problem, all of the area of the query object should be taken into account. In fact, when an object detection search is done, the accuracy increases a lot [19]. Therefore, the spatial weighting scheme should consider all the object. This is why we propose to use saliency measures that splits the image into object and background, such a way that our aggregation scheme could aggregate all of the important features of the query.

3   Image Representation

In this section, we describe our proposal to obtain image representations. Our approach follows the multidimensional aggregation and weighting scheme proposed in [6]. Furthermore, we extend this methodology and adapt it when we use a multi scale partition of the image like R-MAC.

This aggregation scheme, as explained in the Sect. 1 and depicted in Fig. 1, can be applied to any deep CNN. After extracting deep convolutional features from the last convolutional layer of a CNN, activation values are weighted both spatially and per channel before aggregate them to create a final vector. It is important to take into account that the convolutional layer can be of arbitrary size, and therefore avoid resizing and cropping the input image, allowing images of different aspect ratios to keep their spatial features intact.

Being $X \in \mathcal{R}^{M \times N \times D}$, the tensor of activations from a convolutional layer, these are the steps to generate an image representation vector:

1. **Compute spatial weighting factors.** For each location (i, j) in the feature maps calculate a weight, $\alpha_{i,j}$, that will be applied to each channel at that location.
2. **Compute channel weighting factors.** For each channel k, calculate a weight, β_k that will be applied to every location in that channel.
3. **Compute the weighted tensor of activations.** Transform the original tensor of activations X into a new weighted tensor X':

$$X'_{i,j,k} = \alpha_{i,j} \beta_k X_{i,j,k} \qquad (1)$$

4. **Perform aggregation.** Aggregate the new X' tensor of activations by channel to obtain a single vector of dimension $1 \times D$.
5. **Perform vector normalization.** The resulting vector is first normalized (l2-normalization). Then, PCA is applied to reduce the dimensionality and increment the discriminative power followed by a second normalization (l2-normalization).

3.1   Image Representation from Multi Scale Region Partition

In this section we extend the process of computing an image representation from a multi scale partition of a convolutional layer. The process of multi scale region generation of R-MAC [19] is as follows: with a convolutional activation tensor X, sample square regions, R, of specific scales in a sliding window manner with 40% overlap between neighbour windows, for all scales $s = 1, ..., S$. The region size at a specific scale can be calculated as: $R_s = 2\min(M, N)/(s+1)$, where M and N are width and height of each channel of X, respectively. To obtain a final vector representation, basically there is a new step 0 to build the regions and steps 3 and 4 of the process described previously are substituted by the following ones (Fig. 2):

0. **Generate regions** Rs. Generate regions for different scales, usually $s = 1, 2, 3$. For example, a region $R_p = X_{i=x1:x2, j=y1:y2, k=1:D}$ is the following activation tensor:

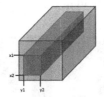

Fig. 2. Region $R_p = X_{i=x1:x2, j=y1:y2, k=1:D}$ from an activation tensor X.

3b. **Compute the weighted tensor of activations.** Transform the original tensor of activations X into a new weighted tensor X':
   a. **Compute the weighted tensor of a region.** Obtain a new weighted tensor Rs' for every Rs of the original activations tensor X:

$$Rs'_{i,j,k} = \alpha_{i,j}\beta_k Rs_{i,j,k} \qquad (2)$$

   b. **Perform region aggregation.** Aggregate the new Rs' tensor of region activations by channel to obtain a single vector of dimension $1 \times D$.
4b. **Perform global aggregation.** Aggregate all of the regional vectors of dimension $1 \times D$ into a single one.

Nonetheless, we would like to remark that R-MAC uniformly treats all regions of an image, even though only specific regions would be helpful to construct a discriminative global feature. We aim to address this issue, by weighting the regions by the spatial factor $\alpha_{i,j}$, and studying different global aggregations as the maximum or the average mean.

3.2   Saliency and Object Detection

It is well known that the accuracy of image search is maximized when object localization of the query Q is done over the original image $\mathbf{I}$. If the similarity is obtained from the region R of maximum similarity, then the corresponding similarity does not take into account all the visual content of image $\mathbf{I}$ and is therefore free from the influence of background clutter. However, the brute-force detection of the optimal region by exhaustive search is really expensive, as the number of possible regions is in $O(M^2N^2)$. Therefore, it is really interesting to obtain a spatial weight $\alpha_{i,j}$, which is able to discard background information.

Taking this consideration into account we propose to use a object detection oriented saliency measure [22], that is able to detect the complete area of the object and discard the background. Such measure, characterizes the spatial layout of image regions with respect to image boundaries and can distinguish between the object and the background at a high precision. The saliency measure is calculated in the original image, and then resized to $M \times N$ (the height and width of the tensor X). We finally apply a gaussian blurring to the resized saliency map to obtain a saliency map $\alpha_{i,j}$ as shown in Fig. 3.

Fig. 3. Saliency map examples. In each row is shown the saliency map generated from the saliency image of a given query.

4   Experimental Results

In this section we present the results obtained in three common image retrieval datasets, Oxford [14], Paris [15], and Holidays dataset [4]. The Oxford Buildings dataset consists of 5062 images with 11 different landmarks, each represented by 5 possible queries, Paris dataset is similar, created with 6412 Paris images, and Holidays dataset with 1491 images and 500 queries.

For each image, the tensor of activations X is the last pooling layer "pool5" obtained from a VGG16 pretrained network in Imagenet dataset (similar to [5,6,19] and [13]). The tensor X is of 512 channels, and proportional to the input image size, because we pass input images through the network with their original size. The tensor is processed following the scheme presented in Sect. 3 resulting in a 512 dimensions single vector per image. In Oxford experiments, Paris dataset is used for PCA purposes, whilst in Paris and Holidays dataset Oxford dataset is used.

For each image query, all of the images of the dataset are sorted according to their euclidean distance. Also a simple query expansion (QE) method is applied in Oxford and Paris dataset.

To evaluate the performance in the given queries of these datasets we use the mean average precision metric (mAP), because it is the standard procedure used in the literature.

4.1   Experiment 1: Global Pooling Aggregation

In this first experiment we evaluate different spatial weighting factors $\alpha_{i,j}$, including: Uniform weights (U), activations based weights [6] (A), our proposal based on saliency measure (SAL) and a Top-Down weighting matrix, in which pixels of the top rows have higher weight than pixels in the botton (TD). Also we evaluate two different channel weighting vectors: Uniform weights per channel (U) and weights based on the sparsity of the map (Sp) [6]. We also test different combination of weighting schemes by directly multiplying their weights.

In Table 1 is presented the performance of different aggregation schemes in the three proposed datasets. We can appreciate that the saliency method (SAL) [22] used as spatial weighting scheme is very helpful to obtain discriminative objects in the images. Moreover saliency can be combined with activations based spatial weights [6] that leads to a great performance improvement. Also we find that a simple weighting scheme (TD) based in the idea that images are taken in vertical position gives a boost when it is combined with any other spatial weight. In fact, the best performance is obtained when the three weighting schemes are joined.

Finally our results are in general better than [13] based also on saliency to weight features, although their approach is not directly comparable because they used a bag of features scheme.

In Figs. 4 and 5 are depicted the performance in all of the Oxford dataset queries and some queries examples with their similar images respectively.

Table 1. Comparison of different global pooling aggregations in Oxford, Paris and Holidays datasets.

Method	$\alpha_{i,j}$	β_k	Oxford		Paris		Holidays
			mAp	mAp (QE)	mAp	mAp (QE)	mAp
ucrow	U	U	0.659	0.705	0.757	0.827	0.811
crow [6]	A	S	0.672	0.715	0.787	0.855	0.825
Top-down	TD	U	0.702	0.756	0.781	0.847	0.789
Act-Top-down-Sp	TD*A	S	0.712	0.771	0.807	0.871	0.819
SAL	SAL	U	0.669	0.718	0.776	0.842	0.804
SAL-Sp	SAL	Sp	0.688	0.746	0.794	0.855	0.818
Act-SAL-Sp	A*SAL	Sp	0.688	0.747	0.801	0.861	0.824
SAL-Top-down	SAL*TD	U	0.710	0.778	0.786	0.853	0.799
Act-SAL-Top-down-Sp	Act*SAL*TD	Sp	0.727	**0.791**	**0.813**	**0.873**	**0.830**
BLCF-SalGAN [13]	SalGAN	U	**0.746**	0.778	0.812	0.830	—

4.2 Experiment 2: Region Pooling Aggregation

In this second experiment, we compare the performance of the spatial weighting methods when they are used in a multi region pooling scheme (Subsect. 3.1). Regions are extracted in three different scales, this results in about 20 regions per image (depending on the size of the image). Each region is transformed in a representation vector and then those vectors are combined. We test two different global aggregations, maximum and average mean to combine the region vectors.

Table 2. Comparison of different regional pooling aggregations in Oxford, Paris and Holidays datasets.

Method	Aggr.	Oxford		Paris		Holidays
		mAp	mAp(QE)	mAp	mAp(QE)	mAp
RMAC[a]	Avg	0.646	0.747	0.763	0.828	0.803
RA-ucrow	Avg	0.660	0.717	0.779	0.843	0.818
RA-crow [6]	Avg	0.674	0.730	0.805	0.866	**0.841**
RA-SAL	Avg	0.650	0.710	0.775	0.839	0.794
RA-SAL-Top-down	Avg	0.710	0.778	0.785	0.848	0.789
RA-Act-SAL-Sp	Avg	0.662	0.730	0.798	0.856	0.816
RA-Act-SAL-Top-down-Sp	Avg	0.697	0.785	0.811	0.867	0.826
RM-crow [6]	Max	0.666	0.724	0.789	0.857	0.825
RM-SAL	Max	0.665	0.733	0.775	0.838	0.799
RM-SAL-Top-down	Max	0.710	0.778	0.783	0.851	0.794
RM-Act-SAL-Sp	Max	0.682	0.756	0.800	0.858	0.818
RM-Act-SAL-Top-down-Sp	Max	**0.724**	**0.799**	**0.813**	**0.871**	0.821
RMAC [19]	Avg	0.661	—	0.83	—	—

[a] the performance obtained in our implementation of RMAC is different that [19] due to the normalization pipeline is different

Fig. 4. Performance comparison for Oxford dataset between Act-SAL-Top-down-Sp and ucrow aggregation schemes. In the title of each image is shown the performance obtained with uniform aggregation (ucrow) and the current performance of the Act-SAL-Top-down-Sp method. The square in the image represents the query region.

The results obtained are shown in Table 2. We can observe that using the multi scale representation in this aggregation scheme do not improve the performance in all of the cases studied. Furthermore it seems that depends on the dataset and the partial weights used. Also we have not a clear conclusion about using the maximum or the average mean as the global aggregation. However the best performance is obtained with the spatial weight as the combination of the proposed saliency, the activations based and the top down mask when the region vectors are combined with the maximum.

Table 3. State-of-the-art results.

Method	Dimensions	Oxford		Paris		Holidays
		mAp	mAp (QE)	mAp	mAp (QE)	mAp
Act-SAL-Top-down-Sp	512	0.727	0.791	0.813	**0.873**	**0.830**
RM-Act-SAL-Top-down-Sp	512	0.724	**0.799**	0.813	0.871	0.820
crow [6]	512	0.672	0.715	0.787	0.855	0.826
BLCF-SalGAN [13]	336	**0.746**	0.778	0.812	0.830	—
RMAC [19]	512	0.660	—	0.830	—	—
CAM [5]	512	0.736	0.760	0.855	0.873	—
SPoC [20]	256	0.531	—	—	—	—
Razavian [16]	32k	**0.843**	—	**0.853**	—	—

Fig. 5. Queries examples, In first row of each example is shown the nearest images to the query obtained with Act-SAL-Top-down-Sp, also in the title o each image is shown its previous rank position with ucrow aggregation. In the second row is shown the spatial weight as the product of saliency and the top-down weight.

4.3 State-of-the-Art-Results

Finally in Table 3, we compare our proposal with state-of-the-art results using off-the-self models. We achieve the state-of-the-art performance in similar experiments with crow [6], BLCF-SalGAN [13], RMAC [19] or CAM [5] or [16]. Another conclusion is that our proposed method is fitted to the Query Expansion process, such a way we obtain higher performance with QE than others methods which are better than ours without QE.

5   Conclusions

In this work we have presented a method to weight most important image regions in the process of obtaining a global descriptor for image retrieval. It is based on robust methodology that is able to split the image into object and background. We have showed that this spatial weighting scheme combined with an activation based measure and a simple top-down filter achieves higher performance (specially in Oxford and Paris) than other pre-trained single-pass methods. However, some future research should be done with respect to the aggregation method followed with a multi regional image representation.

Acknowledgment. This work is partially supported by the research services of Universidad Pública de Navarra and by the project TIN2016-77356-P (AEI/FEDER, UE).

References

1. Cao, J., Liu, L., Wang, P., Huang, Z., Shen, C., Shen, H.T.: Where to focus: query adaptive matching for instance retrieval using convolutional feature maps, pp. 1–10 (2016). arxiv:1606.06811
2. Gordo, A., Almazán, J., Revaud, J., Larlus, D.: End-to-end learning of deep visual representations for image retrieval. Int. J. Comput. Vis. **124**(2), 237–254 (2017). https://doi.org/10.1007/s11263-017-1016-8
3. Itti, L., Koch, C.: A saliency-based search mechanism for overt and covert shifts of visual attention. Vis. Res. **40**, 1489–1506 (2000)
4. Jegou, H., Douze, M., Schmid, C.: Hamming embedding and weak geometric consistency for large scale image search. In: Forsyth, D., Torr, P., Zisserman, A. (eds.) ECCV 2008. LNCS, vol. 5302, pp. 304–317. Springer, Heidelberg (2008). https://doi.org/10.1007/978-3-540-88682-2_24
5. Jimenez, A., Alvarez, J.M., Giro-i Nieto, X.: Class-weighted convolutional features for visual instance search. In: In 28th British Machine Vision Conference (BMVC), July 2017. arxiv:1707.02581
6. Kalantidis, Y., Mellina, C., Osindero, S.: Cross-dimensional weighting for aggregated deep convolutional features. In: Hua, G., Jégou, H. (eds.) ECCV 2016. LNCS, vol. 9913, pp. 685–701. Springer, Cham (2016). https://doi.org/10.1007/978-3-319-46604-0_48
7. Kim, J.: Regional attention based deep feature for image retrieval. In: BMVC, pp. 1–13 (2018)
8. Krizhevsky, A., Sutskever, I., Hinton., G.E.: AlexNet. In: Advances in Neural Information Processing Systems (2012). https://doi.org/10.1016/B978-008046518-0.00119-7
9. Laskar, Z., Kannala, J.: Context aware query image representation for particular object retrieval. In: Sharma, P., Bianchi, F.M. (eds.) SCIA 2017. LNCS, vol. 10270, pp. 88–99. Springer, Cham (2017). https://doi.org/10.1007/978-3-319-59129-2_8

10. Lazebnik, S., Schmid, C., Ponce, J.: Beyond bags of features: spatial pyramid matching for recognizing natural scene categories. In: Proceedings of the IEEE Computer Society Conference on Computer Vision and Pattern Recognition, vol. 2, pp. 2169–2178 (2006). https://doi.org/10.1109/CVPR.2006.68
11. Lowe, D.G.: Object recognition from local scale-invariant features. In: Proceedings of the Seventh IEEE International Conference on Computer Vision, vol. 2, pp. 1150–1157, September 1999. https://doi.org/10.1109/ICCV.1999.790410
12. Mohedano, E., McGuinness, K., Giro-I-Nieto, X., O'Connor, N.E.: Saliency weighted convolutional features for instance search. In: Proceedings - International Workshop on Content-Based Multimedia Indexing, 2018, September 2018. https://doi.org/10.1109/CBMI.2018.8516500
13. Mohedano, E., McGuinness, K., Giro-i Nieto, X., O'Connor, N.E.: Saliency weighted convolutional features for instance search, November 2017. arxiv:1711.10795
14. Philbin, J., Chum, O., Isard, M., Sivic, J., Zisserman, A.: Object retrieval with large vocabularies and fast spatial matching. In: Proceedings of the IEEE Conference on Computer Vision and Pattern Recognition (2007)
15. Philbin, J., Chum, O., Isard, M., Sivic, J., Zisserman, A.: Lost in quantization: improving particular object retrieval in large scale image databases. In: Proceedings of the IEEE Conference on Computer Vision and Pattern Recognition (2008)
16. Razavian A.S., Azizpour, H., Sullivan, J., Carlsson, S.: CNN features off-the-shelf: an astounding baseline for recognition. In: Proceedings of the IEEE International Conference on Computer Vision (2015)
17. Simeoni, O., Iscen, A., Tolias, G., Avrithis, Y., Chum, O.: Unsupervised object discovery for instance recognition. In: Proceedings - 2018 IEEE Winter Conference on Applications of Computer Vision, WACV 2018, January 2018, pp. 1745–1754 (2018). https://doi.org/10.1109/WACV.2018.00194
18. Simonyan, K., Zisserman, A.: Very deep convolutional networks for large-scale image recognition, September 2014. http://arxiv.org/abs/1409.1556
19. Tolias, G., Sicre, R., Jégou, H.: Particular object retrieval with integral max-pooling of CNN activations. In: ICL 2016 - International Conference on Learning Representations, May 2016, pp. 1–12, San Juan (2015). http://arxiv.org/abs/1511.05879
20. Yandex, A.B., Lempitsky, V.: Aggregating local deep features for image retrieval. In: Proceedings of the IEEE International Conference on Computer Vision, pp. 1269–1277 (2015). https://doi.org/10.1109/ICCV.2015.150
21. Zheng, L., Yang, Y., Tian, Q.: SIFT meets CNN: a decade survey of instance retrieval. IEEE Trans. Pattern Anal. Mach. Intell. **40**(5), 1224–1244 (2018). https://doi.org/10.1109/TPAMI.2017.2709749
22. Zhu, W., Liang, S., Wei, Y., Sun, J.: Saliency optimization from robust background detection. In: Proceedings of the IEEE Computer Society Conference on Computer Vision and Pattern Recognition, pp. 2814–2821 (2014). https://doi.org/10.1109/CVPR.2014.360

Impact of Pre-Processing on Recognition of Cursive Video Text

Ali Mirza, Imran Siddiqi$^{(\boxtimes)}$, Syed Ghulam Mustufa, and Mazahir Hussain

Bahria University, Islamabad, Pakistan
{alimirza,imran.siddiqi}@bahria.edu.pk, ghulam.mustufa31@gmail.com,
mazahir1109@gmail.com

Abstract. Recognition of text appearing in videos offers a number of interesting applications including retrieval systems, generation of user alerts on keywords and news summarization systems. Thanks to the recent advancements in deep learning, high text recognition rates have been reported in the recent years. An important step in training such systems is the pre-processing of images for effective feature learning and classification. This study investigates the impact of pre-processing on recognition of cursive video text using Urdu as a case study. The recognition engine relies on a combination of convolutional and long short-term memory networks followed by a connectionist temporal classification layer for sequence alignment. The system is fed with gray scale text line images directly as well as by segmenting the text from background using various thresholding techniques. Experimental study on a dataset of 12,000 text lines in cursive Urdu text reveals that appropriately pre-processing the text line images significantly improves the recognition rates.

Keywords: Cursive video text · Binarization ·
Convolutional neural networks (CNNs) ·
Long short-term memory networks (LSTMs)

1 Introduction

Semantic video retrieval has gained notable research attention in the recent years due to the rapid increase in the digital multimedia data. Typically, images and videos are annotated with different tags or keywords (Fig. 1) which are exploited by search engines for retrieval purposes. A limited set of descriptive tags, however, does not suffice to capture the rich information in images and videos. These limitations served as catalyst to drive the research in content based image and video retrieval systems. More specifically, in the context of video retrieval, smart retrieval systems focus on one or more of the following components.

- Visual content in the video such as persons, objects and buildings etc.
- Audio content such as spoken (key)words.

© Springer Nature Switzerland AG 2019
A. Morales et al. (Eds.): IbPRIA 2019, LNCS 11867, pp. 565–576, 2019.
https://doi.org/10.1007/978-3-030-31332-6_49

Fig. 1. Tags associated with a video are used for retrieval purposes

– Textual content which includes news tickers and subtitles etc.

Among these, we focus on the textual content in videos in the present study. Text appearing in videos can be localized and recognized to support keyword based indexing and retrieval applications. Furthermore, such systems can also be adapted to generate alerts on occurrence of specific keywords (breaking News for example). The development of such systems include two major components, detection and localization of textual content and recognition of text (Video Optical Character Recognition - VOCR), the later being the subject of our research.

Thanks to the recent advancements in deep learning techniques, error rates for tasks like object detection and recognition have dropped significantly. Many of the state-of-the-art object detectors have been adapted to localization of textual content encompassing both caption [27] and natural scene text [32]. The development of large-scale databases with labeled textual content has also been a significant milestone [11]. Likewise, recognition of text has also witnessed a renewed interest of the research community and the latest deep learning based techniques have been employed to develop robust recognition systems [5,8,31]. Despite these developments, recognition of cursive text remains a challenging problem. Characters in cursive scripts join to form partial words (ligatures) and character shapes vary depending upon their position within a partial word. Typical examples of cursive scripts include Arabic, Urdu, Persian, Pashto etc. The complexity of the problem is further enhanced if the text appears in video frames (rather than scanned document images). Typical challenges in recognition of video text include low resolution of text, non-homogeneous or complex backgrounds and false joining of adjacent characters into single components.

An important step in recognition of video text is the pre-processing of images. There has been a debate on whether to feed colored, grayscale or binarized images to the learning algorithm. This paper presents an analytical study to investigate the impact of pre-processing on recognition of cursive video text. More specifically, we employ a combination of convolutional neural networks (CNN) and bidirectional long short-term memory (LSTM) networks for recognition of cursive text. The hybrid CNN-LSTM combination is fed directly with gray scale text line images as well as by segmenting the text from background. For segmentation of text and background, global as well as a number of local thresholding techniques are studied. The study reveals that pre-processing the images appropriately prior to training the models results in enhanced recognition rates. We employ video text lines in cursive Urdu as a case study but the findings can be generalized to other cursive scripts as well.

This paper is organized as follows. The next section presents an overview of video text recognition in cursive scripts followed by an introduction to our dataset in Sect. 3. Section 4 introduces the pre-processing and the recognition techniques employed while Sect. 5 details the experimental setup, the reported results and the accompanying discussion. Finally, we provide our concluding remarks in Sect. 6 of the paper.

2 Related Work

Recognition of text, commonly known as Optical Character Recognition (OCR), has remained one of the most investigated pattern classification problems. Thanks to the research endeavors spanned over decades, state-of-the-art recognition systems have been developed for printed documents [12], handwriting [19], natural text in scene images [21] and artificial (caption) text appearing in videos [3].

As discussed earlier, cursive text offers a more challenging recognition problem due to the complexity of the script. Recognition techniques for cursive scripts are generally divided into holistic (segmentation-free) and analytical (segmentation-based) methods. Holistic techniques employ partial words as recognition units while analytical techniques aim to recognize individual characters which are either segmented explicitly or implicitly [8]. Implicit segmentation refers to feeding the text lines and ground truth transcriptions to the learning algorithm to itself learn the character shapes and segmentation points [14,15]. Such techniques have remained a popular choice of researchers as explicit segmentation of cursive text into characters is highly challenging.

Among notable studies on recognition of cursive video text, Zayene et al. [31] employs long short-term memory networks (LSTMS) to recognize Arabic text in video frames. The technique was evaluated on two datasets, ALIF [28] and ACTiV [30] and high recognition rates were reported. Halima et al. [7] present a system to localize and recognize Arabic text in video frames. The recognition engine exploits a set of statistical features with nearest neighbor classifer to recognize the partial words. In another comprehensive study [9], an end-to-end system is presented for recognition of Arabic text in videos and natural scenes. The system relies on a combination of CNN and RNN for recognition of text. Likewise, Yousfi et al. [28] employ CNNs with deep auto-encoders to compute features using multiple scales. The feature sequences are fed to a recurrent neural network for prediction of transcription. The technique is evaluated on collection of videos from a number of Arabic TV channels and reports promising recognition rates. In another interesting work [29], authors focus on improving the performance of LSTM based recognition engines by employing recurrent connectionist language models. An improvement of 16% in word recognition rates with respect to baseline methods is demonstrated by the introduction of the proposed models.

With reference to Urdu text, a number of robust techniques have been presented for recognition of printed document images. The holistic recognition techniques reported in the literature mostly employ hidden Markov models to recognize partial words (ligatures) [2]. A major issue in holistic techniques is the large number (in thousands) of ligature classes to be recognized. An effective technique is to separate the main body of ligatures from dots and diacritics to reduce the number of classes as a many partial words share the same main body and differ only in the number of positioning of dots and diacritics. After recognition, dots are re-associated with their parent main body component as a post-processing step [5].

Similar to Arabic text recognition, implicit segmentation based techniques have been widely employed for recognition of Urdu text as well. These techniques typically employ LSTMs with a Connectionist Temporal Classification (CTC) layer. The network is fed either with raw pixels [16] or with feature sequences extracted by a CNN [15]. The literature is relatively limited when it comes to recognition systems for Urdu text appearing in videos. A recent work by Tayyab et al. [25] employs bidirectional LSTMs to recognize news tickers in various Urdu news channels. In another related work, Hayat et al. [8] present a holistic technique to recognize Urdu ligatures from video text. Ligature images are first grouped into clusters and convolutional neural networks are trained to recognize the ligature classes. Though the system reports very high recognition rates, the number of ligature classes considered in this study is fairly small (few hundred only).

A critical review of the work on recognition of cursive scripts reveal that implicit segmentation based techniques have proven to be more effective as opposed to holistic recognition techniques. Such techniques not only avoid extraction of partial words from lines of text, they also do not require the training data to be prepared into cluster of partial words. The text lines and corresponding ground truth is directly fed to the learning algorithm making the technique simple yet effective. In our study, we have also chosen to employ an implicit segmentation based recognition technique. Prior to presenting its details, we first introduce the dataset considered in our work in the next section.

3 Dataset

Benchmark datasets have been developed (and labeled) for recognition of printed Urdu text. Two well-known such datasets include CLE [1] and UPTI [20] datasets which have been widely employed for evaluation of recognition systems targeting printed Urdu text. From the view point of video text, datasets like ALIF [28] and ACTiV [30] have been developed for cursive Arabic text. A small dataset of video frames containing artificial text in Urdu is presented in [24]. The number of text lines in the dataset, however, is fairly limited and cannot be employed to train deep neural networks. As a part of our endeavors towards the development of a comprehensive video retrieval engine, we are in the process of developing and labeling a large database of video frames with occurrences of artificial text.

We have collected more than 400 h of video from various News channels and presently, more than 10,000 video frames have been labeled. The ground truth information associated with each frame includes some meta data, location of each text line (bounding box), script information and the actual transcription of text. The dataset will be made publicly available once the labeling process is complete. More details on the dataset and the labeling process can be found in our previous work [13].

For the present study, we consider 12,000 text lines which are extracted from the video frames using ground truth information. Since the focus of this study is on recognition and not on localization, the localization information in the ground truth file is used to extract the text lines. For all experiments, 10,000 text lines are used in the training set and 2,000 in the test set. Sample text regions extracted from the frames are illustrated in Fig. 2.

Fig. 2. Sample text lines extracted from video frames

4   Methods

This section presents the details of the pre-processing and recognition techniques employed in our work. As discussed earlier, the key objective of this study is to investigate the impact of pre-processing on the recognition performance. The recognition engine is fed with gray-scale images as well as by extracting the text using various thresholding techniques. For recognition, a hybrid model of convolutional and long short-term memory networks is employed. Details on pre-processing and recognition are presented in the following.

4.1   Pre-Processing

Presenting the recognition engine with appropriate data is an important step that directly affects the recognition performance. Since the key task of the learning algorithm is to learn character shapes and boundaries, color information is generally discarded as it may falsely lead the algorithm to learn color information rather than the shapes. The idea is further strengthened by the fact that text is readable by humans without color information. Consequently, as a first step, all images are converted to gray scale. A major issue affecting the recognition performance is the non-homogeneous background of text as it can be seen from Fig. 2. Furthermore, the polarity of text can be bright text on dark background or dark text on bright background. The learning algorithm must be provided with images having a consistent text polarity. It is also known that binarizing the text lines can be useful but in some cases imperfect binarization can lead to deterioration in the recognition performance. These and similar issues served to be the motivation of our investigations in the current study.

We start with identifying the polarity of the text. For all experiments, we assume the convention of dark text on bright background. To detect the polarity of a given text line, we apply Canny edge detector on the gray scale image to detect blobs in the image. These blobs correspond to (approximate) text regions in the image. Region filling is applied to these blobs and the resulting image is used as a mask to extract the corresponding regions from the original gray scale image. We then compute the median gray value (Med_{text}) of the extracted blobs as well as the median gray value of the background (all pixels which do not belong to any blob), Med_{back}. If $Med_{text} < Med_{back}$ we have dark text on bright background and the polarity agrees with our assumed convention. On the other hand, if $Med_{text} > Med_{back}$, this corresponds to bright text on dark background. In such cases, the polarity of the image is reversed prior to any further processing. The process is summarized in Fig. 3.

Fig. 3. Identification of polarity of text (a): Original image (b): Gray scale image (c): Text blobs (d): Filled text blobs serving as a mask to extract corresponding blobs from the gray image; In this case $Med_{text} < Med_{back}$ hence the image is not inverted.

Once all text lines contain text in the same polarity, they can either be directly fed to the recognition module or first binarized to extract only the textual information. For binarization, we investigated a number of thresholding techniques. These include the Otsu's global thresholding method [18] as well as a number of local thresholding algorithms. The local thresholding algorithms are adaptive techniques where the threshold value of each pixel is computed as a function of the neighboring pixels. Most of these algorithms are inspired from the classical Niblack thresholding [17] where the threshold is computed as a function of the mean and standard deviation of the gray values in the neighborhood of a reference pixel. Other algorithms investigated in our study include Sauvola [22], Feng's [6] and Wolf's thresholding algorithm [26]. Prior to binarizing the images, we also apply a smoothing (median) filter on each text line to remove/suppress any noisy patterns in the image. Binarization results of applying various thresholding techniques to a sample text line image are illsutrated in Fig. 4. From the subjective analysis of these results, Wolf'a algorithm that was specifically proposed for low resolution video text seems to outperform other techniques. Nevertheless, it is hard to generalize from visual inspection of few sample images and the recognition rates on images generated by each of these techniques could be a better indicative of the effectiveness of the method.

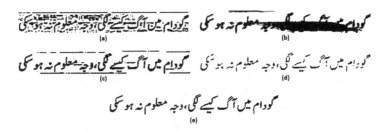

Fig. 4. Binarization results on a sample text line (a): Niblack (b): Ostu's Global Thresholding (c): Feng's Algorithm (d): Sauvola (e): Wolf's Algorithm

4.2   Text Recognition

As discussed earlier, we employ an implicit segmentation based recognition technique that does not require segmenting partial words into characters explicitly. More specifically, we employ convolutional neural networks to extract feature sequences from text line images. These sequences along with ground truth transcription are fed to a bidirectional long short-term memory network. This hybrid architecture is often referred to as C-RNN in the literature [4,10] and has shown promising results on recognition problems [23]. A CTC layer is also employed for alignment of ground truth transcription with the corresponding feature sequences. Figure 5 presents an overview of the recognition engine illsutrating C-RNN with CTC layer.

5   Experiments and Results

This section presents the details of the recognition results using various binarization techniques. As mentioned earlier, for all experiments, 10,000 text line images are used in the training set and 2,000 in the test set. The recognition engine outputs the predicted transcription of query text line. To quantify the recognition performance, we calculate the levenshtein distance between the predicted and the ground truth transcription to compute the character recognition rates.

For a meaningful comparison of various binarization techniques, we employ the same network architecture and the same set of hyper-parameters for each of the experiments. In the first experiment, we compute the recognition rates directly on the gray scale images of text lines and achieve a character recognition rate of 83.48% on the 2,000 test lines. Subsequently, we evaluated the recognition engine with lines binarized through the set of binarization techniques discussed

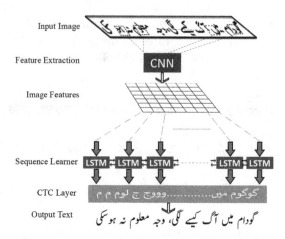

Fig. 5. Recognition of text line imags - C-RNN with CTC Layer

earlier. The recognition rates realized with various binarization techniques are summarized in Table 1.

A number of interesting observations can be made from the reported recognition rates. The gray scale text line images report higher recognition rates once compared to those obtained on text lines binarized using Niblack and Otsu's thresholding algorithms. This observation is consistent with out initial assessment of binarization algorithms where, in general, Niblack's binarization introduces a lot of noise in the binarized images while global thresholding fails once the text images have non-homogeneous backgrounds. The performance of Feng's and Sauvola's binarization methods is more or less similar reading 86.41% and 85.75% respectively. Text lines binarized using Wolf's algorithm report the highest recognition rate of 93.48%. This observation is also consistent with the subjective analysis of binarization techniques where Wolf's algorithm produced relatively cleaner versions of binarized images. Furthermore, the algorithm was specifically designed for binarization of video text (mostly in French) and the current results also validate its superiority over other techniques for recognition of cursive text as well.

To provide an insight into recognition errors, we illustrate (in Fig. 6) the predicted transcription of sample text line binarized using various thresholding techniques. Although all algorithms report recognition errors, it is interesting to note that due to noisy binarization in case of Niblack and Otsu's thresholding, the predicted and the actual characters are very different. On the other hand, the morphological similarity between the predicted and the actual characters seems to be high in case of other techniques, Wolf's algorithm for instance.

We also carried out a series of experiments to study the impact of size of training data on the recognition performance. Keeping the test size fixed to 2,000 lines of text, we varied the number of training text lines from 2,000 to 10,000. The corresponding recognition rates are illustrated in Fig. 7 where it can

Table 1. Summary of Recognition Rates on Grayscale and Different Binarizated Images

Image Type		Recognition Rate
Grayscale		83.48%
Binarized	Method	
	Niblack [17]	81.63%
	Otsu [18]	79.39%
	Feng [6]	86.41%
	Sauvola [22]	85.75%
	Wolf [26]	**93.48%**

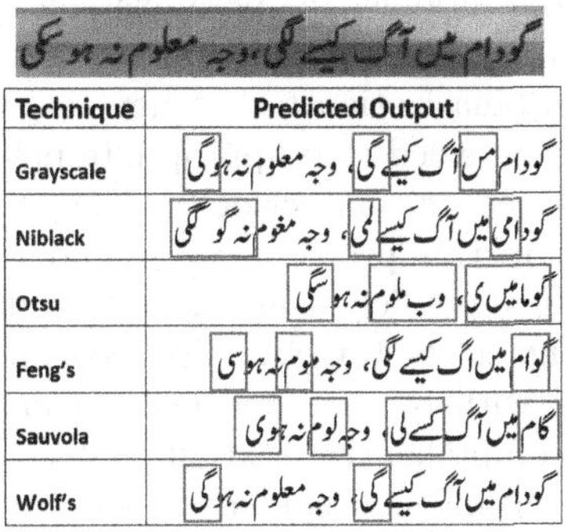

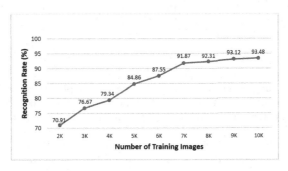

Fig. 6. Recognition errors in predicted transcription of a sample text line

Fig. 7. Recognition rates as a function of size of training data

be seen that the recognition rate being to stabilize from 7,000 lines of text which is a manageable size for such applications.

It can be concluded from the realized recognition rates that pre-processing is a critical step in recognition systems that has a significant impact on the recognition performance. Enhancing this step can lead to improved recognition rates. Binarizing the images appropriately resulted in an increase of 10% (from

83.48% to 93.48%) in recognition rate with respect to what is reported on the gray scale images. While deep learning based recognition systems represent state-of-the-art solutions, it is important to feed these systems with appropriately pre-processed data to achieve the performance that is at par with the expectations of commercial applications.

6   Conclusion

This paper investigated the impact of pre-processing on recognition of cursive video text. We employed Urdu text appearing in video frames as a case study but the findings can be generalized to other cursive scripts as well. The recognition engine comprises a combination of convolutional and long short-term memory networks followed by a connectionist temporal classification layer. The network is trained using text line images in gray scale as well as by segmenting text from background using various binarization techniques. Experiments on a a dataset of 12,000 text line images revealed that appropriate pre-processing of text lines significantly enhances the recognition performance.

In our further study on this problem, we intend to continue the labeling process to develop and make publicly available a large dataset of 30,000 labeled video frames. The present study targeted the recognition part only which is planned to be integrated with the text localization module. This in turn will allow development of a comprehensive textual content based retrieval system. From the view point of recognition, similar to pre-processing, we also aim to investigate the impact of data augmentation on the recognition performance.

Acknowledgment. This study is supported by IGNITE, National Technology Fund, Pakistan under grant number ICTRDF/TR&D/2014/35.

References

1. Center for language engineering. http://www.cle.org.pk, accessed: 2019-04-15
2. Ahmad, I., Mahmoud, S.A., Fink, G.A.: Open-vocabulary recognition of machine-printed Arabic text using hidden markov models. Pattern Recogn. **51**, 97–111 (2016)
3. Bhunia, A.K., Kumar, G., Roy, P.P., Balasubramanian, R., Pal, U.: Text recognition in scene image and video frame using color channel selection. Multimedia Tools Appl. **77**(7), 8551–8578 (2018)
4. Choi, K., Fazekas, G., Sandler, M., Cho, K.: Convolutional recurrent neural networks for music classification. In: 2017 IEEE International Conference on Acoustics, Speech and Signal Processing (ICASSP), pp. 2392–2396. IEEE (2017)
5. Din, I.U., Siddiqi, I., Khalid, S., Azam, T.: Segmentation-free optical character recognition for printed Urdu text. EURASIP J. Image Video Process. **2017**(1), 62 (2017)
6. Feng, M.L., Tan, Y.P.: Contrast adaptive binarization of low quality document images. IEICE Electron. Express **1**(16), 501–506 (2004)
7. Halima, M.B., Karray, H., Alimi, A.M.: Arabic text recognition in video sequences. arXiv preprint arXiv:1308.3243 (2013)

8. Hayat, U., Aatif, M., Zeeshan, O., Siddiqi, I.: Ligature recognition in Urdu caption text using deep convolutional neural networks. In: 2018 14th International Conference on Emerging Technologies (ICET), pp. 1–6. IEEE (2018)

9. Jain, M., Mathew, M., Jawahar, C.: Unconstrained scene text and video text recognition for Arabic script. In: 2017 1st International Workshop on Arabic Script Analysis and Recognition (ASAR), pp. 26–30. IEEE (2017)

10. Liang, M., Hu, X.: Recurrent convolutional neural network for object recognition. In: Proceedings of the IEEE Conference on Computer Vision and Pattern Recognition, pp. 3367–3375 (2015)

11. Lin, T.-Y., et al.: Microsoft COCO: common objects in context. In: Fleet, D., Pajdla, T., Schiele, B., Tuytelaars, T. (eds.) ECCV 2014. LNCS, vol. 8693, pp. 740–755. Springer, Cham (2014). https://doi.org/10.1007/978-3-319-10602-1_48

12. Märgner, V., Pal, U., Antonacopoulos, A., et al.: Document analysis and text recognition (2018)

13. Mirza, A., Fayyaz, M., Seher, Z., Siddiqi, I.: Urdu caption text detection using textural features. In: Proceedings of the 2nd Mediterranean Conference on Pattern Recognition and Artificial Intelligence, pp. 70–75. ACM (2018)

14. Naz, S., Umar, A.I., Ahmad, R., Ahmed, S.B., Shirazi, S.H., Razzak, M.I.: Urdu Nasta'liq text recognition system based on multi-dimensional recurrent neural network and statistical features. Neural Comput. Appl. 28(2), 219–231 (2017)

15. Naz, S., et al.: Urdu Nastaliq recognition using convolutional-recursive deep learning. Neurocomputing 243, 80–87 (2017)

16. Naz, S., Umar, A.I., Ahmed, R., Razzak, M.I., Rashid, S.F., Shafait, F.: Urdu Nasta'liq text recognition using implicit segmentation based on multi-dimensional long short term memory neural networks. SpringerPlus 5(1), 2010 (2016)

17. Niblack, W., et al.: An Introduction to Digital Image Processing, vol. 34. Prentice-Hall, Englewood Cliffs (1986)

18. Otsu, N.: A threshold selection method from gray-level histograms. IEEE Trans. Syst. Man Cybern. 9(1), 62–66 (1979)

19. Plamondon, R., Srihari, S.N.: Online and off-line handwriting recognition: a comprehensive survey. IEEE Trans. Pattern Anal. Mach. Intell. 22(1), 63–84 (2000)

20. Sabbour, N., Shafait, F.: A segmentation-free approach to Arabic and Urdu OCR. In: IS&T/SPIE Electronic Imaging, p. 86580N. International Society for Optics and Photonics (2013)

21. Saranya, K.C., Singhal, V.: Real-time prototype of driver assistance system for indian road signs. In: Reddy, M.S., Viswanath, K., K.M., S.P. (eds.) International Proceedings on Advances in Soft Computing, Intelligent Systems and Applications. AISC, vol. 628, pp. 147–155. Springer, Singapore (2018). https://doi.org/10.1007/978-981-10-5272-9_14

22. Sauvola, J., Pietikäinen, M.: Adaptive document image binarization. Pattern Recogn. 33(2), 225–236 (2000)

23. Shi, B., Bai, X., Yao, C.: An end-to-end trainable neural network for image-based sequence recognition and its application to scene text recognition. IEEE Trans. Pattern Anal. Mach. Intell. 39(11), 2298–2304 (2017)

24. Siddiqi, I., Raza, A.: A database of artificial Urdu text in video images with semi-automatic text line labeling scheme. In: MMEDIA 2012, The Fourth International Conferences on Advances in Multimedia, pp. 75–81 (2012)

25. Tayyab, B.U., Naeem, M.F., Ul-Hasan, A., Shafait, F., et al.: A multi-faceted OCR framework for artificial Urdu news ticker text recognition. In: 2018 13th IAPR International Workshop on Document Analysis Systems (DAS), pp. 211–216. IEEE (2018)

26. Wolf, C., Jolion, J.M.: Extraction and recognition of artificial text in multimedia documents. Formal Pattern Anal. Appl. **6**(4), 309–326 (2004)
27. Yan, X., et al.: End-to-end subtitle detection and recognition for videos in East Asian Languages via CNN ensemble. Signal Process. Image Commun. **60**, 131–143 (2018)
28. Yousfi, S., Berrani, S.A., Garcia, C.: Deep learning and recurrent connectionist-based approaches for Arabic text recognition in videos. In: 2015 13th International Conference on Document Analysis and Recognition (ICDAR), pp. 1026–1030. IEEE (2015)
29. Yousfi, S., Berrani, S.A., Garcia, C.: Contribution of recurrent connectionist language models in improving LSTM-based arabic text recognition in videos. Pattern Recogn. **64**, 245–254 (2017)
30. Zayene, O., Hennebert, J., Touj, S.M., Ingold, R., Amara, N.E.B.: A dataset for Arabic text detection, tracking and recognition in news videos - AcTiV. In: 2015 13th International Conference on Document Analysis and Recognition (ICDAR) (2015)
31. Zayene, O., Touj, S.M., Hennebert, J., Ingold, R., Amara, N.E.B.: Multi-dimensional long short-term memory networks for artificial Arabic text recognition in news video. IET Comput. Vision **12**(5), 710–719 (2018)
32. Zhou, X., et al.: East: an efficient and accurate scene text detector. In: Proceedings of the CVPR, pp. 2642–2651 (2017)

Image Feature Detection Based on Phase Congruency by Monogenic Filters with New Noise Estimation

Carlos Jacanamejoy Jamioy[1,2,3(✉)] (ID), Nohora Meneses-Casas[1,2,3] (ID), and Manuel G. Forero[1,3] (ID)

[1] Facultad de Ingeniería, Universidad de Ibagué, Ibagué, Colombia
{carlos.jacanamejoy,nohora.meneses,manuel.forero}@unibague.edu.co
[2] Facultad de Ciencias Naturales y Matemáticas, Universidad de Ibagué, Ibagué, Colombia
[3] Universidad de Ibagué, Carrera 22 Calle 67 B/Ambalá, Ibagué, Colombia

Abstract. Phase congruency is a relative unknown and powerful image processing technique for segmentation, having been used in diatom image processing, microscopic algae found in water and used to evaluate its quality. However, an important limitation of phase congruence is its sensitivity to noise. To prevent noise from affecting segmentation results, a good noise level estimation is necessary. It can be done with the analysis of the image of local energy. In this paper, we propose the use of the Weibull distribution to estimate the noise profile of the local energy image. The results are compared, in diatom images, with those obtained with the commonly employed Rayleigh distribution and the exponential. The results showed that the Weibull distribution allows a better estimation of the noise level.

Keywords: Image segmentation · Phase congruency · Weibull distribution · Diatom · Noise estimation · Rayleigh distribution · Exponetial distribution · Noise rejection

1 Introduction

The automatic detection of diatoms is a task of great interest for the scientific community, since it allows to evaluate the quality of water. In this field, the ADIAC project stands out, whose work was pioneering in the recognition of diatoms using image processing techniques [4]. Since its inception, the cell walls detection has been an important task, because it is used to locate and separate diatoms from the background [4,9,27]. Currently, it is still a challenge to detect diatoms in water samples that usually include debris and flocs. Therefore, it is a field of great interest that is still being studied [17].

Phase congruency (PC) is a technique used in diatom segmentation [27]. Kovesi was a pioneer in taking the PC to practice in image processing. His contributions corresponded to the possibility of calculating it for two-dimensional

© Springer Nature Switzerland AG 2019
A. Morales et al. (Eds.): IbPRIA 2019, LNCS 11867, pp. 577–588, 2019.
https://doi.org/10.1007/978-3-030-31332-6_50

signals, lower sensitivity to noise and a good location of the regions in which it occurs [15]. This technique allows to weight the important characteristics of the image, independent of the intensity of the signal with values from zero to one, so it is possible to apply a global threshold level to identify the regions of interest.

In previous work, Jacanamejoy and Forero [13] presented a modification of the PC method, where they expand the bandwidth of the filter bank, in order to improve the detection of very close features, which has as a negative consequence a greater sensitivity to noise. For this reason, the noise estimation technique proposed by Kovesi is inappropriate in this case. Therefore, in this work a new noise estimation method is proposed, that is more effective than the previous one, being appropriate in both situations.

This paper presents in Sect. 2 the PC technique proposed by Kovesi. In Sect. 3 the materials and methods, required to define a new way of calculating the noise level, are presented. The results are analyzed in Sect. 4 and the conclusions in Sect. 5.

2   Phase Congruency

The phase $\overline{\phi}(x)$ that maximizes Eq. (1), defined in terms of the Fourier components A_n, of a signal in the position x, allows to determine the PC [23]. Each component defines a different η scale, where the smallest scale, $\eta = 1$, is determined by the largest component, $n = N$. The PC is given by:

$$PC(x) = max \; _{\overline{\phi}(x)\in[0,2\pi]} \frac{\sum_{n=1}^{N} A_n \cos\left(\phi_n(x) - \overline{\phi}(x)\right)}{\sum_{n=1}^{N} A_n} \tag{1}$$

where $\phi_n(x)$ corresponds to the phase of the component n. However, Eq. (1) is not easy to implement, and much more so when it comes to images. Therefore, to solve this problem, the local energy $E(x)$ is calculated instead, which is directly proportional to the PC [29]. Thus, the precise calculation of $E(x)$ is essential.

2.1   Local Energy

Equation (2) shows the existing relationship between energy $E(x)$ and $PC(x)$ in one dimensional signals, proposed by [29].

$$E(x) = PC(x) \sum_{n=1}^{N} A_n(x) \tag{2}$$

To find the PC from the relationship given in Eq. (2), the calculation of the local energy $E(x)$ and the components A_n is done, mathematically expressed as

$$E(x) = \sqrt{\left(\sum_{n=1}^{N} e_n(x)\right)^2 + \left(\sum_{n=1}^{N} o_n(x)\right)^2} \tag{3}$$

and

$$A_n(x) = \sqrt{e_n(x)^2 + o_n(x)^2}. \tag{4}$$

where $e_n(x)$ and o_n are the n-th responses to the odd and even odd quadrature filters respectively [15]. Figure 1a illustrates the geometric relationship between local energy, frequency components and phase congruence and Fig. 1b the representation of the PC as a triangular inequality, where the $\sum_n A_n(x)$ is always greater than or equal to $E(x)$.

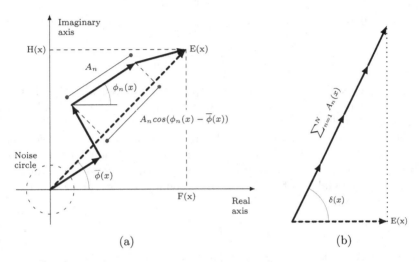

(a)   (b)

Fig. 1. (a) Relationship between phase congruency, local energy, and the sum of the Fourier amplitudes, adapted from [15]. (b) Representation of the PC by a triangle inequality where the $\sum_n A_n(x)$ is always greater than or equal to $E(x)$.

2.2   Calculation of Phase Congruence

The calculation of the components $e_n(x)$ and $o_n(x)$ is the computationally most expensive part of the PC method. Initially, Kovesi used wavelet filters to calculate the PC [15], which is inefficient since a large number of filters are required to obtain the different directions and frequency components. A more efficient alternative was proposed by Felsberg using monogenic filters, which result from the extension of the Hilbert transform to two dimensions [6], although its practical application was not immediate. Later, Kovesi implemented a software version of the PC employing monogenic filters. This code is available on the internet and it is compatible with Matlab and Octave [16]. Likewise, Li Juan formalized the methodology for calculating the PC based on monogenic filters [18]. However, although the PC implementation based on these filters is much more efficient, there are still new publications from different areas that employ the PC implementation based on wavelets [2,5,24,28,30–32].

In one-dimensional signals, $e_\eta(x)$ and $o_\eta(x)$ are obtained as a result of the convolution of the original signal with a pair of wavelets of even and odd symmetry at the scale η [15], then, the conversion between scales and components is given by $\eta = N - n + 1$.

In 2D signals, it is more appropriate to use monogenic filters. In this case, log-Gabor filters are employed, in which the transfer function is mathematically expressed as:

$$G(\omega) = exp\left(\frac{-(\log(\omega/\omega_0))^2}{2(\log(\sigma_o))^2}\right) \tag{5}$$

where σ_0 defines the filter bandwidth and ω_0 the central frequency given by:

$$\omega_o = \frac{1}{\lambda_{min}\, m^{N-n}} = \frac{1}{\lambda_{min}\, m^{\eta-1}} \tag{6}$$

λ_{min} is the length of the signal in the space x associated with the filter with the highest frequency, n the n-th frequency component, η the η-th scale and m the scale factor between consecutive filters.

When the log-Gabor filter is extended to two dimensions, a variable change is done, $\omega = |u|$, where $u = (u_1, u_2)$ is the two-dimensional frequency, and $G : \mathbb{R}^2 \to \mathbb{R}$. Then, $e_n(x)$ is obtained as a result of the convolution of the image $I(x)$ with the log-Gabor filter of the n-th component $G_n(x)$, being $x = (x_1, x_2)$ the image coordinates, ie,

$$e_n(x) = I(x) * G_n(x). \tag{7}$$

Once $e_n(x)$ is calculated by using the two-dimensional Hilbert transform [7], $o_n(x)$ is found from the equation:

$$o_n(x) = -\frac{x}{2\pi|x|^3} * e_n(x). \tag{8}$$

It is important to note that the image $I(x)$ must not have a zero frequency component. To eliminate it, the technique proposed by [21] is employed. Although $e_n(x)$ generates values in $\mathbb{R}$, $o_n(x)$ can take values in $\mathbb{R}^2$. Therefore, when using $o_n(x)$ in Eqs. (3) and (4), only its magnitude should be used, i.e., A_n and E are redefined as:

$$A_n(x) = \sqrt{e_n(x)^2 + |o_n(x)|^2}, \tag{9}$$

$$E(x) = \sqrt{\left(\sum_{n=1}^{N} e_n(x)\right)^2 + \left(\sum_{n=1}^{N} |o_n(x)|\right)^2}, \tag{10}$$

As it can be seen in Eqs. (9) and (10), $A_n(x)$ and $E(x)$ only generate real values. Therefore, all the equations that are defined from A_n and E, that were developed for one-dimensional signals, also works in two dimensions.

In addition to the calculation of $e_n(x)$ and $o_n(x)$, the adaptation with monogenic filters [16] has additional changes indicated in Eq. (11). In this way, the calculation of the PC has three factors: a PC weighting factor fixed according to the frequency band $W(x)$, the simple expression to calculate the PC, and a term to avoid the generation of erroneous PCs due to noise.

$$PC(x) = W(x).\lfloor 1 - \alpha |\delta(x)| \rfloor . \frac{\lfloor E(x) - T \rfloor}{E(x) + \varepsilon} \tag{11}$$

where,

$$W(x) = \frac{1}{1 + \exp\left(\gamma(c - s(x))\right)}, \tag{12}$$

$$s(x) = \frac{1}{N} \left(\frac{\sum_{n=1}^{N} A_n(x)}{\varepsilon + A_{max}(x)} \right), \tag{13}$$

$W(x)$ is a sigmoid function, where $s(x)$ is the measure of the dispersion corresponding to the frequency spectrum of different components, c is the cutoff value of the filter response wideband (spread), below which phase congruency values become penalized, and γ is a gain factor that controls the sharpness of the cutoff [15].

The second term of Eq. (11), corresponding to the simple quantization of the PC, generates values between zero and one, only for small values of $\delta(x)$, the angle of the right triangle formed from the triangular inequality illustrated in Fig. 1b, and α limits the range of $\delta(x)$ that is considered, setting the sensitivity of the PC.

The noise compensation, given by the expression $\lfloor E(x) - T \rfloor / (E(x) + \varepsilon$, causes the term to be zero when the $E(x) \leq T$. The value of T is set according to the image noise level. The constant ε corresponds to a small value that avoids division by zero, and appears in the Eqs. (11) and (13). More detailed information about the first and third factors of Eq. (11) is found in [15], and for the second in [16].

2.3   Noise Estimation

The implementation of Eq. (11) developed by Kovesi [16], and denoted by $PC_k(x)$, estimates the noise ratio as $T = \mu_R + k\sigma_R$, where μ_R and σ_R are the mean and variance of the magnitude of the energy noise vector and k is a factor empirically found to adjust T depending on the case. Kovesi [15] fixes the energy image noise magnitude distribution to a Rayleigh function, to find the parameters μ_R and σ_R.

The probability density function of the Rayleigh distribution is given by:

$$R(x; \sigma_G) = \frac{x}{\sigma_G^2} \exp\left(\frac{-x^2}{2\sigma_G^2}\right), \tag{14}$$

where the mean and variance are given by:

$$\mu_R = \sigma_G \sqrt{\frac{\pi}{2}}, \quad \text{and} \quad \sigma_R^2 = \frac{4 - \pi}{2}\sigma_G^2, \tag{15}$$

and σ_G is the mode of the Rayleigh distribution.

Kovesi proposes to calculate σ_G by using the mode of the component $A_N(x)$, denominated τ [14]. By performing a simple approach, the estimated noise response at successive filters is scaled, inversely proportional to the bandwidth. In this way, σ_G can be expressed by a simple geometric sum:

$$\sigma_G = \sum_{n=0}^{N-1} \tau \left(\frac{1}{m}\right)^n = \tau \frac{1 - (1/m)^N}{1 - (1/m)}, \tag{16}$$

In his webpage, Kovesi proposes two different ways of calculating τ [16]. In the first one, it corresponds to the mode of $A_N(x)$, as it was mentioned before. In the second one, it is assumed that $A_N(x)$ fixes a Rayleigh distribution, so that:

$$\tau = \frac{\text{median}(A_N(x))}{\sqrt{\ln(4)}}, \tag{17}$$

This second form is more robust, since it does not depend on a single value of $A_N(x)$, but on the data set. Thus, to find an adequate value of the noise threshold T, the mode of $A_N(x)$ and the scale factor m between successive filters are taken into account. Therefore, according to (15) and (16) τ, m and k define T.

It is important to clarify that estimating adequate values of T is possible if the following three assumptions are done: image noise is additive, a constant noise power spectrum, and features, as edges, occur only at isolated locations of the image [15]. This latter requirement may not be as strict as the parameters σ_o and α are adjusted, but since there is a compromise between the sensitivity of the PC to nearby edges and the response to noise, the choice of these parameters is not trivial [13]. For this reason, a new method to find a more accurate T to rule out noise is proposed.

3 Weibull Distribution

In many studies, Gaussian, Rayleigh, and Exponential distributions have been used as image models [1]. For example, the luminance within shadow regions in sonar imagery is well modeled by the Gaussian distribution, while the Rayleigh distribution [25], introduced in 1880, is more accurate in the reverberation regions [20], Martin et al. [19] analyzed level set implementation of region snakes based on the maximum likelihood method for different noise models that belong to the exponential family.

These distributions can be worked from a single distribution called Weibull with probability density function (pdf)

$$f(x; \lambda, \zeta) = \frac{\zeta}{\lambda} \left(\frac{x}{\lambda}\right)^{\zeta-1} e^{-(x/\lambda)^\zeta} \tag{18}$$

and cumulative distribution function (cdf)

$$F(x) = 1 - e^{-(x/\lambda)^\zeta} \tag{19}$$

where $\lambda > 0$ is the scale parameter and $\zeta > 0$ is the shape parameter of the distribution. The Weibull distribution becomes Exponential or Rayleigh depending on the parameters in Eq. (18). In this way, if $\zeta = 1$, the Weibull distribution is an Exponential one and, if $\zeta = 2$ is a Rayleigh one [8,22].

It has been proved theoretically and experimentally verified that the first-order derivatives of a wide variety of textures follow a Weibull distribution [1,10,12]. A study on 45,000 photographs [12], taken from the Curet database of natural textures [3], revealed that 60% of all images have strict contrast distributions in the form of Weibull and the remaining 40% has a distribution close to Weibull or is highly regular. In 2009, Scholte et al. suggested the brain models the image information like a Weibull distribution [26], i.e., the parameters of a Weibull distribution inform the brain about the spatial coherence of the perceived scene. However, the model is only valid for a limited amount of natural images [12] and the parameters of the Weibull distribution are sensitive to the conditions of the image such as illumination, enlargement of the camera and resolution power, and texture orientation [11]. Still, the Weibull distribution is considered a good model for image segmentation and versatile enough to represent a wide variety of images [1]. Therefore, the Weibull distribution is a general model that be can used to estimate the background in images, i.e., the Weibull distribution can be used to generalize the different gray levels distributions of the noise in an energy image, being its shape parameter very relevant.

4 Material

To develop and initially evaluate the proposed method the Kovesi code [16] was executed in Octave and 253 images of diatoms, taken from the ADIAC database [4], were used, along with a synthetic image shown in Fig. 2a. The algorithm was implemented in Java, as a plugin of the free access software ImageJ.

5 Proposed Method

The information distribution of an image can be determined by its local energy. If the local energy is represented by means of a monochromatic image, information can be quantified in grey levels, where pixels with the highest values correspond to regions with most information (edges, ridges) and pixels close to zero to regions of little interest, where the ratio signal-to-noise is very low and the PC must not be calculated. Two examples of local-energy images and their histograms are shown in Fig. 2c, d, g and h.

5.1 Weibull Approximation and Threshold Estimation

As it can be seen in Fig. 2d and h, the local energy function shape of the background is either Exponential ($\zeta \approx 1$), when the image has little noise, or Rayleigh ($\zeta \approx 2$), when the image is highly contaminated with Gaussian noise, respectively.

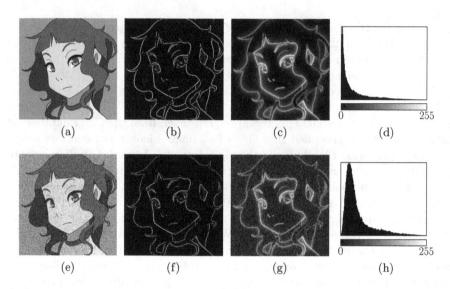

Fig. 2. (a) Sintetic image. (b) PC. (c) Local energy. (d) Histogram of the local energy. (e) Sintetic image with noise. (f) PC. (g) Local energy. (h) Histogram of the local energy.

Once the image representation function is established, it is necessary to find an adequate threshold value to rule out noise variations. As mentioned above, the local energy is higher in the regions of interest with respect to the background. Then, it is possible to determine a threshold value that allows the segmentation of the objects from the background. Thus, the gray level distribution of the local energy image is given by the Weibull distribution that corresponds to the background, and the region of interest that belongs to another distribution, as illustrated in Fig. 2. Therefore, the threshold must be located at an intermediate point between these two distributions.

A quick way to estimate an appropriate threshold, above which phase congruence can be calculated, is to find a value proportional to the gray level mode of the local-energy image histogram. From Eq. (19), we estimate a threshold value depending on the amount of noise we want to eliminate. In this way, we define the threshold level x_u as a product between the factor p and the mode x_m, i.e., $x_u = p x_m$.

$$x_m = \lambda \left(\frac{\zeta - 1}{\zeta} \right)^{1/\zeta} \tag{20}$$

$$F(x_u) = 1 - exp\left(\frac{p^{\zeta}(1 - \zeta)}{\zeta} \right) \tag{21}$$

The amount of noise to be discarded taking into account the threshold x_u, according to the (19) is given by (21). Therefore, to discard more than 95% noise, if $\zeta \approx 1.1$ a factor $p \approx 25$ is required, and if $\zeta \approx 2$ then $p \approx 3$.

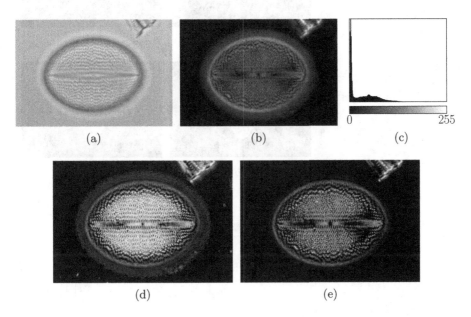

(a)   (b)   (c)

(d)   (e)

Fig. 3. (a) Diatom image. (b) Local energy. (c) Histogram of local energy.(d) PC by noise estimation with Kovesi algorithm. (e) PC by noise estimation proposed in this work.

6   Results

Figure 3 illustrates the results obtained by using Kovesi's method and the technique proposed in this work. In this example, since the background local-energy histogram shape, shown in Fig. 3a, approximates an exponential distribution, a factor $p = 25$ was employed for noise estimation. Other examples are shown in Fig. 4, where the factor values p were chosen according to the background local-energy shape. As can be seen, the proposed method allows obtaining better results. Diatoms are well detected, edges are better defined with a lower amount of noise.

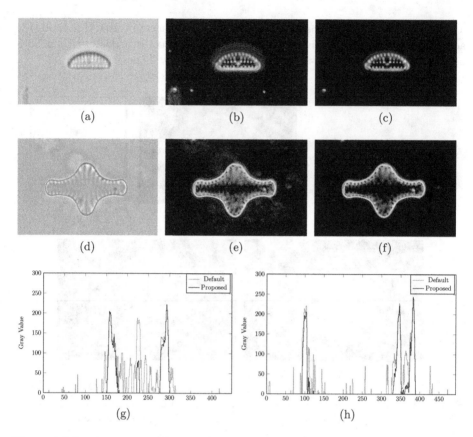

Fig. 4. (a) Diatom image. (b) PC by noise estimation with Kovesi algoritm. (c) PC with $p = 10$. (d) Diatom image. (e) PC by noise estimation with Kovesi algoritm. (f) PC with $p = 4$. (g) Horizontal profile of (b) and (c). (h) Horizontal profile of (e) and (f).

7   Conclusions

Phase congruency is a powerful image processing technique for segmentation. However, an important limitation is its sensitivity to noise. Therefore, to prevent noise from affecting segmentation results, a new noise level estimation method was proposed. The Weibull distribution of the local energy image was employed to estimate the noise profile and a threshold was proposed as a proportion of the local energy histogram mode. The results showed that the Weibull distribution allows a better estimation of the noise level.

By means of the proposed technique, it is possible to accurately identify the amount of noise to be discarded. Additionally, it allows estimating the compromise between the percentage of the region of interest to be discarded against the noise to be handled.

It is also worth mentioning that, in future, an automatic way to find the threshold value could be found by effectively calculating the noise shape parameter from the local-energy image histogram.

Acknowledgments. This work was supported by project 19-488-INT Universidad de Ibagué.

References

1. Ayed, I.B., Hennane, N., Mitiche, A.: Unsupervised variational image segmentation/classification using a weibull observation model. IEEE Trans. Image Process. **15**(11), 3431–3439 (2006)
2. Cinar, A., et al.: An autonomous surface discontinuity detection and quantification method by digital image correlation and phase congruency. Opt. Lasers Eng. **96**, 94–106 (2017)
3. Dana, K.J., Van Ginneken, B., Nayar, S.K., Koenderink, J.J.: Reflectance and texture of real-world surfaces. ACM Trans. Graph. (TOG) **18**(1), 1–34 (1999)
4. Du Buf, H., et al.: Diatom identification: a double challenge called ADIAC. In: 1999 Proceedings of International Conference on Image Analysis and Processing, pp. 734–739. IEEE (1999)
5. Fan, J., Wu, Y., Li, M., Liang, W., Cao, Y.: SAR and optical image registration using nonlinear diffusion and phase congruency structural descriptor. IEEE Trans. Geosci. Rem. Sens. **56**, 5368–5379 (2018)
6. Felsberg, M., Sommer, G.: A new extension of linear signal processing for estimating local properties and detecting features. In: Sommer, G., Krüger, N., Perwass, C. (eds.) Mustererkennung 2000. Informatik aktuell, pp. 195–202. Springer, Heidelberg (2000). https://doi.org/10.1007/978-3-642-59802-9_25
7. Felsberg, M., Sommer, G.: The monogenic signal. IEEE Trans. Sig. Process. **49**(12), 3136–3144 (2001)
8. Ganji, M., Bevrani, H., Hami Golzar, N., Zabihi, S.: The weibull-rayleigh distribution, some properties, and applications. J. Math. Sci. **218**(3), 269–277 (2016)
9. Gelzinis, A., Verikas, A., Vaiciukynas, E., Bacauskiene, M.: A novel technique to extract accurate cell contours applied for segmentation of phytoplankton images. Mach. Vis. Appl. **26**(2–3), 305–315 (2015)
10. Geusebroek, J.M., Smeulders, A.W.: Fragmentation in the vision of scenes. In: Proceedings Ninth IEEE International Conference on Computer Vision, p. 130. IEEE (2003)
11. Geusebroek, J.M., Smeulders, A.W.: A six-stimulus theory for stochastic texture. Int. J. Comput. Vis. **62**(1–2), 7–16 (2005)
12. Geusebroek, J.M., Smeulders, A.W., et al.: A physical explanation for natural image statistics. In: Proceedings of the 2nd International Workshop on Texture Analysis and Synthesis (Texture 2002), pp. 47–52. Heriot-Watt University (2002)
13. Jacanamejoy, C.A., Forero, M.G.: A note on the phase congruence method in image analysis. In: Vera-Rodriguez, R., Fierrez, J., Morales, A. (eds.) CIARP 2018. LNCS, vol. 11401, pp. 384–391. Springer, Cham (2019). https://doi.org/10.1007/978-3-030-13469-3_45
14. Kovesi, P.: Invariant measures of image features from phase information. Ph.D. thesis, University of Western Australia (1996)

15. Kovesi, P.: Image features from phase congruency. Videre: J. Comput. Vis. Res. **1**(3), 1–26 (1999)
16. Kovesi, P.: Matlab and octave functions for computer vision and image processing (2013). http://www.peterkovesi.com/matlabfns/#phasecong
17. Libreros, J., Bueno, G., Trujillo, M., Ospina, M.: Diatom segmentation in water resources. In: Serrano C., J.E., Martínez-Santos, J.C. (eds.) CCC 2018. CCIS, vol. 885, pp. 83–97. Springer, Cham (2018). https://doi.org/10.1007/978-3-319-98998-3_7
18. Lijuan, W., Changsheng, Z., Ziyu, L., Bin, S., Haiyong, T.: Image feature detection based on phase congruency by monogenic filters. In: The 26th Chinese Control and Decision Conference (2014 CCDC), pp. 2033–2038. IEEE (2014)
19. Martin, P., Réfrégier, P., Goudail, F., Guérault, F.: Influence of the noise model on level set active contour segmentation. IEEE Trans. Pattern Anal. Mach. Intell. **26**(6), 799–803 (2004)
20. Mignotte, M., Collet, C., Perez, P., Bouthemy, P.: Sonar image segmentation using an unsupervised hierarchical MRF model. IEEE Trans. Image Process. **9**(7), 1216–1231 (2000)
21. Moisan, L.: Periodic plus smooth image decomposition. J. Math. Imaging Vis. **39**(2), 161–179 (2011)
22. Montgomery, D.C., Runger, G.C.: Applied Statistics and Probability for Engineers. Wiley, Hoboken (2010)
23. Morrone, M.C., Owens, R.A.: Feature detection from local energy. Pattern Recogn. Lett. **6**(5), 303–313 (1987)
24. Mouats, T., Aouf, N.: Multimodal stereo correspondence based on phase congruency and edge histogram descriptor. In: Proceedings of the 16th International Conference on Information Fusion, pp. 1981–1987. IEEE (2013)
25. Rayleigh, L.: XII. On the resultant of a large number of vibrations of the same pitch and of arbitrary phase. Lond. Edinb. Dublin Philos. Mag. J. Sci. **10**(60), 73–78 (1880)
26. Scholte, H.S., Ghebreab, S., Waldorp, L., Smeulders, A.W., Lamme, V.A.: Brain responses strongly correlate with weibull image statistics when processing natural images. J. Vis. **9**(4), 29–29 (2009)
27. Sosik, H.M., Olson, R.J.: Automated taxonomic classification of phytoplankton sampled with imaging-in-flow cytometry. Limnol. Oceanogr. Methods **5**(6), 204–216 (2007)
28. Tian, Y.: Autofocus using image phase congruency. Opt. Express **19**(1), 261–270 (2011)
29. Venkatesh, S., Owens, R.: An energy feature detection scheme. In: IEEE International Conference on Image Processing: Conference Proceedings, ICIP 1989, 5–8 September 1989, Singapore. IEEE (1989)
30. Verikas, A., Gelzinis, A., Bacauskiene, M., Olenina, I., Olenin, S., Vaiciukynas, E.: Phase congruency-based detection of circular objects applied to analysis of phytoplankton images. Pattern Recogn. **45**(4), 1659–1670 (2012)
31. Zhang, L., Zhang, L., Zhang, D., Guo, Z.: Phase congruency induced local features for finger-knuckle-print recognition. Pattern Recogn. **45**(7), 2522–2531 (2012)
32. Zhu, Z., Zheng, M., Qi, G., Wang, D., Xiang, Y.: A phase congruency and local laplacian energy based multi-modality medical image fusion method in nsct domain. IEEE Access **7**, 20811–20824 (2019)

Texture Classification Using Capsule Networks

Bharat Mamidibathula$^{(\boxtimes)}$, Satakarni Amirneni$^{(\boxtimes)}$, Sai Shravani Sistla$^{(\boxtimes)}$, and Niharika Patnam$^{(\boxtimes)}$

Department of Electronics and Electrical Communication Engineering,
Indian Institute of Technology, Kharagpur, Kharagpur, India
bharatmamidi@gmail.com, satakarniamirneni@gmail.com,
shravanisistla1998@gmail.com, niharikapatnam25@gmail.com

Abstract. Texture refers to the natural and external consistency of an object. Classification of images based on texture has always been an intricate problem drawing major research attention. Multiple methods based on image processing and deep learning were developed over the last century. In this paper, we studied the feasibility of solving this problem using capsule networks. Transfer learning was used in which the Xception network trained on ImageNet visual database was used as the primary model. The two layer capsule network served as the secondary model. Experiments on six standard texture datasets namely KTH-TIPS 2b, Kylberg, CURET, UIUC, DTD, FMD were performed. Translational and rotational invariance on the input images was incorporated during the training stage. Our results were observed to be comparable to the state of the art techniques.

Keywords: Texture classification · Deep learning · Capsule networks

1 Introduction

Texture is the intrinsic property of images that plays a vital role in image classification, image segmentation and image synthesis. Texture, as per image processing literature is defined as the spatial variation of pixel intensities across the image. A major problem, however, is that textures in the real world are often not uniform due to variations in scale, orientation, illumination and other visual appearance. Texture classification is concerned with the repetition and flow of patterns within the texture, unlike typical image classification which focuses only on recognizing prominent objects in the foreground of the image. Figure 1 shows the textures of different commonplace objects used in our daily life.

Research on texture classification has received significant attention in recent years because of its applications in various real-life technologies like industrial and biomedical surface inspection, identification of diseases, ground classification and segmentation using satellite or aerial imagery, segmentation of textured regions in document analysis and content-based access to image databases. On

© Springer Nature Switzerland AG 2019
A. Morales et al. (Eds.): IbPRIA 2019, LNCS 11867, pp. 589–599, 2019.
https://doi.org/10.1007/978-3-030-31332-6_51

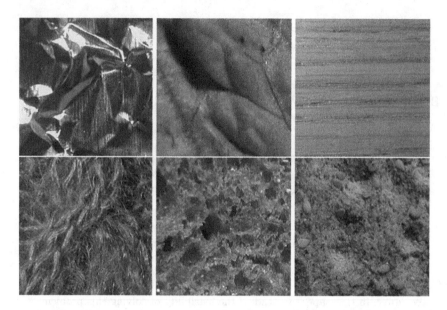

Fig. 1. Examples of different textures taken from KTH-TIPS2b dataset. From top left: Aluminum Foil, Wool, Lettuce Leaf, Brown Bread, Wood, Cracker

the other hand, there exist a few limitations to be considered because of the problems posed by the non-uniformity in the texture surfaces. Differences in orientations, scales and illumination conditions account for significant variability in image textures and addressing it precisely is the challenging task of any texture classification algorithm. Researchers incorporated invariance with respect to properties such as spatial scale, orientation and grayscale. Capsule networks are one of the state-of-the-art methods that explicitly captures the spatial and relative relationships between the extracted features by using vectorial representation. This property of the capsule networks helps in learning the regular patterns embedded in the texture images. In this work, we attempted to study texture classification on various standard datasets by implementing a two layer capsule network.

2   Previous Work

The seeds of the study of texture analysis were sown in 1962 when Julesz [1] proposed the texture perception model which conducted the visual pattern discrimination experiments based on brightness and hue to explain the human visual perception of texture. One of the earliest Texture Descriptor methods - Gray Level Cooccurrence Matrix (GLCM) [2] was presented in 1973 by Haralick. It computed the probability of the joint occurrence of the two-pixel intensities at a specified angle and a specified distance. The statistical measures computed from the co-occurrence matrix serve as the features of the image. In the late 20th

Century, researchers resorted to featuring extraction in texture analysis using filtering approaches such as Gabor filters [3], Gabor Wavelets [4], Differences of Gaussians [5]. Statistical modeling approaches considered that the texture images are derived from the probability distributions on Markov Random Fields (MRF) - MRF texture model [6], Gaussian MRF [7] or Fractal Models [8]. In the first decade of the 21st century, a computationally efficient, gray-scale and rotation invariant texture classification method was presented using the Local Binary Patterns (LBP) [9]. LBPs of an image serve as the texture features. The multiresolution analysis in this work was achieved by combining multiple operators for detecting the LBPs' patterns.

Deep learning methods hegemonized the image recognition research when a major breakthrough occurred when Alex Krizhevsky [10] implemented Deep Convolutional Neural Networks on ImageNet [11] for image classification in 2012. The five layer convolution network with 60 million parameters achieved tremendous results, thus overshadowing the previously existing methods for the design of man crafted texture descriptors. Later on, translational invariance in images was captured by wavelet scattering networks [12]. Scattering representation of stationary processes was used to compute higher order moments and Fourier power spectrum was used to discriminate textures. In 2015, encouraging results for the classification of materials and surface attributes in clutter were obtained when researchers from Oxford put forward a novel texture descriptor using fisher vector pooling of a Convolutional Neural Network (CNN) filter bank [13]. Contemporarily, a deep learning architecture - Texture CNN, specific to the task of texture recognition was demonstrated. It aimed at designing learnable filter banks that are embedded in the architecture. The idea of pooling an energy measure from the last convolutional layer was used to accomplish the task [14].

3   Capsule Networks

3.1   Disadvantages of Convolutional Neural Networks

Geoffrey Hinton's idea in 2012 [10] of using a deep CNN for image recognition laid a strong platform for the deep learning resurgence that took place. CNNs have continued to show their dominance in this area over the past few years.

The extraction of features using a set of convolutional and pooling layers is the principle underlying the working of a CNN. The convolution operations, performed using the weight filters are used to detect the key features in the image. The values of each weight filter are chosen in a way so as to get activated by a certain set of features. Unfortunately, the disadvantage of CNNs lies in the fact that the convolution operations do not consider spatial arrangement and the relative relationship between the features rather, merely look for their absolute presence. The lower level neurons of CNNs fail to send the details only to the relevant higher level neurons.

3.2   Advantages of Capsule Networks

A generic CNN involves the convolutions of scalar quantities namely the features extracted from the preceding layer and the kernel matrix of the present layer. Hinton in his paper [15] suggested that robust image recognition can be achieved by richer feature representation using vectors. More relative and relational information between features can be embedded using vectors.

A generic CNN should be supplied with different variants of the same image in order to classify the image into the correct group. The variant can differ from the original image in terms of size, angle, translation, light intensity, etc. The internal scalar representation of the original image and its variant is differently recorded by a CNN. Hence, the CNN network has to be trained using different variants of the image for it to capture the diversity.

In contrary, a capsule network learns the internal representation of an image in a way to encapsulate the orientation and likelihood of different features. The vectors are capable of learning the general representation of the class rather than memorizing the feature notations of every variant of the image. If all the features are transformed by the same amount and direction during the training phase, these variations are preserved in the vector notation. The constant length vector changes its value as a result of different transformations on the image. This property, which is termed as equivariance is a way of detecting a group of things that can be transformed into one another. It helps capsule networks to classify new and unseen variants of an image correctly. Modified image of the same underlying object can be classified by capsule networks precisely and with high probability. Capsule networks are proved to give accurate results with comparatively less amount of data [10].

3.3   What Is a Capsule?

Every capsule network is initialized with a normal convolutional layer where each pixel of the input image is considered as the input to the first layer. It is convolved with appropriate kernels to extract the corresponding features. Spatial dimension and stride are adjusted accordingly. The resultant feature maps are further activated by rectified linear unit (ReLU) to induce nonlinearity. The number of convolutional layers that precede the first capsule layer is dependent on the problem in consideration.

After the convolution of the feature maps with the required number of kernels in the convolutional layers, the output from each neuron is a scalar, the value of which might represent an internal feature. In a capsule layer, these scalar outputs from the preceding layer are stacked into small decks. Each deck is further split into smaller sets of values termed as capsules, whereas each deck is referred to as a capsule layer. Thus, a capsule is a set of values represented in the form of a vector to store more information about the instantiation parameters like size, angle, hue, thickness, etc. of an object or an object part. This vector is named as the activity vector. The length (norm) of the activity vector gives the probability of the existence of that entity and its orientation gives the details about the parameters.

3.4   Working of a Capsule

The working of an individual capsule layer is explained below with the help of Fig. 2.

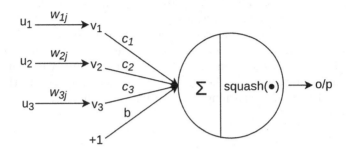

Fig. 2. Internal working of a Capsule showing Affine Transform and Squash Function

Input Vector. A capsule receives a vector as its input and produces a vector as its output. The different dimensions of these vectors correspond to different instantiation parameters. The different capsules are represented by u_1, u_2, u_3 in Fig. 2.

Affine Transformation. As shown in Fig. 2, transformation matrices (w_{1j}, w_{2j}, w_{3j}) of appropriate dimensions are multiplied with the vectors of the previous layer. These matrices can capture the relationships between features which might have gone unnoticed in the previous layer. The purpose of these matrices is to convert the input vector into the position of the predicted output vector representing the next higher level of features. The output vector v_1 represents the predicted position of the next higher feature with respect to u_1, v_2 represents the predicted position of the higher feature with respect to u_2 and so on. The final prediction of the higher level feature is a combination of the outputs v_1, v_2, v_3. If all the outputs make the same prediction, the feature can serve to increase the certainty in the prediction of the next level features. The weighted sum of these output vectors is computed and a non-linear activation function is applied.

Dynamic Routing. Though capsule networks were invented long back, the lack of proper training algorithm hampered their application. The sudden rise in their usage can be attributed to the invention of the dynamic routing method [15], an algorithm to train capsule networks. Thus, it is not the capsule concept that created a revolution rather the training algorithm.

This algorithm is used to compute the weights of the affine transform. It can be viewed as a method which decides on all the output capsules each input capsule has to be mapped to. The lower level capsules compute their different projections onto the higher level capsules and thus optimize the weights in a manner to maximize the fit with the related capsule and minimize the fit with the other capsules in their decreasing order of relevance.

Squashing. Squashing is a new non-linear activation function designed to map a vector to a vector. Since the magnitude of the vector corresponds to its probability, this function ensures that the length of the mapped vector lies between 0 and 1. In order to preserve the direction of the vector, this function has a unit vector in the same direction multiplied with the required magnitude. The mathematical formula is shown below. For j^{th} class, v_j represents the output vector obtained from the squashing function for an input vector s_j.

$$v_j = \frac{||s_j||^2}{1 + ||s_j||^2} \frac{s_j}{||s_j||}$$

$$v_j \approx 0 \text{ when } s_j \text{ is small}$$

$$v_j \approx \frac{s_j}{||s_j||} \text{ when } s_j \text{ is large}$$

4   Proposed Architecture

Transfer learning is a very effective technique in deep learning in which features learned from the first task are re-used in a related second task. The first model is trained suitably to extract the features that are to be transferred. These features are used as the starting point to the second target task. Sometimes, all or only a fraction of all parts of the first model can be used in training the second model. The most important criterion in this concept is that the features are to be general that are suitable for both the tasks.

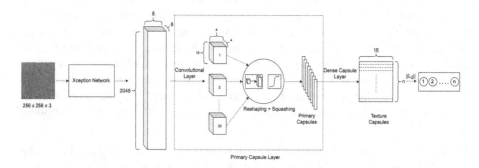

Fig. 3. Overview of the proposed network architecture

Taking the assumption that the features extracted through a series of convolutional layers trained on a particular dataset would be useful for other similar problem statements, we used the Xception network architecture [22] as our base model for the transfer learning task and built upon it. The Xception network uses the concept of spatial convolutions on top of the Inception network for a lighter but more efficient model. The Xception network has been extensively trained on the trimmed ImageNet visual database [11] consisting of more than 1.2 million hand-annotated images. The weights of the Xception network were used as the initial weights for our model. The images from the datasets in use were fed as input to the pre-trained Xception network. The output feature vectors extracted from this network were sent to the subsequent layers namely primary capsule layer and dense capsule layer. The primary capsule layer consisted of a convolutional layer followed by reshaping layer which reshapes the output tensor into a series of capsules of 16 dimensions each. The dynamic routing algorithm is implemented in this layer. The output capsules obtained are then passed through the squashing activation function and lastly to the dense capsule layer to obtain an output feature vector of 16 dimensions for each texture class. The output class is to be chosen as the texture class with the minimum L_2 norm of the error. Figure 3 shows a detailed image of our comprehensive architecture. For all the prescribed datasets, the normalized classification accuracy is used as the primary evaluation metric.

4.1   Loss Function

The cost function or error function that is to be optimized in capsules is called the margin loss L_c for each texture category c and class vector v_c. It is an extension of binary cross entropy used in multi-class classification. The cost function will be a function of the weights whose equation is given below.

$$L_c = T_c \cdot max(0, m^+ - ||v_c||)^2 + \lambda \cdot (1 - T_c) \cdot max(0, ||v_c|| - m^-)^2$$

where $T_c = 1$ corresponds to an image of texture class c, or else $T_c = 0$. We have set $m^+ = 0.9$ and $m^- = 0.1$ throughout our experiments. The 'λ' hyperparameter is set to 0.5 and is useful in stopping the initial learning values from reducing the overall activity vectors of the classes. The total loss is calculated as the sum of the losses of each class.

4.2   Training

We ran our model using the Keras python framework with the Tensorflow backend on an Nvidia GTX 1080 Ti GPU. All the input images were resized to 256×256 prior to being given as an input to the model. All the We trained our architecture separately on the different datasets for 50 epochs to obtain the test set accuracy. For the KTH TIPS 2b database, according to the pre-established norm, we took each sample set as the training set and the remaining three samples sets as the testing set. The Kylberg, UIUC, DTD and Curet datasets were randomly split into the ratio of 0.5:0.2:0.3 to get the training set, validation set, and the test set for each database respectively. The FMD dataset was split into the ratio 0.6:0.1:0.3 for the training, validation, and test set. We used the Adam optimizer for weight updation after every batch input. The batch size used was 16. We used a form of data augmentation while taking a batch by rotating each image by a random angle between $0°$ and $90°$. We used 3 routing iterations for each updation of the capsule layer's weights. We took an initial learning rate of 0.001 and used a decay of 0.9 after every epoch of training. For the KTH-TIPS 2b database, we report the average classification accuracy, sequentially considering each sample as training set and the remaining as the testing set. For the other datasets, we randomly split the dataset five times and report the median classification accuracy. The images in all the datasets were used to train the model for 120 epochs each.

5   Datasets

We performed experiments to assess the texture classification ability using the aforementioned architecture. Our proposed model was trained on different texture databases, namely:

5.1   Kylberg

It consists of 28 texture classes [16] in total. The textures include different types of fabrics, grass, and surfaces of stones imaged in local surroundings. The other textured surfaces are obtained by placing articles like rice, lentils, sesame seeds on a flat surface. Types of ceilings and floors are also considered. Four images of each material were acquired where each image was divided into 40 square patches of 576×576 pixels resulting in 160 unique unrotated samples per class. The patches were saved as 8-bit data in a gray level format with all of them being normalized to have the same mean gray value and standard deviation.

5.2   UIUC

The UIUC [17] database contains 40 images each of 25 distinct texture classes thus adding up to 1000 uncalibrated, unregistered images. These are gray-scale images with an image resolution of 640×480 pixels. The classes include surfaces with textures pertaining to albedo variation (e.g., wood and marble), 3D shape (e.g., gravel and fur), and also a mixture of both (e.g., carpet and brick). The dataset has relatively few sample images per class, but high intra-class variability manifested as non-homogeneity in textures and unconstrained non-rigid deformations. This characteristic feature of the database makes it the most challenging testbed for texture classification. Moreover, viewpoint and scale variations are also strongly evident.

5.3   KTH TIPS 2b

The database [18] comprises of 4 planar images each of 11 different materials namely; linen, wood, cork, lettuce leaf, brown bread, white bread, crumpled aluminum foil, wool, corduroy, cotton, and cracker. Each class has samples with variations in scale, pose, and illumination. 3 different poses - frontal, rotated $22.5°$ left and rotated $22.5°$; 4 illumination conditions and 9 scales equally spaced logarithmically over two octaves are used. At each scale, 12 images are taken in a combination of three poses and four illumination conditions thus giving a total of $12 \times 9 = 108$ images for each of the 44 samples.

5.4   DTD

Describable Texture Database (DTD) [19] is organized according to a list of 47 different categories inspired by human perception, with 120 images per category thus making a total of $120 \times 47 = 5640$ images. Size of the images ranges between 300×300 and 640×640 such that at least 90% of it represents their category.

5.5   FMD

The name Flickr Material Database (FMD) [20,21] suggests that it was collected from the site Flickr.com (under Creative Common License). It is constructed with 100 images per category of 10 distinct categories. Images are pictured to capture real-world appearances of common materials like fabric, foliage, glass, leather, metal, paper, plastic, stone, water and wood.

6   Results and Comparison

As seen in the Table 1 below, we obtained results which are on par with state of the art models. We observed that the accuracy for the KTH-TIPS 2b database was slightly on the lower side when compared to the state of the art [13] due to the fact that the procured images were highly preprocessed by removing background

Table 1. Performance observed for various datasets

Dataset	Training loss	Validation loss	Validation accuracy	Test accuracy
CURET	1.5025×10^{-5}	0.0031	99.62	99.65
Kylberg	3.0063×10^{-4}	9.6577×10^{-5}	100	100
DTD	0.0045	0.1984	76.68	70.98
UIUC	0.0076	0.0037	99.5	99.33
FMD	5.2845×10^{-4}	0.0136	85	80.66
KTH-TIPS 2b	0.0051	0.0044	99.59	71.83

objects. Hence, the advantage of obtained efficient spatial relationships between different objects cannot be observed as clearly as in the case of other datasets. This dataset, however, is not consistent with the real-world natural images as real world images of textures will most likely be present with various other objects. The model for the other datasets produces accuracies that are on par with state of the art results ([13] for DTD, FMD and CURET, [23] for UIUC, [24] for Kylberg datasets respectively as seen in Table 2). Overall, our model has achieved commensurate results for different datasets, compared to other models which showed promising results for a few datasets but not so much for the remaining. The reason for lower accuracies on the DTD and FMD datasets is due to the fact that there is a high amount of diversity in images belonging to the same texture class.

Table 2. Performance observed for various datasets against the existing State of the Art models

Dataset	Test accuracy	State of the art
CURET	99.65	99.7
Kylberg	100	99.7
DTD	70.98	75.5
UIUC	99.33	99.4
FMD	80.66	82.2
KTH-TIPS 2b	71.83	81.5

7   Conclusion

To solve the problem of texture classification, we conducted experiments on multiple datasets to investigate the performance of our proposed model, which comprises of Xception network followed by two capsule layers. Out of all the standard networks used for transfer learning, with proper fine-tuning of weights, we found that Xception network has the best performance to computation ratio. We achieved admirable overall results on all the datasets using our proposed architecture. We also observed that the capsule network can effectively preserve the spatial interdependence between features, thereby subsiding the challenge of data scarcity, highly prevalent in the texture classification problem.

References

1. Julesz, B.: Visual pattern discrimination. IRE Trans. Inf. Theor. **8**(2), 84–92 (1962)
2. Haralick, R.M., Shanmugam, K.: Textural features for image classification. IEEE Trans. Syst. Man Cybern. **SMC–3**(6), 610–621 (1973)
3. Bovik, A.C., Clark, M., Geisler, W.S.: Multichannel texture analysis using localized spatial filters. IEEE Trans. Pattern Anal. Mach. Intell. **1**(1), 55–73 (1990)

4. Manjunath, B.S., Ma, W.Y.: Texture features for browsing and retrieval of image data. IEEE Trans. Pattern Anal. Mach. Intell. **18**(8), 837–842 (1996)
5. Malik, J., Belongie, S., Shi, J., Leung, T.: Textons, contours and regions: cue integration in image segmentation. In: Proceedings of the Seventh IEEE International Conference on Computer Vision, vol. 2, pp. 918–925. IEEE (1999)
6. Li, S.Z.: Markov Random Field Modeling in Image Analysis. Springer, Heidelberg (2009)
7. Chellappa, R., Chatterjee, S.: Classification of textures using Gaussian Markov random fields. IEEE Trans. Acoust. Speech Sign. Process. **33**(4), 959–963 (1985)
8. Mandelbrot, B.B.: The Fractal Geometry of Nature. WH Freeman, New York (1982)
9. Ojala, T., Pietikäinen, M., Mäenpää, T.: Multiresolution gray-scale and rotation invariant texture classification with local binary patterns. IEEE Trans. Pattern Anal. Mach. Intell. **1**(7), 971–987 (2002)
10. Krizhevsky, A., Sutskever, I., Hinton, G.E.: ImageNet classification with deep convolutional neural networks. In: Advances in Neural Information Processing Systems, pp. 1097–1105 (2012)
11. ImageNet Database. http://www.image-net.org/
12. Bruna, J., Mallat, S.: Invariant scattering convolution networks. IEEE Trans. Pattern Anal. Mach. Intell. **35**(8), 1872–1886 (2013)
13. Cimpoi, M., Maji, S., Kokkinos, I., Vedaldi, A.: Deep filter banks for texture recognition, description, and segmentation. Int. J. Comput. Vis. **118**(1), 65–94 (2016)
14. Andrearczyk, V., Whelan, P.F.: Using filter banks in convolutional neural networks for texture classification. Pattern Recogn. Lett. **84**, 63–69 (2016)
15. Sabour, S., Frosst, N., Hinton, G.E.: Dynamic routing between capsules. In: Advances in Neural Information Processing Systems, pp. 3856–3866 (2017)
16. Kylberg, G.: Kylberg Texture Dataset v. 1.0. Centre for Image Analysis, Swedish University of Agricultural Sciences and Uppsala University (2011)
17. Lazebnik, S., Schmid, C., Ponce, J.: A sparse texture representation using local affine regions. IEEE Trans. Pattern Anal. Mach. Intell. **27**(8), 1265–1278 (2005)
18. Mallikarjuna, P., Targhi, A.T., Fritz, M., Hayman, E., Caputo, B., Eklundh, J.O.: The KTH-TIPS2 database. In: Computational Vision and Active Perception Laboratory (CVAP), Stockholm, Sweden, 9 June 2006
19. Cimpoi, M., Maji, S., Kokkinos, I., Mohamed, S., Vedaldi, A.: Describing textures in the wild. In: Proceedings of the IEEE Conference on Computer Vision and Pattern Recognition, pp. 3606–3613 (2014)
20. Sharan, L., Rosenholtz, R., Adelson, E.: Material perception: what can you see in a brief glance? J. Vis. **9**(8), 784 (2009)
21. Sharan, L., Rosenholtz, R., Adelson, E.H.: Accuracy and speed of material categorization in real-world images. J. Vis. **14**(9), 12 (2014)
22. Chollet, F.: Xception: Deep learning with depthwise separable convolutions. In: Proceedings of the IEEE Conference on Computer Vision and Pattern Recognition, pp. 1251–1258 (2017)
23. Sifre, L., Mallat, S.: Rotation, scaling and deformation invariant scattering for texture discrimination. In: Proceedings of the IEEE Conference on Computer Vision and Pattern Recognition, pp. 1233–1240 (2013)
24. Kylberg, G., Sintorn, I.M.: Evaluation of noise robustness for local binary pattern descriptors in texture classification. EURASIP J. Image Video Process. **2013**(1), 17 (2013)

Automatic Vision Based Calibration System for Planar Cable-Driven Parallel Robots

Andrés García-Vanegas[1]([✉]), Brhayan Liberato-Tafur[1,2],
Manuel Guillermo Forero[2]([✉]) [ID], Antonio Gonzalez-Rodríguez[3],
and Fernando Castillo-García[3]([✉])

[1] Semillero MEC-AUTRONIC, Facultad de Ingeniería, Universidad de Ibagué,
Ibagué, Tolima, Colombia
`jorge.garcia@unibague.edu.co`
[2] Semillero Lún, Facultad de Ingeniería, Universidad de Ibagué,
Ibagué, Tolima, Colombia
`manuel.forero@unibague.edu.co`
[3] Universidad de Castilla-La Mancha, Toledo, Spain
`Fernando.Castillo@uclm.es`

Abstract. Techniques commonly employed to calibrate cable-driven parallel robots are manual or use sensors to measure the end-effector position indirectly. Therefore, in this paper, a cable-driven robot calibration system based on artificial vision techniques is introduced, which takes advantage of the available information, which allows calibrating the system directly from the observed video. The proposed method was validated by calibrating a planar cable-driven parallel robot prototype with 2 degrees of freedom. The measured positioning error was lower than 1 mm.

Keywords: Cable-driven parallel robot · Parallel robotic ·
Computer vision · Vision-based control · Robot calibration

1 Introduction

A cable-driven parallel robot (CDPR) is a kind of robot, composed of a mobile platform (end-effector), connected by cables to a fixed one (fixed frame). These robots have a cable collector system composed of: an actuator, a reduction box and a collector mechanism. There are two kinds of CDPRs: planar, with 2 degrees-of-freedom, and spatial, with 3 or more degrees-of-freedom. They can be suspended, controlled and over-controlled. To control the location of the end-effector in the 2D space, the cables length is modified according to a mathematical model, that relates these lengths to the parameters of the robot. These robots can handle high payloads and are characterized by their fast response and improved accuracy [1]. The end-effector is placed on the mobile platform. It can be a clamp for pick-and-place applications, a welding or painting tool, a

© Springer Nature Switzerland AG 2019
A. Morales et al. (Eds.): IbPRIA 2019, LNCS 11867, pp. 600–609, 2019.
https://doi.org/10.1007/978-3-030-31332-6_52

plasma or laser cutting gun, a camera for the transmission of videos (Skycam), an extruder for 3D printing [2], among others applications. These robots are employed in applications such as production engineering, construction, motion simulation and entertainment.

Techniques commonly employed to calibrate cable-driven parallel robots are manual or use sensors to measure the end-effector position indirectly [3–6]. Although several vision-based control systems have been developed [7–9], there is not in the literature any automatic method developed to calibrate the end-effector robotic system. Therefore, in this paper, a cable-driven robot calibration system based on artificial vision techniques is introduced, which takes advantage of the available information, allowing calibrating the system directly from the observed video.

This paper is organized as follows: Sect. 2 details the materials used in this works. Section 3 introduces the calibration and tracking system methods of the CDPR. Section 4 presents the experimental results. The paper concludes with some remarks and suggestions for future works.

2   Materials

In this study, a two-degrees-of-freedom planar cable-driven parallel robot prototype was developed, shown in Fig. 1. The prototype was designed with Solidworks and built with aluminum profiles and 3D printed parts (PLA). The prototype specifications are given in Table 1. As can be seen, the positioning system consists of three red reference squares; two of 80 mm located on the corners of the pulley system, and the other 111 mm located in the end-effector. The robot video input signal is acquired using a Logitech HD Pro C920 webcam with 1080p resolution, located at 1.2 m from the end-effector.

This study used a HP-440 G5 computer with 8 GB of memory, an Intel Core i5 processor (R) CPU @ 1.8, and a Windows 10 operating system. The calibration algorithms were implemented in Python 3.7 using the OpenCV and PyQt5

Table 1. Overview of the CDPR specification.

Parameter	Value/Component	Unit
Stepper motors (NEMA 23)	2	-
Number of cable	4	-
Gear ratio	10:1	-
Drum diameter	63.5	mm
Cable type	Steel	-
Cable diameter	6.0	mm
Degrees-of-freedom	2	-
Size of the robot frame	1.0×1.0	m
Size of the mobile platform	15.0×15.0	cm

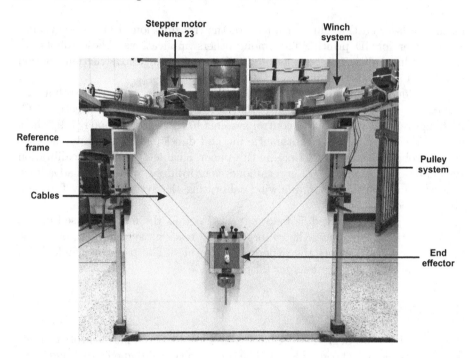

Fig. 1. Prototype of planar cable-driven parallel robot.

libraries. The image processing methods were initially developed and tested using the free access software ImageJ. This application was also employed to measure and validate the trajectories of the end-effector.

3   Methods

The calibration system developed here is based on computer vision techniques. First, the video input is decomposed into frame images. Then, calibration is performed using the red squares, observed in Fig. 1, as landmarks. Red squares were chosen as landmarks because the predominant color in a crop is normally green, and the red color is the opposite one or complementary to the green in the chromatic circle. In this way, a better color separation between the red squares and the background is obtained, making it easier their segmentation. The landmarks correspond to points where excess red is found [10], i.e., where the red intensity is very high and much higher than the intensities of the other two color channels. To find the landmark areas, the red end areas are searched for in images. To do this, a monochromatic image is obtained using the standard BT.601. Then, this image is subtracted from the red channel [11]. Mathematically, this operation is expressed in (1) and the process of identifying objects with excess red color is illustrated in Fig. 2.

As shown in Fig. 4b, most of the image corresponding to the crop remains in the background and areas of extreme red are detected as objects of interest.

Then, the next step is to binarize the image to isolate the pixels whose extreme red values are above a given value. It was empirically found that a value of 38 resulted in the best segmentation between the background and the landmarks.

As seen in Fig. 4c, some isolated pixels are also selected as part of the object; these pixels are produced by noise in the image. To eliminate them, a morphological erosion is performed, so that the final image contains only the regions of interest. The resulting image is shown in Fig. 4d. The results obtained using this method were compared to those of the techniques listed in Table 1, and the precision provided by the algorithm was calculated, comparing the pixels of the images that were manually segmented and those that were chosen via the algorithms.

In this way, a better contrast between the red squares and the background is obtained, making it easier their segmentation. Given that these squares present a very high red value, the detection of these regions was carried out by finding pixels with an excessive red, i.e., pixels where the red value is very high and far from the values of the other two channels. Hence, square pixels are obtained from the red channel by subtracting the original grayscale image [10] obtained by using the BT.601 standard, which generates a monochromatic gray image based on the human vision model [11]. Mathematically, this operation is expressed in (1) and the process of identifying objects with excess red color is illustrated in Fig. 2.

$$Y = 0,701R - 0,5876G - 0,114B \tag{1}$$

where Y is the resulting image and R, G and B are the Red, Green and Blue components of the input image.

Once the excessive red image is obtained, it must be binarized to find the red squares, as it is shown in Fig. 2. A threshold value of 38, found empirically, was employed, as shown in Fig. 3.

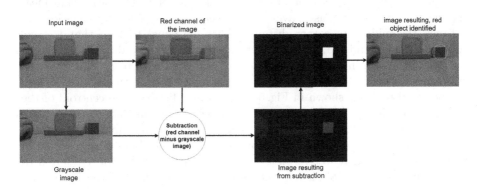

Fig. 2. Identification of excess red color objects. (Color figure online)

The two smallest squares, located on the pulley system (concentric to the upper pulleys), are employed as reference points required to calculate the robot

Fig. 3. Identification of red landmarks. Left. Excess red image. Right. Binarized image, threshold = 38. (Color figure online)

distances. A larger red square is located in it to find the end-effector position. The location of these squares allows calculating the cables length at any point in the workspace.

The landmark on the upper left is employed to measure the sizes of the squares. The square width is computed once the landmarks' four corners are detected. Then, the Euclidean distance in pixels between the landmark centroids is computed in (2). To convert distances from pixels to millimeters, the pixel to millimeter ratio is obtained by dividing the previously calculated distance between the upper left landmark width w that it is known (80 mm).

$$dE_{(p1,p2)} = \sqrt{(x2 - x1)^2 + (y2 - y1)^2} \tag{2}$$

where x_1, y_1, x_2, y_2 are the coordinates of the top corners p_1, p_2 of the upper left landmark.

$$pixels/millimeters = \frac{dE_{(p1,p2)}}{w} \tag{3}$$

Squares must meet two conditions for their correct identification and measurement. First, they must have four corners and, second, the relationship between the midpoints corner distances must be equal to 1. If that is true, edges are drawn, and the dimensions of the square are printed in the developed software, as shown in Fig. 4. If any landmark is tilted with respect to the camera plane, it is not identified as square, because the ratio between its sides will not be equal to 1. As shown in Fig. 5, the distance between the centroid of the upper left landmark (A) and the upper left corner of the end-effector square (B) is calculated by using Eq. 2. The actual length of the cables is calculated and employed to know the localition of the end-effector. As can be observed in Fig. 4, the robot has reflective pulleys located in the end-effector, employed to get a point-to-point cable lenght measures. "The equations of the kinematics and the dynamics of the real system are equivalent to those of the point-to-point model and, therefore, this simplified method can be used without inherent errors" [12].

As mentioned above, the calculation of the cable length is done by the point-to-point model, based on the inverse kinematics of the robot. This means that, both, the steps of the motors and the cable lengths are calculated from the

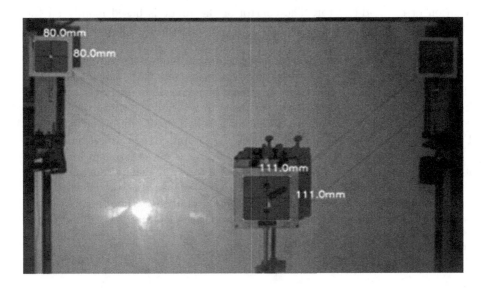

Fig. 4. Measurement of red squares. (Color figure online)

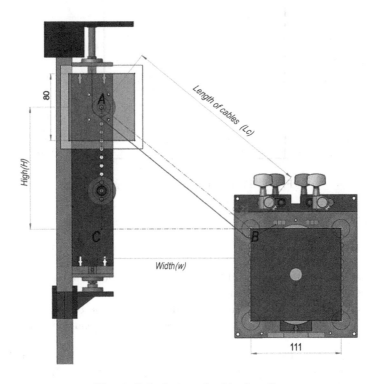

Fig. 5. Calculation of cables length.

location of the end-effector. The control of the robot is based mainly on the aforementioned model and, therefore, the controller input is given by the x, y coordinates of the end-effector.

To generate trajectories using the mathematical model, the movement of the robot must start from the reference point (x_0, y_0), used as the home location. If the robot does not initiate a trajectory from home it will be incorrect or wrong. To determine the robot home, the coordinate in x is half the width between the centers of the pulleys, and the coordinate in y is half the height of the frame, see Fig. 6. This point will be employed as reference point of the calibration system.

Each time the robot is used and its end-effector is not at home, it must store its current position and calculate the distance between that current point and the reference point. Therefore, this will be the distance that the effector must travel to start a trajectory. It must be borne in mind that when this movement is made, it is not starting from the point of reference, hence, this will not travel exactly the calculated distance and must be calibrated several times until the effector is at home. Figure 6 represents the length that the end-effector must move to get home.

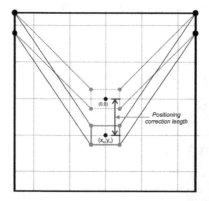

Fig. 6. Positioning correction length.

4   Results

The calibration system was tested by making trajectories of squares and circles, with a repetition of 10 times each. Before performing these trajectories, the end effector was calibrated about 5 times in order to reach the point of reference or home. as shown in the Table 2, the trajectories performed can be seen in Figs. 7 and 8.

As is observed in Table 2, the maximum error was of 0.22 mm, much lower than the error obtained by published methods until now [3,6]. In addition, the performed trajectories are very accurate, despite the vibrations presented by the mechanical system (Table 3).

Table 2. Results of the calibration.

Number of iteration	Home position (mm)	Measured position (mm)	Error (mm)
1	0.00, 0.00	0.22, 0.22	0.22, 0.22
2	0.00, 0.00	0.00, 0.00	0.00, 0.00
3	0.00, 0.00	0.00, 0.22	0.00, 0.22
4	0.00, 0.00	0.00, 0.22	0.00, 0.22
5	0.00, 0.00	0.22, 0.00	0.22, 0.00

Table 3. Comparison of real and desired paths to circle of 100 mm, Square of 100 mm.

Resolution	Size (px)	Software measure (mm)	Real measure (mm)
Test trajectory: Circle of 100 mm			
0.84 px/mm	84 px (Width)	100	100
0.84 px/mm	84 px (High)	100	100
Test trajectory: Square of 100 mm			
0.84 px/mm	84 px (Width)	100	100
0.84 px/mm	84 px (High)	100	100

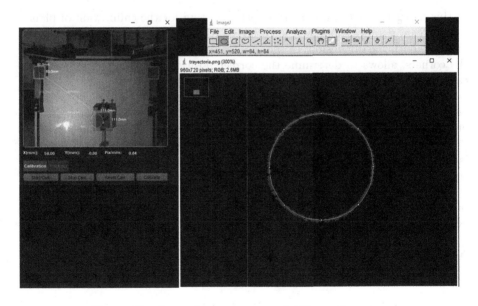

Fig. 7. Circular path measurement of 100 mm diameter.

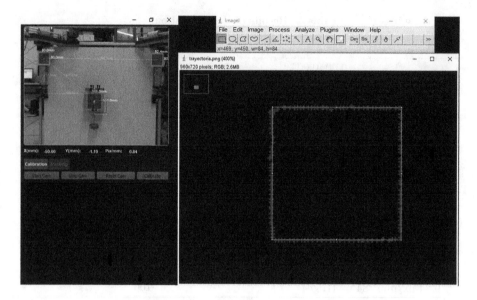

Fig. 8. Square path measurement of 100 mm.

5   Conclusions

In this paper a new computer vision-based system for the calibration of planar cable-driven parallel robot was introduced. It is determined that being able to visualize both the dimensions of the squares and the different distances between the corners, allows to determine the correct positioning and orientation of the camera.

It is essential that the corners or centroids of the squares coincide with the centers of the pulleys, either those of the frame or those of the end-effector, otherwise the measurement of the lengths of the cables will be erroneous.

Since the reference point is located in the middle of the robot's workspace, it is possible to calibrate the robot only with the measurement of one of its cables, since at this point all the cables have the same length.

The proposed method of vision-based calibration along with the reflective pulleys, which eliminate the position error presented in several cable robots, has an error much lower than one millimeter.

Acknowledgment. This work was supported by project 17-462-INT Universidad de Ibagué.

References

1. Pott, A.: Cable-Driven Parallel Robots: Theory and Application. Springer, Heidelberg (2018). https://doi.org/10.1007/978-3-319-76138-1
2. Zi, B., Wang, N., Qian, S., Bao, K.: Design, stiffness analysis and experimental study of a cable-driven parallel 3D printer. Mech. Mach. Theory **132**, 207–222 (2019). http://www.sciencedirect.com/science/article/pii/S0094114X18315568
3. Borgstrom, P.H., et al.: NIMS-PL: a cable-driven robot with self-calibration capabilities. IEEE Trans. Rob. **25**(5), 1005–1015 (2009)
4. Miermeister, P., Pott, A., Verl, A.: Auto-calibration method for overconstrained cable-driven parallel robots. In: ROBOTIK 2012, 7th German Conference on Robotics. VDE, pp. 1–6 (2012)
5. Sandretto, J.A.D., Daney, D., Gouttefarde, M., Baradat, C.: Calibration of a fully-constrained parallel cable-driven robot. Ph.D. dissertation, Inria (2012)
6. Jin, X., Jung, J., Ko, S., Choi, E., Park, J.-O., Kim, C.-S.: Geometric parameter calibration for a cable-driven parallel robot based on a single one-dimensional laser distance sensor measurement and experimental modeling. Sensors **18**(7), 2392 (2018)
7. Bayani, H., Masouleh, M.T., Kalhor, A.: An experimental study on the vision-based control and identification of planar cable-driven parallel robots. Robot. Auton. Syst. **75**, 187–202 (2016)
8. Dallej, T., Gouttefarde, M., Andreff, N., Michelin, M., Martinet, P.: Towards vision-based control of cable-driven parallel robots. In: 2011 IEEE/RSJ International Conference on Intelligent Robots and Systems, pp. 2855–2860. IEEE (2011)
9. Paccot, F., Andreff, N., Martinet, P.: A review on the dynamic control of parallel kinematic machines: theory and experiments. Int. J. Robot. Res. **28**(3), 395–416 (2009). https://doi.org/10.1177/0278364908096236
10. Bose, A.: How to detect and track red objects in live video in MATLAB, Octubre 2013. http://arindambose.com/?p=587
11. Forero, M.G., Herrera-Rivera, S., Ávila-Navarro, J., Franco, C.A., Rasmussen, J., Nielsen, J.: Color classification methods for perennial weed detection in cereal crops. In: Vera-Rodriguez, R., Fierrez, J., Morales, A. (eds.) CIARP 2018. LNCS, vol. 11401, pp. 117–123. Springer, Cham (2019). https://doi.org/10.1007/978-3-030-13469-3_14
12. Gonzalez-Rodriguez, A., Castillo-Garcia, F., Ottaviano, E., Rea, P., Gonzalez-Rodriguez, A.: On the effects of the design of cable-driven robots on kinematics and dynamics models accuracy. Mechatronics **43**, 18–27 (2017). http://www.sciencedirect.com/science/article/pii/S0957415817300156

3D Non-rigid Registration of Deformable Object Using GPU

Junesuk Lee[1] , Eung-su Kim[1] , and Soon-Yong Park[2($\boxtimes$)]

[1] School of Computer Science and Engineering,
Kyungpook National University, Daegu, South Korea
ljs2352@gmail.com, jsm80607@gmail.com
[2] School of Electronic Engineering, Kyungpook National University,
Daegu, South Korea
sypark@knu.ac.kr

Abstract. We propose a method to quickly process non-rigid registration between 3D deformable data using a GPU-based non-rigid ICP(Iterative Closest Point) algorithm. In this paper, we sequentially acquire whole-body model data of a person moving dynamically from a single RGBD camera. We use Dense Optical Flow algorithm to find the corresponding pixels between two consecutive frames. Next, we select nodes to estimate 3D deformation matrices by uniform sampling algorithm. We use a GPU-based non-rigid ICP algorithm to estimate the 3D transformation matrices of each node at high speed. We use non-linear optimization algorithm methods in the non-rigid ICP algorithm. We define energy functions for an estimate the exact 3D transformation matrices. We use a proposed GPU-based method because it takes a lot of computation time to calculate the 3D transformation matrices of all nodes. We apply a 3D transformation to all points with a weight-based affine transformation algorithm. We demonstrate the high accuracy of non-rigid registration and the fast runtime of the non-rigid ICP algorithm through experimental results.

Keywords: 3D reconstruction · Non-rigid registration · Non-rigid ICP · Deformable registration · GPU

1 Introduction

In recent years there have been many studies on the 3D restoration of deformable objects in successive frames [1–4]. However, it is still challenging to reconstruct 3D models of deformable objects from consecutive frames in the field of computer vision and graphics [2]. One of the methods for reconstructing the 3D model of a deformable object is to estimate the transformation matrix for the object's transformed part from a continuous frame. One of the more detailed approaches is to use non-rigid deformation [5–7] to transform the vertices of the model. This approach uses spatial transformations that consist of graph vertices. The transformation for one vertex affects the deformation of the neighboring space because it is associated with the connected node. They solve the non-linear minimization problem and estimate the optimal value of the affine transformation matrix for each vertex. However, because it takes a lot of computation

© Springer Nature Switzerland AG 2019
A. Morales et al. (Eds.): IbPRIA 2019, LNCS 11867, pp. 610–619, 2019.
https://doi.org/10.1007/978-3-030-31332-6_53

time to estimate the transformation matrix for all vertices of an object, most of them work offline or they use the GPU's parallel processing technique to reduce non-rigid registration computation time. Another method is to use only non-rigid parts, except rigid parts like backgrounds [2, 8]. This method can reduce calculation time. Another method [8, 12, 17, 18] is to apply the GPU's parallel processing technique to reduce non-rigid registration computation time. If calculations do not need to be calculated sequentially, the application of parallelism can produce very effective results.

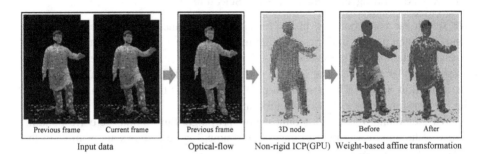

| Previous frame | Current frame | Previous frame | 3D node | Before | After |

| Input data | | Optical-flow | Non-rigid ICP(GPU) | Weight-based affine transformation |

Fig. 1. Overview of the proposed approach

The goal of this paper is to quickly and precisely match sequential 3D data of a dynamically moving whole body model. Our approach does not estimate the 3D transformation matrix for all points to efficiently perform deformable registration. After selecting uniformly sampled points as in [5], we obtain the 3D transformation matrix. Unselected points are related to the movement of neighboring points. This property can have the form of a graph structure [5]. This method results in computationally very efficient and smooth outputs. However, it still requires a high computational complexity to estimate the 3D transformation matrix of all selected points. Therefore, a lot of processing time is needed. We propose a method that a fast and accurate estimation of the 3D transformation matrix of selected points using the GPU's parallel processing.

Figure 1 shows our system flow chart. First, we obtain dynamic full-body model data from a single RGBD camera. Moreover, we use only the non-rigid part by removing the background based on the distance threshold. We use two sequential data as inputs to our system, as shown in Fig. 1. The input data is used as a pair of color and depth images. We use Gunnar Farneback's optical flow [10] to search for the correspondence of sequence data. We used a simple method of selecting pixels at regular intervals as nodes. We project the pixels selected as nodes into the 3D space based on the camera coordinate system. Next, we estimate the 3D affine transformation matrix between the previous frame and the current frame for all nodes through our proposed GPU-based non-rigid ICP algorithm. The 3D transformation matrix of each node has a size of 3×4 in the form of an affine matrix. Finally, we use weight-based affine transformation method we propose to apply the 3D transformation of all points.

The last section of this paper shows the accuracy and runtime test results for non-rigid ICP for all nodes. It also shows the result of applying the weight-based affine transformation method.

2 Corresponding Pixel Search, Node Selection, and 3D Reconstruction [-]

2.1 Corresponding Pixel Search, Node Selection

We search for corresponding pixels for successive frames using Optical-flow algorithm. We then use the uniform-sampling method to select pixels without using all the pixels. Selected pixels are used as nodes. We used a uniform-sampling method to select pixels at regular intervals. The selected nodes estimate 3D transformation matrix using the method in Sect. 3. The unselected pixels estimate 3D transformation matrix using the 3D transformation matrix of neighboring nodes.

We use Gunnar Farneback's optical flow [10] algorithm to find the corresponding pixels of the previous frame and the current frame. Figure 2 shows an example of the Optical-flow algorithm.

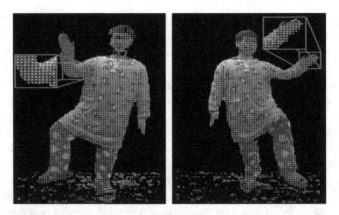

Fig. 2. Corresponding pixel search using Optical-flow algorithm: The yellow pixel is the selected pixel. The red straight line is a straight line that visualizes the vector pointing to the corresponding pixel. (Color figure online)

2.2 3D Reconstruction

In this paper, we aim to do 3D non-rigid registration of deformable whole body model. So we project all the pixels into the 3D space. We transformed the pixels into the 3D coordinate system of the camera reference using Eq. (1).

$$P_{(x,y)} = D_{(x,y)} K^{-1}[x, y, 1]^T \qquad (1)$$

In Eq. (1), (x, y) is the pixel coordinates in the color image. $P_{(x,y)}$ is a 3D point based on the camera coordinate system. That is, $P_{(x,y)}$ is a result of converting a 2D pixel into 3D coordinates. $D_{(x,y)}$ is the depth value for the pixel obtained from the depth image. K is an internal parameter of the camera. The resolution of the color image and the depth image are the same.

3 Non-rigid Registration Using GPU

3.1 Grouping Nearest Neighbor Node

To estimate the 3D transformation matrix between two point groups in 3D space, we must know three or more corresponding points. When the number of corresponding points is less than three, the 3D rotation vector cannot be estimated. In this case, only a 3D translation vector can be estimated.

In this paper, nodes are grouped to estimate the 3D transformation matrix of selected nodes. Our method is as follows. As shown in Fig. 3, we set a distance to a threshold from one node. We have grouped N-closest points within this area. If there are not N-number of nodes in this area, we have chosen the center node. We applied this method to all nodes. If the grouping is successful, the movement of neighbor points affects all neighbor points.

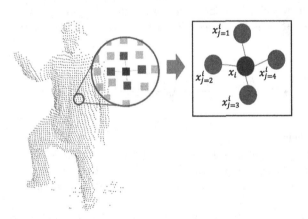

Fig. 3. Grouping the nearest points: We grouped the N-closest points around a point.

When the grouping method is applied as shown in Fig. 3, edges are created between the points. And the overall structure shows the graph form. Therefore, we refer to these points as nodes in this paper. In Fig. 3, i is the index of the selected node, and j is the index of the neighboring node.

3.2   Energy Function

In general, Non-rigid registration algorithm for the deformation model uses a method of defining the 3D transformation matrix as an affine matrix and optimizing the non-rigid ICP energy function [1–3, 5–8]. In this paper, we use the affine matrix as the 3D transformation matrix of each node. The size of the affine matrix is 3×4. We defined the energy function to estimate the 3D transformation matrix of all nodes for the deformation model for the previous frame and the current frame. This section describes how to optimize energy functions at high speed using the GPU. We have defined two energy functions, E_{data} and E_{rigid}, as in Eq. (2). We then use Levenberg-Marquardt (LM) algorithm to optimize the energy function and estimate the affine matrix for all nodes.

$$E_{tol}(X) = \alpha_{data}E_{data}(X) + \alpha_{rigid}E_{rigid}(X) \tag{2}$$

In the Eq. (2), X is defined as $X = \{X_1, \cdots, X_n\}$. X_i is a 3×4 affine transformation matrix for the i-th node. E_{data} and E_{rigid} are called the data term and rigid term. E_{rigid} is also called an orthogonality constraint [2, 11]. α_{data} and α_{rigid} are constant values for weighting each energy function.

3.2.1   Data Term

We define the Data term as Eq. (3). The data term is an energy term for estimating the optimal 3D transformation matrix for a point group corresponding to a specific 3D point cloud. After applying the method in Sect. 3.1, suppose that there is one group of point clouds. In Eq. (3), M is the total number of nodes for the whole-body model, and N is the number of grouped nodes. X_i represents the affine matrix of the i-th node. P is the node of the previous frame, and Q represents the node corresponding to P in the current frame.

$$E_{data} = \sum_{i=0}^{M} \left(\left\| \sum_{j=0}^{N} X_i p_j^i - q_j^i \right\|_2^2 \right) \tag{3}$$

3.2.2   Rigid Term

We define the rigid term as Eq. (4). The rigid term allows Affine matrix to have a property similar to a rigid transformation matrix. In other words, the rigid term is an energy term that causes the affine matrix to have the property of an orthogonal matrix. In Eq. (4), $a_i = (a_{i1}, a_{i2}, a_{i3})$ is a row vector of X_i in Eq. (3). $a_i = (a_{i1}, a_{i2}, a_{i3})$ is shown in Fig. 4. i is the index number of the nodes. M is the total number of nodes for the whole body model.

$$E_{rigid} = \sum_{i=0}^{M} \left(\begin{array}{c} \left(a_{i0}^T a_{i1}\right)^2 + \left(a_{i1}^T a_{i2}\right)^2 + \left(a_{i2}^T a_{i1}\right)^2 + \\ \left(1 - a_{i0}^T a_{i0}\right)^2 + \left(1 - a_{i1}^T a_{i1}\right)^2 + \left(1 - a_{i2}^T a_{i2}\right)^2 \end{array} \right) \tag{4}$$

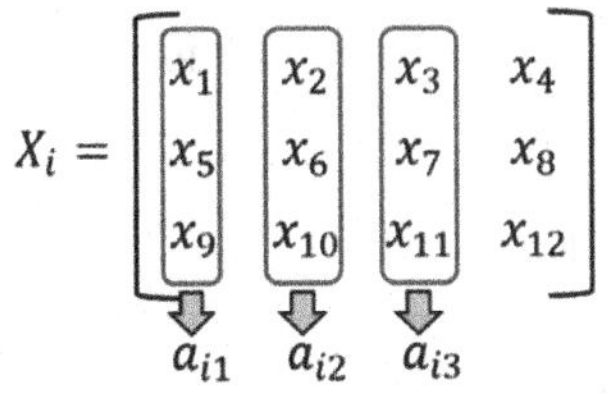

$$X_i = \begin{bmatrix} x_1 & x_2 & x_3 & x_4 \\ x_5 & x_6 & x_7 & x_8 \\ x_9 & x_{10} & x_{11} & x_{12} \end{bmatrix}$$

$$\quad\;\; a_{i1} \quad a_{i2} \quad a_{i3}$$

Fig. 4. Row vector of X_i

3.3   Optimization

3.3.1   Energy Minimization Method

We use a GPU-based optimization algorithm to obtain the X matrix with the size of $E_{tol}(X)$ in Sect. 3.2 minimized. The optimization algorithm as shown in Eq. (5) uses a combination of Levenberg-Marquardt (LM) algorithm and the Gauss-Newton algorithm. In Eq. (5), $\mathcal{J}$ is a Jacobian matrix for $E_{tol}(X)$. λ is a constant value and I is an identity matrix.

$$\left(\mathcal{J}^T \mathcal{J} + \lambda I\right)h = -\mathcal{J}^T E_{tol}(X) \tag{5}$$

$$Ax = B \tag{6}$$

We initialize the initial affine transformation matrix for each node to the Identity matrix. We used Eq. (6) to find h of Eq. (5). A of Eq. (6) uses $\left(\mathcal{J}^T \mathcal{J} + \lambda I\right)$ in Eq. (5). B of Eq. (6) uses $-\mathcal{J}^T E_{tol}(X)$ in Eq. (5). We used GPU based PCG (Preconditioned Conjugate Gradient) algorithm for the linear solver. We applied the variation h obtained from the linear solver for optimization to Eq. (7). Equation (7) is an expression for reaching the optimal solution of X.

$$X = X + h \tag{7}$$

The size of the affine transformation matrix for each node is 3×4. Therefore, we must estimate 12 non-parameters per node through the solver. The larger the number of non-parameter, the larger the number of nodes, the higher the amount of computation required to obtain the Jacobian matrix. Section 3.3.2 suggests how to process Jacobian operations at high speed using the GPU.

3.3.2   GPU Parallelism for Jacobian Calculations

Independent and iterative calculation structures are advantageous for parallel processing systems. Jacobian calculations are dependent on a group of nodes and are independent of other groups. We designed the data term and rigid term as two asynchronous kernels in parallel, as shown in Fig. 5.

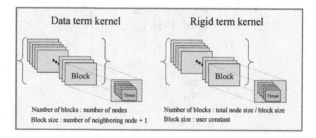

Fig. 5. Asynchronous kernel structure for Jacobian calculations based on GPU

In Data term kernel, we have assigned the number of CUDA blocks equal to the number of nodes. We used GPU shared memory as much as possible by assigning one node group to one CUDA block. CUDA shared memory has the advantage of faster access speed than CUDA global memory. This structure makes maximum use of parallel processing. The number of threads in Data term kernel is 'neighboring node size + 1'. The reason for adding one is because it includes the core node. In Rigid term kernel, the number of CUDA blocks is the total number of nodes divided by the number of threads allocated in a block.

4 Weight-Based Affine Transformation

In this paper, we propose a weight-based affine transformation method to apply the spatial transformation of all points using the affine transformation matrix for each point. Our method is defined by Eq. (8). This method weights each transformation matrix of all points to estimate a 3D transformation matrix of points. We used the exponential function to define the weighted value in inverse proportion to the distance as shown in Eq. (8). The nearest node has a greater effect than the farther node.

$$P' = \frac{\sum_{i=0}^{N} e^{-\lambda d_i X_i P}}{\sum_{i=0}^{N} e^{-\lambda d_i}} \tag{8}$$

In the above equation, P is the point of the previous frame, and P' is the result of applying the weight-based affine transformation. And i denotes an index of a node. N is the total number of nodes. X_i is the affine transformation matrix of the i-th node and λ is a constant.

5 Experimental Results

We used one Intel RealSense D415 camera. All the experiments are worked in a general purpose Intel i7-4790 computer running Windows 10 (64 bit) and an NVIDIA Titan XP graphics card. We evaluated the performance by experimenting with four data sets as shown in Table 1. Table 1 shows information in the dataset and the experimental results. It shows the average number of points and the average number of selected nodes in order. And it shows the calculation time of the non-rigid ICP algorithm and distance error value between nodes. The average non-rigid ICP calculation time was measured at 71.17 FPS. The average distance error of the nodes was measured as 4.24 mm. Figure 6 shows the result of applying our distortion transformation using the transformation matrix obtained from the non-rigid ICP in the previous frame and the current frame. In Fig. 6(a), the red part is the 3D data of the previous frame. In Fig. 6(b), the red color is the result of our proposed method.

Table 1. Experiments dataset

Dataset	#1	#2	#3	#4
Total number of frames	400	1,004	526	552
Average number of points	258,460	119,364	112,560	129,107
Average number of nodes	1,723	2,522	2,030	1,414
Average runtime for non-rigid ICP	71.44	64.84	70.62	77.79
Average distance error for node	2.68	3.17	5.73	5.38

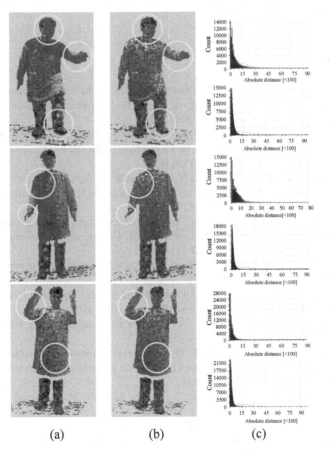

(a)   (b)   (c)

Fig. 6. Experiment results: (a) previous frame + current frame, (b) current frame + our result frame, (c) gaussian distribution based on distance difference: the upper graph is (a), the lower graph is (b).

6 Conclusion

This paper presents a non-rigid registration method for deformable objects and a GPU-based non-rigid ICP acceleration method. To reduce the amount of computation, we first select uniformly sampled points and then estimate the transformation matrix of each point. And we proposed a method of smooth registration of all points through the weight-based affine transformation method. Also, we evaluated the accuracy and speed of the proposed method through experiments.

We used a single camera, and there was an occlusion problem between frames due to the movement of the whole body model. It caused a loss of 3D data. Also, when the deformation of the model between successive frames occurs to a large extent, we have a problem that the error increases. In the future, we will study ways to improve our limitations.

Acknowledgments. This work was supported by 'The Cross-Ministry Giga KOREA Project' grant funded by the Korea government (MSIT) (No. GK17P0300, Real-time 4D reconstruction of dynamic objects for ultra-realistic service).

References

1. Slavcheva, M., Baust, M., Ilic, S.: SobolevFusion: 3D reconstruction of scenes undergoing free non-rigid motion. In: Proceedings of the IEEE Conference on Computer Vision and Pattern Recognition, pp. 2646–2655 (2018)
2. Guo, K., Xu, F., Wang, Y., Liu, Y., Dai, Q.: Robust non-rigid motion tracking and surface reconstruction using l0 regularization. In: Proceedings of the IEEE International Conference on Computer Vision, pp. 3083–3091 (2015)
3. Xu, W., Salzmann, M., Wang, Y., Liu, Y.: Deformable 3D fusion: from partial dynamic 3D observations to complete 4D models. In: Proceedings of the IEEE International Conference on Computer Vision, pp. 2183–2191 (2015)
4. Zeng, M., Zheng, J., Cheng, X., Liu, X.: Templateless quasi-rigid shape modeling with implicit loop-closure. In: Proceedings of the IEEE Conference on Computer Vision and Pattern Recognition, pp. 145–152 (2013)
5. Sumner, R.W., Schmid, J., Pauly, M.: Embedded deformation for shape manipulation. ACM Trans. Graph. (TOG) **26**(3), 80 (2007)
6. Szeliski, R., Lavallée, S.: Matching 3-D anatomical surfaces with non-rigid deformations using octree-splines. Int. J. Comput. Vis. **18**(2), 171–186 (1996)
7. Bonarrigo, F., Signoroni, A., Botsch, M.: Deformable registration using patch-wise shape matching. Graph. Models **76**(5), 554–565 (2014)
8. Newcombe, R.A., Fox, D., Seitz, S.M.: Dynamicfusion: reconstruction and tracking of non-rigid scenes in real-time. In: Proceedings of the IEEE Conference on Computer Vision and Pattern Recognition, pp. 343–352 (2015)
9. Elanattil, S., Moghadam, P., Sridharan, S., Fookes, C., Cox, M.: Non-rigid reconstruction with a single moving RGB-D camera. In: 2018 24th International Conference on Pattern Recognition (ICPR), pp. 1049–1055. IEEE, August 2018
10. Farnebäck, G.: Two-frame motion estimation based on polynomial expansion. In: Bigun, J., Gustavsson, T. (eds.) SCIA 2003. LNCS, vol. 2749, pp. 363–370. Springer, Heidelberg (2003). https://doi.org/10.1007/3-540-45103-X_50

11. Li, K., Yang, J., Lai, Y.K., Guo, D.: Robust non-rigid registration with reweighted position and transformation sparsity. IEEE Trans. Vis. Comput. Graph. **25**, 2255–2269 (2018)
12. Dou, M., et al.: Fusion4D: real-time performance capture of challenging scenes. ACM Trans. Graph. (TOG) **35**(4), 114 (2016)
13. Zach, C.: Robust bundle adjustment revisited. In: Fleet, D., Pajdla, T., Schiele, B., Tuytelaars, T. (eds.) ECCV 2014. LNCS, vol. 8693, pp. 772–787. Springer, Cham (2014). https://doi.org/10.1007/978-3-319-10602-1_50
14. Loke, M.H., Dahlin, T.: A comparison of the Gauss-Newton and quasi-Newton methods in resistivity imaging inversion. J. Appl. Geophys. **49**(3), 149–162 (2002)
15. Hartley, H.O.: The modified Gauss-Newton method for the fitting of non-linear regression functions by least squares. Technometrics **3**(2), 269–280 (1961)
16. Moré, J.J.: The Levenberg-Marquardt algorithm: implementation and theory. In: Watson, G. A. (ed.) Numerical Analysis. LNM, vol. 630, pp. 105–116. Springer, Heidelberg (1978). https://doi.org/10.1007/BFb0067700
17. Zollhöfer, M., et al.: Real-time non-rigid reconstruction using an RGB-D camera. ACM Trans. Graph. (ToG) **33**(4), 156 (2014)
18. Newcombe, R.A., et al.: Kinectfusion: Real-time dense surface mapping and tracking. ISMAR **11**(2011), 127–136 (2011)
19. Yang, Z., Zhu, Y., Pu, Y.: Parallel image processing based on CUDA. In: 2008 International Conference on Computer Science and Software Engineering, vol. 3, pp. 198–201. IEEE (2008)

Focus Estimation in Academic Environments Using Computer Vision

Daniel Canedo$^{(\boxtimes)}$, Alina Trifan, and António J. R. Neves

IEETA/DETI, University of Aveiro, 3810-193 Aveiro, Portugal
{danielduartecanedo,alina.trifan,an}@ua.pt

Abstract. In this paper we propose a system capable of monitoring students' focus through cameras and using Computer Vision algorithms. Experimental results show that our system is capable of identifying students and tracking their focus during a class. At the end of the class, the system outputs graphical feedback to teachers regarding the average level of students' focus. Moreover, it can identify lecture periods in which students were less watchful and the corresponding topics that potentially need extra focus. In this paper we start by presenting the architecture of the system, followed by results obtained both during a small-group workshop and a classroom with a large number of attending students. The main goal of this work is to contribute to the transformation of the classroom as a sensing environment, providing information to both teachers and students about their engagement during the class.

Keywords: Class monitoring · Face Detection · Face Recognition · Face tracking · Focus estimation

1 Introduction

Student engagement is linked positively to desirable learning outcomes, such as critical thinking and grades obtained in a subject [1]. The student engagement and attention depend on several factors, being the teacher one of the most important [2]. Teachers' ability to connect well with students can be beneficial for students' attention. In this paper, we pretend to estimate the students' attention based on Computer Vision algorithms. With our approach, we can suggest that certain student is, in fact, looking to the teacher, to the board or to the projection.

We realize that estimating students' attention is an hard task and cannot be performed only relying on visual data. However, that visual data plays an essential role on determining the students' focus and eventually their behaviour, which then can be correlated with other kind of data in order to get a more

Supported by the Integrated Programme of SR&TD SOCA (Ref. CENTRO-01-0145-FEDER-000010), co-funded by Centro 2020 program, Portugal 2020, European Union, through the European Regional Development Fund.

A. Morales et al. (Eds.): IbPRIA 2019, LNCS 11867, pp. 620–628, 2019.
https://doi.org/10.1007/978-3-030-31332-6_54

accurate estimation of their attention. For instance, that additional data could be a small quiz at the end of the class regarding the studied subjects [3]. However, if we only rely on visual data, we can still obtain satisfactory results about focus of a student. As the study in [4] showed, head orientation contributes 68.9% in the overall gaze direction and the authors achieved 88.7% accuracy at determining the focus. This conclusion implies that head orientation is a powerful method of measuring the students' focus.

In a preliminary work [5] we proposed a system that would in theory be capable of monitoring classrooms. This theoretical proposal was based on the analysis of relevant state of the art techniques in order to find out which methods were the most suitable for each of the blocks of the proposed architecture. The contribution of the current paper is the proof that the theoretical system is in practice capable of monitoring students' focus through cameras and Computer Vision algorithms.

This paper is organized as follows. Section 2 presents the methodology followed to implement our system. On Sect. 3 we present the System Architecture and the developed algorithms. Section 4 provides experimental results. Concluding remarks and the future work are featured in Sect. 5.

2 Methodology

The architecture of our system is made up of several blocks, from image acquisition during a class to the estimation of the students' focus.

2.1 Face Detection

As a first step of our methodology, we need to acquire the regions of interest in the classroom. Those regions of interest are the students' faces, which can be obtained through Face Detection algorithms. This is useful for extracting facial features which are used to estimate the head pose of the students and to identify them throughout the class. We must considerate the working distance in our scenario. Since the cameras need to capture the whole classroom, they need to be placed far away from the students, which leads to low resolutions images as input of the system. Therefore we must build a Face Detector that is efficient in long-range environments.

After the review of state of the art Face Detectors, we proposed in [5] one that fulfills the requirements of our system: MTCNN (Multi-task cascade convolution neural network) [6]. Depending on the used thresholds, this Face Detector is capable of detecting considerably low resolution faces in an image, at the cost of computer performance. Therefore, for different classroom sizes and different cameras, we can adjust the thresholds accordingly in order to detect every single student with a real-time performance. However, achieving the best threshold values for each situation is not straightforward, which may lead to false positives. Our system bypasses this problem by relying on a filter: it only assumes that a detected face is a real face if it detects the same face consecutively over 10 frames.

2.2   Identification and Tracking

Despite the low resolution faces, we must assure a good identification accuracy. This is for the sake of assigning the estimated focus levels to the respective students. It is highly undesirable to assign focus levels to the wrong students, since this could lead to the output of wrong data to both teachers and students regarding their performance and engagement in the class.

For the identification process, we propose a dynamic identification approach. In this approach, the Database is automatically filled during the class, while detecting the students. Through a face tracking algorithm, the system assigns an unique ID to each new detected student and stores several facial features during the class, based on which the Database is built-up. The main reason of implementing a tracking algorithm in our system is to bypass the computational cost of trying to recognize the students in every single frame. However, if for some reason the tracking is lost, the system recovers the students' identification through the Face Recognition, using the facial features stored in the Database. In order to increase the Face Recognition accuracy and avoid having identical identifications in the same frame, our system only compares a detected student with the ones who are not currently in the scene.

The Face Recognition implemented in our system is FaceNet [7] which uses a deep convolutional network and presents a 99,65% accuracy based on the Labeled Faces in the Wild Dataset (LFW [8]).

2.3   Focus Estimation

One way of measuring the students' focus that immediately comes to mind is by analyzing their eyes. However, as [9] mentioned, the accuracy of techniques like Eye Tracking tend to suffer when used on low resolution images.

Nevertheless, as already mentioned, we can rely on students' head pose to estimate their focus. To obtain the head pose we first need to acquire the five facial landmarks outputted from the MTCNN face detector: one in each eye, one in the nose and one in each mouth corner. These landmarks are usually stable, independently on the distance, so they can be trusted to estimate students' head pose. We created a sixth facial landmark in the chin, using the bounding boxes and the mouth landmarks' position, in order to improve the robustness of the head pose.

Lastly, we use an algorithm for head pose estimation [10] available on the OpenCV library [11] to estimate the head pose. This algorithm gives us a line that is drawn to the direction in which the head is oriented to. By comparing the direction of the line with a reference point that is marked by the teacher at the start of the class, it is possible to obtain a focus estimation of each student. This reference point dictates the direction in which the students should be looking at when they are focused.

3   System Architecture

The overview presented in the previous Section led to the design of the following system for monitoring classrooms. In Fig. 1 we present the diagram of its architecture.

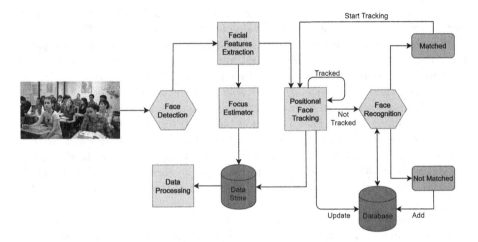

Fig. 1. Diagram of the system architecture, whose main tasks consist in Detection, Identification and Focus Estimation.

The system starts up with an input image captured by the camera. The camera should capture the whole classroom or part of it, depending on the students' acceptance of being recorded. This image is fed to our system, more specifically fed to a block called Face Detection. This block is responsible for detecting all the regions of interest in the image, which are the students' faces. After having these regions of interest, the system feeds them to the Facial Features Extraction block. This block is responsible for extracting the facial features of each student, which are used for the identification and for estimating their focus. Lastly, these facial features are fed to the Positional Face Tracking block and to the Focus Estimator block.

Since the system starts with no information from the past, it is implied that this block can't successfully track the students in the first frame. However, it assigns an unique ID to each detected student and saves their current positions for the next iterations. At the same time, the Database is updated, as it also starts up empty.

When the system already knows the position of each student, it can successfully track them. By comparing all the current positions of the bounding boxes retrieved from the Face Detection block with the positions of the bounding boxes from the previous frame, the system assigns the previous IDs to the closest students in the current frame. If the Positional Face Tracking fails to assign the correct IDs for reasons such as occlusions, the system has a way to reassign the correct ID through a refresh algorithm. This algorithm refreshes all the students' IDs through the Face Recognition block each 9 frames, by comparing the actual facial features with the facial features that are assigned to the respective ID. For instance, if a student takes the ID of other student because of occlusions, the refresh algorithm is going to realize that he/she has the wrong ID because the student who "stole" the ID is only going to be compared with the student who got his/her ID "stolen". In this case, the refresh algorithm outputs a great distance value in the comparison, reassigning him/her the correct ID.

As mentioned in Subsect. 2.2, since the Face Recognition block only compares the students with the ones who are not in the scene for a better accuracy, the student who gets his/her ID "stolen" by other one is not going to be compared with himself/herself, since his/her ID is still in the scene. In order to bypass this problem we set the counter for the refresh algorithm (9 frames) to be lower than the counter for the Face Detection block (10 frames). This will lead to a refresh before the system attributes a new ID to the student who lost his/her ID for assuming he/she is a new student in the scene. Therefore, in this unfavorable scenario, the system is able to reassign the correct ID to the "robber", and the "stolen" student has his/her own ID out of the scene and available for reassignment.

In a scenario where the Positional Face Tracking fails to track certain student, the system goes through the Face Recognition block in order to reassign the respective ID. If the student is correctly matched, the system starts tracking him/her again. If the student is not matched, it means he/she was not detected in the previous frame, therefore the system adds him/her to the Database and assigns a new ID.

While the students are being tracked, the system is constantly retrieving information from their facial features in order to estimate their focus. This estimation is calculated through the algorithm mentioned in Subsect. 2.3. The focus values are stored in the Data Store and, at the end of the class, the Data Processing block is responsible for calculating an average focus for each individual ID. Afterwards, the system outputs this information through graphical feedback regarding the students' focus during the class, which ideally will be consulted by both teachers and students.

4   Experimental Results

In this Section we present the experimental results obtained while testing the developed system in real world scenarios. It is important to mention that, to our knowledge, currently there are no public datasets in academic environments available for testing.

4.1   Ground Truth

Initially, a small-group experiment was conducted with the aim of reaching a Ground Truth of our focus estimator. This served as well as a test to the system as a whole and allowed us to identify potential flaws. Figure 2 shows how the test was conducted.

Fig. 2. Small-group experiment for reaching a Ground Truth of our focus estimator. On top of each bounding box the corresponding person ID is displayed. Below the bounding box the person's focus value is displayed.

This experiment was a small workshop, in which the presenter was substituted by a 10 min video. The circle presented in the right side of the Fig. 2, as mentioned previously, is the reference point to where the participants should be looking at when they are focused.

The system outputted graphical feedback regarding the focus of each participant obtained through the Data Processing block. Afterwards, through manual annotation, it was noted down if each participant was focused or not for each frame of the experiment, over 6522 frames. The annotator marked "1" if the participant was looking to the reference point, and "0" if the participant was not looking to the reference point for each frame. This led to a slight discrepancy between the experimental graphics and the manual graphics. This is due to the fact that the system uses the head pose for calculating the direction of the gaze and the observer used the eyes to understand if the participants were focused or not. As an example of discrepancy, the head pose estimation may be directed towards the reference point, however the gaze is not. Figure 3 shows the obtained results.

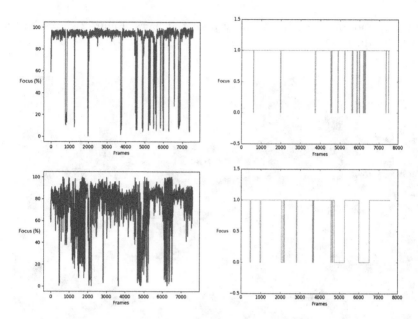

Fig. 3. From left to right, the experimental graphic and the manual graphic obtained for ID 0 and ID 2 (Focus values in the Y axis, number of the frame in the X axis). From top to bottom, the belonging IDs for each graphics: 0 and 2.

The left images are the experimental results and the right images are the results obtained through manual annotation. The Ground Truth was 93.07%, 98.23%, 85.69% and 93.56% from ID 0 to ID 3, making an average Ground Truth of 94.13% for this experiment. While making manual annotations, we deduced that the Ground Truth can never be 100% due to the two dimensional approach limitations in the focus estimator. However, the accuracy is satisfactorily high considering the computational cost.

4.2   Classroom Experiment

A formal experiment was conducted on a real classroom scenario at the University of Aveiro. The class duration was 38 min and 17 s and 60 students attended it. The results were quite satisfactory: the identification block presented an accuracy of 100% during the whole class and the system successfully provided graphics of the estimated focus for each individual ID. Figure 4 shows how the experiment was organized and Fig. 5 shows 2 examples of different focus levels during this experiment.

Figure 5 shows 2 different types of behaviours during the experiment. For this experiment we decided to normalize the focus levels for better analyzable graphics: focus levels less than 50% are converted to "0" and focus levels greater than or equal to 50% are converted to "1". In the left image, we have a student that was focused throughout most of the class, since most focus levels were "1".

Fig. 4. Formal experiment during a class in University of Aveiro.

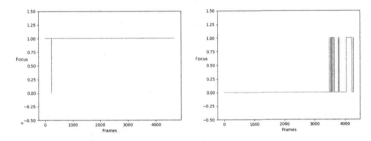

Fig. 5. Different focus levels for 2 students during the experiment (Focus values in the Y axis, number of the frame in the X axis).

In the right image, we have a student that was distracted throughout most of the class, only staying focused a few moments in the end of the class.

This graphical feedback provides identification of lecture periods in which students were less watchful and the corresponding topics that need extra focus. This has the goal of improving academic performance. As future work, we intend to link focus to engagement and classify different types of student behaviours during the class.

5   Conclusion

In this paper we presented a system for monitoring classrooms. After researching about the potentially best state of the art approaches for each required techniques, we built a system capable of transforming the classroom in a sensing environment. This system is capable of running automatically. No registration of the students at the beginning of the class is required, the only requirement being the intervention of the lecturer to instruct the system about the location of the reference point. This is simply done through a mouse click. The results for the Ground Truth of our focus estimator and for our real scenario experiment are satisfactory and encouraged us to follow up with the use of the system in a real classroom environment. As for future work, we intend to add a body pose estimator [12] to calculate the teacher's mood during the class and how it affects his/her performance. Moreover, we are working towards creating a classification of students' behaviour based on their focus and class engagement.

References

1. Carini, R.M., Kuh, G.D., Klein, S.P.: Student engagement and student learning: testing the linkages. Res. High. Educ. **47**(1), 1–32 (2006)
2. Hagenauer, G., Hascher, T., Volet, S.E.: Teacher emotions in the classroom: associations with students' engagement, classroom discipline and the interpersonal teacher-student relationship. Eur. J. Psychol. Educ. **30**(4), 385–403 (2015)
3. Nguyen, K., McDaniel, M.A.: Using quizzing to assist student learning in the classroom: the good, the bad, and the ugly. Teach. Psychol. **42**(1), 87–92 (2015)
4. Stiefelhagen, R., Zhu, J.: Head orientation and gaze direction in meetings. In: CHI 2002 Extended Abstracts on Human Factors in Computing Systems. ACM (2002)
5. Canedo, D., Trifan, A., Neves, A.J.R.: Monitoring students' attention in a classroom through computer vision. In: Bajo, J., et al. (eds.) PAAMS 2018. CCIS, vol. 887, pp. 371–378. Springer, Cham (2018). https://doi.org/10.1007/978-3-319-94779-2_32
6. Zhang, K., et al.: Joint face detection and alignment using multitask cascaded convolutional networks. IEEE Signal Process. Lett. **23**(10), 1499–1503 (2016)
7. Schroff, F., Kalenichenko, D., Philbin, J.: FaceNet: a unified embedding for face recognition and clustering. In: Proceedings of the IEEE Conference on Computer Vision and Pattern Recognition (2015)
8. Huang, G.B., et al.: Labeled faces in the wild: a database for studying face recognition in unconstrained environments. In: Workshop on Faces in 'Real-Life' Images: Detection, Alignment, and Recognition (2008)
9. Krafka, K., et al.: Eye tracking for everyone. In: Proceedings of the IEEE Conference on Computer Vision and Pattern Recognition (2016)
10. Head Pose Estimation using OpenCV and Dlib. https://www.learnopencv.com/head-pose-estimation-using-opencv-and-dlib/
11. OpenCV library. https://opencv.org/
12. Cao, Z,, et al.: Realtime multi-person 2D pose estimation using part affinity fields. In: Proceedings of the IEEE Conference on Computer Vision and Pattern Recognition (2017)

Author Index

Abass, Faycel II-177
Abdelbaset, Asmaa II-169
Abdel-Hakim, Alaa II-169
Abreu, Pedro H. II-322
Acevedo-Rodríguez, Francisco Javier I-77
Acien, Alejandro II-12
Adonias, Ana F. II-247
Agudo, Antonio I-423
Aguilar, Eduardo I-65
Ajami, Mohamad II-497
Alejo, R. I-216
Alén-Cordero, Cristina II-485
Alfaro-Contreras, María II-147
Almazán, Emilio J. I-137, I-329
Alonso, Raquel II-247
Amirneni, Satakarni I-589
Antunes, João I-194
Aouache, Mustapha II-86
Araújo, Ricardo J. II-473, II-508
Ardakani, Parichehr B. II-64
Arens, Michael I-101, I-302
Arevalillo, Jorge M. I-113
Arias-Rubio, Carlos I-161
Arista, Antonio II-239
Arroyo, Roberto I-329
Ávila, Mar I-498
Ayad, Mouloud II-177

Banerjee, Biplab I-472
Baptista-Ríos, Marcos I-77
Baracchini, E. II-520
Barata, Catarina I-239, II-3
Barrenechea, Edurne I-553
Barrere, Killian II-201
Baumela, Luis I-449
Becker, Stefan I-101
Bedoui, Mohamed Hédi II-260
Bellini, F. II-520
Ben Abdallah, Asma II-260
Bengherabi, Messaoud II-86
Benussi, L. II-520
Bernabeu, Marisa I-485
Bernardino, Alexandre I-194
Bessa, Sílvia I-355

Bianco, S. II-520
Bilen, Hakan I-508
Blaiech, Ahmed Ghazi II-260
Blanco, Saúl I-342
Bocanegra, Álvaro José II-359
Brandão, André I-225
Brando, Axel I-29
Brea, Víctor M. II-273
Buenaposada, José M. I-449
Bueno, Gloria I-317, I-342, II-189
Buhrmester, Vanessa I-302
Bulatov, Dimitri I-302
Bustince, Humberto I-553
Byra, Michal I-41

Caballero, Daniel I-498
Calvo-Zaragoza, Jorge II-135, II-147, II-159
Camacho, Camilo II-394
Campo-Deaño, Laura II-508
Cancino Suárez, Sandra Liliana II-465
Cancino, Sandra Liliana II-359
Canedo, Daniel I-620
Cardoso, Jaime S. II-38, II-247, II-473
Caro, Andrés I-498
Caro, Luis I-206
Carvalho, Pedro H. I-355
Casacuberta, Francisco I-16
Castillo-García, Fernando I-600
Castro, Francisco Manuel II-296
Castro, Marina II-508
Cavallaro, Andrea I-239
Cavoto, G. II-520
Cepeda, Karen II-465
Cherifi, Hocine I-170
Chetouani, Aladine I-170
Cleofas Sanchez, Laura II-239
Corroto, Juan Jose II-371
Costa, I. A. II-520
Costa, Joana II-383
Cristóbal, Gabriel I-317, I-342, II-189
Cunha, António II-335

de León, Pedro J. Ponce II-159
de la Calle, Alejandro I-137

Delgado, Francisco J.   I-329
Delgado-Escaño, Rubén   II-296
Demircan-Tureyen, Ezgi   I-89
Deniz, Oscar   I-342, II-371, II-441
Di Marco, E.   II-520
Dias, Catarina   II-335
Djeddi, Chawki   II-177
Dobruch-Sobczak, Katarzyna   I-41
Domingues, Inês   II-322
Domingues, José   II-217
Duarte, Hugo   II-322
Dutta, Deep   I-543

El Hassouni, Mohammed   I-170
El Haziti, Mohamed   I-170
El-Melegy, Moumen   I-270, II-169
ElMelegy, Tarek   I-270
El-Sayed, Gamal   II-169
Escalante-Ramirez, Boris   I-289
Esteves, F. F.   I-461

Fernandes, Kelwin   I-3
Fernandez-Carrobles, M. Milagro   II-441
Fernández-Sanjurjo, Mauro   II-273
Ferreira, Bárbara   II-3
Ferreira, Diogo Daniel   II-404
Ferreira-Gomes, Joana   II-247
Fierrez, Julian   II-12, II-108
Figueiredo, Rui   II-346
Fiori, Marcelo   I-148
Forcén, Juan Ignacio   I-553
Forero, Manuel Guillermo   I-161, I-378,
      I-577, I-600, II-416, II-465
Franco, Annalisa   II-25
Franco-Ceballos, Ricardo   I-398
Fusek, Radovan   II-76

Galeano-Zea, July   I-398
Gallego, Antonio-Javier   I-485, II-135
García, Vicente   I-249
García, Zaira   II-239
García-Vanegas, Andrés   I-600
Garzon, Johnson   I-398
Gaspar, José António   II-309
Gattal, Abdeljalil   II-177
Georgieva, Petia   I-225, II-217, II-404
Gerson, Christian   II-497
Ghosh, Tanmai K.   II-98
Giraldo, Beatriz F.   I-367

Gómez-Moreno, Hilario   II-485
Gonfaus, Josep M.   II-64
Gonzàlez, Jordi   II-64
González-Barcenas, V. M.   I-216
Gonzalez-Rodríguez, Antonio   I-600
Granda-Gutiérrez, E. E.   I-216
Grechikhin, Ivan   II-429
Gruber, Dieter P.   II-453
Guil, Nicolás   II-296
Gupta, Phalguni   II-50
Gutiérrez-Maestro, Eduardo   I-386

Hadjadj, Ismail   II-177
Hamidi, Mohamed   I-170
Heleno, Sandra   I-279
Hernandez, Andrea   II-465
Hernandez-Ortega, Javier   II-108
Herrero, Elias   I-437
Higuera, Carolina   II-394
Horta-Júnior, José de Anchieta C.   I-161
Hurtado, Antonio   I-329
Hussain, Mazahir   I-565

Iñesta, José M.   II-147
Islam, Sarder Tazul   I-543

Jacanamejoy Jamioy, Carlos   I-577
Jafari-Tabrizi, Atae   II-453

Kamasak, Mustafa E.   I-89
Kanagasingam, Yogesan   I-543, II-98
Kerkeni, Asma   II-260
Khatir, Nadjia   I-77
Kim, Eung-su   I-610
Kisku, Dakshina Ranjan   II-50
Korzinek, Danijel   I-41
Krüger, Jörg   II-497
Kurihara, Toru   II-229

Lafuente-Arroyo, Sergio   II-485
Lee, Junesuk   I-610
Lehr, Jan   II-497
Leira, Luís   II-404
Liberato-Tafur, Brhayan   I-600
Libreros, José A.   I-342
Lichtenegger, Hannah Luise   II-453
Lima, S. Q.   I-461
Lopes, Bernardo   II-217
Lopes, G. S. P.   II-520

Lopes, Gabriel   II-38
López, Dolores E.   I-161
López, Juan Manuel   I-367, II-359, II-465
Lopez-Lopez, Eric   II-25
López-Najera, Abraham   I-249
López-Santos, Oswaldo   I-378
López-Sastre, Roberto J.   I-77, I-386
Lumbreras, Felipe   I-423
Lumini, Alessandra   II-25

M. Pardo, Xosé   II-25
Maccarrone, G.   II-520
Maharjan, Samee   I-531
Maldonado-Bascón, Saturnino   I-386, II-485
Mamidibathula, Bharat   I-589
Mansour, Asma   II-260
Marafini, M.   II-520
Marasek, Krzysztof   I-41
Marcal, André R. S.   I-257, II-285
Marín-Jiménez, Manuel Jesús   II-296
Maroto, Fernando   II-441
Marques, Jorge S.   I-239, I-279
Martins, Aurora L. R.   I-257
Mateiu, Tudor N.   II-135
Mazzitelli, G.   II-520
Mejía, Juan S.   I-367
Mena, José   I-29
Meneses-Casas, Nohora   I-378, I-577
Messina, A.   II-520
Mihaylova, Petya   II-217, II-404
Mirza, Ali   I-565
Mohamed, Doaa   I-270
Monteiro, Nuno Barroso   II-309
Morales, Aythami   II-12, II-108
Moreno, Plinio   II-346
Moreno-Noguer, Francesc   I-423
Mucientes, Manuel   II-273
Münch, David   I-302
Murillo, Javier   I-398
Mustufa, Syed Ghulam   I-565

Nagae, Shigenori   II-108
Nait-Bahloul, Safia   I-77
Nakano, Mariko   II-239
Narotamo, Hemaxi   I-53
Neto, Fani   II-247
Neves, António J. R.   I-620
Nin, Jordi   I-182
Nobrega, R. A.   II-520

Nowicki, Andrzej   I-41
Nunes, Afonso   II-346
Nuñez-Alcover, Alicia   II-159

Ochoa-Ortiz, Alberto   I-249
Oliveira, Ana Catarina   II-322
Oliveira, Hélder P.   I-355, II-335, II-473,
    II-508
Olveres, Jimena   I-289
Ondo-Méndez, Alejandro   II-465
Orrite, Carlos   I-437
Oulefki, Adel   II-86

Pagola, Miguel   I-553
Pande, Shivam   I-472
Park, Soon-Yong   I-610
Patnam, Niharika   I-589
Pedraza, Anibal   I-342
Pedraza, César   II-394
Peixoto, Patrícia S.   I-355
Peralta, Billy   I-206
Perdomo, Sammy A.   II-416
Pereira, Francisco   I-279
Perez, Guillermo F.   II-416
Perez, Hector   II-239
Pérez-Palacios, Trinidad   I-498
Peris, Álvaro   I-16
Pertusa, Antonio   I-485
Phong, Nguyen Huu   I-521
Piccolo, D.   II-520
Pieringer, Christian   I-206
Pina, Pedro   I-279
Pinci, D.   II-520
Pinheiro, Gil   II-335
Pinto, João Ribeiro   II-38
Piotrzkowska-Wroblewska, Hanna   I-41
Pires, Pedro   I-225
Pissarra, José   I-257
Pižurica, Aleksandra   I-472
Portêlo, Ana   I-239
Pujol, Oriol   I-29, I-182
Pulido, Sergio David   II-359

Quimbaya, Mauricio A.   II-416
Quirós, Lorenzo   II-123

Radeva, Petia   I-65
Rahaman, G. M. Atiqur   I-543, II-98
Rakshit, Rinku Datta   II-50

Rendón, E.   I-216
Renga, F.   II-520
Reyes, Juan   I-206
Ribeiro, Bernardete   I-521, II-383
Rio-Torto, Isabel   I-3
Robledo, Sara M.   I-398
Rodriguez, Lizeth   II-465
Rodríguez, Pau   II-64
Rodríguez-Pardo, Carlos   I-508
Roldán, Nicolás   II-465
Rosatelli, F.   II-520
Rotger, Gemma   I-423
Ruiz, Angel D.   I-367
Ruiz-Santaquitaria, Jesús   I-342

S. Marques, Jorge   II-3
Saha, Sajib   I-543, II-98
Saini, Manisha   I-409
Sakpere, Wilson   I-125
Salazar-D'antonio, Diego   I-378
Salido, Jesús   I-342
Sanches, J. Miguel   I-53, I-461
Sánchez, Carlos   I-317, I-342, II-189
Sánchez, Josep Salvador   I-249
Santos, Elisabete M. D. S.   II-285
Santos, João   II-322
Sarbazvatan, S.   I-461
Savchenko, Andrey V.   II-429
Sayed, Md. Abu   II-98
Scherer-Negenborn, Norbert   I-101
Segundo, Marcela A.   I-355
Serrador, Diego G.   I-329
Sfeir, Ghesn   I-449
Siddiqi, Imran   I-565, II-177
Siewiorek, Daniel   I-194
Silva, Ana Rosa M.   I-355
Silva, Catarina   II-383
Silveira, Margarida   I-53
Singh, Harbinder   II-189
Sistla, Sai Shravani   I-589
Smailagic, Asim   I-194

Sojka, Eduard   II-76
Souza, D. M.   II-520
Suárez, Iago   I-449
Susan, Seba   I-409
Sznajder, Tomasz   I-41

Tavares, Fernando   II-285
Teixeira, Luís F.   I-3
Tistarelli, Massimo   II-50
Tomassini, S.   II-520
Torres, Fabian   I-289
Torres, Juan Pedro   I-498
Torres-Madronero, Maria C.   I-398
Toselli, Alejandro H.   II-123, II-201
Tovar, Javier   I-137, I-329
Trifan, Alina   I-620

Unceta, Irene   I-182

V. Regueiro, Carlos   II-25
Valdés, Matías   I-148
Valdovinos, R. M.   I-216
Valencia, Mauricio   I-437
Vállez, Noelia   I-317, II-371
Velasco-Mata, Alberto   II-371
Velazquez, Diego   II-64
Ventura, R.   I-461
Vera-Rodriguez, Ruben   II-12
Vidal, Enrique   II-123, II-201
Vitrià, Jordi   I-29
Vujasinović, Stéphane   I-101

Xavier Roca, F.   II-64

Yanai, Keiji   II-239
Yen, Ping-Lang   I-289
Yu, Jun   II-229

Zarzycki, Artur   I-398
Zhan, Shu   II-229

Printed in the United States
By Bookmasters